IN THE THICK OF THE FIGHT

IN THE THICK
OF THE FIGHT

1930–1945

by

PAUL REYNAUD

Translated by

JAMES D. LAMBERT

SIMON AND SCHUSTER
NEW YORK

TO THOSE WHO HAVE NEVER DESPAIRED

The soul of France is not conquered. . . . During the great
ordeals of our history, our people have known days when
faint-hearted counsels have confused them. Their greatness lies
in their refusal to abandon the fight. The day of resurrection
will come.

Tours, June 13, 1940

PREFACE

DURING my long years in prison, I conceived it a duty to my country—provided that the enemy did not bring my task to an abrupt conclusion—to explain to France how she had gravitated into war and why her army had been crushed in 1940.

Before I was deported, I contrived to have the pages which I had already written circulated through the ranks of the Resistance Movement.

When, in 1945, victory snatched me from German clutches, I had already broken the back of my work. Yet, what I had accomplished was only a first rough draft. The most difficult part yet remained: I still had to correlate my impressions, to weave them into a harmonious picture by giving to each its exact value and its true proportion.

I counted on completing this second part on my return to France. The public, eager to learn the vicissitudes of the drama, would not grant me the leisure to do this. How was it possible for me to deny its urgent demand for information?

In such circumstances, and against my own inclination, I consented to the publication of a book which was merely the rough draft of the one I had intended.[1]

Whilst giving way, however, to the impatience of the public, and publishing this book, I privately made the resolution that I would, at my leisure, once more resume my tentative effort, and so provide my country and its Allies with the testimony which it was my duty to offer them.

It is this testimony which I offer today.

I have collated it with the numerous documents published since my first book, and with the testimonies of the other protagonists or spectators of the drama. Of all its great leading actors, Stalin alone did not give his version.

Since my return from captivity, I have made it a point of honour to collaborate in the unveiling of the truth. My co-operation could always be counted on in the inquiries which have taken place (and which still continue) into those very controversial years. At its sitting of May 18, 1951, the Committee of Inquiry, appointed by the French National Assembly, coming to the end of its task, made a point of recognizing

---

[1] *La France a sauvé l'Europe.* This ambitious title was, in my opinion, justified by the fact that Europe would have succumbed to Nazi domination if, on September 3, 1939, France, already exhausted by her appalling sacrifice of blood during the previous war, had not honoured her word.

this fact: 'I wish to place on record', stated M. Dhers, one of the Committee's most valuable members, because of his profession of historian, 'that, of the three last Presidents of the Council, only one has appeared to answer all the probings, even the most intimate, of the Committee with good grace, namely, President Paul Reynaud.'

Here then are my memoirs. They possess originality in that they give, together with my own account, a version or versions which differ from mine, and, in this way, they provide the public with the latest reading of history.

January 1955

LIST OF CONTENTS

MAPS AND FACSIMILES

ACKNOWLEDGEMENTS

A full list of the works referred to, or quoted, in this volume will be found in the Bibliography at the end of the text. To the authors and publishers of these books, the author wishes to express his indebtedness. Special acknowledgement is due to the following:

Eyre & Spottiswoode (Publishers) Ltd., for permission to quote from Paul Baudouin's *Private Diaries 1940–1941*, and from *Hitler Speaks*, by H. Rauschning.

Victor Gollancz Ltd., for permission to quote from *The Fateful Years*, by André François-Poncet.

Wm. Heinemann Ltd., for permission to quote from *Ciano's Diary, 1939–1943*.

The Controller of H.M. Stationery Office, for permission to quote from *Documents on British Foreign Policy 1919–1939*, Third Series, vol. II, ed. Woodward and Butler.

Macmillan & Co. Ltd., for permission to quote from *The Life of Neville Chamberlain*, by Keith Feiling.

The Macmillan Company, New York, for permission to quote from Cordell Hull's *Memoirs*, vol. I (pub. 1948).

INTRODUCTION

IN French public life between the two wars, I was a lone wolf.
On the morrow of the First World War, whilst a young deputy, I
maintained that the only way to make Germany pay was to exact
from her reparations in kind, and I advocated the linking up of France's
heavy industry with that of Germany. After this speech, Hugo Stinnes,
the famous Ruhr magnate, asked for an interview with me. Raymond
Poincaré, who was then President of the Council of Ministers, opposed
our meeting.

I was accused by the extreme Right-wing Press of being the creature
of Germany, and by the extreme Left-wing Press of being that of the
Ruhr capitalists.

As early as 1924, whilst the Socialists preached disarmament and the
other parties pinned their faith on Marshal Pétain, who wished to retain
the cumbersome army of trench warfare, I called for an army which
would be capable of dealing devastating blows, as the only method of
preventing the rearmament of Germany. I added that if we kept our
defensive Army we would gravitate towards another war, this time
perhaps without a 'Sacred Alliance',[1] in which we would see the
German Army 'destroy Poland, and over her corpse offer the hand of
friendship to the Red Army'. Subsequently, we should see 'France
invaded, our factories destroyed, our burial grounds desecrated.'

These prophecies met with nothing but indifference or inspired scorn.
In 1930, as Minister of Finance, I pointed out on the horizon the world
economic crisis which was about to engulf us, and I advised France to
take in her sails.

This created a great scandal. I was sent off to President Hoover, who
himself saw prosperity round the corner, and a newspaper of the
extreme Right accused me of having wished to bring off a coup on the
Bourse.

From 1934, I alone, on the floor of the Chamber of Deputies, begged
our rulers to open their eyes, to realize that they were going to per-
petuate a world crisis if they refused to peg the franc to the pound and
the dollar, both of which had been devalued by forty-one per cent.
I predicted that if we did not carry out this monetary manipulation in
cold blood we should have to do it in hot, and that it would be necessary, consequently, to do it twice as drastically. This, in fact, did happen

---

[1] The term 'Sacred Alliance' (*Union Sacrée*) was applied to the party truce concluded in
France on the outbreak of the First World War, so that a solid national front could be
presented during the struggle [Tr.].

I

when, between the years 1936 and 1938, we had to give way to three successive devaluations.

A President of the Council consulted with his Minister of Justice as to whether I was liable to prosecution, and the extreme Right accused me of acting through base motives.

Our rulers persisted in their policy. Through their error the economic crisis was prolonged. In August, 1934, I stated that the price we would pay at the general election of 1936 would be the victory of the *Front Populaire*.[1] This did, in fact, occur. The franc was devalued by the Popular Frontists who had pledged themselves to do nothing of the kind; but, at the same time, the working week was cut down to forty hours. I demonstrated that this second step would have the effect of destroying the benefit of the first. Moreover, the forty-hour working week was equivalent to destroying one-sixth of French plant, already so inferior to that of Germany, at a time when Hitler was proclaiming with pride, 'The German people are working, night and day, to fashion arms.'[2] This was two years before the war which even the most blind could see approaching.

The majority sided against me with the *Front Populaire* Administration. It was only in November, 1938, that, having become Minister of Finance, I could set afoot—too late, unfortunately!—that recovery which *The Times* was to call 'the French miracle'.

In 1935, when Mussolini became entangled in his Abyssinian venture, I showed, in opposition to Laval, who was working to save him, that, on the contrary, it was imperative in the interests of peace to take advantage of the situation to deal him a knock-out blow.

The majority, now very reduced, it is true, but including most of my friends, sided against me with Laval.

On March 15, 1935, I outlined to the Chamber what the nature of the German offensive through Belgium towards the north of France would be, and I declared that we should only succeed in barring the road to invasion if we reorganized our Army by giving it an armoured corps such as Lieutenant-Colonel de Gaulle had just proposed. I stressed the fact that our defensive Army neither enabled us to honour the engagements into which we had entered with our Central European Allies, whereby we would assist them in the event of a German attack, nor was even fit to prevent the invasion of France. As his sole reply the Minister for War referred me to the Maginot Line: 'Should we not be rather foolish', he said, 'to advance beyond this barrier on some unpredictable venture?' The Chamber of Deputies once more was against

---

[1] The *Front Populaire* or 'Popular Front' was a coalition of parties of the Left [Tr.].

[2] In 1933, a total of nearly nine million working hours was attained in Germany, and eight million in France. In 1937, after Hitler had been in power four years, and the forty-hour week legalized in our country, the totals were sixteen million working hours in Germany against six million in France.

me. My reply to it was: 'We are the only great people whose very existence is at stake.'

On March 7, 1936, I asked concerning the state of our Air Force: 'Can our rulers sleep at night?'

My political career was on the point of being broken. At the general election of May, 1936, it was natural that the average voter, with his respect for the established order, should be apprehensive of a candidate who disagreed with the Bank of France over its monetary policy, the General Staff over its military policy, and the Quai d'Orsay over its foreign policy; a man whose theories the political parties and the important newspapers combined in condemning! Fifteen opponents contested the poll against me.

Between the first and second ballots[1] the Right-wing candidate offered to retire in my favour if I would abandon my theories. I refused. My chances of election were thought to be gone. I was elected by twenty-seven votes.

On January 26, 1937, I predicted to the Chamber that the German Army which would invade us would contrast with that of 1914 'as a train contrasts with a stage-coach'.

On November 3, 1937, I wrote in *Paris-Soir* an article entitled 'Nous sommes entrés dans la zone non sanglante de la guerre'.

I was denounced as a war-monger.

In September, 1938, I protested against the Munich agreement with my friends and fellow Cabinet Ministers, Daladier, Georges Mandel and Champetier de Ribes.

In July, 1939, General Weygand proclaimed, 'If we are forced into winning another victory, we shall win it.' Running counter to such an utterance, I stated on the wireless, 'We are on the threshold of the most perilous period in our history.' A month later came the Hitler-Stalin agreement, the Waterloo of French diplomacy.

On September 3, 1939, we declared war, without a 'Sacred Alliance', without a Russian alliance, without an armoured corps, without offensive aircraft. After the failure of our diplomacy we were to witness the failure of our military leaders, permeated with Pétain's doctrine of the invulnerable *continuous front*.

With the coming of war it was my duty, in my capacity as Minister of Finance, to safeguard the national credit. To maintain confidence in it I invoked the only argument at the disposal of a man who had never stopped denouncing our failure to understand the military problem: the superiority in war potential of the democracies. From this I drew the conclusion, 'We shall prevail because we are the stronger.' Such, in

[1] French national elections were held at this time under the second ballot system. Candidates failing to obtain an absolute majority at the first ballot often attempted to reach an understanding by which they secured the support of other unsuccessful candidates at the second ballot, when a relative majority was sufficient to secure election [Tr.].

the end, was the result. To forestall the jeers which, at a later date, the
German Press of Paris and that of Vichy were to hurl at me, should I
have said, 'We shall be conquered because we are the weaker'?

But in the Chamber I spoke in a different strain. On December 13,
1939, I told the deputies, 'It is easy, very easy for us to lose this war. . . .
It is quite possible for the struggle, which has begun in a kind of apathy,
to finish in a general conflagration. Perhaps, in the darkest days—for
these will come—our ideals of liberty and of well-being will exist only
in our hearts, but they will continue there, deep-rooted and ready to
blossom once more when the days of trial are ended.' Some days later
I warned the Senate that 'France will pay', and I added, 'Time has no
favourites. It will be on the side of the stronger.'

In March, 1940, after the surrender of Finland, I succeeded to the
Presidency of the Council. To sustain French morale, which I could
feel was ebbing, I magnified the Narvik operation, which was to be our
only success during the spring campaigns of 1940. I asserted that the
permanent road to the iron ore deposits, that is to say, the route open
both winter and summer to the minerals which Germany was seeking
in the north of Sweden to supply the steel-works of the Ruhr, had been
cut. It was so, indeed, until the day when the collapse of the French
front forced our Command to recall its troops from Narvik.

To emphasize this naval success, which the brilliant feat of arms by our
light infantry and Foreign Legion was to confirm, seemed an intolerable
thing to those who found in defeat a surly kind of enjoyment. Thence
sprang the silly jestings of Vichy about the road to the iron.

On April 9, 1940, I opposed the plan, settled upon some five months
before by the Allies, to move our defensive Army from its entrench-
ments into Belgium, to face in open country the Wehrmacht[1] and
its Panzer divisions, supported by their Stukas.[2]

The Commander-in-Chief objected that he had himself to shoulder
certain responsibilities. Control of operations was, indeed, by law his
especial province. I decided to relieve General Gamelin of his command. The German offensive of May 10 prevented my doing this, and
it was my fate, as head of the Government, to witness the military
catastrophe that I had described in detail before the Chamber on
March 15, 1935, and January 26, 1937.

The front collapsed. I made preparations to continue the struggle in
North Africa.

On June 10 I telegraphed President Roosevelt: 'We shall fight in
front of Paris. We shall fight behind Paris. . . . We shall go to North
Africa and, if need be, to our American possessions.'

[1] *Wehrmacht*: armed forces. In practice the word *Wehrmacht* was applied to the regular
troops of the ground army.
[2] *Stuka*: dive-bomber.

Pétain and Weygand, to whom I had appealed to restore the morale of commanders and rank and file, wanted France to capitulate.

On June 13 I branded the supporters of surrender on the wireless. 'Our race', I told the nation, 'does not allow itself to be overthrown by an invasion. . . . During the great ordeals of our history, our people have known days when faint-hearted counsels have confused them. Their greatness lies in their refusal to abandon the fight.'

At Bordeaux, three days later, the two men whom I had called upon to take their seats in my Cabinet as Vice-Presidents of the Council, Pétain and Chautemps, placed themselves in opposition to me, heading those who favoured an armistice; these hourly grew more numerous. Further government was impossible with such men. Churchill, in the name of the Alliance, exerted pressure on the President of the Republic to entrust me with the task of forming another Ministry which would strive to keep France in the war. But M. Lebrun asked me to support the proposal of Chautemps, namely that of asking from the enemy his conditions for an armistice. I refused. I repeated my refusal in the presence of the Presidents of the Chambers.

Pétain took over power and asked immediately for an armistice. As we had opposed the armistice, Mandel and I were arrested on a secret warrant issued by the Ministry. We were vilified by the Press and the radio of both Paris and Vichy, without being able to utter a single word in our own defence.

In 1941 Abetz conceived the idea of having us shot. On November 20, 1942, a detachment of S.S.[1] came to the fort of Portalet, where we were imprisoned, and asked for the two prisoners to be surrendered. Pétain handed us over. We were in the hands of the Gestapo.[2]

In July, 1944, the Allied victories were sounding the death-knell to German hopes. Hitler cast about for someone upon whom to revenge himself for his doomed hopes. He thought of Mandel, Blum and myself. He decided upon our death, but intended to let Vichy bear the responsibility for our execution. Why was Mandel his only victim? I do not know.

Such, in brief, were my struggles before and during the Second World War.

[1] S.S., the customary abbreviation of *Schutzstaffel*, security troops: it is well known that Hitler founded his tyranny on the action of praetorian formations who vied with each other in fanaticism and cruelty. The S.A. (*Sturmabteilung*, or storm troops), the Brown militia were, after the bloody June 30, 1934, ousted by the S.S., the Black militia, a real army within the army. To the S.S. fell the duties of executioners to the régime. Independent of the Wehrmacht and in opposition to it, it was their duty to supervise it, to exact from it, if need be, obedience, to permit no flinching on the battlefield, to share in military operations at the most exposed places and at decisive moments, to crush with the utmost brutality any shadow of resistance, whether within Germany herself or in the subjugated territories.

[2] The customary abbreviation of *Geheimstaatspolizei*, the Secret State Police. It is well known that the Gestapo was the most cruel of all the instruments of the Nazi régime.

They were closely linked with the failure to prepare for the war, and with its actual direction.

Thus, they are of interest to history and perhaps offer a lesson for the solution of the grave problems of today.

As a deputy I took part in the great pre-war parliamentary debates.

From April, 1938, to June 16, 1940, the day when the armistice was asked for, I was a member of the Government.

As President of the Council from March, 1940, and responsible through this office for the running of the war, I conferred with Churchill, Roosevelt, Pierlot, Spaak, with the Ambassadors of the Powers, with the President of the Republic, with the Presidents of the Chambers, with Ministers and with our military leaders.

Circumstances have thus willed that I alone should gather within my hands the elements of the decisions to be taken.

The reader will doubtless judge that I owe my testimony to history.

CHAPTER I

THE WORLD ECONOMIC CRISIS CARRIES
HITLER TO POWER

*What was the World Economic Crisis?—The Crisis carries Hitler
to Power.*

WHAT WAS THE WORLD ECONOMIC CRISIS?

I F one were to collect together within a classroom the statesmen of
every country in the world, and give these elderly schoolboys the
task of writing twenty-five lines on the causes of the Second World
War, many of them would answer: 'At Versailles the victors made a
new Europe. After that, they went their separate ways. France remained
alone on the Continent, facing Germany. Each time the Anglo-Saxons
intervened it was to prevent France from compelling the Reich to
honour the promises it had given. The humanitarianism of the French
did the rest. The olive branch of Versailles was thus plucked of its
leaves, one by one. The League of Nations became powerless: it was
unable to oppose the aggression of the Japanese in China; of the Italians
in Abyssinia; of the Germans, first in Austria, then in Czechoslovakia,
and finally in Poland.

'In Germany, Hitler had arisen, a man sprung from the ranks of the
people, who embodied the opposition to Versailles, and promised the
German nation the sweetest of all revenges—the enslavement of
Europe. This powerful nation, proud of having held the world at bay
for four years, humiliated by its defeat and the ensuing abasement,
dedicated itself body and soul to the one who restored to it its strength
and its pride. At the price of immense effort, Germany built up the
most formidable killing machine that the world had ever known.

'Faced with this growing menace the victors remained passive. Hitler
buried Austria, keystone of the Europe of Versailles, then Czechoslovakia. To drive France and England into drawing the sword, he had
to fall upon Poland, and demonstrate to the blindest of eyes that the
independence of Europe appeared imperilled. On September 1, 1939,
the new war, which was to steep the world in blood for nearly six
years, broke out.'

Such an explanation ignores, in my opinion, a decisive factor. That Hitler was the offspring of Versailles there can be no doubt; but he owed his breath to the world economic crisis of 1929.

This is how I depicted this crisis in 1936: 'The oceans were deserted, the ships laid up in the silent ports, the factory smoke-stacks dead, long files of workless in the towns, poverty throughout the countryside. Argentine saw the wheat and livestock prices collapse; Brazil, the price of coffee; America, that of corn and of cotton; Malaya, of rubber; Cuba, of sugar, and Burma, of rice. Then came the stage when wealth was destroyed. The Brazilians threw their sacks of coffee into the sea, and the Canadians burned their corn in railway engines. Just as a man, leaving a house at a moment's notice, burns his papers, civilization seemed to destroy, before disappearing, the wealth it had created. Men questioned the value of what they had learned to admire and respect. Women became less fertile. . . . The crisis was even more general and prolonged than the war. Nations were economically cut off from one another, but they shared in common the lot of poverty.'

What was the cause of the evil? During the First World War, whilst the countries that were fighting had to slow down their production, the young nations developed their own lands to supply the combatants in return for the price of gold. Take as an example the American giant. From 1913 to 1919 the annual production of corn rose in the United States from seven hundred and sixty-three to nine hundred and fifty-two million bushels; that of steel, from twenty-six to forty-two million tons.

After the war Europe rebuilt herself. In ten years she regained her productive capacity of 1913. Failing to appreciate this essential fact, the young countries indulged in the debauchery of stupendous credit transactions. In 1933, the American farmers piled up debts of more than eight milliard dollars in order to improve their machinery and raise their output. Nor was it sufficient to grant huge credits only to producers. These credits were also offered to consumers. Here is one example: the motor industry, the most important in the United States, sold on credit seventy per cent of its output.

In 1929 world production exceeded that of 1913 by fifty per cent. Why should one be surprised, therefore, that from the year before this the price of raw materials, and especially of agricultural products, began to wilt?

Coming back from a trip to America at the beginning of October, 1929, I was interviewed by *Le Temps* about the economic situation in the United States. I replied that a country in which agriculture was not prospering, where the textile industry was having a bad time, where the motor industry was beginning to experience difficulties, and where, as a result, the steel industry, whose principal customer it is, was also beginning to feel the pinch, was a country which could spring any surprises.

A few weeks later, on October 24, came Black Friday[1] on the New York Stock Exchange, when brokers streamed out in confusion, with clothes in tatters and collars torn off. Prices had collapsed. It was the tocsin that heralded the greatest economic crisis in history.

Prices were collapsing; production was to collapse. In 1929, production of steel was around fifty-six million tons. In 1933 it was no more than thirteen. The number of unemployed exceeded twelve million. The price of corn fell to thirty-three cents a bushel. It was, the newspapers stressed, the lowest price since the days of Christopher Columbus. Farmers could no longer meet their financial commitments. Banks became insolvent by the thousand. Poverty stalked the streets. Disorder followed. The evil spread rapidly throughout the whole world. Everywhere, it went hand in hand with the same symptoms and the same effects.

THE CRISIS CARRIES HITLER TO POWER

The crisis was of unparalleled violence in Germany. From six hundred and fifty thousand in August, 1928, the number of workless rose to two million and three hundred thousand in 1929, to three million five hundred thousand in 1930, and to six million by the end of 1932. It was from this mass that Hitler and the Communists recruited their troops. The Brown army of Hitler challenged the Red army. Both deployed in the streets, and fought real pitched battles. Blood flowed.

At the last General Election before the crisis, that of May, 1928, Hitler had still only twelve seats, whilst in 1924 the 'Germany for the Germans' group of Ludendorff had eighty-two. Now on October 13, 1930, a hundred and seven Nazi uniformed deputies, marching in step, were entering the Reichstag. In February, 1932, Hitler gained nearly thirty-seven per cent of the votes. To a correspondent of *The Times* the Führer stated at Munich that his success was due to the economic crisis. The electoral manifesto of the Party ran, 'Hitler is the last hope of those bereft of everything.'

In July, 1932, the Nazi Party was already the most powerful in the Reichstag. To check this advance, the 'red terror' unloosed a series of bloody skirmishes in the country. It turned out to be a stroke of good business for the Nazis, who were able to pose as the champions of order against the Communists.

On January 30, 1933, Hindenburg called Hitler to power. At the

[1] October 24, 1929, was in actual fact a Thursday. But the expression 'Black Friday' is a current phrase in the U.S.A. for a catastrophic collapse in the Stock Exchange prices, to commemorate the 'Black Friday' of American history, or Friday, September 24, 1869, which was indelibly marked on the Stock Exchange by a sudden and exceptionally severe fall in market values.

elections of March 5, the Nazis gained only two hundred and eighty-eight seats, whilst the opposition appropriated three hundred and fifty-nine, of which eighty went to the Communist Party. Hitler did not hesitate: he outlawed the Communist Party, and thus gained, although by only a narrow margin, an absolute majority.

On March 21, the Reichstag met. The very next day Hitler implemented the fine promise he had made to the electorate. He tabled a Bill for the 'alleviation of the poverty of the people and the Reich', and asked for full powers over four years, in order to 'save the German peasantry, and to absorb the unemployed into the channels of productive effort'. Hitler's first task was indeed to fight the crisis. The Bill was passed by four hundred and forty-one votes, ninety-four Socialists voting against it. Hitler turned upon them: 'Now, I have no longer any need of you.' He suppressed all political parties except his own; from that time the Führer held complete power within his hands.

He enacted social measures for the benefit of the workers. He linked the national problem with the social by showing the people that his policy of dictatorship would allow him to raise the nation's standard of living. He gave the worker the stimulus necessary for good morale; first by controlling the management and the profits of the employer, then by exercising his ingenuity to give the worker the benefits of open-air life, physical culture, hydrotherapy, travel. Until then all these advantages had been the privileges of the employer. German labour rolled up its sleeves!

Schacht was given by the Führer the task of putting the German charger on its feet, and at the same time of loading on its back the burden of colossal rearmament.

It was a difficult undertaking.

Schacht was completely successful. He had been making preparations for the task long ago under the Weimar régime. What were his politics? Socialist? Certainly not Socialist; he jealously preserved the powerful incentive of private enterprise; he limited the distribution of profits, but not their reinvestment; he settled labour disputes through the channels of authority.

To arm his country to the utmost, Schacht sealed off its life within a closed cell, and cut it adrift from the rest of the world. The mental state of the German people, to whom Hitler had said, 'Money is filth', made this policy easier.

The Germans heard of nothing but 'sacrifices', and they agreed to tighten their belts. The *ersatz* became the symbol of Teutonic patriotism.

The Army that Hitler forged had a definite objective. It was the instrument with which to achieve the policy laid down by *Mein Kampf*. To fashion this Army, Hitler exacted from the German people more than anyone else had ever done. Whilst William II, in preparation for the previous war, had squeezed the German lemon with his fingers, Hitler did so with a lemon-squeezer supplied with a powerful lever arm. He made Germany become self-supporting. He made her live and toil to attain the end he pointed out to her in *Mein Kampf*.

Thus, German economy was to supply German soldiers with the sinews of modern war; it was ready to stand up to blockade. As for the German soul, *Mein Kampf* and the speeches of the Führer would provide for it. The muscles of the Teutonic athlete had been greased.

CHAPTER II

1933–6. THE WORLD CRISIS WEAKENS FRANCE AND DIVIDES FRENCHMEN

The Crisis hits France.—Georges Bonnet and Germain-Martin imitate Snowden.—Flandin imitates Hoover.—Laval imitates Brüning.

THE CRISIS HITS FRANCE

IN France the crisis, which came tardily, was, through our own fault, aggravated and prolonged. Up to the end of 1938 it had extinguished the blast-furnaces, crippled the mines, sapped our finances, driven abroad our gold, put the brake upon our rearmament, stirred up disorders, disturbed our political life, alarmed our allies in Europe.

How was it that France, though fortunate enough to be affected the last, had not learned a lesson from the experience of so many other countries? Let us go back to 1934, the year in which I put before the Chamber and public opinion the monetary problem which the world economic crisis set our own country like the rest.

We had witnessed many experiments. France had seen the Socialist Snowden in England fail with the policy of 'wait and see' to solve the economic problem, and with his financial reforms to reduce the public expenditure. She had witnessed the Conservative Hoover in the U.S.A. fail in his attempt to exorcize the evil with injections of credit. She had seen Brüning in Germany fail in his effort to reduce cost prices below sale prices. Our French rulers, from all these tragic mishaps, had not drawn any lesson, much less one from the return to prosperity of nations which had devalued their currency.

They had refused to understand that, with us as elsewhere, the solution of the problem lay in devaluation, which alone could revive production by raising prices and thus restoring profits. The sight of thirty-five nations, who had devalued their currency, first convalescing and then recovering, left them indifferent.

At least our rulers might have revealed some shreds of originality in the choice of their mistakes and thus given evidence of some personal attempt to solve the problem in their own way. But, no doubt, this would have been asking too much of them, for, until the *Front Populaire* Administration came into power they were satisfied to copy idly the faults of others, whilst showing surprise, not without an ingenuousness, that these reproduced in France the same results as elsewhere. Georges Bonnet in 1933 and Germain-Martin in 1934 followed in Snowden's footsteps; Flandin, in the first half of 1935, in those of Hoover, and Laval, in the latter half, in those of Brüning. And, because France failed to make a monetary reform with due deliberation in good time, she was panicked into making it willy-nilly in September, 1936, and into repeating it on two separate occasions, until the franc had finally to be devalued twice as much as would have been necessary in 1934![1]

It was through the fall on the Bourse that Frenchmen learned of the existence of the crisis, several weeks after the Black Friday of Wall Street. Our Bourse prices fell like others, dragged down by others, although our economy was not yet stricken. But Frenchmen only saw a phenomenon, purely local and accidental, a problem of internal politics. Bourse prices, they said in 1930, fell because members of the Bourse wished to see the Left in power: the Bourse was a supporter of political cartels.

I was then Minister of Finance. Questioned in March by Marcel Hutin of *L'Echo de Paris* on this alleged support by the Bourse of government by cartels, I replied, 'It is a question of a world-wide phenomenon.' But were the French going to take in their sails before the tempest which was blowing up on the horizon? Oh, no! This interview caused a sensation. I was accused of defeatism. A financial journalist cited for my benefit the optimism of Hoover, who asserted that prosperity was 'round the corner'. Flandin, my fellow Minister of Commerce, became indignant at hearing me talk of a lengthening of the crisis, and concluded, 'The crisis is behind us.' As for *L'Action Française*,[2] it accused me quite bluntly of wishing to bring off some speculation on the Bourse.

Yet, unaffected by this excitement, the crisis got worse. In that same year, 1930, the gold price index of raw materials fell from eighty-three to fifty-nine.

[1] Contrary to widespread opinion, I did not give way to any devaluation during my term of office at the Ministry of Finance, between November, 1938 and March, 1940. I only revalued, on two occasions, the gold reserves of the Bank of France. I had found the franc pegged to the pound, which itself had fallen in relation to gold.

[2] *L'Action Française* was the journal of the *Comité d'Action Française*. This body was founded in April, 1898: it opposed the existing parliamentary form of the Republic, and favoured a strong authoritarian government. Later the movement became Royalist in character, first (1901) favouring the Orléans pretender, and on his death in 1926, the Duc de Guise (who subsequently disavowed it). In the 1930s it was a strong opponent of the *Front Populaire*. It supported the Vichy régime of Marshal Pétain, and was naturally proscribed on the Liberation [Tr.].

The world crisis hit us in 1931. Our colonial empire, the producer of raw materials, had been affected from the start. As Minister of the Colonies I went to Indo-China where the hard times, resulting from the crisis, had aroused, in the north of Annam, riots in which blood was shed.

On the boat the journalists who went with me on my trip told me, on September 21, that the pound had gone off the gold standard. Some of them seemed to think of this devaluation as a kind of revenge for the franc, which had been so badly knocked about from 1920 to 1926. I told them, 'Don't be too pleased about this. It is an event of world-wide importance, pregnant with consequences for ourselves.' French opinion was wrong no less than they were. It believed that British economy alone would be affected by the fall in the gold value of the pound. Our orthodox economists declared that the cost of living was going to rise in England, and that it would be the turn of that country to writhe in the convulsions which are the usual sequel to a rise in the cost of living. The effects were immediately felt by our own economy. Our prices based on gold quickly exceeded those current in England. French economy, sheltered until then by the moderation of such prices, saw the British protective screen collapse, and caught the full force of the world crisis squall.

In 1932 the crisis continued to worsen. The sorely tried taxpayer contributed less to the Exchequer. The problem was to balance the Budget. The Ministers grew alarmed. They proposed economies and new taxes, quite a reasonable thing to do; but people do not like economies or taxes, and deputies have to take heed of the electorate. Ministries fell one after another. There was no question of tackling the evil at its root. One merely confined oneself to noting with a feeling of melancholy that the wholesale prices had fallen by a third after four years, and industrial production by twenty-two per cent.

GEORGES BONNET AND GERMAIN-MARTIN IMITATE SNOWDEN

From 1928 to 1933 the gold index of world prices fell from a hundred to thirty-seven. In November, 1932, Roosevelt came into power. Previous indications foreshadowed the devaluation of the dollar. It was the opportunity for us to depreciate our currency in step with the greatest economic power in the world. If we did not do so, what would happen? Goods, sold for dollars on the world market, would be worth less in terms of gold. World prices would therefore lower *in terms of gold*. Already British prices were lower, *in terms of gold*, than French prices, because the latter were expressed in francs, which repre-sented the same amount of gold as before the crisis. Undergoing the attraction of world prices, French prices were to fall still more. Now, their fall had already eliminated the profit of many businesses. There were to be new bankruptcies, more factories closed down, thousands more workers to suffer unemployment. This was especially so as our exports were to meet greater resistance since, in the world markets, goods sold for gold francs were to be dearer than American goods sold for depreciated dollars.

To keep unchanged the gold parity of the franc, amongst other currencies whose gold parity had been reduced, was the same as increasing the gold parity of the franc amongst currencies which had remained unchanged.

To maintain that the franc could win in a struggle from which the dollar, after three years' resistance, had just withdrawn, was absurd. I offer my apologies for the word, but it is the only one that meets the case.

An exhibition of this absurdity was what we were to give the world in the three and a half years that succeeded the devaluation of the dollar. I never stopped uttering my protests against it.

Let us now see how our rulers went to work. In 1933, Georges Bonnet, Minister of Finance in the Daladier Cabinet, followed the 'wait and see' policy of Snowden.

Roosevelt had understood the situation. On April 26 he announced 'the necessity for an increase in the general level of raw material prices'. And, having understood, he had the courage to act. On May 12 the dollar was unpegged from gold, and after some fluctuation was finally devalued by forty-one per cent, like the pound sterling.

The depreciation of the dollar was to benefit the U.S.A. as much as devaluation in the currencies of other countries had already benefited them. Those who consider that the economic recovery of the U.S.A. was due above all to legislation which followed the monetary operation, part of which was annulled by the Supreme Court, should be reminded that recovery was even more outstanding in Canada, where conditions were identical to those of her great neighbour; yet in Canada no legislative steps were taken.

In Paris our orthodox economists waxed indignant. Joseph Barthélemy, of the Academy of Moral and Political Sciences, prophesied that in eight days Roosevelt's goose would be cooked. But, unintimidated by this prophecy, Roosevelt remained in office, getting ready to beat all records for presidential longevity.

In June, 1933, there was an Economic Conference in London. The countries which had devalued were benefiting from the rise of wholesale prices in their depreciated currency. But there remained a centre of depression in the world. It was the island of blocked gold in which the five countries who had not devalued vegetated: France, Belgium, Holland, Switzerland and Italy. The British Delegation stressed, in its proposed resolution, the need to 'stimulate a recovery in the level of wholesale goods prices, sufficient to give the producer a normal profit,' and it added that, in order to achieve this, 'one of the essential factors is monetary action'. In other words, it counselled devaluation, for was not this the real meaning of the words? Was not this the lesson of experience which, according to the wisdom of nations, surpasses knowledge?

The French Delegation, headed by Bonnet, did not judge the above to be the case. It considered that it was quite natural that the franc should remain divorced from the dollar. The question of finding out if French prices had ceased to be remunerative, if the peasant was forced to sell two beasts instead of one to pay his debts, and if factories were closing their doors when the employer was tired of working at a loss, seemed to it insignificant compared with the sacred duty, as it appeared, of maintaining, whatever might happen or whatever other countries of the world did, the franc at a parity of sixty-five and a half milligrams of fine gold.

In London the Conference broke up without having accomplished anything. The countries who had devalued went back to their growing prosperity; the others to ruin, which increased apace. But in his Report for 1934 the Governor of the Bank of France took a lofty attitude towards those countries which were permitting themselves to avoid ruin and revolution by curtailing the sharply increased purchasing power of their currency, like a surgeon who cuts out a tumour. It was only a case, he asserted, of 'illusory and precarious improvements, soon to be followed by disillusion'.

Yet, our prices having fallen, *in francs*, below the retail price, more factories put up their shutters. And, as our prices were amongst the highest in the world *in gold*, our export of manufactured goods decreased forty per cent in volume, compared with those of 1928, whilst imports of these same goods did not fall. French economy was thrown out of gear.

Two governments were overthrown because they proposed timid economies which, powerless to cure the evil, would only have softened the least of its blows.

As like causes produce like effects, the economic difficulties produced, in France as elsewhere, social unrest. In the political sphere, the suffering caused by the crisis had the result of helping the propaganda of all the enemies of the existing régime.

Rebels arose from both the Right and the Left. The peaceful Conservatives of yesterday became roaring lions. The Right-wing leagues organized great motor-car political rallies.

The former Communist, Doriot, backed by Marion, himself also a former Communist, raised troops.

There was the *Cagoule*.[1] There were the *Francistes*.[2]

Finally, on February 6, 1934, as a result of a scandal implicating a Levantine swindler, Stavisky, and an obscure deputy, Bonnaure, the tradesmen of Paris, exasperated by the crisis, rioted. *L'Action Française* and the Communists came to the point of blows. There were deaths. Daladier resigned office. Capital took flight and, as a result, so did the gold in the Bank of France.

On the morrow of February 6, Doumergue appeared as a saviour, flanked by Edouard Herriot and Tardieu as Ministers of State, and accompanied by Pétain as War Minister and Germain-Martin as Finance Minister. Capital returned, but the economic situation continued to worsen. Doumergue never even asked himself what had been the cause of the rioting.

I went to see Germain-Martin, who in 1930 had been my colleague as Minister of the Budget when I myself was Minister of Finance. I tried to convince him of the need for devaluing the franc. I only succeeded in shocking him. I then saw Tardieu who, satisfied with the re-establishment of order and the return of gold, answered, 'But everything is turning out fine.'

As a last resource, I ended by taking the question to the floor of the Chamber on June 28, 1934. I drew for the Chamber a picture of the revival of thirty-five countries which had devalued. I contrasted their state with that of the increasing poverty of those who at that time I used to call the 'sick men of the "gold-block" hospital'.

I summed up: 'In all the gold-block countries, exports are falling, factories are closing down, unemployment is increasing, tradesmen are going bankrupt, fiscal returns are diminishing; whilst the British Chancellor of the Exchequer has the satisfaction of reducing the burdens of his taxpayers.'

Faced with this situation, what did the Government do? It followed the same policy as its predecessors, namely, 'two contradictory policies: it wished at the same time to bolster up the currency and to keep up prices'.

We were now in utter chaos. It was imperative that we should get out of the mess, and the only means of doing this was devaluation.

'But isn't it a regrettable thing to tinker about with currency?' people said.

[1] The *Cagoule* or *Comités Secrets d'Action Révolutionnaire*, founded in 1936, was a military organization with para-revolutionary aims. It was subsidized by Germany, Italy and Franco Spain. Following acts of terrorism in 1937, the *Cagoule* was broken up, and its leaders imprisoned [Tr.].

[2] The *Francistes* were founded on August 9, 1933. They constituted one of the smaller anti-parliamentarian leagues of the period, and were in favour of a *rapprochement* with Germany. On June 18, 1936, they were dissolved by the Blum Government, but reformed in November, 1938, as the *Parti Unitaire Français d'Action Socialiste et Nationale*, which supported the Vichy régime [Tr.].

Of course it is regrettable. But is it not more regrettable to let bankruptcies pile up, industry come to a stop, workers be thrown on the street?

We had thus a social obligation to perform a surgical operation. Legally we had the right to do it.

But does justice authorize us to do it? My reply was: 'The investor will say, "You are going to plunder me once again. What will be left of my miserable franc which is worth four sous?" It is not a question of that at all. What do we owe in justice to the investor, to the official, to the retired, to the pensioner? We owe it to them—apart from circumstances beyond our control such as war—not to lower the purchasing power of the monetary unit in which we pay them. We do not owe them in any wise a monetary unit whose purchasing power is increased.'

I concluded by warning the Government that 'the policy, followed during the last two years, would lead to a compulsory and not voluntary devaluation, to an operation which would be taken not in a calculated, but in a hasty fashion'. That, unfortunately, is what happened twenty-seven months later.

The French peasant, so calm and restrained, was becoming bitter, for he no longer had the means of keeping his house in order. As for the industrialist, he no longer had the wherewithal to write off his plant: equipment was in a state of utter neglect; specialists were scattered to the winds; a spirit of revolt and rancour was in the hearts of the working masses. The destruction of the country's war potential and the breaking of its morale gave ammunition to foreign propaganda. And at what a time! But the authors of this policy did not believe themselves one whit responsible for our grave lack of preparedness for the war which was coming. War, however, was all the more assured the less we were prepared.

The political parties were of a single mind, for once. All of them exploited the unpopularity of a measure which was so decried. From the Communists to the extreme Right, all vied with one another to fall into line.

Such was, in France, the attitude of the *élite*.

FLANDIN IMITATES HOOVER

By aggravating and prolonging the crisis instead of ending it, the Doumergue Ministry emasculated our industry, precipitated our financial ruin, and thus made more difficult for its successors the task of rearming France.

On November 8, 1934, Flandin came into power. The crisis developed inexorably. Was France at last to understand its nature?

Flandin, also helped by Germain-Martin, decided to boost wholesale prices. What Doumergue had done timidly he was going to do with more boldness and skill. He stepped on the accelerator, and the car set off quickly in the wrong direction. For, to raise French prices in terms of non-devalued francs (that is to say, in gold), prices which were already the highest in the world, was a pernicious step which would lead to inescapable catastrophe.

To raise the level of prices, Flandin resorted to two methods: he cut down French production and the amount of foreign goods coming into France; he prohibited wealth, whether it was produced in France or abroad. That is what he called 'adjusting production to consumption and making the market more healthy'. These were pleasant euphemisms. This was the ideal put before the country: produce as little as possible, and sell as dearly as you can. 'We have too much corn, too much wine, too much meat and too much milk. That is why prices touched bottom,' proclaimed the Minister of Agriculture on December 15, 1934, before the Senate.

And what about industrial prices? Didn't they collapse as well, in francs which had become too dear? In January, 1935, Flandin tabled a Bill the object of which was to reduce industrial production. Here were the aims which he set himself, exactly as he uttered them:[1]

1. The restriction or temporary stoppage of productive methods.
2. The adaptation of these to the internal and external situation of the market.
3. *The limitation of working hours.*
4. *Collective contract of work.*
5. The stock-piling of goods. . . .

He evidently meant to demonstrate in 1937 that on these two points[2] he had been the forerunner of the *Front Populaire*.

So there we were in the full swing of the doctrine of restraint. Two years after Hitler's advent into power Flandin attached such importance to the Bill that he made it a question of confidence before the Chamber. The Senate had the wisdom to bury his proposals. Thereupon, Flandin declared that he was the victim of 'powerful interests'.

Flandin's Bill had foundered, but the spirit of restraint remained in favour. France had an additional ailment.

Still trying to increase prices, Flandin adopted what was later to be called[3] a 'judicious and systematic utilization of quotas and of Customhouse dues'. This policy contributed even more to isolate France from the world. To prevent the flow of goods manufactured abroad at cheaper rates in gold than the French prices, the Customs dues were no

---

[1] *Discours* (collected edition published in 1937), Preface, p. 33. The italics are those of the author.   [2] i.e. those in italics [Tr.].   [3] *Discours*, p. 33.

longer of any avail. We were only taking from each country the quantity of goods they imported from us before the crisis.

The originality in the 'Flandin experiment' consisted in reviving in France the Hoover experiment of 1932, by infusing credit into our economy. For this purpose Flandin placed a new Governor at the head of the Bank of France, Tannery, whom he encouraged to permit a liberal discount on Treasury Bonds.

The real problem did not lie in this. An economic system does not absorb credits, or, at least, does not use them when it does not possess a margin of profit, and such was the case with French economy.

On January 25, 1935, I intervened during a debate in the Chamber on this policy. I remarked that in the France of 1935, as in the United States of 1932, 'it was not so much good debtors lacking credit, it was credit lacking good debtors'. I made a frontal attack on our orthodox economists. 'We have come to a pretty pass when, in official speeches and in the Press, we see ceaseless sympathy being offered to countries who have devalued. Or, if you like—to put it another way—when, looking at their healthy appearance, and noting, for example, that the number of British unemployed has fallen by a third since devaluation in September, 1931, our official "doctors", like Doctor Knock,[1] say to the country "Look out! Good health is a precarious state, and forebodes nothing good."'

I asked, 'Will it be necessary one day to say: "France was ruined because she did not wish to understand."' And I concluded, 'Don't let us wait until the event becomes too imperious a tyrant.'

Flandin categorically answered me that devaluation was only an 'injection of morphine'; and that countries who had given way to it had become caught up in a vicious circle, for each of them would be led to devalue more and more to gain a temporary advantage over its rivals.

He asserted that devaluation would bring an increase in the cost of living, which would arouse 'indignant protests'. And, taking up against me the defence of 'humanity', he indicated to me, not without a trace of demagogy, 'that the world did not live by bankers and their currency exchange transactions, but by the toil of the "unfortunate"'. Profoundly true; but that is exactly the reason why work must be found for these 'unfortunates', instead of following a policy which throws them out of work. Now, the number of unemployed was soaring in France, whilst in Great Britain it was falling. So much for the 'unfortunates'. And the cost of living had decreased in Great Britain since the devaluation of 1931. So much for the 'indignant protests'. Not

---

[1] The chief character in *Knock ou le Triomphe de la Médecine*, a comedy by J. Romains (1923). Knock's principle was that anyone in a state of good health was really without knowing it a sick man [Tr.].

only was the devaluation of the dollar not harmful to British economy, but from 1933 to 1937 the index of industrial production, based on one hundred in 1931, rose in Great Britain from one hundred and seven to a hundred and forty-seven. And the dollar had not been more devalued than the pound. So much for the 'vicious circle'. The Flandin plan was passed by the Chambers, but it had little effect.

As for the reserves of gold and the foreign currency of the Bank of France, they had been falling for three years. They were, in November 1931, ninety-one milliard 'Poincaré' francs.[1] In November, 1934, when Flandin came into power, they had already fallen to eighty-two milliards. It was time to stop this bleeding. Yet it was to become more profuse. In the following June, the reserves were to amount to seventy-one milliards; and in September, 1936, no more than fifty-two milliards. That is what this policy cost us in gold and foreign currency.

The Flandin Ministry was swept out of office on May 30 by this flight of gold, after a pathetic debate during which the Finance Minister resigned without trying to defend a policy which the facts were condemning, and the President of the Council took his place to continue that policy. After this, by entering the Administration of his successor, Flandin identified himself with the policy of deflation, one directly contrary to that he had just been pursuing.

During the debate I informed the Chamber that devaluation was not a policy but the requisite condition of any policy. I had, I believed, convinced the Chamber of the need for devaluation. It overthrew the Government by a large majority, but it did not dare to impose on Laval, the successor of Flandin, a policy which alone could enable us to escape disaster. As for myself, my campaign on behalf of devaluation prevented me from taking office in the Government for several years, and placed my seat in jeopardy during the electoral contest of 1936. During this election one of my opponents had put up a poster showing a gold louis, which a criminal hand had partly clipped. I was narrowly elected on the second ballot by a twenty-seven vote majority.

LAVAL IMITATES BRÜNING

After the set-back of Flandin's experiment, did France see the light? Unfortunately, no! For, if Flandin trod in the footsteps of Hoover, Laval was to follow in those of Brüning. Like the latter, he tried to lower cost prices below selling prices. To do this, he broke contracts, reduced by ten per cent rents, salaries, pensions and even dividends on Government stock.

Flandin's policy had provoked, I have said, a rise in prices which became marked under Laval, and more so under Sarraut on the eve

[1] i.e francs as devalued by Poincaré in 1928 [Tr.].

of the May elections of 1936. So here was the worker, partially employed, totally unemployed, or suffering a cut of ten per cent in his
salary; for the employers had followed the example of the State. What
was more, at the same time, the worker saw meat go up in price.
Never was confusion so much confounded. Lucien Romier wrote in
Le Figaro, 'The Laval experiment will succeed if the cutlet comes down
and incomes go up.' By a distressing interchange of positions the cutlet
went up and incomes came down.

In the midst of this situation, a financial debate took place in the
Chamber on November 29, 1935, several weeks before the resignation
of Laval. I came back once again to the dangers that were inherent in
the over-valuation of our currency. 'Over-valued currency', I said, 'is
followed by a horde of speculators, as wounded game is tracked down
by wolves.' I reminded the Chamber of the warning I had given it on
May 30, the day after the fall of Flandin, and I said: 'I have a profound
belief that we are now rushing headlong into greater perils.'

But the Government continued in the country its campaign against
devaluation. Just as Flandin invoked the defence of the 'unfortunates',
so Laval took up the cause of the 'weak' and the 'humble'.

I replied, 'Stop talking to us about the crushing of the weak and
humble. . . . Has not the British investor—cheated, it would seem
—realized, since 1931, a capital profit as a result of the rise of State
funds, due to a recovery in business, and to Budget surpluses? Has not
this investor gained seventy-five per cent of his capital, whilst his
French counterpart, holding four per cent 1917 stock—protected, it
would seem—lost twenty-eight per cent of his?'

And, as the Governor of the Bank of France had just maintained that
a recovery was about to take place in France as in Great Britain,
because, he said, the same causes produce the same effects, I recalled
the rise in wholesale prices in Great Britain that occasioned no rise in
the cost of living, and added, 'To assert that all this is nothing . . . to
maintain that a forty-one per cent devaluation of the pound is negligible, to assert that the British experiment has only comprised deflation
—in effect to ruin the country—is bad enough; but to cast a slur on its
intelligence, that is intolerable.'

To conclude, I stressed the grave peril to which such a policy was
subjecting the régime, 'We do not want to have our youth in a state of
despair. We do not want to have a weakened France. . . .'

The Chamber applauded, but it did not reverse this policy, as it was
its duty to do. It knuckled under to the pressure of our so-called *élite*.

I was alone in the Chamber in stressing the need for aligning the
franc with the devalued pound and dollar. All the authorities of the
University and the Institute opposed me. I must, however, pay tribute
to the honorary Governor of the Bank of France, M. Charles Rist,

who wrote on August 1, 1952: 'I willingly admit that I was one of those most strongly in favour of maintaining the rate at which, after much hard work and many difficulties, the franc had just been stabilized. When, a little later, M. Paul Reynaud, with remarkable perspicacity, asserted that French economy, faced with British and American devaluation, was on an insecure footing, and that it would be advisable once more to adjust the level of the franc to the new financial rates of the great Anglo-Saxon nations, I made the mistake of not immediately rallying to his support, and not adopting his proposals until some time later when, in 1936, the findings of the Commission on tariffs, of which I was chairman, convinced me of the disadvantageous position in which French economy was being kept by the unreality of the exchange rate.' But that was in 1952.

Through lectures and articles in the Press—in the limited scope to which the pages of the latter were at my disposal, for it was then that I realized how valuable was the floor of the Chamber for free expression of opinion—I was to show the danger of Laval's policy. By cutting down wages whilst causing retail prices to rise, Laval was, I said, making with his own hands an explosive compound.

The explosion took place. The working-class masses began to suffer more and more. They not only suffered in their material life, they also suffered in their dignity, for the worker was, from the nature of the crisis, at the mercy of the employer. To be sacked by him meant certain unemployment. One must understand all this to realize the enthusiasm raised by the advent to power of the Popular Front.

CHAPTER III

HITLER'S PLAN

'Galli ad gloriam, Germani ad praedam.' Tacitus.

*The Germans always give notice of their intentions.—The Aim.—
The Means.—The Causes of the Set-back.*

THE GERMANS ALWAYS GIVE NOTICE OF THEIR INTENTIONS

Wᴴᴀᴛ is pleasant about the Germans is that when they are preparing an unpleasant shock they always give notice of their intentions. Unfortunately this is of no use as a warning to others, because their plan is so stupendous that nobody believes it possible.

In 1862, Bismarck went to London to inform Disraeli of his plans: 'When the Prussian Army is strong enough, I will take the first opportunity to settle scores with Austria, to dissolve the German Confederation and to unify Germany.' Disraeli whispered in the ear of a friend: 'We must keep an eye on that man. He means to do what he says.' But Disraeli failed to draw any useful conclusion from this.

In 1865, Bismarck went to Biarritz to inform Napoleon III of the national mission Prussia had arrogated to herself. Why? The striking down of Austria was an indispensable preliminary, he was to say later, to settling accounts with France. Napoleon smiled, whilst stroking out his long moustache.

Then came Sadowa.

Then came Sedan, and finally the loss of Alsace-Lorraine.

Similarly, on the eve of 1914 Bernhardi prophesied that war which he considered to be 'inevitable and necessary'. The Pan-German Press warned us that the German people were the salt of the earth, and meant to dominate the world. Hitler was to write in *Mein Kampf* : 'The War of 1914 was not, as God is my witness, in any wise imposed upon our people who were, on the contrary, wholeheartedly behind it. In the opinion of the masses, the tone of the ultimatum to Serbia was far too moderate. . . . It was not to the watchword of *Long live universal suffrage and the secret ballot* that the German youth marched to death

24

through Flanders, but to that of *Germany will lead the world*.' But this time, the fight went badly. It ended in Versailles.

We were even more clearly warned before 1939. The plan was written down in black and white in *Mein Kampf*, the 'Bible of the German People'. Betraying the unchangeable instincts which the Germans carry in their hearts, the plan aimed at resuming the secular struggle by which the Teutonic warriors had succeeded in hurling back the Slavs to the Vistula and to the Niemen.

THE AIM

The conclusion of the book laid down the aim to be realized; the German people had one day to becomes *masters of the world*. For that purpose Germany had to expand. Several stages were envisaged.

First of all came the annexation of Austria, the *Anschluss*. 'The welfare of Teutonism requires as a condition the liquidation of Austria.'

Then, Germany would rush into the conquest of new lands. It was necessary 'to ensure that the German people possessed the territory that was their due'. The first objective was the Ukraine. It was a resumption of the ancestral march towards the East, and the sword, as in former times, would open a way for the plough.

There was no question, as one can see, of fighting Russia to destroy the heart of Communism; the aim was to cut out of the midst of Slavonic soil, to snatch from a nation of a hundred and seventy-five million souls, its very own granary. The living space of Germany was in the possession of others.

THE MEANS

Concerning the necessity of reconquering the provinces, lost in 1918 Hitler wrote:[1] '*What can give us back the lost possessions is the victory of our sword. The forging of this sword must be the task of our internal policy. To allow the iron-smith security for this work and to ensure the co-operation of our brothers-in-arms is the task of our foreign policy.*'

In the expression of such an opinion, Hitler was running true to pure Prussian tradition.

Clausewitz used to say, in the last century, 'Germany can only achieve its political unity by the sword.' After him, Bismarck told the Prussian Diet, 'Important questions are only settled by blood and iron.' Such was the continuity of German policy.

Thus, there was but one method—war. But the lesson of a war on two fronts had not been wasted. Hitler meant to strike France down first, and Russia afterwards: 'Inasmuch as we are all, today, convinced of the need to settle our account with France, so we feel such a settlement

[1] The italics are in the text.

would remain fruitless to us if our foreign policy were satisfied with this objective. Such a settlement should therefore be conceived as intended to cover our rear in order that we can enlarge our territory in Europe.'

What means were to be used in cutting down France? First of all she must be isolated; Great Britain and Italy must be detached from her. Above all, the *Entente*, in Hitler's opinion so deadly to Germany, must be broken. Hitler tried to persuade Great Britain that it was in her interests to break French imperialism. An alliance with this country—and with one that could be more easily achieved, Italy—would allow him, totally undisturbed, to take the first measures preparatory to settling the score with France. 'Thus France, our mortal enemy, would be isolated.'

To undermine the morale of France, Hitler kept her on tenterhooks by forcing her to maintain her Army in a state of readiness and to mobilize it permanently. 'This state of mobilization', he said to Rauschning [*Hitler Speaks*], 'can be imposed by my régime upon Germany for years, without my rule running the risk of being over-thrown. The democracies will be forced to follow us in this policy, but the constraint of permanent mobilization will arouse amongst them social disturbances, which will weaken them. It is then that I shall strike.'

Such was Hitler's plan. All the errors committed by French and British rulers, all their vacillations, their false steps, their surrenders, are to be explained only by their ignorance of *Mein Kampf*. This book, they were told, was out of date. Their attitude was reminiscent of that of Napoleon III. Conscription, remilitarization of the Rhine, annexa-tion of Austria, the dismemberment of Czechoslovakia—how many Sadowas, and what Sadowas they were!

THE CAUSES OF THE SET-BACK

On one point alone the plan was not carried through. From this came Hitler's final check. He did not succeed in detaching Great Britain from France. Aware of their interests, and above all faithful to their word of honour, the British people did not allow themselves to be seduced. Left to fight single-handed in the war, they resisted. Hitler was able to convince himself of the truth of Treitschke's prophecy: 'The last account to be settled, that with Great Britain, will take the longest and be the most difficult.'

America in her turn entered the war. On that score Hitler again deceived himself. Relying on the German-American element in the U.S.A., he used to tell Rauschning, 'We have the means of influencing this nation in good time. There will be no new Wilson arising to stir up America against us.' It was Roosevelt who was to come forward.

Finally, Hitler made another blunder. He did not believe in the Soviet power. He pushed on to the Caucasus, but the Russians drove him back to Berlin.

An example dictated the plan of Hitler, that of the survivor of the Horatii against the Curiatii. He attacked in succession each of the countries he wished to make his prey. After the annexation of Austria, the destruction of Czechoslovakia, the invasion of Poland, it was to be the turn of France, and then, of Russia.

We cannot say that we had not been warned, but, once again, it was of no avail.

CHAPTER IV

THE CHOICE: A BALANCE OF POWER IN
EUROPE OR THE 'RESIGNATION' OF FRANCE?

*Hitler initiates the Armaments Race.—The Four Power Pact.—Hitler
anaesthetizes before striking.—Nazi propaganda in Action.—In France,
Public Opinion, the Parties and the General Confederation of Labour*[1]
are divided into two camps.

HITLER INITIATES THE ARMAMENTS RACE

ON January 30, 1933, Hitler came to power. It was an outburst
of national pride, for Hitler was not only the head of a
powerful party, but even more, the prophet who pointed out
to his people the promised land.

Now to work! But Hitler was cunning: 'Let us build', he said, 'the
foundations of the edifice. Let us train the soldiers of tomorrow in
youth organizations. Let us adapt industry to the production of
armaments, and furnish it with raw materials. The day when our tanks
and planes flow from the factories, and when our youth, fanaticized
and militarized, is ready to enter the army, we shall strike our fist on
the table; we shall re-create the national army, whilst the rulers of the
democracies utter speeches of indignation. In a few years, the hour of
Mein Kampf will sound. Whilst we are awaiting it, let us appease the
French, please them with friendly words, with offers of negotiation,
with proposals for disarmament.'

Benoist-Méchin wrote, in his *Histoire de l'armée allemande:*[2] 'A kind
of frenzy was to take possession of German industry. Within a year,
nearly seventy per cent of the factories were to be fitted out for
producing war equipment.' The machines of these factories had to be
fed. Thus the importation of the necessary raw material for armaments
mounted like an arrow. From 1932 to 1933 that of nickel ore rose from
seventeen thousand tons to thirty-four thousand, that of tungsten ore
from one thousand six hundred to three thousand six hundred. From

[1] *Confédération Générale du Travail,* the General Confederation of Labour, or Amalgamation of Trades Unions, then composed both the Socialist and Communist Unions, and
now (1955) only the latter [Tr.].
[2] Vol. II, p. 530.

28

May to July, 1933, that of cellulose increased from a hundred and ten thousand tons to three hundred and thirty thousand, thus tripling in two months. There was a colossal importation of oil for Army vehicles, of wool, cotton, leather for the clothes and equipment of service men. Germany was stretching her muscles.

THE FOUR POWER PACT

The victims, already marked down by Hitler, persisted in closing their eyes to reality. They flattered themselves that they were allaying the impatience of the Führer by concessions. The first act of appeasement was on June 7, 1933. On that date the treaty of understanding and collaboration called the Four Power Pact was initialled[1] at Rome, between France, Great Britain, Germany and Italy. Paul-Boncour was then Foreign Minister in the Daladier Cabinet.

Mussolini was the one who inspired the Pact, which was aimed at opening a way for the revision of treaties. Paul-Boncour told how, in March, 1933, MacDonald, the British Prime Minister, and Sir John Simon, returning from Rome, informed him one fine morning of the proposal the Duce had submitted to them. 'However unexpected it may seem,' he added,[2] 'MacDonald appears to me to be very struck by Fascism and somewhat attracted by Mussolini.'

Revisionism already claimed in France a number of supporters, who, alarmed by the flood of German grievances against Versailles, were worrying their heads about means of appeasing the dissatisfaction before, as they thought, it would be too late. For they had not read *Mein Kampf*. In 1930, the Radical Party held its Annual Congress at Grenoble. It was shortly after the elections in which the Nazis had registered their first success in the Reichstag. The rise of the Hitler movement left no doubt about the orientation of German public opinion. Yet an influential group within the Congress spoke in favour of a policy of revision.

The Four Power Pact was drawn up in such a setting. For France, Henry de Jouvenel, Ambassador in Rome, was the soul of the negotiations. Paul-Boncour relates[3] how he ended up by agreeing with his 'old friend Jouvenel . . . to explore with the head of the Italian Government, as widely as possible, every basis of understanding, which would not imperil our Mediterranean interests and our other alliances'.

In short, France and Great Britain were agreeing to team themselves with Hitler and Mussolini, not in order to share their repast, but in the hope of moderating their voracity.

In attacking the treaties, the two allies used almost the same

---

[1] The Pact was also to be signed in Rome on July 14, 1933.
[2] *Entre deux guerres*, vol. II, p. 340.   [3] *Ibid.*, pp. 338-9.

language. 'These treaties, which are aimed at ossifying Europe, are hindering the evolution of history. Now, everything points to the fact that the expansion of our two peoples is in harmony with this evolution. Have the good sense to agree to it willingly. As the countries which will have to be carved up will never consent to the necessary changes, let us agree upon forcing them to do so.' The Four Power Pact revealed that the map of Europe, as Versailles had drawn it, was to be revised. The first round had gone to the revisionists.

Revision was to be accomplished without the assent of Russia, who was thus held to be debarred from European affairs. It is true there was an attempt later to negotiate with that country an agreement that guaranteed the eastern frontiers of our allies of the East; it is true, Paul-Boncour laid the foundations of an alliance with Moscow; but was it the best method of allaying the mistrust of the Soviets to solve European problems without their collaboration? For Hitler and Mussolini, it was a question of ostracizing Russia from Europe. Was France, which had been saved in 1914 by Russia, going to give this move her support? How imprudent it would be to do so. France did acquiesce to the move. The second round was won.

The countries who felt themselves threatened by the two dictators exchanged terrified glances: 'So this is how France looks after us! France, our Protector and Ally!' The soothing assurances that Paul-Boncour lavished on them were barely sufficient to calm them. Eugène Lautier wrote, 'The Four Power Pact is a club of butchers!' That was certainly the opinion of Mussolini, since the Fascist Grand Council officially decided, on December 6, 1933, upon revision, demanded that the paralysing influence of the small nations should be ended, and, with a brutal irony, stressed the impotence of Geneva to settle anything. As for Germany, she no longer concealed the advantage she intended to draw from the Pact. On September 10, 1933, the Berlin Stadium was the scene of an enlightening demonstration. Before an enthusiastic multitude a huge map of Germany was drawn on the ground with the frontiers of 1914 and those of Versailles. Fifty thousand schoolboys were there; some, in French, Belgium and Polish uniforms, staked out the frontiers of Versailles; others in German uniform, those of 1914. In Europe the conclusion was drawn that the reign of France on the Continent was over, and that Hitler's was about to begin. The Poland of Colonel Beck hastened to veer more decidedly towards Berlin. The third round was gained.

That MacDonald, in agreement, moreover, with Baldwin, should have adopted the views of Mussolini and should have gone as far as accepting responsibility for the Italian plan, and, as Paul-Boncour said,[1] even making it his *own*, was strictly permissible. Great Britain had

[1] *Op. cit.*, vol. II, p. 357.

always refused to undertake the least responsibility towards the small countries of Europe. But with France, it was quite another thing! The Pact ran completely counter to her policy. Paul-Boncour, supported by the Socialists, by Monzie, Caillaux and Henry Bérenger, was to meet the unappeasable hostility of Barthou.[1]

As the Daladier Cabinet had been thrown out, the Pact was not ratified. According to Monzie, the demands of the *Petite Entente*[2] were such that the Pact, practically emptied of its significance, was no longer of any interest. Under these conditions, it was considered better to refrain from putting it into operation. Paul-Boncour[3] contradicted this version: he declared that he was in agreement with Daladier in asking, on the return of the two Chambers, for ratification, and for pledging ministerial responsibility in the matter. The fall of the Government alone was the reason why the Pact was abandoned.

In any case, a blow had been struck both against the morale of our country and that of its friends in Europe. France, indeed, seemed ready to sacrifice them in order to preserve peace.

The hope of disarmament was to justify or rather to explain this policy. In Geneva a conference was meeting which, at grips with the worst possible difficulties, was trying to bring the Powers into agreement on the subject of disarmament. Germany, even before the advent of Hitler, had succeeded in being placed in this matter on an equal footing with the victors of the war. It was clear that, after having pocketed equality of rights, this country would refuse to accept control. This was what Germany did. Joining forces at the conference on September 26, 1933, against a proposal of Mussolini's, who was playing Hitler's game, France, Britain and the United States suggested the establishment of a permanent international control on armaments. If this control proved to be effective, it was later to be succeeded by a general disarmament in stages. Thus, it was a question of effective control. Now, to accept an effective control would mean for Hitler the loss of all hope of putting into effect one day the plan of *Mein Kampf*. As a result he said 'no', and left Geneva, slamming the door behind him. He pretended to believe that the democracies wished to go back on the principle of equality of rights, and he asked his people, through a referendum, 'Will you tolerate being treated like a second-rate Power?' 'No,' was the reply of ninety-five per cent of Germans. With the departure of Germany, there were only three of the seven great Powers left in the League of Nations. One of the three, moreover, was Fascist Italy, whose doctrines and hopes were diametrically opposed to the ideals and principles of Geneva.

[1] *Ibid.*, pp. 349–50.
[2] This was a defensive alliance between Czechoslovakia, Yugoslavia and Roumania for the maintenance of the peace treaties, concluded after the First World War [Tr.].
[3] *Op. cit.*, vol. II, p. 357.

HITLER ANAESTHETIZES BEFORE STRIKING

Is it conceivable that, after having dangled before the eyes of Germany the hope of revenge and of world domination, Hitler was going to give up his plan? 'I will make them believe it,' said he, watching the democracies with their feeble behaviour. The democracies believed in peace because they did not want war. 'Since, before the drive to the East, we must', said Hitler, 'defeat France, I will split up French opinion: I will lull it to sleep.' He would act like those insects who hypnotize their prey before eating it.

Side by side with the hard road which would have saved her, Hitler showed France the easy way that ruined her. He loved France, and only wished her well—so said his propaganda. Let him expand eastwards and he would leave France undisturbed in her domesticity. Did the French love the Bolsheviks so much that they desired to get themselves killed in order to prevent Hitler appropriating a slice of Russia? Did they want to die for the Czechs? For Danzig? Was it not better to let the pressure of steam escape towards the East than to see the German boiler burst? Moreover, was not Hitler, the relentless enemy of Communism, the champion of order in Europe? Was not he, and he alone, the one who could safeguard the French from this Asiatic pestilence? Better to have Hitler than Stalin.

Thus, German propaganda, powerfully backed from 1936 by Italian (cleverer, subtler and simulating a disinterestedness), permeated France.

It was in vain that some clear-sighted Frenchmen objected that Hitler had written[1] in *Mein Kampf*: 'The deadly and pitiless enemy of the German people is and remains France. . . . *This nation, which interbreeds more and more with negroes, and contributes by its sadism and its perverseness to the advent of a Jewish hegemony in the world, endangers the white race in Europe.*' Frenchmen had forgotten the saying of Bismarck: 'He who wishes to buy the friendship of his enemy will never be very rich.' Those who remained unimpressed by German propaganda vainly recalled that Hitler had written in his preface to *Mein Kampf*: 'A doctrine can only preserve its unity and its uniformity if it has been fixed in writing, once and for all.' They added in vain that the official organ of the Nazi Party, the *Völkischer Beobachter* of December 14, 1933, wrote that this book enunciated the definitive principles of Nazi theories. They recalled in vain that the book was so much in demand that its circulation was soaring rapidly, and that in each district the mayor was giving a *de luxe* edition to newly married couples. They observed in vain that Hitler wished to prevent the French from reading *Mein Kampf*, that he was forbidding its translation, that he was prosecuting a French publisher who, out of patriotism, had published an edition of it, and

[1] The italics are in the text.

that he had won from the French courts a ban on the sale of this translation. It was much more agreeable to believe what German propaganda said: 'Mein Kampf is a book which oversteps the limit in some things, but you cannot ask Hitler to revise it. For the Germans it is a sacred book. One does not correct the Koran.'

NAZI PROPAGANDA IN ACTION

Under a totalitarian régime propaganda is one of the essential functions of the State. In a country where a people is not asked its opinion, it must perforce be led to share that of the dictator, failing which the régime would be in danger, and in any case, the power of the State, composed of the effort of all, would be diminished. Every means of modern publicity, every suitable demonstration that would exalt the Teutonic soul was put into operation. Spectacular meetings were held, where the voice of the leader was magnified by loud-speakers, where huge columns of people marched with flags and to music; the newspapers, radio, cinema, theatre and literature, everything combined in a single aim, that of forging the soul of the people by the domination of the mind.

Externally, the effort was more discreet, but none the less formidable. The Reich supported in foreign countries two parallel organizations; its Embassies, which kept up some pretence of respecting diplomatic traditions, and the organizations of the Nazi Party, which waged war in a time of peace. Nazi agents infiltrated into every circle, and concentrated on the work of setting up cells by any means, including that of corruption. Goebbels placed more than three hundred million marks at the disposal of his representatives in France—of whom the best known was Abetz—in order to further the cause of Hitler.

One of the most commonly employed means of action was to invite representatives of French public opinion to Germany. The leaders of ex-soldiers' associations, business men, literary men were received in Berlin, made much of, taken on tours, overwhelmed with consideration, filled with admiration by grandiose meetings to which they were taken. A great success was arranged for the horsemen of the Saumur Cavalry School at the Berlin Horse Show: the Commandant of the School was General Bridoux.[1]

Many Frenchmen, flattered at being received by the rulers of the Reich, forgot what for some years past Hitler had repeated in public to his people. I was curious enough myself to experience one of these

[1] This was a French military academy to which officers graduating from the military school of Saint-Cyr and destined for the French cavalry went. The significance of the reference to General Bridoux lies in the fact that he became (amongst other appointments) Secretary of State for National Defence under Vichy. He was arrested on the Liberation. [Tr.].

conversations which claimed so many victims. Whilst in Berlin in October, 1937, I was received by Goebbels, who said to me: 'What, in reality, are the differences between France and Germany? To what can they be reduced? To a matter of three million Sudeten Germans. M. Paul Reynaud, if we were sitting opposite each other at this table, we would settle the matter in a couple of days. But we don't want any diplomats interfering; above all, no diplomats!'

Nazi agents in France were infiltrating everywhere, even into the University. They succeeded in having distributed in the schools an official book of German propaganda, which denied the responsibility for the First World War, laid upon Germany by the Versailles Treaty. They spoke at political meetings. They practised espionage, sabotage; they encouraged strikes in factories making war material; they subsidized action against France in her colonies. They had a hand in the *Destour* movement in Tunisia. Doriot was bribed by the Germans to publish *L'Emancipation nationale* and *La Liberté*.

IN FRANCE, PUBLIC OPINION, THE PARTIES AND THE GENERAL CONFEDERATION OF LABOUR ARE DIVIDED INTO TWO CAMPS

The near unanimity of those who were collaborating in this propaganda was also to be found in the moving spirits of another class. Amongst the Socialists, some deputies, notably Déat and Marquet, were seduced by the Nazi and Fascist ideology. They left their party in 1933, asserting their faith in an authoritarian régime, and their opposition to any policy which tended to fetter the expansion of Germany and Italy. Other Socialists, who remained in the party, followed Paul Faure, who placed the traditional pacifism of the French Labour Party before the vital interests and the word of France.

On the Right wing, Coty, a perfume manufacturer who had turned himself into a politician, found in the profits of his business the means to found a paper with a wide circulation called *L'Ami du Peuple*. Under the title, 'France d'abord! Avec Hitler contre le bolchevisme', he published, on December 13, 1934, an article in which he showed his indignation with those who preached the encirclement of Germany and an alliance with Russia. He called for an alliance with Italy. He branded the 'short-sighted politicians with their false ideas as a hateful and anti-French sect in the service of the financial-social International, who were proclaiming that there existed in the Italy of Mussolini as well as in the Germany of Hitler, a warlike, formidable and so-called menacing ill-will against France'. From 1936 many of the bourgeois, antagonized by factory disputes, and the five-day working week, did not ask themselves if these strange happenings were not the result of the monetary problem which they had sanctioned, but, seeing with reason a danger for France, embraced as a consequence dictatorial theories, and became susceptible to the slogan of 'Rather Hitler than Stalin'. Nazism seemed to them the antidote to Communism.

Not only was French public opinion divided into two camps, but—by an unprecedented occurrence—each political party was also split into two. In the Chamber, whilst the Right had its hard core of those hostile to Hitler—Marin, Kerillis, Ybarnegaray—it had also its more susceptible members—Goy, Scapini, Tixier-Vignancour. Similarly, whilst the Centre contained Mandel and myself, it had also Flandin, Piétri, Montigny. If amongst the Radicals there was Herriot, on the other hand there was Bonnet, and to the left of the Radicals, Déat and Marquet (whom I have already mentioned), Monzie and Bergery; and to balance Blum, Auriol and Monnet amongst the Socialists there were also Paul Faure, Spinasse and L'Hévéder. Only the Communists, who wished to introduce the Soviet régime into France, and modelled their attitude on that of Moscow, were unanimous. But if they were hostile until the Hitler-Stalin agreement of August 23, 1939, they 'softened up' from the day when that was concluded until the invasion of Russia by the Wehrmacht, when they played a very important part in the Resistance Movement.

There was a similar division in the General Confederation of Labour. Grouped round Jouhaux, the Secretary-General, was the core, unaffected by Hitler's propaganda, which only owed its majority to the support of the Communists. Those who were influenced (with Belin, one of Jouhaux's deputies and his successor to the leadership of the body, at their head) had obtained a strong hold over some of the most powerful federations; for example, amongst the miners, as was the case with Vigne; the teachers, as with Delmas; the postal workers as with Perraud and Giroux. Unfortunately, it was chiefly amongst the young that the pacifists were finding their strength, and this peculiarity was especially marked amongst the teachers. In 1938 the Confederation of Teachers held its annual congress at Nantes. Among the ranks of the opposition spread the infamous slogan—'Slavery is preferable to War' —originated, not as it has been asserted, by Delmas, but by a war-wounded veteran who, in the face of jeers, was forced to retract his words. Jouhaux faced up to the situation, and thanks to the hold which he exercised, rallied behind him three-quarters of the votes.

There was the same difference of opinion in the Press. On the extreme Right, *L'Action Française*, of Maurras and Léon Daudet, which, before and during the preceding war, had denounced anti-French influences, showed the same violence in abusing those who would not subscribe to the enslavement of France in a Nazi Europe. They were, said *L'Action Française*, Jews and people sold to the city and to the Soviets. If there was on the Right, *L'Ordre* of Buré, there was also *Le Jour* of Bailby, which followed in the wake of *L'Action Française*. In the Centre, *Le Temps* was publishing articles by Joseph Barthélemy, wherein was conducted a campaign for the abandonment of Czechoslovakia, our ally. *Le Journal* was printing articles by Flandin. Differences were often appearing in the same paper. In *Gringoire*, Horace de Carbuccia published vehement articles by Béraud, who, like Hitler, wished to separate France and England, whom he even proposed to 'reduce to a state of slavery', and, on the other side, only printed some of the rare articles of Tardieu under the reproving title of *L'Opinion d'André Tardieu*, because he was tied to the latter by a contract. In *L'Œuvre*, where La Fouchardière was opposed to Geneviève Tabouis, appeared, on the eve of Munich, the pacifist proclamations of certain trade union leaders. In the independent pages of *Paris Soir* one could read articles by Blum and others and by L'Hévéder. In *Le Populaire* itself, Blum's own newspaper, a space was kept for Paul Faure and his kidney. In *Le Peuple*, the organ of the General Confederation of Labour, the fighting articles of Jouhaux were followed by the pacifist articles of Belin.[1]

Amongst the scholarly tribe the same division existed. Opposed to the Duhamels and the Maritains, were Abel Bonnard, the disciple of Doriot, Abel Hermant, Louis Bertrand, who, one of his colleagues told me, had often been heard uttering on entering the lecture hall of the Academy, 'Heil Hitler!' Some felt within themselves the urge to play the part of the politician. Having been taken round Germany, they were intoxicated by the virile parades of the Hitler youth. In 1937, Alphonse de Châteaubriant published, in *La gerbe des forces*, the idea of 'a European salvation through the Teutonic renaissance, because civilization sprung from the last parturitions of the Roman Empire, was dead'. France, faced with a choice of Hitler and Stalin, should choose Hitler, whose characteristic was, he wrote, 'an overflowing goodness'.[2]

[1] On the Roll of Honour of papers resolutely and wholly pacifist, Georges Champeaux in *La croisade des démocraties* (vol. II, p. 246) inscribed *Le Temps, Le Journal, Le Matin, L'Action Française, La Liberté, La République, Le Petit Journal, L'Homme Libre*, and out of the periodicals, *Je suis partout, La Flèche*, of Bergery, *L'Emancipation nationale, Pavés de Paris*, etc. . . .

[2] In *Français, voici la vérité* (pp. 177–8), Kerillis, alluding to the 'ravages', caused by the work of Alphonse de Châteaubriant, wrote: 'This book . . . had a tremendous success in student and intellectual circles. At the Académie française, it enlisted disciples, and provoked enthusiastic discussions amongst the distinguished old men. In the industrial sphere, where, in general, books were not read, it penetrated everywhere, and was to be found on directors' tables. . . . It even circulated through the Military Colleges.'

Kerillis continued by relating a personal incident which showed that Weygand, amongst the admirers of Alphonse de Châteaubriant, was one of those who were outstanding because of a proselytizing zeal. He gave me an account of this incident on April 1, 1950, in New York, which contained greater detail than had appeared in his book. Here it is: One day, at the Inter-Allied Circle, Kerillis was approached by Weygand, who, pulling from his coat pocket a copy of Alphonse de Châteaubriant's book, said to him: 'Have you read this splendid book, Kerillis?' Kerillis believed at first that this was a joke. But seeing that it was nothing of the kind, he replied: 'That book makes Hitler out to be an angel of

Before the war a new kind of patriotism had been invented in France: conditional patriotism. Some would say: 'I am a patriot provided that I am governed neither by Blum nor the Communists; otherwise I prefer Hitler.' Others would say: 'I am a patriot, provided France follows Soviet policy; otherwise I prefer Stalin.' And the evil gained ground because disease is more contagious than good health.

peace. It is written with the intention of poisoning French youth.' Weygand put it quickly back in his pocket, and changing the look on his face, broke into this reproach with: 'Kerillis, you were always one to exaggerate.'

The incident had a witness, and one of standing; Weygand at the time he was questioning Kerillis was, in fact, talking to one of his friends, Maître Wateau, a lawyer practising before the civil tribunal of the Seine, and an Air Force general, who enjoyed in military circles an especial esteem, since he was the only officer who, without belonging to the serving forces, had reached the rank of Brigadier-General in the Reserve.

CHAPTER V

A FRANCE WITHOUT ALLIES

I

WHY THE ALLIANCE WITH RUSSIA BROKE DOWN

An alliance which everything dictated.—Edouard Herriot opens the way.—Barthou understands the situation.—Laval only signs the Pact after making it 'innocuous'.—The Moscow communiqué and the volte-face of the Communist Party.—Laval against the addition of a Military Convention to the Pact.—Prague teams up with Moscow.—Fabry shows Potiemkin the door.—Reactions of French public opinion.—What about our glorious military leaders?—Under no circumstances will Poland permit the passage of the Russian Army.—Léon Blum and the Russian Alliance.—My 1937 Campaign.—My 1938 Campaign.

AN ALLIANCE WHICH EVERYTHING DICTATED

WITH whom should a country ally itself? I raised this question in the Chamber on December 27, 1935, when I said: 'We are the only great country in the world whose existence is menaced.'

What did common sense advise? 'One should ally with those who are far away against those who are on the doorstep.' Thus spoke, thirteen centuries ago, the *wisdom of nations*, through the voice of Tai-tsong, Emperor of China. We needed an ally, capable of taking the German Army in the rear on the day it attacked us, or able to resist the Germany Army when we had to attack it in the rear in order to assist an ally which was assailed by it.

What did geography advise? There was, to the east of Germany, a country whose area, under a single rule, was forty times as large as that of France. Its armies had, therefore, unlimited territory into which they could escape, if need be, from the grasp of the German Army. Frederick II feared Russia because, he said, her vastness made her invincible.

What did history advise? Albert Sorel has shown that one cause of the victories of the Revolutionary Armies was the necessity of the King of Prussia and the Tsar to face a Polish revolt, whilst they were at grips with France. For the High Command in Berlin, the memory of a war they had to fight on two fronts from 1914 to 1917 was still a nightmare.

What was Hitler's plan? Hitler, himself, intended to profit by the lesson, and all the more so because he was not in the dark about the industrial progress of the new Russia, because he was aware that the most honoured man there was no longer the Patriarch of the Greek Orthodox Church, but the engineer, because he was informed upon the gigantic development which had taken place in the production of war material. Hitler's plan was to 'settle' first of all with France; then, having his rear free in the west, to cut up Russia. He had never made any secret about this. He had put it down in black and white in *Mein Kampf*. By this very book he was, therefore, with his own hands linking together the two Allies of 1914.

EDOUARD HERRIOT OPENS THE WAY

It is an honourable event in Edouard Herriot's career that he was the first, on the morrow of the First World War, to stress the vital role Soviet Russia was called upon to play in Europe, and that he worked with all his might for the *rapprochement* of France and Moscow.

He has related[1] how 'after a trip to Russia in 1922, and a study on the spot' he was convinced of the necessity of this policy: 'From 1922, I was preaching an understanding between the Soviet Union and France.... From 1924, to the great disgust of certain people, I resumed diplomatic relations with Russia.'

In his *Histoire de la diplomatie*, Potiemkin emphasized the dominating part Herriot took in this vital event. He writes:[2] 'From 1922 to 1923, after his trip to the Nijni-Novgorod Fair, Herriot had warmly advocated the recognition of the Soviet Union. Yet, some months were necessary before he could bring the question on to a practical plane. On October 28, 1924, ... he sent, by dispatch, to the People's Commissar of Foreign Affairs, France's *de jure* recognition of the Soviet Government. "The Government of the Republic," proclaimed the dispatch, "faithful to the friendship uniting the Russian and French peoples, recognizes *de jure* with effect from tomorrow, the Government of the U.S.S.R." Hailing the establishment of friendly relations with democratic France . . . the Central Executive Committee unanimously accepted the necessity of resuming diplomatic relations with the French Republic.'

[1] 'La Politique et l'Intelligence' (*Revue de Paris*, October, 1947).   [2] Vol. III, p. 314.

BARTHOU UNDERSTANDS THE SITUATION

Barthou, whose hostility towards the policy of a Four Power Pact I have mentioned, took charge of Foreign Affairs in 1934 in the Doumergue Cabinet, side by side with Herriot, who was Minister of State. With a keen understanding of the permanent needs of French policy, this Conservative, of whom Potiemkin was to say[1] that he was 'the only constant and active opponent of Fascism' in the Doumergue Administration, and that he was 'the interpreter of French national foreign policy, inspired on the one hand by an accurate estimate of the industrial power of Germany, and on the other, by the patriotic interests of France', was to pursue, without reservations, the path leading to a Russian alliance. Breaking deliberately away from former policy, he proposed to Germany and to Russia the conclusion of a regional Eastern Pact whereby these two Powers, together with Poland, Czechoslovakia and the Baltic countries, would guarantee each other's frontiers, and would promise reciprocal aid against aggression.

Thus, Hitler, who did not hide his intention of devouring a morsel of Russia, was driven into a corner. In September he made known his refusal. Barthou was expecting it: it was the confirmation of *Mein Kampf*. Germany would have nothing to complain about if France now turned to Russia in order to negotiate with the latter an alliance, capable of saving France herself on the day when, as in 1914, she would be at grips with Germany.

Because of the ideology in fashion at the time, the first act of such a policy was to be the admission of Russia to the League of Nations. In agreement with Barthou, Herriot took over the matter; it was he who, as he has insisted upon stressing,[2] had the 'privilege of negotiating' the entry of the Soviets to Geneva. This took place on September 19, 1934, 'through the initiative of French diplomacy', wrote Potiemkin.[3]

LAVAL ONLY SIGNS THE PACT AFTER MAKING IT 'INNOCUOUS'

On October 9, 1934, Barthou was assassinated at Marseilles by the side of the King of Yugoslavia. Doumergue named as his successor Laval, who was to keep the post of Foreign Affairs in the Flandin Cabinet (November 19, 1934–May 31, 1935), and then in his own Administration. It was Laval, therefore, who was to guide our foreign policy until January 22, 1936.

Laval was chosen in order to continue the policy of Barthou. He reconciled himself to following it, but it went against the grain. The

[1] *Op. cit.*, vol. III, p. 508.　　[2] *Ibid.*, p. 7.　　[3] *Ibid.*, p. 517.

negotiations begun with Moscow were in too advanced a state for him to think of breaking them off. An obviously sudden change would put public opinion on the alert. It was more preferable to join in the game in order to be able to give it a twist.

On December 5, 1934, he signed at Geneva with Litvinov a first agreement; it was the 'preliminary protocol to the diplomatic action of France and of Russia with a view to negotiating the Eastern Pact'. Having given this pledge of fidelity to Barthou's policy, he counted on prolonging negotiations and when, forced into a corner, he realized that he could no longer disclaim any competence, he struggled hard to deprive of efficacy the Pact he was about to sign.

Potiemkin, then Ambassador of the Soviets at Paris, wrote,[1] 'The diplomatic collaborators of Laval, who were conducting the negotiations with the Soviet Ambassador in Paris, tried by every means to give the future Franco-Soviet Pact a purely formal character. Thus, they endeavoured to divorce it from everything that could instil into it the vigour of an effective instrument for peace.'

As for Flandin, he stresses[2] the 'ill-will' and 'exceeding bad grace' of Laval. Flandin had to force his hand, to 'make him sign'. He only succeeded in doing this, moreover, thanks to the 'support' which he obtained from Herriot. Laval, he added, only finally resolved to sign from a 'personal electoral interest', in order to keep, at the municipal elections of May 5, 1935, the mayoralty of Aubervilliers, a commune with a 'Communist majority'. Flandin continues: 'It was valuable for Laval to claim there, on the eve of the elections, the friendship of Stalin. This was the reason that inspired him to leave for Moscow. The Parisian Press was filled with accounts and photographs of Laval's interview with Stalin. When he got back, he said to me of Stalin: "He's a good 'scout'. He began like I did. We immediately found each other to be revolutionaries." But, once he had been re-elected at Aubervilliers, he resumed, in relation to the Soviets, an attitude better adapted to the support he was getting from elements that were more Fascist than revolutionary.'

Thus cornered, Laval signed, on May 2, the Pact of Mutual Aid, valid for five years. But he inserted into the alliance a cog-wheel intended to jam the works. The Pact indeed was completed by a 'protocol of signature', whereby aid was only to be given if aggression had been determined by the procedure of the Council of the League of Nations. This, wrote Mr. Nemanov,[3] gave Germany 'in the case of a sudden attack, all the time she needed to conquer the country ... before the said aggression was proved', and, moreover, such assistance had not to be incompatible with agreements formerly entered upon by

---

[1] *Ibid.*, p. 550. [2] *Politique française*, pp. 170 and 194.
[3] *La Russie et les problèmes de la paix*, p. 147.

either of the two parties towards a third, that is to say, as far as we
were concerned, with the Treaties of Locarno.[1] Thus Laval, under the
pretext of interpreting the Pact, 'deprived it of its content and made
it inapplicable', stressed Mr. Nemanov.

Flandin, in his statement before the National Assembly Committee,
entrusted with inquiring into the events which happened in France
between 1933 and 1945,[2] complained that I had written in *La France a
sauvé l'Europe* that Laval had 'cancelled' in the plan worked out by
Barthou the clause which laid down the reciprocal undertaking of
'immediate aid'. Literally, Flandin was correct, but what is 'cancelling'
a clause if it is not 'rendering its content null and void' by neutralizing
it with another which condemns the first to remain a dead letter?
Moreover, Laval himself, through the agency of Fabry, his War
Minister and friend, and of Champeaux, his panegyrist, flattered himself on having succeeded in this very thing. Fabry wrote[3] that Laval
had 'in the articles of the Pact avoided binding France by a too rigid
wording'. As for Champeaux, he praised[4] Laval for having 'refused to
subscribe to the principle of rigid adherence which constituted the
essential claim' of the Soviets, and for having 'succeeded in interfering
with the mechanism of the bomb, made by Litvinov, with the collaboration of Beneš and of Titulesco', and, quite simply, for having
'made the Pact innocuous'.

Did Georges Bonnet mean anything different when he wrote[5] that
the Pact 'in the way in which it had been drafted, had no practical
scope', and gave us a 'feeling of illusory security', or Churchill,[6] when
he said that it was 'nebulous', that it 'contained no engagements binding
on either party in the event of German aggression', and that, in a word,
'no real confederacy was achieved with Russia'?

Laval justified his manœuvre by his desire, so he said, of 'not placing
peace in the hands of Stalin'. Summoning the Supreme Military Committee on November 21, 1935, he spoke about the Pact in the following
terms, which Gamelin said[7] he had noted on leaving the meeting: 'I
have extracted the most dangerous things from it. But, all the same,
I don't trust the Russians. I don't want them to drag France into
war.'

[1] Laval, if he is to be believed in this matter, meant by this reservation to be forearmed
against the risk of seeing Hitler assert that the Pact invalidated the Treaties of Locarno and
draw from that the pretext for declaring that they were a dead letter.

[2] Sitting of July 4, 1947. Later in this book, I shall draw freely upon the depositions
taken by this Committee, which, for the sake of brevity, I shall refer to as the Committee
of Inquiry.

[3] *De la Place de la Concorde au cours de l'Intendance*, p. 75.

[4] Champeaux, *op. cit.*, vol. I, pp. 67–71, *passim*.

[5] *Défense de la paix: I. De Washington au Quai d'Orsay*, pp. 90, 123; *II. Fin d'une Europe
(de Munich à la guerre)*, p. 176.

[6] *The Second World War*, vol. I, *The Gathering Storm*, pp. 121–2 (Second Edition).

[7] *Servir*, vol. II, p. 180.

THE MOSCOW COMMUNIQUÉ AND THE *VOLTE-FACE* OF THE COMMUNIST PARTY

Laval had no difficulty, at the close of his exchange of views, in obtaining the insertion in the Franco-Soviet communiqué, which was published on the 15th, of a paragraph framed thus: 'Stalin understands and fully approves the policy of national defence, drawn up by France to maintain her armed forces at the level necessary for her security.'

This declaration, logical on the part of an ally, stupefied the Socialists and Communists in France, who both still clung to their orthodox pacifism and anti-militarism. Two months earlier on March 15, the former like the latter had voted against a two-year period of military service. But the Communists had gone much further than the Socialists. Then Léon Blum had said to the Chamber, 'I am convinced, and I am choosing my words carefully, that, in order to reply to a characteristic aggression of Hitler Germany, all the workers of this country would rise like all other Frenchmen.' Maurice Thorez, after having declared, in the name of the Communist Party, that the Treaty of Versailles and the alliances of France with Poland and Czechoslovakia were only the manifestations of French imperialism, and were only profiting the armament kings, had added: 'I wish to answer the assertion that has been made on the floor of this House, that the workers of France would rise to resist the aggression of Hitler. We shall not allow the working class to be dragged into a war, alleged to be in the defence of democracy against Fascism.' And he had concluded by saying that it was only the U.S.S.R., 'the fatherland of all the workers of the world', which the working class would agree to defend 'by all means and against all future aggressors'.

Following the communiqué from the Kremlin, there was a complete *volte-face*. Henceforth, the Communists vied with each other in patriotism, and, at the general election of May, 1936, they adorned their posters with the 'Marseillaise' of Rude. In July the Communist group in the Chamber were to demand the summoning of the Parliamentary Army Committee to 'plan the steps necessary to answer Hitler's decision to introduce two years' military service'. The Communists spoke of creating a 'French Front' against Hitler, who was threatening France and Russia, whilst L'Hévéder protested, on August 31, in *Le Populaire*, by declaring that the Socialists did not wish to 'fall victims to the deception of an indescribable, new-fangled "Sacred Alliance", nor to help in spreading the dangerous psychosis of catastrophe which would make possible, and perhaps probable, the bloody conflict'.

LAVAL AGAINST THE ADDITION OF A MILITARY CONVENTION
TO THE PACT

Russia could not be blind to Hitler's threats. At the Seventh Congress of the Comintern, on July 25, 1935, Molotov quoted *Mein Kampf* to his audience: 'When we speak of territories to conquer, we can only call to mind, in the first place, Russia.' Thus, Russia was eager to make her alliance with us something more than Platonic. The Pact, as we have seen, was full of possible loopholes; but, many as these were, it could, on one condition, answer the anxieties from which it sprang: this condition was the conclusion of a military convention. Stalin, moreover, had not hidden this fact from Laval. In giving an account on May 16,[1] of an exchange of views which he had just had the day before with Kalinin, Stalin, Molotov and Litvinov, Laval telegraphed from Moscow to the Cabinet: 'Stalin has declared that he is in full agreement with the peaceful construction I placed, in my toast, on the Pact. . . . He has stated, however, that, in the possible event of peace not being kept, this Pact would be similar to an alliance. Consequently . . . it is necessary to anticipate the worst, and to contemplate immediately technical arrangements which would give it its full effect. I have agreed to this, indicating at the same time that talks between the General Staffs would only be of full value after the conclusion of an agreement between the U.S.S.R. and Czechoslovakia. Litvinov having then told me of the agreement which Beneš and himself had struck, I said that I was ready to propose to the Cabinet the opening of discussions . . . if the usual conditions of discretion were observed.'

Having pocketed the personal advantages he counted on from the signing of the Pact, Laval hoped that it would be forgotten. Any excuse was good enough for him to put the matter off. The Constitution allowed any agreement that did not include surrender of territory or financial undertakings to be ratified by means of decree and not by Parliament. Laval rejected this procedure, which was too expeditious for his liking. According to Flandin,[2] he had been 'informed by Berlin that, if he persisted in a policy of *rapprochement* with the Soviets, an understanding with Germany would no longer be possible'. He had immediately put the Pact 'into cold storage'.

On this matter Flandin is also in agreement with Potiemkin. 'It became more and more evident',[3] wrote the latter, 'that Laval attributed to the document the importance he would to a mere scrap of paper. . . . He had agreed at Moscow that preliminary talks would take place, as soon as possible, between the French and Soviet General Staffs. Laval placed every obstacle he could in the way of carrying out this

[1] Laval left Moscow on the night of the 15th–16th.
[2] *Politique française*, p. 194.   [3] *Op. cit.*, vol. III, pp. 553 and 739.

agreement. . . . Laval had only taken part in the conclusion of the Pact in order that he might the more easily be in a position to kill it afterwards.'

Flandin, as we see, was aware of the importance and urgency of the question. He knew that the only method of making a useful tool out of the Pact was to complete it by a military convention. He was well aware of all Laval's manœuvres, aimed at impeding the opening of discussions on this subject. It was for him, by virtue of being head of the Government, to take action in the matter by asking his Minister of War, General Maurin, directly to negotiate this military convention, the conclusion of which, Russia, our future ally, was justified in pressing upon us. When he resigned on May 31, nothing had been done towards this end. Four years after, when we were to try at last to conclude the convention, it was far too late.

PRAGUE TEAMS UP WITH MOSCOW

On May 16, Czechoslovakia in her turn concluded a Pact with Moscow, the text of which was based on that of our own, but which subordinated the implementation of the undertakings laid down to those already entered into by ourselves. The Article which stipulated this joint liability was as follows: 'The two Governments recognize that undertakings for mutual assistance will only come into effect, if, according to the conditions laid down under the present Pact, assistance to the victim of aggression will be given by France.' After having cited this text which linked together the Russo-Czechoslovak Pact and the Franco-Czechoslovak Treaties,[1] Potiemkin adds:[2] 'By the above formula, the character of a tripartite convention was in effect given to the bilateral Pacts agreed upon by the U.S.S.R. and Czechoslovakia and the U.S.S.R. and France. At the same time, through this clause, Soviet diplomacy, by way of precaution, deprived the French Government of the opportunity, in case of aggression against Czechoslovakia, of itself evading fulfilling pledges provided for in the Franco-Czechoslovak Pact of alliance by throwing on the Soviet Union the responsibility for seeing that help was given to the victim of aggression.'

The Russo-Czechoslovak Pact was ratified without delay by the two parties, and came into force on June 8, 1935. Beneš himself foresaw the importance of Russian intervention in the conflict, the menace of which was looming increasingly on the horizon. In his memoirs,[3] he

[1] We were allied to Czechoslovakia by two Treaties, that of January 25, 1924, and that of October 16, 1925. By the second, signed at Locarno, and parallel to the treaty of mutual assistance between Germany, Belgium, France, Great Britain and Italy, the two parties pledged themselves mutually to 'give immediate help and assistance' if Germany resorted to arms against one or the other, without being provoked.

[2] *Op. cit.*, vol. III, p. 553.

[3] Published in *France-Soir*, March 2, 3, 4, 5, 6, 11, 13, 14–15, 17 and 19, 1948.

gave the reasons that governed his policy: 'I had the impression that, in the struggle which was going to take place, victory would incline to that side which in the end found the Soviet Union as an ally.... We were never forced into this policy by ideological motives, which were inspired by internal considerations. Our opinion on the need of an agreement with the Soviet Union was always exclusively determined by the demands of a policy aiming at world peace . . . I had some reliable information about . . . the Soviet Union. I knew that, for some time, the régime had been firmly seated in the saddle . . . I was not unaware that the Army . . . was powerful, well organized, and still growing. Finally, I had learned, in 1933, that the two Five-Year plans had modified the economic structure of the Soviet Union to the point of making her one of the most powerful industrial countries of Europe. . . .

'After we had concluded the treaty of alliance with Russia in 1935, we remained constantly in touch with each other. In September, 1936, a Czechoslovak military delegation, led by the Chief of our General Staff, General Krejci, was present at the full-scale military manœuvres of the Soviet Army. . . . The delegation returned . . . enthusiastic. . . . The General declared that "the Red Army compelled the admiration of every military expert by its discipline, its morale and its equipment". . . . Stimulated by the preparations . . . of Germany, we had our arsenals execute important orders for certain special arms that the Soviet Army was unable to obtain from France or anywhere else. During the summer of 1937, another Soviet military mission came to Czechoslovakia. . . . We concluded certain agreements, principally in relation to the support which the Soviet Air Force was to bring us in the event of a German attack. Soviet diplomacy, on many occasions, tried seriously to organize conferences, at which views about a common defence of East and West Europe against a Fascist attack could be exchanged. We were always ready to join in such conferences. Nevertheless, until the end of September, 1938, Soviet efforts were broken by the negative attitude of the French and the British.'

Beneš, it is clear, took the matter seriously. In his opinion, there was only one method of countering the German menace: the joint efforts by all those countries that were threatened by Hitler.

FABRY SHOWS POTIEMKIN THE DOOR

Laval succeeded Flandin. Colonel Fabry was Minister of War in his Cabinet. His technical ability, his war wounds, his alert sense of patriotism and anxious eloquence, the confidence Joffre had placed in him, earned him the esteem and sympathy of all.

No one had fewer illusions than he about the danger that German rearmament meant to us. On March 15, 1935, he stated in the Chamber: 'Our military output has been so reduced that, in a few months, Germany has been able to overtake us, and whilst she so insistently demanded equality of rights, she has achieved an inequality of strength. . . . Whereas we are satisfied with two hundred and fifty thousand to two hundred and eighty thousand men, why should Germany have six hundred thousand? . . . This rearmament goes hand-in-hand with zealous physical labour and moral cultivation of patriotic fervour. The only chance we have of avoiding this danger of war is to look things squarely in the face in order to be able to prepare energetically for it.'

Did Fabry fail to recognize the amplitude of Russia's war effort? Not at all. In the same speech he recalled that the military expenditure of this Power had risen in 1934 to five milliards of roubles, and that in 1935 it would reach six and a half milliards. With regard to the strength of the Red Army, this, at the end of 1934, was some nine hundred and forty thousand men. And he paid homage to the morale of the Russian people, ready to 'rise with patriotic faith in the defence of their soil'.

Fabry knew also that, in event of war, the initial effort of Great Britain, a necessary but insufficient ally, would be less than in 1914, and that the increase of the British Army would also be slower. Lastly, he was aware that, fashioned to fight on the defensive, our own Army would be incapable of marching upon Germany, if the latter attacked Poland or Czechoslovakia, and that, under these conditions, we would be left alone against Germany, once she had successively destroyed these two countries.

Now from July, 1935, Potiemkin was pressing Fabry to hasten the conclusion of a military convention of a defensive, but not of an offensive, nature. Was Fabry going to seize the life-line which was offered him? No, he refused it: he showed the Ambassador the door.

This is how he describes[1] his meetings with Potiemkin. 'I received', he writes, 'from M. Potiemkin the renewed assurance that Moscow wished to see the Franco-Soviet Pact completed by a *military convention*. Having avoided, in the articles of the Pact, binding France by a too rigid text, the President of the Council (Laval) had no wish for the categorical automatism of a military convention. I was myself resolved not to take this path, which was too likely to lead to war. As M. Potiemkin quickly noticed this attitude, he ended the second interview by asking me directly: "Why don't you want a categorical military agreement with us? You have plenty with other nations, with the Roumanians, for example." I answered that there was one reason which would absolve me from offering any others. The French Government was sincerely desirous of peace, and any risk of war made it watchful

[1] Fabry, *op. cit.*, pp. 75–6.

and mistrustful. Now, the Soviet Government seemed to accept, without in any way being alarmed, the hypothesis of a European struggle, and considered it, if not desirable, at least inevitable. M. Potiemkin then said to me, point-blank: "Why should a war scare us? A Soviet Russia emerged from the last war. A Soviet Europe will emerge from the next."'

Fabry was right in wishing to bar the road to war. But why did he not see that his attitude, far from eliminating it, was making it inevitable? It rid the High Command of Berlin of the nightmare of a war on two fronts. Hitler could win in Europe the fight of the Horatii against the Curiatii. By his refusal Fabry was opening the road to war.

Bonnet himself wrote in his *Fin d'une Europe* (p. 176): 'It was a grave mistake not to have concluded a military convention, to be put into effect at the same time as the political agreement of 1935. This would have forced us to raise the question of the passage of Russian troops through the countries bordering on the U.S.S.R.; and we should have then perceived both the emptiness of the pact which had just been concluded and its incompatibility with other French alliances.'

REACTIONS OF FRENCH PUBLIC OPINION

If public opinion permitted this sabotage, it was because the majority of the French were hostile to a Russian alliance, some for reasons of an external nature, others for internal ones.

Amongst the first group were the supporters of the policy of the Four Power Pact, one which, in relation to the Russian alliance, represented the opposite extreme. On March 15, 1935, Daladier told the Chamber: 'I cannot acknowledge the reasoning which places the problem of Germany before the existence of a union of other countries.'

Hitler's Germany was complaining, like that of William II, of 'encirclement'. In reality, it was simply a question of making the country innocuous, the very thing that she did not want to be.

On November 21, 1935, the French Ambassador, M. François-Poncet, visited Hitler to tell him of the approaching opening of a parliamentary debate on the ratification of the Pact and to inform him that it was in no wise directed against Germany, that it was of a purely defensive nature, and that it harboured no intention of encircling Germany. In *The Fateful Years*[1] (p. 188) M. François-Poncet tells us of this step. He adds: 'Hitler appreciated the attention our Government had charged me to pay him, but this did not prevent him from launching into a long tirade against the pact he considered criminal. There could be no doubt, he asserted, that this was a military alliance directed

---

[1] *The Fateful Years: Memoirs of a French Ambassador in Berlin, 1931–1938*, translated from the French by Jacques LeClercq.

against him. Russia was a permanent menace to Europe; she did not belong to Europe, and thought only of overthrowing Europe.' Hitler thought that a grave error had been made in introducing Russia to the League of Nations. But such an introduction was a condition of the Franco-Russian alliance.

Part of the Right took up the cudgels on behalf of this complaint of encirclement. On February 18, 1936, in the debate which took place in the Chamber on ratification, Xavier Vallat said: 'Whether you want to or not, you will give Germany the impression of being encircled.' And he added that, if we were attacked, Russia could only offer us 'a tardy, partial help and, I am justified in saying, one which is almost Platonic'. And Montigny went one better: 'It does not seem to me ... opportune that France should be seeking a position in the front rank in this new struggle between Teutonism and Slavism.' In addition this political argument was backed by a military one. Did not a deputy of the Right declare, 'It is an open secret that the Soviets are incapable of supporting war against a first-class Power'?

But the principal incentive behind the opposition to the alliance was that Russia was Communist. Philippe Henriot proclaimed that he rejected an alliance with a country which had decided to 'place French money and soldiers at the service of revolution'.

WHAT ABOUT OUR GLORIOUS MILITARY LEADERS?

In France military circles were well informed about the power of the Russian Army.

On the day after the signature of the Pact, the Soviet Government asked us to send a military delegation to the full-scale summer manœuvres of the Red Army. Our General Staff put General Loiseau in charge of the delegation. The General came back full of enthusiasm. This is what he said, 'The technique of the Red Army has attained an especially high level. . . . The achievement made in equipping the Army during the last three or four years not only reveals the success and power of Soviet industry, but gives the Red Army a tremendous superiority over other European forces which for a long time have often been obliged to use out-of-date material, to the tactical disadvantages of their Armies.'

After having expressed his admiration of the Air Force, the parachutists and tanks, he ended, 'The descendants of Russian serfs, the present defenders of the U.S.S.R., are certainly better prepared than any others to undergo the tests of a new war, in which the principal factor in victory will be, without any doubt, endurance. . . . The Red Army, at the present time, is probably one of the most powerful armies in Europe, and it offers a striking proof of the discipline with which the

Soviet population has submitted itself to the sacrifices exacted by
national defence.' They were prophetic words, which had a resounding
echo in France. On September 20, 1935, *Le Temps* published large
extracts of this report, which Herriot was to cite on February 20, 1936,
on the floor of the Chamber, and added that, at this time, Russia already
had one million three hundred thousand men under arms, and could
mobilize thirteen and a half million.

Gamelin, who in 1934 was Chief of the Army General Staff,
approved the principle of the alliance. During the summer he was at
Geneva with Barthou. The latter told him to find out the opinion of
Weygand, then designate Commander-in-Chief in the event of war,
whom he thought, says Gamelin,[1] 'somewhat refractory'. Gamelin
consulted Weygand. Both agreed that Russia certainly represented 'the
only great eastern counterpoise against Germany'. Without doubt, it
was important to see that our new relations with Moscow had no
repercussions on our internal policy, and hence, on the united morale
of the Army. But, apart from this obvious reserve, Weygand was at
one with Gamelin in recognizing the wisdom of Barthou's policy. The
latter introduced Gamelin to Litvinov at Geneva. 'A short, but interesting, conversation,' continues Gamelin, who adds: 'I told him of the
importance we attached to Franco-Russian military collaboration.'
Paris and Moscow exchanged Military Attachés. The Russians gave the
post to a General. To stress the importance of the event, Gamelin gave
a dinner in his honour, and asked Weygand to preside. The latter
refused, as, moreover, he was repeatedly to refuse to appear at the
Soviet Embassy. An example of internal politics.

Gamelin, who on January 21, 1935, had succeeded Weygand as
Vice-President of the Supreme War Council, and thereby had become
designate Commander-in-Chief in the event of war, was himself to
revise his initial attitude. The change was not long in coming about.
Gamelin himself admits it[2] in his memoirs when telling us the circumstances of it. On October 21, 1935, he had written to the Ministry of
Foreign Affairs that 'the possibility of a repudiation of the Rhineland
Statute should be contemplated before the autumn of 1936, at the
latest'. The threat was indeed becoming a reality. 'In the last few days
of February, 1936, our Intelligence Service [wrote Gamelin] confirmed
the fact that the Germans intended to provide as their motive for entering the demilitarized zone the ratification (which seemed imminent) of
the Franco-Russian Pact: they were alleging that this violated the spirit
of Locarno. . . . On the 25th, accompanied by General Colson, I went
to see the Minister to inform him how matters stood. He wondered,
consequently, whether it would not be advantageous to delay the
voting. . . . But, as the problem was, in fact, one which concerned the

---

[1] *Op. cit.*, vol. II, pp. 132-3.   [2] *Ibid.*, pp. 195, 198 and 200.

Ministry of Foreign Affairs, he wanted the Army General Staff to draft a Note to be handed to the Secretary-General of the Quai d'Orsay, in such a way as not to give the move an official nature. As the matter seemed urgent, the Note was handed to M. Massigli without being submitted to me. The next day I observed a sharp reaction. M. Massigli had me informed that he did not understand our "change of attitude", when we had shown ourselves, till then, ready to reply. Unofficially, I found out that there was some speculation as to whether the Note could be linked with the Press campaign concerning a statement made by General Weygand. He had, it would appear, stated that he was never consulted about the benefits which lay in drawing up the Franco-Russian Pact. I replied to M. Massigli that we had not changed our opinion, but that the Minister wished to see the Ministry of Foreign Affairs informed about the nature and consequences which the coming vote in Parliament entailed. . . . On the 28th, I went to see . . . M. Léger. He thought that we really would not be able to make a gesture which would imply a renunciation of the Franco-Soviet Pact. . . . Albert Sarraut summoned me. . . . He was wondering what was the meaning of the General Staff's intervention with the Ministry of Foreign Affairs. I explained to him the reason and the origin of the matter. Our duty was to inform the Government of German intentions, nothing more. We had not changed our opinion either about the importance of the Pact . . . or about the need for action in case of the occupation of the Rhineland. But Sarraut also thought it was impossible to postpone the debate . . . in the Chamber. . . . For us it would be a retreat and, moreover, it might lead to a dangerous ministerial crisis on the eve of the elections. I assured him that I shared his belief.'

Behind these explanations, embarrassing to say the least, and these euphemisms, it is easy to reconstruct the incident. Indeed, Albert Sarraut reproached Gamelin for playing a political move against the Cabinet, which was based upon a majority of the Left, the Communists having, for the first time, abstained, instead of voting against a bourgeois Government, because of a promise that the Minister would be asking the Chamber for the ratification of the Pact.

In such conditions the task of the Government, it must be admitted, was far from easy. On the one hand, Weygand was denying ever having been consulted about the benefits of an alliance, to which he said he had always been opposed. On the other, Gamelin, taking care not to pledge himself too firmly and leaving himself a loophole, was trying to throw on the Cabinet a responsibility which he ought to have wished loyally to share. Thus, one can appreciate the reflection of Paul-Boncour:[1] 'At this time [that of Laval's trip to Moscow] the Franco-Soviet Pact had few opponents. The General Staff warmly

[1] *Op. cit.*, vol. II, p. 371.

supported it; this was understandable, if we consider the military advantages it was bringing us. Later, . . . Pertinax, . . . complaining to me of certain sudden changes, told me that he had only taken up a definite attitude towards the Pact because he was influenced by General Weygand.'

It seems, in any case, that General Maurin, who, as we have seen, was Minister of War at the time of the signing of the Pact, himself never varied in his opinion. Shortly before the departure of Laval for Moscow, he declared to the Council of Ministers (I have this from Mandel, his colleague in the Government) that, from a military point of view, the Russian alliance would be of no benefit to us.

And how about Pétain? As a colleague of Barthou in Doumergue's Administration, he had certainly been consulted about the alliance, and he had not opposed it. This did not prevent him in April, 1936, from taking a stand against it, when the electoral fight was in full swing. On the 30th, *Le Journal* published this statement by him: 'By holding out a hand to Moscow, we have held it out to Communism, and we have introduced it to a large number of decent people here, who until now fought shy of it. We have admitted Communism into the register of avowable doctrines. It is quite likely we shall have the opportunity of regretting it.' The next day, when I was contesting the second ballot in the second constituency of Paris, *L'Action Française* used the above statement as its headlines, and followed it with a reproach to those who were thinking of voting for 'Paul Reynaud, one of the most dangerous *sponsors* of the Soviet Pact'.

UNDER NO CIRCUMSTANCES WILL POLAND PERMIT THE PASSAGE OF THE RUSSIAN ARMY

However imperfect the Franco-Soviet Pact was in itself, the eventual implementation of the alliance was still more complicated by geographical conditions. Russia had no common frontier with either Germany or Czechoslovakia. If she had to attack the Reich in answer to the latter's aggression against France or Czechoslovakia, or bring help in a like eventuality to Czechoslovakia, she would find in her path the buffer zone of Poland and Roumania. Now both, the first even more resolutely than the second, disliked opening their frontiers to their powerful neighbour who, they feared, could not have sincerely surrendered her claims on certain parts of their territory, and who, moreover, had stated openly that her objective was the propagation and support of Communism abroad.

Gamelin, who, in September, 1937, was present at the full-scale manœuvres of the Roumanian Army, to which King Carol had invited him, received from that sovereign the promise 'that he would let the

Russians go through the northern part of his country to reach Czechoslovakia'. Reporting this promise, Gamelin added:[1] 'But he asked me to keep it a secret, as he did not wish the question to be discussed in Roumania. He was going to take steps at the appropriate moment.'[2] The problem of passing through Poland was complicated in a different fashion. M. Léon Noël, who was our Ambassador in Warsaw from 1935 to 1939, has enlightened us on this subject. 'The conclusion of the Franco-Soviet Agreement', he writes,[3] 'created a scandal in Warsaw. Poland . . . feared that . . . the assistance promised to France . . . would mean for herself a Russian invasion: . . . if Russian troops, even as Allies, entered Polish territory, they would bring revolution and Communism. . . . As at the end of the eighteenth century, once they had entered the country, they would never leave it.' The danger was especially grave for the provinces bordering Russia, peopled with White Russians and Ukrainians, 'the great majority of whom were orthodox, and akin to the Russians in language, customs, and mental outlook'. M. Noël endeavoured, as he says, to put things in a nutshell: 'Never', he declared to his questioners, 'have we seriously thought of requesting Poland to welcome Russian troops into her territory; it would be for her, and for her alone, when the time came, to accept Soviet military help. She would herself lay down its nature and conditions.' And the Ambassador added: 'In my opinion, the only practical possibility of military co-operation between Poland and Russia would be in aerial collaboration.' In Moscow no mention was made of the subject. 'It was known at Moscow', said M. Noël, 'that Poland's consent would never be obtained, and that neither France nor Great Britain would succeed in getting it from her. At the beginning of 1939, a Soviet officer had said to one of the officers attached to my Embassy: "The Poles will never tolerate the entry of a single Soviet soldier within their territory. They would rather perish than consent to it."'

The same reservations were made by Gamelin. In August, 1936, he went to Warsaw. It was certainly an appropriate moment, for Poland had just asked our financial assistance in order to complete her rearmament. Gamelin raised the question with General Smigly-Rydz, Commander-in-Chief of the Polish Army. He asked him[4] 'if he could not visualize a move by the Russian Army through Lithuania upon East Prussia'. 'I found him', wrote Gamelin, 'immediately on the defensive. . . . "If the Bolsheviks enter Lithuania, just as if they enter Poland, they

[1] Op. cit., vol. II, p. 279.
[2] Gamelin disagrees on this point with Paul-Boncour. The latter reports (op. cit., vol. II, pp. 60–1) that, at the beginning of 1936, the King promised him to come to an understanding on this subject, but that, in 1937, he made French passiveness at the time of the remilitarization of the Rhineland the pretext for withdrawing his promise.
[3] L'agression allemande contre la Pologne, pp. 88, 89, 119 and 421, passim.
[4] Op. cit., vol. II, p. 230.

3

will never leave." The only semblance of co-operation . . . with Russia, that I could get him to consider possible, was in the air. In this sphere, he was prepared to study the possibility of supplying airfields which could be used by Russian planes, not as bases, but only for landing in transit.'

This mistrust, in some way instinctive, was not, it must be admitted, without reason. Gamelin relates[1] that in September, 1938, at the time when the Sudeten crisis was reaching its peak, he asked the Russian Military Attaché 'to inform . . . Marshal Voroshilov of the dispositions which we were making'. He adds: 'When I asked him if Russia would, on her side, be ready to move according to events, he did not conceal from me that, in his opinion, there was the possibility that Poland would fight on the side of Germany against Czechoslovakia in order to re-annex Teschen. In that case, the problem for Russia would be to settle accounts quickly with Poland. And it is clear that the idea pleased him. . . . On September 20, the Military Attaché saw my Chief of Staff once again. Marshal Voroshilov thanked me for my dispatch. The Soviets had at the time thirty divisions, a large number of cavalry, numerous tank units and the bulk of the air force ready to strike in the West.'

It cannot be disputed that enmity towards Russia was deeply rooted in the heart of the Polish nation. It is equally certain that the architect of Polish diplomacy, Colonel Beck, far from seeking to dissipate the misunderstanding, did his utmost to aggravate it. It was in our interest that he should be deprived of power. The opportunity for this came to us in 1936, at the time of the opening of the negotiations to which I have just made allusion. M. Noël urged that the granting of the assistance asked for should be conditional upon the dismissal of Beck from the conduct of foreign affairs. The matter, according to him, was easy. 'Beck', he wrote,[2] 'was then very much under fire in his own country. General Smigly-Rydz was filled only with mistrust of him. I had prepared the ground for an approach to the General. . . . The reception which he had given to my hints was sufficient to prove that he would be prepared, without any regret, to agree to use similar words. The Minister (Delbos) approved. . . . He undertook to make the General realize the necessity of getting rid of Beck.'

Gamelin, we have seen, was visiting Warsaw. He took advantage of his friendship with Smigly-Rydz in order to explore the ground. 'I felt at once', he wrote,[3] 'a retreat on the part of my companion. He began to extol the diplomatic virtues of M. Beck. . . . I had, therefore, from the beginning a feeling that M. Noël was under some delusion as to what could be got from the General in this matter. I found out a little

---

[1] *Op. cit.*, vol. II, p. 348.   [2] *Op. cit.*, pp. 140 and 145.
[3] *Op. cit.*, vol. II, pp. 232–3.

later from M. Léger that M. Delbos had met the same reserve as myself, and had not considered it wise that he should be insistent.'

On this point, M. Noël[1] indicts the unconcern of the Government: 'M. Delbos, in opposition to what had been most positively arranged, did not venture to express it (i.e. the political condition), although France's guest had himself, as soon as he arrived, given him the opportunity to do so. During a dinner at the Quai d'Orsay, General Smigly-Rydz had indeed broached the question: "And what about M. Beck?" he asked our Minister without any prompting. Forewarned as he was by myself of the feelings that . . . Beck aroused in France, if Smigly-Rydz expressed himself thus, it was, as one could see with half an eye, not only because he did not fear to hear put forward a demand which he could hardly fail to anticipate, but also because he wished to take back the expression of it to Warsaw, and to profit by it to dismiss a Minister in whom he had not the slightest confidence. Contrary to the pre-arranged "set-up", M. Delbos evaded the issue. To the question . . . he contented himself with an answer: "I know him. . . . He's a very intelligent man." Then he changed the subject. I tried in vain to get back to the theme. The Rambouillet agreement was negotiated and signed without any other mention of Beck or his policy being made. The reasons which led certain members of the Government thus to handle the Minister of Pilsudski remain obscure. The wish to bring negotiations to a successful end . . . was probably not a sufficient explanation. Did the support, which Beck had the skill to draw from certain cliques, turn the scales in his favour? It is quite possible.'

M. Noël gathered the impression that powerful influences, whose co-operation Beck had been able to secure for himself in business circles,[2] came to his assistance. Mandel and myself, thinking it too delicate a subject to discuss on the floor of the House, raised it in the Finance Committee. We were not heeded. Mandel told me at Portalet[3] that Chautemps, a member of the Cabinet whom he met after the sitting of the Committee, asked him: 'Were you trying to bring off a political coup?'

Thus we had missed the last opportunity that presented itself to us of harmonizing the Franco-Polish alliance with those which united us respectively with Prague and Moscow. Much more, the Rambouillet negotiations had the paradoxical result of discouraging, even to the point of disconcerting those in Warsaw who were attacking Beck for

[1] *Op. cit.*, p. 145.
[2] M. Noël (*ibid.*, p. 173) offers, regarding this subject, an indication which gives grounds for reflection: 'A regrettable thing happened in applying the Rambouillet agreement: On the demand of the French Government Poland had to devote the first forty-five millions which were given by France not to the buying or making of war material but to the settlement of a debt claimed by a French national.'
[3] Portalet, the fortress in which MM. Reynaud and Mandel were confined by Vichy [Tr].

a policy contrary to the spirit of the alliance. And because of this consequence, they strengthened the position of the Colonel by giving him the
weapons to intensify his anti-Russian and equally anti-Czech bias. The
bitterness that M. Noël felt in the check to his efforts is consequently
understandable. 'The Poles', he writes,[1] 'were the first to be surprised
by the results achieved. . . . The Commander-in-Chief of the Polish
Army . . . came back to Poland with a success which gained him a
moment of real popularity. . . . But, in reality, the great beneficiary
. . . of the agreement . . . was to be . . . Beck. When he learned that the
French Government had agreed to the advances and the supplies
demanded, without laying down any conditions, without exacting any
political counter-demands, without even expressing the desire for a
change in attitude of Polish diplomacy towards us, Beck felt a real
relief. He saw that France did not bear a grudge against Poland for her
actions, and it was clear that, however disagreeable and embarrassing
these were to French policy, they were not incompatible with the
friendship of our country, with its alliance, with its assistance, and
that these principles which he followed, and the methods which he
employed, were excused, justified, and made legitimate. The criticisms
which a section of his fellow-countrymen levelled against his policy,
and which were directed especially against its effects upon Franco-
Polish relations, lost all their force. The Minister was whitewashed, and
his position was thereby even strengthened. A photograph, published
by the official *Gazeta Polska* the day after General Smigly-Rydz'
return to Warsaw, offered proof of the Colonel's satisfaction: it showed
him on the station platform with a broad smile on his face. He was
happy and triumphant. . . . The Colonel and his policy had been
consolidated by an action which ought to have been made dependent
on his retirement and the serious modification of his policy. The result
could not be more paradoxical or deceptive. It was still assumed at
the time that at least the conversations which General Smigly-Rydz
had had with our Army chiefs had been fruitful, and that his trip to
France had ended in an understanding, if only a verbal one, between
the two General Staffs on the essential questions which would confront
them on the day when they would have to co-operate in the face of
the German Army. The future was to show that nothing of the kind
had occurred and that, however unlikely it seemed, even on the purely
technical level, our responsible Generals had not been able to derive the
least profit from the opportunity which had been offered them.'

During the autumn of 1937, Delbos undertook an official trip to
Prague, Warsaw, Bucharest and Belgrade. Did he profit by it to seize
the chance which he had let go a year earlier? That he did nothing of
the kind is the substance of what M. Noël tells us,[2] when he describes

[1] *Op. cit.*, pp. 146–8.   [2] *Ibid.*, pp. 174–9.

in detail the complaisance with which our Minister, 'with the best intentions in the world' heard Beck, and 'pushed further discretion to the limit by refraining from attempting to do anything to better Polish-Czech relations.' The Ambassador added:

'One cannot be surprised that, in these circumstances, the visit of M. Delbos . . . ended in consolidating the position [of Beck]; . . . at Warsaw—our Minister had made more advances than he himself received. . . . Beck felt himself granted a pardon by the parties which were governing France, and which, until then, had treated him with so little consideration; he had undertaken no liabilities, he kept his hands free, he had acquired more authority in his own country. . . .'

Encouraged by this forbearance, Beck took things easily. In this fashion he was to say[1] to a diplomat, in December, 1938, on the day after the 'annexionist' demonstration at Montecitorio, that 'France would find herself forced to surrender Tunisia to Italy, without a fight, and that she would be committing an error by not at once reconciling herself to this step'. On December 24, the Council of Ministers showed its anger at such talk, which, notes Jean Zay in his *Carnets*,[2] threw into relief the way in which Beck interpreted the alliance and put it into practice. This aroused Marchandeau to the indignant protest: 'Poland supports Italian claims, and we are still giving her money.'

LÉON BLUM AND THE RUSSIAN ALLIANCE

The almost certain impossibility of adapting the mechanism of the Russian alliance to that of our alliance with Poland explains, without justifying, the choppings and changings which I have just described. The irruption of the German Army into the Rhineland had, on the other hand, appeared to corroborate substantially the fears which had been revealed during the debate on ratification. French opinion was bewildered, disturbed. That is why an important element of the Socialist Party was opposed to the Russian alliance, for it saw in this policy an 'acceptance of the idea of war'. On coming into power, Léon Blum had to take into account this division within his own party. His anxiety not to break the Socialist solidarity was certainly one of the motives for the inaction which he showed in this sphere.

As for the essential reason, here it is as he revealed it before the Committee of Inquiry:[3] 'When', he said, 'the *Front Populaire* Government was formed, we were bound to the Soviet Union by a pact of alliance. So far as I was concerned I had recommended it since 1934, that is to say, from the moment when the Polish-German understanding had begun to mature. . . . I had always thought, always

---

[1] *Ibid.*, p. 282.   [2] pp. 41–2.   [3] Sitting of June 18, 1947.

maintained that, as before 1914 and for similar reasons, an understanding between France and Great Britain on the one hand, and with the U.S.S.R. on the other, would end in a later understanding between Great Britain and the U.S.S.R., that is to say a combination which duplicated the *Triple Entente* of pre-1914 years. From 1936, the alliance, which had been signed barely a year before, was already seemingly becoming something of a dead letter. The Russians had earnestly desired that the General Staffs of the two countries should come to some agreement. This had not happened, and the requests of the Russians were met with replies of a generally dilatory nature. Russia was offering, as she did in the utmost good faith, to inform us of the complete position of her military and industrial resources, and of the supplies which she would put at our disposal in the case of a European conflict. She asked in return for similar information, and this information was slow in being produced. I more than once put the problem to M. Daladier, and I realized that M. Daladier, in his turn, ran into—I will not say the opposition of the General Staff—but a reticence on its part. In the autumn of 1936, large-scale manœuvres took place in Russia. The manœuvres were attended by one of the Deputy Chiefs of the General Staff . . . General Schweissguth. I asked . . . for his report. I found out that the report tended to refute that which had been drawn up the previous year by . . . General Loiseau. I then asked for General Loiseau's report. I only got this after some difficulty and some delay. I discovered that contradictions existed in every line between it and the first report. I tried to clear up the reason for this new approach, and I ascertained that at this time our General Staff did not consider military assistance to the U.S.S.R. to be a subject of prime importance. In actual fact, when I tried to restore to the alliance its fullest meaning, I ran into . . . reticence rather than opposition, but this reticence was obvious.

'At the end of 1936, I gave up bringing pressure to bear on the Minister of National Defence and on the General Staff in order to give the alliance its character of military solidarity, . . . [I had just received], in a private and friendly way from my friend M. Eduard Beneš, a piece of advice transmitted by my son who was making a short stay in Prague, which counselled me urgently to take the greatest precaution in our relations with the Soviet General Staff. According to his own intelligence service—the Czech intelligence enjoyed a well-deserved reputation in Europe—those behind the Soviet General Staff were maintaining relations with Germany which gave ground for suspicion. Less than a month later, the trial known as the Tukhashevsky trial took place, which put Marshal Tukhashevsky, head of the Soviet General Staff, in the dock. It was this warning, given at the end of 1936, which crippled in some fashion the tenacious effort that I had been making for several months to invest the Franco-Soviet alliance with all its significance, and profit in the military sphere.'

This incident, as we shall see, had the gravest effect. Beneš, in his memoirs, mentions it in the following words: 'Towards the middle of January, 1937, . . . I was warned . . . in a confidential dispatch that Hitler was pursuing other negotiations at that time. . . . These "other negotiations", as we were to learn later, thanks to an involuntary indiscretion of Count von Trauttmannsdorff,[1] were being held with Soviet anti-Stalinist conspirators . . . Tukhashevsky, Rykov and others. Hitler was convinced that they would succeed. . . . But Stalin took precautions . . . in time. I had, indeed, immediately told the Soviet Minister at Prague . . . of what I had been told in Berlin.'[2]

The end of the incident is well known. Suspended from duty in May, 1937, Tukhashevsky was put on trial, convicted of treason and condemned to death. On June 12 he, together with seven other generals, was shot.

MY 1937 CAMPAIGN

In proportion as German strength increased, the campaign directed in our own country against the Russian alliance became more intense. In May, 1937, I published, under the title of *Le problème militaire français*, a study in which I stressed the peril, the menace of which weighed upon us. 'Let us not forget', I wrote,[3] 'that if, during the last war, the advent on the battlefield of huge British, and later American, armies, from 1917 onwards, allowed us to gain the day, we required other assistance at the outset to avoid losing it, and that immediately.

'Did not Joffre say that we had won the battle of the Marne by a bare division? Now, the invasion of East Prussia by the Russian Armies had diverted three German Army Corps from the French front after Charleroi, in addition to seven held in readiness from the beginning. . . . Today, as in 1914, it is immediate and powerful help of which we are in need from the very onset. . . .

[1] Count von Trauttmannsdorff had been entrusted by Hitler with approaching the Czech Government, in the greatest secrecy, with a view to concluding a pact of non-aggression.

[2] Churchill declares (*op. cit.*, vol. I, p. 258, second edition) that there were grounds for thinking that the Russian Secret Police had already been informed of this plot, but that, wanting to have Stalin told about it from a friendly foreign source, they arranged for Beneš to be entrusted with the revelation.

According to a recent revelation (cf. *Le Monde*, October 23, 1948), the plot aimed at overthrowing the Stalin régime, and was within an ace of being successful. The police only got the wind of the plot at the last moment, thanks to the treachery of General Dybenko, commander of the Central Asia Military Region: he was the last to be admitted into the conspiracy, and lost no time in giving the game away as soon as he got to Moscow, where he went to take part in the revolution. As a reward for his treachery, Dybenko, the only official witness at the trial, was, shortly after the execution of Tukhashevsky and his fellow conspirators, degraded and shot in his turn.

[3] pp. 18–22.

'The truth is that, looking at the map of Europe, it is apparent that an effective alliance with Russia is a geographical necessity for France.

'Once again, what other choice is there?

'There is no doubt that the state of our domestic politics, owing to a foolish economic policy, is greatly complicating the solution of our problem of national defence. . . .

'If Frenchmen subordinate the necessities of their foreign policy to their domestic squabbles, if they imitate the Poland of former days, they will suffer her fate. It is of no avail that frivolous individuals who are governed by their emotions should shed tears of blood on the day when Russia comes to an agreement with Germany; and this is not an imaginary danger.'

It will be seen later that, from 1924, I was haunted by the fear of Germany 'destroying Poland in order to shake hands with the Red Army over the corpse'. Unfortunately, it was not an imaginary danger. But those who had done their best to make this into a real danger were not the only ones to shed tears of blood.

MY 1938 CAMPAIGN

The struggle against the Russian alliance went on increasing. Tardieu, with whom I had been closely connected until his retirement from Parliament to his Aventine on the Côte d'Azur, himself took sides publicly against me. Thus, in *Gringoire*, on April 15, 1938, he wrote of the 'misleading Paul Reynaud, my former Minister of Justice, who has become a friend of the Bolsheviks'.

People would protest to me: 'Ratification by the Chamber was sufficient to make Hitler violate Locarno. The military treaty which you are demanding would be considered by Hitler as a provocation. This time it would be war.' I would reply to this that I certainly did not ask for the signing of a military treaty with a flourish of trumpets, but simply the conclusion of a military convention, without which the Pact could only have an innocuous value. It is customary to give to a document of this kind a secret character. But to conclude such a convention, it was necessary at least to have the will to do it.

On January 28, 1938, addressing the *Société des Conférences*, I said that the country stood in more danger than in the days when the Revolution Government called the citizens to arms by proclamation. 'In this land menaced by so many dangers, all kinds of crises,' I went on, 'a financial crisis, an economic crisis, a monetary crisis, a social crisis, and a political crisis are occurring at the same time.' I raised my voice against those amongst us who put Russia on the same footing as Germany or Italy.

On February 4 I returned to the charge. I showed in a second lecture that, without the assistance of Russia, Czechoslovakia and Poland would succumb soon after the outbreak of war. 'Do you want,' I said, 'in spite of the advice of very competent generals who went to study the tank regiments in Russia and found them outstanding, to judge the Russian Army as worthless? It is said that the Soviet Air Force is most up to date and that it has proved its value in Spain. Do you want us to consider it also as valueless? All right! Even admitting this hypothesis, the very fact of having, in the east of Europe, a country which has the resources of Russia in raw materials and war-potential—that is to say, which has the power of influencing in a decisive way such countries as Poland, herself placed in the uncomfortable position of being between Germany and Russia; or as Roumania, whose assistance from the point of view of supplying petrol would be decisive in a war—would justify the Russian alliance.'

And I ended with this appeal to the French élite, of whom I had many representatives in front of me: 'Alas! Shall we always be too late for everything?'

II

WAS AN ALLIANCE WITH FASCIST ITALY WORKABLE?

Fascist Italy and France.—Laval negotiates in Rome with Mussolini.—The British people, Europe, Abyssinia and ourselves.

FASCIST ITALY AND FRANCE

On March 22, 1927—twelve years before the war—I began a lecture[1] on the 'Black Shirts' at the University of Annales with the following words: 'If I say—and I shall say— that Fascist Italy could constitute a threat of war, I am bound to annoy both the Italians, who know it and who don't want it talked about, and the French, who are asleep and do not want to be awakened.' As a result, the Italian Ambassador made a protest to the worthy guiding spirit of this university, Mme Adolphe Brisson.

This lecture, which I ended by showing 'the peril which Fascism conceals for us', also shocked those French people in whose opinion Fascism was then a safeguard and an example. It was considered a safeguard against Bolshevism which, by way of Italy, could well have been introduced into France. It was considered an example of what a strong

[1] *Conferencia*, October 5, 1927.

Government can do in order to institute at home a discipline which is the condition of a country's greatness. I did not, however, in my lecture, deny that a reform of our political system was necessary. In face of a general scepticism, I stated on the contrary that it was the external danger which made this urgent: 'If we in France cherish our liberties, it is necessary at any cost and with speed to modify, reform and improve our democratic system. In the East, France has two neighbours, two ambitious and prolific nations. These neighbours represent jointly one hundred and five million inhabitants. . . . And they are increasing by more than a million a year. . . . That is why those who say to the French people that, if it be in a state of grace, if it has the will to peace, peace will spread throughout the world, are deceiving themselves and deceiving the French people.'

Those who criticized my denunciation of the Italian danger did not believe in war, and were oblivious to the attacks of the Fascists on the principles of the French Revolution which had built up and still enhance the glory of our country throughout the world; and they shut their eyes willingly to Mussolini's fundamental anti-Christianism. For them there was only one thing to be feared: revolution at home. It was always internal politics which controlled, as one can see, the attitude of most Frenchmen towards foreign policy, whether it was a question of Italy or of Russia. 'Why does he come talking to us about the danger of war!' they would say.

LAVAL NEGOTIATES IN ROME WITH MUSSOLINI

A dictator lives only on prestige. In 1934, Mussolini decided to conquer Abyssinia. But he felt that, before undertaking this distant expedition, it was necessary for him to neutralize France and Britain, or at least one of them. In France, the Flandin Ministry was in power. Laval was at the Ministry of Foreign Affairs. The Duce was aware that the latter wanted to appear in the eyes of his fellow-countrymen as a man of peace, and that, to succeed in doing this, he was open to a generous settlement with the two European dictators. Exploiting this mental attitude, Mussolini approached Laval, not to ask, to be sure, formal permission to attack Abyssinia in defiance of the League of Nations Covenant, but merely to try and get from him the promise of turning a blind eye.

Laval lent himself to this little intrigue. He went to Rome, where he signed with the Duce the agreement of January 7, 1935. In the European theatre it was agreed that France and Italy were to collaborate in opposition to any threat against the independence of Austria. In the African, the two Powers were to settle their old dispute both on the status of the Italian colony in Tunisia and the colonial compensations which we had promised to give to Italy under Article 13 of the Treaty of April 26, 1915. As it appeared in broad outline, the settlement seemed much less disadvantageous to us than the proclaimed desires of the Duce in his unending blusterings would have had us fear. What was the reason for this unexpected moderation? It was because Laval had practically given his fellow-conspirator a free hand in Abyssinia.

On leaving the sitting of the Council of Ministers where he had just given an account of his dealings with Mussolini, Laval was asked by one of his colleagues: 'The Duce asked nothing from you?' 'No ... poor Abyssinia!'

The rumour spread that the fate of Abyssinia had been the object of a secret agreement between the two men. Gamelin relates how[1] during a meeting of the Supreme Military Committee, which took place on November 21, 1935, at the Quai d'Orsay, under the presidency of Laval, the latter said: '... I've got a secret treaty with Mussolini ...' He came back to the subject during the sittings which the Senate held in secret session on March 14 and 15, 1940. The official records of the 15th ascribe to him the following words: 'We [Mussolini and I] came to an agreement—this is the celebrated secret clause which I have in my files, but it's everybody's secret—whereby France henceforth renounced all influence whatsoever in Abyssinia, and abandoned in the economic sphere all the advantages which she could have, to the benefit of Italy. But I said to Mussolini: "Henceforth, you have a free hand, but a free hand in the path of peace."' These utterances could not fail to be of a sibylline nature. Would Laval really have boasted of a Machiavellianism which, in reality, he had not shown?

Flandin, in any case, is explicit. He writes:[2] 'It has often been asserted that these agreements were completed by secret clauses. That is completely false ... Laval, on returning from Rome, gave me the details of his negotiations which, he told me, had been laborious and difficult. A straight talk ... alone had succeeded in smoothing out the differences. Had Laval, as has been said, promised to give Mussolini "a free hand" in Abyssinia? He did not tell me so ... and I must, for the sake of accuracy, bear witness that, when, having succeeded Laval as Foreign Minister in January, 1936, I was embroiled with the policy of sanctions, no Italian authority raised with me the question of any understandings into which Laval might have entered ... other than those which were recorded in the Rome agreements. As I had personally insisted to a large extent on the conclusion of these agreements, and had even forced Laval in the end to leave for Rome in order to put an end to the sabotaging which officials in every quarter of both Ministries of Foreign

[1] *Op. cit.*, vol. II, p. 179.   [2] *Politique française*, pp. 104–5, (2).

Affairs were indulging, I would without doubt have known of the secret clauses, if they had existed.'

This is also the version of M. Charles de Chambrun, who was, at that time, our Ambassador to the King of Italy. In a letter to Gamelin, the text of which the latter reproduces in *Servir*,[1] he writes: '. . . The Franco-Italian agreements . . . *did not contain any secret clauses. Only one article, which I had not negotiated, was not published at the same time as the Treaty.* This Article stipulated that, apart from the interests which we had already acquired, principally our railway . . . *we would place no obstacle in the way of Italian economic development* in Abyssinia. The Article in question, it goes without saying, was duly communicated to the British Government, which was kept informed of all the phases of the negotiations, as well as to the Committees of the Chamber of Deputies and the Senate. The two latter bodies, having examined the question, ratified, by an almost unanimous vote, the whole of the Treaty. Contrary to what one had been led to believe, the Stresa Conference . . . did not discuss the Rome Agreements, which had already come into operation. As for myself, I have never been aware of a secret agreement between Laval and Mussolini. I should add that, during the three days which the Rome negotiations lasted, these two individuals . . . never had a meeting without either myself or M. Léger being present.'

Paul-Boncour's account is more subtly phrased. 'Did the Rome talks', he writes,[2] 'authorize Mussolini to think that he had a free hand for a future conquest? If one sticks to the official texts, indeed they did not. I am not merely talking about the agreements, such as were drawn up and signed, or of the declarations made in public, which commented on them. I am speaking of the very minutes of the talks. Laval wished to communicate them to me one day in the Senate, after a discussion of the Foreign Affairs Committee. . . . I also had confirmation given me by a witness at the talks and by the man who drew up these minutes. He was no other than Léger. . . . But what was said . . . in the confidential talks at the evening party in the Farnese Palace, where one observed the two statesmen withdrawing by themselves in a corner of the *salon*? We shall never know. Perhaps they said nothing to each other. . . . But, even if they spoke of Abyssinia, supposing, with that facile habit of making promises which parliamentary customs in those ill-omened years adopted—by a shrug of the shoulders, or a wink (Vandervelde, who knew both of them well, was convinced that this was how the matter was settled)—Laval was able to convey to Mussolini that he would not be too critical if the latter attempted a military expedition. . . .'

The key to the mystery concerning these sharp practices is supplied

[1] Vol. III, p. 530. The italics are in the text.   [2] *Op. cit.*, vol. III, pp. 14–17.

by Lazareff. He writes:[1] 'Our political editor, who went with the French Minister to Rome, was aware, through one of the close colleagues of the Italian dictator, that the latter had said to ... Laval: "If Italy wants to deal with Abyssinia as France dealt with Morocco, how will France react?"

'"I shall contrive", Laval ... answered him, "that we can look on without saying anything, or only make a protest for the sake of appearances. We are not going to run any risk of falling out on that subject."

'This short dialogue was as important as the agreement. Many journalists got to know about it through some indiscretion. No journalist made any mention of it. Why? Some kept quiet "so as not to hamper the policy of the Quai d'Orsay"; others did so, and amongst them were those most "anti-Laval", because they were, deep down, very pleased to see taking shape a policy opposed to Hitler's Germany. The majority, however, said nothing in order not to displease ... Laval, for ... Laval was able to pull a number of strings. He was the friend or the lawyer of most of the owners or editors of the chief newspapers.'

There you have the mystery cleared up.[2] But this initial mystery was repeated by a second one, which concerned the attitude of Britain. In reference to this, here is what Flandin has said:[3] 'Had Mussolini ... obtained the promise of British neutrality? Throughout this Abyssinian business there were such contradictions between the official and real positions that one is entitled to ask this question. I can only offer, on this subject, the evidence of a conversation which I had with Count Ciano at Paris in May, 1935, towards the end of my term as President of the Council. ... I was determined to find out from him what exactly were Italian intentions towards Abyssinia. Rumours were beginning to circulate about preparations for a military expedition, and the opposition in Parliament, ready to exploit anything against the Government, were already saying that the Rome agreements had given Italy a free hand in the conquest of Abyssinia. I asked Ciano to remind the Duce that the Rome agreements did not in any way authorize armed aggression against Abyssinia. ... I added that he ought, coming

[1] *Dernière édition*, pp. 157–9.
[2] Cleared up at least in this sense that, if it is true that the agreement did not include any secret *written* clauses, it had, nevertheless, been the opportunity for *oral* promises made by Laval to Mussolini, which went further than the undertakings expressly concluded.

Yet it cannot apparently be denied that a Note, marked *Secret*, was appended to the instrument of agreement. Reputable witnesses have stated that M. Léger showed them this sealed note, without, however, revealing to them its content.

If certain rumours are to be believed, the document in question was a personal letter, which at the beginning of January, 1936, Laval, when he realized that his fall was at hand, asked Mussolini to write to him, and in which the Duce, agreeing to this wish, gave him confirmation that no secret clause existed, and authorized him to use this attestation as evidence.

[3] *Politique française*, pp. 177–9.

from London, to have been able to note an undeniable hostility in British circles against any armed intervention by Italy in Abyssinia. To my great surprise Ciano told me that, on the contrary, he did not detect any difficulty being raised by the British. The fact was that the Italian preparations were being made with a maximum of publicity. If the British Government had wished to thwart the Italian venture, it would have been easy for it to begin talks with Rome before Mussolini had committed himself so deeply that he could not retreat without suffering a humiliation which would have been intolerable for a dictator. During the last sitting in April of the Stresa Conference, the final draft communiqué was the subject of debate. Every question in Europe then unsolved had been examined, but no reference had been made to Africa, and Mussolini was no doubt expecting it. When he read the text: "After having reviewed every international problem which has cropped up . . .", he halted and asked: "Should we not add: in Europe?" It was an obvious invitation to the British delegation to speak about Abyssinia. But neither Macdonald nor Sir John Simon moved a muscle. Laval and I, and also no doubt Mussolini, gathered the impression that a tacit acquiescence was being shown by the British Government to Italian ambitions in Abyssinia, even if not to the means whereby these were to be accomplished. These were not to become apparent, as I have said, until after Stresa. At any rate, it was only on June 25 that the British Government asked Italy to give up her demands, already publicly sent to the Emperor, and to accept as compensation a narrow strip of territory . . . in British Somaliland. A stormy interview in Rome between Mr. Eden and Mussolini put an end to the negotiations.'

Flandin himself bears witness, however, to the fact that he was far from being reassured upon the score of the engagements undertaken by Laval with Mussolini. At Stresa, he was waiting for the departure of his Minister of Foreign Affairs in order to negotiate with Mussolini. 'I waited', he writes,[1] 'until Laval left Stresa for Geneva, in order to have a talk with Mussolini. We rapidly reached agreement that the guarantee, renewed to Austria, did not mean anything unless it was completed by military conventions. I indicated that I was ready to have them made the subject of prompt discussions between our respective General Staffs, provided that the Italian guarantee, already given to France by the Treaty of Locarno, was also included within the talks. Mussolini willingly agreed. We even agreed . . . that, in principle, France, if there were the threat of an *Anschluss* . . . would immediately send one or two divisions to reinforce the Italian Army; whilst Italy, if the Rhineland were menaced by a German military reoccupation, would also send several Air Force squadrons to our eastern frontier.

[1] *Politique française*, pp. 172–3.

As soon as I got back to Paris, I sent General Gamelin and General Denain to Rome. The former went on behalf of the Army, and the latter of the Air Force. They easily knocked into shape the verbal agreements concluded between Mussolini and myself. These were even completed, in matters concerning the Air Force, by the exchange of certain technical information of the greatest importance to French aviation. However, curiously enough, a final difficulty arose from the fact that Laval, who was still blinded by his policy of *rapprochement* with Germany (in spite of events which had occurred), was opposed to the agreements being signed by the Chiefs of Staff, in order to avoid awaking in Germany (who might be informed of them) the feeling that a military Franco-Italian alliance was directed against her.'

On his side, Gamelin has related[1] in detail the negotiations which he then undertook with Marshal Badoglio. Both had known each other for a long time, having met at Rio de Janeiro when Gamelin was head of the French Military Mission there and Badoglio was Italian Ambassador. 'We were bound together by ties of friendship', writes Gamelin. In 1935, Badoglio was in Rome, as Chief of Staff for National Defence. On January 21, Gamelin, as we have seen, was nominated Vice-President of the Supreme War Council. Badoglio immediately sent him 'a telegram warmly congratulating him through our Military Attaché at Rome, General Parisot'. We were on the morrow of the conclusion of the Laval and Mussolini agreements. Here is what Gamelin wrote:

On the 25th, I received a letter from Parisot: he had seen the Marshal, who sent me a request to study our possible co-operation in the military sphere, if Germany should take military action against Austria. . . . On February 20, the question was discussed by the Supreme Military Committee, under the presidency of M. Flandin. I was authorized to reply to Marshal Badoglio. The Committee approved the plans that I had worked out for sending a French Army Corps, which would operate on the right flank of the Italian forces to link them up with the Yugoslavs. . . . Similarly, the Committee was in agreement that I should ask the Italians to place at our disposal an Army Corps, which would take up a position on our right, that is between Belfort and the Swiss frontier. Nothing helps to unite our armies so much as rubbing shoulder to shoulder. General Denain, for his part, was to study co-operation between the two Air Forces, chiefly by offering our neighbours bases in the upper valley of Saône and the Doubs, with a view to action against Southern Germany. . . . On March 7, . . . there was another letter from Parisot: Marshal Badoglio and the Duce agreed that conversations between the military leaders should only be fixed up after a definitive agreement between the Governments. I showed my reply, that is to say, my assent . . . to M. Léger. He had . . . the impression that his Minister was not, for the time being, in a hurry to see the matter settled, and hoped we would be able to prolong somewhat any consideration of it.

[1] *Op. cit.*, vol. II. pp. 162–77, *passim*.

He would prefer to obtain first of all some decisions in the political sphere. . . .
On May 4, I again saw M. Léger. He told me that the question of Franco-
Italian military co-operation had been considered by Laval and Mussolini.
They agreed that Marshal Badoglio and myself should investigate the matter. . . .
On June 13, the Italian Military Attaché brought me an invitation, asking me
to go to Rome to settle with him definitely our military collaboration with
respect to the ground forces. I reported the invitation to Fabry. He had me
informed on the 18th that the question had been discussed by the Council of
Ministers, and that I was authorized to go to Rome, but my trip should not
have an official character. On the 25th, I had, before leaving, another interview
with M. Léger. The Government wished my trip to go unnoticed. For the
moment it was not desired that public opinion should see us taking up a too
definite position. . . . Our Ambassador, M. de Chambrun, was waiting for me
at the station in Rome, where Marshal Badoglio himself came to greet me.
The first-named had wanted me to stay with him at the Farnese Palace, so that
we could discuss the matter more conveniently. In such conditions it was
difficult for my presence in Rome to be kept from the public. Moreover, the
Italians wished it to be known. . . . I had a series of private talks with Marshal
Badoglio, in which there was a spirit of mutual trust and affection. We both
felt a deep satisfaction in finding a solution which we had always desired. There
then followed a full meeting with representatives of the Navy and the Air
Force. . . . It was agreed that the complementary and indispensable arrangements would be clarified in these two spheres by General Denain (who was
also expected to arrive in Italy soon), and by Admiral Durand-Viel. In the
minutes which we signed, we gave each other a guarantee covering the whole
of our frontiers: the Alps and Africa. From the outset of any conflict, in order
to emphasize our collaboration, we were to exchange detachments so as to
establish joint stations. . . . The essential thing was that I would send to the
Italians an Army Corps, forming the basis of an Army, which they would
transport to their right flank as far as the Yugoslav frontier. This force was to
act there as a link between the Italian and the Yugoslav Armies, which would
advance together on Vienna in order to support the Austrians and link us up
with the Czechs. In exchange the Italians were to send an Army Corps which
we would place on our right around Belfort. Behind this zone they would
detach Air Force elements to operate against South Germany. . . . The Marshal
had warned me as soon as I had arrived that the Duce wished to see me. M. de
Chambrun immediately agreed to this. . . . Marshal Badoglio had told me that
Mussolini, on leaving his meeting with Hitler at Venice, had said to him: 'You
were right. There are no means of coming to an understanding with that man.
He did nothing but talk to me of the *Anschluss* and of war, in which he wishes
to use all the most brutal modern techniques. He's a barbarian.' I shall always
remember, and have before my eyes the welcome which he (the Duce) showed
me. . . . When about to leave, he concluded: 'To sum up, you are confident?'
'Certainly, I am convinced that you would find again, if need be, the French
Army of the last war.' 'But you are also confident that there won't be a war?'
'That depends, above all, upon our solidarity.' 'Yes, General, you are right.'
On my return, I naturally saw Fabry, M. Léger and . . . Laval, all three of whom
declared themselves to be satisfied. . . . I had invited Marshal Badoglio to our

full-scale manœuvres in September. This provided us with the opportunity for fresh conversations. We were both uneasy about seeing the situation progressing towards a more or less complete break in the close relations which we had desired and established. . . . On September 10, we met at a luncheon in the Italian Embassy, and at the end of the afternoon my wife and I gave a reception in Badoglio's honour. . . . I took . . . my leave of him . . . I insisted that Italy should only take steps in Abyssinia which would respect the framework of the League of Nations. I repeated to him: 'What does the form matter to you if you have the substance of things? The form will come in its due time, and will shape itself on facts. . . .' He assured me that he agreed. But he was not the master, any more than I was for that matter. . . . The crisis broke upon us. . . . The attitude of the League of Nations, encouraged by Britain, is well known. . . . Laval did his best to reconcile the two points of view. . . . A few days later (November 5), a telegram from General Parisot warned me that Marshal Badoglio was uneasy about German intentions in Austria, and inquired of me if anything had been changed in our military understandings. . . . I immediately warned M. Léger. On November 7, I gave the facts to the Supreme Military Committee. . . . On the 9th, the Minister approved my reply to Marshal Badoglio, which assured him of our own fidelity to the engagements into which we had entered. It only remains for me to note a visit from M. François-Poncet on December 30. After our conversation, I went to see M. Léger, who confirmed the points of view which the former had laid before me. Both painted the situation in a particularly gloomy light as regards Germany: 'If France comes to a clear understanding with Russia, Germany will answer by occupying the left bank of the Rhine; if Italy comes out of her present difficulties weakened, there will be the *Anschluss*; if there is war between Britain and Italy, and if we have to join in, Germany is prepared to take action against us. Only a close Franco-British understanding can henceforth ensure peace, and so on. . . .' Thus was heralded the threat which materialized on March 7, 1936. It can be seen that it was not to take us by surprise.

These quotations are lengthy, but how can the state of mind which reigned in our ruling circles in 1935—a year pronounced long before by Mussolini as decisive—be better illustrated than through these texts? They show us our politicians, our military men, our diplomats, collaborating in and yet thwarting, through a mutual distrust, each other's moves, worrying above all over ridding themselves of their own responsibility. Knavery competed in this with incoherence and also with ingenuousness. We know where these *'high'* politics led us.

THE BRITISH PEOPLE, EUROPE, ABYSSINIA AND OURSELVES

On May 25, 1935, before the signatures affixed to the Stresa agreement had had time to dry, the Duce declared at Montecitorio that people nourished strange illusions if they thought that Italy would stay planted on the Brenner, to play against Germany the role of the secular arm of Europe on the Austrian frontier. Autumn came. Certain of himself, Mussolini undertook the conquest of Abyssinia. The Governments of Paris and London prepared to acquiesce. But a giant appeared to trouble the feast: the British people.

Laval had, however, prepared his coup shrewdly. When the Powers assembled at Geneva to prepare, in agreement with the Pact, the sanctions to apply against Italy, he strove to take the problem out of the hands of the League of Nations and to raise the issue outside that body. In this task, he secured, without difficulty, the assistance of his colleague in the British Cabinet, Sir Samuel Hoare. The two Ministers thus drew up, on December 8, 1935, a plan which gave to Italy a large part of Abyssinia. It was the Hoare-Laval Pact. The Prime Minister, Baldwin, supported it, whilst Eden, backed by Duff Cooper and Stanley fought against it. An indiscretion revealed the outlines of the plan. Maps showing the magnificent reward given to the unscrupulous aggressor were published. What had become of the word of honour, of international law, of collective security? The British people, impregnated with Robert Cecil's propaganda on behalf of the League of Nations, rose in indignation. Baldwin had to give way and Hoare to leave the Cabinet.

Arriving on December 19, at the House of Commons to attend that pathetic sitting where, in conformity with British tradition, the resigning Minister opens the debate and indicates the reasons for his conduct, I felt that the M.P.s had been overwhelmed by their constituents, and the Government by the M.P.s. 'Public opinion had not been roused to such a pitch since 1914', General Spears said to me. Baldwin had to make due apology before the House and state that the Hoare-Laval Pact was dead, and he would never permit another Minister to go and pledge his word in imprudent talks at Paris. But before he spoke, Sir Samuel Hoare had declared that, if he had accepted the plan, it was not because of Italian threats; for, if it had been only a question of such threats, the British Empire would have found in its history adequate grounds for feeling reassured. 'What influenced me', he said, 'was the conviction I felt that, if we were attacked, we would go into the fight without the full support of other Powers [read: France], and that this would have caused the downfall of the League of Nations.' Before the silent emotion of the House, Hoare added: 'There was a British Fleet in the Mediterranean: there were British reinforcements in Egypt, at Malta, and at Aden. No other Member State of the League of Nations had moved a ship, a plane or a man.' And he added: 'Without effective co-operation, collective security is impossible, and the League of Nations will perish.' This was the language which France formerly had used to Britain. This time, Britain was using it to France. The leader of the Liberal Party, Archibald Sinclair, intervening in the debate, asked with healthy frankness: 'The question is: does France want to help us?' One of the leaders of the Labour Party, Colonel Wedgwood, put it more bluntly: 'It is impossible to count on people who play hide-and-seek with the League of Nations, who come into the Assembly when their interests are threatened, and keep out when those of others are at stake.' Certainly, talks between British and French General Staffs had taken place, but such talks have value only in proportion to the will of Governments to act. Now, Hoare had just said that it was because he had felt that the French Government would not act that he had accepted Laval's proposal.

I was deeply moved by this declaration. Thus it was, whilst for sixteen years France had striven unsuccessfully to get Britain to put her strength at the disposal of collective security, that now, on the very day when, at the appeal of the League of Nations to defend a country unjustly attacked, Britain was answering 'Present', it was France who was denying her own policy and sneaking away! What moral weakness and what political blundering! They were saying in the corridors of the House of Commons: 'The French Prime Minister is not the man with whom to go tiger-hunting.' Was the situation alarming for the democratic nations because of the menacing attitude of Mussolini? Britain, who had disarmed after the victory of 1918, was not prepared; but Germany, who had just introduced compulsory military service, could not then dream of entering upon a war. She had, on October 4, pledged a benevolent neutrality towards Mussolini. Indeed, Laval was publishing in his newspapers that Italy was more powerful than the British Empire and Russia, and that Italian airmen had sworn to die by diving their planes on the decks of British cruisers. The British fleet was only a collection of scrap iron. L'Action Française and Gringoire embroidered upon these details. One issue of Gringoire was devoted to a justification of Italian claims. This section of the Press stated that, for Britain the League of Nations meant the 'Sources of the Nile'. General Mordacq, former chief of Clemenceau's Cabinet, who was to come to such a bad end during the German occupation, wrote in Vu that it was necessary to come to an understanding with Italy, even at the price of breaking with Britain. And he was hostile to an alliance with Russia! Those who flayed the egoism of Britain during the course of her history refrained from talking about Frederick II and Bismarck who went a little further than egoism. This campaign, designed to divert the French from action, seemed to me deprived of all sense of reality. Mussolini lacked four things to fight France and Britain: coal, steel, petrol and a war-like race like the Germans. Britain needed only to close the Suez Canal to isolate the Italian Army in Abyssinia. Mussolini's capitulation after his boastings would, without doubt, have brought about his collapse. Thus, the prestige of the League of Nations could have been restored, and the small nations would again have reverted to a belief in collective security. Britain would have armed herself, for how, after having thus intervened on behalf of the Abyssinians, could that country have been able to close her eyes when it was a question of the Czechs and the Poles? Now, had not a British M.P., a member of the Franco-British Committee, shortly afterwards answered a talk which I gave in the dining-room of the House of Commons by saying: 'We will not fight for the Czechs'? Such was the tremendous repercussion which the Abyssinian affair had on the security of Europe, on that of France, on her very life, which was menaced.

On leaving the House of Commons I made up my mind to speak in the debate which was going to open in the Chamber of Deputies on this subject. At the moment of leaving London I received an eight-page letter in pencil from Lady Asquith, at whose house I had dined the evening before, in which the widow of the former Prime Minister stressed with a rare political insight the opportunity which was offered to France to conquer once and for all the reluctance of Britain to enter into a system of collective security.

I spoke on December 27 in the debate which opened at the Palais Bourbon.[1] Amongst the complaints voiced against me by German propaganda and by the Vichy Press, none was more virulent than that which this speech aroused. When the Nazis accused me of being 'the tool of Britain', they knew very well that, with the exception of the Abyssinian affair, I had never ceased to disagree with my British friends about the foreign and military policy of their country in the years between the two wars. They knew that, when Lloyd George was in charge of affairs, I said one day in the Chamber: 'Britain does not like other nations to have Gibraltars.' They were aware that I had always represented to the British that, to refuse to intervene on the first attempt by Hitler to break up the Europe established by former treaties, would not absolve them from doing so one day, but in more unfavourable circumstances. They knew also that I was in disagreement with British policy on the necessity of a Russian alliance and on the Spanish war. They knew that I had advised them to create an armoured corps, which France herself refused to introduce. For Britain was no less deceived than France during this interim period between the two wars. If our rulers were less excusable than theirs, the reason is because we were the more in danger. The greatest service which we could do our British friends would have been not to follow their advice. It is true, I did not cease to maintain that for France independence lay only in a close union with Britain, still as powerful by her moral strength as by her material power, and governed, whatever might be the party in power, by *gentlemen*, that is to say by men upon whose word one could rely.

---

[1] The meeting-place of the French Chamber of Deputies [Tr.].

Yet my admiration for this country and my friendship for some of its statesmen never prevented me, despite this, from employing towards it, before as well as during the war, the plain speaking which friends owe to each other.

Regarding my speech of December 27, Champeaux uttered this opinion:[1] 'The event, and one can well call it the climax to the day, has been the declaration of Paul Reynaud, president of the *Centre Républicain* Group,[2] who, to the stupefaction of the members of his group, has violently taken the side of Britain against Italy, quoting *Mein Kampf*, and denouncing the military effort of Germany; in brief, throwing the last-named country into a debate where she had no very clear relevance.' But he was forced to admit 'this speech won him applause from the Left, without the Right being able, strictly speaking, to reproach him with a change of views . . . it kept to the tradition of the Comte de Mun and of Barrès'.[3] Let us therefore analyse this speech, of which it is true to say that it influenced the majority of the Chamber, and provoked a lively discussion in other circles. The resistance to the Italian dictator in the Abyssinian affair was the beginning of the Resistance. I shall give from this speech extracts which should be sufficient to enable the reader to judge for himself, without omitting the comments of the *Journal Officiel*, which will make clear the atmosphere of the debate. It is true that I only treated the question of Abyssinia in relation to the German menace, which the author of *La croisade des démocraties* evidently wished should be left in oblivion.

I began, indeed, by saying: 'Let us try to look beyond the present dispute. Everyone is agreed in recognizing that there is a silent third party present, and it is this which makes the situation a grave one.' (*Applause from a great number of benches.*) After having called to mind the negative results of recent conversations between Hitler and our Ambassador in Berlin, I cited the doctrine of *Mein Kampf*, which I summed up as follows: 'The obstacle to a German war is the alliance between Britain and France', and I added: 'Now, what has become of this alliance?' (*Loud applause from the Left, the extreme Left, from various Centre benches and a few benches on the Right.*) I recalled the estrangement of Britain after the victory of 1918. Of the Baldwin formula, 'Our frontier is on the Rhine', I said: 'This declaration was not enough for us. We reproached the British for short-sightedness. We said to them: "Can't you see that, if the fire takes hold of some part of Europe, Europe herself will be entirely in flames?" But the British politicians resisted this point of view. They remained wedded by a thousand links

---

[1] *La croisade des démocraties*, vol. I, p. 81.

[2] i.e. the Republican Centre, one of the small groups into which the moderate element of the Chamber of Deputies was split [Tr.].

[3] *Op. cit.*, p. 95.

to their traditional conception of insularity. We said to them: "What is essential is that sanctions should be automatic, for, if a discussion occurs on the motives of the aggressor, if there is discrimination upon the faults or merits of the victim, everything is lost." We put forward specific cases: "On the day Germany attacks Austria, she will say: 'But the Austrian people were coming to greet us with open arms.' On the day she attacks Czechoslovakia she will say: 'There exists in Czechoslovakia a German and a Slav minority.' On the day she attacks Yugoslavia she will say: 'The Croats of Yugoslavia are bearing with difficulty the yoke of the Serbs.' On the day she attacks Roumania, she will say: 'There is a large Hungarian minority.'" And we added: "That is why it is necessary to find a formula over which no discussion can arise. Let us put a stop to the aggressor, whoever he may be, or whoever his victim may be!"' (*Loud applause from the Left, the extreme Left and from various benches of the Centre and the Right.*)

I pointed out that it was then that 'a new factor came into being, the greatest since the war . . . the most propitious event since the entry of America into the war in 1917, a factor before which the British politicians were powerless: a powerful, irresistible movement had gathered strength within the depths of the British people.' (*Applause from the Left, the extreme Left and from various benches of the Right and the Centre.*) 'Seeing Imperialism raise its head, an Imperialism which, it had been asserted, had been overthrown; observing that, again on the Continent, *the old and bloody drama* was about to begin anew, that the weak were again going to be brutally crushed by the strong, this people have seen in the League of Nations a means of bringing justice and peace to Europe and to the world.' (*Applause from the Left and from the extreme Left, and from various benches of the Centre and the Right.*) 'That was the significance of the Peace Ballot. All this took place before British public opinion had become aware of the Abyssinian affair.' (*Applause from the Left and from various benches.*) 'Alas! We did not understand the chance which destiny was offering us.' (*Renewed and loud applause from the same benches.*) 'Whilst our rulers still debated, the British people said "yes" to the question which we had been facing for so many years. The problem of peace was virtually settled, and settled—let us be proud of it—by the victory of a French ideal.' (*Loud applause from the Left and the extreme Left and from several benches of the Centre and the Right.*) 'It was a stable foundation for peace because the will of a democracy which endures, is more stable than that of a politician, who passes away.' (*Cries of Hear, hear! from the Left and from various benches.*)

I then revealed why the Hoare-Laval Pact was satisfactory, despite what had been said about it, to the immediate interests of Britain. And, speaking of the movement of revolt by British public opinion which swept this 'Pact' away, I said: 'Therein lies a display of strength.'

(Renewed applause from the same benches.) 'This dismembered victim, this reward to the aggressor which the Hoare-Laval Pact offered, things such as this are what we French have condemned for fifteen years, and are what we have to fear.' *(Applause.)* 'We are forced to recognize that this rebuff to the Hoare-Laval Pact is a victory for French doctrine *(applause from the Left, the extreme Left and the Centre)*, for what we had instilled into the minds of nations at Geneva *(renewed applause from the same benches)*, and it is also thus that the small States of which M. Léon Blum has spoken, have judged. . . . Do not be astonished at the uneasiness of these small nations, of these traditional friends of France who feel that their very life is a gift which the solidarity of various peoples offers them from day to day.' *(Applause.)* I brought to notice the strength of the reaction of the American people, directed, as much, moreover, against Britain as against France over this policy of 'abdication' in the face of violence.

I then indicated to the Chamber the reasons which decided Sir Samuel Hoare to accept the agreement that Laval proposed to him. And also I pointed out the protests of the Liberals and Socialists against the attitude of France. I showed that our relations with Britain were more strained than they had ever been, since the ending of the war. 'Why was this? Because we have not made a choice, and because we seem to the British as if we are about to leave them in the lurch at a time which, for them—as I have just shown to be the case—is the hour of trial. In conforming to our doctrine they have found themselves losing touch with us. Why have we deserted? Why have we jeopardized, by this moral separation, little understood, let us admit it, by the great majority of our fellow-countrymen, our vital interests? That is what I have come to ask, with anguish, on the floor of the House.' *(Loud applause from the extreme Left and the Left.)*

It will be observed that, in the face of this direct attack against the policy of Laval, the Centre and the Right abstained. I recalled that, if Mussolini on four occasions had refused the successive offers of peace which had been addressed to him; that, if he had given the Hoare-Laval Pact the reception which he did, 'it is for a deep-seated reason. It is because there are not only material interests at stake (one could have settled them), but because there exists a deep-rooted opposition between the doctrine of the League of Nations and the Fascist ideology.' *(Loud applause from the extreme Left and the Left.)* I recalled the formula of Mussolini, apostle of violence: 'War is for men what motherhood is for women,' and I added: 'It is this deep antagonism which is fundamental to the debate. It was this antagonism which, in 1923, inspired the bombardment of Corfu, and it was not a question of racial discrimination. This is the dominating idea. One must make a demonstration of force to prove that one is capable of translating doctrine into reality. Fascism has need to conquer. But it is here that the principle of stopping the aggressor comes into play. Thence springs the obligation before which we have hesitated up to now, but which today is imperious. To choose between Italy, who is violating the League of Nations Covenant, and Britain, who is its guardian.' (*Loud applause from the extreme Left, the Left and from several benches of the Centre and the Right.*) Almost all the Chamber appeared again in agreement. Yet this miserable policy was to continue to be that of France! 'Germany, at this moment, is making every effort', I said, 'to conciliate Britain, with the object of separating her from France.' I asked: 'Is there talk of peace being menaced? Is it not in this that the real menace of war lies? In the House of Commons, all the speakers were of the same opinion. All have said: "Abyssinia, for whom we have no sympathy, and whose imposition upon us as a colleague at Geneva was wrong, matters little. What does count is the punishment of the aggressor!" But when for the first time a powerful voice is heard throughout Europe, the voice of the British people, which utters the cry of *Stop the aggressor!* was it to be ourselves, the French, that is to say the beneficiaries in the near future from collective security (*loud applause from the Left and the extreme Left*), who were to rise against this threat to the nations? What a strange confidence in the future those who are in favour of a passive attitude must have, and how little would I envy the *fickle spirit* with which they would assume this responsibility!' To those who said that Britain will always march into the fray because it is in her interest, I replied: 'Do you believe if Britain resolved to wash her hands of the League of Nations, she would intervene the day after in a struggle in Central Europe, in Austria, for example?' To those who said: 'Let us allow Italy to sate her hunger by devouring Abyssinia,' I replied: 'But do you think she will be satisfied tomorrow?' French public opinion was confused, admittedly, by the false 'realists' of the extreme Right, who had become the admirers of Fascism more than of the monarchy, who had only scorn for the ideals of the League of Nations, and only cynicism for respect shown to the pledged word.

This public opinion was vexed with those who were represented to it as being war-mongers. To this I replied: 'It is possible that public opinion has been led astray, but the nobility of our mandate (*loud applause from the Left, the extreme Left and from various benches*), when contrasted with the many small restrictions which are attached to it simply because we are a few months and perhaps a few weeks from elections, lies in the fact that a deputy can rise in a free Chamber in order to say what he believes to be in the best interests of the country.' And I ended: 'In any case, if telling the truth, if exposing a peril which I believe is deadly to the country, is running a parliamentary risk, I, for my part, accept that risk!' (*Loud and repeated applause from the extreme*

Left, the Left, and several benches. The speaker, on returning to his seat, received congratulations.) That speech was not without effect, for several months later I was only elected, as I have stated, at the second voting of the ballot, and by a slender majority.

For those who dabble in a study of mass psychology, this sitting, during which one could see the Right becoming colder and the Left more heated, is full of enlightenment. Why did the Socialists support me so warmly? First of all, it was because their Labour friends had given them the same impression about the revolt of popular British feeling which I had myself gained in London, and which I imparted to the Chamber. Again, it was because they felt that I was filled with a hostility against the Fascist régime which with them was of long standing, and which the murder of Matteotti had rightly turned into something impassioned. Whilst announcing that each country was the only judge of the political régime suitable to it, I had stressed the danger threatening France through a régime which persisted in inciting the Italian people to despoil its neighbours. The Right, on the contrary, was particularly sensitive to the restoration of order in Italy, and it was indulgent to a régime which was credited with working to establish domestic order, and with preserving us from the contagion of Bolshevism. It had also, in so far as the former revolutionary Laval was concerned, the inclination which inspires some to make a gamekeeper out of a poacher.

The next day, Romier wrote in *Le Figaro* this phrase, which I found some weeks later on an election poster of my Right-wing opponent: 'If M. Laval is beaten tomorrow, it will be because of the speech of M. Paul Reynaud.'

Kerillis reproached me in *L'Echo de Paris* with having uttered a deadly speech, which had sown' consternation within the national ranks', in having 'pleaded the cause of Britain with far too much partiality', and he summed up his chief complaint in these words: 'During the whole time he was speaking, the parties of the Left applauded him frantically.' These criticisms weighed all the more on my political friends in that in this article Kerillis recalled warmly his friendship for me.

As for Maurras, he wrote the same day in *L'Action Française*: 'M. Paul Reynaud belongs to that class of questionable politicians: he must be watched, like one watches counter-spies in the pay of a well-regulated international police. . . . But don't be led astray by the word counter-spy. M. Paul Reynaud is not a counter-spy. In his disguise of an Anglophile, he is a German agent. His speech, alleging a German peril (and it is a real peril) has been made in order to threaten with Germany whosoever refuses to serve Britain against Italy. . . . Germany has just found in the pro-British manœuvre of M. Paul Reynaud a precious ally, capable of provoking such an event as the outbreak of war. This alliance of the leader of those who advocate devaluation in France gives Germany a greater chance, which is not unexpected or gratuitous. M. Reynaud's speech is that of a long-standing and perfidious tool of Germany.'

I would not wish to minimize in any way the effect produced on the reader by such a judgement.

Laval got out of the affair in his typical way. Taking an opposite line to the declaration condemning sanctions, which he had made shortly before at the opening of the debate, he replied that France and Britain had concluded military agreements in the three spheres of land, sea and air, and he waxed indignant at the idea that anyone could accuse him of hesitating in his adherence to these agreements. For what, indeed, did one take him? He got a majority of twenty votes, but his Administration was virtually dead. It did expire three weeks later, following upon the resignation of the Radical Ministers within it.

Two days after the vote in the Chamber, I received, and read at the same time in *Le Temps*, a letter in which Tardieu informed me of his resignation from the *Centre Républicain* Group of which I had been chairman since the time he had resigned that post in 1934 to enter the Doumergue Cabinet. 'The position which you have taken', he wrote me, 'on the question of devaluation was already separating us. Your speech and your vote in the last debate on foreign policy throws us still more seriously into opposition. You have presented the problem as a simple choice between Italy, as the violator of the League Covenant, and Great Britain, its guardian. This is not the point. The terrible confusion about the present situation has only one source: it lies in the fact that one has tried to apply sanctions without first having organized them, and from this fact springs their futility and their danger. Now, it is Great Britain who is responsible for the chronic deficiency in the organization of sanctions.... Great Britain... has changed her mind.... It is our duty to recognize that this ... reversal of her opinion means an injustice for Italy; for peace, a danger; for the Covenant, the risk of failure. Indeed the threat of sanctions, organized in advance and thereby impressive, can, when no ambiguity exists about them, prevent war. The application of improvised sanctions on the other hand ... leads to ambiguity and to war.... The Laval Administration tried to ward off this danger. . . . It would be an inopportune time to abandon this Administration.'

On the 31st, I gave him my reply. Stressing the contradictory position in which he had placed himself, I wrote to him: 'It is at a time when Britain takes the road which for fifteen years, we have asked her to tread, at a time when fifty nations are gathered at Geneva to ensure collective security, at a time when the French view is finally triumphing, that you wish to stop this effort, to check its impetus. . . . It is this traditional [French] policy that, keeping faith with myself, I have

defended on the floor of the Chamber, without troubling myself about
any question of praise. On this problem, as on the monetary problem,
I have placed my country before party considerations. . . .'

Sarraut's Cabinet succeeded that of Laval on January 23, 1936.
Delbos, who had a seat in it, had just (on December 17), uttered a
speech in the same strain as myself. But it was Flandin who took over
the post of Foreign Minister from Laval. On March 2, 1936, at Geneva,
he rejected Eden's proposal that oil sanctions should be applied against
Italy. Thus it was Laval's policy which survived. The majority of the
Chamber, which had given Delbos its applause, tolerated the policy
of Flandin! It was a decisive error.

CHAPTER VI

A FRANCE WITHOUT DEFENCES

*'One must be lacking in common sense not to know how important it is
to great Powers to have their frontiers well fortified.'*

Richelieu

*The Classical Route for Invasion.—1922, Pétain makes his choice.
—1934, Pétain as War Minister: Our Northern Frontier will be
'solidly protected'.—June 15, 1934, The system of defensive warfare.—May, 1940, Our light fortifications in the north are pierced
at Sedan, and neutralized elsewhere.*

THE CLASSICAL ROUTE FOR INVASION

IN 1940, the Germans entered our country as though they were
walking over their own threshold.

What was the good of the Maginot Line, 'the buckler of France'?
For ten years the French had been told that, behind the shelter of the
concrete of the Maginot Line they could sleep undisturbed. Who was
it then who had deceived them?

The classical route for the invasion of France is through Belgium
and across our northern frontier: it is the shortest and the least hilly
way to Paris, the heart of the country.

It was from Belgium that the Franks invaded Gaul.

It was from Belgium that the Army of the Emperor Otto IV and
his Allies came, the army which Philip Augustus cut to pieces on
July 27, 1214, at Bouvines.

It was from Belgium that the Spanish Army, in 1636, broke into
France, and penetrated as far as Corbie, creating such alarm in Paris
that the population hooted Richelieu in the streets, whilst the burgesses
of the city fled towards Chartres and Orléans.

It was from Belgium that this 'redoubtable infantry of the Spanish
Army', which the great Condé beat at Rocroi, came.

It was from Belgium that there came, in the reign of Louis XIV, the
Armies of Marlborough and of Prince Eugène, which threatened Paris
and inspired, in 1709, the pathetic appeal of the aged King to his
people.

It was from Belgium that the Austrians, British and Dutch, who
attacked the France of Convention days, came.

It was from Belgium that the Anglo-Prussian forces which entered Paris in 1815 came, after having defeated Napoleon at Waterloo.

It was from Belgium that the German Army came in August, 1914, to reach the very gates of Paris.

'From the Ardennes to Dunkirk, the plain lies open to invasions. Twenty times, a hundred times, the enemy has advanced along it. Almost every hill and every town has the memory of a battle or a siege linked to it. On the very soil there seems to be inscribed a policy, the policy of frontiers, of security, of protection against the Imperial troops,' wrote Pierre Gaxotte.[1] It is not by chance that Laon has suffered forty-two sieges in nine hundred years.

The reason why the Berlin-Paris express passes through Liége and Namur is because that route is the most direct and the least hilly.

Sedan, on the Belgian frontier, is twice as near to Paris as Strasbourg. A hostile army which advances from Sedan could either strike at the heart of France by marching on Paris, or take in the rear the French Army which is defending our northern frontier or which has entered Belgium, or deal similarly with the Maginot Line.

Was this Maginot Line the shield of France? Look at the map. What was the Maginot Line? Two sections, each of seventy kilometres, a total of a hundred and forty kilometres out of the whole frontier of seven hundred and sixty kilometres from the North Sea to Switzerland.[2] And where were these two sections? On the classical route for the invasion of France? Not at all! They lay between the Rhine and Longuyon. It was not one shield, but two bits of a shield, which did not protect the heart!

On June 14, 1934, in the Chamber, the *rapporteur général*[3] of the Budget, asking for a vote of credit for the fortifications, spoke of the Maginot Line in these terms: 'I have been struck, for my part, by hearing M. Fabry, the Chairman of the Army Committee, tell us in the Finance Committee, in order to stress his firm conviction on this point, that he almost wished that the German General Staff had been invited to visit some of these fortified works, because he thought that their strength was such as to discourage aggression.'

They must have laughed very loudly at the Headquarters of the General Staff at Berlin. 'If these French gentlemen think we shall turn aside from the classical route for the invasion of France, in order to

---

[1] *Le siècle de Louis XV*, p. 193.

[2] Add to these hundred and forty kilometres the twenty kilometres around the stronghold of Montmédy, fifteen kilometres around that of Maubeuge and five around that incomplete stronghold of Valenciennes. This, in May, 1940, made a hundred and seventy-five [sic] kilometres of permanent fortifications out of a frontier of seven hundred and sixty.

[3] i.e. the member of a parliamentary committee (in this case, one for discussing the Budget) who was entrusted with giving its report to the Chamber of Deputies [Tr.].

break our skulls on the concrete of their Maginot Line, let them do so by all means!'

And, in 1940 as in 1914, the German Armies came through Belgium, as—I say this without wishing to claim any particular merit—I had prophesied in the Chamber five years earlier. Now, as in 1914, one of them advanced from Sedan, the other from Dinant. And everything was lost, for, since 1914, a new element had appeared on the scene: the German armoured corps, supported and preceded by its Stuka dive-bombers.

Whose idea was this system of fortifications? Who were those responsible?

1922: PÉTAIN MAKES HIS CHOICE

On the morrow of the First World War, a committee was set up for the study of fortified areas, which was placed under the chairmanship of Joffre.

The question was how the frontier should be fortified. Under Louis XIV, at a period when roads, few in number, were the only land communications, Vauban barred the avenues of invasion by constructing isolated forts or strongholds whose garrisons made sorties either against the invading army or against its supply columns, if these passed their way. Thus, the invader, whose artillery was not capable of demolishing these forts, was forced to besiege them, and often for an intolerable length of time, which gave us the opportunity to gather our forces.

After our defeat in 1870, a General of the Engineers, Séré de Rivières, had encircled France with forts and strongholds, which were more powerful than those of Vauban, but which, like them, were isolated and independent one of the other, and whose governors were responsible to the Minister of War, and not to the Commander-in-Chief, who had only the right to link up the mobile element of garrisons with his operations. But, at the beginning of the First World War, the heavy artillery sounded the death-knell of the isolated fort. As for the strongholds, the range of guns had become such that their entire area was brought under fire. Liége, Antwerp, Namur, Maubeuge, Warsaw, all isolated strongholds, fell. If Verdun held out, it was because it was encircled and supported by an army.

After July, 1915, Joffre broke away from this system. In the future, there were to be no more isolated fortifications, but fortified zones which would be controlled by the Command and thus be dependent on the Army which would base its manœuvres on them. There were to be fortified areas at Belfort, Epinal, Toul and Verdun.

This was the plan that Joffre, in 1922, wished to extend to our frontier by creating from the North Sea to Switzerland a certain number of fortified areas, round which the Army would operate: namely at Dunkirk, Valenciennes, Maubeuge, Mézières, Sedan and Belfort.

Pétain, the Commander-in-Chief,[1] was opposed to this plan. Joffre had to resign. What was Pétain's argument? He had formulated it, in 1921, in his *Note sur l'organisation défensive du territoire*. Under the pretext of drawing conclusions from the lessons of war, he declared: 'Modern defensive systems can no longer be other than *battlefields for armies, organized in times of peace*.' And he proposed providing a 'continuous frontier battlefield', the construction of which would be similar to that of the defensive fronts of trench warfare. Pétain, moreover, limited these field fortification works to the north-east frontier, from Thionville to the Rhine, and on the French bank of the Rhine to Basle. As for the northern frontier, he maintained that it was necessary to advance into Belgium to defend it.

Three years after the resignation of Joffre in 1925, the shortening in the length of military service woke up the sleepers for it became more difficult to find a solution to the problem of defending the frontier during mobilization in the case of a sudden attack. The Supreme War Council declared then that the defensive organization of the frontiers must be undertaken without delay; but, in conformity with Pétain's thesis, it added that this should begin with that of the north-east.

A committee, presided over by General Guillaumat, was set up. It concluded, like Joffre, in favour of the creation of fortified regions. It suggested two of them on the Franco-German frontier; the first on the Lorraine front (from Thionville to Saint-Avold), the second on the lower Alsace front (from Bitche to the Rhine). This was to become, after being extended a little later, the two sections which formed the Maginot Line.[2] There was no question at all about our northern frontier.

What was Pétain going to do? This time he gave way. On January 18, 1927, the Supreme War Council, meeting under his chairmanship, accepted the conclusions of the Guillaumat Committee. Two zones were to be fortified. Pétain declared[3] at that time, that they 'locked the gates of France'. But he forgot to say that, at the most dangerous point on our frontier, the gate was going to remain wide open. So the legend of the 'buckler of France' was born.

---

[1] The reader will be aware that the duties of the Commander-in-Chief are duties in time of war, but that the holder of the post is designated in peace-time. In my account, the term has, according to the circumstances, the one or the other significance.

[2] The Committee had decided upon the construction of a third fortified area, which would have covered Belfort. This decision remained in the planning stage. The only thing done was to build round Belfort, after 1930, some light fortifications.

[3] General Laure, *Pétain*, p. 283.

1934: PÉTAIN AS WAR MINISTER: OUR NORTHERN FRONTIER
WILL BE 'SOLIDLY PROTECTED'

The day following the riots of February 6, 1934,[1] Pétain, as we have
seen, became War Minister.

On March 7 he was heard by the Military Committee of the Senate.
Hitler had been in power for three months. Some Senators from the
north were rightly disturbed over the threat of an invasion across our
undefended frontier between Montmédy and the sea. Pétain reassured
them. One reads in the account of his evidence: 'Let us consider the
defensive organization of the northern frontier. This defensive organization is still in a planning stage. It will be organized in sectors. If we
take Dunkirk as a starting-point, of what will this northern frontier
consist? It will be the continuation of the fortified area in the east, which
stops at Longwy-Montmédy. It is a question of continuing this frontier
to the sea.

'From Montmédy, there are the forests of the Ardennes: they are
impenetrable, if one makes special dispositions there.

'As this front would not have any depth, the enemy cannot commit
himself there. If he does throw in his strength at this point, we can
"pinch him off again", when he comes out of the forests. This sector,
therefore, is not dangerous.'

Now, in spite of the special dispositions made by the Belgians, so
little were the Ardennes 'impenetrable' that the armoured and motorized
divisions of the Germans crossed through them in May, 1940. And
we did not 'pinch them off' when they came out of the Ardennes.
Because of an absence of serious defences, they advanced on Sedan,
and from there set out on their course to the sea, taking the Allied
Armies in Belgium in the rear. That was the extent to which this sector
was not dangerous.

Let us resume our examination of the minutes of the evidence.

'*The President of the Military Committee*: Now to pass to the question
of the fortifications on the northern frontier.

'*Marshal Pétain, Minister of War*: Fortifications built on the frontier
would not protect it, because the frontier is too near. It is necessary to
advance into Belgium.'

It is necessary to advance into Belgium!

Let us pause a moment to express astonishment at the declaration
that Pétain made to his biographer, General Laure, as the latter told it
to me on May 18, 1940, when he entered my Cabinet after the disaster
in Belgium. Laure reports it in these words:[2] 'The entry of Allied

[1] The immediate cause of these was the revelation of the Stavisky scandal, a large-scale
fraud in which several politicians were implicated. The riots were initially demonstrations
against the Administration; later they became demonstrations by the Communists and
Socialists against the Fascists [Tr.].   [2] *Op. cit.*, pp. 429-30.

troops into Belgium was a grave error. We should have (as Pétain had always recommended when he was Minister of War) committed only a small number of large units into this action, aimed at supporting and then incorporating our Allies (the Belgians), so as not to run the risk of having to face an encounter battle, and to be able to manœuvre on our fortified positions.' He added in one of the crisp phrases to which he was accustomed: 'We were the victims of neutrals.' If Pétain had spoken to me in that strain, he would have told, as was seen, the opposite of the truth. Laure, who had been his *chef de cabinet*[1] at the Ministry of War, knew this well.

But let us come back to 1934.

Did Pétain's statements satisfy the Senators from the north? The fact was that Pétain tabled a measure proposing a credit of one thousand two hundred and seventy-five million francs, which the *rapporteur général* of the Budget said, when informing the Chamber of the facts as given him by the Government, on June 14, 1934, would permit the 'continuation and completion of the equipping of our land frontiers'. Complete the fortifications? With what? With one thousand two hundred and seventy-five millions? Yet, out of this sum, the greater part—eight hundred and eighty millions—was earmarked for covering the overdraft of credits. There remained three hundred and ninety-five millions, which were to be applied to certain works in the Maginot Line, and which were above all intended for the building of training camps and barracks. In fact, two hundred and ninety-two millions only were to be available for the construction of new works. Where were they to be made? 'From Montmédy to the northern frontier, Montmédy forming the hinge between the Lorraine front and the northern one,' Pétain explained to the Chamber. The hundred and forty kilometres of the Maginot Line had cost seven milliards. And was the intention with two hundred and ninety-two millions to fortify the four hundred and ten kilometres which separated Dunkirk from the Maginot Line, or even only the three hundred and eighty-five kilometres between Dunkirk and Montmédy? For it was a question of 'finishing the equipping of our land frontiers', and not of a first instalment towards this task. Pétain declared to the Chamber: '*This vote will satisfy the deep desire of the people who wish to live in peace behind the shelter of frontiers solidly protected.*'

Until that time, one had spoken of frontiers for reasons that were military in character and not to satisfy the feeling, deep or otherwise, of the population. Rising to speak on the following day, Daladier, who had been War Minister for the preceding thirteen months, said: 'The

---

[1] i.e. the head of his secretariat; French Ministers usually introduced within their Ministries a number of personal and temporary advisers, who formed their *Cabinet* [Tr.].

Supreme War Council . . . was unanimous[1] in giving an opinion which was unfavourable to the fortification of the northern areas and, for myself, I do not oppose in any way the technical reasons which are put forward by the most eminent members of this Council.'

These eminent members were Pétain and the other senior members of the Council.

Why, then, were these fortifications built? Daladier explained: 'But it was realized that, perhaps for reasons more psychological than military, and also for international reasons which were of weight, it was necessary to grant credits to fortify the northern zone. . . .' Thus, it was not for military reasons that, a year and a half after Hitler's advent to power and when he was fully occupied in rearming, France, ruined by the crisis into which she was sinking, France who, for two years, had cut down her military expenses by two milliard francs, was going to lay out the little money which she possessed for her national defence!

What were these pressing psychological and international reasons?

It was a question of reassuring the inhabitants of the north.

It was also a matter of satisfying the Belgians. The latter had just fortified the Antwerp–Liége–Arlon line, of which the first half was made up of the Albert Canal, but the second, that from Liége to Arlon, was so badly planned that a Belgian general, in the rough language of a soldier, declared: 'I p—— on it, and I pass by.' We were pledged to go to the help of the Belgian Army on the Albert Canal, and to take over as our responsibility the defence of the Liége–Arlon line. In reality, the announcement that we had fortified our northern frontier increased Belgian fears; in their eyes it was proof of our intention not to go to their help.

JUNE 15, 1934: THE SYSTEM OF DEFENSIVE WARFARE

Daladier did not stop at giving the Chamber the reasons, other than military, why Pétain said he was going to fortify our northern frontier. The important thing about his speech, which received a great welcome from the Left, was, first of all, that Daladier declared he was speaking on behalf of the Radical-Socialist Party, of which he had been and was again to become chairman; but above all, it was also important because of the fact that he was again to become Minister of War during four years from June, 1936, to May, 1940, and was to play, therefore, a vital role in the preparation for war. Now it is impossible to understand his attitude in 1937 with regard to the armoured corps if one does not know his attitude in 1934 to the military problem as a whole.

Supported by that authority given him as a man who had already

---

[1] Though it was unanimous in 1927, the Council gave an affirmative opinion in 1932 only by a majority of votes.

been Prime Minister and twice Minister of War, Daladier outlined the military policy of his party, which corresponded, it must be confessed, to the feelings of the majority of French people: it was one of systematic defensive warfare. Daladier was sincerely and deeply convinced that fire-power, which was increasing each day, was to make the front of an entrenched army on the defensive invulnerable. This doctrine was inspired by *Le feu tue*[1] of Pétain, and guaranteed by the authority of the 'Victor of Verdun'. Later on, we shall examine this doctrine in detail, but it is impossible to detach it, in Daladier's speech, from the problem of fortifications, since these were presented by him as the essential basis of this question. I am going to speak of the divergence of fundamental views which has existed between Daladier and myself on the military problem; but I would like, first of all, to express the contempt with which the campaign of lies directed against him by the Vichy Press has inspired in me.

There were, Daladier told the Chamber, two systems:

1. 'That of the offensive, as was put into application in 1914 . . . which, alas, would have ended in the final loss of our liberty, but for the amazing recovery which took place on the Marne.'

2. 'The shield or defensive strategy.' This system was inspired by 'the revolution which had taken place in the art of warfare' since the wars in Manchuria and the Balkans, because of the factor of fire-power furnished by automatic arms from the shelter of trenches.

Such were the two systems.

They were, he said, irreconcilable: 'It is impossible to maintain that a system can be found which allows two doctrines so fundamentally different to be harmonized.

'The primary reason which has inspired us, the Radicals, to vote these credits [for the fortifications] lies in the fact that our choice, which was made long ago, is for the organization, behind concrete fortifications, of a powerful network of automatic arms. This, as warfare has shown us, possesses a terrible efficiency against attacking troops.'

In deciding to construct these fortifications, he said, you have chosen the second of these systems, that of the shield. Today, the choice is no longer free. 'You have built, from Dunkirk to Nice, a fortified network . . . you have piled up along your frontiers these blocks of concrete; you have constructed these forts, these casemates, these carapaces which are proof against any gun that has been invented. . . . It is now a protective covering which is the essential element. The provision of this covering we have determined to support. We have taken such steps that it will be unbreakable, and when we vote the credits, it is precisely for the purpose of giving you the means of strengthening it,

[1] 'It is the bullet which kills' was said to be Pétain's motto. See below [Tr.].

of fortifying it still more. If we go into Belgium, it will be to install ourselves on a fortified line, which will shorten the line we shall have to defend.'

This system, which was, as I have said, based on a sincere conviction, was a tempting one, when considered on the political plane. France would be secure behind an indestructible plate of armour, an unbreakable covering. If war broke out, concrete would take the place of bodies; we would no longer be exposing young Frenchmen to the perils of an offensive, which experience during the last war had shown to be futile and dangerous. Unfortunately, this policy was placing us in the position of not being able to attack the aggressor who attacked our allies, and not even being able to defend the national soil, for systematic defensive warfare leads to defeat.

Pétain could not protest since it was his doctrine. The Chamber remained under the influence of Daladier's speech. And the doctrine which it contained continued to be spread throughout the country.

Thus was born the legend of the war of concrete, of the war without suffering, which was to become the 'phoney war'.

What was done in 1934 with the two hundred and ninety-two million francs which still remained available out of the one thousand two hundred and seventy-five millions voted? Organized defensive areas were created on the plateau of Rohrbach, between the two sections of the Maginot Line; the construction of forts was begun at Montmédy; the forts at Maubeuge were patched up, and three small fortifications were placed in front of Condé.

That is the manner in which our northern frontier was 'solidly protected' by Pétain.

MAY, 1940: OUR LIGHT FORTIFICATIONS IN THE NORTH ARE
PIERCED AT SEDAN, AND NEUTRALIZED ELSEWHERE

From Daladier, who had again taken over the Ministry of War in 1936, Gamelin obtained a few months later the extension of this thin crust of fortifications from the west of the Schelde to Dunkirk, because the breaking off of military co-operation with the Belgians had still further exposed our frontier in the north. Thus it was that, between March, 1935 and May, 1940, light fortifications were constructed on our northern frontier, from Montmédy to Dunkirk.

But light fortifications are light fortifications. Having been laid down too late they were, into the bargain, partly incomplete when the war broke out. Thus, the organization of a secondary position, intended to form a supporting line along the whole front, could only be begun on November 15, 1939, two and a half months after the war had commenced. In spite of the unanticipated reprieve of eight months of 'phoney war', the organized defences of Givet where, in May, 1940, we were to see the enemy cross the Meuse, had not been reinforced. As for the other end of the Ardennes front, two members of the Military Committee in the Chamber, MM. Taittinger and de Framond, after an inspection of the sector comprising the area between Montmédy and Valenciennes, pointed out in their report that 'in the region of Sedan, organized defences are rudimentary, not to say embryonic'. And this was in the vital sector of Sedan! They revealed that the concrete had not yet even been poured into certain constructions; that along the approach routes, the minefield areas and the block-houses were incapable 'of holding up the enemy for more than an hour', and that too much reliance seemed to be placed on natural obstacles (forests, the Meuse valley), forgetting that the Marne had, however, been crossed in 1914 by the Germans. These observations were as accurate as they were severe, but the standing of the Military Committee was so paltry that not the slightest attention was paid to it. The report was set aside in the most off-hand manner. General Huntziger, Commander of the Second Army, the one which included Sedan within its sector, indeed replied with a note,[1] the tone of which was as supercilious as it was peremptory, and the matter was shelved.

In spite of everything, this line of light fortifications would no doubt have been effective in the preceding war. But the revolution in the art of warfare about which I had so often spoken in the Chamber and elsewhere was to operate against it. The armoured and motorized German divisions, preceded by their Stukas, cut through it without difficulty at Sedan, as they were, in the following month, to cut through the light fortifications to the south of Saarbrücken, which joined the two

[1] Here is the text of this note:

Headquarters of the Second Army, April 8, 1940.
    The report of M. Taittinger, which you have forwarded to me for some brief reply, informs me:

    1. That the defensive organization of the area round Sedan is rudimentary, whilst that at the bridgehead of Montmédy appears to be redoubtable.
    2. That to the north of the Meuse, the defence consists of block-houses whose resistance, even if it were assisted by minefields, would only last a short while (estimated at the maximum time of an hour), the cavalry of the G.B.D.I. [Armoured Groups of the Infantry Divisions] being destined to be sacrificed on the spot.
    3. That to the south of the Meuse the concrete works can only play their part if they are finished and armed.
    4. That, finally the D.C.A. [Anti-Aircraft Defence] is almost non-existent and that the German Air Force, because of the small number of our fighters, fly freely in the Sedan sector, and at the first appearance of our fighters take shelter in Belgium.
    The remarks of M. Taittinger (who seems, moreover, to be somewhat badly informed, at least on certain points) could have been of great importance if we had awaited them before undertaking the organization of the position.

It will be understood why Huntziger, on becoming Vichy War Minister, tried to remove this letter from the archives. Owing to the watchfulness of an officer in the Historical Branch of the Army it was saved.

sections of the Maginot Line, and as they were, fourteen months later, to cut through at thirteen points and with the same ease, the Stalin Line, covering Russia from Odessa to the Baltic Sea.

The fortifications of the Albert Canal served to no purpose either, for, having called us too late to their help, the Belgians could not hold them.

As to the Arlon–Liége line, it might as well have never existed.

In brief, France had spent milliards in order to protect herself. When she thought she had constructed a shield, she had only two or three pieces of breastplate, sewn on to a jerkin of light fortifications, which broke in the region of her heart.

Thus the drama was played out.

Napoleon wrote: 'It is an axiom of the art of war that the side which stays within its fortifications is beaten. Experience and theory are agreed upon the point.' As he explained in his masterly letter of 1805 to Prince Eugène, fortification is only an element in manœuvre. It is not a wall behind whose shelter one can go to sleep. The theory of the Maginot Line, 'the buckler of France', satisfied the secret desire of a people exhausted by the blood-letting of the previous war. It was popular. The defensive policy was Republican in its implications. We know where this yielding led us.

CHAPTER VII

A FRANCE WITHOUT ARMS

(FROM THE VICTORY OF 1918 TO MARCH 7, 1936)

The nature of the Military Problem on the morrow of Versailles and after Hitler's accession to power.—1924, 'Have we an army suitable to our needs or an army based on our traditions?'—1917–31, Pétain, Commander-in-Chief: 'It is the Bullet which Kills.'—1934, Pétain, Minister of War, and Weygand, Commander-in-Chief, allow our Armament Expenditure to be reduced.—March 15, 1935, I put forward the military problem.—My Counter-proposal to create an Armoured Corps is rejected.

THE NATURE OF THE MILITARY PROBLEM ON THE MORROW OF VERSAILLES AND AFTER HITLER'S ACCESSION TO POWER

IT is an axiom that a country's army is one of the instruments of its policy. A country must, therefore, have an army suitable for its policy. On the morrow of Versailles two policies were conceivable:

1. That of the Wall of China: to build a Maginot Line, stretching from the North Sea to Switzerland, and to place behind it a defensive army, equipped with modern defensive arms.

2. That of a European balance of power: to find allies capable of balancing the German power in the east, and, *at the same time*, to create an offensive army, fit to attack Germany if she attacked our allies. She would thereby be faced with the prospect of a war on two fronts.

Which of these two policies was the right one?

I was hostile to the first. In the first place, this was because it meant leaving the rest of the Continent to Germany, which was a policy unworthy of France. In the second place, I thought it imprudent. Indeed, I stressed the fact, as is known, that the Maginot Line itself would not be impenetrable to the army of a Germany which, at the outset, we would have allowed to seize all the resources of the Continent. We were not, therefore, in a position to do without an army provided with the offensive arms of modern warfare—armoured divisions and dive-bombers—which could repel the enemy by a victorious counter-offensive, after he had broken our line. Now, it was impossible to create at the same time a Maginot Line of seven hundred and sixty kilometres and a modern army. Our resources would not permit us to do this. Finally, to abandon Belgium was, apart from objections on sentimental grounds, to place our richest provinces within cannon-shot of the enemy, to deprive ourselves of the support of the Belgian Army, to allow enemy aircraft to take off from airfields situated within an hour's flight of Paris, and to give our opponent a base for naval and air action against Britain. Because of the rapidity of new instruments of war, Belgium had become, in the military sphere, a border province of France.

This first policy, purely defensive, that of the Wall of China, was, therefore, a bad one, but it was not absurd.

We did not follow it.

But neither did we follow the second.

We compromised, as in all other spheres, with a half and half policy.

As we have seen, we had constructed two sections of the Wall of China between the Rhine and Montmédy, but, on the classical road for the invasions of France between Montmédy and Dunkirk, we had not constructed permanent fortifications other than those of Maubeuge and the little which had been done at Valenciennes. It was not a surrounding wall, but two corner-posts at the edge of a field. Between one corner-post and another we were in the process of constructing, when the war broke out, a palisade of light fortifications. Moreover, we had not even supplied in sufficient quantity the modern arms most necessary for the defensive to our defensive army. We had not thus followed the first policy, the purely defensive one.

Neither had we followed the policy of a European balance of power. Indeed, we had rejected the Russian alliance which was offered to us, although it alone was capable of creating a permanent second front. As allies on the Continent we had only Poland and Czechoslovakia, countries created but yesterday, who, more than all others, had need of being bolstered up. It was necessary, at all costs, to attack Germany on the very same day that she attacked one of them. But we had created a defensive army! And on March 7, 1936, we allowed the Reichswehr to install itself in the Rhineland, through which we could have struck it in the back should it attack our allies in the East. This was allowing Hitler to destroy our allies first of all, and ourselves afterwards. There was, therefore, a fundamental contradiction between our foreign policy and our military policy. The defender of treaties and the protector of small nations to whom these treaties had given birth, the French people were the knights-errant of Europe, the redressers of wrong. But France, a pacific democracy, equipped herself with a defensive army, and thereby deprived herself of the means of intervening in

Europe. She was thus denying herself the essential attribute of a Great Power. Was she at least selfishly securing her own security? Not in the least; for once these eastern allies had been devoured, what would Germany find in front of her, on turning to the West? A French defensive army, which was to advance into Belgium to meet Germany's powerful offensive army. The issue could not be in doubt. When this defensive army had been beaten in Belgium, it only remained for the Germany Army to move straight forward and attack our own unfortified northern frontier. And, for lack of a modern army (armoured divisions and dive-bombers), necessary for a counter-offensive, France was to be invaded.

The historians of the future will be baffled by so much inconsistent behaviour. How can our incapacity to provide ourselves with the army which suited our policy be explained, first of all during the period of implementing the Treaty and afterwards in face of the deadly peril which Hitler's accession to power heralded? How can this lapse of responsible Ministers and of Parliament be explained? Once again we see silhouetted behind them the Marshal of France with the head of marble, the 'Victor of Verdun', the Commander-in-Chief from 1917 to 1931, whose policy was to be continued by Weygand, Commander-in-Chief from 1931 to 1935, then the disseminator, in the *Revue des Deux Mondes*, of official opinion upon the French Army, and the castigator of the non-conformers.

In truth, both knew that the defensive army which they had created would be incapable of going to the assistance of our allies in the East. Pétain was to state in 1935, on the eve of Stresa, that the Army which they had built up was incapable of taking the offensive. These illustrious leaders, therefore, made the decision to abandon the allies of France.

On the other hand, they believed that France was sheltered from invasions. They were unaware of the revolution whereby armoured divisions and dive-bombers had transformed the art of war. They did not know that a continuous front, once it was broken, as it had been on several occasions in 1918, could be fatal if the break-through were quickly and deeply exploited by armoured divisions, linked up with dive-bombers.

It was against these ideas that I raised my voice.

1924: 'HAVE WE AN ARMY SUITABLE TO OUR NEEDS OR AN ARMY BASED ON OUR TRADITIONS?'

We were at the period when the Treaty of Versailles was being put into force. I had just been defeated in the elections of 1924, for having, as a deputy of the Basses-Alpes, voted for the *double décime*,[1] and the

---

[1] The *double décime* was a supplementary tax of two-tenths of a franc imposed by a law of March 22, 1924, on all customary taxes, duties, etc., levied by the State [Tr.].

suppression of small sub-prefectures and courts, which we had demanded of Poincaré in order to 'save the franc'. I did not have the opportunity, therefore, of speaking in the Chamber when Parliament opened. On July 5, 1924, I wrote an article in the *Revue Hebdomadaire*, entitled 'Avons-nous l'armée de nos besoins ou l'armée de nos habitudes?'

I addressed a reproach to the architects of our Army, which they were frequently to hear from me in days to come, that of planning with 'their eyes looking backwards'. I told them that they were deluding themselves if they thought we would again see trench warfare: 'Because at the end of the last war, the British, the Belgians, the Americans and ourselves held a fixed front stretching from the North Sea to Switzerland, and because the final move was carried out supported by heavy and powerful artillery, they have assumed that these circumstances, unique in the world's history, will occur again tomorrow. And they have given us the army which is in line with our military tradition.'

What ought to be the role of our Army in 1924? It should serve the needs of our policy: 'Is the role of our Army, as in 1914, to cover us against any German aggression? No such thing. We are victorious. Its role is to put the Treaty into effect.'

Consequently, I demanded the creation of a 'Treaty Army', whose role and, therefore, whose nature I thus defined: 'Article 178 of the Treaty forbids Germany to take *any measures for mobilization*.

'If Germany violates the Treaty and mobilizes, we need a swift-moving and mobile army, which can fall on the area where the enemy force is concentrated. The distance which separates the two opposing armies will demand speed. Speed and long range are the necessary qualities. It is not a covering army that we need, but an offensive army. It should be an army made up of professional soldiers, within which the three or four first classes of the reserves would be incorporated.'

In the country's state of mind it was, indeed, necessary to avoid a dramatic general mobilization. One can imagine with what a warm welcome I was to receive ten years later the Armoured Corps of the future General de Gaulle, the ideal instrument to carry out the policy of striking 'quickly and deeply'.

I maintained that, by keeping the equipment of trench warfare and enlarging its proportion of unwieldy heavy artillery, we were committing 'in reverse the error of General Percin, who rejected it entirely as being like "leaden boots"'.

In a word, we did not have an army which was suitable to our policy. This was to be the theme of the speeches that I made in the Chamber and country on the military problem after 1935.

I affirmed that, if we showed that we were unable to create an army suited to the Treaty of Versailles, and if we resigned ourselves to our fate, we would march towards a new war and a new invasion: 'You do not wish to profit by the advantages which the Treaty gives you? You are the adherents of passive waiting, of a retreat of ten kilometres and *war on your own soil?* You are perfectly entitled to those views, but recognize and proclaim that it is France which would be invaded, whose factories would be destroyed, and burial grounds desecrated. . . .'

What would happen in this event?

'Will not Germany, armed once more, begin by destroying Poland in order to shake hands over her dead body with the Red Army?'

That is what was to happen fifteen years later, apart from the fact that Germany later turned against the Russians.

'Are you sure, moreover, that there will be the same "Sacred Alliance" in support of mobilizing the war resources of the nation as there was in 1914?'

It was clear indeed that, when Germany should attack Czechoslovakia, or offer her hand to the Red Army across the corpse of Poland, the French people, exhausted by the losses of the previous war, would not have the unanimous urge which carried them in August, 1914, to their attacked frontier. This was well seen in September, 1938, when Hitler threatened Czechoslovakia before partitioning her at Munich, and even in September, 1939, when we honoured our treaty obligations towards Poland.

But no demonstration could influence Parliament, which had the guarantee of our glorious military leaders for formulating a policy that was pleasing to the country.

The country paid the price.

We did not create an army which was adapted to carrying out the Treaty of Versailles. The Treaty was broken. Because we did not fashion an army suitable to our policy, we adapted our policy to the army which we had. We let Hitler rearm, remilitarize the Rhineland, effect the *Anschluss* and drag us into Munich. But all these lapses on our part did not permit us to avoid war. And in May, 1940, we saw 'France invaded, her factories destroyed and her burial grounds desecrated. . . .'

1917–31: PÉTAIN, COMMANDER-IN-CHIEF: 'IT IS THE BULLET WHICH KILLS'

When he was welcoming Pétain under the *Coupole*,[1] the charming and wise Paul Valéry, who was only able, in this sphere, to reflect like a mirror the same praises which Pétain gave to himself, said to the

---

[1] i.e. at the Académie française, to which the term of *La Coupole* was popularly applied [Tr.].

Marshal: 'You have . . . made an important discovery. . . . You have discovered this fact: that it is the bullet which kills. . . .'

And, in order to make such a discovery, added this subtle analyst of dancing, one can be 'nothing less than a man of genius'.

It was an excellent academic meeting.

I propose to show that, in 1940, it was this theory of 'It is the bullet which kills' that killed us.

The legend was spread abroad between the two wars that before 1914, Colonel Pétain, a solitary wise man amid a collection of fools, had observed the effect of the fire of a machine-gun sheltered within a trench on the enemy infantry who tried to take it by assault. No one seems to have thought that this assertion implied an insult to the Joffres, the Fochs, the Fayolles, the Franchet d'Espereys, the Debeneys—in other words, the commanders who led our Armies to victory in 1918.

In 1921, three years after victory had been won, Pétain, who had been given his Marshal's baton and who had continued as Commander-in-Chief, decided to formulate the military principles of the French Army. He had appointed a committee, over which he presided, which was entrusted with drawing up a *Provisional Instruction for the Tactical Employment of Large Units* (Divisions, Army Corps).

The advocate of the systematic defensive began by suppressing the maxim which, until that moment, had never ceased to be the golden rule of our Army, and the wisdom of which military history has constantly demonstrated. 'The offensive alone can produce decisive results.' He replaced it by another: 'Fire power has proved itself to be an overwhelming factor. . . . It has given the strength of outstanding resistance to improvised fortifications.'

From this assertion he concluded that a continuous front was invulnerable. No doubt it could be broken but without any grave consequences for the defender, because 'attack is only made in favourable conditions after the assembly of powerful material means, artillery tanks, munitions, etc. . . . Attack is, therefore, preceded by a period of preparation more or less lengthy, which is devoted to gathering this material together and bringing it into play. . . .' The reserves will have time to concentrate. The continuous front is, therefore, invulnerable.

That was the military doctrine of France as laid down by Pétain in 1921. It was one, as can be seen, which was full of reassurance.

Unfortunately, Pétain did not take into account the revolution in the art of war which had been taking shape in 1917 and 1918 under his very eyes when he was Commander-in-Chief, and the development of which it was easy to foresee.

What does Pétain say about tanks? He devotes two lines to them in the report which prefaces the *Instruction*: 'Tanks assist the advance of the infantry by breaking static obstacles and active resistance put up by the enemy.' That is all he says on the subject.

Tanks are, therefore, one sees, a mere adjunct to the infantry. Thus the *Instruction* only does them the honour of giving them a single paragraph. The first paragraph of the chapter on arms is entitled: 'Infantry and tanks.' We shall see how the function of the first-named is of supreme importance and that of the latter, secondary:

'The infantry has the principal duty in fighting.'

Preceded, protected, and accompanied by artillery fire, and lastly assisted by tanks and aircraft, it takes possession of the ground, occupies it, organizes it and holds it.

'Its task on the battlefield is specially arduous, but it is more glorious than all the rest.

'In battle it is the infantry which expends itself the most. . . .'

In a word, the infantry is, more than ever, the *Queen of the battlefield*. As for tanks, those poor relations, they 'form a sub-division of the infantry arm'.

And what was their function? 'They are intended to increase the offensive power of the infantry by assisting its advance in the fight.'

Finally, Pétain makes a distinction between light tanks, 'whose function is to accompany the infantry and to fight in close liaison with it', and heavy tanks, 'intended to break a way through for the infantry and the light tanks by destroying, through their weight and their fire, the resistance of supporting points which are strongly held'.

Such are the three sections which, out of a total of two hundred and sixty-one in the *Instruction*, speak about tanks.

As regards aviation, whose participation in ground fighting was still modest, but which would certainly increase considerably, the *Rapport au Ministre* said: 'By day, the Air Force will reconnoitre the positions of the troops, on the march or fighting, so as to give their position to the artillery; by night it will itself attack them.' That is all. Aviation, therefore, was to have no direct participation in the battle.

The *Instruction* of 1921 was called provisional. In this there was a gleam of hope! But France is a country where provisional things last a long time. Pétain's biographer writes:[1] 'In spite of this title it has remained the gospel of our Army for fourteen years.' And elsewhere he says:[2] 'The business of the Army has been looked after [for eleven years] by a General Staff whose leaders and personnel are impregnated with its ideas.' Alas! they were so, for more than eleven years.

In reading this *Instruction* again, one cannot help envying the old Austria, who was only 'a year, an army and an idea' behind the times.

[1] Laure, *op. cit.*, p. 268.   [2] *Ibid.*, p. 246.

Such was the state of mind of our Army leaders. Circumstances were, however, grave: we were entering upon a period when the age groups due for conscription were depleted, the five age groups which corresponded to the war years [1914–18]. The logical method of providing for the deficit, which reduced the normal intake by half, would be to double the length of military service by extending it to two years. But we could not face up to doing this, and preferred to fall back upon expedients.

How could we hope to rival Germany in the sphere of numbers? We were beaten beforehand. Thus, we should not have allowed ourselves, at any price, to fall behindhand in the sphere of material. Those who advocated keeping military service at one year kept on repeating: 'If it be a choice between men and material, we are going to vote for material.'

On December 19, 1933, Daladier, the Minister of War, said to the Chamber: 'As far as war material is concerned, we have, you may rest assured, nothing, absolutely nothing, to fear, as you well know. Therefore, let us stop this game which seems to encourage heaven knows what kind of feeling of panic. . . .' It is certainly true there was no immediate danger in December, 1933, but there was a deadly peril on the horizon. Six months later, on June 15, 1934, when his successors, Doumergue and Pétain (authors of the celebrated Note of April 17, 1934, in which they had stated: 'France will henceforth ensure her security by her own means'), did nothing, however, to arm France, Daladier reverted to this question in the Chamber. And was this to reproach Pétain for his inaction? Unfortunately, no! But he did explain his reaction to the rearmament of Germany: 'During the time', he said, 'in which, thanks to the effort of successive Governments after 1932, we reduced the military expenses of France by two milliards, Germany increased hers by exactly that same sum, increasing her military budget from six to eight milliards.' And he added: 'I state these two figures in order to show that I am not allowing myself to be influenced by this systematic campaign, inspired, perhaps, by a quite legitimate desire, which I understand perfectly well, to safeguard French security, but also, perhaps, by other interests. . . .'

Do not let us enrich the 'armament manufacturers'—that was an argument to which the Chamber was not insensible. But the problem continued. We had reduced the duration of military service to one year, and we had promised to 'replace men by material'. If, in order not to put money into the pockets of the 'armament manufacturers', we did not supply the material, what was there left for us except to lose on both accounts?

1934: PÉTAIN, MINISTER OF WAR, AND WEYGAND, COMMANDER-IN-CHIEF, ALLOW OUR ARMAMENT EXPENDITURE TO BE REDUCED

The year 1934 began with the greatest revolution in the internal history of Germany. To mark the anniversary of his accession, Hitler did what William I had not even dreamed of when he had himself crowned Emperor of Germany in the Hall of Mirrors at Versailles. He unified the Reich by tearing away the sovereignty of those countries which composed it. What an increase of power!

For nearly three months Hitler had had a free hand to rearm. On October 14, 1933, he had broken with the League of Nations. The latter continued, none the less, to discuss methods of disarmament for the peaceful Powers. It was to desist from its fatal plan only on the day when France, as a last resort, was to recall it to a sense of reality.

I have already alluded to the Note of April 17, 1934. It was certainly a legitimate move since its object was to affirm the desire of France to provide, by her own means, for her defence; but, at the same time, it was an inopportune move since it offered to a hypocritical propaganda the desired pretext for launching a campaign, charging us with the responsibility for a break which Hitler had completed a long time ago.

It happened, however, that, by an exceptional chance, France had, in 1934, a strong Government, the strongest that she had ever had since the advent of the Third Republic. This Government could at will dissolve the Chamber, instigate a revision of the Constitution, and legislate by virtue of the full powers which it delegated to itself.

In such an atmosphere and conditions, it was only child's play for the Government to obtain from Parliament the means whereby France could ensure her own defence. This was made all the more easy by the fact that, as we have seen, Pétain was its Minister of War. To the prestige given him by his contribution in saving the country, the 'Victor of Verdun' added, in effect, the esteem which he personally enjoyed in political circles, because, unlike most military leaders, he was reputed to be a partisan of the Left. It was for him to determine what France needed to prepare her defence, and to calculate correlatively the total expenses to be employed to this end. The Chamber would certainly not be close-fisted.

There was another point in his favour. Pétain was fortunate in having Weygand, the Commander-in-Chief of the Army, to back him up. Great was the authority of the man who had been the 'right hand' of Foch.

What were these two men, in whom the nation had placed its trust, to do? Were they going to take heed of the peril which the revival of German strength was creating for France? Were they, in short, going to give our country the army necessary to carry out its policy?

No.

What did they do?

Nothing.

Did they increase armaments?

No; on the contrary, they accepted a reduction by a third of the credits of 1934 for new material.[1] Whilst Germany began to build up three armoured divisions as a preliminary step, Pétain ordered seven [sic] heavy tanks in 1934. Laure tells us triumphantly[2] that, before leaving office, Pétain obtained from the Minister of Finance a credit of eight hundred [sic] million francs for armaments, which his successor had voted on January 3, 1935. Now, on the day Hitler began war, he was able to state that Germany had spent ninety milliard marks in rearming. . . .

Were they [Pétain and Weygand] going to increase the number of officers in the regular Army?

No, they reduced their number.

Did they call up more reservists?

No, they called up fewer.

Did they substitute for the one year's service, harmful to the formation of cadres for the Army reserve, one of two years, which in fact the depleted state of the age groups due for conscription made necessary?

No. Pétain's biographer tells us,[3] however, that Weygand, Gamelin and the Supreme War Council, thought that it was 'necessary and urgent' to adopt a service period of two years, 'the only one recognized as sufficient, the only one which would avoid doubling the numbers for yearly call-up, which was so harmful to training and to the organization of the Army'.

Did Pétain doubt this?

Not at all. But listen again to what his panegyrist says:[4] 'The Marshal, in his heart of hearts, was no less emphatic. . . . But he was a Minister, in permanent contact with other Ministers and with politicians, to whom the scheme appeared to be quite revolutionary.'

This is a caricature of a Minister who knows where his duty lies, but who shirks it in order to avoid petty anxieties!

When the two years' service was passed by his successor, was it found difficult to get a majority? Did opinion suddenly harden against it?

Not in the least. The Chamber was to pass it on March 15, 1935, by three hundred and sixty-five votes to one hundred and seventy-six, after the customary display of opposition by the extreme Left and the somewhat feeble opposition of Daladier. As for public opinion, it

---

[1] Two hundred million out of six hundred and ten.
[2] *Op. cit.*, p. 386.   [3] *Ibid.*, p. 393.
[4] *Ibid.*, p. 381. The points of suspension are General Laure's.

understood the necessity of this sacrifice perfectly, and yet, in 1934, despite pressing appeals from the Army leaders, Pétain refused to act. He did worse than this: he compromised the future by declaring that the reduced numbers liable for call-up did not make a two-year military service necessary.

Not only did he refrain from having it voted, but he promised to do nothing about it, and so made the task of his successor more difficult. Listen again to his biographer:[1]

'At the time when the Army Committee was sitting [July 3, 1934], he even consented to make the following statements: "In so far as the length of service is concerned, whilst the depleted age groups still remain to be called up we intend to keep within the framework of the law for one year's service, unless events necessitate exceptional steps for our security."'

The case against the rulers of 1934 is considerably graver than that against their predecessors in 1933. The latter conjured up illusions about the Disarmament Conference, at least until October 14, 1933, and about the Four Power Pact. But the Government of 1934 itself had no excuse, for it was this Government, as we have just seen, which, on April 17, declared that France had decided to 'ensure her safety by her own means'.

Perhaps it can be said Pétain and Weygand underestimated the strength of German rearmament.

Weygand apparently did, if, at least, one accepts as accurate the words which M. François-Poncet[2] put into his mouth at the time. 'You will see how long it will take Germany to catch up with the twenty billions we have spent on armaments.'

Pétain certainly did not underestimate German rearmament. 'When' continues Laure,[3] 'he took over the reins, one fact obsessed him before all others: the military renaissance of Germany, and the danger of an impending disturbance of the peace. . . . In the spring of 1934 . . . the mass of the German people was entirely absorbed in training. . . . Yes . . . we were too far below low-water mark and our safety was gravely compromised.' But, confound it! It was time to act. The reports of our Military Attachés and the information from our intelligence service were unanimous about the frantic moral and material rearmament of Germany. Moreover, Pétain himself was to write in the *Revue des Deux Mondes* of March 1, 1935, about German rearmament. 'The tremendous progress which has been made in this rearmament is the important event of the year 1934.'

This portrait of Pétain, Minister of War, would not be complete if I did not quote a sentence which I heard him utter in the Stanislas

[1] *Ibid.*, p. 388.   [2] *Op. cit.*, p. 179.   [3] *Op. cit.*, pp. 378–92, *passim*.

Square at Nancy before Lyautey's bier. This was on August 2, 1934. At a time when all the General Staffs of Europe were excited by the new possibilities introduced into warfare by the massive use of aircraft and tanks, at a time when France, engaged as she was in an armaments race in which she was handicapped in numbers and weight, could only hope to come successfully out of the business on the score of quality (that is, by imagination and by ideas), Pétain declared: 'France has more need of hard work, conscience and self-denial than of ideas. Ideas too often cause divisions, whilst effort unites.'

No need for ideas! Keep the innovators in the background! The first balloon, the first submarine, the first tank were built by Frenchmen, but that was in the past. Facing the Germany of Hitler, which was frantically arming, Frenchmen, inferior in numbers, had no longer any need of ideas. That is why the French Army was to go into battle without an armoured corps and without dive-bombers.

Effort without imagination? Effort without ideas? What terms were these to address to the France of 1934!

A great Marshal of France—and he was truly great—Foch, said:

'Let us have ideas! Ideas! And imagination! But don't let us forget that two and two make four.'

MARCH 15, 1935: I PUT FORWARD THE MILITARY PROBLEM

In 1935 the debate on the question of two years' military service continued in a pitiable fashion.

The hour of reckoning had struck. The French people had to be awakened, and told that the truth had been concealed from them. Delay could no longer be tolerated, for it was necessary to inform the new recruits that they were to serve more than a year. The Flandin Ministry, instead of tackling the problem frankly, resorted to expediency. Section 40 of the Law of 1928 gave the Government the power, *if the circumstances warranted*, to keep under arms, 'for the time being, a proportion of the intake which had finished its year's service'. This regulation obviously did not allow for the prior extension of the period of service of five complete age groups, none of which had been as yet called to the colours. However, it was adopted. The move was imprudent for the *Front Populaire* was growing stronger as the economic crisis grew worse. Now its three leaders, Blum, Thorez and Daladier, were hostile to a two years' service. If the *Front Populaire* were returned to power by the elections which were to take place in May, 1936, could it not, with a stroke of the pen, abrogate a two years' service, which was thus put into force by an expedient of somewhat questionable regularity? The passing of a law was the only method of forestalling such a danger. A desire to keep in office prevailed over taking this risk, which, moreover, did not materialize because, in France, party loyalty is tempered by disregard for electoral programmes.

On March 15, 1935 Flandin read to the Chamber the Government's statement which put forward the reasons for the return to two years' service. He was silent about the decision of which Goering had just informed the world: Germany was building an Air Force of war strength. He only recalled that 'the effectiveness of the German Army was considerably increased by a unilateral decision, to which the French Government, no more than the British Government, gave its consent'. How sad was this for Hitler! Flandin hastened, moreover, to temper this 'rashness' by declaring: 'France does not wish to question the pacific intentions of anyone.' They must have smiled in Berlin: 'What will he say tomorrow, when he learns that we have re-established compulsory military service?' It must be recognized, however painful it may be, that, in speaking thus, Flandin uttered the words which the Chamber and the country wished to hear.

Would the Chamber vote for the two years' service? The Government knew that the deputies of the Centre and the Right could be relied upon to vote unpopular measures when once they were told that national defence made them necessary. They were to vote the two years' service in 1935, as their predecessors had voted that of three years' in 1913, at the risk of being accused by their opponents in their constituencies of being less republican than those who voted with the opposition. But how would the Radicals vote, who, on June 15, 1934, had so enthusiastically applauded Daladier's threatening words to Doumergue: 'We warn you that we shall not give in to this campaign, which is being waged to abrogate the law for military service of one year.' A courageous speech by Edouard Herriot, Minister of State in the Flandin Cabinet, ensured their favourable vote.

It was during this debate that I intervened in order to put forward the military problem. It can be well imagined that the advent of Hitler to power and his first violations of the Treaty of Versailles had strengthened my opinion of 1924 on the uselessness and incoherence of our military policy. More strongly even than in 1924 I thought that France had not the army which was suitable for her policy. Being a Philistine over our foreign policy, I ought logically to have been a Philistine in matters of a military nature. I deplored more than ever that the architects, who were refashioning our Army, should be planning with 'their eyes looking over their shoulders'. I considered the official point of view, according to which the next war would be a renewal of the previous one, as a challenge to good sense. Indeed, the war which was coming would depend on the inclination of Germany who would wage it in her own good time, as she had done before. Now, Germany knew that she had lost that former war because she had allowed Anglo-Saxon strength the time to marshal itself: it was obvious that she would this time seek a quick decision.

As I had never been a member of a Committee of National Defence I had specialized rather in foreign and financial problems; and above all, I was, at this time, entirely absorbed in my campaign to peg the franc to the pound and the dollar, a condition necessary for the return of prosperity, and thus, for the revival of French strength. I could the less abandon this campaign because it was earning me plenty of harsh words, which there could be no question of my avoiding. It was in these circumstances that I received, shortly before the debate, a visit from Lieutenant-Colonel de Gaulle. He had published a book the preceding year in which he called for the creation of an armoured corps, but which he had the imprudence to call *Vers l'armée de métier.* An armoured corps was the object; the professional army was one of the means of attaining it. His opponents pretended to ignore the object, and criticized the means. They did not speak of the flood of tanks; they saw only the men who drove them. They simulated great indignation; this reactionary was disowning the volunteers of Year II of the Republic, those who answered the cry 'The Motherland is in Danger', the Armies of the Revolution and the glory which they had brought to our flag, equality of obligation to serve in war, the National Army; he wished to return to the professional army of the days of the former monarchy! In reality, Lieutenant-Colonel de Gaulle had limited himself to stating this fact, known from experience, that, to pilot a plane or drive a tank, professional soldiers are necessary; for these are instruments which are too delicate and costly to entrust to a conscript—to a man who is 'serving his time'. The book was received with indifference or hostility by the important Army chiefs, with Pétain and Weygand at their head.

What Lieutenant-Colonel de Gaulle contributed which was original was the idea of an element composed of several armoured divisions, that is to say, an autonomous army, always ready and always capable of decisive action. He advocated, in fact, the equipment of our Army with the means to play the role demanded of it to ensure our security.

Lieutenant-Colonel de Gaulle explained his idea to me so forcefully that an 'armoured corps' seemed to me precisely the instrument for an 'army suitable to the Treaty' which I had mentioned in my article of 1924; so closely did his idea coincide with mine that I decided to speak in its favour.

First of all, I told the Chamber that, from this debate, 'one of the most grave in this Parliament', I drew three conclusions: '1. It was necessary to adopt once more the period of two years' military service;

2. This measure must not be adopted as a stopgap, revocable at any time;
3. It was necessary to recast our military organization if we were to face up to new perils and new demands immediately.'

It was the third point which I developed. The military system, which we were asked to patch up by doubling the length of military service, was old and decaying: 'Indeed, it would be a miracle if any system fashioned to operate in the Europe of 1927 could provide for our safety in the Europe of 1935.

'In 1927, the Germany of Stresemann was going to join the League of Nations.

'In 1935, the Germany of Herr Hitler left it. She created a fanatical youth, inspired by every medium of modern publicity, a youth taught that, if there is no longer any hope in peace, there is perhaps still a hope, an opportunity, in war.'

Léon Blum had just summed up the position of his party clearly: 'We do not believe in the necessity for an armaments race; and we do not believe in the inevitability of the rule of force. We will continue, on the one hand, to think, as Jaurès declared here, twenty-two years ago, that the true military protection of a country lies not in permanent strong forces, or in numerous troops in barracks, serving as the basis of defensive strategy. Rather that it is to be found in what Revolutionaries have called the levying of the masses, in what our old master Vaillant called the general arming of the people; that it is to be found in the inviolable nature of organized defensives, and also—although I recoil from stating this fact, I must however say it—in the terrible nature of reprisals to which every aggressor can today expose himself.'

To this I replied, first of all, that the danger was not in an armaments race, but in the arming of the potential aggressor: 'War would be all the more certain if the peoples who are capable of committing aggression were alone to indulge in the armaments race. When Britain joined in this race by doubling, in 1935, the output of her war-planes over that of 1934, she did not increase the risks of war; she diminished them. If she had been inspired by a similar attitude in the years before the war of 1914, perhaps we might have avoided that struggle. When Switzerland imposes on herself new sacrifices, is she joining in the armaments race? Yes, but only to ensure peace, for by her effort she is helping to strengthen a frontier which, on the French side, is not defended by any military fortifications.

'As regards a solution to the conscription of the masses, M. Léon Blum has called to mind the speech of Jaurès, which evoked it.

'The men of the Revolution, who imposed this conscription of the masses, were perfectly justified in doing so. But don't forget that, at this time, France was the largest country in Europe, that its population was equal to that of all the German States and of Britain combined. The conscription of the masses, at a time, moreover, when armaments were still rather improvised, was a decision which sprang from the national interest, and which corresponded both to our resources and our needs.

'Is it really a policy of quantity which we should follow today? If so, it will be necessary constantly to increase the length of military service, for M. Léon Blum has told us this afternoon that, after 1940, the numerical difference between the French and German military classes of conscripts will be considerable. He has, I believe, said that their numbers will be double our own. If we lean to the side of quantity, don't you see that the people are going to revolt against us because, in order that they can exist, we are depriving them of the reasons for existence? If we disregard quantity, there only remains quality, and it is this card which we must play.'

After having recalled the fact that we had been defeated in 1870 because we had failed to add quantity through compulsory service to the instrument of quality which was the professional army of the Second Empire, I showed that, in 1935, we were facing an inverse problem: 'Today, we have an Army based on a year's military service, which we are going to patch up and mend. . . . But will this military organization suffice for the needs of a transformed Europe? No, gentlemen.' I showed that the country to be assailed must study the weapons which the future assailant was fashioning in order to begin the fight. Now, what weapon was Germany forging for herself? By imposing on her, through the Treaty of Versailles, a professional army, we had endowed her with an army suitable for shock tactics. She needed in addition quantity: 'I would not be surprised if Germany, who, on the morrow of the publication of the British White Book, marked the occasion by informing the world of her creation of a military air force, should reply to our meeting of yesterday by telling us that she has created an army based on compulsory military service.'

[On the very next day, March 16, Germany did in actual fact introduce compulsory service.]

I continued: 'The fact is that, behind this Army designed to employ shock tactics and which can launch a devastating offensive, there is a supporting force, able to carry out the operations necessary to exploit the advantages which have been won.

'You yourselves can read the German Press, as I have done. You are aware that the Germans say: "Thank you, but we do not intend, on the next occasion, to be subjected to a four-years' war. That is the type of struggle which bleeds and exhausts both victor and vanquished alike.

This time, it will be a case of an immediate, instantaneous and devastating attack."[1]

'Whilst we, in France, have had our eyes fixed upon the war of yesterday, the Germans have looked forward to the war of tomorrow.

'It will be through a shattering offensive, with the help of an ultra-modern air force and an army of great mobility capable of a colossal performance, that Germany will carry out this operation.

'Are we equipped to respond to this type of offensive? The problem is for the reactions of the assailed to be as quick as the attacks of the assailant. Are we prepared for this?'

No, this was not so. I demonstrated that our Air Force ought to be 'matched on the ground by an army capable of carrying out a lightning offensive as was the German Army of shock tactics'. Now, we did not have this type of force, and we had to have it. 'The error of the General Staff lies in seeking only the greatest possible number of units, all on the same footing and all incapable of attack. Our General Staff is still back in the 1914 days. Now, we have need of an army capable of shock tactics. Our foreign policy has made this type of army a necessity. Various speakers—M. Léon Blum notably—this afternoon have outlined the function of our Army as being solely one of defence in the interior of our territory.

'But this is not the aim of our policy. And it is necessary to have an army capable of implementing that policy. Is it, by any chance, that we have abandoned our policy of giving assistance? Is it because we conceive assistance as flowing towards, and not from, us—something which we can claim from London, but we cannot give either to Vienna, to Prague or to Brussels?

'Are we, tomorrow, going to conclude a Danubian pact without contemplating the possibility of intervention? If, should the event require, this intervention is not immediately given, a catastrophe might arise and a general war be unloosed.

'That is how, in my opinion, the problem of giving assistance presents itself. Do we wish to change our policy—something to which we are entitled—and leave Herr Hitler to swagger the length and breadth of Europe? If so, we must deny the ideal of the League of Nations and the whole of French tradition. . . . Do you want to change our foreign policy?' It was essential for us to have an army capable of acting quickly, 'for procrastination means war; and if the threat of immediate, rapid and decisive intervention were lacking, there would ensue a conflagration which would spread into a general war'.

[1] We have learnt since from Rauschning's *Hitler Speaks*, published at the beginning of the war, that Hitler had expressed this idea, as early as 1932, in the following words: 'The next war will be quite different from the last world war. Infantry attacks and mass formations are obsolete. Interlocked frontal struggles lasting for years on petrified fronts will not return. I guarantee that. They were a degenerate form of war.'

We had, therefore, to be capable of intervening in Europe, otherwise Germany might destroy our allies and then turn to attack us. And what if she did attack us? This time it would be with an army capable of shock tactics. 'Let us take a case: war breaks out tomorrow, and Belgium is invaded. This event has happened before. If we don't possess the means of going immediately to her assistance and of helping her to cover her eastern frontier, what will happen?

'The same thing will, perhaps, occur, which has already taken place: in spite of its magnificent heroism, it is possible that the Belgian Army will be hurled back towards the sea. This means for us three hundred and fifty kilometres of open frontier in the north of France to be defended.

'For the northern frontier of France is merely a dotted line.

'Is there anyone here who, in advance, is prepared to accept the idea of seeing one of the richest provinces of France once again invaded and torn from the Motherland?

'That is the reason why the German Press shows very little response when there is talk of lengthening the duration of military service, and reacts acutely when one speaks of organized strength like that in the maximum plan of M. Edouard Herriot.'

Once the Belgian Army has been 'hurled back towards the sea' and our open frontier in the north has been attacked, what will happen? If we haven't an armoured corps, *capable of counter-thrusts as devastating as the attack . . . everything will be lost.* That was a definite prophecy.

Was there anything technical in this speech? I would have been completely incapable of this! Were not these arguments based upon mere common sense? Was it not evident that the massive employment of tanks, which had gained us our success in 1918, was bound to increase in the coming war and that, to increase it, it was necessary to create an armoured element? Was it not evident that the other arm of modern warfare, namely, aviation, would have to fight in liaison with it and be accompanied by it on the ground? And was not the correlation of these two newly developed arms, of land and of air, the characteristic feature of the coming war? As to knowing how this collaboration should be effected, I naturally was in ignorance, and it was not my business to know. It was the business of technical experts.

Because we lacked 'an army capable of implementing the Treaty'— that is, one endowed with the arms for modern warfare and capable of rapid and powerful action—did we not have to acquiesce to Hitler sending his Army into the Rhineland on March 7, 1936? Did we not have to agree to his occupying Austria on March 12, 1938? Did we not have to allow him to partition Czechoslovakia at Munich on September 29, 1938? Did we not have to permit him to crush Poland in

September, 1939? And what happened in May, 1940? Was not the Belgian Army 'hurled back towards the sea'? Was not 'our open frontier in the north' attacked at Sedan? Because of the lack of an armoured element, 'capable of counter-thrusts as devastating as the attack', was not 'everything lost'?

Georges Mandel, who was then Minister of Communications, told me in the Fort of Portalet that, during my speech, General Maurin, sitting beside him on the Government bench, said to him: 'So M. Paul Reynaud is now taking an interest in military questions, is he? I wonder what he would say if I busied myself with financial matters?'

'And what did Flandin say about it?' I asked Mandel.

'He said your speech was idiotic.'

But here is what General Maurin said on the floor of the House. Did he deny that our Army would be incapable of advancing to attack Germany if this country committed aggression against any of our allies? Not only did he not dispute this fact, but he declared that, if it did advance, it would be committing a folly: 'How can one believe that we should again think of an offensive when we have spent milliards in order to construct a fortified barrier? Would we be mad enough to advance beyond this barrier on some unpredictable venture?

'That, gentlemen, shows you how the Government are thinking. For the Government—at least, as far as I am concerned—know perfectly well what the plan of campaign will be.'

The French Army was to rest therefore crouched behind the Maginot Line. An army whose leader had said, 'You will never advance to attack the enemy; you will never be victorious; it is the concrete, before which the waves of attacking troops will die, that will gain the victory,' is an army which has lost its soul. And this, whilst our opponent remained faithful to the Napoleonic principle: 'War is an act of force. For reasons of strategy one must seek battle and insist upon it with all one's energy.'

General Maurin took advantage of this plan of war to assert that it would be madness for our Army to advance and fight in the open country. . . . Now, our strategy at the time anticipated that the whole left wing of our forces would advance into the open country of Belgium as far as the Liége–Arlon line. Like Pétain and his predecessors, General Maurin was completely incoherent in his ideas.

The Chamber heard all this. It approved all this. Its Army Committee did the same thing. The explanation was that the Chamber, like the Army, was intoxicated by Pétain's slogan that *Le feu tue*, that, just as he did, it believed in the inviolability of the continuous front, without, moreover, asking itself where this continuous front should stretch. It believed in systematic defensive warfare. It was 'war-mongering' to show the need of being prepared for offensive action in order to honour

our engagements towards our allies, to speak even of a powerful counter-offensive. When opposing a two years' military service, and asking for the recruitment from the unemployed of those who had been professional soldiers, Daladier (who in his speech of June 15, 1934, described the offensive as foolishness) said in the Chamber, on March 15, 1935, 'I would not be seriously opposed to the plan of M. Paul Reynaud so far as it concerns the quality of our Army, although I cannot accept his conclusions, which seem to me to lead to the creation of a professional army for shock tactics, more dangerous for the safety of our country than one realizes.'

Both the Government and the Opposition thus found themselves in agreement against me. But the question had been raised. And I was in future to continue unceasingly to put it before the Chamber and the country.

MY COUNTER-PROPOSAL TO CREATE AN ARMOURED CORPS IS REJECTED

I did not stop at making speeches. I took action. In announcing a period of two years' military service, the Government had tabled on March 15, 1935, a draft Bill lowering progressively the age of calling men to the colours to twenty years.

On March 28, 1935, I tabled an amendment, the credit for which, I repeat, belonged to Lieutenant-Colonel de Gaulle, and whose essential provisions were as follows:

Article 1. There is created, by modifying the laws of July 13, 1927, concerning the general organization of the Army, and of March 28, 1928, concerning the cadres and effectives, a specialized corps, constituted permanently on a war footing, and recruited in principle from soldiers serving as regulars.

Article 2. The specialized corps comprises six divisions of the line, a light division, general reserves and service troops. The proportion of native personnel . . . cannot exceed one-fifth of the total of effectives.

Article 4. The formation of the specialized corps will be begun without delay, and will be progressively continued so as to be completed at the latest by April 15, 1940.

The terminology, I admit, was still uncertain. I called the armoured corps, *a specialized corps*; and the armoured division, a *division of the line*.[1]

[1] It would have been better to say: 'The armoured corps is composed of heavy divisions and a light armoured division,' just as one speaks of *heavy* cavalry and *light* cavalry. The current terminology used armour for the first type (armoured divisions, which existed only in the imagination) and motorized for the second (light mechanized divisions), when

As will be seen, these proposals retained the light mechanized division which already existed (that of Rheims), but created six armoured divisions. I refrained, admittedly, from introducing any technical detail. It was known, moreover—and this was established by the fact that I had laid down a strength of a hundred thousand men in explaining the reasons for this force—that these six divisions ought to have, in my opinion, the composition envisaged by Lieutenant-Colonel de Gaulle, that is to say, five hundred tanks to a division, or a total of three thousand tanks.

The armoured element suggested in my amendment would thus have had a strength superior to that of the ten divisions of the German armoured element which invaded us in May, 1940. And its formation would have been completed *at the latest by April 15, 1940.*

Why ought it to be established permanently on a war footing? The answer is: in order always to be ready to act in full strength at any time of the year—as, for example, on March 7, 1936, on March 11, 1938, and in September, 1938. A corps which was a hundred per cent strong in July and forty per cent in November would not have been suitable to play this role. The primary reason why it had to be recruited, *in principle,* from soldiers serving as regulars, was the necessity of avoiding the periodic disorganization due to the coming and going of groups of conscripts. Another reason[1] was that, 'Modern equipment, which increasingly forms an essential element of manœuvre, is becoming more and more costly and delicate. It would be sheer waste to entrust to conscript recruits the handling of machines which cost a million francs apiece and whose performance will directly determine success or failure.'

I tried in the *Exposé des motifs* to upset the false idea, which had contaminated so many minds, that we were in shelter behind the buckler of the Maginot Line. 'Whatever confidence one may have in the value of our fortifications in the north-east, it would, believe me, be a grave error to see them as a wall which is of necessity unbreakable. Besides the fact that these fortifications leave uncovered the three hundred and fifty kilometres of the northern frontier and the two hundred and fifty of the Swiss frontier, nothing can guarantee that an adversary provided with some means of attack more or less unforeseen would not succeed in crossing them.' Moreover, we had undertaken engagements which the honour and interest of the country demanded

the vehicles in each were both armoured and motorized. In view of this, everyone understood what I wished to convey. I have since been reproached with having spoken of an element which I first called *specialized*, and then *armoured*. The Germans had, however, a Panzer Corps. I should have said *armoured arm*, just as there is an infantry and a cavalry arm, the purists have told me. What is certain is that, by whatever name I called it, no one wanted it at any price. It was the offensive weapon. It was accordingly execrated, just as was the offensive itself.

[1] *Exposé des motifs,* p. 8.

that we keep, and which required us to have an army fit to take the offensive.

I also explained my proposals about the recruiting of personnel and about the employment of material. One will have to admit, in any case, that the armoured corps would have been less costly to us than defeat.

Was that to say that I intended to suppress the National Army in order to substitute an armoured corps for it? Nothing of the sort. I said, 'Thus, the requirements of our policy and those of modern technique are combining together to compel us to *add* a specialized body to the large units supplied by the annual intakes and by the reserves.'

For France it was not a question of denying herself the use of these masses on the day of the fight. 'By no means should France renounce the training for her defence of all the forces which she commands.' If my amendment were adopted, 'we shall find ourselves, in 1940,' I said, 'at the end of the period of reduced numbers of conscript intakes provided with a new military system, in which the specialized corps for manœuvre will constitute one of the essential elements'.

To endow France with a new military system, *to employ by means of reform the tendencies of evolution!* That was precisely what neither Pétain, Weygand nor Maurin wished. It was a strange spectacle. In circles where politicians were eagerly reproached with attaching too much importance to their electoral interests, the present of a deputy who offered an armoured element on a silver platter was rejected. These military leaders seemed to have forgotten the outstanding role of tanks, 'used in massive strength', at the end of the last war. On October 2, 1918, the leaders of the different parties in the Reichstag had heard in consternation an emissary of Ludendorff tell them that the Allies were using tanks in mass surprise attacks. 'Breaking the nerves of our men, these machines', he added, 'are thrusting through our lines, carving a way for the infantry, surging on to our rearward troops, spreading panic, cutting our communications. . . .'

What a lesson for the future! Was it not obvious that it was in this direction that the art of war would develop? Read the last phrase again. It is a picture of what was to be the onslaught of the Panzers in May, 1940. The Germans had understood, the French had forgotten. . . .

Our great leaders were unanimous in speaking against my amendment. On July 15, 1935, in the *Revue des Deux Mondes*, General Debeney, former Chief of the Army General Staff, maintained that the assistance of France to her allies could only be translated into actual fact by an attack of the French Army against the German Army in the Rhineland. 'In this theatre of operations,' he wrote, 'what is the advantage to be gained from a *specialized corps*? It is well known that the ground is very broken, very wooded, and thickly populated: are we going to use the mobility of this body to attempt a thrust in the direction of the Rhine?

In a country which has nothing in common with the plains of Hungary and Poland, where roads pass constantly through villages, and where the ground, except for those roads, is covered with enclosures and trees, cut by deep ravines, the advance of the *specialized element* will not be very rapid; a few improvised obstacles would quickly reduce its possibilities for manœuvre. These obstacles are the least that can be imagined. We should have an excellent communiqué at the start of operations, a few days after, a vain S.O.S.'

The armoured corps, therefore, if Debeney was to be believed, was doomed to misfortune. Let us observe, however, that this very broken, very wooded and thickly populated terrain of Belgium, was to be crossed without any difficulty, in May, 1940, by the German armoured corps, on its way towards France.

'The organization of a certain number of motorized divisions (carried in lorries) would satisfy', continued the writer, 'the function that could be allotted to a specialized element. . . . Thus, motorized divisions have been created.'

Thus, there was to be no armoured corps! Debeney rejected it also for another reason; the armoured element of Paul Reynaud's amendment had, 'in principle', to be made up of regulars, just as were the crews of aircraft and warships. This inescapable consequence of mechanization awoke old images in the mind of the General. 'Let us be satisfied to acclaim the professional army in the glorious chambers of the Museum of the Invalides,' he proclaimed.

In May, 1940, it was, however, not in a museum, but on the Meuse, that we were to need an armoured element.

On March 15, 1936, General Debeney in the *Revue des Deux Mondes* returned to the function of the armoured division. He did not conceive of it as acting in an independent fashion. Like the greatcoated foot soldiers of the previous war, it could not attack without a preliminary bombardment by heavy artillery: 'It is necessary to understand clearly that the really effective support which these divisions need, in order to play their part in an attack on a grand scale, postulates a considerable mass of artillery. . . .'

Yet it was exactly the opposite which took place on the Meuse in May, 1940. This river was crossed by the German armoured divisions unsupported by 'an attack on a grand scale or a considerable mass of artillery'.

'There will be', added the writer, 'powerful attacks on a broad front such as we made during the Battle of France. It is only a matter of amplifying these by throwing in a heavy division.'

Thus, it was a question merely of improving existing things with respect to the First World War.

Regarding anti-tank defence, Debeney continued: 'A deep zone, where the impetuous vehicles would be dealt with successively. . . . The tanks would no longer enjoy the invulnerability of 1918.'

In a word, the heyday of the tank was gone. . . .

Unfortunately the 'impetuous vehicles' of the Panzer Corps, heedless of the false prophets of the French General Staff, were to cross the Meuse and to invade France.

The *Mercure de France* of April, 1936, stated, in an article signed by a three-star General,[1] that Germany, being instinctively prone to the offensive, ought naturally to have armoured divisions, while 'France, peaceful and defensive, could only be "anti-mechanized".'

The objections made to my amendment were four in number:

1. Your armoured corps will skim the cream off the French Army. The best soldiers will go into your armoured corps.

Reply: That is true, but does not the Air Force also attract the boldest and best-equipped men. It also deprives the Army of the cream of the recruits. Do you propose suppressing the Air Force?

2. Your independent armoured corps will advance, like a madcap, into the midst of the enemy, and after several initial successes, nothing further will be heard of it.

Reply: If you had bothered to read the explanation of the reasons behind my amendment, you would have seen that this armoured element is to 'be capable of operating, as an independent unit, and certainly not as an isolated one'. Why should it be taken for granted that the Supreme Commander would be incapable of making use of it? There will be circumstances in which the corps will be split up, and others in which it will be massed.

The action of the German armoured corps which was to invade us in May, 1940, was to be that of 'an independent unit, and certainly not an isolated one'. This corps was to be accompanied by a motorized division for every two armoured divisions. The motorized division, helped by tanks, was to ensure the crossing of the Meuse. Then, when the Meuse was crossed, the armoured divisions were to take the lead, followed by the motorized division, whose duty it was to line the walls of the corridor opened by the tanks. The motorized division itself was to be followed by lorry-borne infantry divisions and some distance behind, by infantry divisions on foot. The role of the infantry masses, as will be seen, was to follow in the wake of the armoured divisions. Hence the bitter reflection, noted down in May, 1940, by a German infantry officer in his diary: 'We are not fighting; we are only occupying.' Obviously we were quite a long way from the infantry being 'the Queen of the battlefield'. A revolution had taken place in the art of war. After having pierced our front at Sedan, Dinant,

[1] i.e. a *Général de Division*, or of a rank equivalent to Major-General in the British Army [Tr.].

then Monthermé and to the north of Namur, the German armoured divisions were to reassemble between Valenciennes and St. Quentin, and, from there, like sheep-dogs herding in a flock, they were to burst on Dunkirk in an endeavour to cut the retreat of the Allied Armies.

If we had had an armoured corps on March 7, 1936, we should have used it in strength in the Rhineland. But, if we had had an armoured corps, Hitler would not have dreamed of re-occupying the Rhineland. And the King of the Belgians would not have broken off military relations with France. And Hitler would not, in 1939, have attacked Poland, because of the risk of being attacked by ourselves in the Rhineland. If we now take as an illustration our front of May, 1940 (Mézières–Namur–Antwerp), half of the armoured corps would have been placed behind Sedan, and the other half behind Dinant, as geography, history and our knowledge about the movements of the enemy dictated. By its counter-offensive, it would have prevented the invasion of France.

3. We do not want a corps 'recruited in principle from soldiers who are regulars'. It would, in addition, be impossible to recruit all those of this category, who would be needed by an armoured corps.

Reply: 'Through what timid reasoning, mental laziness or slavishness to routine should we reject for the ground Army what we accept for the Air Force and the Navy?' I asked the Chamber on March 15, 1935.

If the Government had given me the following answer: 'We accept your armoured corps, but we do not agree that it should be composed of regulars', I would have replied. 'I agree. Let us try the idea out. We shall see. But I warn you: 1. That this corps will be less suitable to fulfil, at any given moment, the function which will fall on it in the case of a sudden attack by France or by one of her allies; 2. That its aptitude for manœuvring—and this is a most important point—will be much less; 3. That, when you have had sufficient tanks put out of action by novices, you will be most eager to ask for the same rule to be applied to the armoured corps as to the Air Force.'[1] But no Government ever used such language to me. Successive Governments all told me: 'We do not want your armoured corps at any price.'

4. The tanks of your armoured corps will be penetrated by anti-tank weapons just as foot soldiers were by machine-gun bullets. For it is 'the bullet which kills'.

Reply: You will lose tanks just as you lose cruisers in a naval battle. Do you intend to do away with cruisers?

The advocates of systematic defensive warfare believed in distributing tanks along the front in order to consolidate it by bolstering it up, whilst their opponents were the advocates of concentrating tanks to achieve powerful action.

---

[1] In actual fact, there was to be no tank in May, 1940, whose crew was not composed of regulars.

I asked for the opportunity of explaining my counter-proposal to the Army Committee. This body received me with courtesy but with coldness. From the very first moment I felt that judgement had already been passed. Had not the Minister of War, who had already been consulted by it, replied that my amendment ran 'counter to logic and to history'? The Committee rejected it. In June, 1935, Fabry, the President of the Committee, became, as we have seen, Minister of War in the Laval Cabinet.

When, on December 26, 1935, the Bill was discussed in the Chamber, my amendment was, therefore, already as good as rejected both by the Government and the Committee. Thenceforth, there was no chance of it being adopted. I should have liked, however, to profit by the debate in order to put forward my case once again. As I was ill that day, I could not do this. My amendment was rejected.

During the course of the debate Fabry made a statement which I do not think he would have been able to do if I had been present. He seemed to believe that seven motorized divisions (carried in lorries) could take the place of the six armoured divisions for which, in addition to the light mechanized division of Rheims, I was asking. This was confusing trucks with tanks! In actual fact we were far from possessing in 1935 the seven motorized divisions about which Fabry was speaking: we were to have only five of them on entering the war in September, 1939, and we had to wait until May, 1940, before getting seven. He counted on, however, what he called the 'motorized corps', composed of these motorized divisions and the light mechanized division of Rheims, 'to sow destruction amongst the enemy'.

Fabry also reproached me with wishing a corps 'held separate from the body of the army'. Is not the artillery an arm which is distinct from the infantry, and is it not held apart from the body of the army? The reproach appeared all the more strange in that Fabry had just congratulated himself on the creation of fortress troops 'an *élite* corps in which it will be considered an honour to serve' and on which he conferred personal privileges and a special uniform. He stated that the 'motorized corps' would possess the advantage of forming the cadres of the army. This is what I had asked for the armoured corps. In order to attack the armoured corps, he attributed to it 'the claim of protecting by itself, national territory'. It is known that I had written expressly to the contrary in the *Exposé des motifs* attached to my amendment.

In a book *Par delà la Meuse*, a German soldier called Maassen, tells of the crossing of the Meuse at Monthermé in May, 1940. He draws a striking portrait of the colonel in command of the sector. 'The colonel is a native of Normandy, a province inhabited by men whose physique has nothing in common with that of their Latin neighbours, of fair-headed men who stand a head taller than their compatriots. . . .

He would not have looked out of place in field grey uniform. . . . He was not one of those who dealt solely in words. . . . He had been amongst the men who had been in favour of the adoption by the Chamber of Deputies of Paul Reynaud's . . . plan to transform the French Army into an offensive weapon. *When this plan received a set-back, the dice were thrown, and the fate of France was settled as regards the next war.* There was the tragic obsession with fortified places, which nourishes a feeling of false security within an entire nation when it abandons itself to it.'

After the Flandin Ministry, it was, therefore, the Laval Ministry which assumed responsibility for rejecting my amendment. I leave it to the reader to judge the nature of this responsibility.

On the next day, December 27, I got out of my bed to speak in the debate about the Abyssinian affair. I took the opportunity of expressing the anguish which the rejection of my amendment had caused me: 'Against whom is Germany arming? Against what powerful army is she in the process of gathering this colossal force, and why are the German people putting their trust today in a single investment, namely that of war? . . . The situation with which we find ourselves faced today is that, as our neighbour, there is a nation with its sinews tautened for war, with a youth twice as numerous as our own—a fanatical youth to whom war is represented as a crusade and a source of hope.'

And I gave this tragic warning to the Laval Government and the Chamber: 'We are the only great people in the world, whose very existence is at stake.'

But my words were in vain.

5

CHAPTER VIII

THE SEVENTH OF MARCH, 1936

Hitler warns us of his Intentions.—Surrender to Hitler.—The Opinion of Churchill.

HITLER WARNS US OF HIS INTENTIONS

HITLER'S plan comprised several stages: the annexation of Austria; the crushing of Czechoslovakia and of Poland, the allies of France; a final settlement with the last named; the conquest of the Ukraine.

This progress by stages was the keystone of the plan. It was its very prerequisite for success.

The first objective was to make it impossible for France to take armed action when Germany indulged, first of all, in the annexation of Austria, and then in the destruction of our Eastern allies.

To do this, it was necessary to install the German Army in the Rhineland, and to bar French access to this region by powerful fortifications. But Articles 42 and 43 of the Treaty of Versailles were categorical: they forbade Germany both to have armed forces in the Rhineland and to build fortifications there. But this was not all. It was not a question of unilateral pledges dictated by the conqueror, of pledges which Hitler had never ceased to condemn. It was a question of obligations freely undertaken by the Reich at Locarno, of obligations which, if their substance was the same as at Versailles, had not become changed in nature since they formed an integral part of a Treaty concluded in a spirit of reciprocity and ensuring the benefit of a guarantee by Britain and Italy to Germany on the same conditions as to France. No examination, however artful it might be in its subtlety, could be successful in discovering the slightest flaw in such pledges. But for months Hitler had not hidden his impatience to repudiate the Treaty and seek some way of evading it. He had, therefore, to find a pretext, an external pretext. Like a good German the Führer had a fertile imagination when it came to inventing motives for a quarrel. The ratification by the Chamber of the Franco-Soviet Pact was to supply him with these.

Hitler conferred with the leaders of his Army. They were unanimous in advising against the operation. They feared in reality any reaction on the part of France, whose military superiority they did not question. This fact was known at the time. The statements of Keitel and his fellow-accused at the Nuremberg trial have merely corroborated it. Thus Albert Rivaud writes:[1] 'At Berlin on March 7, 1936, there was an apprehensive period of waiting in the expectation of a reaction which would then have resulted in capitulation.' And Benoist-Méchin[2] writes: 'The remilitarization of the left bank of the Rhine was an operation whose boldness will appear ever greater with the passing of time. It caused the German Generals legitimate apprehension, for they knew that the Wehrmacht could not resist an answering blow from the French Army.'

But Hitler, with a broader and a clearer vision, calculated on the apathy of our Ministers and Generals. He knew that our country was weakened by an unduly prolonged economic crisis, that it was torn by the resulting social unrest, which was within a few weeks to carry the *Front Populaire* into power, that, into the bargain, it was the eve of General Elections and that already parties were actuated by only one pre-occupation, that of not losing the favour of public opinion. He also knew that the Stresa coalition had not survived the business of sanctions, that Laval, after having sacrificed the intimacy of our relations with Britain for the sake of an understanding with Italy, had managed to lose any benefit from this new orientation. Finally and most important of all, he knew that our Army was defensive as regards equipment and outlook, and that the man who was at the Ministry of War was General Maurin, the same man who, a year earlier, had asked me on the floor of the Chamber if, seeing we had spent milliards in constructing the Maginot Line, we would not be 'rather foolhardy to advance beyond this barrier on some unpredictable venture'.

In any case Germany did not catch us unawares. According to her custom she had abundantly and clearly warned us of her intentions. And, for once, we had taken her warnings seriously.

On many occasions Gamelin, as we have seen, had brought to the notice of the Government information obtained by the intelligence service of the Army General Staff about German military preparations. M. François-Poncet, had already sounded the same warning note. This is to be found in the passage of his memoirs in which he describes his approach to Hitler on March 2, 1936. But as early as November 21, 1935, he had paid a visit to the Chancellor in order to tell him of the imminent opening of a parliamentary debate on the Franco-Soviet Pact, and to remind him[3] that this Treaty was of a 'purely defensive

---

[1] *Le relèvement de l'Allemagne*, p. 391.   [2] *Histoire de l'armée allemande*, vol. II, p. 645.
[3] *Op. cit.*, pp. 188–91.

nature'; that it was only 'one fragment of a whole, inspired by a desire to organize security with the Reich's co-operation', and lastly that 'no notion of excluding or encircling Germany figured in its clauses'.

Hitler's reaction far from reassured him: 'His violence in criticizing the Franco-Soviet Pact . . . left me', he added, 'with no doubt as to his future intentions. If he uttered such an indictment, then he must already have decided to retaliate, and his retaliation could be only the denunciation of Locarno and the occupation of the demilitarized zone.

'I had already instructed the Quai d'Orsay to this effect; I had advised it that Hitler's sole hesitancy now concerned the appropriate moment to act . . . I renewed my recommendations. In a long dispatch on November 26 I requested the Government to consult upon what conduct it should fittingly adopt on the day when Hitler passed from words to action. Personally I suggested we should not wait for this to happen; we should forestall it by openly asking the question, thus forcing Hitler to lay his cards on the table.

'My suggestion was disapproved. . . . Our military high command, which knew of my dispatch, asked in its turn what attitude the Government would adopt if the possibility I indicated were to become a fact. The answer was that in such an event we would depend upon the regular procedure of the League of Nations. Past experience, it would appear, had still left us with illusions about the efficacy of the Geneva system.

'I continued to be so deeply preoccupied by the situation which might face us shortly that I made it the subject of my last telegram in 1935. . . . "In 1936", I wrote, "the efforts of Reich diplomacy will clearly tend to free Germany of a servitude she judges to be too harsh. Invoking the demands of national security, Germany will strive to make possible the establishment of garrisons and fortifications on her western frontier. The means to be employed by the Reich's leaders will depend upon circumstances, the course of events, the dispensations of the League of Nations, the state of our relations with our friends, especially Britain, and the firmness of our attitude."

'On January 1, 1936 . . . Hitler assured me that he had no intention of again bringing up the Locarno question. On January 10 and January 13 . . . I reproached Bülow sharply. "You are behaving", I said, "as though you wished to establish juridicial justification for a future act already planned. This act is, of course, the occupation of the demilitarized zone. . . . You doubtless realize that in such an event the situation would become very serious!"

'Bülow remained evasive and, like his master, protested that Germany had no intentions of denouncing Locarno.'

And M. Noël had reported[1] to the Quai d'Orsay the confidence

[1] Noel, *op. cit.*, pp. 125–6.

which he had received from Beck on his return from Germany where he had an interview with Hitler. 'I don't know exactly what he has up his sleeve, but I am certain that it is now the turn of Locarno and the Rhenish zone. He wishes, no doubt, to rid himself of the servitude of demilitarization.' And M. Noël added that General d'Arbonneau, Military Attaché at his Embassy, had sent to the General Staff 'information which he had obtained from the Poles, and which no longer permitted any misapprehension . . . measures had been taken in the Rhine area to make available the former barracks without delay.'

Was ever a Government more accurately or more fully informed? This time, we were not to be taken unawares. Flandin, who was now Minister of Foreign Affairs in Albert Sarraut's Administration, recognized this fact in his own words: 'It was necessary', he wrote,[1] 'to expect a bad-tempered gesture from the Reich. In my opinion it would be expressed by action in the Rhineland. I resolved, therefore, to take advantage of my trip to London in order to ask the British Government about its intentions if Germany were to violate the Treaty of Locarno.' Flandin put this question to Baldwin, in the presence of Eden.

The Prime Minister [he added] answered me by asking another question: 'What had the French Government decided to do?' I could only give a personal opinion. 'It will oppose the move,' I replied. But as soon as I was back in Paris, I asked the Government to state their position precisely, and I informed Mr. Eden of this at the time of our next meeting at Geneva in February. Indeed, I put the question on January 29, at the first meeting of the Council of Ministers of the Sarraut Administration. . . . I had the impression that my colleagues thought that I was in something of a hurry. I obtained, however, a meeting of the Supreme Military Committee, specially summoned, to examine the future measures to be taken, and to prepare a plan to submit to the Government. The Supreme Committee met[2] several days after. Unfortunately, at the last moment, M. Sarraut, who ought to have presided, was delayed in the Senate. My explanation was received with a great deal of reticence by the Ministers of National Defence and their colleagues. I had put a precise question: 'In the event of German troops attempting to reoccupy the Rhineland, what military measures is it possible to take immediately to oppose such a move?' The Minister of War explained, to my great surprise,[3] that the French Army had been entirely modelled to play a defensive role, and that, it had made no

---

[1] *Politique française*, pp. 194–7.

[2] Gamelin, who was present at the meeting, does not mention a word of this in *Servir*: his silence is all the more worthy of attention, in that the author pushes to minute detail the care which he takes in his memoirs, to leave nothing out about his activities.

[3] This surprise was, in truth, surprising; for, as we have seen, Flandin was on the ministerial bench when I asked his Government to create an offensive army: he had therefore heard the reply which Maurin had made me. Several days later the Flandin-Maurin Ministry, as we have likewise seen, had asked the Army Committee to reject my amendment.

preparations and still less was it ready for a military intervention of the type which I was suggesting. As I turned to the Minister for the Navy (Piétri) to ask him if, in order to bring pressure upon Germany he could, for example, blockade the ports of Bremen and Hamburg, he replied that this seemed to him . . . impossible without the co-operation of the British fleet. The Minister of Air (Déat) put forward the view—which was an accurate one—that aerial reprisals could only be carried out through aerial bombardment, which constituted an indisputable act of war, with all the risks to which civilians would be exposed. I was all the more put out of countenance by the fact that I was counting on a quick reaction by our military men in the face of the threat which the reoccupation of the Rhineland by the German Army would constitute for French security; and, a fact unique, perhaps, in the history of France because the Minister of Foreign Affairs, who was generally inclined towards conciliatory negotiations, was assuming the character of a bellicose Minister in front of the Service Ministers, who were not thinking at all of fighting for the Rhineland. While I was expressing my surprise at the negative position assumed by my colleagues, General Gamelin intervened to state that as the Army General Staff was only an executive body, it was the duty of the Government to make a decision. Any decision taken would be put into execution by the General Staff.[1] I gave an account of the conference . . . to the Council of Ministers. . . . As I had to leave for Geneva . . . I asked: 1st, that the Council should define the terms of the reply which I was to give to Mr. Eden . . . in the name of the Government . . .; 2nd, that in my absence, the Supreme Military Committee should meet again under the high authority of the President of the Council and . . . formulate the measures for execution, which the General Staff would take into account when drawing up their plan of operation. I stressed that these vague decisions were no longer of any current value, and that before the threat of a precise action by Germany, we ought to be ready to offer an immediate reaction. The Council decided . . . that I should be authorized to tell Mr. Eden that the French Government . . . would place its military, naval and air forces at the disposal of the League of Nations, in order to oppose by force the violation of the Treaties and, in consequence, I should be empowered to ask the British Government for its future assistance . . . as was agreed by the Locarno undertakings. . . . The Council decided in addition that a further meeting of the Supreme Committee would be held . . . in order to implement the decision which had been taken. . . . At Geneva, I imparted to Mr. Eden the information which I had been authorized to give him. . . . He confined himself to telling me that he would place it before the Cabinet . . . as soon as he was back in London, and that he would have me informed of the reply through the usual channels. . . . I was never to receive any reply.

And there the matter rested. . . .

The Council had thus given a decision in favour of firmness.

It was, however, obvious that the partisans of inactivity had not given up the fight, and that they by no means considered that their

---

[1] This reply was, it must be emphasized, in conformity with Republican doctrine. The General Staff ought to have urged the Government to act, but it rested with the latter, and the latter alone, to assume its responsibilities.

cause was lost. Gamelin, indeed, says[1] that Maurin had told him that the possibility of the German forces entering the Rhineland had been raised in the Council. The strength of the ground forces on a peace-time establishment would only allow, the Minister of War had insisted, a 'strictly defensive' disposition of troops. He had added: 'For an offensive operation, it would be necessary to order the call-up of our reservists without including the call-up of all classes of men in frontier regions to occupy our defensive organizations serving as a base for our advance. . . . A preparatory . . . step . . . would be industrial mobilization.'

Gamelin took pains to stress the agreement between his own views and those of the Minister. 'Our troops on active service in France do not even by a long chalk equal', he affirmed, 'half of those at the disposal of the Germans.' But what is the good of an army if not to mobilize when the fate of the country is at stake?

During the course of the debate on the Franco-Soviet Pact, the ratification of which was voted on the 27th by three hundred and fifty-three against a hundred and sixty-four, several speakers asked if Hitler were not going to answer the decision of the Chamber by breaking the military restrictions on the Rhineland. Flandin reproached them in the Chamber for 'the dangerous thoughtlessness of their words'. He added: 'What nobody . . . could accept . . . would be . . . a repudiation . . . of a treaty like that of Locarno. It would be to wrong the German Government if one were to attribute to it designs which would provoke a serious conflict, not only with France, but with other signatories.'

Thus we came to the eve of the *coup de force*. We could not have been warned in a clearer and more precise manner. The imminence of the event was disputed by no one. We had time to examine all the hypotheses, to draw up our plan, to hasten on preparations and, finally, to warn Britain, a nation incapable of failing to honour her pledges if a straight answer were asked from her. It was out of the question to do the same for the Italy of Mussolini, the other Power guaranteeing Locarno. On March 7, when the bombshell burst, the explosion, to repeat Gamelin's words[2] had 'long been foreseen'. There was not the slightest surprise amongst the Government, nor amongst the General Staff.

But, from the commencement, the dissent, which we have seen beginning, was to crystallize. The passivity of our military policy was to entail the passivity of our rulers. The latter was the logical conclusion of the former.

---

[1] *Op. cit.*, vol. II, p. 199.   [2] *Ibid.*, p. 200.

SURRENDER TO HITLER

On March 7, during the first hour of the day, the forces of the Reich penetrated into the Rhineland. Neurath informed M. François-Poncet.[1] It was the reply to our overtures, the conclusion that he added to his protestations of friendship! It was only a question, he told the Ambassador, of skeleton detachments, in short, of 'symbolic' units. But M. François-Poncet did not have long to wait to hear from our consuls: 'the "symbolic" units mentioned by the wily Neurath were already nineteen infantry battalions and thirteen artillery sections strong'. Flandin affirmed[2] that there were 'certainly not more than fifty thousand men'.

In Paris, the Government was on its 'last legs'. It deliberated. Of the successive deliberations which followed, we have evidently no minutes, but, thanks to the testimony of the chief actors in the drama, it is possible for us to reconstruct the outlines of these days, which have weighed so heavily on the destiny of France, of Europe, and of the world. For, as we have seen, we could, by a gesture, have overthrown Hitler on March 7, 1936.

Could we at least allege in excuse that we were forsaken by our allies?

Let us look first of all at Poland. M. Noël wrote:[3] 'On March 7 . . . hardly had Hitler's broadcast speech . . . ended, than Beck asked me to go and see him at 5 p.m. In the meantime he had consultations with the President of the Republic, General Smigly-Rydz and the President of the Council. "This time the matter is grave", said the Minister to me. . . . Beck immediately asked me, and not without gravity, to give my Government, in his name and in that of the "governing authorities" of the State . . . the following communication: "Poland wishes, in the circumstances, to assure France that she will carry out, if needs be, the pledges which bind her to your country." It has been asserted, it is true, that, if . . . Beck had spoken to me in [this] categoric way . . . it was because he personally was convinced that France would give way. Whilst admitting that this might be correct, the fact still remains that other responsible authorities, in whose name he had expressed himself as well as his own, were convinced that the French Government would take up an energetic attitude. . . . During the following days, certain facts were unfortunately to reveal in . . . Beck the continuance of his ill-feeling towards France. Perhaps, it is true, he had . . . received information from Paris which caused him to anticipate that we would accept a *fait accompli*, and he thought that, therefore, it was preferable for Poland not to give any grounds for alarm to Germany to no

[1] François-Poncet, *op. cit.*, p. 192.   [2] *Politique française*, p. 198.
[3] *Op. cit.*, pp. 124–9, *passim*.

purpose, and not to allow her to guess that, if the French Government did shew proof of energetic action, the Polish Government would be associated with it in this action.'

On receiving this communication, the importance of which it is a waste of time to stress, what did the Quai d'Orsay do? It neglected to warn Gamelin of it!

'Very courageously she [Poland] had informed us', wrote the latter,[1] 'that, if we thought that we ought to go even as far as armed conflict, she would follow us. Now, it is curious to note that I was not advised of this immediately. I only learned of the determination expressed by Beck to our Ambassador very late, through a report of our Military Attaché in Warsaw. I don't think, however, that they mistrusted me. And the heads of the Quai d'Orsay had appeared to me to wish sincerely for an energetic policy.'

When Beck noted that France was not going to fight, he reverted to his former attitude.

On March 7, we could also count on Czechoslovakia. Beneš wrote in his memoirs: 'On March 7, 1936, Hitler, in reoccupying the Rhineland, dealt a decisive blow at the cause of European peace. Czechoslovakia—and probably Poland also—was ready to march by the side of France against Germany. We had told the French Minister in Prague that we should support France if she decided to reject the consequences which were imposed upon her by Hitler's attitude. The latter had broken the Treaty of Locarno and the Rhineland Pact and, because of this Pact, authorized France and Britain to go immediately to war. The Western democracies would have been able to stop Germany, whilst there was still time, in the pursuit of this criminal war. In my opinion, we were obliged to march at the side of these two Powers and we would have done so. But nothing happened. France thus committed the most dangerous of errors. . . . France did not act, when she had the right to do so in accordance with the terms of a treaty signed by Germany and . . . concluded to provide for this particular case. The Western democracies gave evidence of indecision, of weakness . . . and with a lack of foresight which bordered on frivolity. This important fact was the cause of the tragic collapse of France. It was the first chapter in the story of Munich and of the surrender of June, 1940. In March, 1936, France abandoned herself to her fate: it was thus the easier for her to abandon us to ours in September, 1938.'

This was an implacable judgement, but, unfortunately, one which was well founded.

As for Russia, an important factor in the military sphere, she was entirely with us. In London, where, as we shall see, our vacillation was

[1] *Op. cit.*, vol. II, p. 213.

to lead us, Flandin conferred with Litvinov, who was representing his country on the Council of the League of Nations. Flandin summed up the conversation[1] as follows:

'Litvinov alone was categoric: he promised me his collaboration. . . .'
There remained the Locarno Powers: Italy, Britain, Belgium.

On March 10, Eden representing Britain, Paul van Zeeland, Belgium, and Signor Cerrutti, the Italian Ambassador, met at the Quai d'Orsay. Concerning Italy[2] Flandin writes: 'The Italian Ambassador . . . informed us immediately that he would be present as an observer at the debates, as Italy was still under sanctions, but that his Government still considered itself bound by the Treaty of Locarno, and that it would not fail, if need arose, in its obligations according to the terms of the decisions taken by the conference.'

It was from Britain, supported by Belgium, that the objections to a French military reaction sprang. Flandin relates:[3] 'Mr. Eden made it known that he had been entrusted by the British Government [Baldwin] to repeat to the French Government its request, previously expressed, that no step should be taken against Germany which would create an irreparable situation. . . . The British Government undoubtedly did not dream of evading the obligation imposed by the Treaty of Locarno, but thought that the problem could be settled by diplomatic negotiations, and would willingly take charge of these. . . . M. van Zeeland, [who, also says Flandin[4] 'acted as the intermediary of the British in order to make us give way'] intervened . . . to add his approval of the position taken up by the British Government. He joined his own request to Mr. Eden's that France should not take unilateral action.'

Thus, whilst the German generals trembled before the superiority of the French Army, Poland, Czechoslovakia and Russia were urging us to act, and at the same time promising us military collaboration; Italy was declaring that she would not fail in her obligations; and Britain, however reluctant she might be, declared that she would not dream of failing in the pledge she had given at Locarno.

If, instead of seeking an excuse in the reluctance of Britain, we had made her face up to the pledges inscribed in the Treaty, and had asked her to honour them, she would certainly have acquiesced.

But the will to do so was lacking.

The recital of these sad days has been written in detail by Gamelin,[5] whose timetable of them has no gaps.

On the 7th, at ten o'clock in the morning, Maurin and Gamelin went to the Ministry of the Interior at the request of Albert Sarraut. Paul-Boncour and Mandel were there. Flandin was only present for

[1] *Politique française*, p. 206.   [2] *Ibid.*, p. 202.   [3] *Ibid.*, pp. 203–4.
[4] *Ibid.*, p. 201.   [5] *Op. cit.*, vol. II, pp. 201–2.

a moment at the meeting. Paul-Boncour and Mandel asked us to reply 'with an explicit formal summons, that is to say, by assembling all necessary military means to impose it'. Gamelin writes: 'I remember what M. Paul-Boncour told me: "I want to see you as quickly as possible at Mainz."' The first precautionary methods were decided upon: the recall of those on leave, deployment of covering troops, who were to take up their positions, alerting of railways in the protective zone.

At six o'clock in the evening there was another meeting which took place in Flandin's room. Round Flandin and Sarraut were grouped Paul-Boncour, Maurin, Piétri, Déat, Gamelin, Admiral Durand-Viel, General Pujo and M. Léger. Gamelin notes: 'There was another theoretical discussion, but we did not seem to be able to make any progress, certainly at the moment, towards reaching any definite decisions. I took the opportunity . . . of getting a decision on a new series of measures for the purpose of progressively completing our security requirements. But, for the moment, no decision was taken as to the calling up of reservists.' At the end of the meeting, Flandin, in a communiqué to the Press, refuted the arguments invoked by Berlin to justify the remilitarization of the Rhineland, and announced France's decision to bring the matter to the attention of the League of Nations.

The 8th was to be a decisive day. Did the Government make the Press understand the gravity of the situation? It does not seem so, for the Press as a whole was hostile to any recourse to coercion. The newspapers of the Right threw the responsibility for events on the Government, guilty in their eyes, of having provoked Hitler by the ratification of the Franco-Soviet Pact. Maurras, in L'Action Française wrote: 'We must not march against Hitler with the Soviets', and on the next day, the 10th, he repeated: 'And, above all, we don't want war.' From the Left, there was the same appeal that we should resign ourselves to the situation. Paul Faure wrote on the 7th in Le Populaire: 'It would be madness to believe that a great country of sixty million people would tolerate, seventeen years after the cessation of hostilities, the demilitarization of a part of its territories under the control of its conquerors. . . . The assumption, in any case, and it is one which we refuse to admit, is that war can spring from the diplomatic conflict by this sensational move of Berlin.'

Public opinion, as can be seen, was not in favour of resistance, but the solution lay in the hands of the Government, which itself possessed the means to enlighten public opinion. The Council met, therefore, at ten o'clock on the 8th. 'It would have been necessary', writes Flandin,[1] 'to be ready . . . to put into the field a force corresponding in numbers to the German detachments. But . . . nothing of what had been

[1] Politique française, pp. 198–200.

promised me had been done. The Council met. There was a lamentable confusion. I explained the situation. I informed the Council that I had, without a moment's delay, put the matter before the Secretariat . . . of the League of Nations. It was unfortunately an obligation, which had its source in the Treaty of Locarno, to have Germany's breach of faith established by the Council of the League of Nations. And I knew that in London, even amongst our firmest friends, it was considered essential to respect this procedure in order to put the Treaty into operation. . . . I asked what military steps had been envisaged and when they were to be put into force, whilst bearing in mind that the British Government had expressly asked us to make no move before the meeting . . . of the guarantor Powers. . . . The Minister of War then pointed out, to my profound amazement, that the only thing which had been carried out was to move into their positions in the Maginot Line the troops who were to guard it, and to send back to the frontier . . . two divisions which had been stationed in the Rhône valley. And he added that, in order to intervene . . . in the Rhineland, the General Staff required a general mobilization. This demand provoked an outcry of indignation. . . . General mobilization within six weeks of the elections was madness, declared certain of my colleagues, who were more concerned with domestic than foreign politics. On reflection, is it right to harbour resentment against them for not having understood the importance of the demilitarization of the Rhineland, when the military leaders, entrusted with the security of the nation, seemed themselves so unenthusiastic about it? Finally, we were reduced to four—the President of the Council Sarraut, Mandel, Paul-Boncour and myself—who remained advocates of immediate military action. General mobilization, which the Minister of War did not demand, was not even discussed. The Council was of the opinion that it should await internal and international reactions, before taking a decision. . . . Neither from the Right nor the Left was any request for action made to us. In the ranks of the Centre, where the majority of the Ministry's supporters was to be found, there was uneasiness because of the belief that energetic action might bring about the threat of war at a time when the feeling in the country was, above all, pacific. In a word, each and all felt that the reoccupation of the Rhineland would result in a complication of domestic politics, which would exercise an influence on the elections. I have never felt a more bitter distaste of electoral cowardice.'

That the Minister of War had specifically discouraged any action being taken is unanimously supported by other witnesses.

I have it, indeed, from Mandel that Maurin said to the Council: 'If you issue a decree for general mobilization, you will strike a blow at the morale of the Army, for you know very well that you will not be able to do anything.'

Paul-Boncour[1] writes that Maurin declared that, if we wished to act 'we would have to issue the "white poster" for mobilization, that is to say, the one decreeing total mobilization'. Paul-Boncour added: 'I could only remain astonished ... at the lack of proportion ... between the step proposed and the operation which was to be carried out.' The Minister of War did not budge from the position which he had taken up, and he gave at the same time, by his attitude and his language, the impression of not being 'very much in favour', repeats Paul-Boncour, of the step to which he was subordinating military action. As for Déat, he invoked a clause in a Bill, passed by the Chamber in 1927, concerning the 'general organization of the country in a time of war',[2] and maintained that a modification would only be possible after the League of Nations had voted on the issue. To this Paul-Boncour replied that, the very moment when our frontier divisions, after having been reinforced by the reservists, had crossed the Rhine, we ought to state that we were ready to agree to any decision which was later taken by the League of Nations or the International Court at The Hague. The aim of demilitarization was precisely for the purpose of allowing us to 'oppose immediately, by our own means, any open violation of the demilitarized zone'. And Paul-Boncour concluded: 'To go to the League of Nations before taking action was to invert the order of operations.'

In the presence of such objections upon which he stumbled, what did Flandin do? He leaned over towards Sarraut and, Paul-Boncour tells us, he said to him: 'I see, M. le Président du Conseil, that we must not insist.' Paul-Boncour reproaches him with this fact in the following words:[3] 'In this he was wrong. Would not the President of the Council have been better pleased, on the contrary, if his Minister, who was the most qualified to do so, had insisted, and placed upon his Government the necessity of making a decision. . . ?'

Mandel levied the same reproach against Flandin. He gave me at Portalet the following account: 'Flandin gave a summing up which was in favour of a reaction on the part of France, but on the first objection from Maurin, he closed his file saying: "Well, there we are; I see there is nothing to be done."' And Mandel added: 'That is how, when there yet was time for something to be done, the interests of France were defended.'

Jean Zay wrote:[4] 'The Council of Ministers . . . opened . . . with an account of the situation by M. Flandin. . . . The latter quickly summarized the facts, and made plain their gravity. We awaited, in conclusion, some concrete proposals as to what France should do on the

[1] Op. cit., vol. III, pp. 33-8, passim. The author, through an error, places this important meeting on the 10th.
[2] The draft was later passed by the Senate, and became law on July 11, 1938.
[3] Op. cit., vol. III, p. 35.   [4] Souvenirs et solitude, pp. 65-7.

morrow of the most threatening event which had happened since the end of the war. In a ministerial council and except at a time of Government crisis, there was no precedent for a Minister, who had made up his mind to take a certain line, not, in a matter which fell within his province, to win acceptance for the solution which he had elected to choose. On the other hand, when the Minister had nothing to propose, there was equally no precedent for the Council to come to some decision or other. Now M. Flandin did not propose anything. To be more exact he detailed all the possible lines of action, from the most energetic to the most theoretical, from mobilization and entry into the Rhineland to a mere diplomatic protest by appealing to the League of Nations, without himself making any choice from amongst them. In his cold and impassive voice he confined himself to concluding: "Such are the attitudes which we can adopt. It is up to the Council to make its choice." There was a surprised silence. After a moment or so, someone asked what was the opinion of the Service Ministers. They were questioned. General Maurin . . . said in a stifled voice:

'"The Foreign Minister talks of mobilization, of entering the Rhine. . . . There are risks attached to this."

'"Yes."

'"And these risks, do they entail war?"

'No one replied. General Maurin continued: "The present state of the French Army will not allow us to run risks. . . ."

'M. Déat, Minister of Air, and M. Piétri, Minister of the Navy, expressed in their turn an opinion which was equally reserved.

'It was to no avail that a discussion followed, and that the President of the Council, M. Albert Sarraut, supported by several Ministers amongst whom were M. Guernut, Minister of National Education, M. Delbos, Minister of Justice, and M. Mandel, Minister of Communications, spoke in favour of energetic action. Any spirit of activity was broken. Moreover, though the President of the Council indicated his point of view, he did not try to impose it on his colleagues. M. Flandin, from whom the President of the Republic asked for information upon the reaction of foreign countries, stressed the reserve of Britain and of Belgium, who were ready to collaborate with us in diplomatic action, but would not, in any case, agree to send their troops to support our own in an entry into the Rhineland. Was not Belgium . . . later to denounce her alliance with France, and build fortifications along our frontier? The Council ended by deciding to appeal to the League of Nations.'

These accounts, in their whole, are borne out by those which Albert Sarraut gave at the time, during a dinner to Jean Prouvost. Pierre Lazareff, who was present, reported Sarraut's remarks in *Dernière édition* (pp. 302–5). Emile Buré verified his account in *L'Ordre* on July

25, 1945: 'As Albert Sarraut told me . . . exactly what he said to Lazareff, this account deserves to have some trust placed in it.' Here is what Lazareff says: 'The Council opened in a heavy and nervous atmosphere. . . . I [Sarraut] gave my colleagues a picture of the existing situation. Mandel . . . at the outset . . . stated: "If we refrain from replying to this provocation, Hitler will believe that he can try anything without France stirring a finger. He will try anything. After having reintroduced military service a year ago, he is today wiping out the last of the military clauses . . . in the Treaty of Versailles. Look out! We must make a historic decision, for, if we acquiesce in this gesture of the Chancellor . . . we are barring the road against any interventions. We shall no longer be able to bring help to the States to which we have promised it, and we shall be forced to change our entire system of foreign policy."

'I approved of what he said, as did several other Ministers. . . . Flandin . . . did not oppose us in the slightest. The substance of what he said was: "We ought to throw the German troops out of the Rhineland or cease to try and prevent Germany later falling on Central Europe. Britain will be obliged to follow our lead, as this is formally provided for by the treaties. Yet, I know she will do this with bad grace, and will disapprove of our stubbornness. The United States will accuse us of imperialism, and the hate of the Germans for us will increase."

'"What does that matter?" exclaimed Mandel. "If we do not act, Britain and the United States, revising their judgement, will in a few years' time, accuse us of having ruined Europe through cowardice and perhaps of having ruined the world, which will be a much graver matter. It is, moreover, possible that a military defeat will have in Germany herself serious repercussions on the popularity of Hitler, and may mean for this man the beginning of the end."'

Let us continue Sarraut's account according to Lazareff's version. One will not be surprised to see the role played by Déat. 'But it was Déat . . . who carried the day. . . . He spoke vigorously against the steps proposed by Mandel: "Hitler's decision was inevitable. He had to use his military strength as the mainspring of his policy. If, this very night, two months before the elections, a general mobilization is decreed, we shall be swept out of Parliament, tomorrow, if not before, by a popular revolution. And we shall have given the world the hateful spectacle of war-mongering. Abandoned morally by all the great Powers, we are risking, moreover, if we answer back, the worst of moral and material disasters."

'I [Sarraut] insisted, however, with emphasis on the necessity of replying energetically to the action of the Führer. I begged . . . Maurin to get information again from the General Staff, and I myself telephoned to . . . Gamelin. "I can bring the operation to a successful conclusion", the Commander-in-Chief told me, "but I cannot make certain of doing this if you do not give me the means, and these means entail general mobilization."

'Flandin, in the meantime, had again consulted the British. They were leaning more and more towards an acceptance of Hitler's action. The Council, by a large majority, agreed . . . with this opinion. I should add that Flandin was entrusted with drawing up a speech which I was to make that very evening in order to reassure public opinion, and to answer back to the Germans. . . . It was Flandin who was the author of the famous phrase which was flung so frequently at me about Strasbourg and the "fire of the German guns".'

At the end of the deliberation, a communication to the Press declared that the Council had considered the German memorandum unacceptable and 'approved the decision taken to place the matter before the Council of the League of Nations without delay, and to begin consultations with the signatories of Locarno' at Paris. The Minister of War had 'given an account of the security [sic] measures to be put into force at the outset and the movement of troops ordered by the Government. He has been authorized, together with the Ministers of the Navy and of Air, to prepare the complementary steps which the circumstances require.' Gamelin was to tell us[1] what these measures were: the dispatch of troops to new positions by rail, but only in so far as it concerned units on active service.

On the night of the 8th Sarraut made on the radio the speech containing the famous phrase: 'We are not prepared to allow Strasbourg to come within cannon-shot of the Germans.' Flandin relates[2] that he called the attention of Sarraut to the 'warlike' tones of the text drawn up by the members of his secretariat and especially to this phrase. Sarraut took no notice of his remark. He was right, but he was to blame in not having threatened his colleagues with the collective resignation of the Cabinet unless they followed him on such a vital question.

At a sitting of the Chamber, Sarraut declared: 'France is not taking her stand in the present conflict on wounded egoism or broken pledges. . . . No. She is raising the question of the real value of treaties . . . the problem of the might which is based on right before the right which is based on might.' According to the procedure of the Chamber, only one speaker could follow him. This was the President of the Committee of Foreign Affairs, who approved the action of the Government.

Indeed, at the ending of the meeting of the Council of Ministers everything was 'cut and dried'. After that, what was the use of discussions within a restricted committee about the similar solution to

[1] *Op. cit.*, vol. II, p. 202.   [2] *Politique française*, p. 207.

the seizure of Saarbrücken and Kehl, which raised the same military objections, without settling the problem of the Rhineland? What was the use of the discussions between the signatories of Locarno, who assembled on March 10 at the Quai d'Orsay? Yes, certainly Britain showed herself at this meeting to be in a pettifogging mood, but Britain is an island and, for this reason, she does not run the risk of being invaded as we have been so many times, and were going to be again. What was the use of the discussions in the Council of the League of Nations at London, where it was clear that Britain would, more firmly than at Paris, oppose any action in the Rhineland?

As for saying, as Flandin did, that we would have caused a 'rupture' with London, if we had taken action, this was holding cheaply the time-honoured policy of Britain towards the Continent. If, having acted, France had found herself, by trying to do the impossible, in danger, Britain was bound to intervene, whether she liked it or not. The argument about the risk of rupture was, therefore, a poor excuse.

During these discussions, the German Army installed itself tranquilly in the Rhineland. The negotiations entered into in London had only one result: namely that of acknowledging to Hitler the *fait accompli*. Was I wrong in saying at my lecture on February 4, 1938[1] that the Government of the time had, 'prepared' nothing to stop the execution of the Führer's plan?

The attitude of military circles had been the determining factor. They had committed the supreme mistake of not proclaiming: 'It is necessary to act', and had been content to say: 'This is what must be done if you wish to act.' On March 10, in a report to the Army General Staff, Gamelin stated:[2] 'It must not be possible at any price, for anyone to be able to say that the Army did not dare to march.'

Concerning this attitude of the high military circles, let us quote a book by General Chauvineau published in 1938, *Une invasion est-elle encore possible?* In this book we read[3] that the business of March 7, 1936, 'possessed only an insignificant military interest to us'. And the author made fun[4] of those who had 'exaggerated considerably the really insignificant importance of this event'. As for Maurin (whose close harmony with the Supreme Command, Gamelin, as we have seen, has stressed) he wrote in March, 1938, in *Le Journal* an article called 'La France sut faire la réponse qu'il fallait au geste allemand du 7 mars 1936'. 'In this grave hour', he said, in particular, 'the Army showed itself completely admirable.' These are words which one must read with one's own eyes to believe.

In the military debate of January to February, 1937, when the Blum Administration was in office, Flandin threw a ray of light on the state

[1] *Loc. cit.* (*Revue Hebdomadaire*, February 26, 1938).
[2] *Op. cit.*, vol. II, pp. 203–4.   [3] p. 205.   [4] *Op. cit.*, p. 210.

of mind of the French rulers on March 7, 1936. I had just[1] told the Chamber that one of the causes for our inaction when faced with Hitler's coup was the fact that we did not have the armoured corps whose creation I had demanded: 'A great Power has shown itself incapable of advancing twenty kilometres beyond its frontier in order to seize the pledges provided in the Treaty, without calling up its reserves, because it did not have an instrument fitted to carry out such a mission. Suppose that, in order to send a cruiser to Melilla, we had to mobilize the Navy reserves.'

On my affirmation that, faced with the lack of the armoured element, the Government of the time had been obliged to recoil from a long, costly and dramatic general mobilization—which I still believe to be the truth—Flandin interrupted me to say that, if France had abstained, it was because 'it was her duty to collaborate with the other signatories of Locarno'. And he added: 'It was also her duty not to take up, with respect to the other signatories, an attitude which would have been disapproved by them.' That Britain, a guarantor of the demilitarization of the Rhineland, should not have understood the vital importance to the future of France, and, moreover, to her own future and that of Europe, of chasing the German army out of the Rhineland, and thus overthrowing Hitler, was therefore a sufficient reason for us to accept an obligation to stand aside and do nothing. This was equivalent to saying that the British guarantee was weakening instead of strengthening us. Therefore, I replied to Flandin, 'M. Flandin, like myself, has contacts with British parliamentarians. These gentlemen, at least those to whom I have spoken about the matter, are of one mind on the question. They say to us: "It is true that at that time we did not want to march; it was above all your business, and concerned your safety. But if you had marched, we would naturally have followed you."'[2] I added that the Government of the time had adopted a middle course between action and inertia; it had used words. To this Flandin replied: 'It adopted an intermediary attitude which has led to what constitutes today the most essential, the most decisive guarantee of our safety; the agreement of reciprocal co-operation, complemented by General Staff conversations between France and Britain.'

[1] January 26, 1937.

[2] I was interrupted by Frossard, who ejaculated: 'This is fashioning the story after the event.' When, pray, has one done otherwise than record history after the event? Moreover, was I telling the story after the event when attacking, at the beginning of the month of April, 1936, those responsible for our surrender, I wrote in *Jeunesse, quelle France veux-tu?* (pp. 14–15): 'Do you think that the German Army would have occupied the left bank of the Rhine if we had had the army with the mechanized "shock" element which I was demanding a year ago, in a precisely worded amendment?' And, when persisting during the period of Mussolini's propaganda, in fighting against the advocates of reversal of alliances, I added: 'We have had legitimate reasons for not being satisfied with the British but I regret to tell you that we cannot allow ourselves the luxury of two hereditary enemies.'

Thus it was that the German Army installed itself in the Rhineland. It was, between 1937 and 1939, going to build there the trunk of the Siegfried Line stretching between the Rhine and Trèves and to begin fortifications lining the Luxembourg and Belgo-German frontier right to the Netherlands. What did Flandin do to meet these tragic realities? He concluded an agreement on co-operation, as if there were the slightest doubt about the intervention of Britain in a conflict wherein France would be implicated. Did this agreement on co-operation prevent Britain on the eve of Munich from adopting the same attitude as on the morrow of March 7, 1936? As for the talks between the General Staffs, they had been resumed as early as the autumn of 1935, at the time of the Abyssinian affair. The 'decisive' guarantee about which Flandin spoke did not increase therefore the worth of what we already had.

'Each time I have undertaken a venture, I have succeeded', proclaimed Hitler triumphantly. 'For a State', wrote Richelieu, 'to suffer a wrong without obtaining satisfaction for it, is to invite another.'

France had renounced the defence of her vital interests when she was capable of defending them, and thus Hitler hesitated no longer. Europe, in terror, recognized that he was her master.

The plan of *Mein Kampf* began to unfold.

THE OPINION OF CHURCHILL

Churchill gave an unvarnished opinion on the affair of March 7. Here it is:[1]

MM. Sarraut and Flandin had the impulse to act at once by general mobilization. If they had been equal to their task, they would have done so; and thus compelled all others to come into line. It was a vital issue for France. But they appeared unable to move without the concurrence of Britain. This is an explanation, but no excuse. The issue was vital to France, and any French Government worthy of the name should have made up its own mind and trusted to the Treaty obligations. More than once in these fluid years French Ministers in their ever-changing Governments were content to find in British pacifism an excuse for their own. Be this as it may, they did not meet with any encouragement to resist the German aggression from the British. On the contrary, if they hesitated to act, their British allies did not hesitate to dissuade them. During the whole of Sunday there were agitated telephonic conversations between London and Paris. His Majesty's Government exhorted the French to wait in order that both countries might act jointly and after full consideration. A velvet carpet for retreat!

... There was also great division in France. On the whole it was the politicians who wished to mobilize the army and send an ultimatum to Hitler, and the generals who, like their German counterparts, pleaded for calm, patience and

---

[1] *Op. cit.*, vol. I, *The Gathering Storm*, pp. 174 ff. (second edition).

delay. . . . If the French Government had mobilized the French Army, with nearly a hundred divisions, and its Air Force (then still falsely believed to be the strongest in Europe), there is no doubt that Hitler would have been compelled by his own General Staff to withdraw, and a check would have been given to his pretensions which might well have proved fatal to his rule. . . . In fact she [France] remained completely inert and paralysed, and thus lost irretrievably the last chance of arresting Hitler's ambitions without a serious war. . . .

On Monday, March 9, Mr. Eden went to Paris accompanied by Lord Halifax and Ralph Wigram. The first plan had been to convene a meeting of the League in Paris, but presently Wigram, on Eden's authority, was sent to tell Flandin to come to London to have the meeting of the League in England, as he would thus get more effective support from Britain. . . . Flandin himself arrived late [on the night of the 11th], and at about 8.30 on Thursday morning he came to my flat. . . . He told me that he proposed to demand from the British Government simultaneous mobilization of the land, sea and air forces of both countries, and that he had received assurances of support from all the nations of the 'Little Entente' and from other States. He read out an impressive list of the replies received. There was no doubt that superior strength still lay with the Allies of the former war. They had only to act to win . . . it was evident that overwhelming force lay on our side. . . .

Wigram thought it was within the compass of his duty to bring Flandin into touch with everyone he could think of from the City, from the Press and from the Government. . . . To all whom Flandin met . . . he spoke in the following terms: 'The whole world and especially the small nations today turn their eyes towards England. If England will act now she can lead Europe. You will have a policy, all the world will follow you, and thus you will prevent war. It is your last chance. If you do not stop Germany now, all is over. France cannot guarantee Czechoslovakia any more because that will become geographically impossible. If you do not maintain the Treaty of Locarno all that will remain to you is to await a rearmament by Germany, against which France can do nothing. If you do not stop Germany by force today, war is inevitable, even if you make a temporary friendship with Germany. As for myself, I do not believe that friendship is possible between France and Germany; the two countries will always be in tension. Nevertheless if you abandon Locarno, I shall change my policy, for there will be nothing else to do.' These were brave words; but action would have spoken louder.

. . . I advised M. Flandin to demand an interview with Mr. Baldwin before he left. . . . The Prime Minister received M. Flandin with the utmost courtesy. Mr. Baldwin explained that although he knew little of foreign affairs, he was able to interpret accurately the feelings of the British people. And they wanted peace. M. Flandin says that he rejoined that the only way to ensure this was to stop Hitlerite aggression while such action was still possible. France had no wish to drag Great Britain into war; she asked for no practical aid and she would herself undertake what would be a simple police operation, as, according to French information, the German troops in the Rhineland had orders to withdraw if opposed in a forcible manner. Flandin asserts that he said that all that France asked of her Ally was a free hand. This is certainly not true. How could Britain have restrained France from action to which, under the Locarno

Treaty, she was legally entitled? The British Prime Minister repeated that his country could not accept the risk of war. He asked what the French Government had resolved to do. To this no plain answer was returned. . . . M. Flandin returned to France convinced first that his own divided country could not be united except in the presence of a strong will-power in Britain, and secondly that, so far from this being forthcoming, no strong impulse could be expected from her. Quite wrongly he plunged into the dismal conclusion that the only hope for France was in an arrangement with an ever more aggressive Germany.

Nevertheless in view of what I saw of Flandin's attitude during these anxious days, I felt it my duty, in spite of his subsequent lapses to come to his aid, so far as I was able, in later years. I used my power in the winter of 1943–44 to protect him when he was arrested in Algeria by the de Gaulle Administration. In this I invoked and received active help from President Roosevelt. When after the war Flandin was brought to trial, my son Randolph, who had seen much of Flandin during the African campaign, was summoned as a witness, and I am glad to think that his advocacy, and also a letter which I wrote for Flandin to use in his defence, were not without influence in procuring the acquittal which he received from the French Tribunal. Weakness is not treason, though it may be equally disastrous. Nothing however can relieve the French Government of their prime responsibility. Clemenceau or Poincaré would have left Mr. Baldwin no option.

It is certainly true that this war could have been avoided, as Churchill said to Roosevelt, who asked him one day by what name it would be called.

'The unnecessary war', he replied.[1]

Still it would have been necessary, in order to avoid it, to renovate our Army and not to let Hitler calmly install his own in the Rhineland.

---

[1] Churchill, *op. cit.*, vol. i, *The Gathering Storm*, Preface, p. x.

CHAPTER IX

THE POPULAR FRONT IN OFFICE

The Popular Front takes office.—The forty-hour working week.—
The struggle between the forty-hour working week and devaluation.
—'From Thorez to Paul Reynaud.'—The Daladier Ministry.

THE POPULAR FRONT TAKES OFFICE

AT the beginning of 1936 the electoral campaign began. Springing from a coalition of Communists, Socialists and Radicals, the Popular Front dashed headlong into the electoral campaign. It put the emphasis on increasing salaries and reducing the working period. From an electoral point of view such a programme had virtues which were unrivalled. Victory was certain. But it was the Communists who were the chief victors, whilst the Radicals paid the expenses for this success. The Socialist group became in numbers the most powerful in the Chamber. Intoxicated by their triumph, the working classes demanded the immediate execution of the promises made by the victors. At the end of May, disorders broke out which were especially marked amongst the factory workers. The restlessness increased.

On June 4, Léon Blum formed a Cabinet. The next day, suspending all other business, he broadcast a speech in which he promised the speedy passing by legislation of the essential points in the electoral programme.

THE FORTY-HOUR WORKING WEEK

It was in an atmosphere of excitement, and under pressure from the mob, that Léon Blum gathered together delegates of employers and of workers in the Hotel Matignon. An agreement was concluded, which was based on the promised reforms. It only remained now to secure the approval of Parliament.

The circumstances were unfavourable to the Opposition. Of the Centre, Flandin was away on holiday and Piétri voted with the majority. In the Senate, Laval showed more courage: he abstained. That the reduction in working time should go hand in hand with the development of mechanization, no one would dispute and everyone could only be thankful for it. But were conditions at this moment of a nature to permit this reduction? It is certain that the institution of an eight-hour working day in 1919 had raised unjustifiable opposition, the memory of which still remained alive in labour circles. But, were not those people right who, in 1936, recalled that for three years Germany had been working night and day to forge herself weapons, whilst France stood watching her with arms crossed? Was this the moment for the French to cut down their effort by instituting a forty-hour working week?

In my determination that we should not stray from the technical plane, I said to the Chamber: 'The policy of the Government is running counter to universal experiment. Where, indeed, does the evil lie? It is because selling prices . . . have fallen below purchase prices . . . that a number of factories have had to close down. . . . The experiment made by all other nations has consisted . . . in increasing selling prices, while raising purchase prices as little as possible. You, on the other hand, have raised purchase prices . . . and, whilst everywhere else in the world we can see a considerable reduction in wages . . . what are you proposing that we should do? Increase the hourly wage in terms of gold by thirty-five per cent.'

I concluded: 'We are going to see a rise in retail prices . . . which will be all the more important in the case of monetary devaluation . . . and which is going to decrease to a large extent the purchasing power . . . of the workers. . . . The outflow of gold can only aggravate the existing lack of equilibrium. . . . Devaluation will come one day, for all operations liquidate themselves. But then it will be a collapse in currency. And the devaluation of the franc will no longer be one of twenty-five to thirty per cent, but of fifty to sixty per cent. The expenses . . . of the State and the losses of the railways . . . will be increased by at least four milliards. And how will you find these milliards? With paper money, as you know very well.'

To these gloomy prophecies Léon Blum replied that my speech recalled to him that of M. Purgon in *Le Malade Imaginaire*: 'You will fall from bradypepsia into dyspepsia, from dyspepsia into apepsy, from apepsy into . . .' And, after having stated that his policy was tending to make 'the factories work at a higher percentage than their capacity for production', he concluded, and certainly not without reason: 'The results of the experiment will decide which of the two of us is right, Monsieur Paul Reynaud.' They did, in effect, decide.

Between April and September, 1936, even before the law for a forty-hour working week had been put into operation, wholesale prices had risen by eight and a half per cent, and retail prices by nine per cent, whilst, since September, 1931, the time of the devaluation of the pound, the retail prices in Britain had only increased by three and a quarter per cent. Cash in hand at the Bank of France had fallen from sixty-two to fifty-two milliards. Industrial production had decreased by seven and a half per cent. As concerns the index figure of unemployment, it had increased from a hundred and sixty-three to a hundred and seventy-four. Only my prophecy about the growth of money in circulation had not yet come true, because the Government had just raised a loan, but we had lost nothing by waiting, since, by the time of the disintegration of the Popular Front in April, 1938, this circulation had increased by fourteen milliards.

THE STRUGGLE BETWEEN THE FORTY-HOUR WORKING WEEK AND DEVALUATION

The flight of gold had begun again on an increased scale. Devaluation was to impose itself upon us. (On September 28, 1936, the Chamber met in an extraordinary session to ratify the decision of the Government, which authorized the Bank of France to cease exchanging notes for gold, that is to say, to devalue the franc.)

It was no longer the time for lamentations and regrets. Yet Georges Bonnet, who spoke in the debate, expressed the complaints of the Radicals. After having recalled the phrase of Edouard Herriot during the elections of 1932, 'Either budgetary deflation or devaluation', he showed that, when they were in power, the Radicals had sacrificed themselves to bring about deflation and thereby to avoid devaluation. And, suddenly, the Government, after giving its solemn word not to devalue, was coming to ask the Chamber to endorse devaluation. How were the Radical supporters, who were recruited from amongst the middle classes, going to react under this blow? Was it not true that they, by the very reason of their social condition, would have to suffer severely from the increased cost of living? In actual fact, it was not devaluation, but the increase in the hourly wage, which was going to give rise to distress amongst the middle classes. But Bonnet, who, with the other Radicals, had approved this increase, could not revise his former judgement. His speech, however, embarrassed the Government, which was half composed of Radicals. Bonnet, deep down within himself, had never forgiven Blum for not including him within his Administration. Blum considered it wise to repair this omission by sending Bonnet as far away as possible; he entrusted him with the Embassy at Washington.

For my part, there could not be any question of repudiating what had taken place before, still less of drawing any glory from having been right. Events had, it is true, compelled me to play the role of Cassandra, but be lenient enough to believe me when I say that it was always against my wishes. The essential thing was therefore that devaluation, about whose introduction we had so long delayed making up our minds, should not prove a 'damp squib', and that the country should not be cheated of the advantages that it was reasonable to expect from it. To the Government I said without equivocation: 'The struggle is not between you and me. There is no difference between a devaluation by the Left and a devaluation by the Right. There is a devaluation which succeeds, and a devaluation which has to be renewed all over again. . . . Devaluation will allow a large-scale policy for national recovery at a time when it is fitting that France should be strong. If you make an expedient of devaluation to enable you to continue for a few more months a policy which has been a failure, observe the consequences. . . . In this grave hour I have risen to ask the Government and the Chamber, both of whom are responsible, this question: Is France to be the only country in the world where devaluation has failed?'

The Government was to persevere none the less in the policy upon which it had mistakenly strayed three months earlier. The good fairy of devaluation produced, first of all, a reversal of the economic situation. All the indices took on an upward movement. But, at the end of several months, a wicked fairy arrived on the scene to neutralize this development, and to throw France back into the depths of the abyss of the crisis. In the duel which began between the forty-hour working week and devaluation, it proved to be the first which was the stronger. It broke the back of the recovery inspired by the alignment of the franc.

Salaries soared upwards. The retail price of goods followed them. Retail prices, that is to say, the cost of living, and salaries were plunged into a vicious chase, each in turn outstripping the other without either ever getting out of breath.

In industry, cost prices, thanks to the advantage conferred by devaluation, had fallen in terms of gold to a point where they were level with British prices. From January, 1937, they were higher than these by nine per cent.

Industrial production fell from ninety-four in March, 1937, to eighty-nine in June, and to eighty-two in April, 1938, when the Popular Front split up. It was only to recover a point in October, 1938, on the eve of a reversal of policy.

The index of unemployment rose from a hundred and forty-four in May, 1937, to a hundred and fifty-one in April, 1938, and to a hundred and fifty-six in October.

As national production proved incapable of satisfying the needs of the country, it was necessary to do our buying in foreign markets. Imports increased more than exports. The deficit in the balance of trade increased: from eight hundred and twenty-seven million for each month in 1936, it increased to one thousand five hundred and thirty-eight in 1937.

Alone in the world France had 'foozled' her devaluation.

'There is a devaluation which succeeds, and there is a devaluation which has to be renewed all over again,' I had said to the Chamber on September 28, 1936. We began it all over again. We even did this twice, inflicting each time a new set of regulations on our 'miserable' franc. But nothing was of any avail. It continued to fall until the day when, in November, 1938, I myself, having taken over the Ministry of Finance, was able to attack the root of the evil: the diminution of the production of wealth.

The law of October 1, 1936, which had devalued the franc for the first time, had kept it under the influence of the gold standard. It had fixed, in weight of gold, an upper and a lower limit beyond which it was forbidden that it should pass. To keep it there, it was necessary to hand over such an amount of gold that in June, 1937, the Blum-Chautemps Cabinet had to give way to the Chautemps-Blum one, with Bonnet, called post-haste from Washington, at the Ministry of Finance. It was on Bonnet that Chautemps counted to save the franc. But to succeed in doing this, Bonnet could find no better means than severing the links between the franc and gold.

The dollar, which was equal to fifteen francs nineteen centimes on the eve of the devaluation of October 1, 1936, was worth twenty-one forty-seven on the day after. In the month of June, 1937, it rose to twenty-two, forty-six. In January, 1938, it was worth twenty-nine, ninety-two, and in April, thirty-two, twenty-three. Within the space of a year the franc had fallen in value by forty-two per cent, and the Bank of France had lost five hundred and fifty-seven tons of gold, including gold mortgages abroad.

And the franc continued to decline. France had fallen from brady-pepsia into dyspepsia.

'FROM THOREZ TO PAUL REYNAUD'

On January 13, 1938, Chautemps was himself defeated because he said during a debate in the Chamber to the Communist deputy Ramette: 'M. Ramette wants his freedom. That is his right. As far as I am concerned he can have it.' The Socialist Ministers, not being prepared to stomach the sight of the Communist Party being excluded from the Government majority, themselves left the Cabinet, which handed in its resignation.

On January 14 the administrative committee of the Socialist Party voted in favour of a 'Popular Coalition under Socialist leadership.' This was a subtle type of formula. The political bureau of the Communist

Party demanded an administration which was 'in the image of the Popular Front'; this implied the presence of Communists side by side with the Radicals and Socialists. It was the reverse of their attitude in May, 1936.

On January 16, Léon Blum was entrusted with forming an administration. He adopted the formula 'From Thorez to Paul Reynaud', that is to say, a coalition embracing all shades of opinion in the Assembly from the Communists to a member of the Centre. The proposed coalition did not materialize, and Chautemps formed a purely Radical Administration, as the Socialists refused to serve under him. The crisis over the *Anschluss* began. It ended on March 12 with the invasion of Austria. But Chautemps had resigned on the 10th, and no Government existed in France to react to the crisis. Léon Blum again appealed to me. I replied to him that the circumstances were so grave that they required national unity even more than in the preceding January. Léon Blum agreed upon this, and he had the courage to ask for it on the 12th before the National Council of the Socialist Party, which followed his advice. A meeting of the deputies of the Opposition took place in the Chamber in the Colbert room. I showed how ill-advised it would be to reply by rejecting the attempt which the leader of the Socialist Party had just made to unite all Frenchmen in this tragic hour. Flandin and Fabry opposed the move. The Moderates rejected the hand which was offered them.

Léon Blum formed a Ministry which resembled his Administration of June, 1936, with Chautemps and Daladier in it.

On April 8, the Blum Ministry was defeated in the Senate by two hundred and fourteen votes to forty-seven. On the 11th, Daladier formed a Government, which did not contain the Socialists, but included Mandel, Champetier de Ribes, and myself.

The Popular Front had disintegrated.

THE DALADIER MINISTRY

Daladier had offered me the Ministry of Finance. I believed—and I had never stopped saying so to the Chamber—that the evil from which the franc was suffering was not, really, of a financial but of an economic nature. To save the franc, it was necessary to save French economy; moreover, it was necessary to save it in order to arm France. But, for this purpose, the foremost condition of all was to make the law governing the forty-hour working week more supple. Now, the Radicals had been united, but a short time before, with the Socialists in the Government and in the majority. It would be impossible for them to separate from each other at the very outset on such a burning question. I went, therefore, to see Léon Blum, who, whilst advising me to enter the

Daladier Administration, told me that his Party would not allow the law to become a subject of debate. Under these conditions, I should have entered the Government only in order to overthrow it. Daladier then offered me the post of Minister of Justice, and I accepted this on the advice of Edouard Herriot.

Marchandeau, a level-headed individual, who was an excellent Mayor of Rheims, was put in charge of the Ministry of Finance. He decided, on May 5, to subject the franc, still in a bad state of health, to a third treatment. He had it introduced into the family of the satellites of the pound, and stated that the latter, which just previously was worth a hundred and sixty francs, would never be worth more than a hundred and seventy-nine. The franc profited thereby by immediately losing ten per cent of its value. The pound rose to a hundred and seventy-six francs in May, and to a hundred and seventy-nine in June. A large inflow of gold at first resulted, for, with the pound at a hundred and seventy-nine francs, the franc itself was, after all, not so dear, thought the speculators. But, from the month of July, they changed their minds, for the economic situation, as we have seen, did not improve. From July to November the Bank of France lost six milliards of gold. The dollar reached the rate of thirty-eight francs. The situation was so bad that on October 30, 1938, Marchandeau proposed at a Cabinet meeting that control should be placed on the exchange rates. I made the objection that such a measure would dispel all hope of seeing again the capital which had taken flight, at a time when its return was essential to the economic recovery and to the rearmament of France. I made it plain that it would be impossible for me to stay in a government that pursued a policy against which I had always fought. Around the table, the members of the Administration were obviously wondering if, like all its predecessors of the previous six months, the Daladier Cabinet was, in its turn, going to trip over the monetary crisis. Daladier adjourned the meeting, and, whilst my colleagues smoked cigarettes in what was called the billiard room, because of its long table covered with a green cloth, he had conversations with the two adversaries, as a result of which I became, on November 3, Minister of Finance, and Marchandeau, Minister of Justice.

In the monetary sphere as in the economic, devaluation had thus failed. The franc had lost, in terms of gold, more than fifty-eight per cent of its value in 1928.

A new page of our financial history had been turned. For my part, it was not a question of devaluing the franc a fourth time, but of restoring our economy which had fallen into the depths, whilst, for five years, production was soaring in the German factories, where the arms were being forged for the war which everything heralded as being very near.

CHAPTER X

MUSSOLINI IS OF THE OPINION THAT FRANCE IS 'FINISHED'

1936, Mussolini throws in his lot with Hitler.—1938, The Embassy of M. François-Poncet in Rome.

1936: MUSSOLINI THROWS IN HIS LOT WITH HITLER

WHAT were the results of Laval's policy towards Italy? Did the 'sabotage' of the sanctions demanded by Britain, for the benefit of Mussolini, at least gain us the Duce's lasting gratitude? On the contrary, it was for us that Mussolini reserved his spite. It was against us that he launched his most violent Press campaigns, and it was to Britain that he made overtures. It was with her that, at the beginning of 1937, he signed a 'gentlemen's agreement', and it was again with her at the beginning of 1938 that he asked for conversations. Tardieu himself, who had reproached me for having fought against Laval's policy, complained[1] now of the unhappy position in which France was placed in relation to Italy, because she had 'in M. Laval's time played a double game'.

Moreover, this policy of duplicity only resulted for us in disappointment after disappointment. From September, 1935, Franco-Italian relations, as we have seen, progressed towards breaking-point.

Whatever may be the truth of the matter, our refusal to face up to the situation of March 7 was to be, for Italy, a reason for raising her demands. On May 29 the Italian Military Attaché took 'a step of a very serious character' by pointing out to Gamelin[2] that, if sanctions were not raised, 'grave events might be expected, which could jeopardize our military alliance'. The social disturbances which accompanied the advent into power of the Popular Front increased this arrogance.

On June 9, 'M. Massigli', continues Gamelin,[3] 'had brought me the copy of a Note drawn up on the instructions of M. Léger, which asked the Minister of War to study the consequences to be anticipated on the supposition that the Italians would take measures for mobilization

---

[1] *L'année de Munich*, p. 117. [2] Gamelin, *op. cit.*, vol. II, p. 223.
[3] *Ibid.*, pp. 223-4.

within a brief space of time. . . . And I had received a visit from M. de Chambrun . . . who struck a similar note. Marshal Badoglio had told me in substance: "The Duce, who deceived France in 1935, today believes that she is 'finished', because of the troubles which are materializing everywhere. It is to be feared that he will throw in his lot with Germany." . . . The danger of the situation was made clear for me by a personal letter from Marshal Badoglio, which an officer of his staff brought me on June 13. In the month of October the Marshal sent me confirmation of his impression. Indeed, the Duce was using a more crude expression. . . .'

Mussolini had said, in actual fact, that he believed that France was 'finished'.[1] In the future, there was to be no further contact between the two General Staffs. Mussolini had chosen to side with Hitler.

In the same month of October, 1936, whilst I was at Rome, I had a long, and at times very animated, conversation with Count Ciano, the Foreign Minister and son-in-law of Mussolini. When, after having made several statements to me in the same vein, he launched into a eulogy of Léon Degrelle, leader of the Rexist movement in Belgium, I said to him: 'I perceive what your policy is. Everything in Europe, which is hostile to France, is your ally. I venture to find this an imprudent policy, for I consider the French Army as the bulwark of Italian independence. Kindly tell me what would remain of that independence if France no longer existed?' Ciano answered me that there always would be a France, but he gave me to understand that he would not be sorry to see a diminished France. To this I retorted: 'Allow me then to make you a prophecy. Before two years are out, the German Army will be at the Brenner Pass.' Ciano protested with such emphasis that I wondered if the conversation was not going to be broken off. But seventeen months later the German Army was at the Brenner. . . .

The next day I received a visit from the Rome representative of a friendly country, to whom I imparted my conversation with Ciano, and of whom I asked if reasonable Italians were not alarmed at a policy such as his. He answered me: 'I recently had a conversation with an Italian General, similar to that which you had yesterday with Ciano. He said to me: "Yes . . . but the booty appears so attractive."' Fascism was above all anti-French. Mussolini could tack this way and that, could even make a right-about-turn, but at heart Fascism envied the wealth of France. That is a fact which was as plain as a pikestaff.

In reality, Mussolini knew that he was surrendering the future independence of his country in the hope of its enrichment, an essential factor to a régime which could only endure through prestige. He had read in *Mein Kampf*: 'Never allow two Continental Powers to be created in Europe. See in any attempt which tries to organize on the

---

[1] The French expression is more coarse [Tr.].

frontiers of Germany a second military Power, an attack against Germany. Believe that it is not only your right, but your duty to prevent by all means, and, if need be, by force of arms, the creation of such a Power. If it already exists, destroy it.' This formula was applicable to Italy as well as to France. The loss of Italian independence was the price of Mussolini's policy. We, in France, had placed great hopes on the outcome of the interview between Hitler and Mussolini at Venice in 1934. It was said that when Hitler hailed Mussolini with an 'Ave, imperator', the latter had replied 'Ave, imitator'. It seems that the two men were not compatible. But Mussolini, without doubt, thought twice, for the Italian Press adopted a favourable tone towards Germany. In any case, the same Duce who, on the morrow of the assassination of Dollfuss, on July 25, 1934, had sent two divisions to the Brenner Pass, and had telegraphed to the Chancellor of Austria: 'The independence of Austria, for which Dollfuss has fallen, is a principle which has already been defended, and which will be even more courageously defended in the future by Italy,'[1] this same Duce was not to be found on the spot when the Panzer divisions entered Austria. No doubt, when he asked for conversations two months earlier with Britain, he was playing Hitler's game of trying to separate Britain from France. On September 8, 1938, when the riots amongst the Sudeten Germans of Czechoslovakia had created a state of the gravest tension in Europe, a communiqué from the Italian Government stated that, in a struggle of an ideological nature, Italy would take her place alongside Germany.

1938: THE EMBASSY OF M. FRANÇOIS-PONCET IN ROME

There were numerous Frenchmen who believed that, if our Government recognized Victor Emmanuel as Emperor of Abyssinia by giving him this title in the credentials with which the Ambassador whom we accredited at his Court was furnished, the slackening in tension would be immediate.

M. François-Poncet tells us himself the reasons why, when he had represented our country at Berlin from 1931, he asked insistently for the Rome post. He writes:[2] 'Mussolini had so manifestly dominated his partner, Hitler had so solicitously consulted Mussolini at every juncture, the Duce himself had contributed so usefully to make Hitler accept the final solution, that I concluded that Mussolini had been sincerely won over to the cause of peace. The only influence still capable of acting on the Führer, I thought, was that of his Italian ally. . . . Thus I was led to wish I might be sent to Rome.'

[1] It is true, that, following the interview at Venice, Ciano had stated to the journalists on the subject of Austria: 'You will see that nothing else will happen.'
[2] Op. cit., p. 279.

Indeed, Hitler paid some consideration to his unfortunate accomplice so he invited him to come and see him eat up Czechoslovakia after Austria; but was that Germany of Teutonic warriors and the steelworks of the Ruhr, that Germany of the armoured corps and the Stukas, that Germany of *Mein Kampf*, directed by Mussolini?

I said, at this time, to M. François-Poncet, who informed me of his wish: 'Are you not asking to leave a capital for a provincial town?' Still, the fact remains that on his arrival in Rome, at the end of October, the newspapers were forbidden to publish his photograph and received the order to give the news in four lines, on the third page, as if it were a question of the Minister to represent Liberia. Received by Mussolini, M. François-Poncet told him that Daladier had authorized him to inform Mussolini that we were disposed to make concessions about Djibouti. It turned out to be far from a question of doing this. The Duce dismissed the offer by stating that no talks were possible as long as the matter of Civil War in Spain was left unsettled. On November 30, Ciano's yearly speech in the Chamber of Fasces[1] took place. M. François-Poncet had decided not to be present. Ciano expressed to him his wish that he should be there. He went. Ciano spoke of 'legitimate Italian ambitions'. Immediately, thirty or so deputies stood up and cried, 'Nice, Corsica, Savoy, Tunisia!' The President of the Chamber tapped gently on his desk, and Mussolini remained motionless in his chair. M. François-Poncet left the Ambassadors' gallery. It was obvious that this demonstration had been organized. The French Ambassador had been lured into an ambush. If Mussolini had become so emboldened as to offer insults, it was because, on this very day, the general strike broke out which the General Confederation of Labour had ordered as a sign of protest against the decree-laws which I had just issued, when I took over the Ministry of Finance. It is obvious that, by this news, Mussolini believed more strongly than ever that France was 'finished'. For him the recognition of the annexation of Abyssinia and the dispatch to Rome of an Ambassador were only the equivalent of other indications of weakness.

Some time after, M. François-Poncet asked Ciano what was the meaning of the campaign in which the Italian Press declared null and void the Laval-Mussolini agreements of January, 1935.

'It is because these agreements are only valid', Ciano answered him, 'under a suspensive condition—a Convention regulating the application of the principal clauses, those which relate to the cancellation of Italian claims on Tunisia. Now, this Convention has never been ratified.'

---

[1] This was the *Instituzione della Camera dei Fasci e delle Corporazione* (the Institution of the Chamber of Fasces and Corporations). Actually this body created by Mussolini did not replace the old Italian Chamber of Deputies until January 19, 1939 [Tr.].

Our Ambassador objected:

'But we have handed over to you territories on the borders of Libya, and the shares of the Djibouti railway.'

'That is quite likely, but these are details. The cancellation of our claims on Tunisia presupposed your co-operation in the Abyssinian affair. Now, instead of co-operation, you have applied sanctions against us. I am, moreover, going to send you a Note on this matter.'

Shortly afterwards, our Ambassador did, indeed, receive a Note declaring that the Rome agreements were null and void. The Quai d'Orsay bitterly reproached M. François-Poncet for having raised the question. The latter replied that it was an error to believe that an agreement is void because one of the parties states that it is, whilst the other maintains the contrary. In January, 1939, Chamberlain, the British Prime Minister, and Halifax, the Foreign Minister, went to Rome to woo Mussolini. What did the latter ask of them? To sever Britain from France. It goes without saying that British loyalty remained deaf to such language. Once again, Mussolini was working on behalf of Hitler, who was, seven months later, to unloose war.

Even before signing the Alliance of May 22, 1939, with Germany, Italy was Hitler's tool. The picture which Rivaud[1] paints for us gives an idea of what Franco-German collaboration would have been if we had tried to avoid war through it:

'Germany's grip on Italy was complete from the beginning of 1939, in spite of the resistance of the Royal Family. Engineers, specialists, financial experts at first arrived unostentatiously. Military and financial missions followed. Then came organized formations, brigades and divisions. Artillery equipment, seized in Czechoslovakia, took the road to Italy. The Germans were now everywhere. They controlled all the public services, customs, posts and telegraphs; officers in uniform drove about the streets of Milan and Turin under the surly and often hostile looks of the Italian crowd.' Speaking afterwards of the Treaty of Alliance in which a clause stipulated, he says, that in the event of conflict, the Italian forces would be under the orders of the German Command, the author adds: 'Italy delivered herself, bound hand and foot, to the domination of the Berlin Government. She tolerated a moral annexation which was the prelude to political annexation.' And this prophetic question should have been a warning to our own Conservatives and military men, 'Would Italy bring to the Reich anything else but an element of weakness? No one was ignorant of the fact that the Fascist régime had lost the affection of the Italian people. The existence of the dictatorship was discussed, and threatened, even amongst the faithful who helped it to take root. The Italian nation was rebelling at long last against an effort which was too painful.

---

[1] *Op. cit.*, pp. 422–3.

Would the German cadres be sufficient to move and hold the discouraged masses which were calling for peace?' Finally, this moral was drawn: 'If Mussolini has, as seems certain, agents in Berlin, he must see with what scorn Germany speaks of Italy, of her Army, and her technique. And he cannot be in any doubt as to the deep feelings of the German people about the "traitors" of 1915.' These were the true reactions of Germany towards Italy! And the words which Rauschning ascribed to Hitler who, he said, 'spoke of Fascism with a hateful scorn' corroborate the conclusion of Rivaud: 'Germany would have to fall very low to be reduced to counting on the co-operation of Italy.'

In Rome our Ambassador was held at arm's length by Mussolini. Gamelin, always so discreet in his judgements about men, was bold enough to say:[1] 'M. François-Poncet, after the Munich affair, had, for reasons which I very imperfectly understood, left the Berlin Embassy for that of Rome. He could not win there the happy influence which M. de Chambrun had gained for himself. No doubt the times had changed. But it is certain that M. François-Poncet, a brilliant mind, but theoretical and critical, was himself hardly the type to find a common ground with Mussolini. He really had relations only with Ciano.'

In truth, it did not lie in the power of anyone to succeed. Mussolini clung to the coat-tails of his master. He had put his money on German strength. Through this strength he expected a share of the spoils of France.

[1] *Op. cit.*, vol. III, p. 303 (1).

CHAPTER XI

LEOPOLD III BREAKS AWAY FROM THE POLICY OF HIS FATHER

The Nature of the Franco-Belgian Alliance.—October 14, 1936, Leopold III declares in favour of an exclusively Belgian policy.

THE NATURE OF THE FRANCO-BELGIAN ALLIANCE

A LEVEL-HEADED individual, Robert Schuman, who knew Germany well, said in the Chamber on September 28, 1936: 'There are quite a number of us who have, during the holidays, travelled abroad, and have brought back with us a feeling of sadness, for they have been able to take stock of the disastrous impression that the toleration shown towards the factory workers during the last four months, the impunity granted to certain violations, the sequestrations, the ransoms levied on motorists, etc., have created in all countries, friendly and ex-enemy. . . .'

Coming back to the happenings of March 7, 1936, Gamelin wrote:[1] 'World opinion was then expecting from us an energetic response. Many people were wondering if the absence of this was due to the weakness of our Army, or to a flinching in our policy because of the social crisis which was then imminent and the development of which people were noting. I must say that, when we, General Smigly-Rydz and myself, left Paris by car to journey east,[2] and when, occasionally, we were greeted by groups of people brandishing their clenched fists, I felt in no wise at my ease.'

It is certain that, coming as they did after our refusal to stand up to Hitler on March 7, the disorders which heralded the advent of the Popular Front made a deep impression on foreign nations. France, which introduced the law for a forty-hour working week at a time when Hitler's Germany was stretching her muscles to prepare for the struggle, appeared to some as an easy prey, and to others as an undesirable ally.

As early as June, Badoglio, as we have seen, informed Gamelin that Mussolini considered France was 'finished', and that he was drawing

[1] *Op. cit.*, vol. II, p. 238.   [2] On August 31, 1936.

nearer to Germany who, as soon as she had installed herself in the Rhineland, began the construction of the Siegfried Line.

The German system had a weak point. An offensive starting from the French frontier or from the Luxembourg frontier would run into either the Rhine, or the Hartz Mountains or the Hunsrück and Eifel Mountains. An offensive starting from Liége would strike, on the other hand, into the Rhine plain about Cologne, Düsseldorf and the Ruhr. Hitler decided to extend the Siegfried Line to the length of the Belgian frontier. But, as long as this work was still in progress, the danger continued, and it was made all the more grave, because, by reason of our alliance with Belgium, the defence of the Belgo-German frontier fell jointly upon the French and Belgian Armies.

Let us examine the nature of this alliance. Under the inspiration of King Albert, our neighbours had, on September 7, 1920, concluded with us a military agreement which, signed by Marshal Foch and by General Maglinse, Chief of the Belgian General Staff, constituted an effective defensive alliance. It provided especially for co-operation between ourselves and the Belgians as soon as there was a threat of German aggression. At this time France and Belgium were sharing concurrently in the occupation of the Rhineland, and the General Staffs of both Armies were working in close collaboration. The agreement had for its aim the consolidation of joint action, which until that moment had been sporadic, by giving it a permanent character. The two General Staffs were thus called upon to consult periodically about the problems which a joint defence of the territory of France and Belgium raised. They embodied the results of their exchange of opinions in minutes, which formed the equivalent to annexed agreements. These agreements, which were spread over the period from 1922 to 1933, 'provided', wrote Gamelin,[1] 'that, as soon as a period of political tension came into being, we on the one hand would relieve the Belgian forces . . . facing Luxembourg and Germany on the general front between the stronghold of Arlon and Liége (excluded), and on the other we would send an army . . . as a reserve behind the line of the Liége–Albert Canal, which would be manned by the Belgians.'[2]

[1] *Op. cit.*, p. 85.

[2] In a work called *Les mémoires de P. Reynaud et la Belgique*, M. Wullus-Rudiger disputes the accuracy of Gamelin's assertion. He writes (p. 26): 'Belgium was in no way pledged to call upon the French Army in the event of diplomatic tension.' Gamelin, whom I questioned on the subject, confirmed his statement. He added that, in 1931, when he had just been made head of the Army General Staff and Weygand had succeeded Pétain as Vice-President of the Supreme Council for War, he had, on the instructions of Weygand, drawn up in agreement with the Belgian General Staff a plan for concentrating forces, which chiefly laid down provisions for the use of the Belgian railways by the French Army, which was to advance into Belgium as soon as there was a period of 'diplomatic tension'. In 1932, at the beginning of the second fortnight in August, Gamelin received M. Crokaert, Belgian Minister of National Defence, for whom he arranged visits to a succession of fortifications, then under construction, in the Maginot Line. In *Servir*

OCTOBER 14, 1936: LEOPOLD III DECLARES IN FAVOUR OF AN EXCLUSIVELY BELGIAN POLICY

These are the agreements which Leopold III took steps to bring to an end. The result which this entailed is apparent. Henceforth, the intervention of the French Army in Belgium in the event of political tension, in order to take up a position facing Germany and to attack this country if she herself attacked out allies, the Czechs and the Poles, was to be forbidden. Before calling upon the French Army, Belgium would henceforth wait until she herself was invaded. It was an ideal solution for Hitler. He knew that France would never enter Belgium by force. He could, therefore, with complete safety, strangle our allies in the east. So much for the first stage of Hitler's plan. As for the second, its solution was equally ideal. Hitler was to invade Belgium at exactly the

(vol. II, p. 84) Gamelin alluded to this visit in these words: '[The Minister] showed that he was keenly interested in them. I suggested to him the advantages there would be in his country's organizing the most important part of its frontier on the basis of similar plans . . . and in enlarging the stronghold of Liége on the right bank of the Meuse, by extending, as far possible to the south, the *fortified area* which could thus be created. Equally, I stressed the advantage that we could derive from constructing a strong position at Arlon, which we could unite by Longwy to the left flank of our Thionville-Longwy system. In this respect, it should not be forgotten that the Belgians were then our allies and that we had the right to count on them when they called upon us during a period of political tension.'

It is true that, by an exchange of letters on March 6, 1936, the two parties declared that the Treaty of Locarno had caused certain undertakings, laid down in the agreement of 1920, to become a dead letter, but they declared themselves at the same time resolved to maintain the necessary contact between their respective General Staffs, both for the implementation of the obligations laid down by the above Treaty of Locarno as well as the study of technical conditions for applying those obligations.

No doubt this readjustment was a matter of course. It nevertheless permitted the continuance, although within a refashioned framework, of the co-operation of the two General Staffs. It was this co-operation, a precious guarantee of the solidarity of the two countries for the purpose of ensuring their common safety, which did not survive the step taken on October 14, 1936. Yvon Delbos, Minister of Foreign Affairs at the time, entrusted Gamelin (cf. *op. cit.*, vol. I, pp. 85–6; vol. II, p. 239) to call the attention of the Supreme Belgian Command to the gravity of the repercussions which this change of policy entailed. The Commander-in-Chief designate, acting on his own responsibility, but also with the consent of the Government, revealed to the Military Attaché 'that the Germans were in a position to make a surprise attack, and that, in this case, if the Belgian General Staff did not call us in as a precautionary measure, we could not support the defence of the Albert Canal, of Liége and of the Luxemburg frontier'. He officially warned the Belgian Supreme Command that, as the proclamation of neutrality had practically the effect of denouncing the Alliance, he considered 'as a dead letter' the agreement of the General Staffs, and he was of the opinion that he could 'no longer give any other pledge than that of acting as the circumstances would best permit, and chiefly according to the situation at the moment when Belgium appealed for our assistance'. At the end of November, General van den Bergen, Chief of the Belgian Army General Staff, answered Gamelin as follows: 'Whilst noting my statements, he hoped', wrote the latter, 'that the new situation would not disturb our relations or our future collaboration. I told the Military Attaché who brought me [the] letter: "that my feelings towards the Belgian Army had not changed, that the French Army was going to pursue actively the steps which had been planned for its strengthening, and that it would in any circumstances do all that was possible for its former Allies".'

moment he chose. The French Army was only to enter the country after he himself had done so. Thus, there proved to be insufficient time for it to take up its positions on the Albert Canal. Therefore, as an outcome of this, Hitler's offensive army would advance to meet in open country the defensive army which France had built up for herself.

The Committee of Inquiry set up by His Majesty King Leopold III on July 14, 1946, reproduces, in its *Rapport*,[1] certain statements of M. Spaak's, who became Minister of Foreign Affairs shortly afterwards, which tend to confirm that the latter was himself associated at this time with this reversal of Belgian policy.

As early as April 29, 1936, M. Spaak stated in the Chamber of Representatives: 'In 1925, there existed a demilitarized zone. Articles 42 and 43 of the Treaty of Locarno preserved their full intent. The first article of the Treaty of Locarno referred explicitly to it. The demilitarized zone was for us, in case of a German attack, a military safeguard, whose importance it is unnecessary to stress. In 1936, Germany reoccupied the demilitarized zone, overthrowing previous agreements and confronting us with an entirely new *status quo*. How could we fail to take this into account when laying down our international status? . . . Belgian security in the future could only be attained by a tremendous military effort under a so-called independent régime. . . .' Some weeks later, on July 20, M. Spaak, at a banquet to the foreign Press, after having declared that he intended to stamp the foreign policy of Belgium with the 'impress of realism', added: 'I only want one thing, a foreign policy which is exclusively and completely Belgian.' Finally, M. Spaak had adopted, on September 26, 1936, by the Congress of the Belgian Socialist Party, a resolution, the chief item of which was 'that there has never been and there would never be any question for Belgium of a return to neutrality . . . that her policy must be, to the exclusion of all military alliances and within the framework of the Society of the League of Nations, a policy of complete independence.'

In the speech which he gave on October 14 to the Council of Ministers, the King was to take up these arguments: 'The reoccupation of the Rhineland, by twisting the agreements of Locarno in form and substance, has almost put us back to our international position of pre-war years. Our geographical situation demands of us that we should maintain a military machine which is of a size to dissuade any of our neighbours whatsoever from borrowing our territory to attack another State. In discharging herself of this duty, Belgium is contributing . . . to the peace of Western Europe, and she is creating *ipso facto* a right to the respect and the future help of all States who have an interest in the keeping of this peace. . . . But our pledges cannot go beyond this. Any

---

[1] I shall give later in this book numerous quotations from this document, which, for the sake of brevity, I will refer to as the *Rapport*.

unilateral policy would weaken our position abroad. . . . An alliance, even one of a purely defensive character, will not achieve the end, for, however prompt may be the help of an ally, this ally will only intervene after the onset of the invader, which will be devastating in its character. To struggle against this onset, we would be alone in any event. . . . That is why, as the Minister of Foreign Affairs has recently said, we should pursue a policy which is exclusively and completely Belgian. This policy should aim resolutely at keeping us apart from the quarrels of our neighbours. . . .'

Thus it was that Belgium showed her dissatisfaction with the results of March 7, 1936, when, as we shall see, she persisted in preventing us from reacting to Hitler's blow. And, now when the threat was becoming more pointed and greater, she rejected the co-operation which, by virtue of our agreements, we owed her as soon as a period of political tension began. What was the pretext? We would arrive too late. It was no doubt better, our neighbours thought, to be alone in bearing the brunt of the shock.

Whatever was the case, the Ministers of Leopold III backed his opinion. France and Britain could only state that they continued to consider themselves as guarantors of Belgian integrity. Hitler, as can be well understood, fell into step with them.

Several months after the breaking of the Alliance I had the opportunity of bringing to M. van Zeeland's attention the fact that this rupture would prevent France from stopping the crushing of Czechoslovakia by herself attacking the Reich. The Prime Minister contented himself with answering by this demonstration of trust: 'The Czechs will not be crushed.'

To a Frenchman who deplored in his presence this reversal of Belgian policy, Paul Emile Janson, a great friend of our country, replied: 'Do you believe that the Belgians who were in Paris in 1936, and who were forced to carry their luggage on their own shoulders because of a strike of hotel porters are not to be excused if they possess some misgivings about France?'

It was a reply which, whilst not justifying, explains to a certain degree the development of Belgian opinion, a development which allowed Leopold III to break with the policy of his father.

CHAPTER XII

A FRANCE WITHOUT ARMS
(FROM MARCH 7, 1936, TO MUNICH)

*My Campaign in 1936.—August 12, 1936, Pétain's doctrine is
confirmed.—February 2, 1937, the Chamber decides: France is not
to have an armoured corps.—My campaigns in 1937 and 1938.—
The Key to the problem: Pétain and Weygand are hostile to the
modernization of the Army.*

MY CAMPAIGN IN 1936

ON the morrow of March 7, 1936, I decided to speak directly to
the country in order to adjure it to open its eyes and get a grip
upon itself. Taking up, in *Jeunesse, quelle France veux-tu?* the
problem of collective security, I wrote[1] in the form of a dialogue
between an imaginary questioner and myself:

*Curiosus: Is France in a position to play her part in this new organization
for peace?*

Paul Reynaud: No, because she has no instrument to carry out her
policy. She has kept the defensive Army created by the law of 1927.

Curiosus: How can the situation be remedied?

Paul Reynaud: By building up an army of shock troops, which
possesses devastating speed in action and a formidable fire-power.
Modern assault tanks, which are 'ground cruisers', go at a speed of forty
kilometres an hour in the open country. The specialized striking force
which I asked for in my counter-proposal of March 31, 1935, would
have had double the fire-power of the entire French Army of 1914. It
would have been like a passing tempest. . . .

To have a military system which pins down our forces within our
frontiers means that we are not only made incapable of carrying out
our international engagements, of putting into force, for the benefit of
others, the principle of collective security (from which we ourselves
count on benefiting in the day of danger), but it also means that we are
committing a fundamental error in theory.

[1] pp. 37 ff.

It seems certain that the German Army, preceded by its powerful tanks designed to pierce our front, will pour through Holland on to Belgium, where it is earnestly to be hoped that the Albert Canal . . . will be fortified and held strongly enough to stop it. Failing this, the Germany Army will head for our northern frontier. . . .

It is, therefore, necessary for our own national defence to have an army of shock troops capable of advancing in one leap to the help of the Belgian Army and of repulsing victoriously . . . any sudden aggression.

In addition, how can we fulfil our duty of mutual assistance, honour the signature which we have put to several pacts, without an army which is capable of making a lightning reply to the attack which will be directed against one of the signatory countries to these pacts? It is the rapidity of this future reply which alone can cause the aggressor to hesitate.

Curiosus: Won't the objection be that you are going to create a professional army distinct from the national army?

Paul Reynaud: Do airmen, sailors, the North African and Colonial troops feel isolated from the French nation and from the national army?

Curiosus: Will not the creation of the specialized striking force entail considerable expenditure?

Paul Reynaud: As far as concerns equipment, this expenditure is provided for. The only question is that of knowing whether this equipment will be placed in the general reserve, intended to be portioned out amongst the different armies, or if we can derive the best use from it by creating a 'crack' element.

Curiosus: Yet was not your plan put aside?

Paul Reynaud: Yes, it was, in France. But it has been surreptitiously put into effect in Germany.

Curiosus: Won't we profit by this lesson?

Paul Reynaud: There are no grounds for thinking so at present. [And I concluded] I do not say that Germany is ready. But I do say that she is feverishly preparing, and that she has already eight hundred thousand men (of whom three hundred and fifty thousand are professional soldiers), and the equipment necessary for the thirty-six divisions which she is in progress of creating, and I do say that it is time to oppose the audacity and the accomplishments of her military theorists with something more than our customary routine.

That is the idea I hammered home untiringly in Press articles and in lectures, because the tocsin of March 7, 1936, itself had not woken us from our sleep. I spoke unceasingly of speed to people who were numbed with lethargy.

That year an event occurred which must be stressed, for it was pregnant with instruction. There was an abundance of intelligence in the French Army, but, whilst in the German Army, officers with original ideas were looked upon with favour, it was a tradition amongst ourselves to 'break' them. Long ago Marshal MacMahon said: 'I strike out of the promotion list any officer whose name I have seen on the cover of a book.'

Scharnhorst, who reconstructed the Prussian Army after Jena, stated, on the other hand, that 'without a good military literature, there can be no intelligent army nor any great flowering of military talent'. He added that one should not accept principles which were 'solely based on authority'.

In 1936, because he had written *Vers l'armée de métier*, Lieutenant-Colonel de Gaulle was struck out of the promotion list. The pretext was that, because he had been made a prisoner in 1914, he had to give way to officers who had a better service record than his own. Now, his citations were magnificent. Because of them, he had finally to be put back into the list. Yet he was not to be promoted to the rank of Colonel until December, 1937, after having been posted to the command of the 507th Tank Regiment at Metz in September of the same year.

If I had been in power, I should have formed the armoured corps, because I thought it was necessary as an indispensable instrument to our policy. But I should only have been able to create it because Charles de Gaulle had conceived it. Such should be the collaboration between the politician and the soldier. As I was in the Opposition, I could only try to open the eyes of our rulers, and this I attempted to do for years. It was a hopeless task.

AUGUST 12, 1936: PÉTAIN'S DOCTRINE IS CONFIRMED

In view of these criticisms which were levelled against our military policy, the question arose of finding out if there was not room for a revision of our doctrine of warfare. Was it necessary to abide by the principles laid down in 1921 by the *Provisional Instruction for the Tactical Employment of Large Units*, a work which, as we have seen, was from Pétain's pen.

On August 12, 1936, a new *Instruction* came into force. The Committee which was responsible for the work was presided over by General Georges, who, at that time, was the Chief of Staff of the Army.

In reply to the question 'Has or has not the technical progress achieved since the last war revolutionized the art of warfare?' the *Instruction*, which was to be the Bible of our Army until its defeat, replied: 'No.' The *Report to the Minister*, which served as its preface, indeed expressed itself thus: 'The *Provisional Instruction* of 1921 proposed ... to lay down, according to the lessons of the war . . . conditions for the tactical employment of large forces. Without disregarding the importance of the progress achieved since this time in the sphere of means of combat and transport, the Committee entrusted with drawing up the present *Instruction* has thought fit, nevertheless, to assert that technical progress has not appreciably modified, in the tactical sphere, the essential rules laid down by its predecessors. It has admitted, therefore, that the body of doctrine, objectively laid down on the morrow of victory by eminent military leaders who had just exercised high command, ought to remain the charter for the tactical employment of our large units.'

Thus, nothing had changed since the 'charter' of 1921. And what about the German armoured corps? Was this not intended to strike against us? Was it not the well-forged instrument which was to shatter our front by surprise attack, and speed on to ravage our rear? It was evident, moreover, that it was going to be linked closely with the colossal air force which Goering had been building during the last three and a half years. Was this not a new and considerable factor? The *Instruction* elected to remain in ignorance of this. How was the French Army to face up to this machine which was to become so enormous, since it was developing with every day that passed? This was the enigma. The *Instruction* did not breathe a word about the problem. Neither in the *Report*, nor in the body of the *Instruction* could one find the words 'armoured corps', nor even 'armoured division'. We kept the army which suited our taste, without bothering about the army which our opponent was in process of creating in order to fight against us. Our army would be capable of resisting another French Army which attacked it, but it was to prove incapable of opposing the army which the Germans were busy forging.

Such was the fundamental flaw in the *Instruction* of August 12, 1936.

But did it not contain a chapter called 'The Light Mechanized Division'?

This chapter was there, it is true, but where was it placed? Under the heading of *General Remarks on the Use of Large Forces of Cavalry*. The Light Mechanized Division was a cavalry element. It was suitable for carrying out 'all the functions which developed on large cavalry units'; it could, in particular, ensure 'the supply of information and security necessary for large motorized units'. This was the sole originality of the *Instruction*. This combination of motorized infantry divisions and a light mechanized division which circled around them in order to keep them informed about the enemy and to ensure their safety, inspired, on the part of those who drew up the *Instruction*, this general observation: 'In this organization, the cavalry division has been superseded by the light mechanized division; the infantry division has been turned into a motorized division.' But it is known that, when the foot soldiers of a motorized division put their feet on the ground, they become infantrymen as they were formerly. The truck is only a vehicle which transports them near to the battlefield. It was these infantry divisions, thus informed and protected by the 'cavalrymen' in armoured cars, which continued to be the principal element in the conflict. The light armoured division was only an accessory. On the other hand, the armoured corps, of the type which I had asked to be created, and such, moreover, as the Germans had constituted, was to be the principal instrument of battle. Collaborating on the battlefield with its dive-bombers, it was followed by motorized divisions.

Like the cavalry, our infantry also had their tanks. These were in tank battalions. But these tanks were mere adjuncts to the infantry. They were intended either to 'accompany the infantry' or to 'precede the infantry and the escort tanks on a wide front towards *their* successive objectives', or to 'penetrate into the enemy dispositions as soon as these were sufficiently shaken and to strike thus at the most distant services and the organs of command. *When serious resistance no longer existed*, and when the exploitation of success seemed possible, the tanks could then form the framework of *mechanized detachments*'.[1]

This is something which is totally foreign to the massive use of tanks of an independent armoured corps. In order to prevent any misapprehension being formed upon the importance of their role, the *Instruction* headed the chapter on infantry and tanks with this statement of principle: 'THE INFANTRY IS ENTRUSTED WITH THE PRINCIPAL DUTY IN BATTLE.[2] Protected and accompanied by its own guns and by the guns of the artillery, and eventually preceded by combat tanks and aviation, etc., it conquers the ground, occupies it, organizes it, and holds it. Its task is particularly dangerous, and of outstanding glory.'

For the compilers of the *Instruction* the tank had brought no revolution in the art of warfare, because it was 'guns that did the killing'. Here is the only passage in the *Report* which is in italics: '*As far as the use of tanks is concerned, one cannot sufficiently stress the fact that today, the anti-tank gun is the answer to the tank, just as th e machine-gun was the answer to the infantry during the last war.*' We could, therefore, sleep soundly in our beds.

We had, it is true, just invented the twenty-five millimetre cannon, which penetrated the German tanks and which was to penetrate them effectively in 1940. In a shoot, there are, no doubt, partridges which are brought down, but this does not prevent the majority of the flight from getting through. So it was to be with the armoured division.

If tanks were only an accessory of the infantry, why should one be surprised that, during the war, generals, colonels and even majors, all wished to have their own tanks? General Keller, inspector of combat

---

[1] The italics are in the text.   [2] The capitals are in the text.

tanks, was to give in his report of July, 1940,[1] an account of how tanks had been used during the campaign. He wrote: 'The German attack found facing it forty battalions of tanks, distributed in a ratio of three or four to an army, from the North Sea to Switzerland, and three armoured divisions recently formed and hardly trained. In addition, within each army the tank battalions were distributed company by company, and even section by section, on all the roads and the edges of the woods. They were . . . only a sprinkling of tanks dispersed like dust by every wind, crushed in small units of three by units of twenty, and fated everywhere, under the weight of numbers, to an end which bore no fruit.'

Could such a front be broken? postulated the *Instruction*. Not any more than during the preceding war, for, if it is true that the fire-power of the attacker is greater, defensive systems are also stronger. Therefore these two parallel progresses of the attacker and of the attacked cancel each other out.

And that is why there is no revolution in the art of warfare!

Therefore the *Instruction* only sanctioned the attack of any enemy front *'under the cover of intense action by all the mass of artillery'*.[2] This was indeed the rule from 1916.

As for the close co-operation of tanks and planes on the field of battle, such a thing was not contemplated. The Spanish war, which the Wehrmacht had chosen as the laboratory to make its experiments, showed the usefulness of this collaboration. Also the words 'dive-bomber' are no more to be found in the *Instruction* than those of 'armoured division'.

What was said about the function of aviation on the battlefield? Fighter aircraft, then termed modestly 'light defensive aircraft', can 'at particularly critical moments intervene in the ground struggles with their machine-guns but this mission exposes them to a rapid wastage, and should only be ordered on exceptional occasions'.

The position taken up by the writers of the *Instruction* of 1936 is all the more surprising in that warnings had come to them from abroad as well as from France.

The British *Instruction* of 1927 had already stated: 'The conception that armoured vehicles can only fight in close liaison with infantry and cavalry is out of date.'

At the end of 1935 the *Militaer Wochenblatt* explained that the development of armament led inevitably to a profound change in the organization of the army and imposed specialization on the battlefield.

[1] This document was mentioned during examinations at the Riom trial, as well as during the testimony of General Keller at the hearing of March 31, 1942 (cf. Pierre Mazé and Roger Genebrier, *Les grandes journées du procès de Riom*, p. 260; Maurice Ribet, *Le Procès de Riom*, p. 507).
[2] The italics are in the text.

The armies of the future, it said, will therefore include troops which are solely intended for rapid action, and units which are intended to occupy the ground. The first will be the 'break-through divisions', made up of heavily armoured tank units. The second will be carried in tracked vehicles or trucks. The reservists will be placed in divisions of the old type.

The German military leaders had shown themselves, into the bargain, good friends to ourselves. They had warned even us of the error of our ways, by publishing, in the *Militaer Wochenblatt*, two articles on the doctrine of the *Instruction* of August 12, 1937, and these were quoted in *Le Temps* of August 18, 1937. In them one read: 'The use of armoured vehicles as envisaged by France is a gigantic mistake.' The French method, said the author, could only create 'pockets' in the enemy dispositions, as at Verdun. And he explained the system of lightning attack by successive waves of tanks, followed by motorized divisions. This was the new type of war. . . .

It is true that, disturbed no doubt in having thus put its French colleagues on the alert, *Militaer Wochenblatt* published shortly afterwards the article of a Swiss officer, which said in essence: 'But, not at all. Tanks must remain, as during the last war, the accessory of the infantry.'

'There's a sound fellow,' our General Staff immediately observed in the pages of *Le Temps*, through the pen of General Baratier.

And in May, 1936, the German General Guderian himself was at pains to enlighten our military leaders on the way in which, four years later, he intended to break our lines. In the new German military review the *Militaerwissenschaftliche Rundschau* he wrote that the enemy front was to be torn open by the use of 'heavy offensive and "break-through" weapons', that is to say, dive-bombers and armoured formations. Lorry-borne infantry divisions would then arrive to occupy the conquered territory immediately afterwards, and thereby free the 'mobile' forces, that is to say, the armoured formations, which would continue their course ahead, whilst columns of empty lorries would return towards the rear to load up with more infantry troops. 'The attacker . . . would try to strike by surprise. After having attacked their first objective, the armoured formations, without waiting for the artillery to move forward, or the cavalry to arrive, would exploit their speed to the utmost in order to accomplish the break-through.'

Was this clear? Could we have been warned in a better fashion?

FEBRUARY 2, 1937: THE CHAMBER DECIDES: FRANCE IS NOT TO
HAVE AN ARMOURED CORPS

The most important military debate of the inter-war period was that which took place in the Chamber from January 26 to February 2, 1937.

I have already made some allusion to it. The chief point about the debate was my courteous duel with Daladier about the armoured corps. It seems a dramatic debate when one reads it again today.

At this time Hitler had been in power for four years. On August 24, 1935, he had extended the length of military service to two years. On March 7, 1936, he had sent his troops into the Rhineland, where he began to build the Siegfried Line. On October 14, Belgium broke off her Alliance with us. We knew, as regards Mussolini, that he was preparing to pass over into the enemy's camp.

In France herself, the Popular Front had been in power for eight months. Daladier was at the Ministry of War. In September he had secured the promise of a credit of fourteen milliards to be spread over four years, in order to equip the ground forces, and it had been agreed that tanks should have priority.

The question was what kind of tanks we should have. Were they to be tanks which were constructed to escort the infantry, that is to say, tanks intended to bolster up a continuous front in order to make it more unyielding? Or were they to be tanks suitable for an armoured corps, such as had been suggested in my counter-proposal; for that autonomous element, which ought to be capable of offensive action on a large scale? For one had to be careful about this matter. An armoured division is not simply a collection of tanks. It is a complex organism, whose individual units can be controlled from a distance by radio, and it should be supplied with enough petrol to command a radius of extended action. The tank of an armoured division, compared to an escort tank, is like a racehorse beside the plough-horse. The armoured division has its infantry, which it carries in armoured vehicles. It has its own artillery, made up of self-propelled guns. It has its own engineers, and, above all, its bridge construction unit. And that is not all. It has its Stukas. And there is still more besides. The armoured divisions are integrated with lorry-borne infantry divisions, which can advance at the same pace as the tanks.

Now, it was escort tanks especially that we were building. We had another kind of tank as well, for armoured divisions, but, at the pace which we were building tanks of this type, the armoured corps would be ready, not for the war which was coming, but for the next one.

There was still time to act, but only just time. Once again, I was to remind the Chamber of the need to give our Army an armoured corps.

It was now Daladier who was on the Ministerial bench. I have already said that he had set himself up as the champion of 'defensive strategy', and that he considered as 'dangerous' the offensive weapon which, in my plan, the armoured corps would have been. Into the bargain he now drew from the Civil War in Spain a lesson which left one in no doubt that a defensive army had nothing to fear from an attacker, even if this attacker possessed planes and assault tanks. Thus, he was still rooted in his opinions, and more hostile than ever to the armoured corps, which seemed to him the tool of an imprudent offensive.

For my own part, I had become more strengthened in the opposite opinion. More than ever I believed that the armoured corps, supported by aviation, was revolutionizing the art of warfare. Germany had already three armoured divisions, which she was in the process of doubling. My anxiety was great. It was, therefore, in a more urgent voice than in 1935 that I addressed the Chamber on January 26, 1937.

On November 4, 1936, Daladier had told the Army Committee of the Chamber of Deputies: 'The impression which you form for yourselves of the immediate aim to be attained will govern the organization of the Army and the choice of means. . . . Do you want to carry war straightaway to a distance beyond our own frontiers? . . . Do you think, on the contrary, that a country of forty million people . . . should have, as its foremost concern, the aim of . . . making itself invulnerable, of winning the struggle for the frontiers.'

The debate opened. Montigny, a member of the Army Committee, spoke before myself. He congratulated Daladier in having said, in substance, before the Committee, that the duty of the French Army should be, above all, the protection of the national territory, and that he refused to hazard the future on one cast of the dice in an offensive battle. Daladier had, moreover, added that if Parliament should decide otherwise, 'all our military organization and the psychological attitude of our Army itself must be changed'.

The problem was appropriately crystallized. Was the French Army to be capable of intervening in Europe or not?

Montigny answered this question by advising caution 'in respect of engagements which one could not fulfil except through some kind of rash act'. He concluded: 'I do not know if, in the Chamber, someone will stand up and demand some kind of military revolution, but all of us in the Army Committee have approved the Minister's plan.'

I was to be this audacious man. I borrowed words which Léon Blum, President of the Council, had used two days before at Lyons: 'We cannot remain indifferent spectators in Europe. We have contracted obligations to which we shall remain completely faithful.' So far so good! But were we in a position to honour these engagements?

To do this, I said, it was not enough to have 'the co-operation of Britain, valuable as it may be'. We required, in addition, allies who were capable of giving us 'powerful and immediate help' (Russia), and the military weapon which was fitted to carry out our policy. In effect, it was necessary to have 'the army suited to the policy'.

We had not got this instrument because we had not understood the revolution which had come about in the art of warfare. 'The new factor is speed: speed in the air, on the ground. . . . The German Army of today, contrasts with that which invaded us in 1914, as a railway engine contrasts with a stage-coach.'

Serious as it was for France, this revolution was to create 'a deadly danger for Belgium[1] and our small allies, who themselves have a very limited space within which to withdraw—as the speed of the future aggressor increases: they are in deadly peril if they do not receive immediate help'.

Into the bargain, it was not merely a question of honouring our pledges of assistance to our allies; it was also a question of defending our national soil by a counter-offensive. The only arm which would provide a devastating counter-offensive was the armoured corps.

What had we got in this sphere? A light mechanized division, that of Rheims.[2] But it was only the 'miniature of an armoured division'. No doubt we had modern tanks, but we were less well provided with them than Germany, and, moreover, they were 'not organized', because we were still in the stage of 'groping, trial, and experiment'. The Germans were not, moreover, the only ones who had outstripped us. There were 'several thousand tanks in Russia compared with some hundreds in France'.

The results of this inferiority had already been revealed by events on March 7, 1936, and the breaking off by Belgium of the Alliance.

Thus the question was for us to possess an 'adequate instrument to provide a counter-offensive as savage and rapid as the offensive itself'.

In reply to those who reproached me for asking for the creation of a body which would be separate from the rest of the Army, I replied that the armoured corps would be, on the contrary, the 'point of the lance of which the national army would be the shaft'. The 'point' was to open the way for the 'shaft'.

What was the reason for our backwardness? It was the orthodoxy which prevailed in the military sphere, as it did in all others.

I concluded by stressing the tragic gravity of the debate: 'We have not a day to lose.'

What reply did Daladier make to me? He admitted that Germany had an armoured corps, and that Russia possessed several thousand speedy tanks. But he did not admit the revolution of which I spoke. The Civil War in Spain had seen the 'tremendous hopes which some had placed in certain machines' founder. And this was the reason why: 'Fire-power had been ignored as a factor. Take, for example, Madrid. On all sides, guns, even though they were scarcely protected, prevented the advance of the tanks, which were holed like skimming ladles.'

---

[1] I had in mind the argument invoked by Leopold III to justify his change of policy: 'The shock of the invader . . . will be devastating.'

[2] In actual fact, we had at the time not one but two light mechanized divisions.

He considered as 'illusory' the hope that we could 'avoid wars of attrition, long-drawn-out wars, and would be able to finish the business off rapidly by a conflict which was both short and profitable'.

Daladier then stated that he was 'strongly hostile' to the creation of an armoured corps, because it would be difficult to recruit the necessary volunteers and re-enlisted men; because such a creation, by skimming the cream off the production of our arsenals and the cadres of the Army, would destroy the unity of the latter; and, above all, because he did not believe an armoured corps would be useful.

He became ironical: 'Not so long ago the cavalry stated that at the first alarm, they would be capable, when opposing the enemy cavalry, of inflicting such a heavy blow upon them that the latter would be unable to concentrate, to group together, and to attack.' He went even further. In his opinion the armoured corps would rush forward to its downfall: 'If . . . after several local successes, which indeed, I believe to be possible, the basic law of warfare—that an offensive can only be undertaken after a considerable accumulation of equipment and men—is proved correct, what then would be the fate of the country, with your specialized element and your professional army routed?'

To conclude, Daladier announced the creation of a third light mechanized division as well as the beginning, at the end of the summer, of 'very interesting' experiments in the formation of 'heavy divisions', of which he said he was an advocate.

Thus Germany was to enter the war with an armoured corps prepared by five years of manœuvres, an independent arm which had its own principles of warfare and its own cadres, an instrument both powerful and supple. Such an arm would integrate the Panzer divisions, which were provided with self-propelled artillery and were fashioned to strike into the heart of the struggle, with squadrons of dive-bombers and infantry grouped into motorized divisions. In 1939, we were certainly to have plenty of tanks, but they were to be scattered here and there, like powder, along our front from the North Sea to Switzerland. On the one hand, there was a bludgeon; on the other, there was dust.

Was it not true that, on January 26, 1937, we had no longer 'a day to lose'? But, in order to act, we had to have faith in the massive use of armoured forces. Daladier did not believe in this. Opposed to offensive tactics, he was, of necessity, also opposed to the means of an offensive, and thus, as a consequence, to those of a counter-offensive, for the second means were the same as the first. The conflict which separated the two of us was one which concerned doctrine. Daladier secured the approval of his doctrine by the Chamber, which thus fell into line with the unanimous decisions of the Army Committee.

The concentration of our armoured force into one body which had its own strategy and its own cadres, was therefore rejected. The system of small units was preferred. Thus, when our front, in May, 1940, was 'cracked' at Sedan and at Dinant, armoured divisions, improvised in the full tide of war, were sent to fight as isolated units. Those who had reproached me with wishing to dispatch my armoured corps, like a forlorn hope, into action, sent, as a matter of course, armoured and light mechanized divisions into battle without any kind of support. Yet all the time I was asking, on the contrary, that the armoured corps should fight in 'strict co-operation' with the rest of the Army. As for the tank battalions, which were escorting the infantry, these were spread out along the length of the front, as every unit wished to have its tank.

The Order of the Day, expressing confidence in the Government by 'paying tribute to the efforts it had made, in the sphere of national defence, to place our country outside the danger of aggression', was carried by four hundred and thirteen votes, and, even a majority of the hundred and twenty-four deputies, who, like myself voted against the Government, approved of its military policy.

I was defeated. Germany had its armoured corps. France was not to have one.

MY CAMPAIGNS IN 1937 AND 1938

Three months after the debate of January and February, 1937, I returned to the charge in *Le problème militaire français*.

I warned public opinion[1] that to let Germany gain the advantage in making the destructive machines which modern mechanics have invented was 'to permit the age-long threat which weighed upon us to increase to terrible proportions'.

Running counter to the prophets who proclaimed the invulnerability of defensive warfare, I wrote:[2] 'Only the offensive will secure a decision.'

Of assault tanks, I wrote:[3] The advantage of this weapon . . . whose power is much greater today than it was in 1918, has been relinquished by us to those whom it helped us to conquer.' And I stated[4] that the armoured corps would be 'the hammer . . . which breaks open the gap to victory'. This was with one proviso, however, namely, that we made of it[5] 'not a *pin-cushion*', but 'a *spear-head*'.

I concluded:[6] 'Peace is doomed if France is not ready to fight. . . . There is an urgent need to give the necessary equipment to the specialized ground forces . . . and to the air force.' And, adjuring the country to make a tremendous effort in production 'in order to make

[1] p. 41.   [2] p. 33.   [3] pp. 78–9.
[4] pp. 46–7.   [5] p. 64.   [6] pp. 103–5, *passim.*

up for a shameful lagging behind', I reminded it of Hitler's fateful words: 'For three years the German people have been working night and day to rearm themselves.'

I sent a copy of my book to Weygand. He thanked me for it, but he did not hide from me his disagreement with its thesis.

In November, 1937, I went to Germany. I came back alarmed by the effort which the working classes were contributing to the making of armaments. I again sounded another note of warning. This time it was to the working classes I addressed myself. On the 3rd I wrote in *Paris-Soir* under the title of 'Nous sommes entrés dans la zone non sanglante de la guerre'. 'Once again I have been in Germany. . . . The country offers a Wagnerian sight. . . . Let us admire the spirit of sacrifice . . . of these workers who deny themselves so that raw materials bought abroad can be devoted . . . to supplying the insatiable machines which bring forth German strength. . . . Today, it is impossible to prepare for war without the complete collaboration of the working masses. In Germany, it is the entire population which is devoting itself to this colossal work. . . . With the same action, but unfortunately with a different rhythm, French and German workers are both forging their destiny. . . . Today, to produce is not merely to gain a livelihood for the worker, it is to defend that livelihood. . . . At the present pace of the respective rearmaments of the dictatorships and the democracies, time is working on behalf of the former.'

This was unequivocal, and no doubt harsh language, but it was that, above all, of a man who sees in anguish the approaching battle, to prepare for which he had been exhorting his country in vain for thirty-two months.

The reaction to it was to be found two days later in Doriot's *La Liberté*. Under the title of 'Une campagne alarmiste', M. Alfred Fabre-Luce wrote: '. . . An effort is being made to have us believe that Germany . . . is going to throw herself against the Maginot Line. Evidently it is still an agreeable thing to ascribe complete stupidity to the adversary.' And he jested at the 'thoughtless speeches' of those who 'denounced the dangers on our frontiers in order to fan an obsidional fever which would favour their own designs'.

Those who set themselves up as the defenders of peace joined in the chorus. Hue and cry was raised against the war-monger who was seeking to throw France into war, on account of a hatred towards dictators and some 'ideological' theories.

After the working masses, there was another section of public opinion which I roused in *Le Figaro* on December 23, 1937, under the title 'Pour barrer la route à la guerre, faudra-t-il mobiliser toutes les forces de la nation?'

Once again I propounded the question, where lies the strength of

France? Is it strong enough to bar the road to war? If a war breaks out, is France sufficiently strong to win it?

Once again, March 7, 1936, I deplored the purely defensive character of our Army. I explained the necessity of manufacturing war material. It was the Air Force on which I concentrated this time. 'Our monthly production', I said, 'has fallen from sixty-five to thirty-five planes, whilst that of our neighbours has soared (three hundred and fifty for Germany and two hundred for Italy).' And I ended: 'Can our rulers sleep at night? . . . In the present circumstances, setting about the creation of the French Air Force will brook no more delay. . . . Let us remember that, in great dangers, the only remedy for a great country lies in showing greatness.'

I continued to preach in the wilderness.

On January 12, 1938, I wrote: 'We have come to the point when all our crises must be solved at the same time: economic, social, financial, monetary, that relating to our alliances, and to national defence. Each of these crises aggravates the other. . . . I believe, and I am weighing my words, that the situation is as grave as when the Revolutionary authorities put up platforms at the cross-roads from which they proclaimed that "the motherland . . . is in danger". We must urgently increase our war production as our friends in Europe earnestly advise us to do.' In its issue of February 1, the *Revue des Deux Mondes* reproduced these words, and added: 'They will go down in history. Let us hope they will not feature there as a true prophecy!'

At the *Société des Conférences* on February 4, I uttered a new warning:[1] 'The engine has changed the face of things. . . . Only the *powerful* assault tank is irresistible. In all spheres . . . aviation, tanks, anti-aircraft . . . we are behindhand. . . . We have committed the imprudence of following a lazy policy of pure and simple defence, and of maintaining out-of-date equipment. We have the choice between making a national recovery before the bombs fall, to avoid doing it when they are falling, or of waiting for the bombs in our present state of passivity. . . . When we made small attacking tanks . . . at a time when only the action of the powerful . . . assault tank is irresistible, we did not take into account the evolution which has taken place in the military sphere.' On the necessity of forming an Eastern front, with Russia's help, I said: 'It is no longer a question of finding out if a nation is pleasing or displeasing to us. It is one of saving our skins.'

Our life was at stake. As always, it was a matter of life and death. The months went by. The war was coming nearer. Was any other voice to raise itself in support of my appeals which became more and more anguished in their tone? What did those people who were considered to be our 'great military leaders' think? We shall see.

[1] *Loc. cit.* (*Revue Hebdomadaire*, February 26, 1938).

THE KEY TO THE PROBLEM: PÉTAIN AND WEYGAND ARE HOSTILE TO THE
MODERNIZATION OF THE ARMY

Pétain and Weygand, our 'great military leaders', enjoyed a reputation with the Army which was unchallenged.

We have traced step by step Pétain's theories up to 1936, when they
were crystallized in the *Instruction*, whose broad outlines I have summarized.

Léon Blum, as soon as he came to power, questioned Pétain again
on our military situation. The latter answered him with a letter in
which he affirmed that 'the French Army is in perfect condition, and
can stand up to any army whatsoever'.

In 1938, Pétain informed the country about his doctrine, and revealed
all his theories. General Chauvineau published his book *Une invasion
est-elle encore possible?* He submitted it to Pétain, who, in order to
demonstrate how he approved of the thesis which it contained, took
the trouble to commend it himself to the public in a preface, wherein
he committed himself in unequivocal terms.

Chauvineau, to whom Pétain thus gave the guarantee of his authority,
had been, the latter told us in his preface, a professor, whose ability
was demonstrated by the many promotions of his pupils who had
graduated from the Military Academy. There could be no doubt that
one of his most brilliant disciples was Pétain himself. His book which,
moreover, was to be reprinted in 1940 during the full tide of war,
was a justification of defensive warfare, a panegyric to the invulnerability of the continuous front against which the German armoured
divisions and dive-bombers would break themselves. All this was, in
addition, studded with tasty aphorisms.

This was the work for which Pétain, who was not accustomed to
use his pen prodigally, wrote a preface of twenty-one pages. This
preface, which he took several months to compose, is rather an introduction to which deep reflection has been given, since it bears as a
sub-title the words *Eléments d'une doctrine de guerre*. It was not, therefore,
a question of complacent approval, of an approval which, as Monzie
asserts,[1] Chauvineau had 'tricked' Pétain into writing.

'Generally speaking, the opinions of General Chauvineau about the
commencement of ground operations', wrote Pétain, 'are full of
wisdom. . . . This work will astonish and perhaps even shock the reader.
General Chauvineau has wished, indeed, to get to the origin of causes
without being influenced by ideas which are almost universally accepted.
Often excellent, this method of undertaking an inquiry is at the present
time even more necessary than formerly. . . . It will be to the credit
of General Chauvineau that he has shown that the "continuous front"

[1] *La saison des juges*, p. 145.

is founded both on lessons of history and on the technical properties of weapons and fortifications.'

After summarizing the conclusions which Chauvineau claims to draw about the invulnerability of the 'continuous front', and especially the uselessness of alliances, Pétain expresses his own theory, of which, as one will see, that of his disciple is merely a reflection.

Were we to have in the future, as in the past, an unbreakable 'continuous front'? Yes, replied Pétain, and here was his reason. 'The "continuous front" is not a passing phase of which we can rid ourselves, as if it were a fatal habit.' Why was it invulnerable? The reason was a commonplace one, and one could almost say a sordid one; it was because the human being can no longer run when, enmeshed in a network of barbed wire, he has received in the head or the spinal column a piece of steel launched by an invisible weapon. No patriotic fervour, no moral enthusiasm can be of avail before this fact.

But, confound it, Pétain was drawing us a picture of the 1915 offensive. He was making the mistake of being one war behind. It was now no longer a matter of foot soldiers in greatcoats, mown down by machine-gun bullets whilst they crawled under strands of barbed wire. It was a question of machine crews and gunners travelling at twenty kilometres an hour protected by thick armour plating! As I said to the Chamber in 1937, the German Army which was going to invade us would contrast with that of 1914 as a train does with a stage-coach. Between these two Armies there was more difference than between that of Turenne and that of Napoleon.

Certainly there are two methods, said Pétain, of breaking a continuous front: by tanks and heavy artillery. But then he replied: 'Tanks are few and relatively slow in taking up positions. The rarity of equipment restricts frontal attacks. The time required for the development of their effective action can be used by the defender to bring up his reserves, and this is made all the more easy when the front which is being attacked is more narrow.' Tanks were few! said Pétain. Yet, for two years the German Army had possessed six armoured divisions, of which three were heavy and three were light. I had said this on the floor of the Chamber in 1937. What did it matter? Let the French sleep on in peace.

Between a choice of the armoured corps, such as I was asking for in my counter-proposal, and foot soldiers in trucks, 'including at the same time a few armoured tanks [sic]' Pétain said he would not hesitate. He rejected the armoured corps for five reasons:

1. It was an offensive instrument the result of which 'ran the risk of being short-lived, if no safeguard was prepared against a possible check'. Why should no safeguard be prepared? That is the mystifying thing.

Moreover, was not this instrument as essential to a counter-offensive as to an offensive?

2. A study of the technical implications of tanks had not been pushed far enough.

These had been studied during and since the last war. But evidently it was not a pressing matter!

3. Neither had the possibilities of commanding armoured divisions been sufficiently studied.

But one has to have the divisions in order to learn how to command them! It is only by practice that one becomes perfect. Now, Pétain did not want anything in the nature of such a training. Amongst our neighbours, armoured divisions, which had existed for two years, provided practical instruction by being put to use. We should have followed their example. It was precisely because an armoured division was a difficult instrument to handle that we should have begun training ourselves in their use immediately.

4. On the ground a deadly [sic] barrage which offers opposition to armoured and tracked engines exists: this is the minefield, linked up with anti-tank weapons.

We saw, in May, 1940, how deadly this proved to the Panzer divisions.

5. Our opponent would use his own armoured divisions to counter-attack ours: 'What would happen to an offensive undertaken by armoured divisions if they ran into divisions of the same type, but already placed in position several hours in advance, and deployed along a system of anti-tank defences, linked up with anti-tank obstacles and reinforced with minefields, on a battlefield of their own choosing?'

Pétain acknowledged, therefore, that armoured divisions were an excellent instrument for counter-attacking. Why then refuse to let the French Army have them? The German Army had the right to have them. We knew that it had them. Pétain denied them to us.

What did he say about aerial forces? 'Their direct action in battle is of an ancillary nature, for the troops engaged in ground fighting are prepared for attacks, and ready to reply to them.' Unfortunately, our troops were not prepared to meet them, for our anti-aircraft was entirely insufficient. For what purpose, according to Pétain, should aircraft be used? 'Action by aircraft will most usefully be employed in direct attacks on the rear.... The most worth-while objective to enemy aircraft will be especially the network of communications which links the rear and the front.'

Of the two arms in modern warfare, offensive aircraft and armoured vehicles, Pétain was ignorant of the existence of one, and rejected the value of the other.

His conclusion is full of optimism: 'The likelihood is that our country can certainly halt any enemy wishing to penetrate within our frontiers.'

What did it matter that we should have to fight alone at the start against the Germans! The continuous front was in existence. What did it matter that the British had warned us that they would be weaker than in 1914! Why should we protest and show them the danger of such a policy? What did it matter if our allies in the East were destroyed! What was the good of the Russian alliance! Did it really matter if we did not have an armoured corps and if the Germans had two; if German air strength was twice, three times, ten times that of ours! The continuous front was there!

'We can certainly halt any enemy.' Is it possible that such words could be spoken by such lips at such a time? This was the same language as the 'not a gaiter button missing' used by Marshal Lebœuf on the eve of the 1870 war.[1]

Pétain, who thought of the coming war only as a repetition of that of 1914, was determined to reassure public opinion, which I was trying to arouse. 'Protected by "continuous fronts", the nation has time to rearm in order to resist first of all, and then to pass to the attack.' Pass to the attack? In heaven's name with what? Without an armoured corps? Without offensive aircraft? With what effectives? During the first eight months of the war, Germany created eighty new divisions whilst we only formed sixteen!

As for being in a position to keep our word to Poland, that was the least of Pétain's worries.

It was now Pétain's turn to show the opponent the 'gas flame' over which he would burn his wings if he were to attack us. 'This prospect holds nothing which can gladden the future aggressor: it is the best guarantee of peace.'

To sum up, taking the opposite attitude from that which inspired my campaign in the Chamber and the country, Pétain rejected the arms of modern warfare: armoured divisions and offensive aircraft. Infantry in trucks 'with some tanks' and planes operating 'against the rear' were sufficient for him. It was with these he wished to advance into Belgium, for he did want to go there. Pétain rejected the Russian alliance; he had resolved to allow our allies in the East to be crushed and, when in 1938, I uttered the cry 'The motherland is in danger' he replied with his 'We can certainly halt any enemy.'

Why should one be surprised that, at Vichy, Pétain banned the sale of Chauvineau's book, and that at the beginning of the Riom trial, he had issued to the Press the following orders: 'Number 5. Show that

[1] Lebœuf, Edmond (1809–88), Marshal of France. He was Minister of War on the outbreak of the Franco-Prussian War; and when questioned in the Legislature, declared that 'not a gaiter button of the army was missing' [Tr.].

this trial is not an indictment of the Army, that men and leaders have had to fight without possessing the tools indispensable to a modern war. . . . Number 7. Follow out this order most strictly if it happens to be a question one day of the Marshal himself or of his policy.' But, as I wrote to him from one of my prisons, truth is like a gas which explodes with all the greater force, the more it is compressed.

Pétain was not only writing for the public at large. It is known that the Supreme Council for War had placed before it, as early as October, 1936, the problem of the composition of an armoured division. Pétain had sent to certain members of the Council the artless pages of his preface to show them what he wanted. It remains to be added that Chauvineau's book was widely read by the General Staffs at the front during the long evenings of the 'phoney war'. It was a good preparation for the German offensive of May, 1940! Pétain therefore exerted all his influence, which was considerable, against allowing the Army to become modernized, and towards lulling the nation into a feeling of security. He was completely successful.

He was not the only one to lead the Army and the country astray, by reassuring them without respite. Ranged beside him, Weygand threw all his weight on the same side.

I don't know if Weygand ever had, like Pétain, a personal doctrine of warfare but he had understood the revolution which technical progress had brought into the art of war, no better than Pétain.

On October 15, 1936, in the *Revue des Deux Mondes*, he answered my speech of March 15, 1935, whilst refraining from making any reference to it. He stated: 'It is not a question of opposing quality to quantity . . . but of possessing, at all times, quantity which has quality.'

It is a pity that Weygand did not say how a country of forty-one million inhabitants can prevail, on the score of quantity, over an opponent of sixty-seven million. This numerical inferiority could only be made good by means of the Russian alliance. Now, we have seen what his attitude was on the subject of this alliance.

As for quality, let us see what he thought. Was it necessary to create an armoured element? Weygand, thinking apparently about *Vers l'armée de métier*, replied, 'No, at no price should there be two armies. . . . The French Army should be one, like France herself.' He considered that he was satisfied with the means at our disposal. 'We have', he said, 'a mechanized, motorized and mounted reserve.'

It is known what we really had in this sphere.

And it was on these means that Weygand counted, if the Germans invaded Belgium, to advance 'as far as possible' to offer them battle. It was to be, therefore, a battle in the open country, which we were to offer the enemy. If he attacked our fortified zone 'our mobile covering reserve would have to use its armoured vehicles at top speed in order to bring them to bear on the threatened points'. But we had only light tanks. Were these to be thrown against the German armoured corps? One might as well throw baby 'prams' against motor trucks. With complete intrepidity, Weygand summed up by saying, 'There is no need to construct anything of this kind; it is already in existence.'

That was the only reply which Weygand gave to my warning cries, and here, to conclude, is his lesson read to the politician who allowed himself to criticize our military policy. 'The Command, as is its duty, has not awaited the present time before beginning to reflect about the problem. For a long time plans have been drawn up. For years the General Staff, working silently, stubbornly and often without thanks, has used all its ingenuity and resources to study them.' Let us therefore bow down in respect; let us attend to matters which concern us, and leave the soldiers in peace.

On May 15, 1938, Weygand wrote another article in the *Revue des Deux Mondes*. Optimism was rising. Weygand, in his turn, sang the praises of the 'continuous front'. He said it was capable of 'barring a continent over hundreds of kilometres'. It was necessary for 'diplomacy to ally itself to strategy' in order to go and seek a battlefield elsewhere. Then we should be quite tranquil at home. . . .

And what about the Air Force? Its function remained the same as in the First World War. Of the aeroplane's collaboration in the battle there was not one word.

And tanks? Here optimism overflowed. Weygand consented to a distinction between heavy tanks and light tanks. 'The French Army possesses a striking force, composed of motorized or mechanized divisions which are fit for extensive, rapid and powerful action. The presence of new tanks in the general reserve would allow the formation of heavy armoured divisions.' This was indeed fine news!

But it was false as we have seen.

One cannot go as far as to say that Weygand was hostile to the modernization of the Army. For him the problem did not even arise. On the pretext of 'defending the Army', he defended the traditional order of things. Is this not the place to recall the saying of Gneisenau after Jena:[1] 'War is a serious business'?

On July 4, 1939, Weygand made a speech during a banquet on the occasion of some horse show meeting in the neighbourhood of Lille. 'You ask me', he said, 'what is my feeling about the French Army. . . . I think that the French Army has a greater value today than at any other time in its history. It has first-class equipment and the strongest possible fortifications, excellent morale and remarkable leadership. No one in this country wants a war, but I can say that if we are

[1] Gneisenau, August Wilhelm (1760–1831), Prussian field-marshal. Jena (1806) was one of Napoleon's greatest victories over the Prussians [Tr.].

forced into winning another victory, we shall win it.' This time, both Lebœuf and Pétain were outdone. And Weygand sent the text of his speech to the newspapers! Was this done with the purpose of impressing Hitler? One might as well have taken him for a subscriber to the *Revue des Deux Mondes*.

On July 29 I myself spoke over the radio. What was I going to say to this nation which Weygand had just lulled into a false security? 'It is not merely, unfortunately, a matter of passing through the seas of a dangerous summer. The peril is to last for a long time.' I stated, adding that we were 'on the threshold of the most dangerous period of our history'.

It needed the disaster in Belgium to open Weygand's eyes. On May 25, 1940, he stated to the War Committee: 'France has made a grave error in entering the war, when having neither the necessary equipment nor the necessary military doctrine.' It was the truth at last, but, unfortunately, all was over.

When he was being questioned at Pétain's trial (hearing on July 31, 1945), about his speech at Lille, Weygand replied: 'I had confidence in the French Army and in its leaders. . . . After the enormous expenditure on material which had been made—for credits so astronomically large had been voted that I thought they would never be expended—I could not believe that . . . the French Army would begin the battle in such a state of unpreparedness. I therefore did my duty as a good Frenchman.'

Thus Weygand confessed that at the time he was ignorant of the true state of our equipment, and similarly of how our forces matched up with those of Germany. But this ignorance did not prevent him reassuring in a peremptory tone a public opinion which I was endeavouring to arouse.

Such was the part which Pétain and Weygand played in our race towards the abyss. Chauvineau wrote[1] in his book: 'If the enemy can enter our territory without hindrance, French military leaders will be made ridiculous for ever.' This did not prevent Pétain, after the disaster, from speaking to France in very imperious tones.

[1] *Op. cit.*, p. 132.

CHAPTER XIII

MUNICH

*March 12, 1938, Hitler seizes Austria, and thus takes Czecho-
slovakia in the rear.—September, 1938, Munich: Mandel,
Champetier de Ribes and myself hand in our Resignations.—1938–9,
Recovery in extremis.*

MARCH 12, 1938: HITLER SEIZES AUSTRIA, AND THUS TAKES CZECHO-SLOVAKIA IN THE REAR

HITLER, having protected his rear by the Siegfried Line, could, thanks to Belgium's repudiation of her former policy, begin his meal. Austria was to provide him with the *entrée*.

Once Austria was annexed, the 'Maginot' Line of the Czechs would be turned, and Bohemia would thus be held between the jaws of a gigantic nut-cracker. Everything would be ready for the seizure of Czechoslovakia. Taking possession of Austria was therefore equivalent to removing the keystone of the Europe which had been built upon treaties. Were the Allies prepared to let this happen?

The Power most directly interested in Austria's remaining independent was Italy. As early as May 2, 1925, Mussolini had declared in the national Senate, when speaking about Locarno: 'It is not sufficient to guarantee the frontiers of the Rhine. It is also necessary to guarantee those of the Brenner. Italy cannot tolerate . . . the annexation of Austria by Germany.' Nevertheless, from 1934, the Duce was beginning to waver. On May 5, he received Hitler in Venice. Two months later, Dollfuss was assassinated by the Nazis. Mussolini telegraphed to Prince von Starhemberg, leader of the Patriotic Front, 'The independence of Austria . . . has been and will be defended with . . . the utmost resolution by Italy.' The Duce announced with great ostentation that he was mobilizing on the Brenner. In reality he merely made a semblance of doing so: he held large-scale manoeuvres in the Bolzano area, with all his ministers dressed up in uniform. What clowns they were, thought the Führer.

In 1935 came Stresa: France, Britain and Italy pledged themselves to defend the independence of Austria. But it is well known what value Mussolini attached to this agreement. The Abyssinian affair was to serve as an excuse for his official withdrawal from the Allied front. Mussolini gave up any idea of opposing the *Anschluss*. For his part, Hitler ceased to take an interest in the German minority in Trentino. The Duce still lavished promises on Schuschnigg, the leader of the Austrian Christian Social Party, but these promises were already only empty words. The Nazis were now working in that country in preparation for the great day.

On October 17, 1935, Schuschnigg gave way to Nazi pressure. He reformed his Cabinet, and left Starhemberg out of it. But the majority of the country remained faithful to the conception of a national Austria. Hitler, in any case, was in no hurry. His preparations were far from ready. By an agreement of July 11, 1936, he 'recognized the full sovereignty of Austria', and undertook not to meddle directly or indirectly with the domestic affairs of that country, which agreed, however, to bring its policy into line with that of Germany.

In 1937 Nazi agitation was re-doubled. Schuschnigg was subjected to severe pressure. Mussolini warned him no longer to count on the collaboration of the Italian Army. And yet Badoglio, if M. Noël is to be believed,[1] had 'written . . . [to Gamelin at the end of January, 1938] that the Duce considered that the agreements made by the General Staffs in 1935 were still effective'.[2]

Hitler's Germany was, moreover, making no secret about her imperialistic aims. Churchill relates[3] that in 1937, Ribbentrop, who was then Ambassador in London, asked to see him. The Nazi diplomat explained to him that his mission was principally concerned with concluding an alliance between Germany and Britain. Germany was ready to guarantee the integrity of the British Empire on condition that Britain, for her part, left Germany with a free hand in Eastern Europe. The Reich considered that its future well-being required the absorption of Poland, White Russia and the Ukraine. Churchill told Ribbentrop that his country would never tolerate such an expansion. 'In that case, a war is inevitable', replied Ribbentrop. 'There is no way out. The Führer is resolved. Nothing will stop him. . . .' Churchill then warned Ribbentrop against the danger which Germany ran by misjudging Britain's strength. 'She is', he added, 'a curious country, and few foreigners can understand her mind. Do not judge by the attitude

[1] Noël, *op. cit.*, p. 183.

[2] Gamelin in *Servir* does not breathe a word about this letter. He cites (*op. cit.*, vol. II, pp. 317–18) on the other hand, words which the War Minister in the Chamberlain Cabinet, Hore-Belisha, when he was passing through Paris, April 25, 1938, on returning from Italy, alleged that the Duce uttered: 'In France the generals are very good, but the soldiers are not up to much.' It must be admitted that such an opinion agreed better with the conviction which Mussolini held about the decadence of France.

[3] *Op. cit.*, vol. I, *The Gathering Storm*, pp. 200–1 (second edition).

of the present Administration. Once a great cause is presented to the people, all kinds of unexpected actions might be taken by this very Government and by the British nation. Do not underrate England. She is very clever. If you plunge us all into another Great War, she will bring the whole world against you, like last time.' To this Ribbentrop replied: 'Ah, England may be very clever, but this time she will not bring the world against Germany.'[1]

Churchill has also told us[2] that Roosevelt, alarmed by the growing international tension, thought of inviting the Great Powers to Washington in order to discuss the differences which divided them one from the other. On January 11, 1938, he submitted this plan to Chamberlain, who, said Churchill, advised him against following it up. Léon Blum[3] has stated that he thought he could vouch for the fact that the French Government, then presided over by Chautemps, had no knowledge of the American proposal.

In the meantime Hitler was driving home his advantage. On February 12, 1938, he summoned Schuschnigg to Berchtesgaden. Using threats, he ordered him to fall into line. Schuschnigg was alone in facing Germany. He had to hand over the Ministry of the Interior to Seyss-Inquart, one of the most extreme Nazis. On February 24 he stated none the less in the Diet that Austria would remain Austria, that her determination to defend her independence was unshakable. Two days later Delbos said in the French Chamber of Deputies, 'France cannot ignore the fate of Austria.' 'Mere words', thought Hitler, who was thinking of March 7, 1936.

On March 9, Schuschnigg stated that on the 13th there would be a plebiscite on the question of incorporation within the Reich. On the 10th, the Chautemps Cabinet resigned of its own free will. On the 12th, German troops invaded Austria. Seyss-Inquart seized power. On the 13th, Hitler proclaimed annexation. On the 16th, the Duce, who could not be found during the crisis, declared: 'When an event is inevitable, it is better that it should happen with your consent than in spite of it or worse still, to your own detriment.' This was all that remained of the swaggerings on the Brenner.

Henceforth, one had to be a blind man not to see that war was coming. The Kremlin itself did not fail to see it. The Soviet Government, wrote Churchill,[4] proposed the holding of a conference to discuss with the Powers the means for widening the Franco-Soviet Pact within the framework of the League of Nations. The Russian proposal, continued Churchill, 'was accepted without enthusiasm both in London and Paris'. Paul-Boncour in *Entre deux guerres* makes no mention of such a step. Potiemkin in his *Histoire de la diplomatie* does not speak

---

[1] *Ibid.*, p. 201.   [2] *Ibid.*, pp. 225–6, *passim.*   [3] *Le Populaire*, May 4, 1948.
[4] *Op. cit.*, vol. I, *The Gathering Storm*, p. 245 (second edition).

about it either. But in *Falsifiers of History*[1] one reads: 'On March 17, 1938, Hitler seized Austria without encountering any resistance from Britain or France. The Soviet Union was at this time the only nation to utter a cry of alarm, and to launch a new appeal for organizing the collective defence of the independence of countries which were threatened by aggression. On March 17, 1938, the Soviet Government addressed a Note in which it declared that it was ready to "undertake immediately with the other Powers within the League of Nations or associated with it, the examination of practical steps . . . intended to thwart the development of aggression and to suppress the danger, which had become more pressing, of a new world slaughter".[2] The reply of the British Government to the Soviet Note showed that it did not wish to oppose Hitler's plans of aggression.'

Feiling, Chamberlain's biographer, has revealed the contents of a letter which was addressed by Chamberlain to his sister. It enlightens us as to the Prime Minister's state of mind at this time. Referring to the idea of an alliance between Britain, France and Russia, he writes: 'I talked about it to Halifax, and we submitted it to the chiefs of the Staff and the F.O. experts. It is a very attractive idea . . . until you come to examine its practicability. From that moment its attraction vanishes. You have only to look at the map to see that nothing that France or we could do could possibly save Czechoslovakia from being overrun by the Germans, if they wanted to do it. . . . I have therefore abandoned any idea of giving guarantees to Czechoslovakia, or the French in connection with her obligations to that country.'[3]

In fact Chamberlain, on March 24, stated in the House of Commons:[4] '. . . His Majesty's Government are of opinion that the indirect, but none the less inevitable, consequence of such action as is proposed by the Soviet Government would be to aggravate the tendency towards the establishment of exclusive groups of nations, which must, in the view of His Majesty's Government, be inimical to the prospects of European peace.' If war broke out, it would be improbable that it could be restricted to nations which had assumed contractual obligations. It was absolutely impossible to say where war would stop, or the countries which could be dragged into it.

One can only express surprise that a step of such importance, and one which, as is seen by the above quotation from the Soviet publication, had at the time been a burning topic with the Moscow Press and,

[1] This [Soviet] publication appeared as a supplement to the review, *New Times*, no. 8, of February 18, 1945. It was intended to be a reply to a collection of German documents published in January, 1947, by the U.S. State Department under the title of *Nazi-Soviet Relations during the Years 1939-41.*

[2] *Izvestia*, March 18, 1948 (textual note).

[3] Feiling, *The Life of Neville Chamberlain*, 1946, pp. 347-8.

[4] Hansard, vol. 333, col. 1406.

moreover, inspired Chamberlain's statement in the Commons, should have passed unperceived by the French Foreign Office. Léon Blum, who had then just succeeded Chautemps, stated that the Soviet proposal had not been brought to his knowledge nor to that of Paul-Boncour, who was Foreign Minister. And he added on this subject: 'No dispatch escaped my attention, and the ambassadors of that period knew whether I examined them scrupulously.' What can be concluded from this, but that there was some negligence on part of the Ministry of Foreign Affairs?

At the end of March Churchill came to Paris to establish contact with those responsible for French policy. He took up residence in the British Embassy where he received successively Blum, Flandin, Gamelin, Pierre Cot, Herriot, Marin, myself and, he adds, 'a lot of others'. He brought to Léon Blum's attention the fact that the field howitzer in service with the German Army was reputed to surpass, both in firing power and range, our 75-millimetre gun.

I observed to Churchill, who makes note of my remark in his memoirs,[1] that: 'We quite understand that England will never have conscription. Why do you not therefore go in for a mechanical army? If you had six armoured divisions, you would indeed be an effective continental force.' Since the French Government was deaf to my exhortations, why should not Britain, our ally, fill the breach, left by our default? Did she not combine, moreover, the conditions of financial and industrial strength which were necessary, and had she not a professional army, composed of crack soldiers?

Churchill talked with Flandin for two hours. He found him thoroughly convinced that 'the only hope for France lay in an understanding with Germany'.

On the 28th it was Gamelin's turn to meet Churchill. He jotted down 'on the spot', he writes,[2] Churchill's proposals. The latter told him: 'We have begun the fight and we have just suffered a serious defeat. We British are prepared to draw more tightly our military links with you. I shall work as hard as possible to accomplish this. It is necessary to re-group the Eastern European powers in order to bar Germany's path to the Black Sea and the Eastern Mediterranean (Mr. Churchill seemed to me to include Russia).

'The controlling forces of the world should be the British Navy and the French . . . Army. Each of the two countries should have aircraft but, unless this was of an overwhelming superior strength (and we could no longer hope for this in the brief time left), it would not be the decisive factor in the outcome of the struggle.

'If Italy fought against us, the British Fleet with the help of the

---

[1] *Op. cit.*, vol. I, *The Gathering Storm*, p. 252 (second edition).
[2] *Op. cit.*, vol. II, p. 317.

French, would quickly obtain mastery of the Mediterranean. But we need bases. Malta and Gibraltar are too vulnerable and too confined. In the long run France will have to lend us her bases.

'We have also to prepare air bases in France, where we could be better situated to employ our bombing strength, if Belgium and Holland remained neutral.

'The French Government ought to increase its ground strength as quickly as possible. Your population is obviously greatly inferior to that of Germany, but you have your colonies.

'Finally he thought that "under the threat of events, Britain could be manœuvred into a form of compulsory military service, especially for anti-aircraft defence".'

Gamelin added: 'What a pity it is that the man did not become the head of the British Government earlier.'

For his part, Churchill noted: 'Gamelin . . . was rightly confident in the strength of the French Army. . . .'[1]

As for myself, I considered that we should become more vigilant than ever. On July 8, after a meeting of the Council of Ministers at which a telegram from our Berlin Ambassador had been read, I wrote to Daladier: 'The . . . discussions which took place this morning in the Council of Ministers about François-Poncet's telegram cannot be considered as ending the matter. . . . If it is true that war can break out in ten weeks, it is essential to take immediate and energetic steps . . . to delay . . . works which have nothing to do with national defence . . . to speed up the making of gas-masks, to widen the ways out of Paris . . . to make an inventory . . . of the needs . . . of the three services, from raw steel to cannons, tanks and to . . . aircraft.

'Are there not grounds . . . for diverting other factories to the making of war material? . . . At what stage is the manufacture of modern guns? . . . All these problems . . . should in my opinion be studied . . . in common. . . .

'It is necessary, I think, to give our own and foreign public opinion the impression of France as a strong nation, resolved not to let herself be surprised. . . .'

This letter produced no results.

SEPTEMBER, 1938; MUNICH: MANDEL, CHAMPETIER DE RIBES AND MYSELF HAND IN OUR RESIGNATIONS

Six months after the Wehrmacht had entered Vienna came Munich. Hitler was striking whilst the iron was hot.

In the Europe created by Versailles, Czechoslovakia was one of the new-born States, and delicate like all the newly born. Victorious France

[1] Churchill, *op. cit.*, vol. I, *The Gathering Storm*, p. 253 (second edition).

was her ally. She had signed with France, as we have seen, the treaties of 1924 and 1925.

On Hitler's arrival to power, agitation began amongst the Germans who inhabited the mountainous Sudeten area in the north. Hitler, who controlled the movement, grouped these Germans into a single party, under the orders of a former teacher of gymnastics, Henlein. At the elections of 1935 Henlein gained forty-four seats in the Chamber, out of three hundred. He did not delay in demanding the return of the province to the Reich.

Menaced thus by Germany, whose claims Mussolini now openly supported, Czechoslovakia turned in her anxiety to Moscow in order to ask for help. Russia, as we have said, agreed to give this, but she only pledged herself to act according to how France herself discharged her own pledges towards Czechoslovakia.

In 1938, Nazi agitation amongst the Sudetens was becoming diabolical. The radio played upon the nerves enough to break them. On February 26, Delbos told the Chamber 'France's pledges towards Czechoslovakia would, if necessary, be faithfully observed.' 'Empty words', thought Hitler again.

On March 4, Hodza, Prime Minister of Czechoslovakia, stated that his country, with the backing of France and Russia would defend her frontiers, which he considered sacrosanct, to the last.

On the 11th, Hitler, whilst preparing to enter Vienna, gave Czechoslovakia 'his word of honour that the annexation of Austria was a family matter', and one which would in no wise influence relations between Berlin and Prague. Moreover, the Reich, he stated, had a keen desire to better these relations still further. Goering confirmed these assurances to the British Ambassador, and authorized the British Government to make them publicly known.

On May 22, came the first alert. Gamelin wrote:[1] 'An attack by Germany on Czechoslovakia is thought to be imminent.' European feeling was already resigned. Gamelin continued: 'A very unfavourable note was struck by Belgium. The Foreign Minister, M. Bargeton, told our Ambassador: "We have just carried out manœuvres on the French border to demonstrate that, if you enter Belgium to support the Czechs, you will run into the Belgian army."'

Hitler's plan was ripening. On June 18, he came to a decision. He would attack Czechoslovakia. This was because he was convinced, he wrote on that day to Keitel, 'that France *will not march* and that, as a result, Britain will not intervene any more than she did when the Rhineland was re-militarized or when the Wehrmacht invaded Austria'.

On September 1, Hitler received Henlein at Berchtesgaden.

On the 9th, Prague announced measures in favour of the German

[1] *Op. cit.*, vol. II, p. 334.

minority in the Sudetenland. On the 10th, Beneš said on the wireless: 'Nothing will be changed in the democratic structure of the State, nor in its policy. . . . Our country will come out of the present difficulties victorious.'

On the 12th, Hitler proclaimed at the closure of the Nuremberg congress: 'The Reich will not permit the oppression of three and a half million Germans to continue. . . . If the democracies try to protect . . . those who attack Germans the consequences will be serious.'

Tension was at breaking-point. On the 13th, Henlein, proclaiming that it was the will of the Sudeten people to be rejoined to the Reich, demanded a plebiscite. This was the worst solution of all, the one which Prague feared the most.

On the 15th, Chamberlain took the initiative in proposing an interview with Hitler. The latter accepted. Getting into an aeroplane for the first time in his life Chamberlain went to Berchtesgaden. The Führer asked for a plebiscite amongst the Sudetens to be held. This was also what Runciman asked, who had just made an inquiry on the spot on behalf of the British Government.

On the 16th, Georges Bonnet[1] gave his instructions to M. de Lacroix, our Minister in Prague. He wrote: 'It would be difficult, in any question of war with Germany, for the French Government to get the support of French public opinion, if, on one hand, France was not attacked, and if, on the other, France could not be sure of having Britain at her side in the event of war.' The first of these two conditions resulted in the unilateral breaking of the alliance.

On the 18th, Daladier and Bonnet conferred in London with their British counterparts. We were at the decisive hour. Let us examine the state of mind of the chief actors in the drama. Recent revelations have enlightened us on the subject.

First of all let us hear what Beneš has to say. His bitterness is well understandable:

France [he writes in his memoirs] was already shaping her course towards appeasement. The formation of the Daladier Cabinet, with Bonnet at the Ministry of Foreign Affairs, marked the critical moment. This Government gave a new orientation to French policy, which divorced it from its alliances in Central Europe. . . . Daladier . . . had never failed . . . to observe that he was not present . . . at Versailles . . . that it was necessary to adapt oneself to new situations, and that France could not indulge in the luxury of bothering about the crumbling states of Central Europe. He abounded in ironical criticisms, even scornful, about Poland and Roumania. . . . Bonnet had the reputation of being a gambler and a cynical intriguer, to whom any means were satisfactory, providing that they took him where he wanted to go. In his role as Minister

---

[1] This fact is mentioned by Jules Henry, at that time head of Bonnet's ministerial advisers, in the memoirs (unpublished) which he left.

he sent by telegram or letter, instructions tallying with the official declarations of the Government. At the same time he gave oral directives in a diametrically opposite sense.[1] He was *a priori* opposed to any military or diplomatic resistance to Hitler's policy of expansion. What he would have preferred above anything else was an armed struggle between Nazism and Bolshevism. Thus, it came about that Czechoslovakia and the Soviet Union were completely isolated in the camp of those, who, on principle, were openly and resolutely anti-Fascist and anti-Nazi. . . . Soviet diplomacy, on many occasions, made serious attempts to organize conferences at which views could have been exchanged on the common defence of Eastern and Western Europe against a Fascist attack. We were always prepared to join in such conferences. Yet, up to the end of September, 1938, the Soviet attempts encountered the negative attitude of the French and British. After the mobilization of 1938, I permitted the Chief of my General Staff, General Krejci, to establish direct contact with General Gamelin in order to draw up measures intended to co-ordinate the mobilization of France with that of Czechoslovakia. General Gamelin replied that he had received no instructions on the subject. We did not receive any other reply, and none of our general officers were invited to go to Paris. Therefore, some time before the Munich crisis, we came to the conclusion that the French did not wish, or were not able to enter into common preparations. In September, 1938, we were left alone with the Russians to put our heads together, to devise military steps to be taken in the case of a Nazi attack. At the time Europe was ready in every respect to accept without protest the *Diktat*[2] of Berchtesgaden. When Czechoslovakia energetically rejected the *Diktat*, she received, on September 18, from Great Britain and France a joint Note demanding that she should accept the terms of surrender which had been drawn up by Hitler and Chamberlain on the 15th at Berchtesgaden. When we refused, France and Britain sent us an ultimatum, which told us that, if we did not accept their plan, they would leave us to face the issue alone. . . .

. . . Official circles in Washington were seriously divided. . . . Certain individuals, beginning with Roosevelt, disapproved . . . of the policy of appeasement which was being followed by the majority of European countries. . . . Others . . . defended the policy of Munich, and some even went as far as

[1] Jean Zay in his *Souvenirs et solitude* (pp. 83–4) addressed a similar reproach to Bonnet. He writes: 'One cannot relive in memory this last year of peace . . . without making another observation, namely that amongst certain men, the desire to abandon Czechoslovakia and Poland, should war break out, that is to say, to repudiate pledges solemnly undertaken by all our Administrations from 1920, and the intention of allowing Germany an entirely free hand in the East and in Central Europe as she understood it, were formed well before the crises of September. It was the adoption of a principle previously and carefully deliberated, which found its principal interpreter, within the Daladier Cabinet, in the person of the Minister of Foreign Affairs himself, M. Georges Bonnet. One would not reproach the latter if he had openly proclaimed it. The Council of Ministers would have made its choice in the matter. But he followed this plan secretly whilst proclaiming an apparent fidelity to the official line of conduct pursued by the Government of which he was a member. The speech at Pointe-de-Grave was made, was it not, on September 6, 1938? "France, in any case, will remain faithful to the pacts and treaties which she has concluded," M. Georges Bonnet stated there. This was not his real intention; this was not his desire; this was not his personal policy.'

[2] *Diktat*, dictation. The Germans, as is known, use this word to designate conditions imposed without discussion by the victor on the vanquished. It is in a pejorative sense that the word has been incorporated into international usage.

actively supporting it. Joseph Kennedy, the American Ambassador in London, openly backed . . . the policy of Chamberlain, and the latter, on more than one occasion sought his help. Hugh Wilson, American Ambassador in Berlin, believed, in August, 1938, that a peaceful orientation of German policy was still possible. He . . . paid me a visit on August 6, 1938. I was surprised . . . at the naïve confidence which he had in the peaceful . . . intentions of Berlin. He repeated to me all through our conversation that Goering did not wish for war, and he was undoubtedly working for peace. The American Ambassador in Paris, William Bullitt, did not express his sympathies as openly as Kennedy, but, at the time of the crisis of September, 1938, his attitude to us was unfavourable. He did not hide it. Daladier indicated clearly on several occasions that his policy was in agreement with the views of the Ambassador of the United States, and as a result, with the officials of the State Department. Bullitt himself let it be understood, though feebly excusing himself for the position he took up, that he considered that the Prague Government had not shown itself sufficiently well disposed towards the German minorities, that . . . I [Beneš] was anti-German to the point of being chauvinistic, and that my attitude was threatening the peace of Europe. Bullitt's policy at this time and later was governed by a personal antipathy against the Soviet Union, which he inherited from his term of office at Moscow. His part was later to take on a decisive importance, when, helped by Daladier and Bonnet, he succeeded in driving the Soviets out of the League of Nations, giving as a pretext the war which this power was waging against Finland. It was at this period, according to certain reports, that he sent to Washington his famous telegram which stated that he had at last obtained satisfaction, that is to say, that he considered himself avenged for all the misfortunes which he had suffered at Moscow. He followed out this policy right up to the defeat of France, and then later in the United States. It even seems that he then supported to a certain extent Pétain's régime against that of de Gaulle.

Neither do we lack insight into the London Conference of the 18th. Bonnet in his *Défense de la paix: I. De Washington au Quai d'Orsay* gives (pp. 234–42) a circumstantial account of it. The depositions of Léon Blum,[1] of Daladier[2] and of M. de Lacroix[3] before the Committee of Inquiry, have thrown light on certain controversial points. Let us hear what Léon Blum had to say: 'I received . . . on the day before Daladier was to leave for London a visit from an emissary of Beneš. This emissary . . . was a Social-Democrat member of the Czech Cabinet with whom I had very close relations, and who was called Netzas. . . . [He] came to tell me on behalf of Beneš: "Things have now been so arranged that Britain and France are going to ask concessions from us. I am sending you a map on which Daladier can see, by the very indication of our military works and fortifications, what is the most extreme line, at which, if it is overstepped, we would consider Czechoslovakia as surrendered and . . . ruined." I was not able to see Daladier on the

[1] Sitting of July 30, 1947. [2] Sitting of May 21, 1947. [3] Sitting of March 16, 1948.

morning of the following day when he took off by air from London, but I sent Blumel to him who . . . handed him the document. . . .'

Alluding to this proposal and to the awkward situation in which it placed him, Daladier has stated: 'Was it necessary to show it to Mr. Chamberlain and to try and establish there and then a position on which we could fall back? I made the decision to show it to him, but it proved a further argument in favour of the London thesis. . . . I completely opposed the idea of a plebiscite, because it was a plebiscite for all minorities. I informed Mr. Chamberlain in a private conversation of the proposals about Bohemian salients. . . . He said to me: "You can see clearly that we cannot do anything. Prague recognizes this also." I resigned myself to the idea of recommending the surrender of the Sudetenland, it being understood that it was a question of territories where there was a very clear majority of Germans wishing to become German nationals. I naturally reserved the decision of the French Government. The French Government met the next day, September 19, at the Elysée, and I did not hear one voice raised in opposition—not one. We all deplored what we called the "sad necessity", but no one in the Council of Ministers supported an opposite policy—no one. Therefore, this decision was taken unanimously . . . we gave to the Prague Government—associating ourselves with Britain —the advice which we had decided in London, to offer it.'

Beneš was not satisfied by merely warning Léon Blum. He had tackled the problem with M. de Lacroix. Bonnet relates this fact in the following words:[1] 'On September 15, M. Beneš had another and very confidential talk with M. de Lacroix. He raised . . . the consideration of a plan whose outlines had been sketched at the time of the discussions which preceded the Treaty of Versailles. M. Masaryk himself at the time had already thought of it. M. Beneš suggested, therefore, to the French Minister in Prague the cession to Germany of three of the Sudeten territories, particularly important because they were inhabited by about nine hundred thousand Germans, and because they embraced an area of about eight thousand square kilometres. He had himself indicated in a precise manner what these territories were: one situated in the north-west angle of Bohemia, another in the north-east of the quadrilateral and the third at the border of the Silesian frontier and to the south of the salient of Glatz. M. de Lacroix had warmly thanked M. Beneš. He sent us on the 17th at two o'clock a long telegram in which he informed us of the plan. This could, he said with reason, help us to find a conciliatory solution at the interviews which we would have in London with the British Ministers, and it would avoid the plebiscite so feared in Prague.'

M. de Lacroix, in his deposition before the Committee of Inquiry,

---

[1] *Défense de la paix: I. De Washington au Quai d'Orsay*, pp. 237–8.

stated, on the contrary, that Beneš had asked him 'to beg the French Government not to depend upon' the past proposals which he had just recalled. Our Minister therefore recommended Bonnet to 'keep the secret'. But Daladier, as we have seen, revealed the proposal to Chamberlain. It is true that it had come to him also by another way and without being, in this case, modified by the reservation which M. de Lacroix stresses. The latter in any case has stated: 'I have never forgiven my Government for this indiscretion. Moreover, I have noticed since, in examining the archives of the Ministry of Foreign Affairs, that my telegram had been so twisted that one might believe that the suggestions recalled by M. Beneš were a solution which he was proposing.'

The memorandum which, during the afternoon of the 19th, was to be submitted separately by the representatives of France and Britain to the Prague Government 'without other comment', stresses Bonnet,[1] gave a verdict for the cession of those Sudeten districts, where more than fifty per cent of the population were of German stock. It was a 'peremptory order', to quote the words of M. de Lacroix. The two Powers declared that, in their opinion, the maintenance of peace and the safeguarding of the vital interests of Czechoslovakia could only be ensured at this price. Britain, however, made a statement that she was ready to give her guarantee upon the new frontiers of Czechoslovakia, on condition that the guarantee was the result of a general pledge.

In Prague, there was a surge of indignation; rather than resign itself to subscribe to the 'complete mutilation' of the country, the Government preferred to recourse to the arbitration agreements laid down by the German-Czech treaty of October 26, 1925. But suddenly it changed its opinion. We were now on the evening of the 20th. M. de Lacroix stated: 'I was in the act of drafting a telegram conveying the nature of this reply . . . when M. Hodza . . . summoned me. . . . I immediately interrupted my work to answer his invitation. M. Hodza asked me if I was certain that France would not honour her pledges, if there were a fight. I replied that I knew nothing about the possibility, and I proposed to him that I should telegraph immediately to Paris in order to obtain a definite reply. He objected that this step would take too long, and added: "I admit, *a priori*, that France will not fight and, if you can get from your Government, tonight, a telegram confirming this, the President of the Republic will give way. It is the only way to save peace." M. Hodza added, in reply to my questions, that he was acting in agreement with M. Beneš and with the General Staff, which considered that, without the support of France, a war against Germany would be equivalent to committing suicide. I immediately informed my Government of this conversation. Now, in my examination of the

[1] *Op. cit.*, p. 244.

archives of the Ministry of Foreign Affairs, I have noted that my telegram has had cut out of it the first question of M. Hodza and my own
tentative reply. . . . I believe that this mutilation of my telegram is
a grave act of guilt on the part of the French Government, for it seemed
to imply that, without wishing to confess it, the Government was not
resolved to keep its pledges.'

Was this reproach uttered by M. de Lacroix known to Bonnet? The
fact is that the latter, again in his *De Washington au Quai d'Orsay*, reproduces (p. 248) 'this text of such supreme importance', stating that he
'transcribes it entirely'. Here is the document as Bonnet publishes it:
'The President of the Council had just summoned me. In agreement,
he told me, with the President of the Republic, he instructed me as
follows. If I were to state that very night to M. Beneš, that, in the case of
war breaking out between Germany and Czechoslovakia over the
Germans in the Sudetenland, France, because of her undertakings to
Britain, would not fight, the President of the Republic would take note
of this statement. The President of the Council would immediately
summon the Cabinet, all of whose members were at the time in agreement with the President of the Republic and with himself in proposing
to give way. . . .[1]

'The Czech rulers needed this assurance in order to accept the
Franco-British proposal. They were sure of the Army, whose leaders
declared that single combat with Germany would mean suicide. M.
Hodza stated that the step which he was suggesting was the only means
of saving peace. He wished to have the matter settled before midnight,
if possible, or in any case, during the course of the night. The President
of the Council conveyed the same communication to the British
Minister.'

Whatever be the truth, the move made by Hodza was examined in
Paris. Bonnet relates[2] that he 'insisted strongly to Daladier that the
Council of Ministers should be summoned: the members of the
Government apprised of the situation . . . could only approve our
proposals, and we would thus avoid later criticisms. Daladier shared
my opinion, but he observed to me that it was physically impossible
to assemble the Council. The President of the Republic was at Rambouillet; several Ministers were out of Paris. How much time would
be needed to call the others together? And, on the other hand, the reply
had to be given very quickly, if possible before midnight. Now, it was
after eleven o'clock. . . . After some discussion, we decided that it was
necessary to send M. de Lacroix rather detailed instructions in order to
guide him in the talks he was to have with M. Hodza. . . . However,
before telephoning this message to Prague, the President of the Council

---

[1] The points of suspension are in the text as it is given by Bonnet.
[2] *Op. cit.*, pp. 249–50.

and myself thought it necessary to warn the President of the Republic.
I myself called M. Albert Lebrun at Rambouillet on a direct line. I
insisted, despite the late hour, that the President himself should answer
me. I explained the situation to him. . . . The President . . . gave his
agreement, regretting at the same time like ourselves that we were
obliged to take such hasty decisions.' Half an hour after midnight the
instructions were sent to Prague, whose Government, however, only
gave way at 5 p.m. on the 21st, after having obtained from M. de
Lacroix a written confirmation of the reply, which, in obedience to
Bonnet's instructions, he had only given orally.[1] 'Our friends', the
communiqué of the Czech Government was to state shortly afterwards,
'have advised us to pay for peace with our sacrifice. . . . We have found
ourselves alone.' The Minister for Propaganda, Vavreka, stated on the
radio that the Government had been given no choice. 'Our friends and
allies', he said, 'have forced us to accept conditions that one usually
offers to a defeated opponent. We were not lacking in courage. . . . Do
not let us judge those who have left us in the lurch at this hour of trial.
Let us leave history the task of passing judgement on them.'

On the 22nd Hodza resigned. Chamberlain again took an aeroplane
to go immediately to meet Hitler, who this time received him at
Godesberg-on-Rhine.

On the same day, Mandel, Champetier de Ribes and myself[2] considering that the statement of the Czech radio proved that, contrary to
the decision taken in the Council of Ministers, the Government had
not left Prague free to accept or refuse the Franco-British proposals,
sent our resignations to Daladier, giving him, because of the gravity
of the circumstance, the freedom to choose the moment when he
judged it would be convenient to make them public.[3]

Daladier denied the allegation made by the Prague radio. Bonnet
ought, indeed, to have read to us, at the ensuing meeting of the Council
the telegram by which M. de Lacroix had informed him of the step of
the Czech Government, made with the object of forcing his hand.

During the interview, Daladier added that the first measures for
mobilization were being taken, that war was coming, and that, under

[1] Churchill writes (op. cit., vol. I, The Gathering Storm, p. 272, second edition): 'The
French Government at least was sufficiently ashamed of this communication to instruct
its Minister only to make it verbally.'

[2] Churchill writes (ibid., p. 272, second edition): 'At the height of the crisis (on
September 20) I visited Paris for two days in order to see my friends in the French
Government, Reynaud and Mandel. Both these Ministers were in lively distress and on
the verge of resigning from the Daladier Cabinet. I was against this, as their sacrifice could
not alter the course of events, and would only leave the French Government weakened by
the loss of its two most capable and resolute men. I ventured even to speak to them in
this sense.'

[3] Léon Blum, during his depositions of July 30, 1947, declared: 'There were at least
two members of the Cabinet, whose resignations were only prevented with great
difficulty: Paul Reynaud and Georges Mandel.'

such conditions, our resignations were equivalent to desertion. In the face of these arguments we agreed to withdraw them.

On the 23rd, the crisis again grew acute. Hitler's demands had increased further. With the agreement of France and Britain, Prague ordered a general mobilization. In France, mobilization was taking place by stages.

On the 25th there was a new conference at London.

On the evening of the 26th the Foreign Office authorized the publication of the following statement: 'If, in spite of the efforts of the Prime Minister, Germany launched an attack on Czechoslovakia, France would find herself forced to go to the assistance of her ally, and Great Britain and Russia would take their places by the side of France. . . .' Bonnet allowed certain papers . . . *Le Jour*, for example, to print, despite the evidence, a statement that the communiqué was false.

Certainly Chamberlain's strongest wish was to prevent the outbreak of war. He was never tired of saying so. But Britain had none the less publicly assured us of her determination to come to our help if the execution of our pledges dragged us into hostilities against Germany. And Britain had notified Hitler of this determination.

The latter, moreover, took the precaution of reassuring Poland. At the Berlin Sportspalast he declared on the 26th that Germany was determined to keep up good neighbourly relations with Poland. Moreover, he said that Germany understood Poland's desire to gain access to the sea, that the agreement reached with Pilsudski set aside any risk of struggle between the two countries, and finally that it was only up to both the rulers to improve still further German-Polish relations. In a word, at the same time that he was executing Czechoslovakia, Hitler was giving Poland the same promises that he had made to Czechoslovakia when he was executing Austria.

We gain an insight into the attitude of the United States from *The Memoirs of Cordell Hull*. He writes:[1] 'That same day [September 24] Bullitt telegraphed from Paris his belief that some effort should be made by us to maintain peace, even if it were unsuccessful. He suggested an appeal by the President to the British, French, Italian, German, and Polish chiefs of State to send representatives to The Hague to settle the crisis, and that we should indicate our willingness to be represented. . . .

'The President would be sent directly an appeal to this end by the heads of the interested States.

[1] *The Memoirs of Cordell Hull*, London, 1948, vol. I, pp. 590-3. Appointed Secretary of State on February 11, 1933, Cordell Hull held this post until November 27, 1944. Sumner Welles was himself Under-Secretary of State from May, 1937, to September, 1943. As is known, in the United States the *Secretary of State* and the *Under-Secretary of State* control respectively as chief and deputy chief the *Department of State*, that is to say, the Department of Foreign Affairs. Each of the other departments has at its head a *Secretary*.

'On [the following day] the 25th . . . our Minister to Prague . . . telegraphed a plea from President Beneš that President Roosevelt should urge the British and French not to desert Czechoslovakia.'

The President adopted Bullitt's plan.

'On the night [of September 25] Bullitt telephoned the Department [and advised including in the appeals a "further step"; namely, the suggestion made by Bonnet] that the President should offer to arbitrate. But neither the President nor I was willing to go that far. . . . Then at one o'clock on [the morning of September] 26 he sent [it in] identical messages direct to Hitler and Beneš, and, through me to Chamberlain and Daladier. . . . "I most earnestly appeal to you", said the President, "not to break off negotiations. . . ." [That same day, September] 26, Beneš, Daladier, and Chamberlain stated their complete accord. . . . But Hitler's reply had not arrived . . . Europe was mobilizing. Kennedy telephoned me from London that the British Government had assured the French of its support in the event of war. . . . Bullitt cabled me that Daladier said he hoped the time would soon come when it would be possible to hold a conference to organize a genuine European peace; he thought the call for such a conference had to come from the President. . . . Hitler's reply arrived on the night of [September] 26. It was a long diatribe against the Czech Government, the Treaty of Versailles, and the League of Nations, and it concluded by placing the burden of peace or war upon Czechoslovakia, not Germany. . . . [During the morning of the 27th] Bullitt cabled a suggestion that a second telegram be sent by the President to Hitler requesting him to agree to send a representative to such a conference at The Hague [as Bullitt had previously suggested] Daladier, he said, was "delighted" with the idea. . . . We also sent a telegram to Ambassador Phillips in Rome containing a personal and confidential message from the President to Mussolini asking Mussolini to "help in the continuation of the efforts to arrive at an agreement of the questions at issue by negotiation or by other pacific means rather than by resort to force". [In the evening], President Roosevelt decided to send a further appeal, this time addressed to Hitler alone. . . . It suggested an immediate conference in some neutral spot in Europe, with all nations directly interested in the Czech controversy participating.'

As for the attitude of Russia, it has raised a number of controversies. Moscow certainly did not think of getting out of its pledges to Czechoslovakia, but these pledges were linked, as we have seen, with parallel engagements which France had herself entered upon with Prague. It was natural that the Soviets should recall that any action by them could only be concomitant with that of France, and this concerted action remained in their opinion a natural *sine qua non*. Moreover, the implementation of pledges undertaken by Russia implied in practice, as we have also seen, a passage through Poland and Roumania. The Soviets rejected the idea of entering these countries by force, and only intended to do so if they were legitimately allowed, according to an agreement, that is to say, with Warsaw and Bucharest or, alternatively, and this came to the same thing, at the request of a combination of Powers or, at this juncture, by the Council of the League of Nations.

On September 26 Hitler declared that this time he had come to the end of his patience. He gave Beneš six days to choose between peace and war: 'We have', he proclaimed, 'an armament so powerful that the world has never known its like. Once the question of the Sudetens has been settled, we shall have finished, in Europe, with the last territorial problem.' Finished, yes, until the next time.

However, the French Government never grew tired of repeating to Hitler that, if he persisted in his intentions, war would be inevitable, that this would be madness, but that France would not be able to draw back. Suddenly there came the climax. During the afternoon of the 28th, M. François-Poncet telephoned from Berlin to Daladier that there was to be a meeting on the next day at Munich, to which he, Daladier, was invited.

We now know the reasons and the movements behind the scenes, which brought about this sudden change of policy. Both have been revealed by Ciano in his *Diary*.[1]

The initiative for Munich lay with Chamberlain personally, who consulted neither his own colleagues in the Cabinet nor the French Government, just as several days before he had refrained from informing them of the step he had taken in proposing to Hitler that he should go to Berchtesgaden in order to confer with him.

Whilst events rushed on at this giddy pace, disapproval in France was becoming more marked.

On the 26th, Flandin published in *Le Temps* a letter in which he wrote: 'For every kind of reason . . . I reject . . . the military intervention of France in the struggle between the Sudeten Germans and the Czechoslovak State. . . . I do hope that France will not be faced by the *fait accompli* of a war which has been made inevitable, before the opinion of her legal representatives has been able to find expression in good time. Our British friends should in loyalty be told that the French Army will not be able to bear alone, or even with the support of a small contingent, the burden of land operations on three fronts. . . .' So it was evidently only a matter of a difference between the Czechoslovak State and the Sudetens. . . .

[1] Ciano's two notebooks which concern the years 1937 and 1938 were only made public in 1948, that is to say, two years after the publication of those which dealt with the years 1939–43. Moreover, the pages in the notebook of 1938, which dealt with Munich, had been taken out. They were finally discovered, and then published by *Le Figaro* in its editions of June 26 and 29, 1948.

On the 28th, Flandin went further. He had stuck up on the walls of Paris a placard whose text was, on the following day, reproduced by Doriot's *La Liberté*, a newspaper subsidized by the Reich. This read:

You are being deceived

'People of France, you are being deceived. . . . A cunning trap has been laid for some weeks and months by secret elements in order to make war inevitable. . . .'

What, on reading such a diatribe, could be the impression of young Frenchmen who were being mobilized? If they were the victims of a 'cunning trap' created by diabolical men, would not their first reaction be not to risk raising the butts of their rifles off the ground?

The Government had the placard torn down and seized the issue of the paper. On the spot I sent to Flandin my resignation from the *Alliance Démocratique*,[1] of which he was the President, and with which I had for a long time avoided contact. Several of my friends, amongst whom were Rollin, Jacquinot and Laniel, followed suit.

The pacifist campaign gained both in strength and favour. The headlines appearing on the day of Munich in the Royalist paper *L'Action Française*—a patriotic paper during the First World War—show to what pitch feeling against war had risen in France. They consisted of a verse of the *Internationale* adapted as follows:

> *S'ils s'obstinent, ces cannibales,*
> *A faire de nous des héros*
> *Il faut que nos premières balles*
> *Soient pour Mandel, Blum et Reynaud.*[2]

However, the conference opened at Munich on the morning of the 29th. M. François-Poncet writes:[3]

The meeting began at 12.45 in an adjoining room. The ambassadors were not admitted. Two hours later, as the meeting adjourned, I was informed that the four participants exposed their points of view in turn in general terms. Hitler delivered a diatribe of extreme violence against Czechoslovakia. Thereupon Daladier clearly and vigorously posed the crucial question. Did the Conference wish Czechoslovakia to exist or not? Was the amputation intended to make her healthier and to give her better chances for life in the future? Or was it but a means to weaken her, a mutilation bound to bring about her

---

[1] The *Alliance Démocratique* was a group of parties roughly representing the moderate Right and the Centre. In general it was Republican and Conservative, but differed from the extreme Right in being anti-Catholic and less opposed to the radical Left [Tr.].

[2] 'If they persist, these cannibals,
   To make of us the hero,
   First we must reserve our shots
   For Mandel, Blum and Reynaud.'

[3] François-Poncet, *op. cit.*, pp. 270–3, *passim.*

death? If the point was to prepare the dismemberment and disappearance of Czechoslovakia, then he, Daladier, had no business in this place. He refused to be associated with such a crime and would take his leave. If, on the contrary, the point was to assure Czechoslovakia's future, then he was prepared to concur with the others in a spirit of reciprocal concession and collaboration. The French Premier spoke in accents of a determination and nobility that moved his hearers.

Mussolini declared that Hitler's idea had been misunderstood, and, like the Duce, all protested that they wished to consolidate and to respect the existence of the Czechoslovakian State.

At three o'clock luncheon was served.

There was a second session at the close of the afternoon. This time I entered by permission and sat behind Daladier. The delegates were grouped in a semi-circle around a vast fireplace, the British on the left, the Italians and the Germans in the centre, the French on the right. Within the British group there was scant conversation; within the German and Italian groups there was much. Mussolini was deeply ensconced in his armchair. His extraordinarily mobile features were never at rest for a moment; his mouth would part for a wide smile or contract in a pout; his eyes, generally curious and amused in expression, would suddenly dart lightning.

Standing at his side, Hitler gazed intently upon him, subject to his charm and as though fascinated and hypnotized. Did the Duce laugh, the Führer laughed too; did Mussolini scowl, so scowled Hitler. Here was a study in mimicry. It was to leave me with the lasting and erroneous impression that Mussolini exercised a firmly established ascendancy over the Führer. At any rate that day he did.

No one presided at this session and there was no methodical agenda. For want of directive, the discussion proved difficult, confused, and interminably long. Hampered by the necessity of a double translation, it kept constantly changing its topic and ceased whenever a contradiction arose. The atmosphere grew thicker and heavier. At last toward evening the British produced a type-written memorandum from their files. It had been drawn up by Horace Wilson with Strang's assistance. The debate, which had wavered, now concentrated upon this proposal for an agreement.

At half-past one in the morning the agreement was signed. The Ambassador continued:

We were bitterly aware of the cruelty of the event. Daladier shook his head, muttered, and cursed circumstances. He refused to take part in the congratulations exchanged by the other delegates. Worst, the most painful step had not yet been taken; we had now to break the news to the Czechoslovaks who were awaiting the outcome of the Conference at their hotel. Mastny, their minister in Berlin, broke into tears. I consoled him as best I could. 'Believe me', I said, 'all this is not final. It is but one moment in a story which has just begun and which will soon bring up the issue again.'

Returning to our hotel at 2.30 a.m. I called Bonnet by telephone to inform him of what had happened, while Daladier, still cursing and lost in gloomy thought, weighed the difficulties he was likely to meet on his return to Paris. Bonnet swept aside my detailed explanations. 'Peace is assured,' he said. 'That is the main thing. Everybody will be happy.'

Whatever may be the truth about the meeting, Daladier was resigned to giving way. But in doing so he was the prey of extreme distress. Sadness showed on his face. Peace was saved, but he was well aware of the price of this surrender! We have a noteworthy account of his state of mind at Munich. Causoy, one of the journalists who went with the French delegation, quotes[1] the words uttered by Daladier at the *Quatre-Saisons* on the conference, ending: 'And then, if we had not given way, there would still be a Czech problem; there would have always been Germans in Czechoslovakia.'

As for Hitler, he was triumphant. He had secured complete victory. It seems to be a fact that, in order to carry out his manœuvres, he had to disregard all his advisers, and to ignore the opposition of Goering, Ribbentrop and the generals. The High Command, Brauchitsch and Keitel especially, feared a war, not believing that the Wehrmacht was sufficiently strong to win it. The eagerness of the Allies to 'lick the boots of the Nazis', the ease with which Hitler got out of them much more than he himself dared to hope for, was to exert a tremendous influence on the course of events. Restraint, patience, conciliation were henceforth banned from the deliberations of the Führer. As on March 7, 1936, he had gambled and won. In the future, counsellors and favourites were to vie with each other in the audacity of their recommendations, and to bid for his goodwill by outbidding each other. The reproach which they were to fear above all others was that they possessed moderation or timidity. Because of Munich, Hitler conceived for those whom he had met in conference a feeling of scorn which burst out on occasions in foul expressions. His self-confidence, already tremendous, was to know no limits. He was no longer to have cause to find himself struggling with people who contradicted him. Henceforth, he was liable to be swayed by any mood of exaltation, by any extravagances, by any mania of omnipotence, whose outbursts nothing within him was capable of tempering.

Eva Braun, Hitler's mistress, notes in her *Journal Intime*: 'October, 1938. Three of the *important Four* have left. The fourth, and without doubt the most important, has stayed. For nearly three hours he [Hitler] has talked of the negotiations. "It is only now", he said, "that I know how weak the West is. . . . I shall wage the war which I need to impose my ideas on the world. Now, the difference between Mussolini and myself becomes more and more apparent. He aspires to peace; I, to war."'

In any case Munich made Hitler the arbiter of Europe. Czechoslovakia was harshly punished for having wished to keep men of

[1] *Le Populaire*, March 3, 1948.

German blood under her thumb. The lesson, thought Berlin, would bear fruit. But the Führer had obtained another success, the certain pledge of new victories. He felt sure that he had broken the coalition which threatened, once again, to re-form itself against Germany: between Moscow and the Western Powers he had stirred up mistrust, discord and bad blood.

The Allies themselves laboured under a complete delusion.

Following his dream, whose secret he jealously kept to himself, Chamberlain stayed at Munich until the morning of the 30th. Just before leaving Hitler, he signed with him, without warning Daladier, a pact of friendship. When he got back to Croydon, he stated: 'Peace has been won for a generation.'

On the 30th also, Daladier got back to Le Bourget. He was expecting a hostile reception. Paris, which had just lived through days of anguish, experienced a slackening in nervous tension, and acclaimed Daladier, who crossed the town in an open car, with Bonnet beside him. Michel Clemenceau, son of the 'Tiger', said to me: 'The sight made me weep.' He wrote an article in protest, which he hoped to publish in *L'Ordre*, but Pétain, with whom at that time he was on good terms, advised him not to do so.

I was the only one, I think, of the members of the Government, who did not go to greet Daladier at Le Bourget. It was something which was beyond me. I went to see him at the Rue Saint-Dominique. At the top of the staircase I met Canon Polimann, deputy for the Meuse, who pretended not to see me. This was because the split between those who wished to resist Germany and their opponents, which had long been latent, occurred on the day of Munich. Daladier went with Gamelin and myself into his study. He found it full of baskets of flowers. He said to us: 'It is my policy. It is the Four Power Pact', and he added: 'It is possible to talk with those people. . . . Ah! If we had Ambassadors.' I said to Gamelin: 'You have now only got to find twenty-five divisions.'

During the following two days, Champetier de Ribes, Mandel and myself talked over together the attitude which we ought to take. Here is the account which Francisque Varenne gives of this exchange of views in *Mon patron, Georges Mandel* (pp. 175–6):

'The day following the return of Daladier from Munich, at ten o'clock in the evening . . . Duff Cooper . . . warned Mandel that he had placed his resignation in the hands of Chamberlain, because he did not wish to be associated with the policy of surrender, which had just been sanctioned at Munich. That very evening Mandel gave news of this to Paul Reynaud and to Champetier de Ribes. The three Ministers examined the problem as to what decision they themselves should take. . . . On the next day, there were several meetings at the Ritz of those

Ministers who were opposed to a policy of appeasement. Finally it was decided that resignations would not be handed in. . . . An advocate . . . of resignation, he [Mandel] gave way before the reasons of his friends, and he acknowledged that those reasons were very strong ones. Public opinion, in overwhelming force, blinded by the more powerful newspapers and dominated by a fear of war, did not see in Munich the surrender of France and Britain to Germany. It only saw the dispelling of an agonizing nightmare. The resignation of the Ministers would have been badly received even in Parliament, and would have turned against them anger which would have been long in dying.'

I have no recollection of this interview, which, in any case, could not have taken place at the Ritz. I only recall on the subject these words of Mandel at Portalet: 'A resignation is justified when it is to accomplish something. Our own would have served no purpose.'

On October 1 our friend Jules Julien, Minister of Post and Telegraph telephoned me:

'Flandin has just sent Hitler a telegram of congratulations.'

'Impossible. Make certain about it.'

He did make certain. The telegram[1] had indeed been sent. Here is its text:

'Please accept warm congratulations on keeping the peace, in the hope that out of this historic act will come a trusting and cordial collaboration between those four European Powers which met at Munich.'

This 'historic act' was not to be the last.

On October 2, Hitler thanked Flandin: 'I am grateful for your efforts . . . on behalf of an understanding and complete collaboration between France and Germany. . . .'

On the next day, there were thanksgiving ceremonies at the Arc de Triomphe. In Prague, ex-soldiers threw their Legion of Honour and Croix de Guerre medals on the square in front of the French Legation.

On the 5th, Beneš resigned the Presidency.

Polish troops occupied Teschen. I said to the Polish Ambassador in Paris, who did not hide his satisfaction: 'You are satisfied because Hitler has put you in the refrigerator for his next meal.'

Hitler spoke impatiently about British rearmament. He said on November 2: 'The rearmament of others does not upset me. National Socialist Germany will never eat humble pie.'

On November 20, Hacha succeeded Beneš.

The amputated body of Czechoslovakia was stretched out on the operating table. But Hitler was not to summon the 'butchers' club' again. In future he was to do the cutting up by himself.

[1] Flandin had also congratulated Daladier, Chamberlain and Mussolini.

1938–9: RECOVERY *IN EXTREMIS*

On November 2, 1938, I took over the Ministry of Finance. For seven years France had been struggling in the grip of the crisis. Thirteen plans had been successively tried out. I had fought against these plans one by one on the floor of the Chamber, and had opposed them with my own policy. Naturally, when I stated that I, in my own turn, was going to try out my plan, the fourteenth, the interest with which it was greeted was at least tempered with malice. The omens, whether they came from the Right or the Left, did not fail to predict a set-back for what was called the 'Reynaud experiment'. How was it possible to reverse a tendency of seven years' duration, when, since 1928, one railway truck out of three had stopped moving, when the deficit of our commercial balance had tripled in two years, when the State had been reduced to borrowing abroad, giving as a pledge the gold of the Bank of France, and only continued to live by using paper currency, and when the threat of war did not cease to grow on the horizon?

In this atmosphere, where scepticism vied with hostility, I resolved to find support in public opinion. Breaking away from custom, I was to sound the tocsin, and demonstrate that we were heading for disaster if we did not change our policy.

On November 13, forty-two decree-laws were published in the *Journal Officiel*. They were to be followed two days later by fifteen texts for putting them into operation. The general report in which they were submitted to the President of the Republic was only a summary of the speeches which, for four years, I had delivered on the floor of the Chamber. 'No doubt', I wrote in it, 'there is a problem of production and prices, a problem of credit, a problem of work. They are only aspects . . . of one and the same problem . . . the French crisis.'

Increasing production was my essential aim. This was necessary both for the reorganization of our finances and for the strengthening of our currency. It would also be the result of either. Restoring the profit of the producer, cutting down the rate of interest, increasing the length of working time, restoring to production a part of the labour which it had just lost, these were the means.

The struggles, which I had to undergo, can be guessed. My colleagues, whom I asked to subscribe to my reforms, saw in them so many crimes against their personal peace of mind. The removal of abuses is never popular, for abuses possess in themselves a certain charm. There is no better way of making enemies for oneself than in attacking them. It was not, therefore, without difficulty that, on November 12, I got the consent of the Council of Ministers to my plans.

That same evening I spoke on the wireless to the French people: 'It is a question of the country's fate. . . . In spite of the uncertainties . . .

the deceptions . . . the distress of these last months . . . you have never lost faith in France. . . . You want to know the truth, however serious it may be, so that you can draw from the truth the courage to struggle and to conquer. It is the truth I am going to tell you.' I painted the picture of our economic decline from the beginning of the world crisis. Then I stated my programme: a more liberal régime for prices, credit and work; economies; taxes; considerable sums for rearmament.

The strength of the railwaymen was to be reduced to forty thousand: 'France', I said, 'needs . . . to increase the number of workers in the aircraft industry and to reduce that of its signalmen.'

It was necessary to give the people of France a dose of hard-hitting language: 'However harsh all this may seem, it is only a beginning. I am speaking to you straight from the shoulder, for it is a question of saving the country and not of punishing it.'

I asked my fellow-countrymen these questions: 'Do you believe that, in the Europe of today, France can both maintain her way of life, spend twenty-five milliards for rearmament and go to sleep two days a week? No. What is to be done then? It is action that you want. . . . I announce to you . . . the five-day working week has ceased to exist.'

I concluded by making an appeal to the feeling of national greatness: 'Will there be opposition? When France is in peril, private interests do not have the deciding word. No one has any rights . . . which are prejudicial to the nation. . . . Several weeks ago every man, worthy of the name of Frenchman, made to himself the promise to give back to France all her strength. . . . Today all the nations of the world have their eyes fixed on us. Will France be able, or rather does France want to recover? It is you . . . who are going to give the answer. . . . It is your strength . . . your instinct for preservation, your spirit of sacrifice, your sentiment of greatness, which will conquer. Without your help we are nothing . . . we can do nothing. You will be behind us.'

As one can imagine, this clear reference to Munich was not to the liking of German propaganda. Thus, Champeaux did not miss the opportunity[1] under the Occupation to reproach me in a particularly virulent fashion for this speech.

It is true that my programme meant the reversal of the policy followed for several years. It produced on the whole of public opinion an impression strong enough to prevent the Chamber from repudiating me. But the new taxes were grievous ones, and the statement that the five-day working week had ceased to be provoked a storm from the extreme Left: 'M. Paul Reynaud has raised the French unanimously against him,' stated headlines across the entire front page of an important newspaper of the extreme Left.

The campaign against the taxes knew no bounds. The most moderate

[1] Champeaux, *op. cit.*, vol. II, p. 331.

stated that I had just struck our economy on the head with a club when all that was needed was a stroke from a whip. But the campaign was most formidable on the demagogic level. Certain newspapers strove to show that I had penalized the 'little man' more harshly than the 'big one'.

Speaking on November 17 at a Press banquet in the presence of the President of the Republic, I alluded to these attacks: 'The terrifying figures which I have given, the wear and tear to national capital which I have depicted, the abyss which I have shown to be before our feet, the external danger linked to the internal danger, all these things, it seems, might be effaced. . . . We shall be most feeble spirited if we remain unmoved. . . . Certain people are advising us to moderate our policy. . . . We have need, on the contrary, to strengthen our will power.'

The General Confederation of Trade Unions decided upon a general strike to protest against the decree-laws. Monzie, one of the Ministers who had fought the reforms most keenly, proposed to Daladier that he should make an approach to Jouhaux, who was personally antagonistic to the strike. Daladier, who knew that the fate of the country was at stake, declined the offer. The strike was fixed for November 30.

On the 26th, I spoke on the wireless to all those who were being urged to strike: 'If you stop the machinery one day out of six . . . you are doing the same as destroying one machine out of six. . . .' I refuted the allegation that I was not inflicting a sufficiently hard burden on the rich. Here is the motive which was animating me, and which I wished my hearers to get firmly fixed in their heads. 'A year ago', I said, '. . . the fate of freedom in Europe depended on the production of our war factories. . . . All that I have done. . . . I have done to make you strong. I don't want my country to be for some nations the ideal opponent, and for others an ally whose value is debatable.' Both workers and civil servants understood the significance of my words. The strike was a total failure.

The Chamber had still to be convinced. The extreme Left was obviously hostile. So also were a number of Radicals who were not satisfied with the failure of the *Front Populaire*. Of the Centre, Flandin openly predicted that I would fail, and Piétri gained the applause of the extreme Left by attacking those of our reforms which concerned the law for a forty-hour working week. From his retreat in Mentone, Tardieu rallied the forces of my opponents by asserting in *Gringoire*[1] that it was not possible to make a financial recovery without first having revised the Constitution.

I had to get the Chamber to consent to bending before the tyranny of facts. Rising to speak on December 9 in the Budget discussions, I said:

[1] November 17, 1938.

'The desire which has inspired my actions has been to make France stronger. . . . Indeed the Chamber is debating . . . about the strength of France. This is a subject on which we all should be in agreement.' The Chamber applauded, but, on the vote over the decree-laws, I only secured a majority of seven. The obstacle had, however, been cleared. Success was assured.

I was, however, given a favourable vote in the Senate by almost all its members, when, painting the picture of the situation as I had inherited it, I showed the State ruined by its prodigalities, and stifled by the exorbitant numbers of its civil servants. I recalled, in relation to this latter point, that, in two years, the civilian and military administrations had been swollen by more than two hundred and fifty thousand new employees.

Recovery asserted itself in all spheres. I was not, however, to escape undergoing a number of offensives in favour of a return to the 'five-day working week'. Thus, when the National Federation of Bank Clerks Unions put before the Ministry of Labour a demand for its restoration, the latter backed them in bringing the matter before me. I replied on February 9, 1939, to my fellow Minister by expressing my surprise at seeing him recommend a measure which would have the effect of 'making indispensable the employment of a greater number of men for the same amount of work, that is to say, of making them waste their time'. I added: 'I am put out by the idea that the Minister of Labour can take upon himself the task of organizing . . . the minimum amount of production by each individual inhabitant. . . .' And I reminded him of Daladier's words on August 21, 1938: 'The road to national salvation lies straight ahead of us. . . . It is imperative to increase the national revenue. It is necessary to set France once more to work.'

In March, I undertook to reform the finances of certain large towns, which had been accustomed to leaving to the State the burden of making good their chronic deficit. The municipal administration of Marseilles was as scandalous as it was farcical. I suspended the powers of the municipality, and entrusted a special administrator not only with the task of administering the town, but of reforming the municipal customs which Colbert had already severely criticized.

In this same month of March, 1939, Hitler entered Prague. In the Budget had been included a credit of twenty-five and a half milliards for the purpose of rearmament. The Government decided to increase this amount to forty-one milliards. For the maintenance of the army it asked for an outlay of fifteen milliards. I had, therefore, to find fifty-six milliards for national defence. In the preceding November I had increased by ten milliards the fiscal burdens of the country. It was going to be necessary to ask of it new sacrifices. On April 12 I spoke on the wireless to the country: 'I have the harsh duty of asking you to make new sacrifices. . . . For the last fourteen months great victories have been won in the heart of Europe, solely by virtue of the output produced by our opponent's munition factories. . . . France . . . has decided . . . upon a great effort. This new effort . . . is going to cost us fifteen milliards. . . .'

And, in spite of the burden of these impositions, the franc became once more the foremost currency of Europe. France was settling down to work. The foreign Press, which had doubted our ability to recover, spoke—*The Times* as well—of a 'miracle'. The balance-sheet indeed exceeded all hopes.

I drew up this balance-sheet on July 29 during the last speech which I made in peace-time. I was then completely preoccupied with the approaching war. Once again I stressed the imminence and gravity of the danger. I revealed the scope of the financial effort of the State, which added to its burdens those which were to result from the system of family grants that it had just introduced. 'These', I said, 'would never have been possible without the monetary and financial recovery which the Government has effected in the last nine months.' We had indeed won the battle of production, the battle of exports and the battle of gold.

The last victory was considered the most difficult: 'We were informed', I said, 'that we would at least lose the battle of gold. People were categorical . . . on this point. However . . . gold has not stopped flowing into the Bank of France, so much so that, since March 31 . . . our country has, after the United States, built up the greatest reserves of gold in the world. . . .'

Once again I confronted the French people squarely with their destiny, which, in the future, was to be living dangerously: 'The danger will be with us for a long time. . . . All those who give way to the temptations of an out-dated demagogy will assume a terrible responsibility. France, calm and dignified, the calmest perhaps of all the great peoples of the world, is in the process of adapting herself to her new destiny. Today . . . when we are definitely forced to say farewell to a certain sweetness in life, when we are on the threshold of the most perilous period of our history, I am sure that no one will give way any more to weakening France by dividing Frenchmen.'

I was unfortunately speaking too late!

CHAPTER XIV

POLAND'S TURN

March 15, 1939, Hitler seizes Bohemia and thus threatens Poland in the Rear.—April–August, 1939, Franco-Anglo-Soviet Negotiations; the Hitler-Stalin Agreement; the Waterloo of French Diplomacy.

MARCH 15, 1939: HITLER SEIZES BOHEMIA AND THUS THREATENS POLAND IN THE REAR

THE Munich agreement consecrated a virtual unconditional acceptance of the demands, which Hitler had made at Godesberg. The emptiness of Hitler's alleged concessions sprang from the way in which the Reich applied the clauses concerning the entry of her troops into the ceded territory. The invasion was immediate and spread throughout the whole of the region instead of proceeding in stages over a period of ten days, and, in certain parts, it exceeded the limits laid down. The Allies were nonplussed, whilst the Czechs demonstrated their indignation in the streets of Prague. For Hitler, Munich was only a stage. We know now that the German Government decided, only three days after Munich, to take no notice of the agreement signed and, as early as October 10, to support diplomatically the claims of Hungary against Czechoslovakia.

In Berlin, public opinion and the Press flattered France, who had, at last, associated herself with the institution of a new Europe. Goering said: 'With a man like Daladier it is possible to hammer out some policy.' When he had firmly established himself in Central Europe, Hitler wished to have his hands free in order to follow up his advantages in the East. It seemed to him that the best way of lulling the French to sleep was to throw around Franco-German relations a good-neighbourly atmosphere. That is why I tried to oppose the coming of Ribbentrop to Paris.

In *Souvenirs et solitude*, Jean Zay[1] gives a particularly striking account of the deliberations of the Council of Ministers on this matter:

It was at a meeting of the Council on November 23 that . . . Bonnet spoke for the first time about a future Franco-German statement. It was at that time

[1] pp. 168–70.

so inopportune that the entire Council including the President of the Republic showed some surprise at his words. Hardly two months had elapsed since the humiliation of Munich. The moral and diplomatic isolation of Germany was complete; the persecutions and massacres which she had just perpetrated . . . had inspired the whole world with horror. It was apparent that it was in the interests of the Reich to have herself rehabilitated by France, to demonstrate that she was not treated everywhere as a leper. But it was impossible to find wherein such an action could benefit French interests, for nobody was in the least doubt as to the value of the signature which would be given us. However, once again Bonnet had presented his fellow Ministers with a *fait accompli*, and had acted in such a way as to deprive them of the freedom of decision. He revealed that the initiative had come from Hitler, who, on October 19, in a talk with . . . François-Poncet, had stated that it was necessary to improve Franco-German relations. . . . The subject was not taken up again until three weeks later. Then, suddenly, on November 7, the Ambassador, Count von Welczech, had brought to the Quai d'Orsay, a fully prepared text. Bonnet confined himself to asking for some slight modifications. . . . The document as amended was returned . . . on November 22, brought in haste by . . . Welczech. In handing it over, he had expressed the pressing desire that Herr von Ribbentrop should come in person to sign it in Paris between November 28 and December 3. This insistence was significant.

At a time when British and American public opinion was raging against Germany, whose real intentions it had at last understood, when French public opinion no longer cherished any illusions on the attempts to divide the Allies, which was the principal aim of the Reich, such an unexpected signature and visit could only arouse both surprise and uneasiness. Monzie himself expressed astonishment that the text . . . had not been communicated to Poland. But, if the strain of the document seemed soothing, the coming of Ribbentrop to Paris constituted especially a strange and dangerous idea. About this trip, the feeling of the Council was unanimous. Campinchi pointed out the possibility of popular demonstrations in the streets of Paris and asked: 'Would Herr von Ribbentrop be received in London?' Monzie proposed Strasbourg as the meeting-place. I tried vainly to discover why the agreement could not simply be signed in Berlin by our Ambassador. Reynaud and Mandel demanded that the visit should be postponed. When Bonnet said that Germany had no motive in proposing the agreement, and consented to it solely to show her 'good will towards us', Reynaud answered him that, if the document was for our benefit, the 'purpose of the visit was for Germany's benefit'. Daladier, expressing the feelings of almost all his colleagues, finally stated that, if the Council approved the proposed text, it was 'agreed' that the Foreign Minister, in telling the Ambassador of the Reich of this approval, would point out to him that the visit 'was only possible in calmer circumstances'. This was an adjournment *sine die* of any invitation to Herr von Ribbentrop and . . . Bonnet realized this so well that, on leaving the Elysée, he muttered to Monzie, who has repeated the words: 'We shall tackle the subject again later.'

But why bring up the subject again? It was so simple to override bluntly the will of the Council of Ministers. To do this, the only thing necessary was not to summon it again. Such tactics were a well-tried device. Therefore, the

Council was not called until December 24, or for a month, although during this time the strike of November 30 had occurred. And, during this interval, on the eve of December 6, the Ministers learned, by reading of it in the newspapers, that a Franco-German declaration was going to be solemnly signed in the presence of . . . Ribbentrop, who had come specially for the purpose to Paris.

From that moment German intentions were plain. Our new Ambassador in Berlin, M. Coulondre, in a dispatch dated December 15, laid bare the German plan, which consisted of seizing the Ukraine. Was not this the plan contained in *Mein Kampf*?

As for the international guarantee, when M. Coulondre brought up this subject, he met on December 22 with the smiling refusal of Ribbentrop. 'Cannot this matter', said the latter, 'be forgotten? Is not the guarantee of the Reich sufficient?' The first rent in the Munich agreement was already made. Czechoslovakia was by now virtually reduced to a state of slavery. Ribbentrop informed Prague that Germany could not guarantee 'a State which would not liquidate Jews'. On February 18 the Reich made known its conditions. They were equivalent to complete enslavement.

On March 2 the Wilhelmstrasse told us that the affairs of Central Europe were no longer our concern. Seyss-Inquart and Burckel were sent into Slovakia to foment agitation in favour of independence. The German plan was to divide Czechoslovakia into three parts: Bohemia-Moravia, Slovakia and Ruthenia. Bohemia-Moravia was to be incorporated within the Reich; Slovakia to be declared independent, but placed under German protection; Ruthenia was to be shared between Hungary and Poland.

Monsignor Tiso, the President of Slovakia (which had been autonomous since Munich), demanded complete independence for his country. When he was dismissed by the central Government he appealed to Berlin. On March 14 the Wilhelmstrasse stated that it considered the Tiso Government as the only legal Government. M. Coulondre, in his dispatch of the 14th, described how the operation was to work: 'Action is being staged on the model of that for accomplishing the *Anschluss*, and perfected at the time of the crisis of last summer. . . . In the Berlin newspapers there are the same headlines as in August, 1938, and almost the same accounts.'

Hitler passed to action. On the afternoon of the 14th his troops began to penetrate into Czech territory. Let us reproduce at this point M. Coulondre's dispatch, dated the 16th: 'It was still necessary, however, to secure some semblance of justification, before giving marching orders to the troops ready to invade Czechoslovakia. M. Hacha, President of the Czechoslovak Republic, and M. Chvalkosky, Minister of Foreign Affairs, came to Berlin, where they were received by the

Führer. . . . In a brutal tone the Führer told them it was not a question of negotiations. The Czech statesmen were invited to take note of the decisions made by Berlin, and to acquiesce to them. The slightest inclination to the contrary would be checked. Any attempt to resist the march of German troops would be suppressed by action on the part of bomber aircraft. The Reich had decided to annex Bohemia and Moravia. Prague was to be occupied at ten o'clock the next day. President Hacha, advanced in years and in a serious physical state of health, collapsed and became unconscious. Goering's own physicians intervened and revived him with injections. The old man then signed the document handed to him, by which the Czech Government entrusted with full confidence the destinies of Bohemia and of Moravia into the hands of the Führer.

'On the . . . 15th at nine o'clock, the first motorized elements reached Prague. During the afternoon the Führer himself entered into the imperial castle of the Hradshin, and had the swastika hoisted immediately. Czechoslovakia had expired.

'On the next day a decree of the Führer incorporated Bohemia and Moravia within the territory of the Reich.'

Thus, added M. Coulondre, Munich was only, after all, a means for Hitler to 'disarm Czechoslovakia before annexing her'. And he concluded: 'Germany has shown . . . once again her contempt for any written pledge, and her preference for using brute force and accomplished fact. . . . It is practically the same thing as the morality to be found amongst gangsters and inhabitants of the jungle.'

On the 16th, Bonnet asked M. Corbin, our Ambassador in London, to emphasize to the British Government that an acceptance without protest of such a positive violation of the Munich agreement would lay open to suspicion the good faith with which Britain and France had, on September 29, pledged their word in a political settlement for the purpose of 'safeguarding at the very least the independence and integrity of a more homogeneous Czechoslovakia'.

On the 18th, Baron von Weizsaecker, Secretary of State at the Wilhelmstrasse, to whom (Ribbentrop being for the moment out of Berlin) M. Coulondre objected in the name of the French Government, swept aside this protest, invoking, our Ambassador wrote to Bonnet, 'the verbal assurances, which he alleged had been given in Paris by Your Excellency to Herr von Ribbentrop, at the time of signing the declaration of December 3, and according to which Czechoslovakia could not in the future constitute the subject of any exchange of views'.

On the 19th, Bonnet protested against the allegation of von Weizsaecker, which he declared 'extravagant', and expressed indignation against what he called 'a new proof of the bad faith of the German Government'. But the blow had been struck and no one had stirred a finger. The bastion of Central Europe was German: 'Who holds Bohemia holds Europe', Bismarck used to say.

The road to Warsaw was open.

Moreover, Germany was no longer making any mystery about her intentions. On the 15th, Gauleiter[1] Streicher, during a demonstration organized at Nuremberg, declared, when alluding to the entry of the Wehrmacht into Bohemia: 'This is only the beginning. . . . The democracies will jib against it to no purpose. In the end they will finally succumb.'

Hardly had Czechoslovakia been devoured than Poland felt the breath of the German wild beast on the back of her neck.

On January 26, Bonnet had stated in the Chamber of Deputies that France would honour her pledges to Poland if the latter were attacked. There was no need at all, in any case, to have a gift of divination to realize that Poland's turn was coming. In France, Rauschning's book *Hitler Speaks* (*Hitler m'a dit*) had just been published, in which Hitler stated his territorial claims against Poland. If she resisted: 'I shall always be able to fall back upon a new division.' Here was his grandiose plan: 'In the centre I shall place the steely core of a Greater Germany welded into an indissoluble unity. Then Austria, Bohemia, and Moravia, western Poland.'

On March 30, Ribbentrop summoned Warsaw to enter into negotiations on the Polish corridor, on Danzig, and, in general, on the policy of Poland towards the Axis. The rumour spread that Hitler was on the point of seizing Danzig.

On the 31st, Chamberlain, who felt that his pledged word had been betrayed, showed his teeth. Britain resolved to assist Poland with all her resources, if the latter thought her independence was threatened and considered her existence at stake. The angel of peace had become a lion. Hitler answered Chamberlain in a vehement speech: he would not allow himself to be intimidated or encircled; he would answer force with force.

On April 26, the Reich informed Poland of its views on Danzig. It denounced at the same time the German-Polish Agreement of 1934, and the naval agreement of 1935 with Britain.

On May 11, Chamberlain stated that any attempt to modify by force the *status quo* of Danzig would run into the armed opposition of Britain. Daladier made a similar declaration, and Bonnet repeated to Ribbentrop the determination of France to support Poland, if it was necessary, by force of arms.

On March 22, Germany and Italy signed a treaty of military alliance:

---

[1] *Gau*, district: this is a word which Hitlerian language used to denote the territorial divisions of Germany, as the Nazi régime had defined them. *Leiter*, chief. *Gauleiter*, Governor in the Nazi sense of the word.

it was the pact of steel. On the next day Hitler informed his entourage of his resolution to attack Poland at the first opportunity.

On April 3 the Wehrmacht received the order to take up its positions with a view to the future opening of hostilities against this country. The Army was to be prepared to enter into hostilities with Poland by August 25. Keitel had on this matter stressed the necessity, if this came about, for not beginning the campaign later than September 1, because of climatic conditions.

Events followed each other in rapid succession. In any case each side had clearly defined its respective attitude. If, as Hitler's propaganda claimed, Danzig must at all costs be united with the Reich, the latter ran the risk, this time, of no longer finding scared sheep opposing her path.

APRIL–AUGUST, 1939: FRANCO-ANGLO-SOVIET NEGOTIATIONS; THE HITLER-STALIN AGREEMENT; THE WATERLOO OF FRENCH DIPLOMACY

Chamberlain had, at last, opened his eyes. He understood this time that Britain could no longer avoid fighting. It was, therefore, important for his country and for France to win without delay the collaboration of Powers who were strong in a military sense. Chamberlain naturally thought of Russia. He considered there was no doubt that she would enter the camp of Hitler's opponents. On March 19, Moscow had indeed protested to Berlin against the seizure of Prague. Chamberlain, therefore, took the initiative by asking France to join with Britain in a proposal to the Soviets and to Poland that the Four Powers should sign a declaration, pledging themselves to draw up in common measures suitable to check this new danger to the political independence of a European country.

On April 9, Easter Day itself, Gamelin, on a tour of inspection in the Alps, was urgently recalled to Paris. Bonnet had demanded the summoning of the Permanent Committee for National Defence[1] to examine amongst other things the problem of the Allies' military collaboration with Russia. Daladier, who on several occasions had said to Gamelin that he considered a military *rapprochement* with Russia impossible for political reasons, agreed. Accompanied by Bonnet, he

[1] The Committee had met on February 24 'to examine measures to be taken in North Africa following Italian preparations'. During the deliberations, whose minutes Gamelin publishes in his book *Servir* (vol. II, pp. 391–401), Daladier, who was presiding, made the following statement: 'Germany is in the fifth year of her production of equipment. We, in France, only began in 1937. . . . Thus, we are only in our second year. This is a situation which we must take into account. If hostilities break out in Europe, we shall be inferior in aviation and anti-aircraft. But we shall possess a superiority on land and sea. If we get through the summer of 1939 without war breaking out, we shall have nothing more to fear from the point of view of aircraft, for we shall have regained in that sphere what we have lost. In 1940, our output of material will be considerable.'

presided in person over the meeting, which took precedence of every-thing else in the afternoon of Easter Day. The minutes of the meeting,[1] the importance of which it would be idle to insist upon, were as follows: 'M. Georges Bonnet opened with a rapid account of the diplomatic . . . circumstances. There is no doubt . . . about Britain, who is fully pledged from the diplomatic point of view, and will follow us in military matters. Poland still refuses to enter into any discussions with the Soviets. . . . M. Bonnet has, therefore, adopted a new formula, asking the Soviets to indicate to France what she can do to help Poland and Roumania; her proposals will then be submitted by France to the two . . . interested countries. Discussions on this subject will be begun without delay by our diplomatic representative in Moscow. M. Bonnet will also ask our Military Attaché to have talks on the matter with Marshal Voroshilov. These steps were decided upon.'

Negotiations began in Moscow through diplomatic channels. On April 17 Russia defined her views. She proposed a pact for mutual aid and a military convention between the three Powers.[2] The *casus fœderis* was to apply to any threat to the present state either in Central or Eastern Europe. The Kremlin thus intended that the joint guarantee of the three Powers should cover indiscriminately all countries between the Baltic and the Black Seas, whether or not they were party to it. The question of including the Baltic States, Finland, Estonia, Latvia and Lithuania, was, therefore, expressly raised by Russia. Was it necessary to include them in the scheme against their wishes? Discussions on this point dragged on to the end of June. Hardly was this obstacle overcome on July 2 than another debatable subject came up. The Soviet Government demanded on the next day the exclusion of the Netherlands, Luxembourg and Switzerland from the list of countries covered by the joint guarantee. It also wanted 'indirect' aggression to be treated in the same way as direct, that is to say (according to the Soviet's own definition), any political upheaval occurring in the domestic situation of any of the countries concerned, which would be favourable to any armed attack of the aggressor. Finally, the Soviets asked for the validity of the politi-cal agreement to be subordinated to that of the military convention. It was only on July 23 that, with minor reservations on secondary points, the agreement was at last settled. But the bargaining had been so laborious, had taken place in such an atmosphere of mistrust, that relations between the three Powers, far from becoming improved, ended in being if anything more embittered.

In such an atmosphere were to begin the by far the most difficult negotiations for the military convention. The French Ambassador on July 24 informed Molotov of the approaching arrival of the

[1] Gamelin, *op. cit.*, vol. II, p. 406.   [2] France, Britain and Russia.

Military Mission, to the head of which Daladier had just nominated
General Doumenc. The next day the British Ambassador announced
to Molotov the designation of a British Mission. Bonnet remarks[1] that
Molotov expressed his satisfaction: 'It is understood that our military
experts will arrive in about a week, M. Molotov (our Ambassador
telegraphed on the 24th) having stated, in addition, that a delay of
eight to ten days would suit him equally.' In actual fact the two
Missions did not hurry themselves about setting out for Moscow.
Potiemkin[2] reproached them for their delay in the following words:
'The Missions were in no hurry to leave. . . . They only began to
stir themselves eleven days later.[3] Moreover, they refused to travel
by air (and) . . . embarked in a passenger-cargo boat,[4] whose speed
did not exceed thirteen knots. . . . They took six days . . . to get to
Moscow.'

Actually the Missions arrived in Moscow on the morning of the 11th.
The conference opened on the 12th. General Doumenc, accompanied
by a general of the Air Force and an admiral, represented our country
at it. His duty, such as it was laid down by the order which Daladier
had himself signed, gave him powers to 'treat with the High Command
of the Soviet armed forces in all questions which related to the collaboration that ought to take place between the military forces of the
two countries'. Britain was represented by Admiral Drax, who himself
had no written authority. He was accompanied by General Heywood.
The Soviet delegation was very imposing. Heading it was Marshal
Voroshilov who, from 1924, had been at the head of the War Department. Associated with him were the Commanders-in-Chief of the
Navy and Air Force, and General Shaposhnikov, Chief of General
Staff of the Red Army. Voroshilov was empowered to conclude and
sign military agreements to ensure peace and provide for action against
an aggressor.

At the very first meeting[5] Voroshilov protested against the insufficient powers possessed by the Allied delegations. He agreed, however,
to pass on to an examination of the problem to be discussed: 'We
have', he said, 'a complete plan, with figures. Have the British and
French delegations any?' They had nothing of the kind, so preoccupied
were they, above all, writes Doumenc, with not 'going beyond what
was suitable to be revealed'.

---

[1] *Défense de la paix: II. Fin d'une Europe*, pp. 202–3.   [2] Potiemkin, *op. cit.*, vol. III, p. 707.
[3] August 6.   [4] The *City of Exeter*.
[5] The version which I am giving of these negotiations is based on the account of
Doumenc (*Carrefour*, May 21, 1947) and his statement of February 16, 1948, at Lille
(*Le Monde*, February 17, 1948); the unpublished report of Captain Beaufre, a member
of the Doumenc Mission; Gamelin, *Servir*, vol. II, pp. 443–61, *passim*; Nöel, *op. cit,*,
pp. 420–30; Potiemkin, *op. cit.*, vol. III, pp. 707–10; Bonnet, *Fin d'une Europe*, pp. 275–94;
the deposition of Daladier, May 29, 1947, before the Committee of Inquiry; *Falsifiers of
History*, a publication (previously mentioned) of the Soviet Government.

Doumenc contented himself, therefore, with optimistic generalities on the state of the French Army. This attitude obviously antagonized Voroshilov, who, in the words of an eyewitness, from whom, M. Noël declared, he obtained them, 'answered him with an insolent haughtiness that his statement did not mean anything'. Voroshilov stated that the Soviet Union was ready to place in the line against the aggressor a hundred and twenty infantry divisions, sixteen cavalry divisions, five thousand heavy and medium cannon, about ten thousand armoured vehicles, large and small, more than five thousand fighter aircraft, etc. . . . The British stated that at the beginning of hostilities they could throw into battle five infantry divisions and a motorized division. Doumenc said that the Germans, if they attacked in the East, would only leave some forty divisions facing the West. With reference to the Polish Army, the British declared that, in the opinion of the British General Staff, it was destined, if it relied solely on its own strength, to be crushed in a fortnight. Voroshilov did not fail to take a solemn note of this information, the value of which he was careful not to dispute. Finally the Russians insisted on their need to occupy a certain number of naval bases in Estonia. Admiral Drax could not, on hearing this claim, 'suppress a sudden start'. The Allied Missions evaded the problem.

The conference now tackled the essential question, the one which Voroshilov declared to be of supreme importance. Were Poland and Roumania prepared to allow Russian troops to enter their territory? Voroshilov had raised the problem on the 13th at the end of the sitting. The following day he brought it up more forcibly. 'I want', he said, in substance, 'an unequivocal reply. If the two countries, in question, call Russia in to help them when it is too late, their Armies will be destroyed, and Russia will not be able to bring the Allies any useful assistance.' Voroshilov, therefore, asked that, as soon as hostilities began, the Soviet troops should be able to enter Poland in the Vilna corridor and in Galicia, as well as into Roumanian territory, that is to say, into the zones where their strategy required the advance of their forces. He considered, moreover, that the problem would be the same if Germany began by an attack against France instead of against the East.

The subject was too important for Gamelin, well placed as he was to know the feelings of Poland, to ignore in his instructions. After having recommended to Doumenc that he should try to avoid allowing the Russians to raise the subject, he confined himself to giving an opinion that probably the Poles would consent, when the hour of danger came, to placing bases at the disposal of Red aircraft and perhaps even permitting mechanized units on their territory. But he thought that 'the possibility of their opening their frontiers to all types of Russian forces was improbable'.

On the 14th, there was, in the words of Doumenc, a dramatic sitting. The conference was imperilled. 'The British', writes Doumenc, 'thought that the conference had reached a deadlock; the French that it was essential to come to a clearer understanding.' The two Missions tried to postpone consideration of the difficulty. Voroshilov would not budge from the position he had taken up. He wanted a straight answer. Without this 'the continuation of our discussions', he said, 'would be useless'. Doumenc continues: 'It was a formal summons that something should be done. The two Missions replied by reading a Note which had been rapidly drawn up, but whose words had been well weighed. . . . As Poland and Roumania were sovereign States, their Governments were the appropriate bodies to sanction this authorization. It was a political problem to be settled by Governments! The Missions could refer it back to Paris and London. . . . The Soviet delegation asked for a suspension of the sitting. . . . Again this was put forward by the reading of a written Note, this time by the Soviet delegation. It restated the problem which had arisen, recognized that it was a political one, and asked for it to be settled through the intermediary of the Western nations. Failing a definite reply, the discussions would receive a set-back.' That very evening Doumenc telegraphed to Paris information about the state of the talks. The British Mission, in its turn, gave London the details.

Bonnet discussed matters on the 15th with the Polish Ambassador. He writes:[1] 'I immediately informed him of what was happening. . . . Beck should accept the entry of Russian infantry into Poland, if war were to break out. Failing this, anything was to be feared, including even a German-Russian understanding directed against Warsaw. M. Lukasiewicz replied: "M. Beck will never agree to letting the Russians occupy the territory which we took from them in 1921. As a Frenchman, would you consent to entrust Alsace-Lorraine to the protection of the Germans?"

'"Certainly not," I said, "but don't forget that you have two great Powers as neighbours, both in the East and West. You are now engaged in a trial of strength with Germany, a trial which obliges you to win the support of the Soviets. Three days ago Hitler stated to M. Burckhardt that, within three weeks, he would defeat Poland with his mechanized army of whose strength you have not the slightest conception.

'"On the other hand, it will be the Polish Army which will invade Germany at the outset of hostilities.

'"I sincerely hope that this will be so. . . . But, in the meantime, reply immediately and in the affirmative to the Soviet request. We believe this is of capital importance, for on the success of our negotiations depends peace or war."

[1] *Défense de la paix: II. Fin d'une Europe*, pp. 277–8.

8

'The Ambassador promised me to deliver my request faithfully to Warsaw, but he gave me to understand that Beck's reply would almost certainly be in the negative.

'My conversation with the Ambassador had left me with only a feeble hope. I saw Daladier immediately, and it was agreed that General Musse,[1] who was in Paris, should leave the very same day "in order to approach the Polish General Staff". I immediately asked M. Noël in Warsaw, to support our move.'

On the 17th, the conference adjourned until the 21st. Voroshilov asked for the postponement. The 18th is a bank holiday in Russia, and on the 19th and 20th the Marshal was occupied with other duties. Doumenc, who had asked Paris for authority to send General Valin to Warsaw in order to negotiate, but had received, on the 16th, a refusal on this point, pressed Paris to agree to the Soviet view. He ended his telegram of the 17th with these words: 'To sum up, we note a marked desire not "to be mere observers", but, quite on the contrary, to take as active a part as possible. . . . The U.S.S.R. wants a military pact. . . . She does not want us to give her a piece of paper without substantial undertakings. Marshal Voroshilov has stated that all the problems . . . would be tackled without any difficulty as soon as what he termed the crucial question was settled.'

The decisive moves were to be made in Warsaw. M. Noël and General Musse took the first steps on the 18th. But their attempts met with obduracy on the part of the Poles. The Ambassador telegraphed on the same day to the Quai d'Orsay: 'After having consulted my British colleague, who has received instructions to support my representations and who will see the Minister this afternoon, I have just had a long discussion with M. Beck, whilst General Musse was talking with General Stackiewicz. . . . Whilst making the proviso that he would give me a definite answer tomorrow morning or rather this evening, the Minister has formulated a series of objections of which the following is the gist:

'1. If Poland joined in the proposed alliance, Germany would be informed immediately—the Russians themselves would take good care to tell her—and war would be inevitable.

'2. From the start of the Moscow negotiations begun by France and Britain, the Soviet Government has been manœuvring to make Poland responsible for their failure.'

The last complaint, of which the first two are really only the premises, is worth stressing, for it is symptomatic of the belief held in Warsaw in the duplicity of the Kremlin. The Kremlin, if Beck is to be believed, had neither the intention nor means of keeping the military

[1] Our Military Attaché in Warsaw.

pledges which it said that it was willing to give. The conditions to which the Kremlin wished to subordinate these pledges, he averred, only had the object of allowing it to obtain securities of a political nature.

M. Noël none the less answered his interlocutor on the points which he made:

'1. On the first point, that his reasoning would lose its validity with the strengthening of the peace front . . . that the collaboration of the U.S.S.R., even though it were limited, would certainly, on the contrary, increase the chances of peace, and that, if it were to turn out otherwise, Chancellor Hitler would not manage the U.S.S.R. . . . as he appeared to do so several months previously.

'2. That, if there were any manœuvring on part of the U.S.S.R., the best reply was for Poland to accept. . . .

'3. That, since the rulers of Poland, if war did break out, seemed henceforth to have the intention of entering into discussions with the Soviet authorities to lay down conditions for military collaboration (to which they no longer seemed hostile in principle), it would be infinitely wiser to join in the proposed alliance. They have at the present time the freedom to voice opinions, which they would risk losing under the pressure of events, and the conditions under which the Moscow discussions would be conducted by the Franco-British delegation would ensure for Poland both in the present and future the best possible guarantees.'

On the 19th, Beck gave a definite reply, after having consulted with Smigly-Rydz: 'I do not admit', he said to M. Noël, 'that there can be any kind of discussion whatsoever concerning the use of part of our territory by foreign troops. It is a matter of principle for us. We have not got a military agreement with the U.S.S.R. We do not want to have one.' General Musse and his British colleague tried for their part, as M. Noël also telegraphed on the 19th, 'to overcome the objections of General Stackiewicz, to find with him a compromise and to obtain agreement that the question should at least remain in suspense'. It was all in vain. 'General Stackiewicz', added the Ambassador, 'incessantly invoked one of the watchwords bequeathed by Pilsudski, in other words the dogma: Poland cannot agree to foreign troops entering her territory. This principle, once hostilities have begun, will not have, it is true, the same value.'

On the 20th M. Naggiar, our Ambassador at Moscow, in his turn, urged Paris to 'give a general affirmative reply to the Russian delegation with the object of speeding up the military negotiations.' And he stressed the need for authorizing Doumenc to 'discuss and sign as common interests best demanded, with the reservation that definitive approval must be gained from the Government'.

For his part, Doumenc sent on his own initiative one of his colleagues, Captain Beaufre, to Warsaw, with the mission of influencing the Poles. The reply of Smigly-Rydz was both imaginative and disillusioned: 'If Poland were to fall under the German yoke, she would lose her body; if she fell under that of Russia, she would lose her soul.' The next day he came round to agreeing that the Allied Missions should be allowed to discuss the problem with Voroshilov, but without permitting them to sanction any pledges on his part.

Faced with this stubbornness on the part of Warsaw, Daladier decided to try a last effort. On the morning of the 21st, he summoned M. Lukasiewicz. Since Poland was frightened of seeing Russia profit by any permission which might be given to her to send her troops into the Vilna corridor and the Lemberg area, to install herself there, why, asked Daladier of the Ambassador, should the operation not be supervised by a Franco-British Mission? Could not this Mission take care that the Red Army would not take advantage of the circumstances to get a foothold in the country? 'I added', Daladier stated before the Committee of Inquiry, 'that the situation seemed to me so grave that, if we were determined . . . to avoid war, we had to conclude a military pact, which was the only form of compulsion capable of making Hitler hesitate and reflect. I observed he (M. Lukasiewicz) ought to warn his Government with the utmost speed . . . and that, if, during the afternoon, I had not received a negative reply from him before the end of the afternoon, I would myself telegraph to General Doumenc the authority to sign a military convention with Russia. I gave London a picture of the state of negotiations at the beginning of the afternoon . . . and the British Government expressed itself in agreement with me. It sent at about the same time as ourselves . . . to the British delegation . . . the same telegram as I then sent to General Doumenc. . . . The General only received this telegram, which I had dispatched at quarter past four in the afternoon, at ten o'clock in the evening. It was the first time that a coded cable had taken such a long time to go from Paris to Moscow. Generally, the average time was three hours; this telegram was thus held up *en route* or elsewhere for six hours. . . . Its message was formal and explicit: "You are authorized to sign, in the best interests of all and with the agreement of our Ambassador, a military convention, with the reservation that it must receive the approval of the French Government."'

But the conference had resumed its discussions during the day. Voroshilov, who observed that the Allied delegations had no reply to give to the query which Moscow considered required a preliminary settlement, proposed the adjournment *sine die* of the negotiations. The delegations protested against this proposal: the Soviet delegation could not be ignorant that the problem under examination was of a political nature and that its solution required of necessity some time, but nothing stood in the way of the conference continuing its task while waiting. Voroshilov, after having taken some time to reflect on these considerations, replied with the following Note: 'The intention of the Soviet Military Mission is and remains that of finding an agreement with the British and French Missions on the practical organization as to how the military forces of the three countries can co-operate. As the U.S.S.R. has no common frontier with Germany, she cannot help France, Britain, Roumania and Poland unless her troops have permission to pass through Polish and Roumanian territory, since there is no other way to establish contact with the aggressor. . . . The Soviet Mission does not understand why the French and British General Staffs have not already settled this problem.' The telegram by which Doumenc gave an account of the meeting reached Paris, stresses Bonnet[1] on the 21st at ten thirty-two in the evening, or more than six hours after the dispatch of Daladier's instructions to our Mission.

On the 22nd, Doumenc, primed with his new instructions, attempted to resume negotiations with Voroshilov. In agreement with M. Naggiar and with the British Mission, he informed the Marshal in good time, first by telephone and then by letter, that he was in a position to answer in the affirmative the question which was in suspense. He therefore asked for the discussions to be resumed as quickly as possible, and if possible, in the afternoon. Voroshilov's response was delayed: it only came at six-thirty in the evening, and merely asked Doumenc to come along to see him. The interview took place. A new condition was put forward: the consent of Poland and Roumania was no longer sufficient; it must be accompanied by a corresponding assurance from France. Once Russia had been satisfied on this point, the drawing up of the Pact would take hardly any time. Naturally, added the Marshal, this was conditional on 'the political circumstances remaining unchanged'. Doumenc listened: how could he not be struck by this reservation, which was all the more unexpected because Voroshilov used it as an argument to justify the necessity of postponing the next meeting for a few days. And the telegram in which Doumenc gave an account of the interview ends with this remark. 'From all appearances [the Marshal] is following out orders.'

The version which Captain Beaufre gives of the interview is more full. According to this officer, Voroshilov gave free expression to his complaints, namely: the eleven days' complete waste of time in negotiations; the still unsettled problem of military co-operation with France, which had been under discussion for years and was still no nearer a solution; the rancour of Russia at the time of Munich when she was only awaiting a signal from France to go to the help of the

[1] *Défense de la paix: II. Fin d'une Europe*, p. 285 (1).

dying Czechoslovakia; the tergiversations of France and Britain in prolonging the course of both the present political and military discussions. Finally his decisive argument was: how could it be admitted that Poland and Roumania were really consenting parties to the passage of the Russian Army through their territories when they did not even ask to be present at the discussions.'

All this recital of complaints, detailed one after the other, was designed to prepare the way for a sibylline, awkward conclusion: one could not be surprised if this shilly-shallying had promoted the development of certain political happenings. The Marshal did not clarify any further what he meant by this, but left his colleagues in the discussions the prey to a perplexity which was soon, it is true, to be dissipated. The veil of mystery with which Voroshilov discreetly clothed his words was, indeed, to be torn aside. The dénouement was imminent.

For his part, M. Naggiar saw Molotov. He telegraphed at twelve minutes past midnight on the night of the 22nd-23rd.[1] 'M. Molotov has stated that, at the outset of the meetings of the military delegations, the Russian Mission had been extremely surprised to note that no one was able to supply a reply to the question of the passage of Russian troops for the purpose of making contact with the aggressor. It was only after becoming convinced that nothing positive could be expected on this matter that the U.S.S.R. had accepted the German proposal to negotiate a treaty of non-aggression, and to receive a visit from Herr von Ribbentrop, the initiative for which came from Berlin. I have naturally protested vigorously against . . . the exchange of these views. I have stated, moreover, that I did not clearly perceive the relations between cause and effect, and, moreover, that, upon the problem of troops passing over the frontiers, General Doumenc had been able, in the afternoon of the present day itself, to give Marshal Voroshilov an affirmative reply. . . .

'. . . Regarding the passage of Russian troops, M. Molotov observed that our reply had arrived unfortunately after the visit of Herr von Ribbentrop had been agreed upon; also, he said that the British were not associated with it, and finally that it did not seem that the Poles had consented to it. . . . General Doumenc has given a report of his interview with Marshal Voroshilov. He bears out, in general, my conversation with M. Molotov.'

The Allies had lost the game. On the 21st, during the evening, the official agency of the Reich announced the imminent departure of Ribbentrop for Moscow. On the 22nd, similarly in the evening, the Tass Agency took up, in its turn, the news: 'After the conclusion of the German-Soviet . . . commercial agreement, the question of bettering

---

[1] The dispatch arrived at its destination at four o'clock in the morning of the 23rd.

political relations between Germany and the Soviets was discussed. An exchange of views which took place on this problem . . . has revealed the desire of both parties to diminish the tension in their mutual relations, to banish the threat of war and to conclude a pact of non-aggression.' On the 23rd, in the middle of the day, Ribbentrop, accompanied by an imposing retinue, landed at Moscow aerodrome. That very evening the Hitler-Stalin agreement was signed.

Whilst consternation was reigning in Paris and London, M. Noël telegraphed on the 22nd that 'Beck is quite unperturbed, and does not seem in the slightest worried by this anti-climax. He believes that, in substance, very little has been changed. He observes that, when the Soviet Government brought up the question, as it did, of military collaboration, it knew in advance what Warsaw's reaction would be, and it was preparing the ground to use this as a pretext to break off its negotiations with France after having dragged them out as much as possible.' The same day M. Naggiar telegraphed from Moscow: 'My Polish colleague looks at things with an optimistic eye. He thinks that the German offer and Ribbentrop's visit prove that the Reich is in a desperate situation.'

One remains baffled by such unshakeable blindness. The French Government, however, refused to believe that such a reversal in Russian policy could be effectively implemented. The Council of Ministers discussed the question during the afternoon of the 22nd. It was decided, on Daladier's proposal, notes Jean Zay in his *Carnets* (p. 62) to call upon Warsaw to consent to the passage of Russian forces. Gamelin, who saw Daladier at ten o'clock in the evening, when the Council had risen, notes:[1] 'He [Daladier] told me that he detected two currents of opinion: Paul Reynaud, Mandel on the one hand . . . and on the other Bonnet, Chautemps . . . "the peace-at-any-price brigade".' Bonnet immediately instructed M. Noël about the comminatory step which had just been adopted. He told him to see immediately either Beck or Smigly-Rydz. At ten-thirty in the evening he telegraphed in this strain to our Ambassador: 'Faced with this new perspective which has been created by the announcement of the imminent signing of a German-Soviet Pact . . . the only possible reply lies in the immediate delegation by the Polish Government itself of full powers, which will authorize General Doumenc to go a long way on behalf of Poland with a view to the sole eventuality of a war in which Russia would come to Poland's assistance.' Similarly, on the 23rd, Daladier asked Doumenc to urge Moscow to 'remain in the camp of those who are united against aggression, and to conclude urgently a military agreement on the basic minima of what could be immediately achieved'. M. Noël discharged at once the step laid down. Through

[1] Gamelin, *op. cit.*, vol. II, p. 445.

his insistence, he succeeded in partially overcoming Beck's opposition, and in forcing from Beck the following statement, which was handed to him at the end of the afternoon: 'The Polish Government agrees that General Doumenc can use the following language: "We have become convinced that, in case of common action against German aggression, a collaboration between Poland and the U.S.S.R. in technical circumstances to be determined, is not excluded (or, is possible). The British and French General Staffs consider, therefore, that there are grounds for studying immediately all possible means for collaboration."' This telegram arrived at the Quai d'Orsay on the 23rd at six o'clock in the evening, but M. Noël had taken precautions, before even sending it to Paris, to entrust General Musse with the duty of communicating its contents to Doumenc with the utmost urgency. Even if it had not been too late, the concession to which Beck resigned himself *in extremis* would have far from satisfied the Soviet demands. Bonnet's testimony agrees with that of M. Noël. The first-named writes:[1] 'The Soviet Military Delegation would certainly not be satisfied with this statement. They require a reply from Poland herself about the "passage of troops", and Beck continued to observe a silence on this matter.' M. Noël states:[2] 'All that I could get the Minister of Foreign Affairs to concede—and this almost unhoped for result showed the strength of Polish uneasiness about their Western frontier— was that, once hostilities were begun, Poland probably would not evade a new examination of the problem, nor refuse to consider the eventuality of Polish-Soviet co-operation. For the present . . . Beck held, in a most categoric fashion, to his former point of view.'

Whilst this rearguard battle was being fought, Ribbentrop was at the Kremlin. He was only to leave it with an agreement in his pocket. The terms of this agreement were published by the Department of State in *Nazi-Soviet Relations during the Years 1939-41*. It comprised a Treaty of non-aggression, which was merely the cloak for two additional secret protocols. Of these, the first provided for the delimitation of zones of influence between the two partners. Within the sphere of Russia's influence was allotted Finland, Estonia, Latvia and Bessarabia, and within that of Germany, Lithuania. The second protocol provided for the annexation by Russia of Polish territory situated to the east of a line which was approximately determined by the course of the rivers, Narev, Vistula and San.[3] The question of Poland's survival as an

---

[1] Bonnet, *op. cit.*, p. 296.   [2] Noël, *op. cit.*, p. 423.

[3] On September 19, 1939, Molotov informed the German Ambassador to Moscow, Count Frederick von Schulenburg, that the Soviet Government, renouncing its first intention of allowing an independent Poland to exist, wished for the liquidation of this State, and consequently the distribution between Germany and Russia of the territories which constituted it. On the 20th he suggested the negotiation in Moscow of a definite settlement of the Polish question. It formed the subject of a new Treaty which Ribbentrop signed on the 28th, and which, taking cognizance of the collapse of Poland,

independent State, within frontiers to be laid down, was reserved for future settlement.

The negotiations had taken place, it must be admitted, in an atmosphere free of prejudices, Ribbentrop has stated in substance at the Nuremberg trial: 'Stalin was not slow in giving me to understand that there was no question of settling the German-Soviet dispute in the spirit of the Briand-Kellogg Pact, but that, if Russia were not to get out of the negotiations the Baltic countries and half of Poland, I had better take my leave.' Ribbentrop showed that he understood the situation. The discussions went on late into the night of the 23rd to 24th at the Kremlin. Stalin, Molotov and Ribbentrop dined and drank there in company. They talked freely to each other. Stalin said, according to the German report, that the British Army was weak, that the British Navy no longer merited its former reputation, that the British Air Force was lacking in pilots, that British hegemony in the world only rested on the bluff of Britain and the stupidity of other countries. But he added: 'Britain, in spite of her weakness, will make war with skill and tenacity.' He said that France possessed an army 'worthy of consideration'. He was ironical about the anti-Comintern Pact, which had only served to frighten the City of London and the British shopkeepers. Finally he wished to drink the Führer's health.

The only thing left for the Allied delegations was to take their leave. On the 24th, the leaders of the two Missions asked for an audience with Voroshilov. They were received at one o'clock in the afternoon of the next day. Each of them was accompanied by the Military Attaché of his Embassy. M. Naggiar gives an account of the interview in these words: 'In the name of his Government, Marshal Voroshilov said that Franco-Anglo-Russian negotiations could serve no further object in the political situation which now existed. Nevertheless, he confirmed the pacific intentions of his Government, and no doubt out of courtesy he expressed a wish, particularly to General Doumenc, that one day a contact would again be established, when the political situation permitted it.' M. Naggiar was received, in his turn, the same day by Molotov. The latter expressed his regret at the failure of the

---

sanctioned its disappearance and division. This time it was a *Treaty of Friendship*. This Treaty itself was supplemented by *additional secret protocols*. The first provided for the exchange of the nationals of each of the parties, who were residing in territories placed under the jurisdiction of the other. The second handed over Lithuania, except for a strip bordering on East Prussia, to the Russian zone of influence, and by way of compensation the province of Lublin and part of the province of Warsaw to the zone of German influence. The third pledged the two parties to suppress any Polish agitation in their respective territories. A joint declaration stressed the conviction of the two Powers that it would be in the interests of all peoples to see an end put to the war ... between Germany on the one hand and Britain and France on the other. Finally, the two Governments pledged themselves to encourage their commercial relations. Thus was sealed the alliance between Moscow and Berlin. The Soviet Union affirmed that it considered the existence of a strong Germany to be to her interest.

negotiations, but threw the responsibility for this on Poland, who, in spite of the three Governments' efforts, had persisted in refusing military assistance from Russia. 'A great country like the U.S.S.R. could not', he said to the Ambassador, 'go as far as begging Poland to accept the help… which she did not desire at any price.' As for the Franco-Soviet Pact of May 2, 1935, Molotov stated to M. Naggiar that nothing in the Treaty which the Soviet Union had just signed with Germany prevented it from continuing to be effective. He stressed the fact, however, that 'deprived of all concrete means of application because of the lack of a military convention, this Pact would retain its innocuous character'. When giving an account of this interview, M. Naggiar added: 'I took a verbal note that the Treaty was still considered as effective by the U.S.S.R.'

Such is the story of these negotiations. Were not Molotov's words to our Ambassador sufficient to make plain the gravity of the mistake committed by those who, since 1935, had obstinately turned a deaf ear to the repeated entreaties of Moscow, which had the object of defining in writing the military obligations stemming from the Franco-Soviet Pact? Was it not we who, through our indifference, had condemned the promise of mutual aid, which was the object of the Pact, to remain a dead letter?

How had it thus come about that the Allies allowed Russia to turn aside from them in order to make common cause with Hitler? Albert Mousset who, amongst our historians, is one of the most knowledgeable in Slav matters, did not hesitate to reproach[1] Franco-British diplomacy for having revealed a 'complete misunderstanding of the spirit and aims of Soviet policy', and for having thus assisted the Führer's game in relation to Stalin. The latter, indeed, was not unaware that, to repeat the words of Maurice Baumont,[2] 'there is no lack of politicians either in Britain or France, who would be delighted to see Russia at grips with German ambitions . . . and who would permit full liberty of action to the Germans in the East'. Stalin, at the eighteenth Congress of the Communist Party of the U.S.S.R. (March 10–11, 1939), reproached Britain and France because of their apathy, when faced with a revival of the policy of aggression. He added that Russia ought not to allow herself to be dragged into conflicts in which other nations would try to get her to pull the chestnuts out of the fire. On May 4, Litvinov, a Russian Jew married to an Englishwoman, and who had the reputation, continued Baumont, of being very European-minded, was suddenly dismissed from the post of Foreign Minister.

Germany was obviously going to take full advantage of this suspicious mistrust of the Kremlin. In spite of the hostility which she paraded against Bolshevism, she had always taken care not to compromise

[1] *Histoire de Russie*, p. 300.   [2] *La faillite de la paix*, pp. 756–7.

irretrievably her relations with Moscow. At the beginning of 1938, Berlin had, indeed, proposed to the Soviet Government the opening of commercial negotiations. The two parties broke off negotiations as they were not able to come to an understanding. Towards the end of that year, Germany tried again, and renewed her proposals. Negotiations were resumed at Moscow. Shortly afterwards, there was a new interruption. It was only a brief one this time for Berlin, if we are to place any faith in the statements which were made on March 9, 1946, by Ribbentrop at the Nuremberg trial, had made new approaches to Moscow at the beginning of March, 1939.

Negotiations were then begun, upon which the above-mentioned publication of the Department of State has thrown some light. On April 17 the Russian Ambassador to Germany, Merekalov, who had been accredited to Berlin for about a year, paid his first visit to the Wilhelmstrasse. He went to discuss with Weizsaecker a problem of a technical nature, but he soon dropped this subject to tackle the question of political relations between the two countries. Russia, he stated in substance to his partner in the discussion, had no reason not to maintain normal relations with Germany. Shortly afterwards, Molotov himself informed Schulenburg that the resumption of economic negotiations between the two countries presupposed an agreement between these two on 'the political basis' which such a resumption implied. Hitler listened, but he was still on his guard. The negotiations between the Allies and the Kremlin were indeed in full swing. Was not Moscow trying perchance to obtain new concessions from Britain and France by threatening them with entering into negotiations with Berlin? But the Soviet Government busied itself in reassuring Nazi diplomacy. To this end, the Russians were to use as an intermediary the Bulgarian Legation at Berlin. They let it be understood that their keenest desire was to come to an agreement with Germany. The Bulgarians did not keep this confidence to themselves. They immediately unbosomed themselves to people around Hitler. The ice was broken for the future. On July 27, important Russian personages came to Berlin for talks with Schnurre, who was entrusted by the German Government with economic relations with Eastern Europe. The discussions remained focused on the resumption of commercial negotiations. They continued late into the night, and did not waste time in digressing upon political problems. The Russians made inquiries into the future of the Baltic countries. As for Poland, they had no doubt, they said, that, 'in one way or another' Danzig would return to Germany, and that the question of the Polish corridor would also be settled to the satisfaction of the Reich.

To these overtures, however discreet they were, Hitler lent a complaisant ear. Did they not provide him with the means of ridding himself of the 'nightmare' of a war on two fronts? On August 14, the Führer took the initiative in letting the Kremlin know that the progress of the German-Polish crisis required the rapid adjustment of German-Russian relations and that, for his part, he had no intention of aiming any blow at Soviet interests in Eastern Europe. Ribbentrop was ready to go to Moscow in order to explain the views of his master before Stalin. Molotov left this overture without reply for four days. Hitler felt nervous. On the 18th, Schulenburg was received by Molotov; he found him well disposed. On the 20th, Hitler took the initiative. He wrote Stalin a personal letter in which he begged him to receive Ribbentrop. A reply came from Stalin by the next day: he would expect Ribbentrop. Molotov put in Schulenburg's hands the proposed terms of the non-aggression Pact. On the 22nd, Ribbentrop was received with great ceremony in Moscow.

In *The Falsifiers of History*, the Kremlin defends itself against the charge of having deceived the Allies. The Soviet Government advances in justification the shilly-shallying of the Allies, Poland's refusal to permit the Red Army to enter into her territory, the paucity (which it terms as 'derisory') of the ground forces which Britain was putting into the line, in order to justify in its turn the accusation that Britain and France were guilty of duplicity. 'The treacherous plan of Anglo-French policy', thus runs the publication, 'was to give Hitler the impression that the U.S.S.R. was isolated, that Hitler could attack the U.S.S.R. without running the risk of meeting any opposition from Britain and France. . . . The Western Powers . . . were proposing . . . to wreck the discussions. The truth is that, at the same time as they were publicly negotiating with the Soviets, *the British were, behind the scenes, conducting with Germany discussions to which they attached an infinitely greater value.*'[1]

Let us finish with this lamentable controversy. Let us confine ourselves to noting that the negotiations in Moscow were undertaken in a spirit of mistrust for which the attitude of Britain and France towards Hitler before the Prague coup sufficed to account. Both had snapped their fingers at Russian help when it was offered to them. When, finally, they wished to secure it, it was too late. Stalin lived in apprehension of a new lapse on the part of the Allies, of a new veering towards the policy of Munich. It was to safeguard himself against the renewal of such a risk that he decided to negotiate with Hitler over the body of the unfortunate Poland, a victim of her own blindness. France and Britain paid bitterly for their mistake. But Stalin himself has

---

[1] The italics are in the text. No doubt the document meant to allude to the negotiations at Nuremburg, which London and Berlin held at the last moment through the mediation of official and well-intentioned emissaries, and whose object was a pacific settlement of the Danzig question and of connected problems, and in particular to talks in which a Swede, Herr Dahlerus, an influential businessman, and Goering played an important role.

revealed that at no time had he been duped by the promises of the nation whose health he had certainly only unwillingly pledged. It is true that Hitler himself never believed for a moment in the solidarity of the unnatural alliance which he had concluded with Bolshevism.

In any case the Allies did not lack warning nor indications. Let us reveal some of those which came in good time to the notice of the French Government.

M. Ristelheuber, French Minister to Bulgaria, gave an account on December 16, 1938, of an interview which he had just had with M. Kiosseivanov. The Prime Minister of King Boris considered a 'rapprochement possible between the U.S.S.R. and the Reich'. This, 'the dream of a section of the German General Staff', would provide the opportunity for 'a fourth partition of Poland'.

Certain indications inspired reasons for fearing that a change in policy was in the process of taking shape. On January 1, 1939, the Chancellor received, as was customary, the diplomatic corps. Observers noted that he chatted longer with the Russian Ambassador than with any others. In his speech on April 28, Hitler refrained from any mention of the Soviets.

According to her custom Germany herself gave us a warning. On May 6, one of Hitler's intimates spoke to a colleague of M. Coulondre in terms which gave food for thought. Hitler, in his last speech, as we have said, had made no reference to Russia. 'Have you not noticed', stressed the speaker, 'the understanding way in which the Press this morning speaks of Molotov and Russia? You have certainly been given an indication about certain negotiations that are afoot and about the visit of the Soviet Ambassador and the Military Attaché to Moscow. These two were received the evening before their departure, the first by Ribbentrop, the second by the *Oberkommando*[1] of the Wehrmacht, and have been . . . informed of the point of view . . . of the Reich. I cannot . . . tell you any more, but you will learn one day that something is brewing in the East.' In answer to his interlocutor, who asked him how he reconciled this new orientation with the recent declaration of the Führer that there was only one country with which he could never come to any understanding—the Russia of the Soviets—the German replied that it was not a question of fine words. In such matters 'it is not', he added, 'juridical or ideological considerations which are important. . . . Moreover, are the two régimes really different? Are they not almost identical in the economic sphere. . . ? Hitler . . . no longer thinks today of settling the German-Polish dispute without consulting Russia. . . . There have already been three partitions of Poland. Very well, believe me, you will see a fourth!'

Did not the cynicism of these words corroborate those which

---

[1] *Oberkommando*: High Command.

Hitler, in the spring of 1934, had already employed to Rauschning: 'Perhaps some day I shall not be able to avoid making an alliance with Russia. But I am reserving this possibility as my last trump card. The unexpected move may be the decisive act of my career but . . . for the time being, let us continue to see in Bolshevism our mortal enemy.'?

On May 9, M. Coulondre reported that 'for the last twenty-four hours, the rumour has been spreading through the capital . . . that Germany had made or was going to make to Russia . . . proposals aimed at a partition of Poland'. The rumour took on substance. On the 22nd, our Ambassador attributed the idea of a partition to Ribbentrop, who was combining it with one for a German-Russian *rapprochement*,[1] such an understanding being itself, in the opinion of the Foreign Minister, a condition for settling the Polish problem. 'The Führer', wrote M. Coulondre, 'still put up some personal opposition to the plans . . . of the Minister. . . . He seemed to consider it . . . very difficult, because of ideological reasons, to direct German policy in such a direction. . . . Ribbentrop appeared to find supporters, chiefly in the High Command and . . . in big business. The Chancellor . . . has, it seems, already to a certain extent taken heed of the tendencies of his Ministers.' On June 1, M. Coulondre dispatched information to Paris which revealed that the question of German-Russian relations was more and more governing Hitler's policy. 'It is known . . . in high quarters', he wrote, 'that if an armed conflict breaks out with Poland . . . a general war will result. The Führer has asked Generals von Keitel . . . and von Brauchitsch . . . if, under present conditions, a general conflict would turn out to be an advantage to Germany. Both have stated that their replies are conditional on Russia not taking part in the fight . . . Keitel has said *yes* and . . . Brauchitsch . . . *probably*. Both have declared that, if Germany has to fight against Russia, she will have little hope of winning the war.' And the Ambassador concluded by giving the opinion which was prevailing at the Wilhelmstrasse: 'Hitler will risk war if he has not to fight against Russia. On the other hand he will retreat rather than expose his country, party and himself to ruin.'

On May 31, Molotov presented to the Third Session of the Supreme Soviet of the U.S.S.R. his report on foreign policy. Alluding to the discussions taking place at Moscow between the three Powers, he said

---

[1] It was also in May that Beneš learned from Prague and Moscow of the opening of economic negotiations between Germany and Russia. He tells us of this in his memoirs. On July 19, he was to learn that discussions were actually taking place. Between August 10 and 12 he finally found out that German-Soviet discussions had taken place during the night of 3rd-4th of this month. 'Ribbentrop, Goering, Goebbels, Jodl and some others had met at the Ministry of Foreign Affairs to decide if Germany was or was not to sign the agreement with the Soviet Union. Hitler, who was at Berchtesgaden, was in direct communication with the room in which the meeting was being held. Discussions went on until the small hours of the morning of the 4th. . . . Hitler intervening incessantly by telephone. Finally, he gave his consent to the agreement, and Hilger his special envoy, took a plane shortly afterwards for Moscow, carrying the reply of the German Government.'

that the last proposals of Britain and France were a 'step forward' but he added that they were hedged with such reservations . . . that it might well turn out to be that this was only a 'fictitious step forward'. Molotov concluded by speaking on this subject in these words, which, one must agree, were very significant: 'Whilst carrying out our negotiations with Britain and France, we consider that we are in no wise bound to abstain from having business relations with such countries as Germany and Italy.'

Portents were henceforth to multiply at an ever-increasing pace. Coming from a different source, they reinforced those which M. Coulondre had received in Berlin.

Now it was the turn of our Consul-General in Hamburg, M. Garreau, to raise facts which were especially disturbing. Marc Rucart gives information of outstanding importance on this subject. 'June 4 was', he writes,[1] 'a Sunday. Berlin was on holiday. At the Lustgarten, Hitler was receiving the Condor brigade, that is the German soldiers who had fought in Spain for Franco against the Republican Army. In a café M. Véquaud, French Vice-Consul at Hamburg was talking with an S.A. officer whom he knew very well. The S.A. . . . gave vent to his disgust. "Hitler is shaking hands with the widows of those who have fallen fighting against the Spanish Bolsheviks. It is a shame, for, at the same time, he is offering his hand to Stalin." M. Véquaud could not believe his ears. He asked some questions. "They are", replied the other, "in the act of preparing a pact of non-aggression for ten years. It is not you French who will succeed in the negotiations. Have you not noticed how your Delegation is being treated?" But M. Véquaud wanted more precise details which could put him on the track. He asked who had served as the go-between. The S.A.—who was in the confidence of the highest people, as it was possible to verify later—gave this information. "The intermediary is the former chief of the Czech Army, General Sirovy. He has already made several trips between Moscow and Berlin."'

On the 7th, M. Garreau sent this story to the Embassy, which passed it on immediately[2] to the Quai d'Orsay without any alteration being

---

[1] *La dépêche de Paris*, August 8, 1946.

[2] The text of the Berlin telegram to Paris is not to be found in the *Livre Jaune*. On June 13, M. Coulondre wrote to Bonnet that Ribbentrop had still not given up the idea of a partition of Poland, and that to this end he continued to treat with the Soviets. 'The return of the Condor brigade', he adds, 'would normally have furnished the opportunity for diatribes against Bolshevism. . . . Ribbentrop took good care nothing should be said in the speeches made which was offensive to Russia. The Führer . . . when he addressed the brigade . . . did not utter a word against Bolshevism or against Communism. It was against the "democracies", the "warmongers" and "war profiteers" . . . that he launched his thunderbolts. The reserve which he observed in regard to Russia was obviously not a chance effect. It was due to the influence . . . of Ribbentrop, who preserved . . . the hope of "winning over" the Russians or at least of seeing them hold aloof from the bloc set up under the aegis of Britain and France.'

made in it. The alarm was given. But the news encountered the incredulity of Paris. M. Garreau was informed of this reaction, with the result that he hesitated subsequently to report information which, coming to him from other sources, tended to confirm the rumour which he had passed on. Indications, however, became more precise. The negotiations for a pact of non-aggression were thought to be taking place. Certain circles of the Press knew about them. M. Véquaud, always on the watch, got wind of them. Invited, on the 25th, aboard the steamer *Robert Ley* anchored in the port, he bluntly questioned a correspondent of the *Fremdenblatt*, and learned from him that Berlin, without denying the mysterious discussions, had just given an order to the Press to keep silent about the matter. M. Garreau, who had already burned his fingers, refrained from passing on this new piece of information, which, however, agreed with the first. He could not be persuaded to return to the subject, until he had received a warning on July 4, from M. Bassaget, commercial agent at his Consulate, that rumours were reaching him of the negotiation of an economic agreement between Germany and Russia. M. Garreau then decided to break his silence, regardless, as he told himself, of any consequences. Stressing the items of information which he had received, and which in their entirety, corroborated each other, he was going to seize upon this opportunity, as Marc Rucart says, 'to try and get his teeth into the business again'. The very same day he telegraphed Paris, this time directly and not through the intermediary of the Embassy. 'The German Press are not giving any information about the German-Soviet commercial negotiations now in progress. Trade circles in Hamburg, usually very well informed, believe, nevertheless, in the fact that, if an agreement is not shortly concluded between London, Paris and Moscow, the Soviet Government would be ready to sign a pact of non-aggression for five years with the Reich.' Marc Rucart resumes his account: 'Once again the Quai d'Orsay did not "catch on". . . . I should say that the responsibility for the "blocking" of the information, or at least the scorn or disbelief with which it was treated, lay at the door of M. Léger, Secretary-General for Foreign Affairs.'

From Moscow came no less disturbing indications. On June 29, *Pravda* published an article by Zhdanov entitled 'The British and French Governments do not want a Pact concluded on a footing of equality with the U.S.S.R.' The conclusion to be drawn was an obvious one. '. . . The British and French do not wish to conclude with the U.S.S.R. a pact which is based on the principles of equality and reciprocity. . . . The U.S.S.R. whose strength, power and merit are known throughout the entire world, cannot accept . . . such a pact.' Quoting this text, Potiemkin writes:[1] 'This article created a sensation in

---

[1] *Op. cit.*, vol. III, pp. 706–7.

diplomatic circles and had a wide repercussion throughout the
world. . . .'

On August 1 came a new warning from our Embassy at Berlin:
'There is cause to wonder . . . whether, in view of the delays in the
Anglo-Franco-Soviet negotiations, the rulers of Hitler Germany will
not be tempted to fall back on the idea of some devastating action
which, in a few weeks, would eliminate the Polish Army . . . the risks
of seeing Germany resort to such a solution cannot by any means be
ignored whilst the Russian puzzle remains to be solved.'

On the 15th M. Coulondre expressed himself more urgently: 'I
consider it essential . . . to speed up as much as possible the conclusion
of an agreement with the Soviets. I can never say too often how much
this represents an important psychological factor for the Reich.'

Finally, on the 16th, came a last cry of alarm from M. Coulondre:
'It is necessary at all costs to come to some solution in the Russian
business as quickly as possible.'

Jules Henry relates, in the memoirs from which I have quoted above,
the remarks which M. Cabestan, Press Attaché to our Moscow
Embassy made to him at this time. He writes: 'M. Cabestan, who was
an intelligent, enterprising and well-informed man, speaking both
Russian and German, reported, on returning from a trip in Germany:
"I know that Molotov has had conversations with Berlin. Pay very
great attention to them, and do it quickly. If you don't sign pretty
rapidly, it will be the Germans who will do so with the Russians."'

Another testimony comes from one of our representatives in a
country of Eastern Europe. Warned by the highest authority of the
country about the imminence of an agreement between Hitler and
Stalin, this diplomat came to Paris to tell M. Léger about it. The latter
received him on August 11. He had barely finished listening to his
colleague than he took him familiarly by the lapels of his coat and
asked if he had lost his head. He assured him that 'not a comma was
now lacking in the draft Convention with the Russians'.[1] He added:
'Come back tomorrow. The Convention will then be signed.'

Everything points to the fact that the Quai d'Orsay remained
obstinately deaf to all these warnings, which were as circumstantial as
they were corroborative. M. Léger, who wielded a despotic authority
over our diplomatic service, peremptorily refused to take these items
of information seriously. He had received the above-mentioned report
of M. Véquaud with obvious irritation. This had been so strong that
the latter, when visiting Berlin on June 11 had received orally from
our Ambassador the advice to 'refrain in future from sending such
unlikely dispatches'. M. Dejean, a colleague of M. Coulondre, had
explained to the individual concerned that his report had 'put out' the

---

[1] M. Léger was evidently referring to the political convention

Quai d'Orsay and even made M. Léger 'furious'. M. Léger merely saw in all these stories misleading reports which were being deliberately put out by the Nazis. Shortly afterwards, M. Garreau, when visiting Paris, received the same reprimand from M. Hoppenot, Deputy-Director for European Affairs. The latter told him in effect that he did not attach the slightest importance to the rumours of German-Russian discussions, so convinced was he of the imminence of the conclusion of the Pact under discussion at Moscow.[1] Now, M. Hoppenot was 'the most intimate colleague of M. Léger'. Eight years later in 1947 he was to testify to this fact in his deposition at Baudouin's trial before the High Court.

We had, therefore, been grievously deceived. Both sides were disputing for the support of Russia. Retracing this rivalry between the Anglo-French and German-Fascist blocs, Potiemkin begins his account[2] with the following introduction: 'For both camps it was a matter of exceptional importance to discover on whose side the Soviet Union would be in the next conflict.' The scales tipped in Hitler's favour. Potiemkin adds:[3] 'On July 22 . . . negotiations . . . were resumed. On August 19, they were completed by the conclusion of a commercial and financial agreement. . . . It was clear that German-Fascist diplomacy was not only interested in using the Soviet markets into which they could pour the products of German industry, and in receiving from the U.S.S.R. indispensable raw materials. The Germans were obsessed by the fear of a war on two fronts. That is why they sought the good favour . . . of the U.S.S.R. in the hope of preventing her concluding a pact of mutual assistance with Britain and France. German diplomacy did not confine itself to consolidating economic relations with the U.S.S.R. In the summer . . . the Germans proposed to the Soviet Government the conclusion of a non-aggression pact. The Soviet Government accepted the German proposal.' We know the sequel.

Hitler, I have said, does not seem to have cherished any illusions about his partner's feelings towards him. In the hour when he turned against Stalin, he was to write, on June 21, 1941, to Mussolini, that, in taking a decision to attack Russia, 'the most grave', he stressed, in his life, he felt 'his mind relieved of a burden'. 'By marching side by side with Russia, I had', he adds, 'the impression of breaking away from my very past, my conceptions and my former pledges. I am happy to be delivered from this torture.' There can be no doubt, indeed, that he shared Ribbentrop's opinion of Stalin. Ribbentrop on the eve of the conclusion of the pact said to Ciano[4] that, however execrable

---

[1] Cf. Marc Rucart, *op. cit.* Later M. Véquaud had supplemented his first account with the details which I have inserted above.   [2] *Op. cit.*, vol. III, p. 701.

[3] *Ibid.*, p. 711.

[4] On March 16, 1940, Ciano reported the words to Sumner Welles, who was then on a mission to Rome (cf. *The Time for Decision*, 1944, p. 137).

Communists might be, there was not a worse specimen than Stalin. The personality of the latter impressed Hitler no less. On August 22, 1939, just before the signing of the monstrous, but, as Goering justly calls it, inspired agreement, he informed the High Command: 'I have decided to march with Stalin, for there are only three great statesmen in the world: Stalin, myself and Mussolini. Mussolini is the weakest.' Therefore, he kept the last-named outside his grandiose scheme. He and Ribbentrop confined themselves to telling Ciano on two occasions that, to hamper the Anglo-Franco-Russian negotiations, they were trying to conclude a commercial agreement with Russia, but that it was only 'a trivial matter'. The Italian Government was not to be advised of the signing of the alliance before August 21,[1] when the Führer telephoned the news to Ciano.

Daladier, in summing up the negotiations writes:[2] 'Since May the U.S.S.R. had been conducting two negotiations, one with France, the other with Germany. She preferred to divide Poland rather than to defend her. This was the immediate cause of the Second World War.' The democracies' military weakness and lack of resolution, it must, however, be recognized, also played their part.

As for M. Noël, he described Moscow's manœuvre in the following words:[3] 'In actual fact the Soviet Government had been simultaneously conducting two contradictory sets of negotiations: one in public . . . with the Western Powers; the other in secret with Germany. There had been much rumour of commercial negotiations . . . intended to throw a smoke screen over the political discussions. When he was questioned on this subject by Count Szembeck, M. Sharonov (Russian Ambassador in Warsaw) went as far as to deny them. . . . In actual fact . . . the discussions . . . were then taking place. . . . It is, therefore, inaccurate to assert . . . that the Soviet Union had only decided to come to an understanding with Hitler because it was faced by a refusal on the part of Poland to accept the demands . . . of Voroshilov put during the conversations with the Doumenc Mission. Russia . . . had made up her mind long ago about the position of the Poles, and it appears that she only entered into discussions with France and Britain in order to lead Hitler into concluding an agreement with her. This would gain for her the respite of which she was still in need, it would allow her to keep out of the struggle for a certain length of time, and would bring her, moreover . . . an advantage . . . that nothing led her to anticipate from the Allies: a jumping off ground to recover the east of Poland and the Baltic countries.'

[1] On February 26, 1940, Ciano also reported this fact to Sumner Welles (cf. *ibid.*), showing indignation at the free and easy manner of Berlin. 'There is an example', he said to his interlocutor, 'of the way in which Italy is kept informed about Germany's foreign policy.' This is quite different from the consideration which Hitler showed Mussolini at Munich. [2] *Minerve*, April 19, 1946. [3] *Op. cit.*, p. 426.

For her part Moscow did her best, from this time, to throw the responsibility for failure on the Allies: 'If the military negotiations with Britain and France', declared Voroshilov in an interview published on August 21 in *Izvestia*, 'have been interrupted, it is not because the U.S.S.R. has concluded a pact of non-aggression with Germany, but quite to the contrary; the U.S.S.R. concluded this pact, because her negotiations with France and Britain had ended in a deadlock. . . .' Let us note, however, that, when the Wehrmacht attacked Russia on June 22, 1941, Stalin himself experienced the need of excusing himself from being allied to the man who had announced this act of aggression in *Mein Kampf*. In his speech over the wireless on July 3, 1941, he said: 'How did it come about that the Soviet Government agreed to conclude a Pact . . . with such monsters as Hitler and Ribbentrop? . . . Was not this an error on part of the Soviet Government? . . . I believe that no peaceful nation can refuse to subscribe to a peaceful agreement with a neighbouring country, even if this country is administered by cannibals . . . such as Hitler and Ribbentrop. . . . What profit have we derived from concluding a pact of non-aggression with Germany? We have ensured for ourselves a spell of peace for a year and a half, and the possibility of preparing our forces for the day when Germany . . . would take the risk of attacking us in defiance of the Pact.'

Whatever be the truth of the matter, once the agreement had been signed the Fascist camp exulted. The Italian Press overflowed with joy at the news of this 'bitter surprise' for the Allies. Gayda, in the *Giornale d'Italia* of August 22, stressed the importance of a pact which had so happily completed the system of which Italy had laid the foundations. He added: 'There is nothing surprising about the fact that, in such a grave hour of European history, the totalitarian peoples feel the need to use their elbows.' The same day the *Lavoro Fascista* wrote that the time had come for a revision of the existing situation, and if it were opposed, the Axis would not hesitate to unloose 'a rapid and total war'. 'The Fascist régime', it added, 'is certain that Italian claims against France will be completely satisfied. A peaceful solution to the Danzig question would serve no purpose, because a solution to Italian claims must be found.' The same day the Berlin correspondent of the Brussels *Soir* telegraphed: 'The certainty of no longer having to fight the Red Army gives the German masses a complete confidence in being able, with Italy, to conquer the democracies one day.' On the next day the same paper published an article by Roland de Marès, an habitual caller at the Quai d'Orsay: 'We must', wrote this journalist, 'put aside the fanciful idea of a German-Russian pact of non-aggression. . . . In its present state of social and political decadence, Stalinist Russia is incapable of playing a European part of such amplitude.'

Coming as a veritable thunderbolt, the agreement stupefied public opinion equally in Britain and in France. In the opinion of some, of Gamelin for example, the *volte-face* of Russia, by leaving us practically alone to face Germany, made us powerless. Would it not be courting disaster to risk war with our neighbours under these conditions? Was it not essential to warn the Government whilst there was time to do so? But we were in honour bound to Poland. And above all, a new withdrawal would be the final abdication for us. It was a cruel dilemma for his conscience to face. Gamelin opened his heart to Georges, his *alter ego*. They both were aware of the responsibility which rested on their shoulders. They both chose to remain silent.[1]

Braving gibes and rebuffs, our representatives abroad tried in vain to put Paris on its guard against the threatening schemes which were being woven in the shadows. Nothing succeeded in shaking the pedantic impassiveness of M. Léger, any more than the self-confidence of his followers. The permanent regent of the Quai d'Orsay remained deaf to all warnings and to all appeals. He denied that any danger threatened. He was to go on denying it until the end. Was ever a great country fobbed off to such an extent? Had ever diplomacy known such a Waterloo. 'How', exclaimed Marc Rucart,[2] 'could we have remained in ignorance of the discussions between Hitler and Stalin? How was it, consequently, that we could be driven, during the period when the storm was breaking, to reverse every shred of policy brought to the point of realization and the final exchanges of mutual trust?'

The reply, and one that is saddening, we unfortunately possess! But the country must atone for its sins, because the incompetence of the Quai d'Orsay had long been apparent. Indications of it were manifold. Here is one example out of numerous others. M. Noël[3] writes that, on the eve of the *Anschluss*, he came from Warsaw to Paris to call the attention of the leading people in the country to the danger which was threatening us. 'Chautemps . . . the President of the Council, gave me his full approval. The President of the Republic did the same, but neither was strong enough to make his views prevail over the views of officials who were in charge of the Quai d'Orsay, and who, to put it mildly, cold-shouldered my intervention in a marked manner.'

Mandel's words are now understandable: 'If only the Quai d'Orsay had been shut up between the two wars!'

[1] Cf. Gamelin, *op. cit.*, vol. I, p. 41.   [2] *Loc. cit.*   [3] *Op. cit.*, p. 184.

CHAPTER XV

THE WAR

September 3, Britain and France honour their Signatures.—The 'Phoney War'.—The Belgian Operation: When and How it was decided.—The Alert on January 10, 1940.—The Soviet attack on Finland and the prelude to the Norwegian operations.

SEPTEMBER 3: BRITAIN AND FRANCE HONOUR THEIR SIGNATURES

As soon as the news of the Hitler-Stalin agreement was known, Bonnet asked Daladier to summon the Ministers for National Defence and the Chiefs of the General Staff to a conference. Mandel who, however, was responsible for the defence of our colonies, was not asked to be present, nor was General Bührer, Chief of General Staff for the Colonies. The meeting took place on August 23 in the Rue Saint-Dominique in Daladier's study: it lasted from five minutes past six to seven-thirty in the evening.

The secret of the deliberations was well kept at the time, for Mandel, always accurately informed, nevertheless did not know, as I myself did not, that this Council had been summoned. Both of us only learned about it in December, 1940, when *Gringoire*, inspired by Bonnet, published the minutes of the meeting.

No one had dared during the meeting of the Council of August 23 to mention that France ought not to carry out the pledge which she had given to Poland.

The Council of Ministers met on the next day. No one there either dared to suggest that France should seek to escape her obligations. But experience had made certain Ministers distrustful.

Mandel asked that, if the German-Polish dispute were to be submitted to a conference similar to that which had taken place at Munich, the country chiefly concerned should not this time be left out of the discussions. There was a unanimous agreement on this. When he got back home Mandel—from whom I have received this information—was called to the telephone by Monzie who had just made an official trip to Poland, and who was eager to congratulate him on his intervention on her behalf. The same person, in 1941, was to denounce in *Ci-devant*,[1] the 'secret influences' which were being exerted on the President of the Council and were leading to a war, the 'tragic gravity' of which was realized by the latter.

During the sitting of the Council of Ministers, Daladier made no reference to the discussion of the previous evening. He asked, finally, for authority from the Council to make Poland heed advice to act with moderation, and above all, not to take the initiative in hostilities even if Germany were to proclaim the annexation of Danzig.

On the 29th, Hitler, wishing to strike the same blow against a representative of Poland which he had dealt on March 14 against the unfortunate Hacha, summoned Warsaw to send to him within twenty-four hours a plenipotentiary who would have authority to treat with him 'without referring back to his Government'. The Führer thus thought that Poland was at his mercy.

On the 30th, Ribbentrop read to the British Ambassador the conditions which Hitler had decided to dictate to Poland. The reading was made at break-neck speed. Ribbentrop refused to allow the Ambassador to have a copy of the document.

War seemed on this occasion inevitable. On the 31st, Ciano told M. François-Poncet: 'Mussolini is offering, if France and Britain will agree, to invite Germany to a conference, which would meet on September 5. Its aim would be to examine the Articles of the Treaty of Versailles which are at the root of the present trouble. An invitation would only be sent to Germany at the last minute, after France and Britain had given their assent.'

To all appearances a new Munich was being prepared, this time with the body of Poland as the prey.

On the same day there was a meeting of the Council of Ministers. Bonnet proposed the acceptance of the Italian plan. According to him the British would agree to it. Daladier said brusquely to Bonnet: 'It is necessary to say under what conditions the British will accept it.' They would only accept it on condition that mobilization was stopped. Now, we had taken important steps for mobilization and it was not as easy for a democracy to countermand them as it was for Nazi Germany, if the case should arise.

Finally, the Council agreed to accept, but on condition that Poland, and eventually the other interested countries should be present at the conference. Daladier had brought in during the sitting a personal letter from our Ambassador in Berlin, telling him that the German conditions were unacceptable, and letting it be understood that Hitler was down on his knees, and that he was bluffing. This letter had a deep influence on Daladier.

[1] p. 135.

At three o'clock in the afternoon Ribbentrop dismissed the Polish Ambassador, who had not plenary powers to negotiate.

At eight o'clock the German wireless stated that the conditions laid down by Germany had been handed to the British Ambassador, and that the German Government considered that they had been rejected by Poland because she had failed to send a plenipotentiary within the time permitted.

At ten o'clock the German wireless announced a Polish attack against the wireless station at Gleiwitz.

On September 1, at dawn, the Second World War began. Without any declaration of war, Germany attacked Poland. The Reichstag met at ten-thirty in the morning. Hitler stated: 'Last night the Polish Army opened fire.' He was lying as we shall see.

The Council of Ministers met. Bonnet declared that he had tried to telephone Halifax, but the latter was at his dentist. He wanted to tell him that we would accept the Italian proposal. At a quarter to twelve in the morning he telephoned M. François-Poncet to ask him to tell Ciano that France would accept Mussolini's offer.

Daladier said that he had ordered a general mobilization. Bonnet asked leave to state that France had accepted the Italian offer. This was an idle gesture for the British had already refused it, or rather they had made their acceptance conditional on the withdrawal of German troops from Polish territory. 'Bonnet was working for the *Livre Jaune*', Mandel told me. Jean Zay and Guy La Chambre stated that they were off to join the forces. Daladier asked the latter to stay at his post.

At a quarter to one in the afternoon, M. François-Poncet informed Ciano that the French Government accepted his proposal. Ciano replied that he did not know if any reason for it still existed, and if, therefore, there was any object in putting it to Hitler.

At ten o'clock in the evening, our Ambassador told Ribbentrop 'that, unless the German Government was prepared to give the French Government satisfactory assurances that it would suspend any aggressive action against Poland, the French Government would not hesitate to fulfil the pledges which it had given to that country'.

At eleven o'clock, Ribbentrop replied to M. Coulondre. He denied that there had been on the German side 'any aggression against Poland'. 'It is the latter', added Ribbentrop, 'who, during these months, has given continual provocations, by stifling Danzig economically, by ill-treating minorities, by perpetrating incessant frontier violations. The Führer has endured these provocations with the greatest patience, hoping that Poland would come to her senses. But it has turned out the opposite way. Poland, who has been mobilizing for months, last night ordered a general mobilization. The Poles attacked German territory at three points.'

We know now the truth about Germany's innocence. The Nuremberg trial has established it. On August 22, Hitler informed his entourage of his decision to find a motive for his aggression against Poland. 'It matters very little', he said in substance, 'whether the pretext is a convincing one or not. The strongest are always in the right.' And he added that he was certain that, if Germany did take action against Poland, France would refrain from engaging in a general offensive. He was thinking to himself of March 7, 1936, and of Munich. This is what our pacifists of the period earned for us. A few days later the Gestapo was put in charge of the business. The incident which was to supply the *casus belli* was carefully arranged. Himmler himself ordered the Polish uniforms which were to be used in the staging of the incident. He selected from a concentration camp a dozen wretches who, after having been drugged, were rigged out in Polish uniforms in order to attack a train within German territory near to the frontier. When the job had been done, the Gestapo shot down the twelve individuals on the spot. But, if the Gestapo were the instrument used to carry out this machination designed to place the responsibility for having violated German territory on the Polish Army, the brain which conceived it belonged to Hitler. Since the Ems dispatch, Germany had made progress. One can understand the passion with which the Reich was later to try and throw the responsibility for the war on France! But it is not so easy to understand how some of those who formerly advocated that France should shirk her responsibilities and had opposed the modernization of our army (the only way to avoid war), today accuse their country of making a mistake in not avoiding the struggle.

During the night of September 1–2, Bonnet issued the following Havas dispatch: 'The French Government was yesterday informed, as were also several other Governments, of an Italian step to ensure the settlement of European difficulties. After having discussed this, the French Government has given an affirmative reply.'

On the 2nd at one o'clock in the afternoon our Ambassador in Poland telegraphed: 'Violent fighting is continuing . . . along the whole of the German-Polish frontier.'

At ten minutes past one our Ambassador in Rome telegraphed that Mussolini was hesitating considerably about informing Berlin of his proposal because he feared that Hitler would accuse him of trying to frustrate his victory.[1]

At one forty-five our Ambassador in Warsaw sent this telegram: 'German aviation continues to be extremely active. Civilian victims are numerous.'

---

[1] At seven-thirty in the evening Ciano was to inform M. François-Poncet that, because the British Government required Germany to recall her troops within her own frontiers, Mussolini was obliged to give up his attempt to arrange a conference.

At three o'clock Daladier read a statement in the Chamber, in which he said: 'Poland is our ally. We have given, between 1921 and 1925, certain pledges to her. These pledges have been confirmed. At the price of our honour we would only buy a precarious peace, which would be revocable and, when we have to fight tomorrow, after having lost through it the esteem of our allies and other nations, we would only be a wretched nation, sold to defeat and to slavery.' The Chamber rose, and cheered him.

Then it voted, as in 1870, the necessary credits for the opening of hostilities. The vote was unequivocal. It was indisputable that it sanctioned a declaration of war according to the procedure laid down by the Constitution. A new deliberation on the subject would, therefore, have been merely a waste of time. To the Finance Commission Daladier said, however, that he was ready to return to Parliament in order to obtain expressly from it a vote declaring war. But, after the sitting, he changed his mind. Nothing, he then thought, would justify a second vote. The Chamber, therefore, would not have to take up the question again.

As for Gamelin, he asked Daladier not to hurry things. He was frightened indeed that aerial bombing might hamper mobilization. 'The British', he writes,[1] 'were insisting that hostilities should begin as soon as possible in order to give some useful assistance to Poland without delay. . . . I turned, I must confess, a deaf ear to this demand, for we had to gain time for our preparations, *which would in no wise delay the hour when we would be able to attack*.[2] At the end of the morning of the 3rd . . . Daladier asked me . . . to begin hostilities at five o'clock in the evening. I could no longer refuse. In actual fact, I still managed to delay doing so until the morning of the following day.'

But it was against Bonnet that the Polish Ambassador inveighed for this delay. In his suspicion, the words of the diplomat took on an insulting tone. Bonnet replied: 'Do you then want the women and children of Paris to be massacred?'

Yet these delays were severely criticized in London. M. Corbin passes on an echo of these criticisms in his dispatch of September 7: 'Whilst the Chamber of Deputies . . . and the Senate were meeting in Paris, the House of Commons was itself sitting. This time along all the benches of the House an excitement was manifest which the statements of the Prime Minister did not succeed in calming. Mr. Neville Chamberlain naturally could not be precise about the time which would be granted to the Government of the Reich to reply to the ultimatum of France and Britain. He alluded to the Italian proposal for a Five Power conference as one of the reasons for delay, as well as the difficulty of synchronizing British action with that of France. These

[1] *Op. cit.*, vol. II, p. 456-7.   [2] The italics are in the text.

arguments, instead of appealing to the House, raised vehement protests from the Labour benches as well as from many Tory ones. The head of the Government had to promise a statement of a more definite nature for the next day; even this did not prevent the House from adjourning in a mood of storminess and exasperation. . . .

'At the Embassy, where I returned for a few minutes, I could discern echoes of the emotion which was stirring parliamentary circles. . . . Members of Parliament and journalists were besieging the Embassy with questions. In the end I had to adopt a peremptory tone with some of my questioners, asking them to compare the British effort, which was revealed above all in the factories, with the great national up-heaval, which was going to call six million Frenchmen to arms. One of the most animated was Mr. Winston Churchill, whose barks made the telephone vibrate. He reminded me that he had always striven for a Franco-British alliance, and added that this was the last occasion, perhaps, when France and Britain would be called upon to join forces. . . . . If they were divided in such grave circumstances, Britain would isolate herself within her island and would defend herself bitterly, but she would no longer want anything to do with European affairs. I ended up by calming him, and he promised me to do his utmost to speed up the military development of his country to the maximum.'[1]

At ten-twenty on the morning of the 3rd, Bonnet telegraphed our Ambassador in Berlin: 'You will notify the Minister of Foreign Affairs of the Reich or his representative that the French Government is, from the nature of the German reply, obliged to fulfil, with effect from today, September 3 at five o'clock, the pledges which France has given to Poland and of which the German Government is aware. You may at this time ask for your passports.'

The feeling aroused in the House of Commons had forced Chamberlain to speed up action. The British Government notified Germany that Britain considered herself to be in a state of war with Germany from midday.

The Polish Ambassador, who had come to see me on the preceding evening, had received my assurance that France would keep to her word.

In any case, the dice were thrown. Hitler had been warned on several occasions and in the most solemn manner that, if he attacked Poland, he would unloose a general war. He had not withdrawn before this danger. He provoked the struggle knowingly, voluntarily, because, he said to the British Ambassador, 'he preferred to make war when he was fifty rather than when he was fifty-five'. Goering, during the examinations at the Nuremberg trial, was to relate that Hitler believed that he

[1] Churchill told me on July 16, 1946, that M. Corbin had understood this telephone call imperfectly, and that Britain in his opinion should have gone to war—even alone—by the side of Poland from the moment she had pledged herself towards that country.

had cancer of the stomach, and that the hypochondria which this obsession aroused in him made him determined to launch into this mighty adventure. Convinced of his approaching end, and permeated with the idea that he was destined to ensure the welfare of Germany, he feared that he would not have time to fulfil his mission. In any case he waited, before throwing himself into the struggle, until the military conditions which he considered essential to success were all realized. He had concluded a treaty with Russia. He had thus dissipated the nightmare of a war on two fronts. The way was open to him.

THE 'PHONEY WAR'

'It is easy, very easy for us to lose this war.'

Chamber of Deputies, December 13, 1939.

It was only after war had been declared that I uttered any optimistic words. As Minister of Finance I had just made, on July 29, a speech over the wireless in which I said that we were 'on the threshold of the most dangerous period of our history'. When war broke out, I took the responsibility for not declaring a moratorium, which was contrary to the procedure my predecessor in 1914 had adopted. It was a bold decision, if one recalls the psychosis created by numerous financial disasters which had happened since then. But it was such an advantage for the national credit to avoid a moratorium that, considering this psychosis healed, I took the risk of not enacting one. The Paris Stock Exchange was not closed one single day. And the prices of Government stock rose.

When speaking over the wireless on September 10, I considered that my duty as Minister of Finance was to bring reasons for hope to those who were prepared to save money. After having asked them 'to refrain from underestimating the strength of our opponent', I stressed the fact that in several months our reserves of gold, that treasury of war, had increased by nearly thirty per cent, so that France possessed twice as much gold as she did in 1914. On the other hand, I had not drawn on the twenty-five milliards which the law allowed me to borrow from the Bank of France. I announced that there would be a control on purchases of foreign currency during war-time, that fifteen per cent of the wages of workers mobilized in the factories would be retained, and I spoke about the necessity of producing. 'Today, even more than in 1914, the wife of the peasant called to the colours, who courageously drives the plough, the father of the industrial worker now at the front, who goes back to work at the factory to prevent it from closing down, the young scouts who harvest or carry dispatches, all these Frenchmen, young or old, are indispensable in maintaining the life and vigour of

France. Those who are capable of producing, and evade this duty, merit the name of deserters.'

Finally, refraining from comment on our military strength, I expressed my hope in the superiority of the 'war potential' of the democracies, and I finished with this sentence which, after being criticized, turned out to be accurate: 'We shall prevail, because we are the stronger.' . . . Indeed, was it not the superior war potential of the democracies which allowed them to collaborate in the arming of all the Allies at the same time as they were providing for their own Armies?

Since this phrase has been criticized, I shall make the observation that the only known method of conquering is by being the stronger, and that it is not customary for the Government of a country at war to say: 'We shall be beaten, because we are the weaker.'

On the other hand, as soon as I saw the danger of the 'phoney war', I did not stop warning the country, and sometimes even our Allies, for I said on November 14, 1939, over the B.B.C. in London: 'Our enemy is a formidable one. He is making frantic efforts. Time will be on our side if we know how to use it to our advantage.'

Before the Chamber on December 13, 1939, when I was moving the Budget, I painted the following picture of France's situation when she entered the war: 'When war broke out, our country was far from having recovered her losses in men and wealth, resulting from the last war and from the seven years' economic crisis which had been badly handled. The value of her currency had been cut by four-fifths because of that war, and the last fifth had itself been reduced by more than half because of the crisis. On the other hand, in 1914 we had just enjoyed a period of one hundred and twenty years' monetary stability. There was no longer any recollection in the mind, or rather in the history books, of any inflation other than those of the National Convention and Directory periods. None of the ills recorded in our agonizing balance-sheet of November, 1938 had been entirely remedied. . . . It was, therefore, a reviving country, but one which was still very far from giving its best effort, which found itself last September abruptly thrown into the war.

'It is true that we are carrying out a blockade, but it is the blockade of a country which, for six years already, has trained itself to live as though it were a besieged stronghold . . . a nation which is encircled by five other countries, Russia, Roumania, Serbia, Italy and Belgium who, during the last war, were its enemies and today are neutral.

'The truth . . . is that we have the choice between two policies. The first might be called the policy of safeguarding the morale of the country. Its supporters say to us: "Since it is a question of a psychological war, the only problem is to keep up the morale of the country. Therefore stop imposing privations, restrictions, taxes. . . . Suppress legal action against those liable to taxation, property owners and shop-keepers. Stop persecuting the employers with your decree taxing war profits; stop irritating the workers by considerable deductions from their salaries. Don't you understand that allowing war profits and high salaries to flourish during 1914–18 was one of the factors which kept up the morale of the nation, and consequently contributed to its victory? . . . What do a few milliard receipts less or expenses more matter? . . . Sacrifice everything to maintaining morale and you will win victory."

'Thus spoke the apostles of freedom from restrictions. I answered them: "Yes, but how long can such a policy last? . . . If it could last a long time, a very long time, there would not be any reason for possible hesitation. . . . It would then be proper to get rid of the Minister who subjected the country to useless sacrifices as being a dangerous man. Unfortunately, the truth is more difficult. Here is the position. The demands which one meets, the salaries which are rising, the civil works which are increasing, all this means that paper currency is becoming more abundant and prices are rising. . . . What is the balance-sheet of this policy? A population thrown into want—one which lives on a fixed income; a growing distress; a land ripe for revo-lutionary propaganda and, in the near future, labour disputes. . . . Do you not realize that the economic disorganization which would ensue would bring about the social disintegration of the country?"'

I then explained the policy of the Government:

'I have been reproached for making a fifteen per cent levy on the wages of workers mobilized in the factories. My answer is "I have recently been told a fact by which I do not think the Chamber will remain uninfluenced. There were, in a certain part of Paris, two neigh-bours of the same age. One is at the front; the other in a factory. The wife of the factory worker has left for the country with her children to seek fresh air and to be far away from the bombs. The wife of the soldier has not been able to get out of Paris. She will stay there in the hovel in which she lives, and wait for the bombs. Do you think that some steps should be taken to remedy this? . . . Don't you think that, when one is talking about morale, the morale about which we should think first is that of the soldiers? . . . The soldiers want neither a comfortable living for their wives nor war profiteers.'

The return of capital was an important factor in the strength of the country. I revealed this figure to the Chamber; it seemed an incredible one—sixty milliard francs in thirteen months.

I pointed out that family allowances would come into force during the height of the war, from January 1, 1940.

Whilst, during the preceding war, it had taken us three years to set up a war-time fiscal system, this time 'our fiscal tools were ready'.

I explained the significance of the Reynaud-Simon Agreement of December 4, 1939, which was to inspire so many foolish remarks in the Vichy Press.[1] Did it not go as far as asserting that I had promised to pay forty per cent of all British war expenditure!

My words on this subject, however, left no room for any ambiguity:

'No doubt, in the sphere of military preparedness, the two democracies are behindhand, because their eyes have been opened too late. But look at the map of the world which we have posted up on all the walls of France. What an immense reservoir of men and of wealth these large red patches represent. Possessing a third of the surface of the civilized world, with four hundred and fifty million inhabitants, these two mother countries are the richest in the world after the United States. You know our Empire. . . . But the British Empire, with her bankers, with her coal, her ships, with her resources . . . of raw materials with her Dominions, peopled by her British stock, is the greatest in the world. . . . Can these two Empires, powerful in a varying degree, but both very powerful, remain unlinked? Can their currencies remain independent?

'The Agreement which we, Sir John Simon and myself, have signed is a good one because it is profitable to the two nations. It affirms to the world their solidarity and their common intention to fight until victory is won.'

Analysing the Agreement, I explained that the purchases of Britain from our Empire would be covered by credits which we would place at her disposal and vice versa; that all raw materials and all manufactured products would be shared between the two countries *pro rata* to their respective needs, and the one which received more than its share of the quota would have to indemnify the other by payment of a sum in gold or currency. Common expenses, such as the upkeep of the

[1] On the day after the conclusion of this Agreement, Lucien Petit, a former Governor of the *Crédit Foncier* and a writer upon the finances of the preceding war, wrote to me: 'I learnt only too well, during the course of the last war, what financial difficulties can arise, and also the way in which the British Treasury defends its interests, not to realize the authority, will-power and subtle and tenacious intelligence which was required of you in reaching the agreement which is announced in the newspapers. Permit me to express to you my deep admiration, and all the gratitude which the country owes you. . . .

'You have succeeded, Mr. Minister, in creating at the first attempt an agreement which appears so well fashioned, so solid, complete and advantageous, when contrasted with all that others have been able to do, in a laborious and precarious fashion, during four years of anxious efforts. . . .

'You have said in your magnificent speech: "We shall conquer." You will have certainly played a great part in the victory.'

To give the reader an idea of the 'financial difficulties' to which Lucien Petit refers, I will quote the following extract from a letter which Alexandre Ribot, Minister of Finance, wrote on September 18, 1914, from Bordeaux to the Government: 'It seems as though it will be a long war, and we shall have to fall back on the Bank to support it to the end. . . . The issuing of National Defence Bonds will only provide us with a feeble part of the resources which we shall need.'

Polish Army in France or those of the blockade, would be borne by Britain and ourselves in the proportion of three to two.

Here are my concluding words, in which is revealed the anguish of a man whose words have not been heeded: 'The democracies will conquer, but they will only conquer at the price of sacrifices which, perhaps, they do not yet conceive. If we do not enter the struggle, prepared to bear everything, it is easy, very easy for us to lose this war. It is possible for the struggle, which has begun in a kind of apathy, to end in a general conflagration. Perhaps, in the darkest days—for these will come—our ideals of freedom and of comfort will exist only in our hearts, but they will remain alive and ready to flourish once more when the days of trial are ended. Today is a testing time. France has experienced in her history more pathetic times. She has never known any more grave.

'I have finished. I shall sum up in a word all what I have said to you: "We shall conquer. But, to conquer the enemy, we must first conquer ourselves."'

This speech earned me the rare honour of seeing the President of the Chamber, M. Herriot, after having adjourned the sitting, come and shake my hand on the Ministerial Bench. But censorship, anxious about our morale, cut out the last two phrases of my speech in the cinematograph recordings.

Speaking, on December 28, 1939, before the Senate about the Budget, I stated:

'France will pay, do not forget this fact. . . . There will be strict economy and privations, such is the law of warfare. . . . Time has no favourites. . . . It will be on the side of the stronger.'

THE BELGIAN OPERATION: WHEN AND HOW IT WAS DECIDED

The operation, which consisted of moving, on May 10, 1940, the Allied Armies from their line of light fortifications on the Franco-Belgian frontier to meet the invader, was one of the causes of defeat. Let us examine the conditions under which this decision was taken. We shall see later on that, when I had become President of the Council, I tried to oppose it, and why I did not succeed in stopping it.

During a conference held at London between the French and British General Staffs on May 5, 1939, four months before the war, 'eventual' intervention in Belgium had been 'considered', but no decision about it was taken.

This intervention was, however, necessary, for the Allies could not go to the assistance of Poland on the day she was attacked by the Wehrmacht, unless they decided on an offensive against Germany through Belgium.

At the Nuremberg trial, the German General, Jodl, stated: 'In 1939 catastrophe was only avoided because one hundred and ten French and British divisions remained inactive against our twenty-five divisions in the West.' And Field-Marshal Keitel said: 'We were surprised not to see France march against Germany during the Polish campaign. Such an attack would have only encountered a screen of twenty-five divisions, including reserves, and we could have only put up a weak resistance. Our astonishment in only having to participate in minor skirmishes within the zone between the Maginot and Siegfried lines was, therefore, great. We could not understand why France did not seize this unique opportunity, and her failure confirmed our belief that the Western Powers did not want to make war against us.'

The Supreme Franco-British Council met on September 22 at Brighton. Chamberlain raised the problem of Belgium. Great Britain had urged the Belgians to enter into Staff discussions with the Allies. But M. Spaak, the Kingdom's Foreign Minister, had replied to the British Ambassador that the Belgian Government did not think there was any imminent danger of seeing Germany attack Belgium, 'but that on the contrary the Reich entertained serious fears of an attack mounted by the Allies against Germany through Belgium'. It was necessary, therefore, Brussels concluded in substance, to avoid the possibility of the Germans seizing the pretext of conversations between the General Staffs for invading Belgian territory.

In the last day of October and the first ten days of November, Germany massed considerable forces on the frontiers of Belgium and Luxembourg: five armoured divisions and three motorized were distributed between Clèves and Trèves. German aircraft repeatedly violated the neutrality of both countries. The tone of the German Press became menacing. Indications that an attack was imminent multiplied. The Dutch authorities believed themselves in a position to state that this would begin at dawn on November 12.

The Belgian Government tried to divert the storm. On October 30, General van Overstraeten, aide-de-camp of the King, summoned, on the orders of his sovereign, the Military Attaché of the Reich to make to him the following communication:[1] 'During the course of a recent conversation between the German Ambassador and M. Spaak, it was mentioned that the Minister of Foreign Affairs of the Reich had explained troop concentrations on the Lower Rhine by pointing out, on the one hand, that there were large Franco-British concentrations facing Belgium, and, on the other, that there had been a Belgian redistribution of forces, which was more clearly aimed against Germany.

'What I am about to tell you is neither an excuse, nor an explanation.

[1] *Rapport*, pp. 27-8 (see fn., p. 154).

9

I would earnestly ask you to regard it only as information, and information of a friendly nature, which His Majesty the King thinks it is proper that I should give you.

'It is true that, for a month, we have reinforced our dispositions facing Germany. The reason for it is simple. During the first weeks of the war, a great number of our available forces were placed facing the south. But, as soon as the Polish campaign was finished, we had, of necessity, to anticipate the flow of the majority of the Germany Army towards the west. Thus, we had to take proportionately a series of precautions on our eastern frontier, which conformed to the essential spirit of our policy.

'I am telling you about this quite frankly. We have allotted to the above duty much more than half of our strength, and we have set about organizing, with the greatest possible energy, a powerful defensive system, which is already in a satisfactory stage. . . .

'I would also like to draw your attention to the state of Belgian public opinion, that is to say, the opinion of the bulk of the population, and not of a few persons, of a few cliques or of certain newspapers. If ever the German Armies were to penetrate into Belgian territory, the whole nation would rise against you as a single man. Take my word for this fact. We are an independent people, and we shall not tolerate being dragged into the war against our will by any side whatsoever.'

But preparations, far from slackening off, were quickening. There was alarm in Brussels. It was then that the King decided to ask the Allies what were their intentions. The *Rapport* says on this subject:[1] 'The event provided an opportunity for asking the Supreme Commander of Franco-British troops for some information on the intervention of Allied Forces in the case of German aggression.

'When receiving our Military Attaché in Paris (Colonel Delvoye) on November 10, General Gamelin replied: "Taking into account new types of weapons and the experience offered by the war in Poland, we think it is necessary to oppose a continuous front to the adversary, a wall which advances at night along the roads, with the troops halting during the day to receive an enemy attack.

'"Even light mechanized divisions will move under the shelter of a defensive disposition to protect them from planes, and they will not, therefore, be sent far in advance.

'"To sum up, the advance of the Allied forces will be very methodical, and governed by the speed of infantry elements, from one battlefield to another, and care will be taken on each of these to establish anti-tank defences.

'"If the Germans . . . take the initiative . . . there can be no question

[1] pp. 29–30.

of sending only isolated divisions to the Albert Canal. If the supporting operation unfolds normally, the right wing of our Armies in movement would be, at a certain time, at Namur, and their left wing in Zeeland; and our front line would pass through Wavre–Louvain–Lierre–Antwerp. Then, according to the state of the situation, we shall realize the support which it will be necessary to give to the defenders of the Albert Canal and the Liége–Namur line. It would be hazardous to send the Allied forces forward to defend Luxembourg or to support you on the Ourthe. We must wait until the Germans have created a large pocket in the Ardennes."

'The King thanked the Supreme Commander for this information, stressing how much he appreciated the frankness and trust which characterized it. He repeated that: "Our dispositions were such that, if the intervention of the guarantor Powers were invoked, it could be carried out without the possibility of a surprise on land".

'Information on the military intentions of Germany continued to be alarming for several days, and appeared to confirm the fact that an attack was imminent. Then suddenly, plans for a German onslaught appear to have been abandoned.'

The Allies themselves were keenly on the alert. The Supreme Council met in London on November 17. Chamberlain did not hide his fears at the idea of seeing the Germans occupy Belgium or Holland. To forestall such an occupation was vital to Britain, as much from naval and air considerations as from economic. It was, therefore, necessary not only to go to the help of Belgium if she were attacked, but even to advance as far eastwards as possible. The Council agreed with these opinions. It decided that in view of 'the importance that existed in keeping German forces as far to the east as possible, it was imperative to try by all possible means to hold the Antwerp–Namur line, if there were an invasion of Belgium by the Germans'.

Gamelin,[1] who was in touch with the Belgian General Staff through Colonel (later General) Laurent, our Military Attaché in Brussels, and Colonel (later General) Delvoye,[2] Belgian Military Attaché in France, appointed to deal with future problems raised by the eventuality of military co-operation between the Allies and Belgium, an 'officer for personal liaison . . . attached to the High Command'. This liaison officer was Lieutenant-Colonel Hautcœur, whom Gamelin accredited to General van Overstraeten. Gamelin proposed, moreover, 'to send, as soon as the Belgians called for our assistance, a full mission headed by one of our most distinguished leaders, General Champon'. He informed the latter that he would be entrusting him with this possible

[1] Gamelin, op. cit., vol. III, p. 147.
[2] Gamelin writes of him (ibid., p. 143) that he was 'a sincere friend of our country'.

mission, and asked him, whilst he retained provisionally the command of the VII Corps, to come frequently to Supreme Headquarters, 'in order to familiarize himself with the business concerning the role which he would have to play'.

The British appointed, as head of a similar mission to the King, Admiral Sir Roger Keyes, the hero of Zeebrugge, who was a personal friend of Leopold III, and enjoyed a very great influence with him.

If we were to advance on the Schelde, from our frontier to Ghent, and along the canals from Ghent to the sea, we would be in a position, it was certain, to gather up the remains of the Belgian Army, which, after the first attack, would be fighting in retreat. But such a solution would only be, it was obvious, a makeshift one. The left wing of the Allied Armies, in actual fact, would have to fight with its back to the sea. The line of the Schelde and of the canals was, moreover, little suited to resistance, because the right bank of the river dominated the left bank, and because the obstacle formed by the canals was one which could be easily overcome. The outcome, in the end, meant the surrender of Brussels and of Antwerp.

The Allies, therefore, dismissed this solution. They were, it was decided, to advance to the Meuse–Antwerp line. They informed the Chief of the Belgian General Staff, and through him the King, of this decision. But it was to be understood that the Belgian Army would be kept on a war footing; that it would organize the so-called Dyle line (see map) by the immediate flooding of the valley of this river, as well as that of the Nèthe, and by the fortification of the left bank of the first river; that it would immediately construct anti-tank defences between the Dyle and Namur; and, finally, would fortify the Namur–Givet line. Alluding to the step which I have mentioned above, Gamelin writes:[1] '(Colonel Delvoye came to see me) in order to inform me, on behalf of his General Staff: "If Belgium is attacked, under what conditions could you come to support us on the Albert Canal?" . . . On the 13th I had a personal assurance that the Belgian General Staff intended to fulfil the conditions which seemed to me necessary so that we could advance beyond the Schelde without meeting any delay which could prejudice everything.' It was, therefore, to the Namur–Antwerp line that the left wing of the Franco-British forces was to advance, if Belgium were attacked.

As regards Holland, it was arranged that, if she herself were attacked, the Allies would take possession of the Walcheren and Beveland islands, the southern islands of Zeeland, in order to ensure possession of the estuaries of the Schelde.

[1] *Op. cit.*, vol. III, p. 143.

THE ALERT ON JANUARY 10, 1940

Yet the position of Belgium remained governed by the decision made on October 14, 1936. It was a vital mistake, and one which M. Spaak, with a commendable nobility, admitted when making a public declaration to the Press. He stated, January 25, 1948, that the Belgian policy of independence and neutrality had been an 'error on a national scale' and that it had 'been a failure' for it had not 'prevented Belgium from being dragged into the war'.

Winter came. The Western front continued to be peaceful. This stagnation prompted reflection. Was Belgium at last going to open her eyes and change her opinions? Was she going to understand that, whether she liked it or not, her cause was indissolubly linked to our own? A fortuitous incident which occurred in mid-January gave hope for a moment that this might be so.

On the 10th a German plane was obliged because of engine trouble to land in Belgian territory. Two officers were aboard. The papers which they were carrying were seized by the Belgians. These documents contained plans of a German offensive between the North Sea and the Moselle. The King was informed of them on the 11th at twelve-thirty midday. He instructed General van Overstraeten to send an abstract of these documents to Lieutenant-Colonel Hautcœur, who took them in all haste to Gamelin. The Belgian High Command was frightened that the attack was imminent. Gamelin would have liked the originals or at least photographs of them to have been sent to him. The Belgians refused to do this. In any case, Gamelin took the necessary steps. On the 14th at twenty minutes past one in the morning, General Delvoye went to see Gamelin. He warned him that there would 'almost certainly' be an attack on the next day.

Gamelin writes:[1]

We replied to him: 'Are you calling on our help?' He had no instructions to this effect . . . M. Spaak asked our Ambassador: 'If a German attack takes place, will it result in the help of France and Britain?' At three-fifty in the afternoon Daladier telephoned me. He had been informed by . . . Chamberlain that . . . Keyes . . . had seen the King. *The latter declared that he was prepared to call in our help.* He asked, however, . . . if France and Britain would pledge themselves to guarantee the frontiers of Belgium and the Congo in the peace treaty. In addition, would they promise financial help? The British Government met to discuss the questions. The President of the Council wished to know our feelings, especially in the military sphere. My reaction was immediate. I did not believe that the Germans were in an effective state of readiness to attack. It was snowing, and aviation could not do much. These were not favourable conditions for offensive operations by our opponents. *It was, however,*

[1] *Ibid.*, pp. 156–9. The italics are in the text.

necessary to seize the opportunity. I asked the President of the Council for a quarter of an hour in which to come to some agreement with Georges, who was responsible for the operations of the ground army, and to advise Darlan and Vuillemin. All three agreed with my opinion, and I told the President that, in order to stress unmistakably our wish to act, and not to lose a minute, the order was going to be given to our troops to close up to the frontier that very night, despite the bad weather. They were to enter Belgium on the following morning as soon as we were given the authorization to do so. We waited for this impatiently. The President stated that he was satisfied with our decision. He was going to tell London that it was necessary to give Belgium all the logical guarantees. He would do it without even consulting his Council of Ministers, who would certainly endorse his decision. I added, for my part, that, in the present circumstances, I did not want to enter into Luxembourg, where there was no adequate line of resistance. For the time being, leave the Germans the responsibility of taking the initiative in this. . . . At quarter to five in the afternoon Georges called me . . . to tell me in a rather embarrassed fashion: 'I've thought things over. Don't you think it would be better to advise the Belgians not to call on us for help? We are not entirely ready. Would it not be better to wait until our Air Force was quite ready, and our forces reorganized?' Although, generally speaking, I have my feelings well under control, I lost my patience. I replied, first of all, somewhat sharply: 'I have committed myself. I cannot go back on what I've said. One must make up one's mind. Otherwise it's better not to go to war.' Then, taking a grip on myself, I repeated the arguments which came surging into my mind. Georges . . . appreciated them. . . . The exchange ended in a mutual understanding. The matter, which was perhaps only a misunderstanding, was over and done with. . . . The night was curiously tranquil. The die seemed to me to have been cast, and in favourable circumstances. . . . It kept on snowing. . . . In the morning, although they had taken away the barricades at certain points, the Belgians still would not let us enter their territory. . . . During the night I sent one of my officers to see General Delvoye on my behalf. I wanted His Majesty to be personally informed about my situation. On the morning of the 15th we were told by the Quai d'Orsay that the British Government had not accepted the demands of the King unreservedly. . . . It considered that it ought to give the guarantees asked for only 'in so far as was possible'. However, General Ironside had told me that, personally, he shared . . . my feelings. It was known that the Belgian Government had met. At the beginning of the morning, I sent a note to the head of the President's military secretariat, dated the 15th, eight-thirty: '. . . In response to the appeal which we have been led to expect, French troops last night closed up to the frontier. . . . Because of the cold, the troops are in a bad way. . . . The enemy is certainly going to discover our movements . . . through his spies. We are, therefore, losing the start which we could have gained. . . .'

Daladier summoned the Belgian Ambassador, M. Pol Letellier. In his statement to the Committee of Inquiry[1] he has related what was said in the following words: 'I asked the Belgian Ambassador to come and see me, and I spoke to him in approximately these terms: "You

[1] Sitting of June 4, 1947.

must know from the plan, of which you have been informed, what
Germany's true intentions are; yet your Government and yourself
seem, in my opinion, to nourish singular illusions about them. According to international law you are being threatened. You can therefore
make an appeal to France and Britain immediately. In which case, we
shall come to your help without delay. We shall advance even as far
as your northern frontier, to the banks of the Albert Canal. We have
time to do this." M. Letellier . . . stated that he was in agreement with
me. He set off himself to Belgium, and various long and lively discussions, according to what I learned, crystallized the opposition between
the different currents within the Belgian Ministry. But finally the
Belgian Government, after having given us its thanks, stated that it did
not want to assume this responsibility. Things remained as they were.
I told the Ambassador . . . who came to give me an account that,
henceforth, the French Government, and, above all, the French military
leaders would resume an entire freedom to form their appreciations
of the situation.'

Daladier informed Gamelin, who writes:[1] 'At eight-thirty in the
evening M. Daladier, the President of the Council, telephoned me:
"The Belgium Government has rejected the King's proposals. It does
not think that it should assume the responsibility for permitting Allied
troops to enter Belgium. . . ." On January 16 a personal telegram from
General Lelong (French Military Attaché in London) informed me:
"Through the agency of Sir Roger Keyes, Lord Halifax received,
during the evening of the 15th, King Leopold's reply on the Belgian
affair. Hardly bothering to discuss the British Note, the King confined
himself to stating that he could not definitely assume the responsibility
for advising a step which would infallibly lead to the invasion of his
country by Germany. . . . The initiative taken by the King, the day
before, appears, therefore, to be incomprehensible. The questions put to
Great Britain were drawn up in his own hand. The most probable
explanation, in the opinion of the Foreign Office, is that the Palace and
the Government . . . at first concerned about the imminence of an
attack, have been reassured by subsequent events."'

After the event, came the justifications. M. Pierlot writes in *Pages
d'histoire*[2] that he examined with M. Spaak and General Denis[3] the
documents taken from the German officers, as well as the reports about
troop movements on the German-Belgian frontier: 'The three Ministers', he writes, 'made no proposal either to the King or to their
colleagues that our frontiers should be opened, and our country thrown
into a state of war.' But the King, without consulting any of his

---

[1] *Op. cit.*, vol. III, pp. 159-60.   [2] *Le Soir*, July 9, 1947.
[3] Baron (later Count) Pierlot was Prime Minister, and Lieutenant-General Denis,
Minister of National Defence.

Ministers, 'took it on himself', adds M. Pierlot, 'to ask the British Government through Admiral Keyes, what guarantees they would give to Belgium if she called upon Franco-British help. This request was made by the Admiral to Mr. Chamberlain on the morning of the 14th. The King received through the Admiral the reply of the British Government on the morning of the 15th. The British stated that they were ready to enter Belgium, and added that, according to their information, so also were the French. The reply contained the enumeration of the guarantees: no peace negotiations without Belgium, the political and territorial integrity of Belgium and of her colonies, economic and financial assistance. The British Government added that Belgium's appeal would lose its force if it were not made as soon as possible, to be in time to secure for the Allies the advantage of the initiative. . . . The King's questions had been construed, both in London and in Paris, as the announcement of an immediate appeal. Allied troops had begun a movement to close up on the Belgian frontier. . . . M. Daladier, during the 15th, questioned, M. Letellier. . . . The Ambassador knew nothing about the matter. He telephoned M. Spaak, who expressed surprise at a communication, of whose cause he was ignorant.'

The three Ministers discussed the matter amongst themselves, and then with the King. 'It was decided', continues M. Pierlot, 'that we should reply that Belgium thought she should adhere to the line of conduct which she had adopted, and only count on making an appeal to the guarantees of the Allies, if she were attacked. The Council of Ministers, meeting on the 15th at seven in the evening, immediately gave its agreement on this draft reply. . . . Shortly afterwards the King received M. Spaak, and informed him with some annoyance of the approach which he had made to London. The Minister respectfully pointed out that his action was unconstitutional. Disturbed about the consequences of his step, the King asked the Minister to take charge of the matter.'

The official explanation was later to be that there had been a misunderstanding. General van den Bergen, Chief of General Staff, who had decided on the evening of the 13th to take away the barricades which obstructed roads to the frontier, and gave the command that Allied troops, if they arrived, should be allowed to pass at one o'clock on the 14th, was told through the instructions of his superiors to cancel his own order. The Government was not content to let the matter rest there. It opened an inquiry into the origin of the instructions which had been given without its knowledge. General van den Bergen was to be the scapegoat. He was disavowed because of his unpardonable 'lack of coolness', and relieved of his command. General Michiels succeeded him.

The reader will be convinced without any difficulty that my conclusion remains a valid one: the opportunity which was offered was certainly lost. The Allied Armies made a right-about turn and took their stations up once more. The Germans naturally were informed. Through this they learned from ourselves the dispositions which the Allies would take up on the day they entered Belgium. This was no doubt the aim which Hitler had sought to achieve in manipulating the faked accident which was at the root of the affair. Thus the Belgian Government which, on October 14, 1936, had rallied round the King when it was a question of breaking the alliance with France, disavowed him when it was a case of putting right this error in so far as this was possible. This Government was to await the day when it would please Germany to invade Belgium, before inviting the Allies to advance and meet the Wehrmacht under the worst possible conditions. What more could our common enemy wish than that?

The explanation given in the *Rapport*[1] is worthy, however, of being reproduced: 'It was necessary to let the matter rest there, for this singular episode could only be a trick intended to throw on our guarantors, called prematurely to our assistance, the responsibility for violating Belgian territory and to justify an invasion coming from the East. The King held, therefore, to this theory, although forty-eight hours later a message from our Military Attaché in Berlin made it appear that an invasion was imminent. Our troops were, however, put in a state of alert, the Commanders-in-Chief of the Allied forces were warned, but entry into Belgium remained forbidden. Events were to justify this prudence. Realizing that his designs were thwarted, the Führer countermanded the movements which had been set afoot. The *Generalstab*[2] had to reshape its plans. Thus, an additional respite of four months was gained for us.

'From this moment, we were, in any case, at pains to reveal clearly our military position. Thus, the main weight of our defensive organization was deliberately turned towards Germany without regard to her protests. The relations linking us with the Allied Supreme Commands were maintained. Moreover, on the orders of the King, General van Overstraeten established contact with the Military Attachés, Hautcœur and Blake, which, whilst respecting our neutrality, and without giving any pledges or reciprocity on our part, established a liaison with the Allied Supreme Commander with a view to eventual intervention on our behalf. . . . '

THE SOVIET ATTACK ON FINLAND AND THE PRELUDE TO THE NORWEGIAN OPERATIONS

When the Soviets attacked Finland on November 30, 1939, French public opinion took sides with the latter country and demanded that

[1] pp. 30–1, *Annexes*, pp. 24–5.   [2] *Generalstab* (General Staff).

the Allies should go to her assistance by sending her arms and also troops. Those in Parliament and the country, who were the most bitter advocates of coming to blows with Stalin, were the pacifists, namely those who, three months earlier, were seeking every means of avoiding fighting against Hitler. Today, it was not enough that we should have the Germanic colossus on our hands. They wished to give themselves the luxury of adding to our burden the Muscovite colossus.

On December 19, Daladier informed the Supreme Council of a plan for giving military assistance to Finland. In substance, he stated that relief forces were necessary for those Finnish divisions, which were fighting without respite, without an hour's rest.[1] But Britain feared that Russia would react against assistance of this nature by breaking off diplomatic relations or even by military action. Now, London did not want at any price to hear any talk of dangerous complications. In its opinion, the assistance of the Allies should be hedged by discretion, and at all costs it should be confined to supplying equipment.

Daladier, however, gave instructions on January 8 for equipping a mixed brigade, the basis of which should be composed of Alpine battalions, with the object of eventually conducting operations in Arctic territory. On January 28 this formation was put on a war footing.

From that moment the problem of finding ways through to Finland was under study. The most practical one was that which left Narvik, a Norwegian port on the Arctic Ocean, and went by rail to Luleå, a Swedish port on the Gulf of Bothnia, through the north of Norway and Sweden. The way was all the more important to the Allies, because it served the celebrated mines from which Sweden derived nine-tenths of her mineral ore, the mines of Kiruna and Gellivare. Now, these deposits were the ones which supplied Germany with nearly half of the ore which fed her blast-furnaces. Cutting the Reich off from Swedish iron ore was, therefore, a counter-blow which would reduce to a considerable extent the productive capacity of the arsenal in which Hitler was forging his arms. Thyssen, the Catholic magnate of the Ruhr, who, at the beginning of the war, had left the country to avoid Nazi persecution, had in a report which, at that time, created a great stir, laid bare this chink in the German armour.

There is no doubt that the Allies had good reasons to put forward when asking from Norway and Sweden the use of the Narvik to Luleå road. But Nordic solidarity came to a stop when it was likely to meet the threat of danger, either from Russia or the Reich. The obstacle of Scandinavian neutrality would certainly not be easy to overcome.

[1] Cf. Daladier's statement, on February 9, 1940, to the Chamber, when it met in secret session. Against the thirteen divisions which Finland had placed in the field, the Russians sent forty.

Wisdom counselled one, therefore, not to count too much on the possibility, by means and under the cover of a transit operation, of seizing the mining basin and thus preventing Germany from gaining supplies. There was another solution: intercepting the transport of the mineral by sea. It was obviously no use thinking of attacking the route passing from Luleå and through the Gulf of Bothnia, which entered the Baltic Sea. For the waters of the gulf froze in winter. Now, we were in the depths of the worst season, and thus, until spring at least, it was sufficient to blockade the Norwegian waters which themselves were always free of ice. By stopping entry to and exit from Narvik to German shipping we were effectively cutting the 'permanent road of iron'.

The Allies were all the more determined to do this because, disregarding international laws, the ships which were plying from Narvik under the Reich flag were keeping within Norwegian territorial waters, and by thus avoiding the high seas were foiling the Franco-British blockade. On January 17 the Allies took the opportunity arising from the disadvantage which this violation was causing them to declare their decision not to consider themselves bound, in the like case, by international law. But, at the request of King Haakon, and in spite of Daladier's protests, Britain immediately revoked, in so far as she was concerned, the decision which had been taken.

On January 15, Gamelin called Daladier's attention to the advantage of establishing a new 'front of attrition' against the German Army by opening a theatre of operations in Scandinavia, which would also have had the effect of depriving Germany of the Swedish mineral ore. Rejecting any intervention which was contrary to the will of Norway and Sweden,[1] he concluded: 'It seems, as much from the point of view of running the war as from the physical factors governing any intervention, that the Allies should be ready to exploit all the possibilities which would be offered to them as soon as an error of tactics by Germany created a favourable political atmosphere. There is even an advantage

---

[1] The Germans were not themselves handicapped by this honourable scruple. The examinations of the Nuremberg trial have revealed that, from October 1, 1939, Grand Admiral Raeder was insisting to the Führer on the importance of occupying Norway. Admiral Doenitz, then head of the submarine arm, had given, the day before, a top-secret report to his superior, Raeder, about the advantages which the establishment of bases at Narvik and Trondheim would present. On December 22, 1939, the occupation of Norway was envisaged in a conversation between Raeder and Quisling. Two days later, the Führer gave the Army High Command the order to begin preparations for it. According to the *Journal* of Colonel (later General) Jodl, Hitler had decided in February, upon conquering Norway. Preparations begun on March 5 were finished by the 20th. It has been said at Quisling's trial that the date fixed originally was March 25, 1940, but that it was delayed because the Skagerrak was not then entirely free from ice. It was Quisling who, on behalf of the Germans, had contrived the entry of picked soldiers of the Wehrmacht, concealed in the holds of merchant vessels, into the port of Oslo. On April 9, Quisling, whilst the disembarkation was in progress, installed himself at the Grand Hotel, Oslo. He was already forming his Government.

in going further, and in trying to create this favourable political climate, namely, by provoking this tactical error on the part of our adversary. In this respect, the pressure exerted by the British Government on Norway to obtain a reduction in the export of mineral ore to Germany appears to offer, if skilfully handled, the possibility of provoking an armed reaction, which would justify our own intervention. Similarly, any violation by Germany of another country's neutrality . . . would provide a favourable occasion and should inspire on our part, as an immediate counter, and, in agreement with Sweden and Norway, an Allied expedition to Scandinavia in order to cut the road supplying minerals. The French Command should then be ready to undertake, in collaboration with British troops, the occupation of ports and airfields on the west coast of Norway. The action should utilize for its operation the few winter months, which we have before us and from which it can more easily benefit.'

Thus, on the next day, Daladier instructed M. Corbin to press the British Government for an assent to the blockade of Norwegian waters on the one hand and to an expedition to Petsamo for direct assistance to Finland on the other.

On February 5 the Supreme Council decided to send to Narvik, copying the example of the Italians in Spain, a body of volunteers numbering thirty thousand men, of whom each Ally was to provide half. The French contingent was to include our mixed Alpine brigade, a Polish brigade and a foot regiment of foreigners. Daladier had agreed that the two divisions which Britain would supply should be drawn from the contingent intended for the French front and even, if numbers were still lacking, from troops already in France.[1]

When the body had been raised, the Allies, after having persuaded Finland to call them to her aid, would use this appeal to ask Norway and Sweden to permit the passage of troops. If this was rejected 'there would be grounds', stresses Daladier, 'for ignoring the refusal and carrying out the operation despite it'. But the British remained reticent. If the Norwegians were to blow up the railway from Narvik, how could we carry help to Finland? On the 16th there was another violation of Norwegian waters, this time by the German ship, *Altmark*. Daladier proposed on the 21st that the Norwegian ports should be occupied 'by a sudden operation'. The British again rejected the proposal, basing their refusal once more on international law and on

[1] With reference to this matter Daladier stated, during the above-mentioned sittings of February 9: 'I have heard . . . certain objections. They are weighty ones . . . But . . . my opinion prevailed. . . . To the question "Do you want everything which is available to come to you, to join your soldiers in the battle against the common enemy, or would you prefer that an important part should be raised for other countries?" I answered: "They should be raised for other countries. . . ." I added: "I will collaborate with you so that together we may conduct the same battle. It is not an easy expedition. It is not without danger, but come what may!"'

the dangers of complications with Russia.[1] But, as Finland had signed peace on March 12, the second argument lost its validity. Therefore, in a telegram of the 14th and a memorandum of the 15th, Daladier repeated his demand, to which he added a new argument: the advantage there would be in 'the eventual launching of a German attack, which could provide us with the justification for wider enterprise in our war effort on the Norwegian and Swedish territories'.

Such was the situation when, on March 21, I took over the Government. The Russo-Finnish war had ended. The Scandinavian operation was only of future value in so far as it would permit us to cut off effectively Germany's supply of mineral ore. This, therefore, quite naturally found a place in the plan of the campaign which the Allies were conducting against Hitler. It was to be the Norwegian expedition. I was, as will be seen, to concentrate my attention on it.

---

[1] Referring to the British attitude, Churchill writes (*op. cit.*, vol. 1, *The Gathering Storm*, p. 516, second edition): '. . . We had been able . . . only to send from our own scanty store contributions insignificant to the Finns. In France . . . a warmer and deeper sentiment prevailed, and this was strongly fostered by M. Daladier. On March 2, without consulting the British Government, he agreed to send fifty thousand volunteers and a hundred bombers to Finland. We could certainly not act on this scale, and in view of . . . the [ceaseless] intelligence reports of the steady massing of German troops on the Western Front, it went far beyond what prudence would allow. However, it was agreed to send fifty British bombers. On March 12 the Cabinet again decided to revive the plans for military landings at Narvik and Trondheim . . . at Stavanger and Bergen, as a part of the extended help to Finland into which we had been drawn by the French. These plans were to be available for action on March 20, although the need of Norwegian and Swedish permission had not been met.'

For his part Daladier, when speaking to the Chamber of Deputies, assembled on March 19, 1940, in secret sitting, alluded to the procrastinations of Britain: 'The reason', he stated, 'which prevents the French Government . . . from being able to go to the limit of its help lies in the fact that neither Britain nor Turkey wish to take the slightest responsibility for a military or diplomatic rupture with Russia.' These words, it is true, had only a retrospective significance, since, at that date, Finland had a week before laid down her arms.

Whatever be the truth of the matter, the help given to Finland by France and Britain in war material was far from being negligible. Our own contribution was, in round figures, one hundred and seventy-five aeroplanes, five hundred pieces of artillery; five thousand sub-machine guns and machine-guns. Daladier himself gave this enumeration to the Chamber during the above sitting of March 19. The same day, Chamberlain declared to the Commons that Britain had sent Finland a hundred aeroplanes as well as more than two hundred guns (especially anti-tank ones).

CHAPTER XVI

FULL TIDE OF WAR

March 21, 1940, I take over the Government.—I make a Choice between two War Policies.—The Norwegian Expedition: 'The permanent road to the iron supplies is cut.'—France secures possession of the Norwegian stocks of Heavy Water.—April 9, My opposition to the Belgian Operation.—May 9, I ask for Gamelin to be relieved of his Command; I resign; on the following day the German offensive obliges me to remain in power.

MARCH 21, 1940: I TAKE OVER THE GOVERNMENT

THE Government, under pressure from Parliament, had promised to intervene in Finland. Now, on March 12, Finland signed peace with Moscow. This was the cause for the downfall of the Daladier Administration about which a lot of stupid things have been said. As Mandel often used to say, a government is only overthrown in time of war because of a military event. The day following the Moscow Treaty, the Senate discussed it in a secret sitting, and only gave Daladier two hundred and thirty-six votes on the Order of the Day. There were sixty abstentions.

On the 18th, Mussolini met Hitler at the Brenner.

The next day the Chamber also discussed, in secret, the defeat of Finland. Louis Marin tabled a motion which asked 'that the war should be prosecuted with increasing energy' and that 'the Government should organize itself into a War Government, determined to employ, with method and energy, the total resources of the nation'. The motion of confidence, tabled by Chichery, President of the Radical Socialists, won two hundred and thirty-nine votes.[1] But three hundred deputies abstained. Amongst them were the Socialists, ten Radical Socialists, twenty-nine members of the *Alliance Démocratique* and thirteen members of the *Fédération Républicaine*. The Government therefore no longer had the confidence of the House. On the 21st, Daladier resigned.

During the crisis, the Italian Press raised its tone: 'Let us finish holding out the olive branch,' exclaimed the *Giornale d'Italia*.

[1] Only one deputy voted against it.

On the 21st, President Lebrun invited Daladier to form a new administration. When he refused, he summoned me at 5 p.m. and entrusted me with this responsibility.

A plenary meeting of the leaders and rank and file of the Radical Socialist Party passed a motion of confidence in Daladier, which praised, according to Le Temps, 'his never-failing energy to increase the moral and material strength of France', and which said that 'for six months he had conducted the war with wisdom and firmness'. Rightly or wrongly, the word 'wisdom' was interpreted as evidence of mistrust in relation to myself. For several years, the advocates of a systematic defensive type of warfare had been prosecuting a campaign against the man who had demanded an offensive army, which would permit France to honour the pledges that she had given to her allies. For several months they had been stating that, if, by some misfortune, I took over the government, I would indulge in thoughtless offensives, which would lead us into catastrophe. On the other hand, those who had been in favour of Munich considered me as the leader of the war-mongers. In other words, the hostile factions who united against me were inspired by the same frame of mind.

It was learned in the Chamber that the Radical Socialist Party had decided to press Daladier to resume power if I did not succeed in forming an administration, or alternatively, to urge that he should keep the post of Minister of Defence in the Government which I was forming.

I tried to get Daladier, who since September, 1939, had also been both Minister of Foreign Affairs and Minister of Defence, to keep the first post and hand over the second to me, for I considered that, in time of war, the head of the Government should be in direct contact with the Army chiefs. Daladier, who had been in charge of National Defence for nearly four years, refused to leave the post. I would, therefore, have refused to accept the task of forming an administration had not Herriot insisted that I should try to do so, and leave Daladier in the Ministry of Defence whilst I, myself, took that of Foreign Affairs and Chautemps kept the Vice-Presidency of the Council.

I appealed to the Socialists for support, as I thought that such an important party ought not to be deprived of a share in the Government, when it was a question of waging total war. This is what Churchill was to do, several weeks later, in Britain. I want to say immediately that I had no more loyal and devoted colleagues.

Because of the state of public opinion, I had to give up any thought of inviting Léon Blum to accept office. In order to maintain a balance, I refrained, therefore, from including Louis Marin. Nothing more than this was needed to prompt the Fédération Républicaine to refuse me its support. The members of the Centre to whom I appealed only gave me, to start with, their individual collaboration, as their leaders, with

Flandin at their head, decided to oppose me because of my 'war-mongering'.

I was in a difficult position. I had not been able to achieve national unity. I found myself leading a Government which was more to the left than that of Daladier.

My Cabinet included six Socialists, five Radical Socialists (from the Chamber), six members of the *Gauche Démocratique* (or the Radical Socialists of the Senate), three of the *Union Socialiste et Républicaine*, five of the *Alliance Démocratique*, five of the Independents, two members of the *Union Démocratique* of the Senate, and one deputy who was unattached to any group.[1]

I introduced a double innovation. On the one hand, I formed within the Government a War Cabinet,[2] presided over by myself, and similar to that of the British, with a secretary to compile the minutes of the deliberations. In addition, I created an interministerial Economic Committee, presided over by Chautemps.[3]

My arrival in power was favourably received in London. On March 22, Churchill, still First Lord of the Admiralty, wrote to me: 'I cannot tell you how glad I am that all has been accomplished so successfully and speedily, and especially that Daladier has been rallied to your Cabinet. This is much admired over here, and also Blum's self-effacing behaviour.

'I rejoice that you are at the helm, and that Mandel is with you, and I look forward to the very closest and most active co-operation between our two Governments. . . .

'I look forward to an early meeting of the Supreme Council, where I trust concerted action may be arranged between French and English *colleagues*—for that is what we are.'[4]

---

[1] Because of the attitude which I had adopted in the Abyssinian affair, I took good care not to offer Mussolini any pretext to take umbrage against my Administration. That is why, whilst leaving out Georges Bonnet, I decided to give Monzie the strictly technical portfolio of Public Works.

[2] My Administration was therefore composed of: *President of the Council and Minister of Foreign Affairs*, Paul Reynaud; *Vice-President of the Council*, Chautemps; *National Defence and War*, Daladier; *Justice*, Sérol; *Navy*, Campinchi; *Air*, Laurent-Eynac; *Munitions*, Dautry; *Blockade*, Georges Monnet; *Finance*, Lamoureux; *Information*, Frossard; *Interior*, Roy; *Commerce and Industry*, Rollin; *Supplies*, Queuille; *Agriculture*, Thellier; *Merchant Navy*, Rio; *Colonies*, Mandel; *Communications*, Julien; *Public Works*, Monzie; *National Education*, Sarraut; *Labour*, Pomaret; *Public Health*, Héraud; *Pensions*, Rivière.

Undersecretaries of State:
To the President of the Council, Champetier de Ribes; *To the Vice-Presidency*, Robert Schuman; *Of National Defence*, Ducos; *Navy*, Le Cour Grandmaison; *Information*, Février; *Finances*, Laniel; *Aircraft Production*, Colonel Mény; *Munitions*, Blancho; *Interior*, Jacquinot; *Public Works*, Albertin; *Merchant Navy*, Pinelli.

[3] This should not be confused with the War Committee, a body provided for by law, and presided over by the President of the Republic. It comprised the President of the Council, the Foreign Minister, the Ministers of National Defence, the Colonies, and the Commanders-in-Chief.

[4] Churchill, *op. cit.*, vol. 1, *The Gathering Storm*, p. 519 (second edition).

Need I say that Churchill's friendliness was a great comfort to me? Alluding to the formation of my Administration, he writes:[1] 'My relations with M. Reynaud stood on a different footing from any I had established with M. Daladier. Reynaud, Mandel, and I had felt the same emotions about Munich. Daladier had been on the other side. I therefore welcomed the change in the French Government. . . .'

On the 23rd I faced the Chamber with my Government. As one can guess, it was received without enthusiasm, if not with hostility, by a part of the Centre of the Right and the Left.

My ministerial statement was short. I confronted Parliament with its responsibilities: 'The stake in total warfare is the whole stake. To conquer is to save everything. To succumb is to lose everything. . . . Parliament, expressing the national will, has weighed these terrible realities in all their significance. Therefore, the Government which is before you has no other reason for its existence and it wishes to have none other than the following: to arouse, assemble and direct all sources of French energy to fight and to conquer; to crush treason, wherever it may spring up. Thanks to your confidence and with your support, we shall achieve this task.'[2]

Speakers from the Right criticized the composition of my Cabinet and, in particular, the choice of such or such a Socialist Minister. Radical Socialists speakers accused me on their own behalf but not without sympathetic echo within their party, of having seized power as the result of complicity with the Socialists; this inspired Léon Blum to utter an eloquent protest.

I replied: 'We wish to make war, because it is only a will to war which will result in the durable peace we desire. If this will to war is disapproved by you, the enemy will understand. . . . If you grant us your confidence, we shall have to suffer, probably in the near future, terrible ordeals. We shall hold to our course, with teeth clenched, and deep in our hearts the will to fight and the conviction of conquering.'

On the division I gained two hundred and sixty-eight votes, of which a hundred and fifty-three were Socialists,[3] who thus constituted the greater part of my majority, against a hundred and fifty-six; there were a hundred and eleven abstentions. Out of a hundred and sixty-six Radicals, seventy abstained, thirty-three voted for me and ten against me. Out of forty-three members of the *Alliance Démocratique*, twenty-four voted against me and twelve abstained. On the Right,

[1] *Ibid.*, vol. I, *The Gathering Storm*, p. 518 (second edition).
[2] At a Cabinet meeting which I had called in the morning to submit my ministerial declaration, Mandel had demanded the insertion of a sentence 'stigmatizing' the conduct of the Soviets. I had immediately agreed to this.
[3] Out of a total of a hundred and fifty-five, two of them abstained.

the *Fédération Républicaine* opposed me,[1] a fact about which I have no grounds for complaint, since they had refused to join my Government.

When I was speaking to the Chamber, the President of the *Gauche Radicale* came to tell me that his party considered that it had been badly treated because none of its members were in my Cabinet. Opposed for my 'war-mongering' by the leaders of the Centre, I could not even rally the support of the majority of my own party to my Administration. It was true that the leaders of the Centre were not in my Cabinet. There was a more serious handicap. The Radical Socialist Group, which was second only in importance to the Socialists in the Chamber, revealed its hostility to me as much by its attitude as by its votes, even when three of its members, Daladier, Chautemps and Sarraut (all former Presidents of the Council), were sitting by my side. It was clear that a number of the Radicals were not prepared to admit that their party should lose the post of President of the Council. Chichery did not conceal the ill-temper of his colleagues from me. 'You can do no more than resign', he told me after the vote. This is what I would have done if there had been in Parliament any personality other than his own who had claims on the Presidency of the Council. But this was not the case. The President of the Chamber thought that I should stay in office.

In any case, I then thought that I had no right, especially in time of war, to leave my Government exposed, to perish from backstairs intrigues, and I resolved to drain any abscess immediately. I called my colleagues to a Cabinet meeting in the large dining-room (which was that day very chilly) of the Finance Ministry, which I still occupied. The three former Radical Socialist Presidents of the Council sat opposite me. I called to mind the attitude which their friends in the Chamber had just taken up, and I asked them: 'Don't you find this embarrassing?' I added that, knowing the authority which they exerted over their party, I wished to know if I could count on them. They answered that they must consult with the other Radical members of the Government. I invited them to withdraw into a neighbouring room. After half an hour's consultation they came back like a jury at an assize court. Their verdict was shaded in its meaning. Chautemps spoke on their behalf. His colleagues, he said, thought that my own capabilities could not be questioned; but they wondered if, in time of war, there did not exist a danger to a Government which was supported by such a weak and therefore precarious majority. It was not for the Radicals to decide this question. It was for the leader of the Government himself. In brief, it was a question of inviting me to interpret the division in the Chamber

[1] Fifty-one members of this party voted against me out of a total of fifty-four; one abstained and two were on holiday.

as an indication that I should resign, but without the Radicals assuming any responsibility for the crisis.

I replied that the duty of the entire Government was to consider what would be the consequences of a new crisis in the present circumstances. Marcel Héraud on the one hand, and the Socialists, Sérol and Rivière on the other, supported me. Sérol, especially, demonstrated the danger that existed in opening the way during war-time to a succession of crises. Whilst reserving the rights of his party to have the final word, Chautemps finally assured me of the support of his colleagues.

'The Chamber is looking for someone to guide it', said Mandel. 'Are we prepared to do so?'

'Let us do so and we shall stem the tide', was my reply. At the conclusion of the meeting the following communiqué was issued: 'A meeting of the Cabinet took place at the Ministry of Finance under the presidency of M. Paul Reynaud. It examined the situation created by the vote of the Chamber. All the Ministers have assured the President of the Council of their loyal co-operation. In such circumstances the leader of the Government has considered that, because of the gravity of the present situation, the duty of the Cabinet, which has obtained an absolute majority of the votes of the Chamber, is to stay in office. The War Cabinet will assemble tomorrow.'

My Cabinet appeared, therefore, to be a very weak one, but it kept on gathering strength. On the 25th, the Radical Socialist newspaper L'Œuvre wrote that Goebbels, turning his wishes into realities, had announced on the wireless the fall of the Government; but his hopes were cheated.

A few days after the creation of my Ministry, I asked Paul Baudouin, Governor of the Bank of Indo-China, to take office as Under-Secretary of State to the President of the Council. According to certain accounts, he was forced into my Cabinet by underhand influence. As usual, the truth of the matter is less diverting than the legend.

Baudouin, a former member of the *École polytechnique* and an Inspector of Finance, had been prominent in circles which bordered the political world from the time Léon Blum appointed him as a colleague of M. Charles Rist, to the head of a committee for controlling the exchange of currency. In the previous month of October, Daladier had offered him the post of Under-Secretary of State to the Ministry of Finance, which he had refused. A subordinate at the same time both of Mandel, Minister of Colonies, and myself, the Minister of Finance, he had supported my financial policy in circles where my campaign on behalf of devaluation had done me harm. He had expressed a desire to serve under me if I took office one day. When I formed my Government, I offered Colonel de Gaulle the post of

Secretary to the War Cabinet, a body which, as I have mentioned, I had just created. The difficulties of his relations with the Ministry of War caused him to decline the post. I then asked Baudouin to accept it, and he agreed. Shortly afterwards Mandel, under whom, as I have said, Baudouin also came, observed to me that I would create some difficulty if I did not nominate Baudouin Under-Secretary of State, because the objection would be raised that the post of Secretary to the War Cabinet could only be occupied by a civil servant or a member of the Government. I told him that I would willingly nominate Baudouin, but that I had heard it said that, in an article in the *Revue de Paris*, he had supported views on foreign policy which were at variance with our own. Mandel told me that Baudouin had, indeed, written such an article, but that he had just made to Mandel the most categoric statements about the war. Thus it came about that Baudouin was nominated, shortly after the formation of my Administration, as Under-Secretary of State to the President of the Council. So it will be seen what truth there was in the stories to which I have referred.

I MAKE A CHOICE BETWEEN TWO WAR POLICIES

When I came into power I had to choose between two war policies.

We have seen that, in the opinion of our Supreme Command, the Allies had the means of beating the Reich through military strength. In Gamelin's opinion,[1] the problem was one of forcing Germany to fight, of forcing her both to take the offensive on our own front and to open new theatres of operations. How was this to be done? By operating against sources of raw material which were necessary to her for the prosecution of the war.

In the West, it was necessary to tighten up the blockade to deprive the enemy of any motive for dealing tactfully with Holland and Belgium. In other words, it was necessary 'to incite Germany to bring matters to a head, and to compel her to invade Holland and Belgium, who would no longer possess any very useful advantage to her from an economic point of view'.

In Scandinavia it was necessary to stop the supplying of Germany with Swedish mineral ore: 'Faced with such a situation', wrote Gamelin, 'Germany might make the decision to react and march into Sweden.'

In the Caucasus 'the bombing of oil wells at Baku and Batum would probably impose a considerable handicap on German supplies of petrol'.

Finally, 'it was important to begin, as soon as possible, the sowing of mines in river waterways by aircraft'.

As will be seen, Gamelin considered that he was ready. He was in

[1] *Note sur la Conduite de la Guerre* submitted to Daladier by Gamelin on March 16, 1940.

a hurry to cross swords with his opponent, in circumstances which he considered the most advantageous, that is, as the assailed. Was not this, moreover, the logical outcome of our military doctrine?[1]

But I had never ceased to oppose this doctrine and to explain the danger which the Panzer Corps, accompanied by its planes, held for us.

On the other hand, an inventory of the military situation, which I had just had drawn up, emphasized the increasing superiority of German strength over that of the Franco-British Armies.

Because of this last reason some took the opposite point of view to that of our Supreme Command. They maintained that the Napoleonic principle of 'victory goes to the largest battalions' was more true than ever. So strongly did they hold this to be true that, in their opinion we had no chance of winning a military victory, whilst we lacked the help of a new ally.[2]

How, they asked, did we win the First World War? It came about solely because the gap between a hundred and seventy-five Franco-British divisions and two hundred and seven German ones on the Western front was made up by the reinforcements of the American Army. Now, today, this lack of proportion was even greater. What could we oppose to the hundred and ninety divisions which the Germans would have formed by the coming month? A hundred French and ten British divisions. And this discrepancy would continue to increase; French potentialities in man-power had almost touched their ceiling; the British could only form between now and the end of the year another ten new divisions, whilst the Germans would not be long in passing the figure of two hundred and forty-eight divisions, which marked their peak in the last conflict. If, therefore, we could not hope, as in 1918, for the assistance of a third army, it was completely useless to think that we could supply a military solution to the war. Now, was it not true that this third army was nowhere in sight?

Therefore, we had to try and settle with the Reich by suffocating her. But the blockade of the First World War had had no deadly effect on Germany. Why was this? It was because we confined ourselves at that time to intercepting the flow of supplies, a form of blockade which can never be decisive. It was necessary, therefore, to capture these

[1] It will be seen later that the Spanish Foreign Minister, Colonel Beigbeder, said to one of our countrymen in March, 1940, that the German armoured divisions would burst through our front 'like a thunderbolt'. On his return to Morocco, the latter reported this conversation to the 'appropriate authorities'. He was given to understand, he says, that he was being 'to say the least, naïve, and that our own authorities knew better than anybody the relative value of the German armoured divisions; that we were just waiting for their attack to achieve their destruction, and, after this, passing over to the offensive, we would soon bring about the capitulation of the enemy'.

[2] This thesis was, as far as I know, first propounded by Lieutenant-Colonel de Villelume. He was the liaison officer between the Ministry of War and the Ministry of Foreign Affairs in military matters. I was to include him on May 10 as head of my secretariat at the Ministry of National Defence.

supplies. Let us seize the supplies of iron, the only important 'strategic raw material' which was within our reach. That step would be, moreover, the only means of reinvigorating that strength (already in a state of semi-lethargy) which came from our mastery of the sea; of finding a use to which British help could be put, a help which, for a long time to come, could only be powerfully applied in this way.

Such was the thesis which I adopted, for, without being a supporter of the quantitative theory, I noted that our opponent had both quantity and quality. The Chamber and the Senate, to whom I explained the idea at a secret sitting, gave me their unanimous approval. I received the support of the British Goverment as regards the Norwegian operation.

THE NORWEGIAN EXPEDITION: 'THE PERMANENT ROAD TO THE IRON SUPPLIES IS CUT'

For four years the Vichy Press stated that the Norwegian expedition had no strategic importance, and accused me of having committed the country to this adventure merely for the sake of consolidating my Administration. It did not stop deriding my statement in the Senate, 'The permanent road to the iron supplies is definitely cut.'

Hitler has chosen to differ on this first point with the strategists of Vichy. He was to say in his speech of March 16, 1941: 'On April 9, thanks to our gaining a few hours' advantage over the enemy, Britain's most dangerous attempt failed; the attempt to strike us to the very heart in the North.'

He returned to the subject in his proclamation of May 4, 1941: 'The German Government learned that a plan was going to be put into execution against the Reich, which would have given it a decisive blow. . . .'

A blow to the very heart: a decisive blow. Hitler himself is speaking.

We have seen what the situation was like when I came to power.

On March 14 and 15, Daladier had repeated his demands to the British: it was important, he stressed, no longer to delay the execution of an operation intended to gain for us the mastery of Norwegian territorial waters and the possession of certain ports in that country.

For my part, I had submitted on the 25th to Chamberlain a memorandum to stress the fact that I myself fully accepted this step of Daladier. But London still did not seem to have made up its mind to take action. We had, however, to finish with these delays. The two Governments agreed, therefore, to proceed to a detailed study of the problem at the next meeting of the Supreme Council; this was fixed for the 28th.

Now I had to ask myself the following question. Would the reasons which were causing the British Government to hesitate take precedence over the stakes involved in the struggle to be undertaken?

Gamelin, as we have seen, had his own theory. He stuck to it, even after operations had begun in Norway. On April 21, that is to say after the opening of the campaign, he was indeed to write to Daladier: 'The French Supreme Command considers that the Scandinavian business must have the most serious effects on the outcome of the war. It comes within the framework of the plan, which the Command outlined, of opening new theatres of operations, designed to pin down and wear out the enemy. This has always been the rational conception of conducting operations, such as that of a battle against a powerful adversary. On the other hand, the Scandinavian business may have reactions on the attitude of all the neutral Powers, and on Italy in particular. The greatest moral importance is attached to our success. Finally, it is necessary to add the importance that exists, both for the conduct of the war as well as for the blockade of Germany, in the mining basins of the north and centre of Sweden.

'However, if in this theatre of operation there is one of the elements of victory, it cannot lead our troops victoriously into the heart of Germany, for it is bounded by the Danish straits. Both for ensuring the indispensable integrity of our national territory as well as for enabling us one day to attack the left bank of the Rhine, and threaten the nerve centres of German strength, the north-east theatre of operations remains the principal one, unless, because of the entry into the war on our side of Italy, ways into Germany are opened in the south and along the Danube.'

As will be seen, the iron ore was only the last argument of our Supreme Command.

I have said that, for myself, it was the decisive argument. It was decided, therefore, to enter and win the battle of iron. Since I considered this to be essential, I went to London on March 27, where, as I have said, the Supreme Council was to meet on the next day.

It is now time, therefore, to cast an eye on the nature and chances of success of the entire operations, which have been called the Norwegian campaign.

Certain people will object that it is unreasonable for the weaker adversary to create a new front; by doing this his own forces will be thinned out, and the enemy permitted to increase his relative superiority at the point which he has chosen to attack. This is perfectly correct in principle. In the present case, however, the weakening was to be insignificant: forty-five thousand men out of two million five hundred and seventy-five thousand then under arms. And these were not raised from the north-eastern front.

Others will also say that we would, inevitably, find in the new theatre of operations that superiority in men which the enemy placed against us in France. But this reasoning is not valid. On foreign fronts, in actual fact, the importance of troops who can be engaged depends much less on the total forces and material available than on the opportunities which are available for their transport and supply. Now, in the Scandinavian campaign, if it had been carried out in a normal way, Germany above all would have been handicapped in these respects. These handicaps would have prevented her from intervening in time with sufficient forces to prevent our weak forces from putting the iron mines out of service.

But, some will say again, the Germans would have been able in the long run to transport into Sweden enough forces to drive our own out of the country. That is possible, but repairing the installations necessary for the production and transport of the iron ore could not have been accomplished before the return of cold weather. Germany would, therefore, have been totally deprived of Swedish ore for a year, and this would have had a considerable effect.

On my arrival in London, I found Gamelin, Vuillemin and Darlan at the Embassy. They told me that, in the military sphere, a complete agreement had been reached between the British and themselves but that, in the political, the consent of the British Government had still to be obtained. After dinner I received a visit from Chamberlain and Lord Halifax. I informed them that I would be unable to answer, before a parliamentary committee, the question of how we could win the war in the present circumstances, unless some action aimed at depriving the enemy of his supply of Swedish iron ore were undertaken.

The Supreme Council decided, therefore, that on April 5 mines would be sown in Norwegian waters, and that before doing this, we were to warn the Scandinavian Governments. British consent, which had been refused us for four months, was given.

This was, however, only at the price of a slight concession in another sphere. For some months also we had opposed, from a fear of reprisals, a British plan for sowing mines in the Rhine and other German waterways. Churchill was insistent on this. With the agreement of Gamelin—Daladier had not been able to come—I consented, with the reservation that the War Committee should approve to link the two plans in spite of their extremely unequal importance. There was to be no placing of British sea mines unless mines were also sown in rivers.

The War Committee refused unfortunately to endorse my acceptance. On the 3rd the British Government therefore informed me that the operation scheduled for the next day in Norwegian waters would not take place.

Churchill arrived in Paris on the 5th. Finally, the British Government decided that sea mines would be sown. But this operation was delayed until the 8th, and this time-lag had been used by Hitler to find out about the business and to prepare his reply.

In the evening of the 8th, Reuter issued a dispatch that German convoys were crossing the North Sea. I immediately telephoned the news to Gamelin, who did not know about it: 'I hope', I said to him, 'that you have prepared a thunderbolt in reply.'

I also had a colleague telephone Darlan, who did not hide his astonishment. The following dialogue took place between my colleague and Darlan:

'How do you know?'

'I've just read it in Reuter.'

'Then I'm going to make inquiries.'

On the following night, the invasion of Denmark and Norway was an accomplished fact.

At seven o'clock in the morning the three Ministers for National Defence, Daladier, Campinchi and Laurent-Eynac as well as Gamelin, were gathered in my room at the Quai d'Orsay. The Commander-in-Chief informed me that the only body of troops trained for the Scandinavian theatre of operations was the Audet division which, moreover, was not at Brest but in the Juras. It would take it two days to get to Brest from where it would embark for the Clyde; from there it would sail for Norway where the Germans had already disembarked the previous night. We were, therefore, anticipated, although it was ourselves who had taken the initiative for an operation which we had devised for our convenience. It was a cruel surprise. Gamelin made the objection that it was the British who were in command of the expedition.

'Have you given the British leave to have you defeated?' I replied to him.

The fact that the British were in chief command of the expedition placed the onus for faults committed in its execution on their passivity. But the faults in planning lay at the door of the two Allied Supreme Commands, who had drawn up the schemes in common. One of the aims was, according to Gamelin, to lure our opponent into a trap by provoking him to invade Norway. Now, far from falling into a trap, he had forestalled us by seizing Norwegian ports and placing his planes on aerodromes near to these ports, from where he bombed Allied warships and thus thwarted our expedition into central Norway.

I immediately asked for a meeting of the War Committee. With M. Lebrun in the chair it included Daladier, Campinchi, Laurent-Eynac and Mandel, as well as Gamelin, Vuillemin, Georges, Bührer, Darlan and myself. I expressed the opinion that it was necessary to take immediate action in the neighbourhood of Narvik as iron ore was of supreme importance to the outcome of the war. I asked for the dispatch of the mixed brigade at Brest, which had been originally formed for Finland, to be speeded up, and for arms to be immediately taken on board. I emphasized that it was a *race* between Germany and the Allies, which had begun. Darlan proposed that we should reply to German aggression by sending our troops into Belgium, by local attacks on the north-east front and by sowing mines in the rivers.

For the time being I will ignore the discussion concerning the Belgian operation. As far as the Scandinavian campaign was concerned it was finally decided that we would promise help and assistance to the Norwegian Government and that I would go, with Daladier and Darlan, the same day to London.

At the Supreme Council which met in the afternoon, a decision was taken to send help to Norway at last.

But what were the forces to be?

The only units which had been placed on a war footing were those which had been prepared for Finland, and the two British divisions which it was intended should be sent there, had been subsequently shipped to France. They were no longer available.

Britain had, since February, on the first appeal from Helsinki and with a view to occupying Stavanger, Bergen and Trondheim, prepared seven battalions. There was not one more. For three days even these would be five short. These five had in actual fact been embarked on cruisers, when the mines were being laid. But these mines had not been guarded, and the Germans had swept them. The British therefore sent these same cruisers at full speed to the spot, after, having hastily disembarked the five battalions . . . but, without thinking to unload their equipment also.

We know the state in which we French found ourselves.

There had been, however, no lack of warning. Darlan, whom I was reproaching one day because of the inefficiency which had characterized the organization of the Norwegian expedition, answered: 'Ask Campinchi to let you have my letter to Daladier.' He had indeed written a letter to Daladier and Gamelin on March 30, which I got to know about ten days later when I asked for it. In it he stated: 'It would be foolish to imagine that Germany will passively look on whilst we intervene in Norwegian waters. Recent information reveals that she has gathered the material for an expedition against bases in south Norway . . . or Sweden. It is not unreasonable to think that she will react the day after our diplomatic move or after sowing the mines, that is to say, April 3 or 6, by invading the Scandinavian peninsula, or marching on the mineral supplies. If, therefore, we do not want to run the risk of losing the benefit of the step which we are preparing, we must be ready to disembark in Norway. . . . The assembly of a Franco-British expeditionary corps and the means for appropriate transport seem to me an indispensable complement to the inter-allied decisions of March 28. I have brought the fact to the attention of General . . . Gamelin . . . on this very same day.

'[When it was a question] of the Finnish operation, a delay of a fortnight had been allowed for assembling in the embarkation ports the maritime means necessary for an expedition of the same kind. I am taking steps to cut down this time to a week. I propose, in brief, that a Franco-British expeditionary corps be held ready to operate against Narvik as soon as possible after the Note of April 2 has been sent. Every day gained will be of importance. . . . A commander should immediately be appointed for this impending expedition. So that French maritime resources for transport can be assembled in a week, an immediate decision in principle, authorizing the Navy to proceed with immediate requisitioning, is necessary. . . .'[1]

My mental attitude on receiving this tardy communication can be well imagined.

On April 5, I had warned Gamelin of the impending sowing of these mines, and I had asked him to hold himself in readiness. Finally, on the 8th, I had telephoned to him about the departure of the German transports.

As for the preparations for embarkation, they were in a more than neglected state, in spite of the efforts of Darlan. Though the latter had raised the question of requisitioning ships on the 2nd, it was only on the 9th, when the Germans were already in Trondheim, that he was given the authority to proceed with this. Fortunately he had, to a certain degree, anticipated the authorization.

Therefore, here we were at the outset, heavily handicapped. It was essential to make up the leeway.

On the 11th, I wrote to Daladier: 'During a conversation which we had yesterday with the Commander-in-Chief and the Admiral of the Fleet, we agreed on a certain number of principles to be followed and steps to be taken for prosecuting the war in the Norwegian theatre of operations. . . .

'1. The conflict which has begun is one for iron. On the outcome of the struggle will depend the fate of the war. . . . The campaign . . . is of vital importance.

'2. The objective of France . . . should not simply be the clearing of

---

[1] Gamelin told me in Germany that Darlan, who had control over the operation, did not play a fair game. He was evasive about the choice of an embarkation port; either Brest or Cherbourg; and asked for the troops not to be sent in advance so that the attention of the enemy would not be attracted. The latter showed less scruple and more efficiency. Similarly, the British Admiralty did not wish, so Gamelin told me, to have our troops earlier. A fine organization for defeat!

the Norwegian ... coast. The only serious action is a rapid disembarkation of considerable numbers of troops in Norway, ready to occupy
the Swedish iron ore mines. ...'

And I concluded by asking for the Audet division to be embarked
the following day, even if the transportation of this division had the
effect of seriously disturbing rail traffic; and, within a fortnight, for
two or three other divisions to be 'assembled in some spot, ready to
leave in case there was a lack of British troops'.

But it was urgent that we should decide and act. On the next day,
the 12th, at six o'clock in the evening, I called the War Cabinet. This
discussion is of such great interest, both from a psychological as well as
a political point of view, that I think I should give the minutes of it.

M. Paul Reynaud explained under what conditions and according to which
directives he had, during the last few days, pursued diplomatic action and laid
down the outlines for France's military action. He began by pointing out that
an attack against the Siegfried line could not be contemplated at the present
time; that the best means of acting effectively against Germany were to strike at
her supplies of iron and oil. To take action against these raw materials it was
necessary to intervene either in the north of Europe, or the Black Sea and the
southern Caucasus. During a preceding War Cabinet, General Weygand had
approved the general lines of preparation for an action in the oil region. Today,
it was a question, said M. Paul Reynaud, of examining the present situation in
the struggle, now begun in Scandinavia, and of formulating directives for
future action, which should be prompt and powerful.

The President of the Council recalled the circumstances in which, on the
morning of April 8, minefields had been sown as the result of the decision
taken by the Supreme Council on March 28, and of Mr. Churchill's visit to
Paris. He demonstrated on the map the principal results of the German reaction
of last Tuesday and of following days. Repeating the words of his recent
explanations in the Senate and the Chamber ... he pointed out that it was the
battle of iron supplies which was being waged, that this battle could have a
considerable importance on the outcome of the struggle, and that it was, therefore, essential to win it. To do so it was necessary to strike strongly and quickly
by disembarking a force as considerable as possible at Narvik, ready to move
very rapidly on the mining basin of north Sweden before the thaw had freed
the port of Luleå from ice. One might anticipate indeed the arrival in this port
of German forces during the last days of April. He had the War Cabinet
approve the written instructions given to the Ambassador, M. Coulondre, who,
accompanied by General Mittelhausser, had left on Thursday morning by
plane, and arrived at Stockholm a few hours before the meeting of the War
Cabinet.[1]

---

[1] The mission was entrusted with the duty:

1. Of giving the Swedish Government the assurance that, in case of an attack by the
Germans, the Allies would stand by Sweden.

2. Of asking it to mobilize its military resources and of pointing out the danger of a
German attempt on Luleå.

He read a letter which he had sent on April 11 to the Minister of National Defence to point out that the battle which had begun was above all one requiring speed and audacity. On this subject M. Paul Reynaud read part of a letter addressed on March 30 by Admiral Darlan to the Minister of National Defence, which anticipated a German reply to the sowing of mines, and which asked General Gamelin to prepare steps in order to ward off this counter-stroke. M. Paul Reynaud had no hesitation in calling this letter prophetic, in that it anticipated the events of April 9 and of following days. But, on the contrary, the President of the Council regretted that he had to point out the apparent failure of the Supreme Command to follow the advice of Admiral Darlan and to take steps to overcome the German reply. The President of the Council considered that there had been an authentic failure on part of those entrusted with planning French and British counter-measures and with preparing them. He gave numerous details about this matter: in particular, he said that the units embarked for Norway were still in the Juras on the 10th, and that the transport convoy had not been completely assembled.

All these reasons inspired the President of the Council to stress particularly to the War Cabinet the importance of taking some decision, designed to speed up military disembarkations in Norway, and to provide for their reinforcement in the same proportion as the enemy developed his action. . . . He asked the War Cabinet if the latter was . . . in agreement with this policy . . . and if it approved of the instructions which he had given the day before in his letter to the Minister of National Defence.

No member of the War Cabinet answered the request of the President of the Council.

After a long silence, M. Daladier . . . intervened to state . . . that, in his opinion, no criticism could be levied against General Gamelin, and he would, moreover, like the latter to come immediately to the meeting to give any explanations himself. M. Paul Reynaud replied that it was preferable for the members of the Government to begin the discussion amongst themselves before hearing General Gamelin. M. Daladier pointed out that the operations undertaken during the last days in Norway and those which were to begin in the near future and continue for several days, according to a plan drawn up by the British General Staff in agreement with the French, were above all naval operations, that, moreover, British contingents would be engaged before French ones, and that, in the present state of things, the participation of British soldiers would be more important than that of French. He added that, in agreement with a plan adopted by France and Britain which laid down that, whilst operations in France and the western Mediterranean were to fall under French command, those in the north Atlantic and the eastern Mediterranean were to

3. Of persuading it to refuse the Germans, should they ask for it, the use of Swedish railways for their Norwegian operations.

Chamberlain, whom M. Coulondre had seen in London, had approved this step.

The mission had found the Swedish Government and public opinion deeply alarmed by the German successes.

The Swedish Minister of Foreign Affairs stated that he had full confidence in the Allies, and that Sweden would refuse, if it were necessary, the use of Swedish territory to the Germans, and that a strong force would be posted at Luleå in order to oppose any attempt to seize it.

come under British, it was Britain who had assumed control of operations in Norway. M. Daladier added that he thought the criticisms developed by the President of the Council were unjustified, for, in his opinion, General Gamelin had given all the backing which the suggestions offered by Admiral Darlan in his letter of March 30 deserved. He considered that the plans for Anglo-French action had been laid down, and that there was not, at the present time, any criticism to be made or modification to be introduced.

M. Dautry, Minister for Armaments, indicated that in his opinion time was pressing, and it was essential not to lose sight of the final objective of the Anglo-French operation in Norway, which was to seize hold of the iron ore mines or, at least, to prevent the Germans from exploiting them. Consequently, it was necessary to destroy quickly the railway line to Luleå, the electrical power station, and finally, to advance on the mines by a bold movement which would either occupy or destroy these centres vital to the German iron industry.

The President of the Council pointed out that he was not in agreement with M. Daladier, because he found that the present plans, drawn up before German aggression against Denmark and Norway, were partly forestalled by the very fact of this aggression. He insisted on action without delay and without hesitation, a single quick campaign which would ensure success . . . in Scandinavia. He thought that the French Supreme Command was not sufficiently inspired by this need for prompt action, and did not seem convinced of the fact that, because of the impossibility of taking action on the western front, only battles on the wings were possible. Now, Scandinavia presented a battlefield on the northern wing, which could be decisively important in the war. . . .

At ten minutes past seven General Gamelin and Admiral Darlan were brought into the Council.

M. Paul Reynaud asked General Gamelin to sum up the situation. General Gamelin pointed out that Admiral Darlan was in a better position to give the latest information.

Admiral Darlan indicated, according to the latest news received, the position of German naval and land forces along the Norwegian coasts, and gave details of the counter-operations begun by the British Navy.

M. Paul Reynaud asked General Gamelin to give details of the measures which had been planned in case of a German reply to the sowing of mines, and to give an indication of the pace at which these would be carried out. The question of *speed* seemed to him essential at the present time. General Gamelin said that the campaign was being directed by the British General Staff, that it was under the command of General Ironside, and it had been studied in collaboration with representatives of his own General Staff, but that, at present only the British Command had charge of the Norwegian operations. He did not think it was possible to intervene at the present moment with this Command, for a plan had been laid down which did not provide for the employment of French troops except as a support.

M. Paul Reynaud was insistent on the need for pointing out to the British Command to what degree the French Government, responsible towards its own country for the general handling oft he war, was convinced that it was necessary to strike quickly and strongly. Would it not be possible to speed up the operations laid down by the plan of which General Gamelin had spoken, for increasing the forces before disembarking on the Norwegian coasts? It was important to go to the help of Norway, and also to bolster up thereby the morale of Sweden, who was, possibly, on the verge of receiving a German ultimatum, and who would, perhaps, give way to that ultimatum if she were not backed by the firm intention, already translated into vigorous action, of Britain and France, to assist her. General Gamelin, supported by brief remarks uttered from time to time by M. Daladier, pointed out that his conception of command together with the responsibilities which it implied did not coincide with the wishes expressed by the President of the Council, who desired to modify a military plan when its implementation had been scarcely begun. In his opinion, continued General Gamelin, the only attitude to take was one of trust in the British Command. He stated that, for his own part, he had taken the steps suggested in Admiral Darlan's Note of March 30, and that there was no need for planning a more rapid concentration and hasty embarkation, since the British plan did not provide for the precipitate entry into action of French troops.

The President of the Council pointed out that he had never meant that the plan drawn up by the British Command should be discarded or profoundly modified, but it seemed, nevertheless, to him that it should undergo certain changes, if only by reason that it provided for the occupation of the Norwegian coasts without these being previously seized by the enemy. Now, the Germans were at Bergen and Narvik. In such circumstances, continued the President, should not some modifications be made in the plan? Should not events be speeded up, the execution of this plan pressed on, and more important forces provided with which to intervene?

Admiral Darlan broke in to point out it did not seem possible to him to speed up the plan for throwing in more forces[1] and that, on the contrary, the presence of the enemy would, it was to be feared, prolong its execution by three or four days. Moreover, increasing the number of French troops was a very difficult problem since the British Admiralty had asked the French Government to provide for the transport of its own troops. Now, France had very few ships available, and an increase in troops to be transported to Norway would cause a grave disturbance in supplying France by sea.

M. Chautemps intervened to state that, in his opinion, the present discussion had lost any motive as a result of explanations given by General Gamelin and Admiral Darlan. In reality, the War Cabinet had met only to find out if some plan for going to the assistance of Norway had been laid down. Now that an affirmative reply had been given by the responsible military commanders, the only possible thing seemed to be to allow this plan to develop according to the lines laid down.

The President of the Council stated that the game which was being played in Norway was so important to the outcome of the war, so decisive as regards the German steel industry, that he, for his part, could not be satisfied with an affirmation that the existing plan was satisfactory, and that it should be allowed to develop without bothering about modifications which could be made in it.

[1] If this were true, it is apparent what a grave mistake was made in evolving, with the collaboration of the British Command, a plan which was insufficient to meet the danger pointed out by Darlan in his letter of March 30. I gained the suspicion at this time that Darlan was not without some ulterior motive. Gamelin's complaint on this matter has been mentioned above.

He believed that it was essential to insist to the British Command that the naval and military attack which the British proposed to begin in the near future should be pressed with an especial vigour. He added that he was ready to inform the British Government that France was prepared to offer, if it were necessary, a considerable contribution to the effort which the Allies were about to undertake in Scandinavia. It was in this sense that he had given instructions to M. Coulondre, who had gone to Stockholm. France and Britain must persevere along this avenue of action or we should lose the game in the North.

M. Dautry and M. Campinchi broke in to ask a certain number of questions about the composition of the expeditionary corps. M. Dautry insisted on the need for destroying the mines and the electric power station as quickly as possible, for he feared, and M. Campinchi supported him . . . on this point, that, when we got to the mines, we might already find them guarded by the Germans who had arrived secretly on the spot. Would the expeditionary corps include sappers of the engineers, supplied with explosive charges capable of blowing up bridges, etc., and factories? General Gamelin replied that the British detachments included engineers, capable of carrying out destructions. When asked by the President of the Council where the electrified section of the Narvik–Luleå line was, whether on the Norwegian or Swedish side, General Gamelin stated that he was unable to answer.

After a rather lengthy exchange of views about the lapse of time required by the British plan and on the methods of its implementation—and the War Cabinet was unanimous in approving that action should be taken initially at Narvik—the President of the Council intervened to sum up the discussion and to detail the decisions which, in his opinion, might be taken. He proposed, with the natural reservation that these decisions met with the agreement of the British Government, to:

1. Ask M. Coulondre to approach the Swedish Government in order to persuade the latter that, if Sweden were attacked by forces of such strength that she could not hold out for long, she would herself destroy the equipment of her iron ore mines in the south and north; France and Britain would state that they were ready to pay the Swedish Government an indemnity corresponding to the damage;

2. Ask Admiral Darlan to approach the British Admiralty in order to obtain the promise for the transportation of additional French troops which the French Government was prepared to send to Norway. Admiral Darlan was, in addition, asked to explain to the British Admiralty how strongly the French Government felt that there was need to retake Narvik promptly;

3. Ask the Military Command to study the organization for a raiding force capable of destroying part of the iron ore installations in the north of Sweden— this, naturally, in the event of Sweden herself being previously attacked—before the expeditionary corps arrived on the spot.

The Cabinet approved these proposals.

Gamelin told me that, after the meeting was over, he offered his resignation to Daladier, who refused it.

Daladier answered, on April 13, my letter of the 11th: 'The General Commander-in-Chief and the Admiral of the Fleet know that events

in Norway are of vital importance, and understand as well as anyone else, from having devoted their attention to it, the major importance of the rapid disembarkation in Norway of a Franco-British
expeditionary force, capable of occupying and holding successfully the
Swedish mines against any German or Russian threat. In this race
between Germany and the Allies, neither the Minister of National
Defence, nor the Commanders-in-Chief of our Armies have been
surprised by events. The French expeditionary force has been recruited
and quickly armed and equipped for the Scandinavian campaign,
thanks to steps which I took a long time ago. . . .'

On the 15th, I again wrote to Daladier in the same strain. I pointed
out to him that the trial of speed between Hitler and ourselves in
Norway was not turning out to our advantage. On the other hand, I
told him, 'to send insufficient forces there would be worse than sending
nobody'. I concluded: 'You will certainly consider, like myself, that
the plan, envisaged up to the present and now being put into execution,
is insufficient, and bears no relation to German activity.'

The fact was that, whilst the Germans were disembarking a division
each week in Norway, we still had not a man there.

On the 18th, I wrote to Chamberlain: 'It is the pace of enemy
reinforcements which should control the pace at which our own
troops arrive. . . . I am, therefore, asking you to try to make the
necessary effort to place at our disposal the tonnage which we
need.'[1]

On the other hand, the British Fleet gained a great success. During
fights which took place up to the 13th, the Navy of the Reich suffered
heavy losses. The Vichy Press has scoffed at me for having called the
sailing of the German Fleet into the North Sea a strategic error. It is
true that the Reich forces established themselves in the port of Narvik
on the 9th at a quarter past five in the morning and that they held on
there until May 28, the day when the Allied troops finally succeeded
in dislodging them. Nevertheless, the fact still remains that the British
Fleet, after having destroyed, during engagements between April 10
and 13, ten of the most modern and speedy torpedo-boats of the Kriegs-
marine—which were escorting General Dietl's convoy—blockaded
closely all the fiords around Narvik. Not another German boat could,
from that date to the end of May, the date of our voluntary evacuation,
enter the port. In the excellent account, which Lieutenant Torris, who
died in action in 1945, has devoted, under the title of *Narvik*, to
this campaign, in which our troops covered themselves with glory,
the author puts into the mouth of Admiral of the Fleet, the Earl of

[1] A military critic has reproached me with intruding into the sphere of operational
activities in Norway. Should the Head of a Government, responsible for the fate of his
country, have had to remain passive, because of some intricate formalities when the threat
of defeat loomed on the horizon, due to the Germans having forestalled us?

Cork and Orrery, who commanded all the Allied Forces in the Narvik sector, the following words:[1] 'The British Fleet from April 13 established a mastery over the fiords. Not a German ship sailed there any longer.' It was therefore merely a matter of prestige for Hitler to continue holding Narvik. This was why he clung so desperately to it. On April 20, Mussolini wrote to him. . . . 'If you have any means whatever to help you to hold on to Narvik, you must use them. If the evacuation of Narvik took place it would become the subject of noisy exploitation by Allied propaganda.'

The future expeditionary force was being organized at this time. If my suggestions were not entirely followed, it was at least decided to form three light divisions (with two infantry regiments) and the equivalent of a fourth (Polish and Foreign Legion). Unfortunately each of these divisions was only to be supplied with very insufficient equipment: an artillery group, two companies with 22-mm. guns for defence against low-flying aircraft, but none which had a range above one thousand metres, a company of out-of-date tanks (except that of the 1st Division), and finally as the sole 'recce' element for all the expeditionary corps, a squadron of machine-gun carriers, which, however, was to be dispersed within the different sectors. The Germans were less parsimonious. It seems probable that they sent a dozen infantry and two armoured divisions into Norway.

Were these slender resources at least compensated for by our rapidity in preparing our troops? And, if we had been forestalled in seizing the ports, was the pace of our movement going to allow us to reconquer them rapidly? Unfortunately the timetable laid down was not in the least inspired by the battle for speed which I had never ceased to advocate. The 1st Light Division (six battalions), the Polish brigade (four battalions) and the two battalions of the Foreign Legion were to embark between the 12th and the 23rd. The first echelon of the 2nd Light Division was in its turn only to embark on the 24th and the second echelon did not leave Brest. As regards the 3rd Light Division, its departure was dependent on the British providing the necessary ships. In actual fact it was destined never to leave Brittany.[2]

Finally, on the 19th, ten days after the first German landing, the first French troops disembarked in Norway. The port chosen was Namsos, from which the Wehrmacht was still some distance, and which was the terminus of roads leading to Sweden. But, though our troops were able to disembark there without interference, they were completely incapable of moving off or of offering any action whatsoever. Their

[1] p. 21.
[2] The 3rd Light Division was later placed completely and solely at the disposal of General Georges. It was the same with the 2nd Division, whose first echelon was brought back from Norway after the evacuation of Namsos.

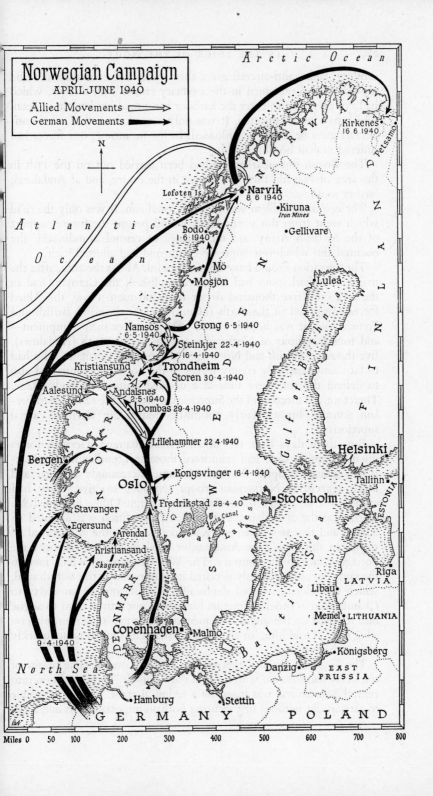

Norwegian Campaign
APRIL-JUNE 1940

Allied Movements ⇨
German Movements ➤

N

Arctic Ocean

Atlantic

Ocean

Kirkenes
16·6·1940

Petsamo

Lofoten Is.

Narvik
8·6·1940

Kiruna
Iron Mines

Gellivare

Bodö
1·6·1940

Mö

Mosjön

Lulea

Grong 6·5·1940

Namsos
6·5·1940

Steinkjer 22·4·1940

16·4·1940

Kristiansund

Trondheim

Storen 30·4·1940

Aalesund

Andalsnes
2·5·1940

Dombas 29·4·1940

Lillehammer 22·4·1940

Bergen

Kongsvinger 16·4·1940

Oslo

Fredrikstad 28·4·40

Helsinki

Tallinn

Stockholm

Stavanger

Egersund

Arendal

Kristiansand

Skagerrak

Gota Canal

ESTONIA

Riga

LATVIA

Libau

Copenhagen

Malmo

Memel · LITHUANIA

Königsberg

9·4·1940

Danzig

EAST
PRUSSIA

North Sea

Hamburg

Stettin

GERMANY

POLAND

Gulf of Bothnia

FINLAND

Baltic Sea

DENMARK

Kattegat

SWEDEN

NORWAY

Miles 0   50   100   200   300   400   500   600   700   800

artillery, tanks, anti-aircraft guns, their mules and even their skis and snowshoes had remained in the auxiliary cruiser *Ville-d'Alger*, which had not been able to enter the harbour because of her length—a detail which had been forgotten. It was only a week later that some anti-aircraft guns began to be unloaded. In the meantime, our forces had suffered violent bombing raids.

The British disembarkations had been carried out on the 13th in the area of Narvik, then at Namsos in the centre, and at Andalsnes, farther south.

The essential problem was to free Trondheim. It was only the road which went from this port, which would permit the future support of the Swedish Army and the defence of central Scandinavia, the essential aim which our Supreme Command had allotted itself.

The operation should have been successful. About the 20th, after the major disembarkations had been accomplished, the Germans had in the area only five thousand or six thousand men. Now, the Allied forces comprised in the north (Namsos), eight thousand British and French who, it was hoped, would finally recover their equipment—and four battalions of Norwegian troops; in the south (Andalsnes), five thousand British and Norwegian troops. The Germans, who had to face simultaneously enemy forces to the north and south and also to defend the sea, were thus at a decided numerical disadvantage. Therefore, at a meeting of the Supreme Council on the 22nd, Chamberlain revealed himself fairly optimistic despite the Germans' aerial superiority.

But, three days later the situation had changed. German forces disembarking at Oslo had reinforced those at Trondheim. The Luftwaffe, which occupied the bases, became increasingly stronger and more aggressive. Norwegian troops remained inactive. They had carried out no destructions. Thus the Foreign Office informed M. Corbin on the 26th that the Trondheim expedition was doomed to failure, and that it was necessary to take steps for the withdrawal of troops in this area. Our Ambassador tried in vain to convince the Foreign Office to the contrary. The War Committee, which met on the same day, unanimously declared itself opposed to this withdrawal, which Gamelin considered deplorable. I wrote on the same day to Chamberlain in order to instruct him about our attitude and to advise him to speed up the dispatch of men and material. 'One must plan on a big scale', I told him, 'or abandon the struggle. One must act quickly or lose the war.'

The Supreme Council met on the 27th in London. The results of our delay had become worse. I told the Council: 'The expedition into central Scandinavia was based on a technical error. It was impossible to carry it out without first securing both an important port and aerial bases. Even without one of these things, the operation would have been difficult. But, lacking both, one has cause to wonder if the Allies have the slightest chance of success.'[1]

On the other hand the occupation of Narvik was attainable and of the utmost importance since it was the exit door to the mineral iron. Chamberlain stated that the capture of Trondheim was no longer possible, and that he thought this point of view was shared by Gamelin, who, however, insisted upon the importance to the Allies of holding Namsos in order to advance from there on Narvik, occupying different points along the coast. The British Government thought we should continue to fight at Namsos, but it believed that it was scarcely possible to keep a foothold there for long. At Narvik, on the contrary, Chamberlain continued, steps had already been taken to seize the port as quickly as possible when weather conditions would allow, and then to push to the Swedish frontier. But would the Swedish Government, intimidated by German successes, allow us to advance to the iron ore mines? The result, moreover, he added, 'would not be as immediate as that resulting from action against the German reserves of oil'.

I myself asked in the first place that at least we should save our face by not evacuating central Scandinavia before having attacked Narvik and, subsequently, that we should defend vigorously the road from Namsos to this port. During the night, the only wharf available at Andalsnes was destroyed by an air raid. The War Office ordered evacuation. 'Lord Halifax', M. Corbin wrote to me on the 28th, 'has assured me that it is only the prospect of not being able to supply the Allied contingents at Andalsnes and Namsos any longer, which has brought about the present situation. . . . It is none the less true that the British military leaders have almost completely readapted their plan . . . the first step of which has thus been organizing the withdrawal of half of the expedition.'

With this inglorious page we must contrast the glorious capture of Narvik on May 28 by our troops and those of our Allies, although they had received the order of evacuation from London on the 26th. On the 30th, the Allied forces pinned the enemy on the Swedish frontier. The examinations at the Nuremberg trial have proved[2] that, at this time, Hitler considered the Allies to have won the battle at Narvik,

---

[1] On my arrival in London I found at the French Embassy Gamelin and Darlan, who had just been conferring with British military and naval authorities. M. Roland de Margerie, director of my diplomatic secretariat (who, in passing, together with M. Dejean his deputy, rendered me outstanding service), has kept a record of the dialogue which then took place between Gamelin and myself. Here is an extract from his notes:

'*Paul Reynaud:* How does the problem of anti-aircraft defence present itself?

'*Gamelin:* I think it will be quite easy to solve. In the valleys, low-flying aircraft are scarcely to be feared, if one places gun sites on the mountain-sides. In such a case, the German Air Force could not continue to operate as it is now doing.'

[2] Cartier, *Les secrets de la guerre, dévoilés par Nuremberg,* pp. 152–3.

and that the Dietl corps was lost. It was Dunkirk that saved Dietl and his troops.

The disaster of Flanders entailed unfortunately a confirmation of the order for withdrawal. This was done at the request of Churchill, by the Supreme Council, which met in Paris[1] on the 31st. Until our voluntary evacuation, 'the permanent road to iron ore supplies', was, I repeat, well and truly cut. The 'madcap enterprise' was based, therefore, on a healthy inspiration. It could have been realized, but its execution was defective.

FRANCE SECURES POSSESSION OF THE NORWEGIAN STOCKS OF HEAVY WATER

In any case we succeeded in foiling Hitler's design to seize hold of one of Norway's most precious possessions: the one hundred and eighty litres of heavy water which constituted the total stocks of this country.

It was France who ensured possession of these stocks, held by the Norwegian Company of Azote. A mission of four officials was entrusted with the operation by Dautry. Dividing themselves into two teams, in order to distribute the risks, the mission, during the last days of April, succeeded under the very nose of the Germans in carrying off the heavy water from the place where it was produced to Stavanger as a first stage, then to Scotland and finally to France. Though the adventure[2] is less romantic than legend would have it, it was of a type to strike the public's imagination.

As soon as he had returned to France, M. Aubert, an official in the Explosives Department, who was leading the mission, came to see me at the Quai d'Orsay. This was at the beginning of May. He told me of the adventures of his team. He informed me of the far-reaching researches which this precious material would allow him to carry out. But, for this, considerable expense would have to be undertaken. The support and protection of the State would be necessary over a certain number of years. He asked me to arrange this collaboration for him. I promised him that I would set about doing this.

APRIL 9: MY OPPOSITION TO THE BELGIAN OPERATION

The question of the Allies entering Belgium was raised, as we have seen, at the War Committee on April 9. It was Darlan who proposed answering the attack against Denmark by sending our troops into Belgium.

It was obvious that, if the operation was one day to take place, it

---

[1] The evacuation took place on June 8. It was carried out in four convoys. The Allied forces (French, British and Polish) of twenty-four thousand men were all re-embarked, as well as large quantities of provisions and equipment.

[2] Cf. Le Monde, April 28, 1948.

would be better for us to choose our own good time rather than allow the enemy to do this. But the problem was to know if, on April 9, we had the means of undertaking such an operation. This was the reason why I asked our military leaders whether our twofold inferiority in troops and material ought not rather to persuade us against the enterprise.

'I have taken up my responsibilities', Gamelin gravely answered me. I understood by this that he was using the powers which he legally possessed. The argument was unanswerable; or rather the only reply to it by the Head of the Government was a decision to relieve him of the post of Commander-in-Chief.[1]

Georges, whose opinion I asked because I thought he was against the operation, declared that he was in agreement with his superior. I had therefore to give way.

In addition, here is a passage from the minutes about this matter: 'Admiral Darlan proposed advancing into Belgium and proceeding to sow mines in the rivers as well as making local attacks on the north-east front.

'The President of the Council asked General Gamelin for his opinion about these proposals. General Gamelin stated that he was in favour of action in Belgium. After the President of the Council pointed out to him that the enemy was twice as strong as we were in aircraft and men,[2] General Gamelin reiterated his affirmative reply, and General Georges supported him in it.

'The Minister of National Defence and War gave an opinion which was wholeheartedly in support of the operation.

'It was unanimously decided:

'1. That the Government would try to obtain the consent of the Belgian Government for carrying out the Belgian operation;

'2. That if this were granted, the operation would be undertaken;

'3. That if the operation were undertaken, the rivers would be mined;

'4. That the Government should inform the Belgian Government that France would give her help and assistance;

'5. That the President of the Council, the Minister of National Defence and War and Admiral Darlan should proceed that afternoon to London.'

Thus, after having repeatedly said during the years preceding the war: 'If you wish to advance into Belgium, arm', I said on April 9, 1940: 'Since you have not armed, do not advance into Belgium.'

[1] At this stage the difference may be pointed out between ourselves and Britain, where, in time of war, the military steps are decided by the Committee for Defence, presided over by the Prime Minister.

[2] It goes without saying that the superiority of the enemy in armoured divisions, which the minutes do not mention, was amongst the most considerable of my worries.

As this meeting of the War Committee had been hurriedly called, it was Gamelin who, in the absence of the Secretary of the Committee, sent me a draft of the minutes, which omitted my opposition to the Belgian operation. I demanded a correction which would clearly emphasize the importance that I attached to my attitude.

Let me observe that, a month after the publication in Paris of these amended minutes in *Les Nouvelles Continentales* of July 5, 1941, Déat stated in *L'Œuvre* of August 7, that one of my crimes was to 'have thrown our best Army into Belgium instead of leaving it to defend our lines'.

At the Supreme Council which met that afternoon in London, I explained the thesis of the War Committee as to the advantage of the shortened front which the Belgian operation would entail. The decision was taken. The two Governments would urge the Belgian Government to delay no longer in asking the Allies to enter Belgium, and thus no longer to wait, before doing this, for a German invasion. They emphasized the gravity of the responsibility which the Belgian Government would assume, if it persisted in refusing to agree. The step would be supported by a parallel one in which the French Supreme Command would approach its Belgian counterpart.[1]

The approach proved once more to be fruitless. During the evening of the 11th, M. Spaak told our Ambassador that, 'in the present state of affairs, the Government did not believe itself justified in appealing to the guarantee of France and Britain'. General van Overstraeten, after having seen the King, stated for the Belgians that 'the reply is in the negative'.

MAY 9: I ASK FOR GAMELIN TO BE RELIEVED OF HIS COMMAND; I RESIGN; ON THE FOLLOWING DAY THE GERMAN OFFENSIVE OBLIGES ME TO REMAIN IN POWER

I have spoken of the mistake in planning which had hampered the organization of the expedition to central Norway. The Germans had been quick; the Allies had been slow. The latter had allowed themselves to be forestalled in an operation, undertaken though it was, in their good time. From that time, Gamelin's hope of opening a theatre of operations in Scandinavia was to be reduced to naught.

From the time of the meeting of the War Committee on April 9, I found myself, as one has seen, in conflict with Gamelin on this subject. It was a difficult situation for me, because I was not the

---

[1] Churchill also asked the Supreme Council to agree that the Belgian operation would be carried out automatically if Holland were invaded. I offered no opposition to this, because the hypothesis of an invasion of Holland alone seemed to me purely theoretical. The Belgians informed us, moreover, that, in this unlikely event, they would call in our assistance.

Minister of War, and Daladier who held this post, had made common
cause with Gamelin. I had not ceased from that time protesting against
the delays which were to end in the check to the Scandinavian expedition.

I was, therefore, in disagreement with Daladier and Gamelin at the
same time about the Norwegian expedition and the future operation
in Belgium, as I had been for several years over the organization of
our Army. I had the alternative of giving way or provoking a certain
ministerial crisis. Indeed, it was no longer possible for me to exercise
power in such circumstances. If, on the other hand, I was entrusted
with forming a new Government, I would begin by taking over the
Ministry of War and by asking for Gamelin's resignation. I decided,
therefore, to assemble the Cabinet Council on May 9, and during the
meeting I would explain the reasons for replacing Gamelin, and, if,
as was certain, Daladier opposed the step, I would announce the
resignation of the Government.

I imparted my determination to several of my colleagues, who
showed their distress about it. Of especial significance was a visit
which I received on the eve of the Council meeting from Campinchi,
who represented to me the danger which this decision held for me.
He brought to my attention the fact that, because Daladier was the
leader of the Radical Socialist Party, the Radical members of the
Cabinet and himself [Campinchi] would therefore be obliged to fall
in behind him. It would be impossible for me, if this were the case,
to form a new Government. I replied to him that I was not unaware
of this risk, which was purely a danger to myself, but that I could not
put this in the balance against the danger to the country which supporting Gamelin, in my opinion, entailed.

If I had been in need of strengthening in my design, I would have
been so by a letter which I had just received from Colonel de Gaulle.
Here is the text of the document, the perspicacity of which it would
be idle to stress:

Sector 100   May 3, 1940
Monsieur le Président,
     The events in Norway, coming after those in Poland, have proved
that there is today no longer any possible military operation except
through the use of and according to the degree of mechanized strength.
If, tomorrow, operations spread to Swedish territory, the day after
to the Balkans, later to the Ukraine, and then to Belgium and finally
to the West (whether against the Siegfried or the Maginot Line)
this same evident truth will be established.
     Now, the French military system is conceived, organized, equipped
and commanded contrary in principle to the law of modern warfare.

There exists no more absolute and pressing need than that of radically reforming this system. The most important problem of the war for us is today and will be tomorrow, just as it was yesterday, 'the French military problem'. But reform, and through reform, victory, is becoming all the more difficult the longer we put off making a decision and taking action.

Let me repeat that the military organism, because of the inherent traditionalism in its very nature, will not reform itself of its own accord. It is a matter for the State, a matter which takes precedence over all others. A statesman is necessary for the task. In France the great leader of this war will be a Carnot, or there will be no great leader.

You alone . . . by virtue of your position, your personality, of the stand which you have taken in regard to this problem—and taken alone—for the last six years, can and ought to achieve the task. I venture to add that, in making this problem the most important one for your Government, you will transform the internal and external circumstances, and you will place in your hand trump cards which it is at present lacking. Each day which passes after today, each event which occurs, proves the value of our doctrine, whilst, unfortunately, at the same time the enemy puts it in practice.

Naturally I covet no greater honour than that of serving you in this work of such supreme importance as soon as you judge it convenient to undertake it.

I beg you to accept, Monsieur le Président, an assurance of my respectful and faithful devotion.

Charles de Gaulle

When on May 19 I finally took over the Ministry of War it was, alas, too late to 'reform the system radically'.

I went to see the President of the Republic early on the 9th, and I informed him of my decision to bring about a ministerial crisis. He advanced with warmth the popularity of Daladier in the Army, and of 'our Gamelin' with Hore-Belisha.[1] I answered him that, having assumed responsibility, I intended to possess the power to make a decision which I considered to be of vital importance.

The Cabinet Council met at the Quai d'Orsay at ten-thirty in the morning. I explained the problem raised by the Norwegian expedition; I demonstrated the errors which had been made, and I concluded with the need for relieving Gamelin of his command. At the end of a minute's heavy silence, Lamoureux, who appeared to voice the opinion of most of our colleagues, stated that he was convinced by my explanation and he was in agreement with its conclusions. But Daladier thought

---

[1] Hore-Belisha had left the War Office on January 6, 1940.

that the step which I was proposing was unjustified, as the British had been in command of the expedition. I recorded our disagreement, and I stated that the Cabinet would resign, asking my colleagues to maintain secrecy about the decision, which was only to be revealed when a new Government had been formed.

The President of the Republic summoned Herriot, who was at Lyons, the next day, in order to consult with him, according to tradition, about the solution which would resolve the crisis.

But, during the night, the German offensive was unloosed. It was no longer a question after that of replacing the architect who had built up the structure for the Belgian operation. Neither could I myself, without being a coward, shirk responsibility in the face of the peril which I had denounced five years earlier in the Chamber.

I wrote to Gamelin:

'General. The battle has begun. One thing only counts: to win the victory. We shall all work in unison to this end.'

He answered me:

'Monsieur le Président. There is only one answer to your letter of today. France alone is of importance.'

Louis Marin, President of the *Fédération Républicaine*, and Ybarnegaray came into my Government, in which, from now on, the Right was also represented.

CHAPTER XVII

THE DISASTER

May 10, The Manstein Plan.—May 10, The Wehrmacht passes over to the attack.—The Gamelin Plan.—The first Set-backs.—The Mistakes of our Command.—May 12, The Allies organize their Command.—May 13, Huntziger's Front is Broken at Sedan.— May 13, Corap's Front is Broken at Dinant.—What was Happening between Namur and Antwerp?—What would Georges do?— The Attitude of Leopold III: 'No, not southward; northward.'— May 16, Churchill in Paris.—My Disagreement with Churchill over the theory of War.—The Disaster, described by the enemy.— If we had not advanced into Belgium. . . .—The Truth about the Armoured Forces of the Wehrmacht.—The conflict between Leopold III and his Ministers.

MAY 10: THE MANSTEIN PLAN

ON March 16, 1940, Ciano told Sumner Welles about the imminence of the German offensive in the West. Ribbentrop had himself come to Rome to tell Mussolini and also, it would appear, the Pope, about it. The Reich counted on crushing France within five months. Then she would deal with Britain.

Naturally the Quai d'Orsay of that time had no inkling of this information.

In 1914, the Schlieffen plan aimed at enveloping the left wing of the French Army. The German Army had therefore to cross Belgium and Luxembourg to carry out the plan. Joffre brought about its failure on the Marne.

The plan of 1940 also comprised the invasion of these two countries to which the Netherlands were joined on this occasion. The object was no longer to envelop our left wing, but to pierce the very centre of our battle line.

The Wehrmacht had massed a hundred or so divisions, of which twenty were held in reserve[1] for this decisive operation.

[1] Ten Panzer divisions and a hundred and thirty-five Infantry divisions were to join in the campaign.

Eighty were concentrated on the north-west frontier of Germany: they were spaced out behind each other back to the River Weser. 'This disposition of troops in such depth was unparalleled in history', the spokesman of the Wehrmacht's High Command was to write.[1]

At the head there were the Panzer divisions. They numbered ten (see map). One was to advance on Breda through the Brabant plain; two were to cross the province of Limburg, striking towards Maastricht; the other seven, that is to say by far the larger element, were to thrust towards Dinant and Sedan, to the north and to the south-east of the Ardennes massif.

At dawn on the appointed day, the tanks were to vibrate under their armoured covering whilst the Netherlands, Belgium and Luxembourg were lulled in the deep sleep of neutrality. Linked to this irresistible advance guard, a gigantic block of seventy infantry divisions was to begin its forward march. Just as in Poland, as in Norway, this was once more to be the *Blitzkrieg*, the lightning war.

What about the Dutch Army? In the twinkling of an eye, it was to be driven into capitulation.

What about the Belgian Army? Through the morning twilight we shall, decided the German Command, burst on the bridges of the Albert Canal, after first having sown the fortifications which flank them with our parachutists. Our armoured column will debouch from these bridges, supported by a motorized infantry division, and will 'roll up' the Belgian forces, which we will surprise in their stations along the canal.

What about the French and British Armies? They were to be defeated in two stages. We know, they said at the German General Headquarters, that these forces will advance into Belgium on the Namur–Antwerp axis. We know this because, for some months, the Belgians have inscribed it on the ground by constructing from Namur to the River Dyle a futile line of anti-tank defences and by flooding the low ground which forms the valley of this river. We shall let the French and British advance without being disturbed into the trap. Our fine French gentlemen are convinced that their continuous front is unbreakable. We shall crack it for them in its very middle. They imagine that their front cannot in any case be torn open except through employing the massed strength of our artillery, and they believe in this so strongly that they count on having adequate time to bring their strategic reserves to the spot. We shall defeat them by speed. From the frontier seven Panzer divisions will crash like wild horses through the Ardennes. Above them will fly their eagles, the Stukas, and in their wake will come motorized infantry divisions. These will be the advance guards which will force the Meuse at Dinant and Sedan. And what about the

[1] Murawski, *Der Durchbruch im Westen*, 1941.

artillery of these advance guards? Except for that of the armoured and motorized divisions, it will be an aerial artillery which will precede our Panzers. Our shells will be the bombs of the Stukas. The aim is speed!

When the 'point of the lance' has opened a breach, the shaft will follow, that is one motorized division for each two Panzers, then the body of the infantry; but this will be composed of foot soldiers trained to march, carrying a light equipment so that they will easily be able to make from thirty to forty kilometres a day. The aim is speed, and still more speed. This mass will plunge into the breaches and will spread destruction in the rear. It will be a *débâcle*.

Such was the plan which the Wehrmacht was to put into application. The strategic conception which inspired it was audacious in its nature. Who was its author? The first enlightenment on this subject has been given us by the preliminary investigations and the examinations at Nuremberg. Interrogations, depositions, inquiries, agree with documents from private sources[1] on this point. The plan had been conceived by Hitler, and imposed by him on the High Command. Certainly, this was hardly the time for the German Generals to glorify the memory of the dead leader. The Führer, who had the happy idea of burying himself under the ruins of his work, had a broad back on which to plant the blame. The sudden and unanimous modesty of these military leaders was, in these circumstances, to appear due to self-interest, and therefore at least in need of some confirmation. When Goering, in a bantering tone, depicted the 'blue funk' of the Generals, who already saw the French in Berlin,[2] others wondered if this was not again an exaggeration, itself also tending to show that, from the outset, Hitler had found opposition and resistance from his entourage.

Official or private researches have subsequently been made, which have amplified the information obtained at the judicial inquiry. Archives have been ransacked and studied in a most exhaustive manner. New items of evidence have been asked for and collated in a calmer atmosphere. Men who were intimately associated with the conception and execution of the operation, Field-Marshals von Rundstedt and von Manstein, and General Guderian, to cite only the front-rank leaders, have supplied information gathered in circumstances which, unlike those wherein the accused of Nuremberg found themselves placed, are a guarantee of sincerity. Comparisons, collations, all the methods of historical scholarship have been employed in this investigation, which, because of its objectivity, does honour to those who have undertaken it. From this new study, which raised again the doubts that the Nuremberg trial had created, it turns out that, contrary to the deductions generally drawn from evidence at this trial, Hitler was not the

[1] Such as the previously mentioned diary of Jodl.   [2] Cf. Cartier, *op. cit.*, p. 130.

author of the plan put into execution by the Wehrmacht. But he deserves the real credit for adopting it as soon as it was submitted to him by a subordinate, and, in making it his own, for having imposed it (on this point, the Nuremberg version is confirmed) on his timorous and recalcitrant Generals. Thus is exploded the myth of a Hitler who was a strategic genius. Moreover, in order to credit such a belief, it would be necessary to forget that this same Hitler, overriding the opposition of Field-Marshal von Brauchitsch a second time, had in the following year forced the latter to undertake the campaign against Russia. It is well known where this new initiative of the Führer led the German Army.

We are indebted to Liddell Hart[1] for information which throws a startling light on the operations of May and June, 1940. Here is a summary of the facts which he has obtained.

Hitler was not slow in seeing that a war of attrition was unfavourable to him, and that time was working on behalf of the Allies. He had no confidence in Russia who, he feared, was only awaiting a convenient hour in order to stab Germany in the back. Thence arose the urgency for him to crush us and to impose peace on us. Once France had been vanquished, the British, he thought, would agree to come to terms. The Führer considered that the Wehrmacht was of a sufficient stature to defeat us. It was necessary to profit from this superiority as soon as possible. Hitler, on October 9, 1939, ordered the elaboration of a plan of campaign against France. The German Generals were far from sharing the Führer's confidence about the outcome of an offensive in the West. Von Brauchitsch, Commander-in-Chief, expressly advised against the undertaking. Hitler had to override him and impose his own wishes. Preoccupied with the vulnerability of the Ruhr industries, he never ceased to dread seeing us forestall and impede his plans by taking the offensive through Belgium and the Netherlands against the basin of the Ruhr. The supreme leaders of the Wehrmacht pushed their opposition to the point of collaborating on the means to thwart Hitler and to overthrow him. It is true that they never got beyond this.

The Führer had made up his mind. He feverishly consulted meteorological forecasts so that, as soon as they turned out to be favourable, he could give the order to attack. Between November and April, the order was given on eleven occasions, but was annulled each time before H-hour.

The plan drawn up initially by the High Command was based on the Schlieffen plan. Thus the principal strength was to be concentrated on the right wing. Facing the Ardennes, the centre under the command of von Rundstedt, was to play a secondary role. It had the simple task of protecting the flank, and was not to cross the Meuse. The dispositions

[1] Cf. *The Other Side of the Hill*, 1948, pp. 114 ff., *passim* (first edition).

adopted by the Allies show that the latter considered it an established fact that the German Army would repeat the manœuvre of August, 1914.

If the Wehrmacht wished to gain an advantage through surprise, it had to refashion its plan. Already during the winter, the High Command had been inspired to recognize the need for increasing the importance of the role of the centre. Von Rundstedt who, in the original plan, was not to have any Panzer divisions (the bulk of the armoured element being allotted to the right wing) received a corps of Panzers in January. His mission became no longer one of a protective nature, standing at readiness on the Meuse, but an active one of carrying out a flanking movement on a broad front beyond the cutting formed by the valley of the Meuse. But the right wing still preserved the principal role. Liddell Hart writes:[1] 'It is clear now that if that plan had been carried out it would have failed to be decisive. For the British Army and the best equipped part of the French Army stood in the path. The German attack would have met these forces head on. Even if it had broken their front in Belgium it would merely have pushed them back on their fortified line in Northern France, and closer to their bases of supply.'

It was to Erich von Manstein, then a Brigadier-General and chief of von Rundstedt's staff, that the upsetting of this plan of operations was due. It was he who insisted on the need for making surprise a factor of supreme importance. The battle envisaged by the German Command was to be an encounter battle in the Brabant plain where the British Army would be massed, which, von Manstein considered, would be 'more capable of resistance' than the French. In addition, the Panzers, which would have to fulfil a decisive role, would have to manœuvre in a region which, though it was flat, was intersected by waterways: 'a serious handicap in a struggle wherein everything depends on speed'.

Von Manstein, having made this astonishingly penetrating criticism of the plan drawn up by the High Command, did not stop at that. He proposed that the chief effort should be brought to bear on the Ardennes. The French would certainly not expect the massive action of Panzers in an area which lent itself so little to the development of tanks. It was therefore certain that the Panzers would not run into serious opposition. It would be sufficient for them to cross the Meuse in order to debouch into the plains of northern France, an ideal terrain for their sweep towards the sea. It is useless to remark that the audacity of this plan aroused resolute opposition from the High Command. Von Manstein anticipated this organized challenge. He realized that the only chance which he had to secure the acceptance of his plan was to explain it to Hitler. But how could he break through the barrier

[1] *Op. cit.*, p. 118 (first edition).

which prevented him from gaining access to the master of the war?
In the end he succeeded in doing this. He was not mistaken in believing
that the Führer would be won over by the audacity of the plan.
Indeed, Hitler adopted it on the spot, and made von Brauchitsch
accept it.

MAY 10: THE WEHRMACHT PASSES OVER TO THE ATTACK

On May 10, at half-past one in the morning, the French Command
learned that the German forces were standing to arms, and that columns
were beginning to move towards the west. About four o'clock in the
morning, the Belgian Ambassador telephoned me to inform me that
his country was being attacked, and he was appealing for French help.
At the same hour Gamelin received the same information from the
Belgian Military Attaché.

Georges telephoned to him. He seemed uncertain.

'Is it clear that it is a move against the Dyle, and not one against the
Schelde?'

'Since it is the Belgians who are calling us, do you see how it can be
anything else?'

'Evidently not.'

The anticipated manœuvre began to unfold. At seven o'clock in the
morning, German troops began to move.

THE GAMELIN PLAN

Gamelin, as I have said, was not surprised by the event. Nay more:
if Hitler intended to assist the plans of the Allies, he could not have
adopted a more suitable line of action than he was doing.

Our Supreme Command was, therefore, convinced that the German
Army was running into disaster by taking the offensive. Far from
dreading the German initiative, Gamelin asked for it in his prayers.
From that date our Supreme Command considered that, if Hitler
fell into the trap, that is to say, if he took the offensive, the Allies
were of sufficient strength to inflict a bloody check on him. Gamelin
was, therefore, not surprised, and he insisted on stressing this fact:
'We have been told: "You allowed yourself to be surprised." All
the documents which I have reproduced in this account reveal the
opposite. From the end of the winter we expected the German attack
any day.'[1] I must point out, however, that Gamelin had on May 7
restored army leave.

---

[1] Gamelin, *op. cit.*, vol. III, p. 389. On March 20, M. Yves Bouthillier, who was at this
time Secretary-General of the Ministry of Finance, received from Gamelin an explanation
of his views on this subject. In *Le drame de Vichy: I. Face à l'ennemi, face à l'allié* (p. 19), he
writes: 'On March 20 I was the guest of General Gamelin . . . at Vincennes. He had

Gamelin had reflected deeply on the Belgian operation. He had drawn up its outlines and worked out its smallest details a long time previously.

We know that he had told Leopold III about his plan. The King considered the sector which Gamelin allotted to the Belgian Army on the battle-front to be too restricted and asked him to enlarge it by allowing it to take in at least Louvain and Brussels. By doing this Gamelin would be better able to bolster up the system between Wavre and Namur, and especially that running from Namur to Montmédy. It turned out that the offer inspired no result, and when it was repeated on May 12 by the sovereign, it was to be declined a second time.

The King went even further. At the beginning of March, he formed, on the evidence of information secured by his Intelligence Service, a conviction that the Germans would try their decisive blow in the Givet-Longwy sector. He entrusted General Delvoye with the task of warning Gamelin about this.

During the morning of April 30, our Military Attaché in Berne learned from an authoritative source that the Wehrmacht would pass over to the attack between May 8 and 10, with Sedan as the 'principal axis of the movement'. He immediately warned the Intelligence of the Army General Staff, which at once passed on this precious information to G.H.Q. The deputy of the Military Attaché was passing through La Ferté on May 3. He made certain that Gamelin and Georges had been told the information.[1]

Gamelin remained deaf to this warning. He stuck to his plan. Nothing could influence him to change it in the smallest particular. He was so certain about his business that it was with obvious joy that he received the news of the enemy offensive. 'In the afternoon of this fatal May 10, I received', writes M. Bouthillier,[2] 'a visit from my colleague at the Ministry of War, the Controller-General of the Army, Jacquinot, a conscientious administrator with whom I was on the best of terms. He told me in some detail about the imprudent manœuvre which had been ordered that morning. Because I expressed my astonishment, as one who was not in the "know", at this strange

explained to me with great lucidity why it was certain in his eyes that an enemy offensive (towards the west) would begin during the spring. Such an attack, which he anticipated would be powerful, was not, according to the Commander-in-Chief, a probability, but a necessary and inescapable fact. He talked about it with calm lucidity in the best of faith!'

[1] Cf. L'Aurore, November 14, 1949. Another indication of the same mental attitude is revealed by the following. Some twenty days before May 10, Huntziger received a visit from Jacquinot at his headquarters. The latter asked him:

'In your opinion are the Germans going to attack?'

'Certainly not. On the contrary they are frightened that we are going to do so! Come back in a fortnight. You will see the sector in more detail; you will thus be able to note for yourself how uneasy they are.'

[2] Bouthillier, op. cit., p. 19.

strategy which consisted in deploying before a line of fortifications after having built them, the Secretary-General of the Department of War answered, "If you had seen, as I have done this morning, the broad smile of General Gamelin when he told me the direction of the enemy attack, you would feel no uneasiness. The Germans have provided him with just the opportunity which he was awaiting."'

THE FIRST SET-BACKS

During the day of the 10th, the advance forces of our motorized elements, Giraud's Army (Seventh Army), the British Army (under the command of Gort), and Blanchard's Army (First Army), reached the Antwerp–Namur line. The cavalry of Corap's Army (Ninth Army) established itself on the Meuse from Monthermé to the south of Namur, and pushed its reconnaissance units on a broad front beyond the Semois. Huntziger's Army (Second Army) followed it. These two armies took up positions at right angles to each other on the Meuse and the Chiers (see map).

Giraud's Army concentrated in the area of Antwerp. It was covered by the 1st Light Mechanized Division, which had the task, in addition, of ensuring liaison between the Dutch and Belgians. But the German parachutists had already seized the bridge of the Meuse at Maastricht and two of the three bridges of the Albert Canal. As for the Eben-Emael fort, which covered these passages with its guns, it was attacked by Stukas, then assaulted by parachutists, who blew up the turrets and casemates, and put the fortifications out of action. Two Panzer divisions advanced from the bridges, followed by a motorized division and burst upon Tongres. A Belgian Army Corps, commanded by General Bogaert, was in position astride the Albert Canal and it ensured liaison with the Dutch brigade under Colonel Schmitt, which was holding the line of the Peel.

Hardly had the 1st Light Mechanized Division established liaison about three o'clock in the afternoon with General Bogaert, than the latter withdrew his troops on the west bank of the Canal. Seeing that, because of this withdrawal, his right wing was uncovered, Colonel Schmitt withdrew in his turn. On the 11th at ten o'clock in the morning, Colonel Schmitt's brigade was approaching Breda in its retreat, whilst German parachutists were seizing the Moerdyk bridge over the Meuse. Giraud's Army, in its turn, was running the risk of finding itself uncovered. On the 11th, Gamelin asked Georges to advise Giraud to be careful:[1] 'General Giraud', he ordered Georges, 'must not commit his forces too strongly beyond Breda. . . .' On the 12th, Giraud ordered the 1st Light Mechanized Division, in contact with superior forces, to retreat.

[1] Gamelin, op. cit., vol. I, p. 99.

Gamelin had counted on the Dutch to hold out for three days or, at least, for two on the line of the Peel marshes, and on the Belgians to delay the German advance for several days. On both these points he was completely deceived.

It was the same in the Belgian Ardennes, from Liége to Arlon. The Belgian forces carried out all or part of the planned destructions which, according to the calculations of the Belgian Command, ought to have held up the enemy advance for four days. It took the latter several hours to advance beyond them. But the Belgian troops did not hesitate to speed up in their retreat, without fighting, to the north of the Meuse between Liége and Namur. They did not even leave a rearguard to ensure a cover for the cavalry (four light divisions and two independent brigades) which the armies of Corap and Huntziger had pushed forward to meet them through the Ardennes massif. It had, however, been agreed that, during their retreat, Belgian forces should place themselves for the time being under the respective commands of the Army in whose zone of action they would find themselves. General Blanchard has spoken[1] bitterly about this indifference of the Belgian Army: 'Having on the 10th . . . in the afternoon, passed the Ourthe, the Colonel of the 4th Regiment of machine-gun carriers established contact at Marche with a Belgian General who had several divisions under him. . . .[2] This officer congratulated his colleague on arriving so quickly, and ordered his General Staff and troops to make way for our troops. The French Colonel remarked with surprise that he had only some light and mobile elements under his command, and that the bulk of French forces would only be able to get up in two or three days. The Belgian General replied that he had his orders, and that, pivoting on his left wing, he was going to retreat on Namur.' Another set-back.

The business was beginning badly. There was a danger of the battle being engaged in unfavourable circumstances. In any case it was too late to throw overboard the plans which had been drawn up. On the 12th, Georges and Billotte went, in company with Daladier, to confer with King Leopold at the Château de Casteau.[3] They confirmed the fact that Gamelin intended to offer a pitched battle on the Antwerp–Namur–Meuse line.

THE MISTAKES OF OUR COMMAND

We have seen that Gamelin had decided to stand fast and wait for the Germans in the Brabant plain between Wavre and Namur. This is one of the classic routes along which Germany falls on France.

---

[1] Ribet, op. cit., p. 495.
[2] There were two: the 1st Division of Ardennes Chasseurs, and the 1st Cavalry Division.
[3] Casteau is situated at about ten kilometres to the north-east of Mons.

There he concentrated the flower of his troops. He had refused to allow
Leopold a sector on this battle-front. The Belgian Army was to man
the line from the Antwerp valley—the Nethe valley—the Dyle to
below Louvain. Gort's Army would then occupy the line up to Wavre.
These two sectors were easy to defend as they were covered by artificial
flooding—in the valley of the Nethe as regards the first sector, and in
the valley of the Dyle as regards the second. There was no risk of
seeing the Panzers throwing themselves on the stronghold of Antwerp
or getting bogged down in the low-lying areas which bordered these
two rivers. The gap extended from Wavre to Namur. Blanchard's
Army (our First Army) had the honour of defending it. This was our
best Army: it was composed of two light mechanized divisions, the
2nd and 3rd forming the cavalry corps under the command of General
Prioux; eight infantry divisions of which six were regular (three of
them motorized), one garrison (the 101st, forming the garrison of
Maubeuge, which was its base), and finally a Class A reserve division,
the 32nd (in reserve).

Two other corridors of invasion were left, that from Dinant to the
north of the Ardennes massif, and from Sedan to the south-east.

The defence of the first was entrusted to Corap's Army. This Army
remained in the positions which it occupied from Mézières to
Monthermé, and, to the west of this latter position, its troops which
were situated on the Franco-Belgian frontier extended along the
course of the Meuse. The Dinant corridor was held by a force whose
troops and equipment were insufficient, and whose quality was
mediocre. Here there were two Class A reserve divisions, that is to
say units which, although composed of the youngest reservists and
having, except for trifling differences, the same establishment as regular
ones, only possessed a partial anti-tank and anti-aircraft armament. To
crown the misfortune these troops were not to arrive in time to line
the Meuse.

It was worse still at Sedan. The hinge of the Armies of Corap and
Huntziger was here. The gap was manned by three Class B reserve
divisions; that on the left was attached to Corap's Army, the two others
to Huntziger's. Divisions of this class were formed by the reservists of
older call-ups. Their establishment was poor. They were almost
entirely without anti-aircraft and anti-tank equipment. Finally, one of
these divisions, the 71st, which was attached to Huntziger, and which,
because it was one of the two placed to the south of Sedan, found itself
in the thick of the battle, relied for its recruitment on the north-east
suburb of Paris. As half of its effectives comprised men who had been
recalled to the colours after March, 1939, this division seems to have
been contaminated by Communist propaganda. In any case the morale
of the rank and file was low.

And what about the reserves of Corap and Huntziger? The first-named was to place his, a regular division, the 4th North African, at Philippeville, thirty-five kilometres from the front. Huntziger placed his on the outskirts of Verdun.

That is how the gates of France were to be guarded! But had not Pétain said, in 1934, that the Ardennes sector was not dangerous? The Allies were, therefore, to be strong where they might have afforded to be weak, and they were weak where every consideration required that they should be strong.

MAY 12: THE ALLIES ORGANIZE THEIR COMMAND

On the 12th, the troops had accomplished their approach movements, and taken up their positions.

There remained one question, as delicate as it was important, to be settled—that of organizing the command. Gamelin was Commander-in-Chief of the Allied forces in France. By virtue of this title, the British Expeditionary Force[1] came under his orders. The British were puncti-lious on this point. They lost no opportunity of stressing the necessarily restrictive nature which this subordination had to maintain. Viscount Gort, Commander-in-Chief of the Expeditionary Force, consented to carry out the instructions of Georges, Commander-in-Chief of French forces on the north-east front, to whom Gamelin, at the beginning of hostilities, had delegated his powers as far as concerned operations. But the Army of Gort 'cannot', wrote Gamelin[2] to Georges on March 5, 'be placed under the orders of the commander of an Army Group'.

As for the Belgian Army, it provided a source of embarrassment. We have seen that, at the beginning of November, the Allies had, to repeat the words of Gamelin,[3] 'arrived at an agreement with the Belgian General Staff', although the Belgians refused to enter into 'any signed agreement' for fear that such a pact would come to the know-ledge of the Germans and furnish them with an excuse for invading the country. In order to ensure the secret of Belgian relations with the Allies, the King of the Belgians, Commander-in-Chief of the Army and the Belgian General Staff, had 'expressed the desire to have no contact'[4] except with Gamelin. The latter in his above-mentioned Note of March 5 stresses this to Georges: 'The Belgian Army will be under the authority of the King who, for the time being, only agrees to follow out my personal directives.' It was imperative to settle the question.

On May 10, Gamelin sent[5] a ciphered message by telephone to the King: 'As General Joffre did in October, 1914, to General Foch, I have delegated to General Georges my authority to settle with the Belgian

---

[1] B.E.F. is the customary abbreviation.   [2] Gamelin, *op. cit.*, vol. III, pp. 173–5.
[3] *Ibid.*, vol. I, pp. 84–7.   [4] *Ibid.*, p. 318.
[5] *Ibid.*, p. 317.

Army problems concerning the direct co-ordination of the Allied forces in the present battle as we have planned it. This delegation of power already exists in so far as concerns the British forces. General Champon will, therefore, represent General Georges as well as myself with Your Majesty. . . .' 'On the 11th', continues Gamelin, 'I was instructed that the step had been accepted by His Majesty. I immediately informed . . . Georges about this. . . . He told me that he was going to ask the King as well as Lord Gort to agree to General Billotte taking control of operations along the whole of the Allied left wing.' On the 12th, Georges went, as we have seen, to meet the King, who received him at three o'clock in the afternoon at the Château de Casteau. Leopold stated that he considered the proposed organization as an 'obvious necessity'. Georges gives an account of this negotiation:

What was the organization of the northern front on the morning of May 10? [he writes]. General Billotte was in command of the First, Ninth, Second Armies. On his left the British, who agreed to obey my orders as the delegate of General Gamelin, refused, however, to be placed under the command of a French Army Group commander. Farther to the north, the Belgians only had relations with General Gamelin. Finally, on the extreme left the Seventh Army continued to be subordinated to me. Definitive arrangements were to be settled later. It was fortunate that this was so, for this temporary organization (if it can be called by such a name) was in truth chaotic! And then the events of May 10 burst upon us! Still nothing had been settled.

During the evening or perhaps it was the night of the 11th, I received in the form of a simple memorandum the copy of a telegram addressed (by General Gamelin) to the King of the Belgians. . . . It contained no particular instruction which concerned me. And yet the situation was quite different from that in 1914. Then, Foch was the deputy of Joffre and therefore unattached, and he could be entrusted with a special duty on the northern front. But since January, 1940, I was no longer the deputy of the Commander-in-Chief. On the other hand, I was responsible for the north-east front, from Dunkirk to the Lake of Geneva. The attack, which was unloosed on May 10, was just beginning. It extended to the outskirts of Metz. It could even extend to new sectors. I could not be in command of both the whole and of part of the battle.

It was essential that we should act quickly. I abandoned the idea of discussing the question with Vincennes. I telephoned to General Champon to request him to ask an audience for me with the King of the Belgians. It was granted. Early in the morning, I left for Billotte's headquarters, where I summoned General Gort. As he was ill, he sent his Chief of Staff, General Pownall, whom I knew well. I explained my proposals to him: the need for ensuring the co-ordination of Allied operations on the spot; my intention of entrusting this duty to General Billotte, who for several months had been in command of a group of armies in the north, who knew the area and who was in touch with the Allies. Then I met President Daladier,[1] who was making a tour of the northern area.

---

[1] Daladier was at this time Minister of Defence; the term President is given as an honorary title to him as a former head of the Council of Ministers [Tr.].

I informed him about my proposals. He approved of them. Then I asked him to go with me to the King to back me up. He agreed very willingly. We went then to the Château de Casteau. The King received us in company with General van Overstraeten. The Chief of the Belgian Staff was not there! I explained my proposals; these President Daladier warmly supported and General Pownall accepted in the name of General Gort without raising any difficulties. The situation was grave. Our experience in the last war, when we had lost so much time in settling the organization of our command, was cited with useful effect. In a few moments the problem was settled. An official report of the meeting, which was drawn up on the spot, ratified the agreement which we had reached. Because of the new and delicate task which had fallen on General Billotte's shoulders, I thought, in agreement with him, that it was necessary to lighten his duties as much as possible. For this purpose, Huntziger's Army was to be directly under my control. I would be better able to reinforce it, for it was near to Prételat's group of armies,[1] from which any levies that were drawn could be more rapidly moved to the appropriate spot.

Georges, therefore, withdrew Huntziger's Army from Billotte's command, and left him Corap's Army. It was a disastrous readjustment of forces. It affected, in fact, the *hinge*, that hinge which the enemy had committed himself, as a primary objective, to break by sheer force. One could have understood if, in this sector, Georges had restored unity of command. But on the contrary, he broke it, and to crown the misfortune the order was only in actual fact given on the 14th,[2] that is to say at the decisive point of the battle.

As for the two divisions which were in the line, one at Dinant and the other at Givet, the commander of one (who was on sick leave) was replaced by the General commanding the infantry division; the commander of the second was on leave and only rejoined his unit at the height of the battle.

The co-operation of British aircraft stationed in France also raised delicate problems. Only part of this force was under the orders of Gort. The rest was under the direct command of Air Chief Marshal Newall, who had his headquarters in England. The latter, however, in the end agreed to have a deputy in France in the person of Air Marshal Barratt. He set up his headquarters very close to that of the Commander-in-Chief of our Air Forces in order to be in close liaison with the French Command. As for the aircraft which remained based on England and which comprised the bulk both of fighters and bombers, Barratt could call on them at the request of our Supreme Command. At first the British had intended, when Belgium was attacked, to bomb the Ruhr. Gamelin asked them to abandon this plan in order to use the planes in co-operation with the ground battle. Newall objected, thinking that his craft were not suitably adapted for intervening on the battlefield.

[1] This group of armies held the sector between Montmédy and the Rhine.
[2] Commandant Lyet, *La bataille de France (mai–juin, 1940)*, p. 56 (note).

A compromise was finally agreed on: British bombers were to operate in the rear of the battlefield at the request of the Commander-in-Chief of the north-east front. To implement this agreement, it was arranged between Vuillemin and Barratt that the bombers based on England would operate over the rearguard to the north of the Namur–Liége line; French aircraft were to do the same to the south of the line.

MAY 13: HUNTZIGER'S FRONT IS BROKEN AT SEDAN

During the evening of the 12th, the Panzers made contact with the bridgehead at Sedan.

At one o'clock on the morning of the 13th, Gamelin issued a new Order of the Day to his troops: 'We must now stand firm against the onslaught of mechanized and motorized enemy forces. The time has come to fight to the end in the positions laid down by the Supreme Command. We no longer have any right to retreat. If the enemy makes a local breach, it must not only be stopped up, but counter-attacked and retaken.'

The battle which had been so long awaited was at last to be joined. In the account which I am going to give of it I can only use items of information which our Supreme Command received as the operations succeeded each other.

On the 13th, in the morning, Gamelin was at Ferté-sous-Jouarre[1] with Georges, when the news came that the enemy was attacking at Sedan. Within a few hours disaster had befallen.

We had created, I have explained, a defensive army. But where were the arms for defence? Where were the mine-fields, which should have halted or slackened down the enemy's advance? Where was the armour plating for the new fortifications and for our numerous old ones? Where were the fighter planes which should have brought down the Stukas? Where were the anti-tank guns and the anti-aircraft guns, which should have stopped the tanks and brought down the bombers? Where were the dive-bombers which should have stopped the Panzers? Nothing existed of these arms, or not enough. We have seen why.

Our troops had the impression of fighting an altogether too unequal battle. On the 13th, a Panzer division crossed the Meuse. During the morning of the 14th, Gamelin was back again at La Ferté. Huntziger had just telephoned to Georges that certain of his troops were not holding out, that men were to be seen leaving block-houses with their arms raised, and that he had given orders for them to be fired on. General Grandsart, commander of an army corps, has stated in the

---

[1] La Ferté was the seat of the headquarters of the north-eastern front. Georges had established his Command Post, and also his residence at Bondons, a country house which had belonged to Georges Ohnet, and which was situated about twenty kilometres to the east of La Ferté.

Riom Court that his two Class B divisions, the 55th and the 71st, were not 'up to scratch'. The commander of the neighbouring infantry division and other officers alleged, moreover, that these divisions possessed a low morale, which some of these witnesses have put down to Communism. They have stated that, even before the offensive, their men did not train, that many did not salute their officers. When the attack took place, they have informed us, men were seen with their helmets turned round (a rallying sign of the Communists), running through the ranks, shouting: 'Here come the Boches. Beat it!' There can be no doubt that the morale of these two divisions was bad. But one must take into account the nervous shock which surprise at the first contact with the Stukas and the Panzer divisions produced on troops, who felt that they were being left unprotected by their own aircraft. Indeed, we had no fighter aircraft, with the result that the Stukas bombed our troops, the combatants have told us, with the tranquillity of hunters who expend their cartridges on surrounded game.

One can assert that, despite the warnings of our Supreme Command, part of our troops did not suspect the character of the war to which they were going. One of our most energetic leaders, General Touchon, was to say in effect to the Riom Court: 'When, during my inspections, before the German offensive of May 10, I used to say to the officers: "Be careful. Remember what happened in Poland. The attack will be a formidable one and will come in new ways", I would see a smile of incredulity, not only on the faces of the older ones who were thinking "We were at Verdun", but also on those of the younger.' All of them had been more or less contaminated with the idea that the continuous front was unbreakable, and that one was safe behind concrete. It appeared that it had not been explained to the rank and file what this new form of warfare would be: a combined onslaught by Panzers and Stukas. It appeared that it had not been explained to the older ones *why* this would not be the same thing as at Verdun. Let us note, moreover, that when, after the German armoured corps had broken through towards the sea, Huntziger's Army was attacked by artillery and infantry, it stood up to the attacks of the infantry. For we knew how to do this from the preceding war.

The sudden revelation of modern warfare was a frightful surprise. There was stupefaction amongst the front-line soldiers, bombarded by the Stukas, whose whistling bombs, they afterwards said, created more fear than actual harm, but which killed the gun teams. There was stupefaction amongst the garrisons in the fortifications, who saw the guns blown to pieces by shells from armoured self-propelled guns, which, under the protection of planes and tanks, approached to within a short range in order to fire directly on the embrasures. There was stupefaction amongst the artillery-men who saw the Panzers come up to the muzzles of their guns, although these had continued to fire since they were several kilometres away. There was stupefaction amongst the military leaders, who saw the Panzers surging upon their command posts, and learned that their front was broken. This was another type of war. . . .

Witnesses were also to tell of officers belonging to these divisions who, according to them, left their men. The excuse would appear to be that, since the situation was desperate, the least possible number of prisoners should fall into enemy hands. But let us not stress this. Let us simply observe that it is improbable that there were many Communists amongst the officers. These reports of eyewitnesses raise the problem of finding out to what degree a weakening in the morale of the Army —and therefore of the nation, since it was a question of reservists— contributed to the defeat. Gamelin told me, when we were in Germany, that, in his opinion, Communist propaganda had not been an important factor in our defeat. The campaign for inducing France to shirk her responsibilities, which went as far as prompting certain people to say, 'Rather Hitler than Stalin!' and others, 'Die on behalf of Danzig?' had certainly substantially contributed to lower the morale of the middle classes, and, as a consequence, of the reserve officers. Maurras, who, on the eve of Munich, urged soldiers to keep their bullets for the war-mongering Ministers, and who, a week before the war, accused these Ministers of offering 'a violent opposition to the peace of the world', was to confess after the Armistice that the morale of the combatants belonging to the *Action Française* was not so high as in 1914. The contrary would have been surprising. It was not in this direction that the Riom Court focused its dark-lantern. It was a court with discreet intentions. By expurging school textbooks, after our victory in 1918, of anything which prepared our youth for sacrifices, for the day when the Motherland would be threatened (and it was so once every generation after 1870), it is probable that we had, to a certain extent, weakened the morale of our soldiers of 1940.

And finally can it be denied that the idea that one could no longer fight except behind the shelter of concrete had blunted the pugnacity of our Army, which was subsequently deadened by eight months of 'phoney' warfare? Against our soldiers advanced a fanatical youth, trained for combat, which went even as far as abjuring the Christian religion in order to harden its soul, which went into the attack with a song and linked arms.

Yet, on the eve of this offensive, Billotte, Giraud, Blanchard and Corap were saying in their reports that their troops were 'full of fight' and burning to enter Belgium. Blanchard's Army fought very well between Namur and the Dyle, and in the Alps five Class B reserve divisions, amalgamated with two fortress divisions, inflicted a severe lesson on the Black Shirts of Mussolini, who were six times as strong as they were. I shall not talk about individual and collective deeds of valour, such as the defence of the Loire crossing by the cadets of Saumur during the battle of France. Moreover, were there not instances of weakness at the beginning of the First World War, when the first contact was made with the enemy? Everyone is aware of those shown by a regular corps at Dieuze in the battle of Morhange, and of the Valabrègue reserve divisions which gave way to the south-west of St. Quentin. These units were none the less able to pull themselves together in admirable fashion afterwards. In May, 1940, the speed of the enemy gave to these weaknesses a decisive significance, because the troops who gave way were holding precisely those points which it was essential to preserve.

The inexcusable fault was in having entrusted the defence of France's two gateways to troops who—especially those at Sedan—were in all respects of an inferior quality. How can one ignore the fact that, to the south of Sedan, one of the regiments of the 55th Division was reduced to firing on the Panzers with its machine-guns, because it had no 25-mm. anti-tank weapons? The wounded colonel of this regiment was even seen firing with his revolver at a Panzer in order to save his honour.

Did aviation play a decisive role in the defeat? It would appear that the reason why the artillery, which, from the heights of the Marfée where it was placed, commanded the right bank of the Meuse and thereby the routes along which the Panzers raced, remained silent was because it had been put out of action by enemy aircraft.[1]

The infantry, seized by the impression that it was being sacrificed without any defence to the hostile planes, was no doubt very demoralized as a result. General Grandsart told an officer of General Headquarters that, when he asked Huntziger for fighter protection, he received the reply: 'Your troops can stand up to the bombs. We stood firm at Verdun.'

However, the only order which Vuillemin issued, according to the records of Riom, was for the protection of Sedan, but it was on the evening of the 13th. This proved too late. As Georges said, our planes although they were helped by British squadrons, could only operate against the exits of the town to the west of the Meuse. And Georges added in substance: 'Moreover, what did we have to oppose the Germans along the whole front? Four hundred fighters, and as for bombers modern enough to offer combat during the day-time over

---

[1] An eyewitness was to state at Riom that the artillery ran out of ammunition. If this fact were true, those responsible for it deserve severe censure, after the unexpected respite that the 'phoney' war gained for us.

the battlefield, thirty-one. But we had not a single dive-bomber. As for obsolete bombers, they had been ordered by Vuillemin to stay away from daylight operations, because they were immediately shot down. On the other hand, the British Air Marshal Barratt proved to be a magnificent colleague, who always gave the utmost of which he was capable.' The deficiency of our aircraft was noted by everybody, and seen by everybody. Nobody will dispute the fact that this had the gravest consequences. Nevertheless the fact remains that, however important a factor the air was, an army provided with a modern armament should be capable of resisting an attacker who commands air superiority, even if this superiority is overwhelming. The proof is seen in the fact that Blanchard's Army held out. In 1944, when the balance of air strength had swung against them, the Germans at Monte Cassino and later at Caen demonstrated in their turn that resistance under such conditions was not impossible.

MAY 13: CORAP'S FRONT IS BROKEN AT DINANT

Corap's task was much more difficult than that of Huntziger, because, firstly, instead of staying on the spot, he had to extend his left wing into Belgium to take up a position on the Givet–Dinant–Namur line, which was not fortified. Secondly, the left bank of the Meuse was much more difficult to defend there than at Sedan, for, though the cliffs are much steeper, artillery fire is much more difficult to organize because of the narrowness of the valley, the height of the right bank slightly dominating in places that of the left. Finally, Corap had not been given enough troops to hold the sector.

Corap had received, like Huntziger, an order from Georges to send his cavalry—which was also composed of two light divisions and an independent brigade of Spahis—in the direction of Liége–Arlon to meet the 1st Division of Ardennes Chasseurs and the 1st Belgian Cavalry Division.

On the morning of the 10th he launched his Brigade of Spahis through the Belgian Ardennes, and sent his two infantry divisions, flanked on their left by a motorized division, to occupy the Givet–Dinant line south of Namur. Such was the best solution, but this line would have been occupied in time and better supported, if the cavalry had waited there for the infantry. Having adopted this solution, Corap should have held to it. But he did not do this. The advance towards Namur was only a demonstration, a symbolic taking of possession, for, on the orders of Georges and in conformity with a plan which he had drawn up with Corap some weeks before the attack, the two divisions advanced in another leap to meet the Belgians whom they did not find, for the reason we have already mentioned. The first advance towards Namur lost them twenty-four hours, which would have been most precious in slackening down the advance of the enemy, in so far as cavalry can impede the progress of armoured divisions. The cavalry, which had anti-tank weapons and 37-mm. cannons on their gun-carriers, fought, however, for a day against the Panzers, and came back in a state of good morale.

After having retreated, Corap's cavalry regrouped behind the front, and only a part of its elements was able to take part in the defence of the Meuse, so rapid had been the advance of the enemy. On the 13th, in the very heart of the Ardennes massif, a Panzer division forced a passage, and gained a footing at Monthermé, but could not advance from there.

In the turning movement of the Allied Armies about the hinge of Monthermé, Corap's Army had the advantage of being nearest the hinge. It did not, however, carry out the orders which were given in good time. In the area of Dinant two Class A infantry reserve divisions, entrusted with occupying the sector, arrived, said a witness at the Riom trial, tired out; some witnesses stated that they busied themselves with their billets, others that they saw the advanced elements of the enemy on the opposing heights. In any case they gave up the idea of occupying the bank of the Meuse and setting up a system of gun positions, with the result that the German infantry crossed the river during the night of the 12th to 13th, and built bridges over which two Panzer divisions crossed. Panzer divisions, having crossed the Meuse, helped in 'cleaning up' the depths of the valley. During the day of the 13th, the river was also crossed at Givet. In the morning of the 14th, the two Panzer divisions which had crossed the Meuse at Dinant debouched on the plateau of the left bank and grouped together, as if at manœuvres, under an enormous covering of planes.

What was Corap doing whilst these dramatic events were taking place? He kept his headquarters at Vervins instead of advancing it to Chimay as had been agreed, and he spent the 11th and 12th in a car on roads which were jammed with traffic. This prevented him from giving any orders. It is before the battle that a leader should go to see his troops, and especially so in a war of speed as this one was. But Corap, ignoring this factor, believed that he had sufficient time. Some timid local reactions took place. During the morning of the 14th a battalion of R.35 tanks counter-attacked the enemy infantry who advanced from the woods crowning the cliffs of the Meuse's left bank abreast of Dinant, and hurled it back into the woods. But our infantry was not thrown into this counter-attack, and the regained territory could not be held. The other tank battalions were split up in the action. Indeed, Corap only used two companies of his tank battalions.

During the evening of the 14th and the night of the 14th to 15th, the

18th Division, which was at Givet, the 22nd which was at Dinant, and the right wing of the 5th, which was to the north of Dinant, had 'faded away'[1] under the attacks of the Stukas and Panzers.

The general situation was then as follows: the front was broken at Sedan, Givet and Dinant. One of the three Panzer divisions which had crossed the Meuse at Sedan drove straight to the south. The two others burst towards the west and crossed the Ardennes canal. Shortly afterwards the 53rd Division, which had received an order from Corap to take up its position on this line, arrived. It ran into the two Panzer divisions, who cut it to pieces. The regular 14th Division, brilliantly commanded by General de Lattre de Tassigny, only arrived in time to gather up the remains of the 53rd. The Panzers continued their advance towards the west. Corap's right wing was turned.

At three o'clock on the morning of the 15th, a disastrous decision was taken. Corap, in agreement with Billotte, ordered the units[2] who were still holding the left bank of the Meuse from Mézières to the south of Givet to withdraw. Because of this withdrawal the Panzer division which was marking time at Monthermé could advance on the plateau. It took the road to Mézières and swung towards the west, cutting off the retreat of our troops who, by the end of the morning, were in full rout. Corap's Army now no longer existed. At Compiègne more than fifty thousand men belonging to these two divisions and to the 53rd were gathered up. The disintegration of Corap's Army recalls Hugo's verses on Waterloo:

> There faded away this noise which was a great army.

From the east of Sedan to the north of Dinant there was a breach in our front of nearly a hundred kilometres. It was quite a different thing from the reversal which Lanrezac's Army suffered at Charleroi in August, 1914. This Army, after fighting in retreat, turned at Guise to face the enemy and inflict on him a crushing set-back.

At Sedan and Dinant the events occurred so rapidly that neither Huntziger nor Corap could throw their personal reserves into the battle, because they had placed them too far back. Again it was a matter of speed.

On this same 15th, in the morning, Daladier and Gamelin were with Georges at La Ferté. Georges received a telephone call from Billotte, asking him to relieve Corap of his command, and to switch him over

---

[1] The expression was used by Weygand, in the deposition which he made on August 26, 1940, at preliminary investigations of the Riom trial.

I shall frequently make reference to this deposition, which, instead of being, as was customary, oral and therefore spontaneous, was in the form of a note written out of the presence of the magistrate and therefore at full leisure. This peculiarity gives the text an authority which must be accepted by its author. One is completely justified, therefore, in confronting him with it.

[2] The 102nd, which was a fortress division, and the 61st.

with Giraud, because, he said, Corap was not capable of facing up to the situation. Nominations to the command of army groups and armies fell to Daladier. In agreement with Gamelin he consented to Billotte's proposal. During the afternoon Gamelin sent one of his colleagues, Lieutenant-Colonel Guillaut, to Corap's Army. He returned on the 16th with the report that: 'The disorder of this Army is beyond description. Its troops are falling back on all sides. The Army General Staff has lost its head. It no longer knows even where its divisions are. The situation is worse than anything we could have imagined.' Guillaut had seen Giraud, who came to take command[1] of this disintegrated army, arrive on the spot.

On hearing this news, Gamelin asked Daladier to relieve Corap completely of his command. On the other hand, Gamelin told me, on the 19th, that the bridges of the Meuse had not all been blown up. This was an inaccurate statement, which Weygand repeated to me, formally promising me to take disciplinary action. Because I was only too pleased to be able to tell the Army and the country that, if our front had been broken, it was due to an accidental fact and not to the irremediable inferiority of our forces, I gave the news on the 21st to the Senate. To this body I also pointed out that Corap's Army 'composed of less adequately established and less fully trained divisions, whose best troops had been placed at the disposal of the wing advancing into Belgium', had arrived too late on the Dinant front.

As we have seen, this was due to the initial personal failure of Corap himself. Moreover, he had not, as he should have done, asked for the strength of his Army to be increased, when, if it were not reinforced, it would be powerless to ensure the defence of the Dinant gap.[2]

[1] Giraud took command of the Ninth Army on the 15th at four o'clock in the afternoon. The Panzers did not give him a moment's respite. At nine forty-five on the morning of the 18th he decided to withdraw his Command Post from Wassigny to Le Câtelet. The movement was to begin at one o'clock in the afternoon. He himself was to stay with the rearguard, whose resistance he wished to stimulate. But Wassigny was encircled. At four o'clock Giraud had to follow the retreat. Accompanied only by two officers he set out for Le Câtelet, already occupied by the Panzers. However, the three men succeeded under cover of night in getting through. Then, trying to reach Cambrai, they ran into a German outpost picket with whom they exchanged shots. Giraud ordered the two officers to cross the fields to join the rear of the Army. Remaining alone, he stopped behind a hedge at the side of the road. When daybreak came, a column of French trucks, headed by a machine-gun carrier, which had succeeded in passing round Le Câtelet, arrived. Giraud got into the machine-gun carrier. He opened fire on the first Panzer which came along and put it out of action. Three others appeared. He dashed into a farm which the three Panzers surrounded, whilst an enemy column came to help and guarded the road. That was the end. At six o'clock on the morning of the 19th, Giraud fell into the hands of the Germans.

[2] Gamelin had inspected Corap's Army before the German offensive. He deposited on the file of the Riom Court a note from his General Staff, summarizing the demands sent to the Supreme Command by Corap as a result of this inspection. None of them concerned an increase of effectives. According to Georges, however, Corap's Army had always been treated as a poor relation. At the beginning of the war it was simply an army detachment. Corap, backed by Georges, had not ceased to ask for this detachment to be raised to the status of an army by the addition of the indispensable units necessary. This change was

Moreover the inquiry, which was ordered by Weygand and to which General Dufieux went, established that all the bridges of the Meuse had been blown up, contrary to the statement which I had made public—and which I regret having done—because I had it from two successive Commanders-in-Chief, both equally categoric about this point.

Georges proposed to Gamelin that Huntziger should be relieved of his command after the front had been broken at Sedan. Gamelin objected to this.

WHAT WAS HAPPENING BETWEEN NAMUR AND ANTWERP?

What was taking place to the north during these tragic days? Behind the Dyle, the Belgians were not attacked, and the British were hardly probed by the enemy. The existence of Blanchard's troops between Dyle and Namur was more full of incident. In the first place, to cover his Army while it was taking up positions and to strengthen the Belgians, as had been promised, Blanchard sent his two light mechanized divisions in advance of his front, the 3rd to the north and the 2nd to the south. But the Albert Canal had been forced, and there again, contrary to agreement, the Belgians had not joined with our forces in any common action, but had merely retreated rapidly towards the rear. The light mechanized divisions thus formed the only covering for Blanchard's Army which would not be completely in its positions until the 14th. Therefore, Billotte ordered Prioux to hold on at all costs until that date. This obliged the latter to throw in the whole strength of his light mechanized divisions and to spread them over a front of forty kilometres instead of keeping them concentrated. The bulk of two Panzer divisions, which had crossed the Albert Canal, together with a motorized division and the vanguards of following lorry-borne divisions fell on Prioux's northern division, which had only its own infantry and artillery. It suffered severely. The division to the south was less sorely tested. When they had carried out their mission the two divisions fell back within the lines during the night of the 14th to 15th, and proceeded to string out and to thin themselves along the whole front in order to bolster it up with escort tanks.

The density of troops was very great on the front held by Blanchard's Army, where one division held on an average a sector of five kilometres, whilst on Corap's front a similar unit held fifteen. Moreover, Blanchard's men were, as we have said, of high quality; they held out under the combined assaults of Panzers and Stukas. But the three

finally made, but slowly and somewhat parsimoniously because the means were lacking. It therefore seems that the strategic importance of Corap's Army was only tardily and incompletely appreciated.

divisions were only clinging to the front line, and we have seen that the two light mechanized divisions were sorely tried. When a general retreat was ordered, Blanchard's Army fell back into the British zone, carrying disorder and confusion there. It was a false move, and one, no doubt, which contributed towards the set-back of Weygand's later plan; this was set afoot to disengage the northern Armies by means of an attack in the direction of the Somme, that is to say, the south.

WHAT WOULD GEORGES DO?

Thus our lines were broken both at Sedan and at Dinant. What would Georges do in his capacity as Commander-in-Chief? 'The presence of the General', Napoleon used to say, 'is indispensable. He is the head, he is the sum total of any army.'

For five months Georges had known that his Armies would man the front between Montmédy–Sedan–Mézières–Dinant–Namur–Antwerp. For five months he had the leisure to reflect on the dangers which this front offered, and on the means to ward off these dangers. What was his reply to be? Would he take up a position from which he could counter-attack the enemy if he happened to advance through the corridors of Sedan? Was he going, on the other hand, to mount a total offensive like Joffre conceived shortly after Charleroi?

In the sphere of aerial warfare we know the slender resources at Georges' disposal. But what about the sphere of ground operations? The weapon of the Commander-in-Chief consists in the reserves which he can throw into action at a time and place chosen by himself. That is why his first duty is to form and re-form without respite a pool of reserves as they are progressively absorbed by the battle. At the end of 1915 Joffre had created a reserve which comprised half of the French Army—forty-seven divisions out of ninety-eight. Certain of these reserve divisions were for the time being at the disposal of army group commanders, but Joffre could withdraw them at will. This allowed him the following year to hold out at Verdun and to attack on the Somme. Before the offensive on May 10, Georges had not profited from the security which the Maginot Line and the Rhine gave him to create a body of reserves by means of withdrawals from his eastern Armies. His excuse was that he wished to send as many divisions as possible to that part of the front where we were in contact with the enemy.

'Prételat (commander of the army group in the Maginot Line) was opposed to withdrawing troops from the line', he answered Gamelin, who was pressing him to do so.

'Tell him that I myself require it.'

'Please let me tackle him. I shall manage to convince him.'

But how can one convince a general responsible for a battle-front that he has too many men? All that was required was to sign an order to that effect, and everything would be settled. Georges did nothing about it. Thus the Maginot Line was of little use to us during the battle of Belgium, since we had the same number of divisions immobilized on this front and that of the Rhine as our opponent had (each side had forty). During the battle of France this renowned line was even detrimental to our cause because we did not dare to abandon it in order to shorten our front. Georges recognized that he lacked an army of general reserves in the centre of the front. There had been one in the initial concept of the plan, he said, but it had been sent to the extreme left of the front in order to advance into Holland. He added that on two occasions, December 5, 1939, and April 14, 1940, he had stressed to Gamelin the need for re-creating a general reserve, but Gamelin had preferred to replace it by 'a sixth army which, in reality, was only an organ of command on May 10'.

According to the Franco-British Order of Battle on the north-east front, May 9, 1940, the eve of the German offensive, the reserves of the Commander-in-Chief were as follows: he had, under his personal command, eleven infantry divisions, one of which was motorized, and three armoured divisions. Where were these eleven divisions? Two were behind Corap's Army, one was at Vitry-le-François, and eight 'behind the Lorraine and Rhine fronts'. Was this not a very long way from the Belgian front, where the danger lay? Gamelin stated at Riom that he thought the disposition of the reserves was logical because of the railway system. Very well. The fact remains that we did not see these reserves join in the battle to the rear of Sedan or of Dinant.

What was the state of these three armoured divisions? The first two had begun to be formed on January 16. Georges thought that the 1st alone was, because of its equipment and training, fit to fight on May 10. He had been present at exercises of the 2nd in the area of Châlons some days before the German offensive, when the division had scarcely been brought up to strength, and when it had, as he put it, 'no dynamic training'. As for the 3rd Division, which was scattered in the area of Rheims on May 10, General Devaux, its Chief of Staff, stated to the Committee of Inquiry (sitting of December 21, 1948) that it was a 'unit of incomplete strength', and it 'lacked indispensable equipment in certain essential spheres'; that it was in particular without any 'unit of command, of petrol supply and breakdown services', which was 'only beginning to be knocked into shape'; that it had only begun its training as a complete unit on May 1, and thus, in a word, it was not fit 'to take on the duty' which the Command was going to give it.

That left the 4th Armoured Division which still did not figure in the Order of Battle and the formation of which was to be feverishly carried out in a few days.[1]

The reserves were not included in the Order of Battle as all those which were available for the operation were attached either to each of the Armies or Army Groups on the north-east front, or alternatively to the Commander-in-Chief of the ground forces, that is to say, to Gamelin himself. On this score Gamelin controlled on May 10: (*a*) three infantry divisions which were stationed about the plateau of Langres, and which could advance in case of urgency towards the north-east, the Swiss frontier or the south-east; (*b*) two light infantry divisions, intended for Norway; the 2nd, which was on the point of embarking, and the 3rd held in reserve at Brest. From May 10, Gamelin placed the three infantry divisions at Georges' disposal, and a short time afterwards the two light divisions. As a result Georges controlled a reserve totalling twenty-eight divisions and including the three armoured divisions.

In any case, if our front were broken, *everything was lost*. There was no question of a repetition of the battle of the Marne. We had cast our lot in favour of a continuous front. We had to abide by such a decision. It was therefore vital that we should prevent the enemy breaking our front.

Where was it possible to break it? We have seen that, of the three corridors which offered a possible route for invasion, the two most threatened were those of Sedan and Dinant. Georges therefore ought to have used his available forces to stop the enemy forcing them, and the Panzer divisions crossing through them and deploying out of them. It was in the rear of these two corridors that he ought to have thrown his reserves on the dawn of the 10th, without losing a moment. Did Georges see that the danger lay here? One can well ask the question, since it was not to Corap that he sent the two divisions which were held in reserve behind this latter's Army. He sent them behind the north part of the front, which was already reinforced by Giraud's Army in reserve, and by two British divisions which were also in reserve. Maassen, in *Par delà la Meuse*, recounts that, during the attack on Monthermé, 'aerial reconnaissance showed that the roads for a long distance from Laon were free of troops'. Therefore, he notes, 'the enemy had thrown all his forces towards the north . . . when the centre of gravity of our attack was here in the south'.

It was all the more necessary to use the reserves to reinforce the defence of these two corridors of invasion because the bulk of the Panzer divisions—the stations which they had taken up (known by us

---

[1] We should add that all the armoured divisions had been quartered in Champagne, where they were using training camps which were suitable for joint manœuvres, especially those of Sissonne, Mourmelon, Suippes and Mailly.

before the 10th) were sufficient to prove it—were directed against them. It was obvious that they would be followed by the main body of the forces allotted by the enemy for the offensive. Now, the fronts of Corap's and Huntziger's Armies were manned by thirteen infantry divisions and five cavalry divisions, without a single armoured or light mechanized division. Why was this? Why did our Air Force concentrate on bombing the bridges of the Maastricht and of the Albert Canal over which only two Panzer divisions had passed, whilst seven divisions rolled, with headlights switched on and their instructions coming over the wireless in clear, towards the corridors of Sedan and Dinant? It has been said that this was because the British, who had promised to do this, had preferred to go and bomb objectives in the Rhineland. But it was to the south of the Meuse where the danger lay!

How can one explain this attitude of Georges? Had he forgotten that, in August, 1914, the Third German Army had crossed the Meuse at Dinant and the Fourth at Sedan? It is clear that, although he rebuts this, Georges believed in the efficacy of Pétain's continuous front, and that he was convinced that his front would only be attacked after a powerful concentration of artillery had been assembled. He believed that he had enough time, and this was not so.[1]

On the other hand, he did not proceed to concentrate his own forces. Because he had failed to use them in time, he had left out of the battle almost all the infantry divisions at his disposal for tactical use. Eight of these, out of the eleven in his general reserve, were *behind the Lorraine and Rhine fronts*. Neither does he seem to have drawn on the general reserve[2] to reinforce the artillery and machine-guns of Corap's and Huntziger's Armies at the beginning of the offensive. On the 13th, noting that Georges' divisions and Vuillemin's air squadrons were remaining a long way from the front, Gamelin expressed his surprise to both of them, and asked them to *close up their reserves*. He had all the more reason to be surprised, he notes, because, in his Note of September 21, 1939, he had drawn from the Polish campaign the lesson that the first echelon of reserves ought to be placed 'in more or less immediate proximity to the front, according to the rapidity with which the enemy could reach the different parts of the front'. But, on May 13, it was too late. The Meuse had been crossed that very day at three points by enemy infantry.

At Sedan a Panzer division had already cut the 55th and 71st Divisions to pieces, when Georges gave Huntziger the order to counter-attack.

---

[1] Georges did, however, note that, according to the latest information concerning the dispositions of the Panzer divisions, an attack could take place to the north of Namur. In any case, this could only be to the south of the Dyle.
[2] Whilst the German Army reinforced all its divisions as much as possible, the French Army kept in general reserve the means to reinforce with artillery and machine-guns those divisions engaged in battle.

General Flavigny in command of the 3rd Mechanized Infantry Division, the 5th Light Cavalry Division and the 3rd Armoured Division was in charge of the operation, which according to orders was to begin around midday on the 14th. But the armoured division could not take up its position before four o'clock in the afternoon. General Flavigny called off the counter-attack, which was put back to the following day at three o'clock in the afternoon. However, as the armoured division only seemed to him to be capable of going into action with accompanying infantry, he placed it at the orders of a motorized infantry division. A few tanks did, indeed, set out, but as they were not followed by infantry, they soon called a halt.[1] That was all which was done. However, the Panzers had increased the pace of their advance; on the 16th it was definitely to be too late for any attempt to contain their flow.

As for the two other armoured divisions (the 1st and the 2nd) Georges sent them towards Namur. But they also joined in the battle too late. The 1st, indeed, was only on the spot at Charleroi on the 14th. Billotte allotted it to Corap, who placed it under the orders of General Martin, commander of the Eighteenth Army Corps. It is true that this corps, which held the Dinant–Givet sector, had lost, as we have seen, its two Class A divisions, yet General Martin still had under him the 4th North African Division which was still waiting, arms at the order, in Philippeville—as well as the two light cavalry divisions who, having accomplished their mission, had withdrawn to the rear. But instead of massing his forces, General Martin, who had, nevertheless, been Inspector of Tanks, threw the armoured division into battle alone on the 16th, that is, without the support of infantry and artillery. By doing so, he sent it headlong into disaster. Cut off from its rear and encircled, it fought valiantly, but could not escape its fate. It left a great part of its equipment on the field of battle.

The 2nd Armoured Division which had been diverted when on the road from Valenciennes and Hirson was in its turn only able to join in the battle after the 16th. Once again, it was in a piecemeal fashion (as its tanks arrived on the scene) that this division was thrown into the furnace of battle. It was the same old story: too late, always too late.

The 4th Armoured Division which, under the command of General de Gaulle was grouped around Laon, was given the task on the 16th of attacking the enemy who, advancing from the breach of Sedan, wheeled right and drove towards the sea. But the Germans, who were

[1] Huntziger immediately wrote to General Flavigny: 'I learned with indignation that my orders have not been carried out, that the counter-attack from which we might have expected great results has not taken place, because the commander of the 3rd Armoured Division has not given the general commanding the 3rd Mechanized Infantry Division sufficient support. I would like you to make a personal inquiry immediately into these sorry facts.' On the 16th, General Brocard, commander of the 3rd Armoured Division, was, at the request of General Flavigny, relieved of his command.

still pushing towards the west, guarded the left flank. A Panzer division, supported by infantry divisions, opposed the 4th Armoured Division, and forced it to retreat.

A tardy engagement with troops thrown in piecemeal—such was the nature of the strategy which characterized the employment of our armoured divisions. What exactly was the nature of the instrument?

First of all, what was the equipment worth? Less manœuvrable and less speedy perhaps than the Panzers, our tanks were superior to them in the resistance of their protective armour and the power of their engines. But, for various reasons, they commanded a less extensive radius of action. Wireless communication was not up to the mark. Anti-tank armament was of unequal value, for a number of tanks were still equipped with 1916 model guns. Finally, anti-aircraft equipment was to a large degree insufficient. General Bruneau, who commanded the 1st Armoured Division, offered the following explanation for this state of things to the Committee of Inquiry (sitting of July 6, 1948): 'I must say, with complete frankness', he has stated, 'that I was utterly unable to understand the situation . . . which resulted from the fact that the Command had not realized what life in tanks was like.'

But our real inferiority lay in the conception which our Supreme Command had formed about the use of the armoured element. 'I consider', General Bruneau has stated, 'that . . . our inferiority . . . was due less to a lack of tanks than to the fact that these weapons were not organized in a suitable fashion. This arm had not been given an indication of what its role was, it had not been equipped, trained, or mobilized to conduct a war of movement. On the contrary . . . there was a desire to turn its tanks into escort vehicles.'

In brief, we had not wanted an armoured corps, and we were paying the penalty for it.

In the enemy camp, on the contrary, it constituted an arm which was organically, tactically and strategically independent, and whose employment was linked with that of dive-bombers in massive strength and rapid action.

It was the enemy who had understood Napoleon's words to Lauriston: 'Always remember: concentrate your strength!'

Thus, the Wehrmacht, when it took the offensive, found our front of seven hundred and fifty kilometres, from Antwerp to Basle, sprinkled with tanks. It massed its Panzer divisions to launch them into the attack. And the blow of this battering-ram was to be decisive.

In a lecture at the *École Supérieure de Guerre* on the engagement of the 1st Armoured Division in the battle of the Meuse, Major Ornano expressed himself as follows: 'Those, who before the war did not believe in large independent armoured units and who did not create them, must have had a heavy burden on their conscience when they were obliged, after two days of warfare, to assign them to duties which for years previously they had not thought necessary.' How can we avoid echoing the opinion quoted by General Bruneau during his evidence before the Committee of Inquiry?

THE ATTITUDE OF LEOPOLD III: 'NO, NOT SOUTHWARD; NORTHWARD'

The King of the Belgians set up his General Headquarters in Breen-donck Fort.[1] On the 14th he received Billotte, who did not 'conceal his anxiety' from him; then, shortly afterwards, Gort,[2] who 'did not hide his lack of confidence'. He [the King], on the 15th, sent for his Prime Minister and his Minister of National Defence. He received them at three o'clock in the afternoon.

We have an account of this audience based on the King's notes.[3] Would it not be best to reproduce this text?

'After having pointed out that the French battle-front between Namur and Sedan seemed to be endangered, the King inquired of his Ministers what were the Government's intentions. . . . The King observed . . . that Brussels appeared, at the moment, to be the town which was least exposed to bombardment. . . . The Ministers . . . had that very day decided against leaving Brussels. In the event of its being necessary to evacuate Brussels, the King insisted on the Government's undertaking to remain in Belgium. They had to prevent, at all costs, the separation of the Government, should it move to France, from the King and the Army. The latter, with the British divisions, might find itself cut off from the rest of the Allied Armies, following the break-through at Sedan and the rapid advance of the German Armies in the direction of the Channel. The Prime Minister, appalled at the prospect, agreed that this had to be avoided at all costs, and that taking every possibility into account, the King could not run the risk of allowing himself to be captured: "We must manœuvre in such a way as to lead our Army towards France and not towards the North Sea." The King remarked that our Army's tactics depended, before everything else, on the development of events, and General Denis added that they were equally dependent on the general conception of operations as a whole and on the orders of the Commander-in-Chief. The King asked the Ministers to insist . . . with the authorities in Paris and London on obtaining from France and Britain a written declaration giving the fullest guarantees to Belgium when peace should be signed. He drew the Government's attention to the danger of wishing to incorporate or

---

[1] One of the forts within the fortified area around Antwerp.
[2] *Rapport*, p. 35.   [3] *Ibid.*, *Annexes*, pp. 46–7.

of allowing Belgium to be incorporated in the Anglo-French Alliance on any grounds imaginable. The greatest caution was required in view of the uncertainty of events. The Prime Minister replied that certain agreements had urgently to be concluded with France and Britain, notably in respect of the exchange of the Belgian franc against the pound and the French franc, and of supplies and equipment. The King insisted that, in no circumstances, should an alliance be made: Belgium should preserve her liberty of action, the more so since neither London nor Paris up till now seemed inclined to give the guarantees required as regards the future of Belgium.'

From his side, M. Pierlot has given his version of the audience. According to him,[1] the King, commenting on the break-through at Sedan, showed the Ministers the map, observing: 'They will be there within eight days.' On the subject of the direction in which the Belgian Army was going to make a fighting retreat, M. Pierlot indicated that this should be to the west, and then to the south. The King's actual reply was: 'No, *not southward; northward.*' He explained: 'The culmination of the retreat, if it were prolonged, should not end on French territory, but result in a position based on the coast.'

Thus it will be seen that the King wanted neither an alliance, nor a unified operation with the Allied Armies. A Belgian writer, M. Marcel Thiry, has provided a commentary, as seen from the King's point of view, the importance of which needs no emphasis. The operational plan, drawn up by the King, at General van Overstraeten's suggestion, consisted, he wrote, in 'regrouping the Belgian Army northward, under the shelter of prepared defences. The idea of maintaining a cohesive Belgian Army, of preserving for Belgian executive power, on Belgian territory, a proper military force assembled on this territory, took precedence over the idea of sharing, first and foremost, in the common victory of the Allies, even if this meant sacrificing national pride and territory, even at the cost of retreating beyond its frontiers. And how could the second idea be taken as an aim, when, according to the King's thoughts and words, even after the invasion, we had no *allies*, but only *guarantors*? It is much more than a subtle difference in meaning: with allies you wage war to the end, whatever the cost; while guarantors are under a unilateral obligation to come to your assistance with all their resources, without any obligation on your part towards them.'

This view, we find officially stated by Count d'Ursel, the Belgian Minister at Berne, in a letter of September 12, 1940:[2] 'We have never admitted the Pierlot Government's thesis, according to which an alliance existed between France and Britain. Those two countries were our guarantors, who came at our call, according to their promise. Our part

[1] Pierlot, *op. cit. (Le Soir,* July 10, 1947).   [2] *Rapport,* p. 208.

of the bargain was an undertaking to defend our territory. But there was never a common cause, nor a promise to link our fate with theirs.'

The doctrine is clear. According to this theory of 'neutralism', the guaranteed is in no way linked with his guarantor. He has rights, but no duties. He is justified in acting from a military point of view with complete independence. It is in the name of this principle that the Belgian Army saw eight thousand of its men fall in vain on the battlefield.

Let us revert to the day of the 14th. Accompanied by M. Gutt, Minister of Finance, M. Spaak came to see me in Paris. According to the latter,[1] 'the Quai d'Orsay persisted in leaving unanswered (the Belgian) request for guarantees for the future'.[2] Commenting upon his interview with me, M. Spaak declared on July 3, 1947, in the Belgian Senate: 'When I saw M. Reynaud in Paris, on May 15,[3] our discussion was not very satisfactory. I noticed that he was ignorant of all the meetings between General Gamelin and the Belgian authorities and that perhaps this ignorance of certain important facts could have put him in a frame of mind which was unfavourable to our country.' It is correct that I was not made aware of these exchanges. Gamelin, in *Servir*, carefully notes the fact.[4]

But how could I have not already failed to get a bad impression, even a gloomy presentiment? The same day, the 15th, at the Council of Ministers, the question of Belgium had been raised. Marcel Héraud, in the notes which he took during this meeting, wrote:

'*Daladier*—The Belgian Army began to fall apart from the very outset. Fragments of it are to be found everywhere, which we collect and which are placed under French command. . . . I noticed in many

---

[1] *Rapport, Annexes*, p. 48.

[2] This problem of guarantees, which, as we have seen, already arose at the time of the alarm on January 10, had been raised both in London and Paris by the Belgian Government on May 10, or the very day on which Belgium was invaded. Negotiations immediately opened between the Foreign Office and the Quai d'Orsay. On the 25th, officials of the Ministry submitted a Note to me in favour of conceding the guarantees which were asked. I wrote in the margin of this Note the following annotation. '*Accepted*. If we win the war we can carry out our pledges. If we lose it, our pledges will not matter.' As a result the Quai d'Orsay replied to the Belgian Ambassador with a letter (of which only an undated copy remains in the archives). In this the Government of the Republic, renewing certain pledges given to Belgium during the First World War, gave her an assurance that the French Government would wage war against Germany in full association with the Belgian Government without opening negotiations for a separate peace, not doubting that the Belgian Government would enter into a corresponding pledge, that the French Government would do all within its power to maintain the territorial integrity of Belgium and its colony, and finally that Belgium would receive after the war economic and financial assistance of which she was in need.

As will be seen, it does not appear that France's attitude in this matter can be open to criticism.

[3] It was, as we have seen, on the 14th and not the 15th that I received MM. Spaak and Gutt.

[4] Vol. III, p. 351.

Belgian villages the presence of numerous young men who were not mobilized. I have the impression that the King and the Government ... are soon going to leave Brussels. There have been discussions with the British Navy about evacuation.

'*Paul Reynaud*—I have insisted that they shall not leave Belgium. The news I have about the behaviour of the Dutch Army is entirely praiseworthy in character.

'*Lebrun*—Ninety thousand out of three hundred thousand have been killed.

'*Daladier*—During a two-hours' audience which I have had with the King of the Belgians, he did not mention Holland once. He spoke only of Belgium. I was tempted to ask him: "Whose fault is it?"'

Daladier, who himself knew about Gamelin's talks [with the Belgians], clearly thought little differently from me. M. Spaak himself, on May 31, at Limoges, told the Belgian M.P.s: 'Although I was not present at this meeting (on the 15th, at the King's General Headquarters), I can say that it was on that very day that our first doubts were born.'

MAY 16: CHURCHILL IN PARIS

When our front had been broken, the enemy clearly had two courses open to him: either to drive on to Paris, which was unprotected by any formidable defences or by any army, or to deliver the feint blow on the North Sea. Since our Supreme Command thought the first course the more likely, I sent Churchill,[1] on the 14th at 5.45 p.m., the following message by telephone:

'Having just left the War Committee, I am sending you, in the name of the French Government, the following statement:

'The situation is indeed very serious. Germany is trying to deal us a fatal blow in the direction of Paris. The German Army has broken through our fortified lines south of Sedan. Should it succeed, it will be due to our inability to resist the combined attack of heavy tanks and bombers. To stop the German drive, so long as there is still time, and to allow our counter-attack to succeed, the German tanks must be isolated from their supporting Stukas. This is only possible through a considerable force of fighter aircraft.

'You have already willingly sent us four squadrons,[2] which represents more than you promised.

'To win this battle, which could well be of decisive importance for the whole war, it is essential that you send immediately ten additional

---

[1] Churchill had succeeded Chamberlain on the 10th as Prime Minister.

[2] *Squadron*. The English term is used here in order to stress the fact that it was a question of a British formation with the organic establishment which it comprised.

squadrons. Without such a contribution, we cannot be certain that we shall be able to stem the German advance.

'Between Sedan and Paris, there are no defences comparable with those in the line which we must restore at almost any cost.

'I have confidence that, at this critical hour, British aid will not fail us.'

Churchill replied the same evening, at 8.30 p.m.:

'The British War Cabinet and General Staff have given the most careful consideration to the request which you addressed to me this afternoon, and we are losing no time in studying the means of meeting the situation.

'We have called in Staff Officers who are in position to give us details of the last-minute state of affairs, so that we can be sure that all available resources are employed to the utmost in the common cause.'

On the 15th at 7.30 a.m., I called Churchill, who was asleep (as he tells us), to the telephone. I renewed the request I had made to him a few hours earlier. The air strength stationed in England was indispensable to us. Its intervention had to be both powerful and immediate. Churchill seemed so surprised that I repeated to him:

'We are beaten. We have lost the battle.'

'Impossible! Experience shows that, at the end of a certain time, all offensives peter out by themselves. In five or six days, they will be compelled to stop in order to get supplies.'

'All is changed. A torrent of Panzers is bursting through.'

'Will you let me telephone Georges?'

'Certainly.'

Churchill was thinking that we were still in the First World War. I knew that we were concerned with an entirely different war.

Churchill ended by saying that he would come to Paris the next day.

During the afternoon of the 15th, Churchill sent a telegram to Roosevelt, in which he painted the situation in a particularly alarming light. He emphasized the demoralizing effects on the French of the technique introduced by the Wehrmacht: powerful attacks by Panzer divisions, in conjunction with squadrons of Stukas. 'The battle', he wrote, 'has only begun. I am waiting to see the full strength of the forces thrown in.' After having predicted Mussolini's entry into the war to make sure of his share of the booty, he added that Britain awaited her turn, soon to come, to be attacked by bombers as well as by parachute or airborne forces. Turning to the possibility that Great Britain might, alone, have to continue the struggle, he emphasized that it was high time that the United States brought its material strength to the help of the Allies, if she did not want Europe shortly to become 'Nazified'. And Churchill listed the immediate needs of Great Britain:

forty to fifty obsolete and uncommissioned destroyers[1] to be drawn from the reserve of disarmed units of the American Navy and temporarily leased to the Royal Navy; several hundred aircraft of the latest type; anti-aircraft material; and steel. Believing in the possibility of a landing in Ireland by parachute or airborne troops, he asked for a squadron to be dispatched to Irish waters, which it should patrol for a considerable time. Lastly, he begged Roosevelt to watch Japan and placed the base at Singapore at his disposal.[2]

Again, on the 15th, following a telephoned SOS from Daladier at quarter past six in the evening, I returned to the charge by sending Churchill, at ten past seven, the following message: 'We lost the battle last night. The road to Paris is open. Send us all aircraft and troops you can.'

[1] I had forestalled Churchill on this point by asking the American Government, on the 14th, to let us have, if only on a temporary basis, fifty of the ships in question. Cordell Hull in his *Memoirs* alludes to this step (vol. I, pp. 831–2):

'[The sale or loan of the destroyers had first been broached by the French] Premier Reynaud on May 14, only four days after the invasion of France, and by Mr. Churchill on the following day.

'. . . the President opposed the proposal. On May 16 he cabled Mr. Churchill that . . . a step of that kind could not be taken except with the specific authorization of Congress . . . He said furthermore that, in view of our defense requirements of this hemisphere and with our obligations in the Pacific, he doubted whether we could dispose even temporarily of the destroyers. He added that, even if we were able to take the steps Mr. Churchill suggested, it would be at least six or seven weeks as a minimum before the destroyers could undertake active service under the British flag. . . .

'On the same day we cabled Ambassador Bullitt . . . saying that the question would have to go to Congress and that Congressional permission at this moment seemed unobtainable. Also, we had no excess naval tonnage. . . . A fortnight later, on June 1, we cabled Bullitt again . . . as a result of further requests from the French Government. The President believed that an exchange of American destroyers would probably be inexpedient because of the enormous sea area we had to patrol. It would require Congressional action which might be difficult to get. Our old destroyers could not be sold as obsolete because they were now in commission or were being reconditioned for commissioning. He suggested that destroyers might be obtained from some of the South American Republics.'

[2] According to Cordell Hull (*op. cit.*, vol. I, pp. 765–6), Churchill, when handing the message to Mr. Kennedy, which he asked to be cabled directly to the White House, told him that he considered the chance of the Allies winning would be slender if Italy came into the war and that the French were asking for reinforcements but that he refused to send them any, as he was convinced that, before a month was out, Britain herself would be violently attacked. He ended by declaring the determination of Britain, even if the country were reduced to ashes, never to give in, at least, as long as he was in power. 'The Government', he asserted, 'would move to Canada, take the fleet with it, and fight on.'

Roosevelt replied by emphasizing, as we have just seen, the constitutional bonds which placed an obstacle in the way of handing over the ships of the American Navy, but assuring Churchill, however, of his wish to give the Allies as much help as was possible within the framework of neutrality. He also professed himself ready to study the question of sending a squadron into Irish waters, and, as regards Japan, he recalled that the American fleet mounted guard at Pearl Harbour. It was only after nearly four months, on September 3, that the U.S.A. was to agree to handing over to Britain the destroyers in question, but in exchange for the ceding by Britain of bases in Newfoundland and the British Antilles for a duration of ninety-nine years.

As the Supreme Command stated that it could no longer be responsible for the security of Paris after midnight on the 16th, General Héring, Military Governor of Paris, sent me, on the morning of the 16th, the following letter:

Mr. President,

In the present circumstances, I deem it wise, for the purpose of preventing any disorder, to suggest that you order the evacuation of the Government—except the National Defence Department, or at least, their senior grades—the Chamber of Deputies and the Senate to the pre-arranged evacuation areas. I should be obliged if you would inform me of your decision as soon as possible.

On the 16th, at the Quai d'Orsay, I held a meeting which was attended by the Presidents of the Chamber, several Ministers and the Director of National Security. I acquainted them with the communication which I had received from the Military Governor. Herriot raised the question of whether the inhabitants of the capital ought not to be warned, to which Monzie replied that we had not at our disposal the means of transport needed for the evacuation of all who wanted to leave. In fact, this evacuation of the population, even on a limited scale, would have rendered the scheme for evacuating the services impossible. This scheme (it had been planned in peace-time) was spread over seven days. It was decided to reduce evacuation to a minimum, in order to preserve what was essential. It was agreed that the Minister of Public Works should inform the Presidents of the Chambers and the Ministers at 2 p.m. about the number of lorries which each could count upon. I stated that, so far as the Government was concerned, it ought to remain in Paris, no matter how intense the bombing might be, but that it should, however, take care not to fall into the enemy's hands: it ought to leave the capital only if a threat of this nature should materialize, and, in that event, at the last moment.

The next day I received a second letter from the Military Governor.

Mr. President,

It was my duty, yesterday, to suggest to you the departure of the Government and the Chambers from Paris. You have decided to remain. My heartiest congratulations. Yours respectfully,

Héring.

On that very day, the 17th, I summoned Weygand to Paris. During the Pétain trial[1] he stated that it was during the 'great anxiety of May 16' that I had sent for him.[2] Here is the truth. That pessimism was general

[1] Hearing on July 31, 1945.
[2] Daladier to whom Weygand (according to the hierarchy) was subordinated through the intermediary of Gamelin did not object to this summons. However, he asked me to carry it out myself.

I do not deny. I learned, indeed, that an armistice was already being talked about at General Headquarters. 'Armistice means *capitulation*,' I replied.

Churchill had arrived in Paris on the 16th. It was his first visit to the French capital in his capacity as Prime Minister.

At twenty minutes past five in the afternoon, seated round a large-scale map placed on an easel, Churchill, with General Sir John Dill, Vice-C.I.G.S., Air Marshal Joubert de la Ferté (himself assistant to Air Chief Marshal Newall), and General Ismay, Assistant-Secretary to the War Cabinet, Daladier, Campinchi, Laurent-Eynac, Gamelin, Darlan and General Bergeret, Deputy Chief of Staff of the French Air Force, deputizing for Vuillemin, who was detained elsewhere, met in my office. M. de Margerie drew up the following report of the discussion which ensued:

Mr. Winston Churchill began by saying that he was not entirely clear about the position, nor did he quite understand what stage had been reached when he heard that the Government was thinking of leaving Paris.

M. Paul Reynaud remarked that it was the Military Governor of Paris, General Héring, who had asked for this departure, which, it should be added, was not for the moment going to take place.

General Gamelin spoke next, and gave an account of the situation. In the main, the front from Switzerland to Montmédy, along the length of the Maginot Line had not moved. It was from Montmédy that its hinges had been broken off by the German drive. The latter had made a deep pocket at two points between Rancourt and Anor. (Questioned by the Prime Minister, the General made it clear that we no longer held Mézières, although encircled French elements in the area were still resisting.)

M. Paul Reynaud remarked that German tanks, followed by lorry-borne infantry, had been thrown into this gap and were now fanning out in three directions towards Paris.

General Gamelin added that these forces consisted of two tank divisions, and two or three infantry divisions in lorries. General Giraud had taken command and was trying to restore the situation.

The President of the Council emphasized the fact that the German Army was attacking the hinge of our front in the direction of the capital with all its strength.

General Gamelin thought that there were nearly eighty German divisions between the Moselle and the Schelde, of which at least fifty had already been thrown into action as a first stage, and that the remainder were being held in readiness to increase the pressure.

Questioned by Mr. Churchill, the General made it clear that, at the northern-most end of the front, the French Army, which had penetrated as far as Breda and Tilburg, was making a fighting retreat towards the Schelde.

Mr. Churchill then stated that he could not understand how an order to retreat, which involved the abandonment of Brussels and Louvain, could have been contemplated: according to him, the Anglo-Belgian Armies which were in Brabant were in a position to make a strong counter-attack against the flanks of the German Armies which were driving on Laon, and it seemed absurd to him to abandon all that terrain.

M. Daladier rejected that idea: the French Army had nothing left which would enable it to cover Paris and, in the circumstances, in order not to remain completely unsupported, it had to fall back on the Sambre.

The Prime Minister thought, on the contrary, that this was the time to hold fast; to this M. Daladier retorted that to do so would require reserves and supplies, when we had no more.

M. Paul Reynaud added that the enemy enjoyed numerical superiority and that he could throw in the considerable number of tanks he had. This had resulted in a local break-through, which now threatened the stability of the whole front. The tanks . . . were now spreading out in every direction.

Mr. Churchill hesitated to take the threat presented by the tanks so seriously. So long as the latter were not supported by strong infantry units, they were only a limited force; so many little flags stuck on the map. But they would be unable either to support themselves or to refuel.

General Gamelin observed that it was hoped to check the advance by ordering Giraud's Army to counter-attack tomorrow. But he felt that he ought to point out that the French armoured divisions had sustained heavy losses, and had suffered greatly during the operations of the last few days. A third of the heavy tanks, and two-thirds of the light tanks were now out of action. The French heavy tanks, from experience, had shown themselves to be of better quality than the corresponding German tanks, but the latter had the advantage of numbers.

Mr. Churchill repeated his previous contentions and declared that he refused to see in the German tanks' spectacular dash any real invasion.

'Yet it is an invasion', retorted M. Daladier, 'because a breach has been made, through which the whole German Army is trying to force its way. Because of this very fact, the disposition of the Anglo-Franco-Belgian Armies in northern Belgium is powerless to do anything in the matter.'

'Not a bit of it', asserted Mr. Churchill. 'This is the moment to advance and not retreat.'

General Gamelin, in this connexion, observed that it was General Gort himself who wanted a retreat.

General Dill said that he had been able to talk with Lord Gort over the telephone during the day and that, though speaking guardedly, they had managed to understand each other. With the arrival of German units in the south, General Gort thought it would be better to fall back on the canal which ran behind Brussels.

General Gamelin saw the advantage in thus having the front shortened, and added that it would be most important for us if the British Army extended its dispositions, so as to hold a front corresponding to that occupied by the French Army.

M. Paul Reynaud supported this request, observing that at this very moment, six French divisions were holding a front corresponding to one held by nine British divisions.

'That ought to be quite easy to do', added M. Daladier, 'since there does not appear to be much pressure at the moment in the north.'

Mr. Churchill still could not see the need for retreat in Brabant. He was constantly told that in moving the Armies towards Amsterdam, they had the support of the Belgian Army and so an economy was being made to the extent of some twenty divisions. In his view, it was better for them to fight where they stood, and to drop the idea of bringing men from the north to reinforce the Armies in the south.

General Gamelin stated that four divisions had already been drawn from the reserves which were in the north and they had no hope of finding more in that area. Moreover, the cutting of the Belgian railways was hampering troop movements. . . .

Mr. Churchill continued to question the wisdom of giving up Louvain. To this, General Gamelin replied that the essential thing was to stop the gap leading to Paris, which was made much more difficult by the fact that our best means of action—that is to say, our armoured forces—were all but exhausted. It was for the purpose of stopping this gap that the French Government had asked, with so much insistence, for the support of the British Air Force.

Mr. Churchill gave his opinions on this point. Great Britain had thirty-nine fighter squadrons, whose maintenance in the British Isles was absolutely vital to the country. This was, in fact, the force which kept the German Air Force away from British war industries, whose working was essential for the continuance of the war. So long as British fighters were there, the German squadrons would have to rely upon night raids, the results of which were necessarily uncertain, in view of the difficulty of clearly picking out their targets. By contrast, daylight raids, which could become possible if the defence of the United Kingdom were to be weakened, would, most certainly, have disastrous results for the very outcome of the war. It was with this consideration always in mind that the Prime Minister and his colleagues had studied the possibility of giving France the air support asked for by M. Paul Reynaud and General Gamelin. Four British fighter squadrons were sent at once. They went into action near Sedan. He was bound to say that, out of sixty-seven aircraft, thirty-six did not return. Now, the foot-bridges over the Meuse could be rebuilt in a short time. It was sad to have to cast into the furnace combat units of such importance for results which could not have the slightest permanence. On the other hand, such sacrifices were justified if the purpose were to strike against essential targets, the destruction of which affected or threatened the German war potential. Therefore, the British Air Force had attacked the interior of Germany, bombing factories and oil refineries in the Ruhr, with results which were certain. Now, out of a hundred and twelve aircraft which took part in this night operation, only two failed to return. That was the kind of operation which paid, which earned dividends. The British Air Force was going on in that way and, in Britain, it was hoped that this would incite the Germans to reprisals—that they would attack the British Isles and that this would relieve some of the pressure from the air, which was now being exerted on the French front. But they had to make sure that German aircraft could only come at night, unless they wanted to see them attack really important targets.

This morning, four additional squadrons provided by the British Government should have arrived on the French front, to be put to the best use on the orders of the Command. This made a total of eight [squadrons], i.e. a hundred and eight aircraft, excluding some twenty aircraft sent to replace those destroyed. Here, then, was a force to be reckoned with, and one which ought to get results. But it was impossible to expect air forces to fight tanks. Tanks could only be fought on the ground and by infantry.[1]

Late in the evening, Churchill came to my private house. He read me the admirable telegram he had sent to London after our talks, describing France's situation. In it he gave the picture of the Quai d'Orsay burning its documents on the lawn. He also brought me the answer: the R.A.F. was prepared to place ten squadrons at our disposal, that is to say, a quarter of the defensive forces of the British Isles. I thanked him warmly. He expressed a wish that Daladier should be told the good news—the only good news we had had since the beginning of the German offensive. The discussions were renewed. On the arrival of the Minister of War, Churchill re-read his message. Daladier rose, moved towards him and gripped his hand without a word. The Prime Minister then delivered a forthright harangue on carrying the war to the enemy and revealed, amongst other thing, that the R.A.F. would set fire to the German harvests and forests.

In fact, the Wehrmacht had chosen the scythe-like drive on Dunkirk. Paris was respited. It was a mere respite.

It was also on the 16th that I told my colleagues of the possibility that, at a moment's notice, the Government might find it necessary to go to North Africa and to carry on the war from there. At the end of the afternoon M. de Margerie unburdened himself to Churchill. On the 31st, the latter, who had come to Paris for a meeting of the Supreme Council, again mentioned a question which had been raised during one particular conversation he had had, at a quarter past six in the evening at the British Embassy, with M. de Margerie. He asked him point-blank: 'Was that some kind of a jest of yours, when you told me, fifteen days ago, that France might have to fight successively on the Seine, the Loire, the Garonne, and that the Government would be forced to go to North Africa, in order to continue the struggle?' M. de Margerie explained the reasons which justified the proposals of the 16th, and expressed his deep conviction that it was France's duty to

---

[1] The account which Churchill gives in his memoirs (*op. cit.*, vol. II, *Their Finest Hour*, p. 42) of this Conference brings additional light to this exchange of views which took place: 'The General [Gamelin]', writes Churchill, 'talked perhaps five minutes without any one saying a word. When he stopped there was a considerable silence. I then asked: "Where is the strategic reserve?" and, breaking into French, which I used indifferently (in every sense): "*Où est la masse de manœuvre?*" General Gamelin turned to me and, with a shake of the head said "*Aucune*".' Gamelin, adds Churchill, then resumed his explanation. He examined the means of cutting in two the armoured column which was pushing to the sea. Churchill asked him where and when he counted on attacking the flanks of the 'bulge'. . . . His reply was: 'Inferiority of numbers, inferiority of equipment, inferiority of method.' And Churchill notes: 'And then a hopeless shrug of the shoulders.'

Gamelin states (*L'Aurore*, November 21, 1949) that he did not answer, 'There are none' but 'There are no longer any.'

push on with the preparations in the event of such a possibility. Churchill ended by saying: 'When you put forward these proposals fifteen days ago, I wondered whether you had not fallen a victim to an attack of madness, but I now fully realize the extreme gravity of the situation.' If we are to believe him, he was even then not wholly convinced: indeed, he relates, in his memoirs, that on June 11 he discussed this hypothesis with Georges and admitted that barely a week earlier he believed it to be impregnated with a spirit of defeat.

Churchill returned to London. Three days later he addressed his compatriots in the magnificent language which was to become one of the ingredients of victory. He told them: 'I speak to you for the first time as Prime Minister in a solemn hour. . . . I have invincible confidence in the French Army and its leaders. . . . I have received from the Chiefs of the French Republic, and in particular from its indomitable Prime Minister, M. Reynaud, the most sacred pledges that whatever happens they will fight to the end, be it bitter or be it glorious.'

I was grateful for that speech, which was as valuable for French morale as it was for that of our ally.

MY DISAGREEMENT WITH CHURCHILL OVER THE THEORY OF WAR

I certainly disagreed with the Prime Minister about the scope of the disaster following the piercing of our front, but, at the time, I was far from imagining that my disagreement was as marked as is shown by Churchill's memoirs.

It will be recalled that, on the 15th, at three o'clock in the afternoon, Corap's Army was ordered to fall back. From Sedan to Dinant a gap of nearly a hundred kilometres had been made in our front.

My telephone conversation with Churchill, four and a half hours later, will also be recalled, in the course of which he challenged both the nature and extent of the disaster. We now know that, during the afternoon of the same day, he telegraphed to Roosevelt: 'The battle has only begun. I am waiting to see the full strength of the forces thrown in.'

What is this but an expression by Churchill, who enjoyed the confidence and friendship of some of the high officers of the French Army, showing that he had been quite naturally led to an acceptance of their idea of war? It was they who had inculcated the idea that a continuous front was impregnable; that indeed it might be pierced, but in this case reserves would be hurried to the scene to contain the attacking force and reduce the breach as a surgeon remedies a rupture. This was, in fact, the experience of the First World War. But, on the other hand, it was not so during the final months of this war.

According to this thesis, the piercing of our front bore the same characteristics as the 'break-throughs' of the earlier war—that of March 21, 1918, for instance. Accordingly was it not a clear indication of weakness to contemplate the possibility that the Government might, very soon, be compelled to withdraw to North Africa to continue the war from there, as though all hope of containing the enemy drive in metropolitan territory had been lost?

On both sides of the Channel the official doctrine was therefore the same. Nothing better demonstrates that it was also solidly entrenched in Britain than the indifference which Liddell Hart, the distinguished military writer, had run into when he undertook to focus attention on the revolution which the large-scale employment of armoured forces was bound to bring about in the art of war. Alluding to this blindness, Liddell Hart, who, it is true, has had a most striking revenge since Guderian, creator of the German Armoured Corps, stated that he was a disciple of Liddell Hart, wrote to me on March 8, 1949, following an article which I published[1] on the 2nd in *Le Figaro*, the *New York Times*, the *Daily Telegraph* and the *Corriere della Sera*, in reply to Churchill's memoirs:

'I have read your article with the greatest interest. . . . Indeed, Mr. Churchill reveals in his account that he has not always understood the situation. . . .

'I am in a position to know that, among the statesmen of our two countries, you were almost the only one, before the war, to recognize the importance of armoured units. Your warnings on the subject of the part which this new weapon would be called upon to play and your approaches to the French Government in favour of the formation of an armoured corps awakened my interest at the time. You may remember that, on several occasions, I drew attention to your campaign in *The Times*.

'In 1936, in *The Times* as well as in discussions with the Ministers and military heads in my country, I emphasized the necessity, in the country's interests, of devoting their efforts to the formation of armoured divisions and the development of the air strength, for the purpose of supplementing France's deficiencies in one or other of these spheres. Mr. Chamberlain told me, at the beginning of 1937 (accordingly, on the eve of his taking office), that my arguments had convinced him. In fact, as soon as he had been appointed Prime Minister, our military policy was imbued with my views. I was, at that time, Hore-Belisha's personal adviser: the plan for the reorganization of the British Army, which had been laid down, envisaged the development of armoured units, which were regarded as the backbone of our expeditionary force. . . . But this policy did not commend itself either

---

[1] I had sent my article to Churchill on February 28. He telegraphed me on March 5 that he had found it *very interesting*.

to the views of the French Government, or to those of the military heads, who, on the contrary, insisted on the necessity of sending a large number of infantry divisions to the Continent. Above all, it was under their pressure that the policy, which I had so strongly advocated, was abandoned during the winter of 1938-9 to make way for a plan which postulated the raising of large forces of infantry. . . .

'The efforts you made before the war threw into relief . . . the foresight with which you grasped what was the essential factor of military superiority. The tragedy of Europe and particularly of France lies in the fact that the words you spoke were addressed to men determined to remain deaf to your arguments.'

In each of the two countries, the leaders were clearly infected with the same error. It was an error which led our Supreme Command into massing its best troops on the wings: Giraud's Army, on the left wing, at the mouth of the Schelde, and our light infantry divisions, on the right wing, in the Vosges, when it should have disposed its reserves on the spot at the northern and southern defiles of the Ardennes massif, i.e. in the rear of Dinant and Sedan, through which the Germans had passed once before in August, 1914. But, let us make no mistake, the onslaught of the Panzer divisions could only have been checked by a lightning attack by an armoured corps. But we lacked the weapon needed for this movement.

THE DISASTER, DESCRIBED BY THE ENEMY

As for the decisive character of the role of the German Armoured Corps in our defeat, the German communiqué of June 5, 1940, which gives the account of the first phase of the German offensive, proves the point again: 'The armoured units, forging ahead of the infantry divisions, had, by May 13, reached the Meuse between Dinant and Sedan. . . . Contrary to all the hitherto accepted tactical ideas and despite all the calculations of the enemy Command, these units, accompanied and followed by the infantry divisions (which themselves reached this point by forced marches) and, continuously supported by the Luftwaffe, made themselves in a single day masters of the river and its defences, crushed the defenders as well as all counter-attacks, and opened the road to the Oise. In this way a breach was made in the enemy's front.'

Was that not 'an iron hammer smashing open a breach on the road to victory'?

Alas! On the 25th, I received a postcard at my address, found on the body of an officer of Corap's Army, who had just committed suicide in Le Mans station. He wrote: 'I am killing myself, Mr. President, to let you know that all my men were brave, but one cannot send men to fight tanks with rifles.' How bitter for one who, for so long, had begged for an armoured corps!

IF WE HAD NOT ADVANCED INTO BELGIUM . . .

'How did it come about that you opposed the Belgian operation?' I have been asked. 'Such an attitude is strange in a man who for five years kept on asking for an offensive army.'

'It is precisely because, though demanding it, I never succeeded in getting it', is my reply. 'Our Army was neither offensive in its structure, nor, and this is more serious, in its mentality. Do you recall what Daladier said to the Army Committee of the Chamber before the debate of 1937, about the psychological state of our Army?'

'You cannot dispute, however, that we had the strongest possible reasons for advancing into Belgium. There were sentimental reasons to start with—these sprang from four years of joint struggle during the previous war. There were reasons of a strategic nature—we could not afford to give the enemy this spring-board for his attacks against Britain. There were reasons of a national character—we had to avoid allowing our frontier regions to become a battlefield. There were reasons of an economic nature—we had to preserve in Belgium and France the mines and industries serving our war effort. And finally there were political reasons—we could not offer to neutral countries a new demonstration of Allied weakness by allowing Belgium to be occupied after we had permitted the destruction of our Polish friends and the occupation of their territory.'

'You are right a hundred times over,' I answer. 'Everything you say is perfectly just, but, above all, it was essential that we should not succumb. Now, we did succumb.'

'You would have abandoned the Belgians?'

'By receiving the Belgian troops on our frontier, we would on the contrary have saved them from captivity, and we would have given them the opportunity of fighting at the side of their Allies as their fathers, the men of the Soldier-King, had done. The interests of the Allies were the interests of Belgium. The destruction of the French Army was a disaster for that country as well as for us. It was not our fault if the Belgians refused to let us go to their assistance at the appropriate time, and if they even formally forbade us to do so on two occasions.'

'But you would be forfeiting the advantage of having eight Dutch divisions and running the risk of losing twenty-two Belgian divisions?'

'In actual fact you are aware that the Dutch divisions did not play any part and you know the part played by the twenty-two Belgian divisions. Flanked by the Allies on our frontier, the Belgian divisions of 1940 would have fought as brilliantly as the ten Belgian divisions of the previous war, for I cannot believe that the Belgian Army, twice as numerous as in 1914 would have allowed its country to be invaded without declaring war.'

'Would not Britain, feeling herself threatened by the presence of the Germans in Belgium, have abandoned the Continent to concentrate only on the defence of her island?'

'She did not do so in 1914 when the Germans were not on our northern frontier but at Noyon. How, in her own interest, and without taking into account her lofty sense of honour, could she have abandoned us when this entailed the risk of seeing the enemy seize Dunkirk, Calais, Cherbourg and Brest, which would become so many pistols pointed at her heart? Moreover, the eleven divisions she still had in France would have been trapped by the enemy. These eleven divisions comprised the cadres of that great national army which she was in process of raising as she did in the previous war. Britain could not abandon them to their fate.'

'Was not the Monthermé–Namur–Antwerp line more easily defensible from a military point of view than that from Monthermé to Dunkirk?'

'That is true. First of all it is shorter. From Monthermé to Antwerp is only a hundred and seventy kilometres. But, by advancing to Antwerp, we had to either effectively support the Dutch Army or occupy Zeeland, and, in any case, the coast facing it, so as to avoid the risk of having our flank turned by an enemy landing. It is none the less true that the Antwerp front was shorter than that of Dunkirk. What is more important still is that, thanks to the flooding of the Dyle valley and the existence of the stronghold of Namur, there were only two corridors of invasion to be defended between Monthermé and Antwerp, those of Dinant and of the Brabant plain. On the other hand, except for Maubeuge, Valenciennes and the flooded Yser valley, the Franco-Belgian frontier was only defended by light fortifications which, we have seen, had not been reinforced during the eight months of "phoney" war except in a very insufficient fashion.'

'And then?'

'Then, as opposed to this policy of action, there was a passive policy, and experience has proved that it was an awkward one. First of all the British, when they had agreed to a reasonable distribution on the Franco-Belgian frontier, demanded a disastrous one on the Belgian battle-front. They only consented, in fact, to hold an extremely small sector from Louvain to Wavre, protected by the flooding of the Dyle river.[1] The result was that the British Expeditionary Force, which was equipped with good material and whose morale was high did not play any part. Neither did Giraud's Army. Both watched, arms at the order, while the enemy invaded France. On the other hand, if the divisions of Corap's Army which had advanced to fight at Dinant had remained on the frontier, they would not first of all have run the risk of getting there too late; moreover, they would have been better placed—entrenched as they would have been behind fortifications, however insufficient—than in the open country. It was not without adverse effect that our soldiers had heard from their earliest childhood that henceforth concrete would replace their breasts. To send soldiers, amongst whom, according to doctors, alcoholism was rife, to fight in the open country, was imprudent. As for our generals whose patriotism obviously was not in any degree suspect, they were for the most part as unfit as the rank and file to undertake the Belgian operation, because, permeated with Pétain's doctrine, they had failed to understand that the essential nature of modern warfare was mainly speed. Moreover, the Belgian operation resulted in the profitless waste of our three light mechanized divisions. Now, unlike our armoured divisions, these were in perfect trim, with well-trained troops and good commanders. Finally the Belgian operation rendered four of our seven motorized divisions unavailable. These were one of the two belonging to Giraud's Army, and three of Blanchard's, in other words, excellent regular divisions which remained pinned down in the north.'

'But even if we had not advanced into Belgium, our Command would still not have realized that we needed good troops at Sedan with reserves in close proximity.'

'Admittedly; but no other sector was held by such inferior troops, and the very fact of distributing to the rear of the front three light mechanized divisions, three armoured divisions and seven motorized divisions would have allowed us to entertain some hope of repulsing the enemy as he advanced from Sedan, instead of permitting him to proceed without hindrance right to Dunkirk. The Belgian operation lost us the means for a counter-offensive, and at the same time made us more vulnerable. That is why it was a factor in the disaster. I should also add that a check to the first German attack would have raised the morale of our troops considerably.'

---

[1] Of the ten infantry divisions which composed the Expeditionary Force nine were massed in the north and the tenth was allotted to the Second Army which held the line from Saint-Avold to Longuyon. The forces which advanced into Belgium were distributed as follows: four divisions in line, two in reserve around Brussels, two at more than a couple of marches from the front (these were still at the base). As for the armoured division, this element, after it had disembarked at Le Havre, remained to the south of the Somme, and only joined in operations after May 25. Gamelin emphasizes in his *Servir* (vol. I, p. 332) Gort's 'reservations' when Georges asked him to 'extend his front to the south of the Dyle'.

'Did not the Germans already have a hundred and forty divisions against the hundred and twelve Franco-British ones? Did we not face the threat of seeing the number of their divisions increase more quickly than ours?'

'Our numerical inferiority was an additional reason for staying within our defences, and avoiding an encounter in the open country. After that the British would have speeded up their preparations, and the Maginot Line, unless we accept in principle that it ought not to be put to any use at all, would have allowed us to draw reinforcements from the troops who manned this part of the front, even though we would have had to abandon the territory which forms a slope in front of it. Finally our situation as regards armoured strength would have rapidly improved. After May 16 we would have had at our disposal a fourth armoured division, and, a little later, a fourth light mechanized division, as well as two British armoured divisions. This would have given the Allies a total of ten armoured or mechanized divisions.'

'Is it certain that we would have been able to hold out?'

'I think we would have had a chance to hold out. I only know one thing which is certain. The French Army sealed its fate by advancing into Belgium.'

THE TRUTH ABOUT THE ARMOURED FORCES OF THE WEHRMACHT

Free rein has been given to speculation about the armoured forces which faced each other in the battle.

A similar controversy has arisen about the armoured forces of the enemy. Let us examine the question.

Estimates which our specialist services gave to our Supreme Command on this subject ranged, roughly speaking, from one extreme to another. Gamelin emphasizes the divergence in this sphere between the General Staff of the north-east Command and the Intelligence Service. The latter according to Gamelin[1] put the number of Panzers thrown into the fight against us at four thousand. According to the calculations of Georges' General Staff, the Wehrmacht had employed on May 10, between seven thousand and seven thousand five hundred tanks on all its fronts.[2] 'These', says Commandant Lyet,[3] 'were divided into from twelve to fourteen armoured divisions, and some fifteen independent regiments or battalions.' But he adds, 'It has often been assumed that the German Army had actually engaged in the western campaign a total of seven thousand to seven thousand five hundred tanks.' Between these two extreme estimates lies that of our own Command of Armoured Forces which, according to Colonel Ferré,[4]

---

[1] Gamelin, *op. cit.*, vol. III, p. 281. [2] *Ibid.*, vol. I, pp. 277–8.
[3] Lyet, *op. cit.*, p. 33. [4] *De défaut de l'armure*, p. 113.

'puts the number at about four thousand five hundred or five thousand tanks'.

In the confusion of defeat, imagination has still further magnified these figures. We shall see a figure of ten thousand Panzers constantly quoted by the most authoritative circles without it ever being contested. And Pétain, in his speech to the nation on June 25, 1940, was to appear a realist when he only attributed eleven Panzer divisions to the Wehrmacht.

We now know the truth. General Guderian has told it to us. There could be no better qualified authority. On the eve of the war, Guderian, in actual fact, was Inspector-General of Armoured Forces to the German Army. It was he who, during the campaign, was to be entrusted with the decisive movement, namely, the forcing of the Meuse at Sedan. Guderian states that the forces thrown in against us comprised ten Panzer divisions and six motorized. The Panzer divisions had a total number in each ranging from two hundred and fifteen to three hundred and twenty-four tanks, and not four hundred to five hundred as was estimated in 1940 by our experts. The number of Panzers came, therefore, to three thousand and three at the most. To this figure must be added eight hundred and forty-eight heavy armoured cars. Thus there was a grand total of three thousand eight hundred and fifty-one vehicles, of which a certain number took no part in the battle. Colonel Ferré writes:[1] 'Guderian gives a definitive figure of two thousand eight hundred tanks and seven hundred armoured cars. Commandant Lyet estimates[2] for his part that the total was three thousand. A figure', he adds, 'slightly higher than that of the Franco-British forces.'

'Thus', writes Gamelin, 'is exploded the myth of a crushing German superiority in tanks.'

Is it not now a convenient time to recall once again that, materially speaking, it was not the number of vehicles but their organization, as I had emphasized so often to the Chamber, which was the decisive factor? A collection of tanks was not, I was never tired of explaining, an armoured division. The German Army had an *armoured corps*. We had not.

Did we not see our leaders, opposed to the massive use of armoured forces, deny that these contained a danger in an assault against a continuous front? When, on the morrow of the Polish campaign, General Billotte and Colonel de Gaulle each in his turn recommended, because we were lacking armoured divisions, the integration of infantry escort tanks as armoured divisions, our Supreme Command would not listen to their proposal. It is true that this proposal would have been of no avail unless we could have been certain that the enemy would give us the necessary respite to establish the divisions, whose creation

[1] *Op. cit.*, p. 112.   [2] *Op. cit.*, p. 33.

was proposed. In actual fact there could have been no question of 'improvising' armoured divisions.

On this subject we also have the opinion of General Bruneau, who, as we have seen, led the 1st Armoured Division into battle, the only division which, as we have also seen, was capable of standing up to the Panzer divisions. He gave his opinion to the Committee of Inquiry in his deposition, cited above, of July 6, 1948. To one member who asked him if it were 'technically possible' to form divisions out of battalions of escort tanks, General Bruneau replied: 'No; a large armoured unit cannot be improvised.'

THE CONFLICT BETWEEN LEOPOLD III AND HIS MINISTERS

On the 16th at two o'clock in the afternoon the King of the Belgians gave another audience to the Prime Minister, who was accompanied by M. Spaak and General Denis. The meeting again took place in Breendonck Fort. The French Army was making a fighting retreat. Billotte had just begged the King to follow him in the withdrawal which he had made with his own army groups. Let us turn to the account of the audience,[1] based on the King's notes. The King explained the situation to his Ministers as follows: 'Either the Belgian Army will be able to withdraw towards France, or else the speed of the German thrust will isolate it from the Allied forces, and prevent it from making a fighting retreat with the French Army. In the latter case it would not be able to resist alone, and would be compelled to capitulate sooner or later, when it was forced back to the sea. On this day the possibility of capitulation would have to be considered.' [To this the Ministers replied that] everything should be done to prevent the Army being immobilized on Belgian territory and cut off from the Allied Armies. They thought that the possibility of surrender was just as calamitous from a political as from a moral point of view. . . . The Ministers' opinion was based on the conviction that France would never give up the struggle, and that the French Army would resist even if it had to retreat beyond the Loire. M. Spaak recalled a phrase of Mandel: 'The Allies will march to victory, through disaster upon disaster.' The King replied 'that every hypothesis had to be taken into account, and not merely the hypothesis that the French Army would resist to the uttermost'. The account continues: 'The Ministers seemed to gather, from this recital, that the King, from that moment, had made up his mind about the outcome of events and the attitude to adopt. On the contrary, the King told them that, as yet, he had formed no definite opinion whatsoever.'

M. Spaak's speech at Limoges, in the main, corroborated the King's account. But he gave details which make the King's reactions easier to understand. With regard to General Headquarters on the 16th, M. Spaak declared that 'it was pervaded by an appalling atmosphere of defeatism'. 'From that time', he added, 'the High Command of the Army was convinced that there was nothing more to be done, that not only was the Belgian Army beaten, but also the Allied Armies. . . . The King . . . with a perspicacity which today seems almost frightening, had predicted the military events which were to take place. He was convinced that the German columns would not march on Paris. He foresaw the drive towards the sea and sensed that, not only his own Army, but the Anglo-French Army were going to be encircled. . . . The King asked us: "What has the Queen of Holland done?" We told him that the Queen of the Netherlands was in London, surrounded by her Government, and that she intended continuing the struggle. The King then said: "Do you think she did right?"' M. Spaak continued: 'The King still claimed that, despite the appeal made to the French and the British, he was under no obligation towards them. We told him: "Sire, once you promised to ask for assistance, you were united to them. If you desert their cause [that of the Allies] you are a traitor and dishonoured."'

Events moved quickly. That very evening, the Government left Brussels for Ostend. Informed by M. Pierlot of the misgivings with which the King's attitude filled him, the Council of Ministers was unanimous in deciding that, at all events, the Army must avoid being cut off, and that the King, whatever happened, must leave. The Prime Minister, taking account of the gravity and urgency of the decision which had to be made, considered it essential to put the matter before the King in writing. 'The Government's primary consideration', he wrote to him on the 17th, 'is to see that the Belgian Army shares the fate of the Allied Armies and does not allow itself, in any circumstances, to be isolated from them. This question is intimately connected with that of the King's personal security. . . . The unanimous opinion [of the Ministers] is that the King must, at all costs, get away in time from the danger of being captured. If the Belgian Army does not share the same fate as that of the Allies, this would provoke feelings of an extremely grave nature, as much abroad as in Belgium. . . . A peace treaty could, under such conditions, only prove fatal to us. Lastly, quite apart from all the foregoing considerations, such events and the interpretations which they would bear, would make the reconstruction of Belgium within the framework of her institutions impossible. This would put an end to our national existence. Such a problem is not exclusively confined to the military sphere. It is not solely a question of the conduct of operations, but of the political aspect of the war and of all the consequences of the decisions which will be taken. We find ourselves thus bound by those constitutional responsibilities which are imposed on the King's Ministers. It is thus their duty, in so important a matter, to speak with complete frankness, as indeed the King has always authorized them to do.'

On the 18th there was another audience, this time at Saint-Denis-Westrem,[1] where the King had moved his General Headquarters. The same participants were there. M. Pierlot had already taken the initial steps towards evacuation: the Government had moved to La Panne as the first stage. The talks were renewed. They soon became lively. The King had carefully examined the problem presented by M. Pierlot. In his notes, he repeated his view:[2] if the Allied Armies were beaten or on the point of being beaten, Belgium was not under 'the slightest obligation to link her fate with theirs'. He added: 'Belgium entered the conflict because she had been invaded and in order to defend herself, and had undertaken no other engagement in respect of her guarantors except that of defending her territory.' In front of his Ministers, he returned to the question of his military responsibilities: the movements of the Army did not depend upon the Belgian Command, but upon the orders of the Commander-in-Chief, which the Belgian Command has undertaken to obey.

And here is the conclusion of Leopold III's statement:

'As for the King's personal situation, the Ministers expressed the view that his position as Head of the State took precedence of his position as Commander of the Army, and that, therefore, he could not link his fate to the latter office, and run the risk of being captured. Their opinion was that, since retreat into France was impossible, the King ought to relinquish command of the Army, and take refuge in France with the Government. The King contested this view. He maintained, first of all, that, if the fortunes of war compelled the Army to surrender, honour demanded that its Commander should not abandon it. He further stated that, from a political point of view, it was implicit in the interests of Belgium for the Head of the State to remain on national territory and not take refuge abroad. It was, indeed, necessary to consider every hypothesis. The only one which the Ministers were considering assumed that the Allied Armies would be able to stabilize the front, continue the struggle and fight on until there was peace, when, as victors, they would retake territories temporarily abandoned. But the King, basing his views on the military information in his possession, insisted on taking into account the hypothesis in which the Allied Armies would be defeated, cut off from the Belgian Army and compelled to lay down their arms. In this event, how, if the Head of the State had taken refuge abroad,

---

[1] Near Bruges.   [2] *Rapport, Annexes*, pp. 51–4.

could he defend Belgian interests? What authority would he have when negotiations were begun, whether from an international or a national point of view? And what would the Belgian Army think of a Commander who had abandoned it? It was at this point that the marked differences of opinion between the King and his Ministers were revealed. The latter believed that, whatever the circumstances, the entire Government should remove to France. They had already made it clear that, if the King refused to accompany them, they could constitute an autonomous Government in France without him, which would not recognize acts done in Belgium. The King, on the other hand, had not yet come to any definite conclusion. He did not feel able to make an immediate decision. Moreover, he thought it unnecessary to make a hasty one, for, if, at any given moment, his departure should be decided upon, he could always leave, *in extremis*, in an aircraft. Being out of touch with the Supreme Commander-in-Chief of Allied Forces, the King sought to maintain contact with him, while bearing in mind that the former's chief preoccupation was the consolidation of the French Armies, badly disrupted by the break-through at Sedan, before attempting to maintain or restore contact with the Belgian Army, whatever importance the position of this Army might have for him. The interview came to an inconclusive end.'

On his part, M. Pierlot underlined the fundamental aspect of the disagreement. 'The King', he wrote,[1] 'envisaged from that moment [the 18th] the defeat of the Allies.' As for M. Spaak, he declared again in his explanation at Limoges, that the Ministers resorted to every argument in the talks. 'I dare say', he added, 'that we even resorted to insult and that, before you yourself were uttering the horrible words of dishonour, desertion and treachery, these words had been used by us in the very presence of him who was going to accomplish this act. I do not think an argument exists which was not used. . . . The King told us something which gave us a ray of hope: "I am aware of the difficulty of the decisions to be taken. I am aware of the responsibilities which will weigh upon me. I request that some Ministers come to me at General Headquarters." He indicated the Prime Minister, the Minister of National Defence, M. Vanderpoorten, Minister of the Interior, and myself. . . . We returned to La Panne to tell our colleagues: "The decisions have been taken. We are going to rejoin the King. . . . We are still hoping to succeed."'

In fact, the four Ministers, in deference to the wish of Leopold III, took their places, at his side, at Bruges.

[1] *Op. cit.* (*Le Soir*, July 1, 1947).

CHAPTER XVIII

I STRIVE TO STIFFEN OUR RESISTANCE

May 18–19, I take over the Ministry of War; Pétain joins the Government; Weygand succeeds Gamelin; Mandel is transferred to the Ministry of the Interior.—May 18, M. Léger's Disgrace.—May 19, The Secret and Personal Instruction of Gamelin.—May 21, Weygand confers with Leopold III at Ypres.—May 21, 'Whatever happens, I shall not surrender'.—May 22, Weygand explains his plan in the presence of Churchill and myself.—The Gort Report.—May 24, Pétain and Weygand begin to talk of an Armistice.—The meeting of the War Committee on May 25.—The Minutes of the War Committee of May 25 are false ones.—March–June, Attempts made with a view to preventing Italy from entering the war.—Badoglio's Revelations.—May 27–8, Leopold III capitulates.—May 29, The First Weygand Memorandum.—May 29, My reply to the first Weygand Memorandum.—May 29, I prepare for the continuation of the War in North Africa.—May 27–June 4, Dunkirk.—June 5, I reshuffle my Cabinet.—June 5, I telephone to Roosevelt.—June 5, The Battle of France begins.—June 10, Second Weygand Memorandum.—June 10, Mussolini stabs France in the back.—June 10, Message to Roosevelt.—June 10, Departure from Paris.—June 11–12, Meeting of the Supreme Council at Briare.

MAY 18–19: I TAKE OVER THE MINISTRY OF WAR; PÉTAIN JOINS THE GOVERNMENT; WEYGAND SUCCEEDS GAMELIN; MANDEL IS TRANSFERRED TO THE MINISTRY OF THE INTERIOR

OUR front had been broken from Sedan to Dinant; Corap's Army had 'faded away'; the Allied Armies in Belgium were in full retreat and threatened with encirclement; the onrush of the German Army, with Panzers and Stukas in the van, was invading France. What was to be done in the presence of such an overwhelming disaster?[1]

Were we to wait for the arrival of a new British Army? There was

[1] 'The art of conducting a retreat is more difficult with the French soldier than with the soldier of northern lands. A lost battle deprives him of confidence in his leaders and pushes him into insubordination.' Napoleon.

339

no equipment in Britain. Were we to hope for the support of the United States? I was to ask this from President Roosevelt, and he was to promise it to me, but only in so far as he had power to do so. Were we to call up new classes of conscripts? I wanted to raise two more, but the General Staff replied, 'It will be useless! You have no rifles with which to equip them.'

First of all, I insisted on taking over the Ministry of War from Daladier who, thanks to President Lebrun's pressing intervention, agreed to be transferred to the Ministry of Foreign Affairs. To restore the morale of the Army and the country, which were struck with stupefaction, to try to obtain some recovery, and, to save, at all events, the honour of the Army, I decided at the same time to make Mandel Minister of the Interior, to appeal to Pétain, who was Ambassador at Madrid and to Weygand, who was at Beirut.

It needs a great effort on the part of Frenchmen today to conjure up the image which these two military leaders presented to them in May, 1940. The first had laid down the command of the Army nine years, and the latter five years, previously. But the French like old men, and although they detest war, they love the glorious soldier. As the Marshals who had given France victory in 1918 passed away, the figure of the 'Victor of Verdun', the Marshal of France with the marmoreal head, who shrouded himself in silence, grew in stature. He seemed to everyone like a living symbol of victory and honour. Amongst our great leaders, he possessed his own especial place. Whilst the others commanded above all the attention of the Right in our assemblies and in the country, he, as we have seen, had the reputation of being a man of the Left. We all have to bear some responsibility for the deification of Pétain before the war, but it is the Left which contributed to it in the greatest degree, by believing that the only strategy which could spare our country wholesale slaughter, and which was thus reconcilable with democratic principles, was that of systematic defence. The Left revered in Pétain the leader who incarnated this doctrine and who, to husband the blood of his men, had known how to shield them against that 'insane theory' of an all-out offensive. Thus, it was thanks to Painlevé that he was to be promoted in 1917 to the position of Commander-in-Chief, and eight years later, to be put in charge of the campaign against Abd-el-Krim. It was this same Painlevé who, using the language of Bossuet's funeral orations, had bestowed on Pétain, 'Victor of Verdun' and then 'Pacifier of the Rif', the justly celebrated citation:

'Marshal Pétain,
    'Although not being able to increase the glory of a career crowned by the victory of 1918. . . .'

The favour, which both the Left and Right bestowed on him, never ceased to increase from the time that he first appeared to be like an isolated giant.

'The Marshal stepped on to the tribune, acclaimed by the Assembly from Left to Right', writes his biographer,[1] when describing Pétain's first appearance before the Chamber as Minister of War on June 14, 1934. Speaking from the tribune on the next day, Daladier said of him: 'Monsieur le Maréchal Pétain, to whom yesterday the Chamber gave a welcome which expresses the feelings of admiration and gratitude felt by the whole country. . . .' It will also be remembered that, in the military debate of 1937, Daladier invoked 'the well-tried skill of our most illustrious soldier'. Several months before the outbreak of war Daladier nominated him Ambassador to Madrid.

At the beginning of the war Daladier asked him to enter his Government. In his deposition at Pétain's trial[2] Léon Blum made the following statement: 'Edouard Herriot had advised Edouard Daladier to include Marshal Pétain in the new Government. . . . Herriot had said to Daladier: "The war may begin with a serious reverse. It is possible that, at some time we may need a tremendous effort to maintain a warlike enthusiasm in this country and a will to continue the struggle. Include Pétain in your Government. If there is one man who is capable of speaking in language suitable to this purpose, if there is a man in whom the country has confidence when he does employ this language, it is Pétain."'

Although he had refused Daladier's offer, Pétain had, just like an Allied Power, a personal liaison agent with Gamelin. When I became President of the Council, and informed the Senate, of which a majority were of the Left, that Pétain had entered my Government, one heard amongst the acclamations which greeted the announcement the cry of 'At last!' from numerous benches.

I must say, as far as I was concerned, that, during several talks which I had had with him at rare intervals before the war, and which had created between us a sympathetic understanding, it had appeared to me he was becoming something of a symbol. But one sees that it was a far cry from the Pétain whose likeness legend of that time had transformed into a popular hero, to the Pétain whom Vichy has since revealed to us: a man of limited intelligence, deprived, on his own confession, of memory and imagination, a dried-up individual, a pessimistic soul, the originator of a military policy which ruined us. I confess that I was ignorant of his responsibility for the lack of French preparedness for war. The reason is that I had never belonged to the Committee for National Defence whose members are called upon to establish contact with Army circles. In 1935, when I had tabled my

[1] Laure, *op. cit.*, p. 384.   [2] Hearing of July 27, 1945.

amendment for the creation of an armoured corps, I tried to convince Gamelin, the Commander-in-Chief, and not his predecessors, Pétain and Weygand. Moreover, even if I had been well informed of the facts, I should have realized that it was equally necessary to solve the question of morale which was gravely impaired both in the Army and the country. What counted in this matter was not the value of Pétain's military doctrine. French people were unanimous: amongst the living, Pétain was the national glory of France.

Weygand, who had retained an astonishing vigour of body and mind, was surrounded with the halo of Foch's glory. To him was attributed the credit for the victory of Poland over the Russian Army in 1920. As Commander-in-Chief from 1931 to 1935 he had never ceased to pose as the defender of the traditions and of the rights of the officer element. At the beginning of the war Daladier had nominated him, at the request of Gamelin, to be Commander-in-Chief of our Army in the Near East. This was because he rightly judged that Weygand's personal prestige would secure for France the command of the Allied Armies in the East if the Balkan countries with their hundred divisions joined us in the war. In this former capacity Weygand came to Paris in April, 1940, to explain lucidly the situation in the East to the War Cabinet. He showed in his exposition such a fighting spirit that I thought to myself while listening to him, 'This is in the Foch tradition.' Mandel, who was present at this meeting, gathered the same impression as myself, and I know that M. Massigli, who had received a visit from Weygand at Ankara, also shared this feeling. Weygand had the reputation of being reactionary, but was not Foch as well?[1]

When we faced disaster, he seemed to me the only one with the requisite authority over our Army and those of our Allies to restore the situation in so far as it was capable of being restored.

Hence the reproach which M. Kammerer, a French Ambassador, addressed[2] to me after the event for going to seek out 'the Marshal, an old man who was always a defeatist', and for having 'recalled from Syria another old man who was equally past his prime . . . [who] had not been tested as a war leader'. Who, then, had been so tested, and whom had Foch stated that he bequeathed to France?

On May 8 Pétain joined my Government as Minister of State and Vice-President of the Council. The military situation was then as follows: the German forces had crossed the Rethel–St. Quentin–

[1] During the autumn of 1914, at the time of the 'drive to the sea', Foch knocked at the door of the Cistercian monastery of Mont-des-Cats. 'We are', he said to the Reverend Father, 'in a difficult position. I am coming to "requisition" the prayers and penances of your monks for a week. I am going to try some dodges. If I don't have the help of God, I shall never pull them off.'

[2] Kammerer, *La verité sur l'armistice*, p. 146 (first edition).

Brussels–Antwerp line. The bulk of the Panzer divisions was grouped in an arc to the west of St. Quentin, preparing for their scythe-like sweep on Dunkirk in order to capture the Allied Armies in the north of France and in Belgium. On his side, Georges was trying to reform a front on the Aisne and the Somme with the divisions which he had gathered from the east. The movement of these troops towards the west had been slowed down by the cutting of the railways, carried out by German aircraft. The enemy had mastery of the air, and this allowed him to keep an eye on all our movements.

Pétain, therefore, could not be deceived about the extreme gravity of the situation. He did not ask me a single question about my war policy, which was, however, well known. Into the bargain, the Press had published the agreement which I concluded on March 28 in London, whereby the Allies promised each other to remain side by side in the struggle.[1] Pétain did not breathe a word about this to me. I should have considered it an insult to him to ask him if he were, like myself, resolved to abide by the word of France. Rumours had represented the defeatist clique, headed by Laval, as having a plan to make use of him. I thought that, by joining my Government, Pétain had made his choice and taken a stand against these defeatists. In announcing his appointment, I said on the wireless: 'Marshal Pétain is at my side. He will stay there until victory.' I am not aware that he protested to anyone against this solemn and public statement.

On the afternoon of the 18th we went together to visit Georges at his Headquarters at La Ferté, which was such a distance from Paris and also from the front. He explained the situation to us on a large

---

[1] This agreement was drawn up as follows: 'The Government of the French Republic and the Government of the United Kingdom enter into mutual engagements not to negotiate nor conclude an armistice or treaty of peace during the present war unless by common consent.

'They undertake to discuss peace terms only after a complete agreement has been reached between them about the necessary conditions to ensure both of them respectively, effective and lasting guarantees for their security. Finally, they undertake to maintain, when peace has been restored, collaboration in their actions within all spheres as long as this will be necessary to safeguard the security and ensure the reconstitution, with the collaboration of other nations, of international order in Europe, which will guarantee the liberty of Nations, respect for law and maintenance of peace.'

Is there any need to stress the agreement? Was it not, in substance, only another edition of the Pact, concluded on September 5, 1914, by France, Britain and Russia? Thus, Daladier and Chamberlain had entered into negotiations for this purpose on the outbreak of hostilities. But the negotiations, which were based on a draft coming from the pen of M. Léger, dragged on because London on the one hand invoked the political autonomy of the Dominions to restrict the scope of the agreement for the United Kingdom, and on the other was loath to subordinate her acceptance to the stipulation of the guarantees which we asked. 'We must have a system of effective guarantees', Daladier had declared to the Supreme Council on December 19, 1939.

When we had obtained satisfaction about the question of guarantees, that is, on the most important point, I submitted the text to the War Cabinet, which approved it unanimously. Daladier, who, as we have seen, had begun the negotiations, was, one feels sure, the first to give his consent.

map, which, with his hand covered by a grey glove, he pulled up and
down on its roller. We saw on the map the positions of the Armies,
and, prominently marked, those of the ten Panzer divisions. Two or
three times he broke off his account to tell us, his brown eyes brooding
sorrowfully on us: 'It is a difficult situation.' We then went to the
Château of Vincennes, Gamelin's Command Post. He was waiting for
us there[1] with Daladier, whom I did not replace as Minister of War
until the next day. Affected but always elegant and fluent—the
Commander-in-Chief of the ground forces gave us an explanation of
the situation, during which I must say I did not note in him that
'deep dejection', of which Weygand was to speak in his evidence at
Riom.

On Sunday the 19th, I arrived at the Rue Saint-Dominique, and, for
the first time and at the height of disaster, established contact with the
Ministry of War, about which I knew nothing and which I bitterly
regretted not having taken over two months earlier. Weygand, whom
Daladier had asked me to summon myself, arrived by plane at the
beginning of the afternoon on that same day. I offered him the succession to Gamelin, who seemed to all of us responsible for the disaster.
I added that it was my intention to give him the fullest powers by
appointing him Commander-in-Chief in all theatres of operations, of
the ground, sea and air forces. Weygand himself also knew the extreme
gravity of the situation, the reciprocal pledges undertaken by the
Allies, and my position as regards the conduct of the war. The idea
did not pass through my mind to say to this man, who was as lively
as a fighting cock, when offering him the post of Commander-in-
Chief: 'It is clearly understood that there is to be no thought of
capitulation.' He made not the slightest reference to the subject, any
more than Pétain had. He asked my permission to go and find out
something about the situation from Gamelin and Georges. After having
been to see them, he came back in the evening to the Rue Saint-
Dominique, and told me that he would accept command.

I had the necessary decrees prepared, and sent for the signature of
the President of the Republic. I also drafted a letter to Gamelin
including a copy of these texts. Whilst this was being prepared, I
mechanically opened the drawer of the desk at which I had seated
myself for the first time that morning, and I found in it the file on
Gamelin. The first remarks which it included fell under my eye. The
writer spoke in them with praise of this young second lieutenant with
the boyish face, who had passed out of Saint-Cyr as the best cadet. I
had my letter to Gamelin redrafted in order to add to it the thanks of

[1] Pétain had undertaken to warn Gamelin and Georges of our visit. His orderly officer
made a mistake in the order of these visits, with the result that Daladier and Gamelin
were waiting at Vincennes whilst we were at La Ferté.

the Government for the long and loyal services which he had given the country. Here is its text: 'I have the honour to bring to your notice two decrees which the President of the Republic has just signed. I am sending you the thanks of the Government for the services which you have given the country during a long and brilliant career.'

The first decree suppressed the functions of the Commander-in-Chief of the ground forces.[1] The second appointed Weygand Chief of General Staff of National Defence and Commander-in-Chief of all theatres of operations, ground, sea and air. He received, therefore, over the Navy and the Air Force an authority which Gamelin had never been able to secure.

The attitude of Pétain and Weygand, in accepting, in these dangerous circumstances, the one a share in the responsibilities of the Government, and the other, those responsibilities of supreme command, aroused in me a keen feeling of gratitude towards them. They seemed to me to be nobly sacrificing themselves for their country.

The effect of these measures was considerable. *Le Populaire* wrote on the 19th: 'With that spirit of decisiveness which is typical of his character, M. Paul Reynaud has today carried out a ministerial re-shuffle which, in the present circumstances, can only increase in the greatest degree the war potential of the country.'

The appointment of Pétain and of Weygand, and the substitution which was to take place of M. Charles-Roux for M. Léger, prompted *L'Aube* on the 21st to utter this thanksgiving: 'Three men have been called to share the responsibilities of the Government. All three seem to have been marked out by destiny to fulfil the mission of France: Pétain, Weygand and Charles-Roux. . . . Pétain and Weygand were amongst the greatest architects of the victory of 1918. Today, events are shaping as if God were saying to them: "The victory of 1918 is not complete; it is for you to round it off. I have given you the necessary blessing to rise to the level of your destiny. I will grant you my help."'

Kerillis in *L'Epoque* wrote: 'At the side of Paul Reynaud in charge of the Ministry of War, and of Georges Mandel at the Ministry of the Interior, appears the noble and grave figure of Marshal Pétain, the "Victor of Verdun". In all the capitals of the world, neutral, allied or enemy, it will be realized that something new is happening in France . . . that France has found herself capable of rising to those heights which she has always achieved in the most tragic hours of her history.'

I have never heard anyone dispute the fact that my aim of restoring the morale of the country and the Army had been attained. And I remember having received at that time a visit from Herriot, who said to me: 'Without you, it would already be all over.'

---

[1] Although they had been laid down by the law of July 11, 1938, which dealt with the 'organization of the country in time of war'.

On the 22nd I stated to the Senate in the following words that Pétain and Weygand had answered my appeal:

'Amidst the misfortunes of our Motherland, we feel a pride in thinking that two of her children, who have the right to rest on their past laurels, have come to place themselves in this tragic hour, at the service of the country: Pétain, the "Victor of Verdun", the great leader who has known how to be humane, who knows how victory can be wrested from the depths of disaster: Weygand, the disciple of Foch, the man who stopped the German onslaught when our front was broken in 1918, and who then was able to change our destiny and lead us to victory.' The Senate unanimously acclaimed these words.

MAY 18: M. LÉGER'S DISGRACE

When, on the 16th, I told the Chamber that I was going to change methods and men, the deputies rose to their feet and applauded my statement. We had been beaten because we had, according to the phrase which was used by Pétain on June 16, 1940, 'too few arms and too few Allies'. It seemed to me, therefore, that my taking over the Ministry of War, and Weygand, the Supreme Command, of necessity required, as a corollary, the dismissal of the Secretary-General of the Ministry of War and the Secretary-General of the Foreign Office.

The first accepted the step with great dignity. It was not the same with the second, M. Léger, whom it was, however, much less possible to keep in his post.

I have already spoken of this individual, with his wily ways, who had devoted most of his time to enmeshing France in the pacifism which Stresemann profitably put to his advantage and to our detriment.

In 1938 he agreed to go to Munich with a definite mandate for supporting the dismemberment of our ally. Having done this, he permitted the dismissal of his rival, M. Massigli, then Political Director, who was notoriously anti-Munich and treated for this reason as a 'war-monger'. As a result of all this, M. Léger received from Bonnet the medal of Grand Officer of the Legion of Honour. The wind having changed, he began to support the opponents of Munich and to try to earn a reputation as a 'war-monger'.

M. Léger contrived to acquire political support for himself by giving a small number of privileged journalists 'inside' information on State matters.

The régime which he had instituted at the Quai d'Orsay was based on the principle of setting civil servants who were making their career in Paris (and thus more anxious for position than for material results) in opposition to those who were posted abroad. Our Ambassadors were not kept in touch with general policy, because, they asserted, M. Léger feared to see them given any credit.

What inspired my decision of May 18 with respect to him was that his reign had culminated in the diplomatic 'Waterloo' of which I have spoken above. The blindness of M. Léger, as we have seen, had passed all limits. But, because of the lustre which he succeeded in gaining from his display of a warlike policy,[1] I was weak enough to believe that I was bound to provide him with a 'graceful exit'. I offered him an alternative post of importance: the Embassy at Washington. I did not refrain, however, when doing this, from telling him how much it cost me to think of dispensing with the eminent services which M. de Saint-Quentin had given us in this post, and I warned him that, in any case, my offer required immediate acceptance, for there could be no question of entrusting a mission of such importance to a man who, it might seem, had been demoted. Because of his annoyance, M. Léger refused the offer. A few days later he communicated to me through one of his friends, Elie-Joseph Blois, his desire, after due reflection, to withdraw his refusal. I replied in my turn that it was too late, and recalled the condition which I had attached to my offer.

In June, 1940, M. Léger spent several days in London, where M. Paul Morand reveals him taking up a disapproving attitude towards the policy of resistance and setting out as quickly as possible for America.

Months passed by. When autumn came and Pétain seemed to have consolidated his dictatorship, M. Léger came out into the open. Through the intermediary of our Washington Embassy he addressed a lengthy supplication to Pétain for pardon. He tried to secure forgiveness for his departure by representing himself as being my victim. He added that, relieved through this fact of any administrative duties, he had left for the purpose of using his enforced leisure to visit his relatives in Guadeloupe. Finally, he offered his services to Pétain. The latter turned them down, and Léger took up residence at Washington, where he gave a final proof of his political intuition by adopting an attitude of haughty indifference to General de Gaulle.

As for the intrigues in which M. Léger was to indulge at Washington, it will suffice for me to quote the words in which Marc Rucart has denounced them:[2] 'The step taken by M. Paul Reynaud had important

---

[1] In the United States M. Léger later strove to give pledges to public opinion. In a speech which he made on March 28, 1942, at the University of New York at the commemoration of the eightieth anniversary of Briand's birth (*Les cahiers de la quinzaine*, *été–automne*, 1950, pp. 158–65) he stated: 'It was the London Conference in March 1936, and not Munich, which really gave birth to the Hitlerite excesses. Briand had never abandoned nor allowed to be abandoned, the application of the sanctions laid down against a violation of his Rhineland Pact . . . [nor] committed the mistake . . . of following out at an unseasonable hour the so-called policy of appeasement.'

Obviously embarrassed by the part which he had taken in the responsibility for the 'desertion' of London, and the 'mistake' of Munich, M. Léger resorted to a trick which deceived no one.   [2] *Loc. cit.*

repercussions in America where M. Alexis Léger went, full of rancour: Press campaigns, film productions, the publication of the very tendentious and even more fantastic work of Pertinax, of which the Communists made special use during the debate on the electoral campaign in the Nord Department.'[1]

MAY 19: THE SECRET AND PERSONAL INSTRUCTION OF GAMELIN

On the 19th, at eight o'clock in the morning, Gamelin and Vuillemin[2] were with Georges at La Ferté. I have mentioned that this was the line reached on the evening before by the German Armies. Gamelin revealed the vital importance which lay in preventing the enemy from encircling and capturing the Allied Armies of the north.

At nine forty-five he sent his *Personal and Secret Instructions No. 12* to Georges and Vuillemin. Here is its text:

'Without wishing to interfere in the conduct of the battle now being waged, which is in the hands of the Commander-in-Chief of the north-east front, and in giving my approval to all the arrangements which he has made, I consider that, at the present time:

---

[1] M. Léger did not stop at this open propaganda. In the influential circles of the country whose hospitality he was enjoying, he spread the most malevolent statements about me. There was also a deputy ready to echo these insinuations during the course of the debate about my competence, which took place in the Constituent Assembly on June 5, 1946. Flying to the help of his Communist friends, this parliamentarian rose to state that in a book (whose title he did not mention) an American politician (whose name he did not give) had reproached me as having shown a 'tragic weakness'.

The American personality was, according to the Communist statement, Mr. Sumner Welles. Unfortunately for my calumniators, Mr. Sumner Welles himself has inflicted on them a stinging denial. Here, indeed, is a letter which Mr. Sumner Welles sent on September 18, 1948 to M. André David to thank him for his proposal to entrust me with the duty of presiding over a lecture he was to give at the Ambassadors, and which a sudden deterioration in his mother's state of health finally forced him to cancel.

Bar-Harbour (Maine), 18th September, 1948.
Dear M. André David,

I received your letter of the 14th September a short time ago. Although, in the times in which we live, every man who has to do with public affairs must expect to note that the number of inaccurate rumours circulating about him is even more increased than in normal times, the report which you mention in your letter is nevertheless of a character to cause me surprise. All the passages in my writings about President of the Council, Paul Reynaud, are there to bear witness to both the sincere admiration and the personal regard which I have for him. In my book, *Time for Decision*, I have in actual fact tried to prove that, of all the men who came to power in France during the most critical years that this country has known, there were only two, Paul Reynaud and Georges Mandel, who showed themselves to be real *statesmen*. In these circumstances, any rumour of the kind which has reached you can only appear to be inexplicable.

To conclude I wish to tell you that all the arrangements which you desire to make for my introduction seem entirely satisfactory to me.

May I assure you of my deepest regards, Sumner Welles

[2] Vuillemin's General Headquarters were situated near to Saint-Jean-les-Deux-Jumeaux between Meaux and La Ferté.

'1. We should continue, as has been initiated, to extend the front of our Eastern Armies and those covering Paris towards the west, and to maintain the link with Number 1 Army Group (Billotte's group of armies).

'2. That, as regards Number 1 Army Group—rather than let it be encircled—we must take the boldest course, first by forcing, if necessary, the road to the Somme, and secondly, by throwing in particularly mobile forces against the rear of the Panzer divisions and the motorized infantry divisions which are following them. It seems that there is, at present, a vacuum behind this first echelon.

'3. To prepare with all available resources an offensive against the bridges at Mézières.

'4. The complete strength of French and British aviation must now devote itself to joining in the battle:

'(a) As regards fighter protection: fighters must preserve the mastery of the air; priority in this is to be given to the front of Number 1 Army Group, and, as far as is possible, protection is to be given to our movements behind the front.

'(b) As regards bombing: bombers must operate against the German columns marching towards the west, by attacking their rear and stemming their progress towards the west. Such action should be especially directed against the southern concentration of Panzer divisions.

'(c) Finally and at the appropriate moment, this aerial force must be ready to support the action of the Second Army.

'(d) In the meantime, it should operate against the Meuse bridges by bombing and by sowing mines in the river.

'5. *Everything depends on the next few hours.*'

MAY 21: WEYGAND CONFERS WITH LEOPOLD III AT YPRES

When Weygand succeeded Gamelin, did he give orders that the *Personal and Secret Instruction* of May 19 should be executed more rapidly? He has related, in his deposition at Pétain's trial:[1] 'During the day of the 20th, I worked. I saw General Georges. I confirmed the orders which had been judiciously given for an offensive that alone could make good the time which had been lost. I telephoned to General Billotte, who was in charge of the offensive, that he was to take most energetic action, and I decided to leave on the morning of the next day to visit the leaders entrusted with conducting it, for when one is in command, it is not simply a question of covering sheets of paper with orders. One must go as well to those who are leading, to encourage, direct and convince them. That is what I did.'

[1] Hearing of July 31, 1945.

Such were, indeed, excellent principles. I must say, however, that, on my return from captivity, I took down the following notes during a conversation with Georges, which have a slightly different ring:

'During the evening of May 19, Georges said to Weygand:
'"I should like to explain the situation to you."
'"No, tomorrow."
'The next day Georges explained the situation to Weygand. Weygand replied: "I must go and see on the spot what the situation is."'

But Weygand had more urgent cares. He spent the best part of the daytime of the 20th in paying visits. Mandel was one of those he hurried off to see, as I learned later from Mandel himself.

It was only towards the end of the afternoon that he asked me to approach Churchill to secure the stronger co-operation of the British Air Force. I immediately drafted a personal message for the Prime Minister, which M. de Margerie handed to the British Ambassador at 6.45 p.m. The latter sent it in all haste to its destination. 'General Weygand,' I said to Churchill, 'faced with the necessity of stopping with all means possible the advance of the German armoured divisions towards the sea, asks that Air Chief Marshal Sir Cyril Newall be requested by the British Government to carry out such bombing missions over the battlefield which might be required of him by General Billotte, who is co-ordinating the operations of the French, British and Belgian Armies in Belgium.'

On the following day, the 21st, Weygand went to confer first with Billotte and then accompanied by the latter, with Leopold III. He had first of all to get to Béthune, where Billotte had his headquarters. It was a trip which proved to be full of incident, a 'veritable Odyssey' Weygand himself said, on his return, to Baudouin, who quoted this phrase.[1]

It was indeed an Odyssey. Bourget[2] describes it in these words:

The journey by rail and road, such as it had been planned at the beginning, soon proved to be impossible. The General's transport was sent to Abbeville during the afternoon of the 20th to take him, on his arrival there by his special train, on to the north the next day. It found the place in flames, and narrowly escaped from the Germans, who had established themselves on the Somme. We were obliged, therefore, to organize the journey by air. The General . . . took off from Le Bourget at dawn on the 21st, with a flight of fighters for protection. The first sign of the enemy's presence came to him from anti-aircraft fire, which burst round the plane when passing through the valley of the Canche. A little farther on, the escort planes had to meet Messerschmitts which dived on the Commander-in-Chief's aircraft. The landing took place near to Béthune on the airfield of Norrent-Fontes, as had been planned. What

---

[1] *Private Diaries, 1940–1941*, translated by Sir Charles Petrie, Bt., p. 37.
[2] *De Beyrouth à Bordeaux*, pp. 34–8.

we had not foreseen, was that the airfield would be cleared of all aerial formations by the morning of the 21st, and that it had already been evacuated on
account of bombing. Moreover, the motor car ordered for the General ... [to
take him] to Calais failed to turn up. On this deserted and 'unhealthy' aerodrome there only remained one truck for carrying petrol, which was under
the orders of an N.C.O. Thanks to it, the officers accompanying the General
were able to reach a telephone and get some information, as a result of which
it was decided to continue the flight to Calais aerodrome, although it was
known that this field, damaged by bombs, already offered a devastated appearance which made landing rather ticklish. ... The plane landed undamaged.
By good fortune also, the General was able, on the telephone of the airfield
commandant's office, to get hold of General Champon at Calais town hall.
The latter told him that the King of the Belgians was going to Ypres, and
would receive him there at 3 p.m. General Weygand was finally provided with
a car, picked up General Champon at Calais and went with him to Ypres,
where the King ... arrived shortly after, accompanied by General ... van
Overstraeten.... The Commander-in-Chief, joined in the meantime by General
Billotte, was able to give the latter his orders. ... Time had passed quickly: it
was 5.30 p.m., and the General had to be making his way back. Journey by air
had become out of the question because of the state of airfields in the region,
which were being constantly bombed. Admiral Abrial (Commander of the
Naval Forces of the North, called the 'North Admiral') who had arrived in
his turn on the spot, offered to place at the Commander-in-Chief's disposal the
torpedo boat, *Flore*. His proposal was accepted and the General ... went to
Dunkirk to embark. As if they had been informed of the presence of the
Supreme Commander, German planes, in heavy waves, came to bomb the
port during the embarkation. This was carried out under a hail of bombs,
which continued even after the torpedo-boat had crossed the harbour bar at
full speed, amidst fountains of water thrown up by bombs falling in the water,
and alongside the quays set alight by incendiaries. After a detour by Dover the
ship entered the port of Cherbourg, when dawn had broken (Wednesday,
May 22). From there, the General and his entourage reached Saint Lazare
station [Paris] by rail at about 10 a.m.[1]

We have King Leopold's version about this meeting at Ypres. Here
it is:[2]

At 3 p.m. on May 21, the King met General Weygand at Ypres town hall.
When the King arrived the Supreme Commander was talking in the office of
the mayor with the Ministers, Pierlot, Spaak and Denis, who had already

[1] In his deposition on March 8, 1949, before the Committee of Inquiry, Weygand has
emphasized the hectic nature of his trials: '. . . I had', he stated, 'many set-backs'. The
airfield at Norrent-Fontes, on which he landed 'had been evacuated two days before by
the British and no one knew this fact'. He added: '. . . I travelled the countryside to try
and find a telephone. After some time and with great difficulty I got into touch with
General Billotte's Headquarters. He, in his turn, was searching for me. Everything had
been badly organized. The confusion of the moment explains this failure. Finally, I
arrived at Ypres for my meeting with the King of the Belgians at 3 p.m., after having
landed at 9 a.m. or 9.30 a.m. on this northern airfield. That shows you the time I wasted.'
[2] *Rapport, Annexes*, pp. 56, 59, and 67-8.

arrived. The King and the Supreme Commander withdrew alone into the hall of the town hall, and afterwards . . . called up several general officers. . . . It appeared from this interview that no well-defined plan for resistance existed, and that the Supreme Commander was not aware of the situation; he was even in ignorance, that at that very moment, Abbeville was in the hands of the Germans. He learned this fact during the interview through the King's A.D.C. He could only give very general outlines of the operations to be undertaken, and declared that action should be restricted to movements which might contain, or, at a pinch, slow down the German advance, but with no immediate hope of repulsing it. The different possible movements were considered.

After the adjournment of the meeting, during which MM. Pierlot, Spaak and Denis again had the opportunity of talking with General Weygand in the burgomaster's office, General Billotte, accompanied by General Fagalde arrived. Another military discussion was immediately begun.

General Billotte emphasized the irresistible power of the Panzer divisions which permanent fortifications alone could stop. In the open country, the Allied divisions were routed within an incredibly short time. The French divisions had been sorely tested and were very tired. The British Army, as yet intact, could still constitute a powerful offensive instrument. . . . Coming back to his plan he [General Weygand] agreed that it would be difficult to withdraw the Belgian Army behind the Yser, and suggested that the British divisions should be released for action by substituting Belgian ones in their place. The King immediately agreed, and even offered to put the Sixteenth Army Corps at the disposal of the French Army. It was, therefore, necessary to invite Lord Gort to join the conference. But he could not arrive before 7 p.m. General Weygand had left by this time, after confirming General Billotte in his powers.

A third meeting began as soon as Lord Gort arrived. It finished at 9.30 p.m., having agreed that a British attack might be able to bring a decisive influence to bear on the situation; but neither Lord Gort nor General Pownall seemed to believe in any favourable outcome.

These three meetings, of such vital importance, failed to give the King any precise guidance on the march of events, and left him with a very strong impression that the Allied Armies were not in a state to retrieve the situation nor to re-establish contact . . . by an offensive action. An immediate offensive action by French and British forces would alone have been capable of restoring the situation by breaking the German front. But there could be no illusions in this respect.

After the meeting . . . the King ordered the General Staff to get everything ready for an eventual retreat to the Yser in order not to incur any reproach from the British and the French.

In the interval between the second and third meetings the King had the chance of talking with MM. Pierlot, Spaak and Denis. They adopted at this time an aggressive and disagreeable attitude. They complained of being left in ignorance about the progress of military operations, and of not having been allowed to join in the meetings with the Supreme Commander. Whilst they acknowledged that the conduct of military operations lay outside their jurisdiction, they thought it necessary for them to follow the progress of operations for which, according to them, they bore, constitutionally, a responsibility, just as they had a responsibility for all the other actions of the King. . . . They criticized the situation of the Army, refusing to admit that it was essential to await the orders of the Supreme Commander, and asserting that it was necessary, if need be, to take the initiative by retreating towards France. The King explained to them, by demonstrating . . . on the map, that the Allied deployment would not permit such a manœuvre. . . . During the interview at Castneau, the King had signified his willingness to fall in with the orders of General Billotte. Only one order had been received; that to fall back on the Schelde. The King could not decide on this withdrawal without the agreement of the Supreme Command. The Ministers, however, indulged in tactical and strategical considerations which were not founded on any established facts, and expressed their opinion about the possible ways of using the Army. They seemed to suspect the King of having desired to jockey the Army into a position which, by cutting it off from the Allied Forces, would oblige it to capitulate, and thus make a separate peace with Germany inevitable. . . . However, on May 22 at 10 p.m., the King had an interview with General Denis at General Headquarters in Saint-André-lez-Bruges. Maps in hand, the King explained to him the situation of the Army, and the General offered no objections. He undertook to explain it to his colleagues. The attitude of MM. Pierlot and Spaak during this interview on the 21st, had been so aggressive that the King deemed it necessary on the 22nd to send the Prime Minister a letter written in unequivocal and definite language, which made the position quite clear.

To gain an accurate opinion of the views and words which were exchanged that day, it is essential to match up the version which the King has given us, with that of M. Pierlot.[1] Here is the latter's account:

On May 21, the Ministers learned by chance, during a conversation with the Ambassadors of France and Great Britain, that the King was going to meet Generals Weygand and Gort at Ypres. I told the King of our wish to be present. The King only put up a brief opposition, and we went, M. Spaak, General Denis, and myself, to Ypres.

The King would not allow us to be present at any of his conversations with the Allied Generals. In spite of the humiliating position in which the Ministers were thus placed, it was not the time for withdrawal from the meeting. The stake was too important and, although any hope of inducing the King to share the views of the Government seemed to be largely doomed to disappointment, we did not wish to abandon it by hurrying things. Any public difference between the King and his Ministers was, moreover, at this time likely to arouse an uneasiness which we wished to avoid.

Different and somewhat contradictory accounts, both from French and Belgian sources, have been given about these interviews at Ypres. I shall content myself with stating what my colleagues and I have seen, heard and said.

We arrived at Ypres at 3 p.m. We immediately met Generals Weygand and Billotte.

The Supreme Commander, questioned as to what he thought about the shape of things, stressed the importance which he attached to communications being

[1] *Op. cit.* (*Le Soir*, July 12, 1947).

re-established between the Armies in Flanders and those on French soil. He then expressed his astonishment at noting that the retreat of the Belgian Army had not been more speedy in spite of the danger that its southerly withdrawal might be cut off.

I replied that my colleagues and myself had been for many days the prey to an increasing anxiety, because we had observed the same danger; but that, to be fair, it should be added, as the Belgian Army was part of the whole and had to conform with the orders of the Supreme Command, it was from this Command that the order should come.

The proposal was not taken up.

Generals Weygand and Billotte insisted on the urgency of an attempt being made to break off contact with the enemy, and on a more decided movement towards the south with a view to reopening the road in this direction. The Ministers did not conceal that these aims coincided exactly with what they were thinking.[1]

In the midst of all this, the arrival of the King was announced. The Ministers only caught a brief glimpse of him. He immediately went into conference with Generals Weygand, Billotte and van Overstraeten, and they were all joined from time to time by other military leaders. General Gort had been given a very late notice of the meeting, and his summons had not found him at his Command Post.

Whilst the Ministers waited in a neighbouring room to that in which the conference was taking place, General van Overstraeten joined them for a moment. They spoke to him of their anxieties. General van Overstraeten gave them to understand that, for the Belgian Army, the end of the campaign was drawing near.

'But', asked the Ministers, 'can't the retreat be speeded up? Why should the Army delay so long on the Terneuzen canal?'

Reply—The troops are too worn out.

'In spite of their fatigue', I observed, 'we noticed, when visiting their positions, that they are in no wise unfit to continue their march, after a few hours of well employed rest. Is not a withdrawal in stages to the Yser possible?'

Reply—Why should we abandon so much ground?

When they heard such a reason given, the Ministers showed their astonishment. It was no longer the temporary possession of several kilometres, more or less, that mattered, they said, but the preservation of the Army. It was better to retreat than to be captured.

Reply—But we are trapped.

I answered, unable to suppress a sign of anger. 'No, we are not trapped; we shall be, if everything possible is not done to avoid being so; but one is not trapped whilst one has arms and can manœuvre.'

General van Overstraeten left without saying a word.

The meeting between the King and the Generals went on until seven o'clock.

---

[1] In his above-mentioned deposition of March 8, 1949, before the Committee of Inquiry, Weygand gave an account of this interview which corroborates the general lines of M. Pierlot's: 'All of them asked me', he stated, 'what I thought of saying to the King. I told them. They looked at each other and I saw that what I intended saying to him was nothing like what he would be expecting, but that it suited them because I would be asking the Belgian Army to link up with the main body of the Allied Forces.'

The Ministers then had a brief conversation with General Weygand. They asked what decisions had been taken and what he thought of the situation.

'We have', replied General Weygand, 'met from the start with opposition from General van Overstraeten. The Belgian Army intends to withdraw, and take up a semi-circular position, based on the coast, and to defend itself there as long as possible. Naturally, I have not accepted this proposal, which separates the fate of the Belgian Army from that of the Allied Armies, and contains an implication that it will cease to fight alongside the latter.

'I have recommended that the Belgian Army should, without delay, resume its retreat, and take up positions behind the Yser. Having thus shortened its front, it can spare a number of its divisions to co-operate with Franco-British forces alongside it in the counter-attacks which must be launched towards the south in order to re-establish communications in this direction and to avoid encirclement.

'The King told me that, at the present time, a retreat of the Belgian Army could not be considered. The troops are worn out, their morale would break if they had to surrender more ground and if they were faced with the prospect of fighting outside their own land. These are factors on which the Belgian Command is better informed than I am. I must, therefore, defer to it as to the importance which is to be given to these considerations.

'Accepting these factors as a basis', concluded General Weygand, 'the King has proposed that the Belgian Army should hold its present positions on the Terneuzen canal and to the south of Ghent. It would, he suggests, extend its front towards the frontier, so as to release part of the British troops, which would thus become available for the proposed counter-attacks. This proposal has been accepted.'

'Does it satisfy you?' asked the Ministers.

'I have just told you', replied General Weygand, 'that my plan was different, and that I have given way to the objections which were placed before me. The dispositions which have been laid down can be justified, and I have accepted them.

'The solution adopted is similar to General van Overstraeten's in that the whole of the Belgian Army will keep to its positions. It differs in that these positions will be extended farther south. The lines occupied by our troops are disproportionately lengthened by about ninety kilometres, an obvious cause of weakness.'

Without such an arrangement the glorious and worthwhile battles along the Lys would not have taken place. Unfortunately, General van Overstraeten's plan remained the decisive element in it, and the positions adopted led as a consequence to the separate capitulation of the Belgian Army. The constant preoccupation of the Government had been that, in defeat as well as in battle, our Army should remain tightly linked with its neighbours, and share the same fate as befell them. Such a result was certainly more important than the illusory preservation of part of our country. In a military situation which was perhaps already desperate, something remained to be salvaged: the political and moral position of Belgium.

After General Weygand's departure, the Ministers were shown into the King. They complained about the inadequate way in which they were being kept in touch with the progress of events. M. Spaak keenly reproached the King with the lack of confidence which he was showing towards his Ministers. The King protested, saying that the Ministers possessed his confidence, but that he himself had his own particular duties as regards the conduct of military operations.

As regards what General Weygand had said, the King briefly informed the Ministers of the decisions which had been made. The impression which he gave his listeners was very different from that which General Weygand had conveyed to them. The King considered the situation of the Armies in Flanders as leaving little if any hope. As for the manœuvre recommended by the Supreme Commander, it was necessary, before taking a decision, to obtain the consent of General Gort. When the Ministers asked: 'Has the French Supreme Commander, therefore, not the right to order this counter-attack?', the King gave a negative answer, and emphasized that, in actual fact, unity of command did not exist.

The Ministers again expressed their astonishment that the retreat had not been carried out more rapidly. The King replied, as General van Overstraeten had done, that the troops were worn out. Struck by this insistence on invoking —whether it was a question of the capacity of our troops or their physical state—every argument which could be used in favour of keeping them in the positions which they held, I replied by telling the King of the conclusions which my colleagues and myself had drawn when we visited the units guarding the Terneuzen canal. They were tired, but in no wise worn out; their morale appeared to be good; provided one took the precaution of giving them a short rest, one could still ask of them an effort, which would avoid disaster. The King did not reply, but he seemed to be very annoyed.

The conversation then slackened off and even completely ceased. The King, nevertheless, kept the Ministers in attendance, whilst waiting for General Gort's visit. When the latter arrived, he was received only by the King and General van Overstraeten.

At the end of the meeting we were given a second and very curt interview with the King, who told us in substance: 'General Gort has agreed to attack towards the south according to the recommendations of General Weygand. As for the Belgian troops, they are to extend their front as had been agreed, but, instead of continuing to hold the line of the Schelde, they will man the line of the Lys. This position is less advantageous from several points of view, more particularly as regards the direction of the river, but it is impossible to do anything else because the Schelde position is, according to General Gort, already too deeply penetrated. The British General considers that the chances of the manœuvre in which he is going to take part are practically nil. The situation is desperate.'

The Ministers went back to Bruges, whilst the King returned to his headquarters. The return journey, made in darkness along roads encumbered by traffic, proved fatal for General Billotte. He died several hours after having been involved in a motor accident.

In the *Annexes* of the Report of the Committee of Inquiry one reads (p. 58), that, after the Ypres meeting, 'the King ordered everything to be prepared for an eventual retreat to the Yser in order to avoid the risk of incurring the reproaches of the British and French'. This part of the account, taken from the

King's Notes, is difficult to understand after what was said to prove the impossibility of this solution. In any case, the eventuality of a retreat to the Yser failed to materialize.

Finally, let us give the text of letters exchanged on the 22nd and 23rd between the King and M. Pierlot. We shall see each of these two opponents, after having again taken up and summarized his line of argument, defining, with due deliberation, his own position regarding the matter. Here, first of all, is Leopold III's letter:

G.H.Q., Saint André, 22nd May, 1940.

My dear Prime Minister,

I shall not hide from you the fact that our interview yesterday at Ypres, at which M. Spaak and General Denis were present, has left me with a very painful impression. I do not think that I deserve the reproaches which the Government levied against me, of following a policy which aimed, it is implied, at leading the country to conclude a separate peace with Germany. In carrying out my constitutional duties as Commander-in-Chief of the Army, my first and foremost aim has been to defend the national territory, whilst attempting to co-operate so far as is possible with the fight waged by the Allied Armies, and avoiding anything which might endanger the fate of our Army.

Thus, the conduct of Belgian Army operations is subordinated to two factual circumstances:

Collaboration with the Allied Armies, which makes the Belgian Command subordinate to the plan laid down by the Supreme Commander;

Flanking of the Belgian Army by the sea to the north, and by the British Expeditionary Force to the south.

This situation leaves us with no choice. No other line of action is possible.

I should add that the policy of evacuation, to which I am still opposed, will still further restrict our troops' liberty of movement.

These reasons in themselves are sufficient, in my opinion, to refute the remarks addressed to me.

I cannot admit, moreover, that the Ministers, whose competence does not extend to the conduct of military operations, should pass judgement on the capabilities of the Army, by coming to any conclusions, for example, as to whether the Army is or is not in a state to carry out a retreat.

In addition, you reproach me with keeping the Government in ignorance of how the military situation is developing, and you assert that the political consequences of this situation justify the Government's keeping a close watch upon it. This assertion is contrary to actual fact. Already at Breendonck, I drew your attention to the fact that the march of events was taking on a character which might result in a situation quite different from that which you considered as the only probable one. The sole difference in views, which has become apparent between us, lies in the fact that you consider, whatever the circumstances, there can be no question for me of linking my fate with that of the Army. I have replied to this objection by saying that it is impossible to exclude a hypothesis justifying such an attitude. . . .

May I now inform you, my dear Prime Minister, what the Head of the State, in the present circumstances, expects of members of his Government. . . .

If, in the military sphere, I try so far as possible to keep you in touch with the general picture of operations, I have the right to expect from you and, in particular, from the Minister of Foreign Affairs, to be constantly informed about political events, which, at the present time, I am unable to follow with close enough attention. I can easily understand that the ridiculous haste with which all the Government Departments and a section of the Provincial and Communal services have been transferred to France places you at the present time in a difficult position. This inexcusable failure of the civil authority leads to this conclusion: since the beginning of hostilities the Government has not possessed the means of governing.

Léopold.

M. Pierlot replied on the 23rd to this letter:

Sire,
 . . . I have never concealed from Your Majesty that I am unable to share your opinion concerning the scope of the constitutional provision which entrusts the command of the Army to the Sovereign. The text of this provision does not impair the general principle, which is unchallengeable, according to which the Government alone bears the responsibility for the actions of the Head of the State. . . .

In actual fact there can be no watertight division in this matter between military questions and political problems. The conduct of the war has a direct influence on the future of the country. Making due exception for the technical aspect of operations, whose appreciation common sense demands should be left to the Command, the Government will have to bear responsibility. In fact, the workings of our institutions allow Ministers alone to be accountable for their actions.

 . . . Since the conversations at Breendonck, to which Your Majesty refers, I confess that I have experienced a distressing anxiety about the decisions which I believed that I dimly apprehended. I had gathered, from these two visits to Breendonck, the impression that the retreat of the Belgian Army into a redoubt backed by the sea and separated from the Allied Armies, without any other future than capitulation, was intended. This was not only to be an eventuality which the course of events might force upon us, but also an outcome which was preferable to the disadvantages of leaving Belgian territory. My colleagues and myself have said everything in this matter, which springs from the convictions that we hold. We have none the less stressed the vital importance to the country of not seeing the King link his fate with that of the Army, to the point of surrendering his liberty. It appeared at the audience which the King granted us at Saint-André, that we have not quite understood what was in his mind. I offer my excuses for this misunderstanding, which has caused Your Majesty some pain, and I sincerely regret the displeasure which Your Majesty has felt. I should add, in extenuation of this, that, if our points of view now appear similar, we have had legitimate grounds for believing that, at first, there were fairly considerable differences between them, and these, because of the gravity of the subject, were enough to make us believe that it was our duty to reveal to the King everything which inspired us with concern.

I should not be expressing all I thought if I did not add a word about the meeting at Ypres. In view of the supreme importance of the decisions to be taken, I did express the desire that my colleagues and myself should be present at the disposal of Your Majesty, at the place where this interview was being held. I did not expect to attend a discussion of the military situation, but I should have considered it appropriate . . . that the Minister of National Defence be called. I should have wished to be present at the conclusion of the interview and to hear the Supreme Commander sum up his point of view. However accurately Your Majesty has informed us about this, it is obvious that nothing can replace the explanation that a man can give of his own ideas. I should then, in addition, have taken the opportunity, if possible, of putting a question, of asking for certain elucidations. Instead, we have left Ypres full of the uncertainty which a summary account was inevitably bound to implant in us. I shall not hide from Your Majesty that we experienced there one of the most cruel hours of our life, and that this impression has not risen solely from the consequences of events. To it was added a feeling that we were not entirely carrying out those duties which are within our province.

I believe that I am correct in saying that this method was not the one which was followed during the last war, and not that which is still practised by other belligerent countries. By that method the Government or, on its behalf, those Ministers who are best qualified by the character of their duties, whilst not meddling with the control of operations, are not kept apart from Councils where the general conduct of the war is being decided.

We regret that we have not been able, during these last days, to keep Your Majesty in better touch with the state of our foreign policy. This is due, not to a lack of personnel in the Ministry of Foreign Affairs, but to difficulties of communication.

We have no direct contact with Paris and Le Havre; we are not receiving any messages; we can only telephone to London. We are very grateful to Your Majesty for having authorized us to stay with you, but inevitably a flagging in Government activity will be caused by this. Such an inconvenience has not caused us to regret this decision, for we believe that our place is in Belgian territory as long as our presence is possible there.

. . . As for my colleagues who have left Belgium, I do not think any reproach can be levied against them on this score. If this reproach were well founded, I would, moreover, be the only one to merit it, for they have left at my request. May I point out that the Government only left Brussels on the day before the enemy arrived. I could no longer delay in sending my colleagues and their staffs to Le Havre unless I was to run the risk of seeing them thrown into confusion and endangered within the zone of operations.

Let us stop for a moment to consider these testimonies.

Weygand, says the King, was even ignorant that at that moment Abbeville was occupied by the Germans. Van Overstraeten, in his account of the interview, for his part writes:[1]

'*The A.D.C.*—"Is not the Supreme Commander aware that the Germans have been in possession of Abbeville since this morning (the 21st), that the occupying elements have stated this to be so in clear over the radio, and that the British believe the information to be accurate? The front is broken."

'*The Supreme Commander*, taken aback—"I was unaware of the fact."'

This ignorance on the part of Weygand appears, to say the least, surprising since, as we have seen in Bourget's account, Weygand's journey was to be taken by rail exactly as far as Abbeville and, from there, by road, and that the plan had to be abandoned because 'the General's transport sent to Abbeville during the afternoon of the 20th' had found the town in flames, and the Germans installed on the Somme. The King writes that 'Weygand agreed that it would be difficult to withdraw the Belgian Army behind the Yser'. We shall see that, on

_____
[1] *Rapport, Annexes*, p. 27.

this point, Weygand disagrees in his account completely with Leopold III.

M. Pierlot has told us what the King said at the interview on the 15th. 'They will be there before a week is out.' M. Spaak, who on the 16th first established contact with the General Headquarters of the King, informs us that 'a shocking atmosphere of defeatism reigned there'. On the 21st the Prime Minister notes that this atmosphere had become worse: 'General van Overstraeten . . . let it be understood that the end of the campaign was drawing near for the Belgian Army.' Then there are the words: 'But we are trapped' from this same van Overstraeten. And finally the King's remark: 'The situation is desperate.' And Baudouin writes[1] in his turn: 'Captain Gasser, General Weygand's A.D.C., told me that at Ypres last Tuesday the King's brother, the Count of Flanders, informed him that within eight days the struggle would be over.'

MAY 21: 'WHATEVER HAPPENS, I SHALL NOT SURRENDER'

It is known why I had entrusted the supreme command to Weygand. I knew the hostility of the Foch 'school' for the Pétain 'school'. On the day Pétain joined my Government I said to him: 'I have summoned a man whom you do not like, but the hour is not one when our personal sympathies or antipathies count. Weygand is arriving tomorrow from Syria.' Pétain kept silent.

Pétain asked that we should meet each morning, all three of us, in my room to examine the situation together. Both Weygand and I agreed to this.[2] Pétain's and Weygand's arrival had the effect on the morale of the Army and the nation which I anticipated it would. Hope revived in their hearts. For a time the wave of defeatism which, since May 16, threatened to submerge the country, was arrested. It was none the less clear that this benefit was a frail one and that, if I wanted it to be unaffected by new reverses, it was essential that nobody in France should be able to cast doubt on the unshakeable determination of the Government to fight to the last.

On May 21, I received M. Charles-Roux, who had taken up the post of Secretary-General in the Ministry of Foreign Affairs. What did I say to him? Here are my words:

[1] Op. cit., p. 60.
[2] Weygand was to state at Pétain's trial (hearing of July 31, 1945) that I took the initiative in proposing this daily meeting which, he said, proved a great nuisance to him, but whose importance, he added, he was not long in appreciating.
Darlan shortly afterwards asked to join in these talks. Pétain and Weygand as well as Darlan, from the day when this last-named joined us, waited in Baudouin's room before coming into mine. Baudouin would come in at the same time as they did, but he merely played the role of a silent onlooker.
It had been agreed that, unless there was a change in time, the meeting would be held at 11 a.m.

'My third visit', he writes,[1] 'was to M. Paul Reynaud. He led me to a large map ... pinned to the tapestry in his room, and explained briefly the state of operations. The Germans had encircled the armies ... fighting in Belgium. All hope of breaking their ring had not vanished. But there was only a chance and one in which we could not place too much faith. The President of the Council ended, emphasizing his words: "Whatever happens, I shall not surrender."'

Two days later the War Cabinet met at 10 p.m. Marcel Héraud was present because one of the problems which was under consideration fell within his province; the evacuation of refugees. I have already quoted a passage from those very vivid notes, which he took from day to day, of the deliberations in which he took part. He has kept the remarks which, at the end of this meeting of May 23, several Ministers who were lingering in my room exchanged with me.

Dautry, he writes, declared that our Supreme Command still believed in the infantry as the 'queen of the battlefield'; Chautemps, that Gamelin had extended his front excessively and neglected the armoured divisions, thus doing exactly what he had reproached the Poles for doing; and I, that when Weygand arrived, the General Staffs were already talking of an armistice.

Marcel Héraud added:

'Mandel said ironically: "Under the stimulus of invasion we must begin to prepare for war."
'Paul Reynaud expressed his bitterness in having foreseen such a state of affairs, and in having failed to get anyone else to do so. . . . He declared, moreover, that all these retrospective considerations must not prevent us from resisting. The Government would remain in Paris, even if it were bombed. If Paris were taken, it would go elsewhere. If it were necessary, we would get on a cruiser, and patrol with the fleet in sight of the coasts of France.
'To conclude, he uttered a phrase of Churchill, about the British Army, at present isolated in the north: "It is like a cut flower in a vase."'

To each and all, it will be seen, I spoke in the same strain.

MAY 22: WEYGAND EXPLAINS HIS PLAN IN THE PRESENCE OF CHURCHILL AND MYSELF

Weygand had now drawn up his plan. On the following day he was going to explain it to Churchill and myself.

The British Prime Minister arrived in Paris during the morning.

[1] *Cinq mois tragiques aux affaires étrangères, 21 mai–1er novembre, 1940*, p. 4.

At midday we went together to the stronghold of Vincennes under a sky whose very beauty seemed implacable in those tragic days. There Weygand, who had come two hours before to inform me of what had transpired when he met the King of the Belgians, was waiting for us with Sir John Dill. Dill, who was about to succeed General Ironside as Chief of the Imperial General Staff,[1] was accompanied by Air Vice-Marshal Peirse and General Ismay.

First of all, let us remember that Corap's Army had ceased to exist. As for Giraud's Army, the Seventh, this originally had possessed a front line strength of four infantry divisions, two of which were motorized (the 9th and the 25th) and two were Class A (the 4th and the 21st), and, a second line strength of two Class B divisions (the 60th and the 68th). It was entirely covered by the 1st Light Mechanized Division (pushed forward as far as Breda). All of it had been dispersed and broken up on the 15th, the day when Giraud had gone, as we have seen, to take over the command of the Ninth Army from Corap. Its General Staff and the organic elements which were attached to it had since left by road to place themselves under the command of General Frère,[2] who was busy forming, to the south of the Somme a new Seventh Army, the nucleus of which was constituted by troops brought up hastily from Alsace-Lorraine. One of the two motorized divisions, the 25th, was sent to join the First Army, as well as the 1st Light Mechanized Division, and thus General Prioux was, henceforth, to include all our three light mechanized divisions in his Cavalry Corps. The second of the two motorized divisions, the 9th, had been, on the 15th, thrown by Giraud into the conflict in order to support the debris of Corap's Army, which was flowing back to leave a gaping hole on the River Oise. That left two Class B divisions which formed

[1] With reference to the replacement of Ironside by Dill, Churchill offers the following explanation (op. cit., vol. II, Their Finest Hour, pp. 64–5):
'There was a very strong feeling in Cabinet and high military circles that the abilities and strategic knowledge of Sir John Dill, who had been since April 23 Vice-Chief of the Imperial General Staff, should find their full scope in his appointment as our principal Army adviser. No one could doubt that his professional standing was in many ways superior to that of Ironside.

'As the adverse battle drew to its climax I and my colleagues greatly desired that Sir John Dill should become C.I.G.S. We had also to choose a Commander-in-Chief for the British Island, if we were invaded. Late at night on May 25 Ironside, Dill, Ismay, myself, and one or two others in my room at Admiralty House were trying to measure the position. General Ironside volunteered the proposal that he should cease to be C.I.G.S., but declared himself quite willing to command the British Home Forces. Considering the unpromising task that such a command was at the time thought to involve, this was a spirited and selfless offer. I therefore accepted General Ironside's proposal; . . . Sir John Dill became C.I.G.S. on May 27. . . .'

Though the appointment only became effective on the 27th, Dill, in actual fact, took over his new post on the 22nd.

[2] This magnificent soldier, seriously wounded during the previous war, was arrested on June 13, 1943, by the Gestapo because of his participation in the Resistance Movement. It was he, who, in 1942, had assumed charge of the Organization of Army Resistance (O.R.A.). Imprisoned in Struthof Camp (Alsace), he died in 1944 as a result of his cruel treatment.

the 16th Corps, which, under the orders of General Fagalde,[1] continued to hold its positions on the estuaries of the Schelde.

Let us consider the exposition of the situation given by Weygand, as we can reconstruct it from the minutes of the Supreme Council, drawn up by M. de Margerie:

The German Armoured Corps had opened a gap of about twenty-five kilometres in breadth between the Somme and Arras. It had established, in its crossing of the river, bridge-heads to the south, notably at Amiens and Abbeville. A Panzer division, skirting the coast, had already reached Etaples and was pushing on to Boulogne, where two battalions of the Guards, the last two units of the Regular Army still remaining in Britain, had just disembarked. Thus, the encirclement of the forty-five divisions, which comprised the Allied Armies of the North, was being rapidly carried out.

From left to right our forces were disposed in echelon in the following positions:

1. At the estuaries of the Schelde were Fagalde's two divisions, which were, however, on the point of falling back on Dunkirk in order to ensure its defence.

2. Lining the left bank of the Schelde, from Neuzen to Oudenarde, were the twenty divisions of the Belgian Army.

3. From there to the confluence of the Schelde and the Scarpe were six British divisions, of which two were in reserve.

4. From there to the confluence of the Schelde and the Sensée, then along this latter river to Arleux, then from there to Biache, and finally along the Scarpe to the outskirts of Arras, lay our First Army with its Cavalry Corps on the right. This was a powerful Army both as regards its effectives and their quality. In addition to the two light mechanized divisions and the eight infantry divisions which, as we have seen, it originally included, there had been added, at the beginning of the German offensive, two infantry divisions which Georges had raised from his general reserves, and later the 1st Light Mechanized Division, and the motorized division which it had, as I have said, inherited when Giraud's Army was dispersed. In all, this First Army comprised fourteen divisions, from which, it is true, we must deduct at the present time two divisions, the 101st Fortress Infantry Division and one of the two divisions raised from the general reserves which had just been, the first completely and the second partly, annihilated in the forest of Mormal.

[1] For a number of years Fagalde had been Military Attaché in London. Married to an American and very well known in London society, he was *persona grata* in the upper circles of the British Army. He was an acquaintance of Churchill, and on terms of close friendship even to a point of familiarity with Spears.

Billotte was in command of these three Armies. Churchill had told me that Gort was complaining of having been left by him without orders for four consecutive days. But Billotte, during the night of the 21st to 22nd, had just been mortally injured in a car accident. He died on the 23rd. He was to be replaced, as we shall see, by Blanchard, whom Prioux himself succeeded as commander of the First Army. But this accident was only known to us after the meeting: I was not to learn of it until 7 p.m. Such, therefore, was the situation of the Allied Armies of the north on the 22nd.

To the south of the Somme, Frère's Army, as we have seen, was taking up its positions. It comprised eight divisions, and was extending its front progressively towards the estuary. Farther to the east, to the south of the Aisne, was Touchon's Army; this was linked up to that of Huntziger and thereby to Montmédy and the Maginot Line.

The German infantry was pouring onward behind the motorized divisions which were following the Panzers. Large bodies of infantry were already in contact with Huntziger's Army.

Having explained this, here is Weygand's plan: 'The Commander-in-Chief considers that there can be no question of asking the Anglo-Franco-Belgian body of troops, which is still in the north and which comprises more than forty divisions, to fight purely and simply in a defensive withdrawal to the south in order to join up with the main element of the French Army. Such a manœuvre would be doomed to failure, and these troops, in such an event, would incur certain disaster. The situation demands, on the contrary, that, under the protection of the Belgian Army which would act as a cover, first of all facing the east and later the north, the French and available British forces should take offensive action in the Cambrai and Arras area and in the general direction of St. Quentin, so as to fall on the flank of the German armoured divisions which are, at the present time, engaged in the St. Quentin-Amiens "pocket". At the same time the French Army of General Frère, concentrated to the south of the Somme in the Beauvais area, should push northwards so as to increase pressure on the enemy armoured elements which are in the vicinity of Amiens, Abbeville and Arras. The essential thing is to subject these elements to a constant pressure, to allow the German armoured divisions no opportunity to act on their own initiative but to keep them perpetually on the move, to inflict losses on them, and to threaten their rear. It is only by fulfilling such conditions that the withdrawal of the Armies in Belgium can be carried out.'

Thus, as affairs turned out, it was no longer a case, on the 22nd, of resisting the advance of the Panzer divisions as Gamelin had suggested on the 19th. On the other hand, they were to be attacked in their rear in order to attempt to separate them from the rest of the German Army which was following them at a distance, as Gamelin had also laid down in his *Instruction* of the 19th. As for attacking them in the flank as Weygand planned, was not this too late? Were they not already switched towards the north?

Whilst the Franco-British Armies, which were sustaining the shock of the German Armoured Corps, found themselves given, into the bargain, the duty of attacking in a northerly and southerly direction, the Belgian Army, whose strength was, however, practically equivalent to that of the Franco-British forces, was only asked by Weygand to withdraw behind the flooded Yser, which had saved them in 1914. Its duty was to cover Dunkirk, the supply base of all the Allied Armies, against enemy attacks coming from the north. Had Weygand secured satisfaction about this point in his conference with the King of the Belgians? We have read Leopold III's account. Here now is that of Weygand as it is to be found in the minutes of the meeting: 'As far as the role of the Belgian Army is concerned, the Commander-in-Chief was faced with two differing conceptions on which the King at the moment did not come to any decision. One, that of General Weygand himself, is to ask the Belgian Army to withdraw progressively from the Schelde to the Yser, whilst ensuring cover for the Franco-British forces which are to operate against St. Quentin. In reality, the Belgian Army, from the estuaries of the Schelde by way of Ghent to Oudenarde, is in an exposed position where it is running grave risks. The support which it has to give to the remaining Armies of the western front could quite as well be given on the Yser with the help of its inundations (which General Weygand had, moreover, ordered to be executed immediately).

'The other [conception] has been advanced by General van Overstraeten. . . . The role of the Belgian Army should be rather to stay in its present position and, if need be, to separate itself from the rest of the Allied forces in order to cover the coast in an extensive semi-circle, with its supplies being ensured through Ostend and Dunkirk. To justify this plan General van Overstraeten has emphasized the fatigue of the Belgian troops, who have not stopped marching since Maastricht, and the state of their morale, which has naturally suffered from this long retreat. Since the Army arrived on the Schelde and after a rest of twenty-four hours, it has pulled itself together, and has proved this by repulsing brilliantly during the day of May 21 two German attempts to cross the Schelde. To ask these troops to resume their withdrawal and to abandon almost every yard of national territory would, according to General van Overstraeten, expose them to a new wave of demoralization.

'General Weygand protested very strongly against this plan. He pointed out that the Allied forces constitute a whole, that the French and British had advanced to the help of the Belgians in Belgium and that now the Belgians ought to continue fighting at the side of the British and French. He added that the supplying of the King's Army, in the circumstances envisaged by General van Overstraeten, would be impossible, and that the Belgian forces would very rapidly find themselves, in such a case, condemned to capitulation. The King took no definite stand in the discussion.[1] It was only on returning from the Belgian Headquarters . . . that General Weygand learned that the Belgian Command had agreed to his opinion and had decided to retreat to the Yser in two stages, the first of which would be a withdrawal to the Lys.'

Weygand concluded by asking of Churchill the greatest possible co-operation of the British Air Force.

The plan proposed by Weygand received the complete approval of Churchill, Sir John Dill and myself. Churchill stressed the fact that the re-establishment of communications between the Armies of the north and of the south by way of Arras was indispensable, that General Gort's British forces had only four days' provisions, that all the supplies and war material of the British Expeditionary Force were in ports from Calais to St. Nazaire, and that the chief preoccupation of General Gort had been to keep open these lines of communication, which were vital to him.

After the meeting the three of us went together to my room where Churchill drew up a summary of the decisions which had just been made. These he immediately telegraphed to his Government in London. This summary was approved by Weygand, to whom

---

[1] Weygand was to show himself more affirmative on this point in the hearings of the Pétain trial: 'I had', he stated at the hearing of July 31, 1945, 'the opportunity of being able to convince the King of the Belgians that the strategy which he was contemplating did not seem to me good, because he had thought, first of all, of leaving the Belgian Army rather isolated. I asked him to lead it on the contrary towards the west in order that it might link up with the Allied Armies.'

It is true that, in his previously mentioned deposition of March 8, 1949, Weygand was to be more evasive. He stated: 'I . . . told the King that this Allied group of Armies was still powerful, for, if the First French Army had had to stand up to a great effort on the part of the Germans, the British Army had hardly fought at all, and the Belgian Army had not, up to that time, had to meet a heavy attack. What I was asking of this group of armies was perfectly feasible. I required it to attack towards the south, and in this attack, I asked the King that the Belgian Army should protect the eastern and south-eastern front of the attack against a German advance. . . . The King . . . asked the opinion of General van Overstraeten, who had more influence over him than his General Staff. . . . The General . . . in suitable academic language said he proposed a line of action whereby the Belgian Army, positioning itself with its back to the sea, should wheel on its left flank which was at Ghent near the Dutch frontier, and that it should fight in such circumstances. After listening to him, I told the King that I could never agree to such strategy which would leave the Belgian Army isolated from the others, and that, in my opinion, his plan would lead to the capitulation of the Belgian Army, for it would not be able to defend itself under such conditions. The King told me he would give me his reply, and indeed, I received it on the morning of the following day. He informed me through General Champon . . . that he had come round to my own plan of action.'

Churchill remarked: 'There is only one fault in you; you are too young.' Thus, he paid a tribute to the alertness of bearing in this man of seventy-three years of age.

The substance of the decisions agreed upon was as follows:

(a) The Belgian Army will withdraw to the Yser, whose lock-gates have been opened, and will hold on to the positions which it takes up there.

(b) The British Army and the French forces in the north will attack as soon as possible, and in any case by tomorrow, the 23rd, at the latest, in the direction of Bapaume and Cambrai, with a strength of eight divisions.

(c) Inasmuch as the battle to be fought possesses a vital importance for both Armies, and that the maintenance of British communications is dependent on the liberation of Arras, the R.A.F. will give, both night and day, its utmost possible support during the whole period of the battle.

(d) The new group of French Armies, which has been put into the line along the Somme and is progressing towards Amiens, will advance northwards to meet the British divisions marching towards Bapaume.

From that time I considered it my duty to back the execution of the Weygand plan with all my authority. Our weakness lay in the lack of an armoured corps and aviation, those two arms of modern warfare. I could do nothing in May, 1940, about giving my country an armoured corps, but to the end, I never ceased urging Churchill, at the repeated requests of Weygand, to intensify the collaboration of the British Air Force in order to compensate for the inferiority which resulted from the deficiencies of our own. What did lie within our power was to rid the Army of all those Generals who, in the struggle, had shown that they were not up to their task. By the 25th, sixteen of them had been relieved.

On the 23rd at 4.20 p.m. Weygand telephoned to the office of the President of the Council to say that he was 'very satisfied with the progress of operations since the morning'. He added that 'our troops were approaching Amiens', and that, having received a message from Churchill, he was happy to record once again his 'complete identity of views' with the Prime Minister.

Why did the Weygand plan fail? It is necessary to have the text of the orders which were given to state the reasons with certainty. No doubt the French soldier in the field has spoken bitterly of the British retreat on Dunkirk. But it is important to remember that the bulk of the Panzer divisions were concentrated, on the 18th, to the west of St. Quentin and that, if one part did swoop on Boulogne and Dunkirk, the other tried, on the one hand, to contain the Allied Armies, and on the other, to pin them against the sea. The only help that I can offer is to give the text of messages which I exchanged with Churchill on this subject.

On the 23rd at 4.50 p.m. Churchill telephoned to say that Gort had received no information from Blanchard. He added that, because of the position of the German armoured divisions, he was wondering whether it would not be better if the British Army fought in retreat towards the coast.

I answered him: 'Weygand is satisfied. We ought not to change anything. We must follow the path which we have traced out. (*We must go on.*)'

During the night of the 23rd[1] Churchill sent me, for transmission to Weygand the following telegram, a translation of which made by my secretariat, is more accurate than that in the German White Book:[2]

'General Gort wires that co-ordination of northern front is essential with armies of three different nations. He says he cannot undertake this co-ordination, as he is already fighting north and south and is threatened on his lines of communications. At the same time Sir Roger Keyes tells me that up to 3 p.m. today (23rd) Belgian Headquarters and King had received no directive. How does this agree with your statement that Blanchard and Gort are *main dans la main*? Appreciate fully difficulties of communication, but feel no effective concert of operations in northern area, against which enemy are concentrating. Trust you will be able to rectify this. Gort further says that any advance by him must be in the nature of sortie, and that relief must come from south, as he has not (*repeat* not) ammunition for serious attack. Nevertheless, we are instructing him to persevere in carrying out your plan. We have not here even seen your own directive, and have no knowledge of the details of your northern operations. Will you kindly have this sent through French Mission at earliest? All good wishes.'

On the 24th I received the following letter from Weygand.

'I have the honour to inform you that, as a result of the withdrawal during the night of May 23 to 24 of the British Army on the Haute-Deûle Canal, the importance of which I realized this afternoon, I have directed the Commander of Number One Army Group, if he considers the manœuvre previously ordered can no longer be carried out, to form a bridge-head as extensive as possible in front of the three northern ports.

'In spite of violent enemy attacks we still hold these ports, and it is essential at all costs to reinforce them.

[1] The telegram only reached me at 5 a.m. on the 24th.
[2] The text given here is that given by Sir Winston Churchill, *op. cit.*, vol. II, *Their Finest Hour*, p. 61 [Tr.].

'I have, therefore, this morning asked the British Command to continue sending troops there and to place for the same purpose, if possible, at my disposal that half of the 5th Light Brigade which is still in the Clyde.

'I am asking Admiral Darlan, in addition, to reinforce the sea defences. . . . I am also requesting him to carry out quickly the supplying by sea of the northern troops, despite any difficulties that may exist.'

On the same day at 12.15 p.m. following a conversation with the British Ambassador, and then with Weygand, in Pétain's presence, I telegraphed to Churchill about the information which Weygand had received that Arras had been evacuated the night before.

'1. General Weygand explained to you, the day before yesterday in my presence at Vincennes, a plan which met with your entire approval, as well as that of the officers who were with you.

'2. This plan was summarized by you in writing. General Weygand informed you that he agreed with this summary.

'3. General Weygand knows all the difficulties of the situation, but he believes that no other solution is possible except through the execution of this plan even if it has to be adapted to the exigencies of the moment as, for example, by inflecting the advance towards the southwest so that the right wing would make for the Somme below Amiens. Thus, he repeated this morning the order to carry out this plan. The encircled Armies ought, therefore, to make a desperate effort to advance and effect a junction with the French forces which are marching from the south to the north, by trying to issue forth from along the Somme, and especially from Amiens.

'4. It is imperative that Gort's Army, which is covered by two of Fagalde's divisions, should be supplied through Dunkirk.

'5. It is most desirable that you should send troops to these ports as you did yesterday to Calais.

'6. General Weygand has noted with surprise that, contrary to this plan, Arras was evacuated yesterday by British troops.

'7. General Weygand's liaison with the Belgian Army is established. He learned last night that the Belgians have repulsed minor attacks and that their morale is excellent.

'8. The impossibility of communicating directly with Blanchard, Commander-in-Chief of the three Armies, those of the Belgians, of Gort and of Blanchard, makes it impossible for General Weygand to give you an answer about the lack of liaison between Blanchard and Gort. But, when communicating directly with the Belgian Army, he was convinced that his orders have reached Blanchard, and through him, Gort. Proof of co-operation between Blanchard and Gort appears to be offered by the fact that last night a French division relieved a British division.

'9. General Weygand has just learned of the evacuation of heavy units of the British Army at Le Havre, which is having a serious effect on the morale of the rear areas. He is surprised, as I myself am, that he was not previously advised of this.

'10. You will agree with me that a single command is more than necessary in these tragic hours, and that General Weygand's orders should be obeyed.

'11. General Weygand is convinced that his plan can only succeed if the Belgian Army, and those of Blanchard and Gort are inspired by a grim intention to make a sortie, which alone can save them.'

At this moment we learned that the British troops had withdrawn forty kilometres towards the ports. The question was raised at Vincennes whether or not Gort had received from London different orders from those which were laid down in the Weygand plan. That is why I sent during the evening of the 24th the following telegram to Churchill, which Vichy propaganda has pin-pointed and emphasized in such a way that it can be inferred from it that France's ally was guilty of treachery towards her. This is an absurdity when one knows the facts which I have just related. I am happy to say, on the contrary, that, during these tragic days, the friendship which united Churchill and myself did not suffer in the slightest. Here is the text of the telegram which I sent to Churchill:

'You telegraphed me this morning that you had instructed Gort to persevere in carrying out the Weygand plan.

'General Weygand now tells me that, judging from a telegram sent by General Blanchard, the British Army has, contrary to formal orders, which he has himself renewed this morning . . . decided on and carried out a withdrawal of forty kilometres towards the ports, at a time when our troops, moving up from the south, are gaining ground towards the north in their advance to meet the Allied Armies of the north.

'This withdrawal has naturally compelled General Weygand to modify his arrangements. He believes that he must, as a result, give up any idea of closing the gap and of re-establishing a continuous front. I need not lay stress upon the gravity of the consequences which can result from this.'

The same evening I received a reply from Churchill to my telegram of 12.15 p.m.

'We are in agreement on points 1, 2, 3 and we shall keep on trying to do our best.

'Point 4: We are pleased to hear that Fagalde has taken over

Command from Blanchard, but your telegram is ambiguous on one point. For the present the road to Dunkirk is open and we are sending Gort supplies by this route.

'Point 5: Unfortunately we have no more troops.

'Point 6: We know nothing about the evacuation of Arras. Such a withdrawal would be entirely contrary to our views.

'Point 7: The only material evacuated at Le Havre consists of gas shells which it seems inopportune to leave there. As a precautionary measure we have also transferred a part of our supplies to the south bank. In any case it is a matter which concerns us.

'Point 8: I am a believer in unity of command, and we have faithfully conformed to this rule, but believe me, my friend, since the beginning of the retreat, there has not been in the north any command worthy of the name until the day Weygand took things in hand.

'We have sent General Dill on to the Continent today to see the Belgians, Blanchard and Gort. As soon as I receive his report, I shall telegraph you.

'My best wishes, and excuse my bluntness.'

On the 25th at 1 p.m. I received the following telegram (dated the 24th) from Churchill:[1]

'We have every reason to believe that Gort is still persevering in southward move. All we know is that he has been forced by the pressure on his western flank, and to keep communication with Dunkirk for indispensable supplies, to place parts of two divisions between himself and the increasing pressure of the German armoured forces, which in apparently irresistible strength have successively captured Abbeville and Boulogne, are menacing Calais and Dunkirk, and have taken St. Omer. How can he move southward and disengage his northern front unless he throws out this shield on his right hand? Nothing in the movements of the B.E.F. of which we are aware can be any excuse for the abandonment of the strong pressure of your northward move across the Somme, which we trust will develop.

'Secondly, you complained of heavy materials being moved from Havre. Only materials moved away were gas shells, which it was indiscreet to leave. Also some of the stores have been moved from the north to the south side of the river at Havre.

'Thirdly, should I become aware that extreme pressure of events has compelled any departure from the plan agreed I shall immediately inform you. Dill, who was this morning wholly convinced that the sole hope of any effective extrication of our Army lies in the southward move and in the active advance of General Frère, is now with Gort.

---

[1] The text given here is that given by Sir Winston Churchill, op. cit., vol. ii, Their Finest Hour, p. 64. Sir Winston Churchill dates his telegram May 25 [Tr.].

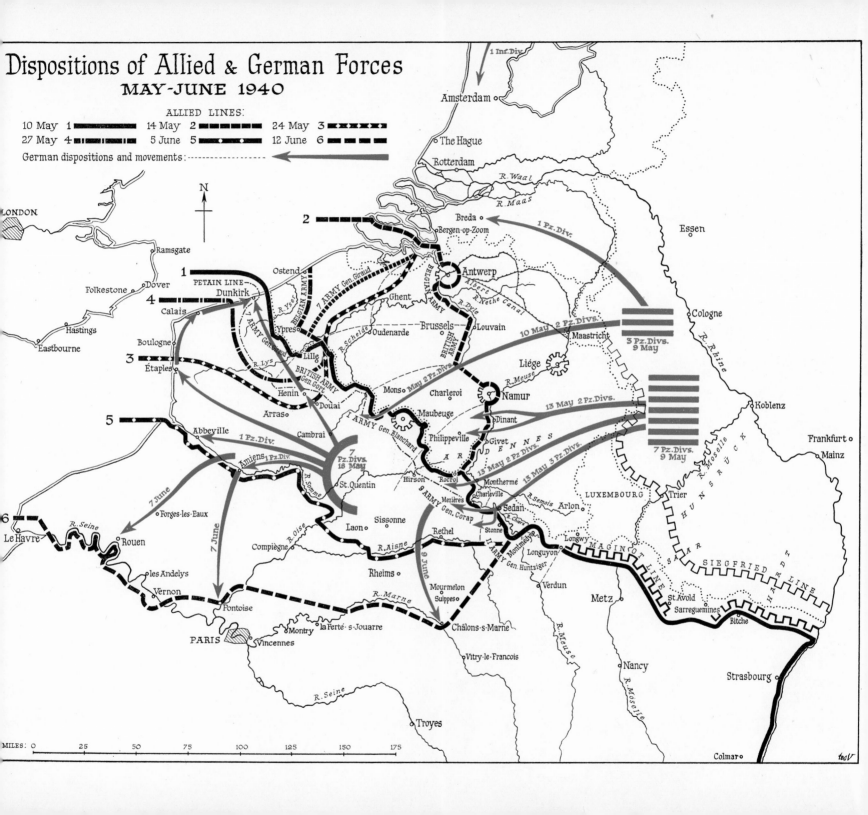

Dispositions of Allied & German Forces
MAY-JUNE 1940

ALLIED LINES:
| 10 May | 1 | ━━━━━ | 14 May | 2 | ━━━━━ | 24 May | 3 | ×××××× |
| 27 May | 4 | ▬▬▬▬ | 5 June | 5 | ━●━●━ | 12 June | 6 | ▬ ▬ ▬ |

German dispositions and movements: -----------

N

LONDON
Ramsgate
Folkestone · Dover
Hastings
Eastbourne

Amsterdam
The Hague
Rotterdam
R. Waal
R. Maas

Essen

Breda
Bergen-op-Zoom
1 Pz. Div.

Cologne

PETAIN LINE
Dunkirk
Calais
Boulogne
Étaples
Henin
Arras
Abbeville
Amiens 1 Pz. Div.
1 Pz. Div.
St. Quentin

Ostend
R. Yser
Ypres
R. Lys
Lille
Douai
Cambrai

BELGIAN ARMY
7 ARMY Gen. Giraud
7 ARMY Gen. Giraud
Ghent
Oudenarde
R. Schelde
BRITISH ARMY Gen. Gort
BRITISH ARMY Gen. Gort
Mons
Maubeuge

Antwerp
Albert Canal
R. Nethe Canal
R. Dyle
Brussels
Louvain
10 May 2 Pz. Divs.
Maastricht
3 Pz. Divs. 9 May

Liége
R. Meuse
13 May 2 Pz. Divs.
Koblenz

BELGIAN ARMY
16 May 2 Pz. Divs.
Charleroi
Namur
Dinant
7 Pz. Divs. 9 May

Frankfurt
Mainz

7 Pz. Divs. 18 May
Hirson
Rocroi
Montherme
13 May 2 Pz. Divs.
13 May 3 Pz. Divs.
R. Semois
Arlon
LUXEMBOURG
Trier

7 June
Forges-les-Eaux
Laon
Sissonne
R. Somme
Philippeville
Givet
ARDENNES
I ARMY Gen. Blanchard
9 ARMY Gen. Corap
Mezieres
Charleville
Stonne
R. Chiers
Sedan
Longwy
MAGINOT LINE
Longuyon
II ARMY Gen. Huntziger
Montmédy

6
Le Havre
R. Seine
Rouen
les Andelys
Vernon
Pontoise
PARIS
Vincennes
Montry
la Ferté-s-Jouarre
Compiègne
R. Oise
Rheims
R. Aisne
Rethel
9 June
Mourmelon
Suippes
Châlons-s-Marne
Vitry-le-Francois
Verdun
R. Meuse
Metz
St. Avold
Sarreguemines
Bitche
Nancy
R. Moselle
Strasbourg

7 June
R. Marne
R. Seine
Troyes
Colmar

HUNSRÜCK
SAAR
SIEGFRIED LINE
HARDT

MILES: 0   25   50   75   100   125   150   175

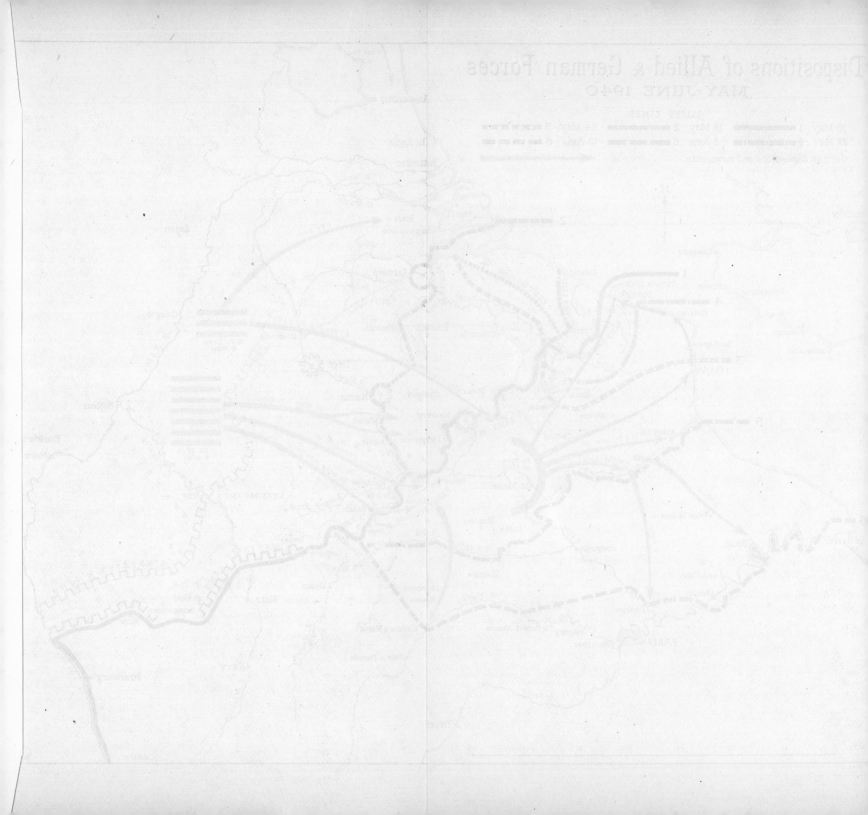

You must understand that, having waited for the southward move for a week after it became obvious[ly necessary], we find ourselves now ripped from the coast by the mass of the enemy's armoured vehicles. We therefore have no choice but to continue the southward move, using such flank guard protection to the westward as is necessary.

'General Spears will be with you tomorrow morning, and it will probably be quickest to send him back when the position is clear.'

In actual fact, General Spears arrived that day. . . . I had known him for a long time. As President of the House of Commons' Franco-British Committee, he had long been linked with me on terms of friendship. He was well qualified to fulfil the liaison duties with which Churchill entrusted him. The latter accredited him to me in the following letter:

24 May, 1940.

My dear Reynaud,

As we agreed last Wednesday, it is most essential that you and I should collaborate as closely as possible on military problems. It is not easy for either of us to take time off frequently in order to visit each other for discussions. That is why I have nominated Brigadier-General Spears, one of your old friends, as a personal liaison officer between us for military problems.

This appointment does not alter the existing liaisons which we have already, between ourselves, between our Supreme Commands, as well as between our respective naval, army and air forces.

In my opinion General Spears should take up permanent residence in Paris, and come to London any time you or myself wish.

Knowing as you do the special qualifications of General Spears for this mission, you will, I am sure, place your full confidence in him. He is leaving tomorrow at dawn to report to you.

Yours sincerely,
Winston S. Churchill.

As soon as he arrived on the 25th, Spears came to see me. At 1 p.m. I gave him the following telegram for Churchill:

'1. The Commander-in-Chief of the three Armies, Belgian, British and French is General Blanchard.

'2. General Prioux has taken General Blanchard's place as commander of the First French Army.

'3. The retreat of some British units from the Arras area towards the Deûle Canal caused General Weygand, yesterday, Friday, at 4 p.m., to send the following order to General Blanchard: "If you think that the British withdrawal from the Arras area means that an offensive by you towards the south is impossible, it is necessary that, at the very least, you should make certain that your group of Armies retreats towards the sea, and that you keep Dunkirk, which is essential for its supplies."

'4. This morning, at one o'clock, General Blanchard telegraphed to General Weygand, without making mention of his telegram of 4 p.m. yesterday, that, in conjunction with certain British units, he would attack in order to obtain today a jumping-off base delimited by the line from Marquion-bois to Bourlon-Cambrai. It was his intention to push this attack, during the following day, Sunday, in the general direction of Bapaume.

'5. On receiving this telegram from General Blanchard, General Weygand answered him with the following: "I approve of your arrangements and I am happy that, in spite of the situation which I described in my telegram of yesterday, you consider that you are in a position to attack.

'6. On arriving in Paris at midday[1] General Weygand received a senior officer of General Blanchard's staff, who had left his Head-quarters twenty-four hours before, this officer gave him a map, showing the present position of the group of armies.[2]

'7. General Weygand sent this senior officer to General Blanchard, and telegraphed to him that, in the difficult situation in which he was placed, and of which we were fully aware, General Blanchard was the sole judge of the decisions to be taken, and that the honour of the Army was in his hands.'

At 6.55 p.m., five minutes before the War Committee were to meet at the Elysée, I received from Churchill the following telegram:[3]

'My telegram last night told you all we knew over here, and we have still heard nothing from Lord Gort to contradict it. But I must tell you that a Staff officer has reported to the War Office confirming the with-drawal of the two divisions from the Arras region, which your telegram to me mentioned. General Dill, who should be with Lord Gort, has been told to send a Staff officer by air at the earliest moment. As soon as we know what has happened I will report fully. It is clear however

---

[1] As we have seen earlier, Weygand came from Vincennes to consult with me every morning in Paris.

[2] This was Major Fauvelle, whom Blanchard sent by air to Paris to report on the situation. I received him at midday in the presence of Pétain, Weygand, Darlan, Spears and Baudouin. According to him, there was no longer any hope of Blanchard's being able to carry out the offensive movement that Weygand had ordered. The First Army had, in actual fact, only three divisions left, which were in a fit state to fight. These only had a day's artillery ammunition in addition to that in the boxes of the batteries, and a day's provisions. Major Fauvelle added that the British Army seemed to be preparing for its re-embarkation, and that the Belgian was slipping away. 'I think surrender is very near', was his conclusion, according to Baudouin (*op. cit.*, p. 49).

[3] The text given here is that given by Sir Winston Churchill, *op. cit.*, vol. II, *Their Finest Hour*, p. 63 [Tr.].

that the Northern Army is practically surrounded and that all its communications are cut except through Dunkirk and Ostend.'

Military historians will relate why the Weygand plan had to be abandoned. Already the reader knows enough to form an estimate of the worth of German and Vichy propaganda, which attributed this set-back to 'British treason'.[1]

THE GORT REPORT

Here are the essential passages of General Gort's Report[2] on the operations of the British Expeditionary Force during its campaign in Flanders:

The Weygand plan, as it came to be known, was for a counter-offensive, on a large scale.

From the north the French First army, and the B.E.F. were to attack south-west at the earliest possible moment with about eight divisions and with the Belgian Cavalry Corps supporting the British right.

The newly formed Third French Army Group was reported to be organizing a line on the Somme from Amiens to Péronne with a view to attacking northwards.

A new cavalry corps was assembling south of the Somme near Neufchâtel and was to operate on the line of the Somme west of Amiens, in touch with the British Armoured Division on their left.

I fully appreciated the importance of attacking early before the enemy could bring up his infantry in strength, but facts had to be faced. The 5th and 50th Divisions were on this day (May 23) still closely engaged with the enemy, and 2nd, 44th and 48th Divisions, would not become available for a further forty-eight hours, since the French and the Belgians, though they had arranged their relief, could not complete it earlier. The ammunition immediately available to the B.E.F. was of the order of three hundred rounds per gun and with communications cut with the main base, the prospect of receiving any further supply was remote.

The French light mechanized divisions and our own armoured units had already suffered serious losses in tanks which could not be replaced. Such information as I had received of the Belgian cavalry did not lead me to take an

[1] No doubt it was to put a stop to this grievance of desertion at the height of battle that Churchill, when speaking on December 30, 1941, to the Canadian Parliament in Ottawa, stated that the French Army 'had collapsed', not without adding, however, 'it was the duty ... of the French Government to withdraw into North Africa. ...' This earned him the following reply in an official Vichy communiqué of January 1, 1942: 'Mr. Churchill ought to remember quite well that, if there was a collapse of the French Army, he had a lot to do with it. There was in actual fact during those tragic days of May, 1940, some hope of stopping the German advance; this lay in the British Army having the firm intention of fighting. By withdrawing to re-embark, without the French Command being aware of this, and despite the order to attack given by the French Command, the British divisions nullified completely this last opportunity of putting up any resistance.'

[2] Supplement (Friday, October 17, 1941) to the London Gazette of Friday, October 10, 1941. The Report itself is dated July 25, 1940.

optimistic view of the prospect of their being able to engage, at short notice, in a battle forty miles away and on French soil.

Experience had already shown the vital importance of close co-ordination of the allied armies in any operation. General Billotte had been appointed the co-ordinator at the conference at Mons on May 12, but in practice, the measure of co-ordination fell far short of what was required if the movements of the three allied armies were to be properly controlled.

Except for the issue of orders to retire from the Dyle (obtained only after I had sent Major-General Eastwood to General Billotte's headquarters to represent my views), I received no written orders from the French First Group of Armies, though at the meetings between General Billotte and myself which took place from time to time, we always found ourselves in complete agreement. Unfortunately, however, General Billotte had been seriously, and, as it turned out, fatally injured in a motor accident returning from the conference which he and I had attended at Ypres on the night of May 21. General Blanchard succeeded him in command of the French First Group of Armies, and presumably succeeded to the function of co-ordination although this was never officially confirmed.

I telegraphed to the Secretary of State pointing out that co-ordination was essential with armies of three different nations, and that I personally could not undertake any measure of co-ordination in the forthcoming operations as I was already actively engaged on my Eastern and Southern fronts and also threatened on my Lines of Communication.

Nevertheless, I saw General Blanchard and proposed to him that to implement our part of the Weygand plan, we should stage an attack southwards with two British divisions, one French division and the French Cavalry Corps. So far as we were concerned the attack could not take place till the 26th at the earliest owing to the reliefs which were in progress, and the need to assemble 5th and 50th Divisions. I also asked General Blanchard to enquire from G.H.Q how such an operation could be synchronized with the attack from the line of the Somme which was said to be in process of preparation. These negotiations, as will be seen, were later continued by Sir Ronald Adam on my behalf. I emphasized, both to the Secretary of State and to General Blanchard, that the principal effort must come from the south, and that the operation of the northern forces could be nothing more than a sortie.

I never received any information from any source as to the exact location of our own or enemy forces on the far side of the gap; nor did I receive any details or timings of any proposed attack from that direction. . . .

On May 23 Calais was finally isolated. . . .

Information received at this time indicated that two enemy armoured divisions were converging on Calais and two more, supported by a motorized S.S. [*Schutz-Staffel*] division, on St. Omer. A fifth armoured division appeared to be moving on Béthune. . . .

During May 24, I had simultaneously to prepare for a counter-attack southwards on the 26th and also to press forward with the strengthening of the canal line.

To make the detailed arrangements for the counter-attack I appointed the Commander of the 3rd Corps, Lieutenant-General Sir Ronald Adam, who on my behalf, continued negotiations with General Blanchard, and with the Commander of the French 5th Corps, General Altmeyer. [*sic*.]

The final plan was for a counter-attack with three French and two British divisions under the command of General Altmeyer. As a first stage, on the evening of May 26, bridgeheads were to be established south of the Scarpe, and the main attack was to start the following morning, with the objective Plouvain–Marquion–Cambrai. Sir Ronald Adam with three divisions (two British and one French) was to advance east of the Canal du Nord, and General Altmeyer with two French divisions to the west of the Canal du Nord, his right being covered by the French Cavalry Corps. This attack was never carried out for reasons which will presently appear. . . .

On May 25, enemy activity intensified. . . .

At about 7 a.m. on May 25, news was received that in the late evening of May 24 the enemy had attacked the Belgian 4th Corps on the Lys with a force reported to be of four divisions, supported by tanks. The attack penetrated to a depth of one and a half miles on a front of thirteen miles between Menin and Desselghem.

It was fast becoming a matter of vital importance to keep open our line of communication to the coast through a corridor which was hourly narrowing. It was no longer possible to count on using the main road Estaires–Cassel–Dunkirk, while the news which had just been received made it certain that before long, the whole area east of the Yser canal would be in the hands of the enemy, since there was, in fact, no satisfactory defensive position between the Lys and the Yser canal. There seemed, therefore, to be a serious risk of the Belgian right becoming separated from the British left at Menin, and of the Belgian Army being forced to fall back in a northerly, rather than in a westerly direction. I considered it vitally urgent to prolong the British front without delay northwards to Ypres, along the old Ypres–Comines canal, now practically dry, and round Ypres itself to the line of the Yser canal.

As an immediate step, 12th Lancers were sent off early on 25th to watch the left flank of 2nd Corps on the Lys, and gain touch with the right flank of the Belgians.

The remaining infantry brigade of 48th Division (143rd) was later placed under 2nd Corps, and a pioneer battalion sent to begin preparations for the defence of Ypres in case Belgian measures for the purpose should prove inadequate.

The Belgians had at this time one division in reserve between Menin and Ypres, and this was ordered to counter-attack at 2 p.m. However it is doubtful whether it was found possible ever to launch this counter-attack. Orders were also issued for the Belgian 1st Corps to come into line on the right of their 4th Corps between Ghelewe and Ledeghem; this move was carried out on May 26.

Sir John Dill (who had now become C.I.G.S.) and whom I had asked to visit me, arrived on the morning of May 25, and I explained the position to him. He then telegraphed to the Prime Minister and to the Secretary of State, that there could be no disguising the seriousness of the situation. He added that in his opinion the proposed counter-attack to the south could not be an important affair in view of the enemy attacks which had penetrated the Belgian defences.

General Blanchard arrived during Sir John Dill's visit and took part in our discussions.

During the day the Belgians continued to withdraw in a north-westerly direction under enemy pressure. Reports also indicated that a fresh enemy attack would take place next day on the northern end of the Lys position. . . .

By 6 p.m. that night (May 25) I was convinced that the steps I had taken to secure my left flank would prove insufficient to meet the growing danger in the north. . . .

The gap between the British left and the Belgian right which had been threatening the whole day, might at any time become impossible to close; were this to happen, my last hope of reaching the coast would be gone. At this time, it will be recalled, I had no reserves beyond a single cavalry regiment, and the two divisions (5th and 50th) already earmarked for the attack southwards.

The French First Army, which was not affected in the same way as the B.E.F. by the situation which was developing on the Belgian front, had, it will be remembered, agreed to provide three divisions and the Cavalry Corps for this attack. Therefore, even if no British divisions could be made available, the possibility of carrying out the operation would not be entirely precluded. I did realize however that the French were unlikely to take the offensive unless British support was forthcoming.

Even so, however, the situation on my northern flank was deteriorating so rapidly that I was convinced that there was no alternative but to occupy, as quickly as troops could be made available, the line of the Ypres–Comines canal and the positions covering Ypres. . . .

I immediately communicated my decision to the headquarters of the French First Group of Armies, but I was unable to get into personal touch with General Blanchard that evening as he was visiting the Belgian G.H.Q. at Bruges. However, I went to see General Blanchard at his headquarters at Attiches early next morning (May 26). . . . I found that General Blanchard also feared the collapse of the Belgian Army and felt that the time for a counter-attack southwards was past. Indeed he had already decided that the situation on both flanks made it necessary to withdraw.

After an hour's discussion, we arrived at a joint plan for the withdrawal of the main bodies behind the line of the Lys. These arrangements were subject to there being no further deterioration in the Belgian situation.

With this decision, there vanished the last opportunity for a sortie. . . . I had not so far discussed with General Blanchard a further withdrawal to the sea. However, the possibility could not have been absent from his mind; nor was it absent from mine, for although up to now no instructions had been given authorising me to undertake such an operation, I had, as I have said, foreseen the possibility of such a move being forced upon us.

I returned from the conference at General Blanchard's headquarters at about 10.30 a.m. on May 26 to find a telegram from the Secretary of State which read:

. . . I have had information all of which goes to show that French offensive from Somme cannot be made in sufficient strength to hold any prospect of functioning with your Allies in the North. Should this prove to be the case you will be faced with a situation in which the safety of the B.E.F. will predomi-nate. In such conditions only course open to you may be to fight your way back to West where all beaches and ports east of Gravelines will be used for embarkation. Navy will provide fleet of ships and small boats and R.A.F. would give full support. As withdrawal may have to begin very early preliminary plans should be urgently prepared.

. . . Prime Minister is seeing M. Reynaud tomorrow afternoon when whole situation will be clarified including attitude of French to the possible move. . . .

I replied that a plan for withdrawal north-westward had been agreed with the French that morning; I added that the news from the Belgian front was disquieting, and concluded by saying:

. . . I must not conceal from you that a great part of the B.E.F. and its equipment will inevitably be lost even in best circumstances.

Later in the day, I had a further telegram from the War Office which read as follows:

. . . Prime Minister had conversation M. Reynaud this afternoon. Latter fully explained to him the situation and resources French Army. It is clear that it will not be possible for French to deliver attack on the south in sufficient strength to enable them to effect junction with Northern Armies. In these circumstances no course open to you but to fall back upon coast. . . . M. Reynaud communicating General Weygand and latter will no doubt issue orders in this sense forthwith. You are now authorized to operate towards coast forthwith in conjunction with French and Belgian Armies.

MAY 24: PÉTAIN AND WEYGAND BEGIN TO TALK OF AN
ARMISTICE

The two men on whose collaboration I had believed that I could count to stimulate the spirit of the nation were not long in adopting a language quite different from that which I was hoping to hear from them.

During the evening of the 23rd the situation of the Northern Armies became, as we have seen, suddenly worse. Gort relinquished his hold on Arras, and withdrew towards the coast. The Weygand plan collapsed. From that moment the idea was born in the mind of Weygand, and *a fortiori*, in that of Pétain, that the hour was approach-ing when France ought to lay down her arms. It was on the 24th, during our daily conference that the plan, against which I was to have to struggle, was revealed to me. Baudouin was there. Here is his account:[1]

Friday, May 24, 1940

At 10.30 a.m. General Weygand came into the Prime Minister's room, and found Marshal Pétain already there. I remained throughout this meeting, which lasted until a quarter to one.

[1] *Op. cit.*, pp. 43-5, *passim.*

On entering, the General whispered to me, 'The situation is very serious, for the English are falling back on the ports instead of attacking to the south.' He told the Prime Minister that . . . the English had abandoned Arras without being compelled by the Germans to do so, and appeared to be retreating in the direction of the ports. This was contrary to the formal instructions given by General Weygand to the British Army according to the plans shown on Wednesday the 22nd to the British Prime Minister and approved by him . . . General Weygand . . . went on, 'It is impossible to command an army which remains dependent on London in the matter of military operations. Lord Gort has certainly not taken it upon himself to modify the strategy of his forces, and the order must have come from London. All this is the more regrettable in that yesterday and during the night Besson's army group, coming from the south, reached the Somme, while Colonel de Gaulle's armour is at Boves, ready to issue forth to assist the southern army to move north.' . . . General Weygand estimated that if the junction of the forces in the north and south was not effected rapidly it would be very difficult to avoid the capitulation of the Allied Armies in the north. . . .

The Prime Minister asked General Weygand what view he would take of the situation in the event of these divisions being compelled to surrender. The General declared that all the French troops would be in position on the Somme, the Ailette canal, and the Aisne, . . . it would be very difficult to resist the German drive. . . .

. . . M. Paul Reynaud said that even if the armies in the north surrendered, and even in the event of war with Italy, his fixed determination was to fight on to the end. . . . He asked General Colson if it would not be a good idea to call to the colours the remainder of the classes 1939 and 1940. The General replied that there would be neither arms, clothes, nor blankets for these young recruits. He further stated that there was a lack of equipment for the remnants of Corap's army which was in process of being reorganized in the interior. Not even enough rifles were available; at the outside there were five thousand, and they were of an old pattern. . . .

Thus, when Weygand told me that it was going to be very difficult 'to resist the German drive', did I think that there was the slightest reason for flinching? Did my tone of voice become less firm? My reply is there: 'Even if the northern Armies capitulate, even if Italy declares war, it is my fixed resolve to fight on to the end.'

Throughout his account, Baudouin carefully refrains from placing the word 'armistice' in Weygand's mouth.

Yet, during the evening, Weygand summoned Baudouin to Vincennes. The situation had become still worse.

'The situation is very bad,' Weygand told him.[1] 'Early this afternoon I had a telegram . . . to the effect that the English army had adopted, and put into effect, the strategy of a retreat of forty kilometres. In these circumstances I was compelled to abandon Wednesday's plans. . . .'

[1] Weygand, *Rappelé au service*, pp. 45–7, *passim*.

'General Weygand', adds Baudouin, 'seemed to me overcome by the defection of the English. . . .' 'Overcome', he also was overcome!

This alleged defection, which supplied the Vichy anti-British propaganda with one of its favourite complaints, was the result, Weygand now tells us,[1] of the withdrawal under enemy pressure of our 1st Light Mechanized Division which was covering the right of the British forces occupying Arras. General Franklyn, who commanded these forces, pointed out to Gort the danger of encirclement which threatened him, and in the evening received the order to retreat. It is a strange thing that Gort, in his report, is less categoric about this point than Weygand is in his book. On the other hand, Weygand reproaches Gort with not having warned him of his withdrawal. The reproach, it must be admitted, is a grave one.

Let us take up Baudouin's account again. After complaints about the British 'defection', the two men exchanged opinions. They revealed to us what lay within their innermost hearts.

The General [continues Baudouin] repeated to me what he had said that very morning in the Premier's room, namely that France had gone to war without the means of carrying it on, without tanks, anti-tank guns, aeroplanes, anti-aircraft defence or a solid Eastern Front. There was neither military nor diplomatic preparation. 'It was criminal', he said, 'in these circumstances to have declared war on September 3rd. It is inconceivable that whoever was responsible for the French Army at that time did not tell the Government that the state of the army did not permit it to fight.'[2]

I told General Weygand that it was not only the material means that were lacking but also the soul. . . . I added that I was impressed by the faltering which I saw on all sides, and by the collapse of that false governing class which was at the head of the French administration. I wondered if the morale of the army and of the country was good enough to withstand a surrender on the part of the forces in the north. . . .

I said to him, 'We have only one object—to get France out of the ordeal which she is undergoing so as to allow her, even if defeated in the field, to rise again. Perhaps the terrible evils which she is suffering will in the end turn out to have been to her advantage. Out of evil may come good.' With tears in his eyes the General told me that he shared my fears. . . .

The significance of these sentences which were exchanged certainly needs no commentary. But once again a word is missing in Baudouin's account, that of 'armistice'. We shall see later why this is so. The Committee of Inquiry, struck by the omission, thrashed the matter out in its sitting of July 26, 1949. The truth has been revealed in a dialogue between one of the commissioners, M. Dhers, and Baudouin.

[1] *Ibid.*, p. 118.
[2] To form an estimate about their author, from these words, one must compare them with what we have heard Weygand say in public before July 4, 1939, at Lille: 'I believe that the French Army has a greater value than at any other time in its history: it possesses first-class material . . . an excellent morale and a distinguished Supreme Command.'

M. Dhers: '. . . Your reply has already been that, in your opinion, defeat was practically a foregone conclusion after May 16.'

M. Paul Baudouin: 'That is quite correct.'

M. Dhers: 'Therefore, on May 24, the date of your conversation with General Weygand, you were already reconciled to an armistice, before General Weygand had made an official request for it. I even recall . . . that I had asked you: "But, tell me, what prompted you at that time to be in favour of an armistice?" . . . You answered me: "General Weygand convinced me that it was necessary. The military leaders convinced me of it."'

M. Paul Baudouin: 'I was certain . . . on May 24 that the struggle was lost. In actual fact, it can be said that everyone, all those who were in touch with M. Paul Reynaud, were certain about it. M. Paul Reynaud himself on May 24 was certain that we had lost the fight. He kept talking about fighting on to the end, of fighting to save our honour, but the battle itself, the battle of France, was lost. . . .

'This May 24, if I am not mistaken, was . . . the tragic day on which he (Weygand) saw the orders which he had given, not carried out, and that his intention of crushing . . . the German advance in a vice, which was to be screwed tight around Bapaume . . . was impossible. That was our last hope. He knew that this thin barrier which he was erecting on the Somme and the Aisne could not stem the German flood for long, once the Germans threw themselves in assault against the slender and too thinly manned French line.

'Can you, therefore, find something unusual in the fact that a man, who was probably the best informed of all, because he was the first to be informed and at the hub of all military information—that was my daily task, my job, I could say—should have anticipated on May 24 that the fight was to come to an end? Yes; it was certain that it had to do so.'

Such is the testimony of Baudouin. This testimony is as decisive as regards its fundamental significance as it is irrecusable in so far as concerns its author, since the latter has never ceased to take a pride in having joined his fortunes with those of Weygand.

Thus, I knew on the 24th that Weygand, and with him Pétain, were to form a coalition in order to demand an armistice, if, as unfortunately there was reason to believe, the battle which was to be waged on the Somme were lost. It was a cruel betrayal for a man who had just, a few days previously, placed his confidence in them!

It was in vain that I pointed out to them that we ought not at any price to be separated from our Allies; that the only possible independence for France was in a close union with the two great Anglo-Saxon democracies; that France could, with all the less reason, prove to be the only enemy of Germany which capitulated; that she still retained intact the second empire in the world and the second largest fleet in Europe; that, finally and most important of all, France had pledged her word—and her honour forbade her to break it—to refuse to enter into a separate armistice. To this Pétain replied in a soft and somewhat quavering voice: 'You are considering things from an international viewpoint, and I am looking at them from a national one.'

As if the honour and independence of France were not essentially questions of national importance! Pétain maintained that the defeat of France would reverse the European situation to such a degree that an armistice would be inevitable. 'In any case, it is impossible for the Government', he said 'to flee from danger by abandoning the French people and leaving it at grips with the enemy.'

This thesis was supported by Weygand, but with a characteristic twist. It was necessary, he added, to preserve the Army intact so that it could maintain order. The duty of the Government, he stated, was, should the enemy enter Paris, to await him there, just as the Roman senators formerly awaited the barbarians, seated in their curule chairs. It goes without saying that, if we had followed this advice, Hitler would have thrown us all into prison so that he could immediately replace us in power with his own creatures. Nothing could have served his plans better. Is it not a fact that Rauschning, in *Hitler Speaks*, had warned us of the Führer's intention to wage a political war at the same time as a war of arms?

Pétain and Weygand seemed to me patriots who were deceiving themselves. They seemed solely concerned with immediate interests, and were refusing to place the abiding interests of their country in the foreground. I was struck by the off-hand manner which these two men (whom a popular referendum would, without doubt, have considered as the men most qualified to represent French honour) treated the plighted word of France. But, it will be said, why in these circumstances did you not summon them to give way or to resign? What stopped me was not the gratitude which bound me to them, but the overriding interests of the country. I had just replaced one Commander-in-Chief. Was I going within five days to appoint another to the French Army? And that at a time when the crucial stage, on which hung the invasion of the whole of France, was about to begin! And, above all, could I run the risk of dealing a deadly blow at France's rising morale!

On whom, moreover, could I confer the succession of Weygand? Except for Georges, the unlucky leader of the north-east front, three names at that time carried any prestige with the Army: Huntziger, who, because he had allowed his front to be broken at Sedan, was the initial cause of the disaster; Giraud, who had the most fire, but had just been made prisoner; Billotte, who had just been killed in an accident. A great leader is a rare and fortunate discovery. He must be at the same time an intellectual and a fighter: 'When I go into battle, I take my big stick with me', Foch used to say. We fell far short of having that galaxy of stars we had in 1914, such as Joffre, Foch, Gallieni, Fayolle, Franchet d'Esperey, Sarrail, Dubail, Maunoury, Castelnau, Mangin, Maistre, Guillaumat. Contrary to Germany, France, during the previous war, had wasted the blood of the *élite*, and many of those who could have become great leaders had fallen. In September, 1939, Gamelin was the only one of our generals who had reached the rank of battalion commander in 1914. All the rest were then captains and lieutenants, and it is known what an enormous percentage of losses we incurred amongst subaltern officers.

And, above all, this war was quite different from the preceding one! The Imperial Germany of William II only waged upon us the traditional war of arms. Now Hitler was waging a total war. He was proving a powerful political agitator, whose fifth column had penetrated everywhere, and who was using every method of modern publicity against us, from the illustrated picture postcard showing a British soldier inviting a French soldier to be the first to plunge into a bath of blood, to the most powerful of all—unknown in 1914 and which, in the sphere of morale played a decisive role in the present war —radio. This was a terrible weapon of war, which Hitler used against France, and Mussolini against our North African colonies. The war which Nazi propaganda had begun in 1933 kept on striving unceasingly to sow division amongst the French, and to lower their morale. If I had put my disagreement with Pétain and Weygand to the Council of Ministers, the rumour of our conflict would soon have spread throughout Paris. Berlin would have immediately got to know about it, and would have put it out on the radio. To French public opinion the problem of knowing if it was or was not necessary to fight on would have seemed to be one of a military nature. Which men were the more qualified in its eyes, both in the sphere of military competence and as regards the honour of the nation, than the two glorious leaders of the French Army? What profit would the gentleman, who over the Stuttgart wireless was trying every day to undermine French morale, have drawn from this? He would have denounced this 'war-monger sated with French blood', who, after having thrown us into war, was now trying to prevent us getting out of it! 'He no doubt considers', he would have added, 'that not enough French blood has flowed to suit the taste of Mr. Churchill.' What a wave of demoralization would have submerged the country!

Pétain and Weygand knew exactly the support which they could draw from this situation and from the eulogies which I myself had just heaped upon them before the country. Whoever is ignorant of this state of affairs cannot understand the development of the events which were to follow. That is why I drew up the following plan: I would avoid a rupture by postponing any discussion on an armistice, and would prepare, with the Army General Staff which was directly under me, to continue the war in North Africa. I would reshuffle my Cabinet by getting rid of such members whom I had reason to fear would vote in favour of an armistice on the day when the question arose.[1] This was to be the second surgical operation, which I intended to perform only a few days after that which I was going to carry out on the Supreme Command. I informed the President of the Republic, the Presidents of the Chambers and in addition Mandel and Chautemps who had shown themselves to be loyal to me on the occasion of my first Cabinet difficulties. I hoped that, if we were defeated in the battle of France, the patriotism of Pétain and Weygand would be convinced by the unanimous decision of my reorganized Cabinet, and that I would thus avoid a rupture which I considered to be disastrous. Up to the end I tried to avoid this rupture which, by my opposition to our 'glorious military leaders', would have cut France into two.

THE MEETING OF THE WAR COMMITTEE ON MAY 25

We have seen earlier that, on the morning of May 25, Major Fauvelle brought us in Paris the news that the capitulation of the Northern Armies was imminent.

Our morning conference opened that day with this sombre threat hanging over it. The reaction of Pétain and Weygand was to become more marked: it would be necessary to ask for an armistice, and thus contrive the means to retain an army with which to maintain domestic order. The Government must stay in Paris, and surrender to the enemy.

But, on this subject again, I ought to give the reader other evidence than my own statements. The language which Pétain and Weygand used to me on the 24th and 25th, they used again before several witnesses on the 26th, whilst I was in London, that is to say, on the very day following the War Committee which met in the evening of the 25th. In my absence Pétain, Weygand, Baudouin and Chautemps spoke freely to each other, and during their conversation revealed their innermost thoughts. We have the irrecusable testimony of Baudouin on this point.

Before coming to his account, let us quote the version which Rollin gives in his *Journal* of his visit on the 26th at eleven in the morning to Vincennes. Weygand said to him: 'Do you remember Titus Livy, the

---

[1] It will be seen that, amongst the Ministers whom I did not include in my new team, were several about whom I entertained no suspicions as regards this question.

Roman senator? . . . When the Barbarians—and we were the Barbarians then—invaded Rome . . . the senators remained on their curule chairs and continued to deliberate. . . . I well remember that, after a Gaul pulled the beard of a . . . senator and the latter struck him with his rod, all the Senate . . . was massacred, but . . . this attitude possessed a certain grandeur.'

In his deposition of July 28, 1949, before the Committee of Inquiry, Rollin alluded to this interview. Here is an extract from his statement:

'General Weygand—and this shows clearly that he was harbouring mental reservations of a political nature, and reservations concerning capitulation and an armistice from this time—spoke in the following fashion to me personally when I went to see him at his Headquarters at Vincennes. I clearly recall his words. He said to me: "You know, I have not slept the whole night. I have spent a long time in thought. There can be no room for hesitation. The Government must remain in Paris, and allow itself to be captured. There can be no alternative course of action." . . . I was so surprised by these words when he uttered them to me that I thought it was my duty to give an account of them to the President of the Republic. He will perhaps remember this. I went to see him and said: "Listen, I am quite astounded. Here is what General Weygand has been saying to me." I still remember President Lebrun, throwing up his arms and saying to me: "But whatever does he want? He must be mad. What is at the back of his mind? It is incomprehensible. Where does he want to lead us?"'

And in his *Journal* Rollin attributes to M. Lebrun the following words: 'Does he want to allow me to suffer the same fate as Schuschnigg? How can a Government, which is a prisoner, freely act in the conduct of a war?'

Weygand used the same words on the same day and also during the morning to Baudouin, who writes:[1]

'General Weygand asked me to go and see him at . . . Vincennes. . . . "My opinion is [the General said] that if the Government wishes to preserve intact the morale of the army, which is improving every day, and if it wishes to avoid the growth of a revolutionary movement in Paris, it ought to announce that it will remain in the capital come what may, and that it will retain control even at the risk of being taken by the enemy. It is a matter of the maintenance of order and the preservation of power. Let us remember that when we entered Rome—and we were the barbarians in those days—we found the senators sitting in their curule chairs."'

Thus as the morale of the Army was growing better, it was necessary

[1] *Op. cit.*, p. 56.

to preserve this Army in order to maintain order amongst the French people! To complete the recovery in the morale of the Army, the Government had to deliver itself into the hands of the enemy! Unless this were done there would be revolution!

Weygand understood imperfectly the mentality of the nation. And, moreover, had the German Army tolerated revolutionary disturbances in Belgium, in Holland or in any of the countries which it had occupied?

'The General confirmed', continued Baudouin, 'that our troops were fighting well on the front of the Somme and the Aisne, but that if we succumbed to superior numbers and weight of material it would be a terrible task to hold the Germans. "I met them at Rethondes twenty-two years ago. Shall I have to meet them again with the parts reversed?"'

Thus it had become a question of an armistice after the politicians had been got out of the way.

And what about Pétain? Baudouin met him at the Rue Saint-Dominique after having left Weygand at 11.30 a.m. He also confirmed to Baudouin the statements that he and Weygand had made to me during our talks of the 24th and 25th.

'At midday', writes Baudouin,[1] 'Marshal Pétain came to see me. . . . The Marshal told me that he did not believe in a fight to the finish. . . . A part of the army must be saved, for without an army grouped round some leaders to maintain order a true peace is impossible. . . .'

'A true peace.' We shall see later that the Pétain-Weygand Government was indeed to try and get out of the enemy a peace treaty.

This was far from being the whole story. These gentlemen proceeded openly in their designs, for Baudouin went at four o'clock to sound Chautemps. Matters were already in a very advanced stage. Indeed, Baudouin found a Chautemps who was immediately agreeable upon the need of forming a military government to negotiate with the enemy: 'No civilian,' said Chautemps, 'will have the requisite authority to negotiate, and we shall have to do that soon.'[2]

An unforeseen disagreement, however, took place. Who was this military leader to be? Pétain? Weygand? Chautemps had already chosen his man, and Baudouin also. Chautemps was in favour of Pétain; Baudouin in favour of Weygand, whom he considered much superior in character to the Marshal.

This is what was being debated in Paris amongst certain of my

[1] *Ibid.*, p. 57.
[2] *Loc. cit.* Here is the passage from which I have taken this extract, *in extenso*: 'I saw M. Chautemps at 4.0 p.m. He was very alarmed at the situation, and wondered if there was any point in carrying on the struggle much longer. He stated his dislike of Daladier, whom he considered unworthy to be at the Quai d'Orsay, and he declared to me that it was necessary for France to rally round Marshal Pétain for "no civilian will have the requisite authority to negotiate, and we shall have to do that soon". I replied that I thought General Weygand a much stronger character than the Marshal. "The General is out of the question", he answered quickly.'

colleagues—notably by our two glorious military leaders and a former President of the Council—whilst I was in London pleading the cause of France! These men, it will be seen, were preoccupied with a quite different matter from the business on which I was to bring back a report.[1]

That evening, at seven-thirty after this busy day, Baudouin punctually welcomed me when I arrived by plane at Le Bourget. Naturally, he told me not one word of his conversations, which he was to hide religiously from me, and which Mandel, in spite of intelligence services, did not himself know.[2]

Having now revealed to the reader the state of mind of Pétain, Weygand, Chautemps and Baudouin, let us go back for twenty-four hours. The War Committee met at the Elysée on the 25th at 7 p.m. At this moment, if I did not know all, at least I knew, as we have seen, that Pétain and Weygand were in favour of asking for an armistice on the day the battle of France was lost, and of allowing the Government to be captured in Paris. The tragedy of the situation was, therefore, increased for me by the preoccupation about the need to frustrate, without breaking with these individuals, the manœuvre which the meeting of the War Committee was going to give them the opportunity of putting into execution. Who in France would have forgiven me for depriving the Army at such a time of the leader whom I had just given it five days previously, and who had really succeeded in restoring to our troops the faith which they had lost in themselves? And, with even more reason, who would have forgiven me for quarrelling with the 'Victor of Verdun'.

The War Committee opened with a report by Weygand. He painted a most gloomy picture of the situation which, although justified by the event, contrasted nevertheless with the confidence which he paraded when he was describing a little while later the tactics which he had worked out to resist the Panzers, a confidence which he was to parade again, as we shall see, on June 11 before the Supreme Council at Briare. He reproached France with entering the war without having 'the equipment which she needed, or the military doctrine which was necessary'. 'It is probable', he prophesied, 'that she will pay dearly for this imprudence.' This was an audacious complaint in the mouth

[1] In a memorandum which he was to draw up in the United States in September, 1945, and which he later secretly circulated through France, this same Chautemps related that, on May 27, 1940, or the day after that on which he pronounced in favour of a government of 'negotiation', I told him that I had resolved to carry on with the struggle, whatever happened, by the side of the Allies. But he added,' I was completely in agreement with the decisions of my Prime Minister'.

[2] Baudouin writes (op. cit., p. 58) that he 'dropped me a word' about his conversation with Pétain. If he had done so, it could only have been to confirm to me what Pétain and Weygand had told me on the 24th and 25th about the need for keeping an army which to maintain order and to ask for an armistice, as soon as the battle of France was lost. It is a great pity that he did not 'drop me a word' about his talk with Chautemps.

of a man who only came to understand our plight, unfortunately, when everything was over, but who took good care not to recognize the responsibility which he bore for the 'great mistake' which he denounced.

Continuing his report, Weygand showed our Armies on the eve of having to hold the line of the Somme and the Aisne, against three times their own strength, and having only a fifth of their armoured forces left. This was the conclusion of his first explanation: it was necessary to fight until the line was completely broken in order to save our honour. But what was to happen if the battle which was to be engaged was lost? Weygand stated that he had 'the right to anticipate the worst, that is to say, what would happen if we no longer had at our disposal the northern group of Armies', and that he had 'anticipated' this 'in conversations which he had had with me'. Indeed, we have seen what his solution was. Baudouin, alluding to these conversations with Weygand and me, declared on July 12, 1949, to the Committee of Inquiry: 'General Weygand had raised the problem on the evening before—and *a fortiori* that very morning—to the President of the Council. . . .'

My reaction to the question propounded by Weygand has been summarized by M. Lebrun in the account which he has published of this discussion.[1] Here it is:

'M. Paul Reynaud, anticipating the case . . . in which we would have reason to fear a German advance on Paris, consulted the Supreme Command about the attitude which the Government should take.'

Weygand's reply was prompt, and it was categoric. M. Lebrun has recorded it: 'General Weygand said that in his opinion the Government should not leave the capital.' M. Lebrun adds: 'And this was what he [Weygand] was later to recall before the Riom Court.'

Thus, what Weygand was asking for was an armistice, and, as a corollary, the capture of the Government.

I cut short all discussion on this subject with a brief sentence. 'There can be no question', I said in substance, 'of allowing the Government to fall into Hitler's hands.' Reviewing then the places to which the Government could transfer its seat, I pronounced in favour of Bordeaux, a step towards North Africa. This is recorded by Rollin in his *Journal*, 'The question of the future departure of the Government was raised, and even, if circumstances required, of transferring it outside Metropolitan France.'

The matter was, therefore, settled. The agenda had been dealt with, and it only remained to close the debate. M. Lebrun, who was presiding, reopened it. Obviously impressed by Weygand's account, he came

[1] *Témoignage*, pp. 72-3.

back to the problem which, I believed, had, once and for all, been put aside. But it was in no wise, as Weygand has asserted, to ask for an armistice. The hypothesis which he contemplated was quite different: 'Suppose', he said,[1] 'that after his initial successes in France, the enemy renews his proposal to cease hostilities as he did on the morrow of the Polish campaign, the Government must be in a position to examine the proposal, even if it is only for the purpose of rejecting it at their leisure, that is to say, outside the grasp of the enemy. We should not, therefore, hesitate to leave Paris if the circumstances require it.'

This observation revived the discussion which I had done my best to silence. Seeing it thus digress, I recalled the formal pledges which bound us to Britain, and I stressed the determination of Churchill to fight to the bitter end.

Weygand admitted that we were pledged to Britain, but demanded an immediate examination of the problem with her. At the same time, he changed his attitude about the struggle to safeguard our national honour. The gist of what he said was that we must open the eyes of our Allies to the peril which France was running, if the Army, because it had been sacrificed to save our national honour, was not strong enough to ensure the maintenance of public order.

This, as we know, had become an obsession with Weygand. It was a fear which was to recur as a perpetual refrain in his statements.

Pétain, for his part, compared the military effort and the sufferings of each of the two Allies, and concluded by raising doubts upon the equality of their respective obligations. He tried to dissipate the idea of national honour.

I had decided to go to London on the following day in an attempt to obtain from Churchill, on the promptings of our Ambassador in Rome, certain concessions in order to prevent Italy falling on us. Later I shall give an account of this interview. I was certainly to use Pétain's state of mind as an argument with Churchill and his colleagues. It goes without saying that I refrained from taking the step demanded by Weygand.[2] My final words to the War Committee were, moreover, that they should remember that we were pledged to Britain.

On the following day Weygand passed, according to Baudouin,[3] the following judgement on the meeting: 'The discussion', he

[1] These are his own words, as he gives them himself (*op. cit.*, pp. 72–3).

[2] This was what Baudouin was to note as soon as I had returned to Paris that evening. Here is what he said about it to the Committee of Inquiry on July 28, 1949:

'When I went . . . towards the end of the afternoon to meet M. Paul Reynaud at the airport, the first question which I asked him was, "What were British reactions to the report which you were to make on the probable event that we would not be able . . . to continue the struggle?" . . . I was astounded to hear the President of the Council tell me that he had not tackled the problem, that he had spoken chiefly of the problem of Italy.' To be astounded, he must have known me very imperfectly.

[3] *Op. cit.*, p. 56.

commented, 'lacked constructive ideas. In particular the removal of the Government to Bordeaux seems to have been insufficiently thought out and not even thoroughly understood.'

This is the impression which Weygand had retained of our deliberations but a bare few hours after the meeting. It is, therefore, quite natural that he should sum it up in his deposition at the Riom trial in the following words:

'On May 25 General Weygand was present at the Elysée from seven p.m. to nine-thirty p.m. at a meeting of the War Cabinet. There he made a complete report on the situation. This report inspired the Government to discuss forthwith the methods of its departure from Paris.'[1] That is all. Nothing unusual, therefore, impressed Weygand in my attitude or, moreover, in that of my colleagues.

THE MINUTES OF THE WAR COMMITTEE OF MAY 25 ARE FALSE ONES

To produce 'wittingly . . . a false document',
Charles Serre, Rapporteur Général of the
Committee of Enquiry.

Five years later Weygand was to switch the parts which had been played. By then victory has been assured. It was no longer he who had demanded an armistice. It was the other members of the War Committee: myself, for example!

At the hearing on July 31, 1945, of the Pétain trial, he employed a phrase which he had extracted, according to him, from the minutes of the War Committee of May 25. This phrase, which was attributed to me, runs as follows: 'It cannot be said that our opponent will grant us an immediate armistice.' And Weygand ejaculated: 'Thus it was, gentlemen, that I heard the word armistice spoken for the first time, a word which I had never uttered up to then, for there was not any occasion to use it.'

This was the beginning of a campaign against me which gained ground even abroad. Thus, Mr. Langer, Professor of History at Harvard University, was to write in Our Vichy Gamble, which appeared in 1947, that at this critical hour (May 25) every problem was examined during an important consultation by the War Committee; that Weygand stressed the gravity of the situation, but recognized with myself that the French Army ought to fight to the death to save its honour. 'Then', he writes, 'the President of the Council thought for a while, and from his own lips fell for the first time, the fateful word, Armistice.'

The Committee of Inquiry set up by Leopold III was in its turn to

[1] Let us ignore the confusion which Weygand makes between the War *Committee* and the War *Cabinet*.

take up this thesis of Weygand. In its *Rapport*, also published in 1947 the Committee observed:[1] 'And it should be noted that already at this time, in the French War Committee, the word "armistice" had been uttered. Indeed, M. Reynaud continued: "Taking this into account, it cannot be said that our opponent will grant us an immediate armistice. Is it not indispensable to avoid the capture of the Government if the enemy enters Paris?"'

And the authors of the *Rapport*, laying bare their own motives, add: 'These words and the date on which they were uttered must not be forgotten; they must be compared with the angry and unjust speech which this same Paul Reynaud uttered over the wireless on May 28 to abuse the King and the Belgian Army, and place on them the responsibility for defeat.'

Now, this phrase, which Weygand was using against me, I had, as he himself knew, struck out with my own hand from the draft minutes which had been drawn up by Baudouin, and which the latter, conforming to practice, had, immediately he had drafted them, subjected to my approval. Indeed, Baudouin himself gave evidence on July 12, 1949 before the Committee of Inquiry that he had at that time informed Weygand of my corrections. Weygand was not, therefore, ignorant of the fact that the phrase in question had been struck out by me, and that it ought not, consequently, to have appeared in the minutes. Weygand was able, at the Pétain trial, to call *minutes* a document which was only a *draft* of them, and it was just the same as if he was thus able to produce 'wittingly . . . a false document'. To this, Baudouin, who was obviously ill at ease, answered: 'I don't think that General Weygand has wittingly produced a false document. I've seen him since, a long time afterwards, and I said to him: "Here is what happened." He was very surprised at my words, and told me that he was entirely ignorant of the second version of the minutes.'[2]

Whatever be the truth of the matter, Weygand submitted, on May 24, 1949, to the Committee a photostat of the minutes, bearing my written corrections of Baudouin's draft. Why did he do such a thing? The reason is because, in June, 1948, or eleven months before the above-mentioned book of Baudouin had appeared in which the latter revealed the text of the *draft minutes* as these texts emerged after my corrections.[3]

---

[1] p. 50.

[2] Is it necessary to observe that the expression is incorrect? A *War Committee* is, in this respect, comparable to a diplomatic conference. The secretary of a meeting of this kind has the duty of summarizing the discussion, but the document which he draws up is simply a *draft*. He should submit it to everyone who has spoken. It is only after having incorporated the corrections on the latter that the text of the draft becomes authentically *minutes*. Later it will be seen that the aforesaid *draft* was not sent to M. Lebrun or to Campinchi, both of whom joined in the discussion.

[3] Baudouin, *op. cit.*, pp. 50–6.

Baudouin was, moreover, to admit without demur that the draft which he drew up had only a relative authority. When he was questioned on this point on July 19, 1949, by the Committee of Inquiry, he stressed in these words the subjective nature of this tentative document: 'I have given, according to my impression (and it is only my own opinion), an exact account of the meeting.'

Was Weygand, who was not ignorant of this aspect of the problem, prepared, as in all honesty he should have been, to profit by the occasion offered him to disabuse public opinion which he had misled by his statements to the High Court? Was he going, before the Committee, to re-establish the truth, that is to say, to withdraw the accusation which he had made against me at the Pétain trial, using as his authority a document which he knew to be apocryphal? Not in the least. Commenting on my correction, he was this time to say, that he had 'heard' the phrase, which I had struck out. 'Someone', he said, 'mentioned armistice at that time.' Who is this 'someone'? He is careful not to say.[1]

But, it will be asked, why at the Pétain trial did you allow the phrase which Weygand extracted from the alleged minutes to use as a weapon against you to pass unchallenged? The explanation is simple. Here it is.

The Germans had discovered amongst the documents which our G.H.Q. had abandoned on June 15, 1940, in the station of a Charité-sur-Loire, a copy of the Baudouin *draft*. They quickly published it in the White Book which the Wilhelmstrasse issued in 1941.[2] As I was certain that I had never uttered the notorious phrase—for it clashed fundamentally with what I was thinking and doing both before and after May 25, 1940—I felt consequently sure that, if at the time, the document in question had been submitted to me, I would not have allowed the words which it falsely placed in my mouth to have remained. This is what I said in *La France a sauvé l'Europe* (vol. II, p. 181). What strengthened me in this conviction was that M. Lebrun also disputed the veracity of the *draft*, which he complained had not, contrary to the rules, been communicated to him.[3]

---

[1] In a new *volte-face* Weygand later wrote in *Rappelé au service* (p. 147): 'I remember (and the item of the minutes which were sent to me records it explicitly) that the President of the Council uttered a doubt on the willingness of the enemy to grant us "an immediate armistice". I noted that he had struck out in his own hand that part of the phrase in the item of the minutes which referred to an armistice.'

[2] White Book, No. 6: *Les Documents Secrets de L'Etat-Major Général Français*. German propaganda services had, moreover, published in the Press during the summer of 1940 most of the documents concerned.

[3] Baudouin stated to the Committee of Inquiry on July 12, 1949, that M. Lebrun had asked him to submit the aforesaid *draft* only to himself, Weygand and myself. He added that this draft had received the approval of Weygand, who had telephoned him in person to this effect, and that M. Lebrun, for his part, had sent a telephone message through M. Magre, his secretary-general, that he also approved it.

M. Lebrun disputed this assertion. Thus the controversy arose again before the

It goes without saying that, if I had remembered having corrected this text, I would have routed Weygand on the spot at the Pétain trial by showing that he was basing his account on a false piece of evidence. But those who are aware of the life which I was leading during those dramatic days[1] when the Wehrmacht was encircling our Northern Armies, and when Italy was preparing to throw herself on us, will not be surprised that something which was entirely personal was entirely obliterated from my mind.

My friend Campinchi, who was present at the War Committee as Minister of Marine, has been in his turn the victim of a no less odious manœuvre. In actual fact, *the draft of the minutes* ascribes to him the following statement:[2]

'It is for the military leaders to enlighten the Government and to advise it to yield with the words: "We can go no farther." . . . If the present Government has given its word to England, another Government would experience less inconvenience in signing a treaty of peace

Committee of Inquiry during the sitting of July 26, 1949, presided over by M. Louis Marin. Here is an extract of the discussion which took place upon this subject:

'*The President:* . . . As regards the very serious business of the minutes of the War Committee of the 25th, you have told us, to explain the three copies, that it was the President of the Republic, who asked you not to have too great a number typed. . . .

'*M. Michel Clemenceau:* . . . M. Baudouin has explained to us that these famous minutes or a draft of them was submitted to President Lebrun, who ordered him not to circulate more than three copies: one for him, one for General Weygand, and one for the President of the Council. . . .

'*M. Paul Baudouin:* . . . On leaving the War Committee, I went to see M. Paul Reynaud. He was talking to the President of the Republic. I said to him: "I am about to make a draft of the minutes, and I will submit them to you. Then I shall send the draft to the members of the War Committee." At that moment the President of the Republic said to me: "Make only a few copies, because we must be careful about leakages of information in war-time, and send me a copy. You will give one to the President of the Council and one to General Weygand." I was under the impression, moreover, that he mentioned the name of the President of the Council and that of General Weygand because it was these two who had spoken the most.

'*M. Michel Clemenceau:* . . . We have questioned M. Lebrun. He has made a formal and definite statement to us. He never gave an order to anyone to circulate the minutes to this or that individual. He is categoric on this point.

'*M. Paul Baudouin:* I sent him a copy, and I received through M. Magre the agreement of the President of the Republic.

'*M. Michel Clemenceau:* M. Magre is dead.

'*M. Paul Baudouin:* I can only tell you what happened!

'*M. Michel Clemenceau:* Yes, but M. Lebrun is categoric in his statement. He never saw the minutes, and he never gave any instructions about their circulation.

'*M. Paul Baudouin:* Well, what of it?'

[1] Rollin, alluding before the Committee of Inquiry (sitting of July 28, 1949) to the state of excitement in which I was living, ejaculated: 'All the more reason for this since at the time it was not minutes which counted, but seconds.'

I still remain perplexed, indeed, how, in this tragic tumult, I succeeded in snatching, out of the time at my disposal, the seconds necessary to correct the passages which concerned me.

[2] In the document this statement occurs on the last sheet, which is not reproduced in the White Book.

without that country's previous consent. The present Government has no other course but to resign.'

In his deposition of March 8, 1949, before the Committee of Inquiry, Weygand quoted the above statements, and added:

'I did not realize at the time that this was to be the policy. We saw it carried out later.'

How distressing it is to see the man in whom the French nation had, on the morrow of the Meuse disaster, placed its hope, descend to perverting the truth in such a degree!

Everyone who knew Campinchi was indignant at this piece of calumny, and the use to which it was put. This was so with other Ministers who were present at the War Committee: Louis Rollin and Laurent-Eynac.

When he was being heard by the Committee, the first stated on July 28, 1949:

'I must say that truly I have no kind of recollection that Campinchi ever uttered such words. Campinchi was a most scrupulous and loyal man. He was first and foremost so, and I cannot see how this honest and upright man could say: "We are pledged to Britain. We must get out of our pledge, but let us do it in a roundabout way. Let us perform the operation by indirect means." This was absolutely out of tune with Campinchi's character and with his whole behaviour, for he had been, from the outset, one of the most decided and resolute of those who opposed Hitler. . . . I certainly have the impression that he spoke, but it was certainly not to say what has been attributed to him. Decidedly not.'

As for Laurent-Eynac, whom I asked in October, 1949, to send me his recollections about the alleged utterances found in the *draft of the minutes* of this now historic sitting, he forwarded to me the following note.[1]

'I was present in my capacity of Air Minister at the War Committee of May 25, 1940.

'I was very surprised to learn from the reports of the Pétain trial that alleged minutes of this meeting were said to have attributed to M. Paul Reynaud words which would lead me to believe that he was entertaining the idea of an armistice. Not only have I no recollection of such a thing happening, but the President of the Council never stopped struggling to the very end against the advocates of an armistice.

'I have learned with a still greater astonishment that these same

[1] This note is dated October 25, 1949.

minutes attributed to my colleague, Campinchi, Minister of Marine, statements which represent him as harbouring the idea of an armistice, and suggesting that it should be begged by another Government of which we should be members. Such duplicity was quite contrary to his character. M. Campinchi also never ceased to oppose the idea of an armistice. He was, moreover, one of those who did so with the greatest energy and even with hot temper.'

When it was his turn to be heard by the Committee, Laurent-Eynac stated on November 29, 1949:

'[The] statements [of Campinchi] at previous meetings and at all the Councils of Ministers which followed give . . . a formal denial to the words . . . which have been attributed to him.'

On this point, M. Matteo Connet, who was at this time the head of Campinchi's secretariat, was also heard by the Committee. In his deposition of January 12, 1950, he indignantly protested against the words which his former chief is alleged to have uttered, and quoted in support details of actions which revealed him to be violently and unremittingly opposed to any idea of an armistice.

Why did Baudouin, breaking the rule, refrain from submitting to Campinchi the *draft* which he had drawn up? Pressed, on July 12 and 26, 1949, by the Committee of Inquiry to give an explanation on this point, he found himself incapable of offering a satisfactory reason.

Let us examine his statements. As we have seen, he alleges that M. Lebrun asked him to restrict the number of copies of the document to three. These were to be sent respectively to himself, to me, and to Weygand. Now, M. Lebrun has stated that he gave no such order, and that, moreover, he never saw the aforesaid draft. He has confirmed this statement orally to me. I have not, moreover, any more than he has, the slightest recollection of such an instruction being given.

Baudouin alleges then that it fell to me, as President of the Council, to review the whole of the text.[1] This is a strange idea. Each person is responsible for the words which he utters at a meeting of this kind. Does the President of the Council revise the reporting of the speeches and statements of Ministers even in a parliamentary debate?

Let us leave the matter there. But let me add, however, that I have been more distressed by the slander placed on the memory of that unyielding patriot, Campinchi, who was my friend, than by any intrigue woven against myself.

[1] Baudouin's text could certainly not fail to be improved by such a revision. Incidentally, I have pointed out in *La France a sauvé l'Europe* (vol. II, p. 189) one of the mistakes which is to be found there. This consists in placing Sedan in Corap's sector, when it was common knowledge that it lay within Huntziger's.

As regards my attitude concerning the armistice, we shall read later of the text of a telegram which I sent, a fortnight later, to Roosevelt, informing him of my intention to continue the war in North Africa, and even, if need arose, in our American possessions. We shall later see Weygand give an account himself of the disputes which I had to the very end, when at Bordeaux, about this question. And, finally, we shall see that my opposition to an armistice cost me fifty-six months in prison and nearly my life.

Finally, let us observe that it was only after victory had been won, when he was summoned before the High Court, that Weygand thought of his plan, which consisted in trying to implicate me in his own culpability, by making use, to my detriment, of a text which he knew to be false. During his long, written deposition at the Riom trial, whilst the event was fresh and thus the smallest details of this sitting of May 25 were still in his memory, Weygand did not utter a word about this incredible reversal in my attitude, of which he was to accuse me, five years later, at the Pétain trial.

Whatever be the truth of the affair, it was not without a feeling of stupefaction that I saw Weygand, in 1950, push his manœuvre even further in his book, *Rappelé au service*. Giving an account of June 16, 1940, the day on which I notified President Lebrun of my refusal to sue for an armistice, he quotes the statement attributed by Baudouin to Campinchi, whose apocryphal character had, however, been proved several months before by the Committee of Inquiry. But this time, in order to make the reader believe that the text is my own, he refrains, in citing this infamous phrase, *from naming Campinchi*: 'If the present Government has given its word to England, another Government would experience less inconvenience in signing a treaty of peace without that country's previous consent. The present Government has only to resign.' (*Minutes of the War Council* of May 25, 1940.)[1]

Such was the policy which, according to him, I was to carry out.

But three lines later he abandons this accusation, so unsupportable does it appear even to him, and he writes:

'One has just cause for thinking that the time came when M. Paul Reynaud, *after having opposed an armistice for a long time*,[2] judged that this decision in favour of it was absolutely necessary.'

Is it possible to reverse one's judgement to such a degree? If it were true that I had been, on May 25, a supporter of an armistice, how could Weygand write, in speaking about my attitude on June 16, that, until then, I had been opposed to it? The *volte-face* is as brusque as the contradiction is complete. Let us pass on. . . .

[1] pp. 234–5 (I).   [2] The italics are those of M. Reynaud.

MARCH–JUNE: ATTEMPTS MADE WITH A VIEW TO PREVENTING ITALY FROM ENTERING THE WAR

' . . . what he [Mussolini] wants is war, and, even if he were to obtain by peaceful means double what he claims, he would refuse.'   Ciano, Diary, May 27, 1940.

M. François-Poncet,[1] who, as we have seen, was our Ambassador to Rome during the eighteen months which preceded Italy's entry into the war, made, in 1945, a revelation which throws a sinister light on the intimate designs of Mussolini. He stated[2] that, during the 'phoney war', when the treacherous Italians only thought of enriching themselves by selling us war equipment,[3] Ciano did not hide from him what were 'his Master's ultimate intentions': 'When he saw me trying, in accordance with my instructions, to pin Italy down to a state of non-belligerency, and even to convert this into one of declared neutrality, he said to me with a frightful cynicism but not without frankness: "Don't waste your time in propaganda efforts. Your only propaganda is victories! If you win victories, we shall be on your side. If you don't we shall be against you."'

This cynicism must, indeed, have distressed our Ambassador, who, as I have said, had been transferred at his own request from Berlin to Rome because the considerations lavished by Hitler on Mussolini at the Munich Conference inspired in him the belief that Rome was the city in which to work for the promotion of peace. But M. François-Poncet was not the kind of man to be discouraged. He gave tit for tat. On March 20, the morning after the interview at the Brenner he said to Ciano, who notes it down in his Diary (p. 225): '. . . the Duce has put his money on the wrong horse, and now he is doubling his bet. But

---

[1] With praiseworthy scrupulousness M. François-Poncet had not hesitated to ask me, when I took over power, to nominate to his post another person whom I thought would have more influence with the Rome Government than he had. In my opinion no other Frenchman possessed this. Therefore, I rejected this very disinterested offer, and at the same time assured him of my confidence in him.

[2] Le Figaro, July 17, 1945.

[3] When war broke out, Hitler, making the best of Italian reservations, abstained from pressing Mussolini to enter the fight. Once war had been declared Italy accepted several orders for military equipment from France. Simple individuals allowed themselves to be deceived by this ruse. The way in which negotiations were carried out was unusual. Mussolini demanded that the most complete secrecy should be observed, and that dealings should be entrusted to a single representative of each Government. The two negotiators were to meet at San Remo. Representing Italy was the banker, Giannini, an individual who carried out all kinds of jobs for the Duce.

At the beginning of the war I met Count Volpi in Paris, a member of the Grand Fascist Council, with whom I talked about the later attitude of his country. I reminded him that Mussolini had solemnly proclaimed that, when Italy had taken Abyssinia, she would be a 'satisfied Power'.

'Yes, he said that . . . but it was not true.'

This was a categoric confirmation of what I had stated to the Chamber four years earlier; it was a categoric denial to those who asserted that this acquisition, so unscrupulously gained, would appease the Italian dictator.

the Franco-British horse, even if at the beginning of the race it may lag behind, will win in the last lap.' Mussolini was therefore only waiting to stab France in the back on the day when she 'was biting the dust', that is to say on the day when he thought Germany had secured victory, and when, consequently, he could throw himself on our country without running any risk. The Duce's personal correspondence with Hitler reveals that he had taken this decision a long time previously. It was part and parcel of the Fascist régime to attach value to an acquisition only if it were snatched by force. There are some natures to whom the morality and immorality of actions are words empty of significance. In a celebrated sally Bismarck defined Italian policy as that of a 'jackal'. Mussolini ran true to tradition. But at least he made no pretence about it.

On April 11 he wrote to the Führer:

'I am very grateful to you for having told me about the opening of operations in the North. . . .

'I am confirming to you that, as from tomorrow, the Italian Fleet will be on a war footing, and that I shall speed up the pace of the mobilization of my other forces. I don't know whether the French have ever seriously entertained any illusions about Italy's intentions. If they have done so, they will soon have them shattered. The Italian people, although they wish to gain time in order to be better prepared, are now convinced that they cannot avoid entering the struggle.'

Another letter from the Duce to the Führer, this time undated, but subsequent to May 10, runs thus:

'I think that time is pressing for Italy as well, and I am deeply grateful for the promise which you have given to keep me informed of the development of operations, so that I can make my decisions in full knowledge of the facts.

'As far as Italian armed forces are concerned, the Navy is ready, and by the end of May, we shall have two army groups prepared to advance either to the west or east, as well as air and anti-aircraft formations

'It is unnecessary for me to tell you that I am personally following the progress of your forces in a comradely spirit.'

Ciano writes[1] that the Duce told him on May 13, the very day on which our front was broken on the Meuse: 'Within a month I shall declare war. I shall attack France and Great Britain in the air and on the sea.'

The approaches made, therefore, in April and May by the Allies to Mussolini and the repeated interventions of the two highest moral authorities in the world, the Pope and Roosevelt, to try to prevent him

[1] *Op. cit.*, p. 249.

from entering into the war were doomed to failure. The only effect which they had was to give the Duce the impression that he had to deal with opponents well aware of their own weakness.

Thus Ciano relates[1] that Chamberlain had transmitted to him on April 5 'a useless and very general message . . . one of those messages of goodwill destined from the start to remain unanswered'.

For a long time, as is known, I entertained no illusions about Fascism in general or Mussolini in particular. Convinced that Fascist Italy would enter the war, I decided, as soon as I came to power, that I would force Mussolini to put himself in the wrong. I, therefore, summoned Signor Guariglia, the Italian Ambassador on March 25.

Here is the memorandum of the interview which was drawn up after our meeting:

'M. Paul Reynaud began by explaining to his visitor his complete faith in the final victory of France and Britain. He compared the struggle in progress to a boxing match between a heavy-weight, representing the two Western Empires with all their wealth and slowness, and a light-weight, skilful and trained for the fight but whose only hope in winning was at the start of the contest, and who would be lost if he did not gain victory in the first few months. The war had now become a long drawn-out affair; thus, there could be no doubt about its result.

'The President of the Council then took up the theme that, to a people endowed with the political insight of the Italians, it was apparent that there could be no conceivable balance of power in Europe if France were beaten. The power of the Allies precluded in advance this hypothesis. The result would be none the less very serious for Italy if France were defeated.

'If, on the contrary, France was victorious, Italy had nothing to fear from such a victory, for it was also in France's interest to see Italian influence in Europe increase. The triumph of the Allies would, therefore, be doubly profitable to Italy, by the effect which it would have on the European balance of power as well as by the expansion of Italian interests.

'Signor Guariglia, whilst stating that he was in agreement with the views put forward by M. Paul Reynaud, and whilst agreeing that in his opinion the situation was not developing favourably to Germany, nevertheless emphasized the dangers which a continuation of the war held for Italy. There was the risk that she would become involved; there was a general uncertainty, a stoppage of business, all reasons which could inspire Italy to desire a rapid conclusion of peace. The Ambassador did not linger, however, over this brief allusion to the

[1] *Op. cit.*, p. 231.

peace offensive, and the President of the Council answered him that his country would realize one day how dangerous it was to have Germany for a neighbour, an experience which France had suffered for a long time.

'Signor Guariglia improved on this by alluding to the difficulty that the Italian Government was meeting at the present time in South Tyrol. The Reich was encouraging all its nationals to leave the country so that they could draw in Germany a financial compensation for the property which they were giving up, but it was at the same time giving them to understand that, later, they would in any case get it back there. Italy found herself compelled to stop this emigration for she was already a debtor of the Reich to the tune of eight milliards, and the day would not be far distant when the bill would come to twenty milliards.

'The President of the Council then alluded to the interview at the Brenner, and to the change of tone in the Italian Press about the Allies following this meeting.

'The Ambassador was obliged to minimize the importance of this development by observing that a nation which is not at war, after having been for a long time keyed up to a high pitch, can only be exaggerated in its reactions. He stressed the fact that, barring a new move such as Russian intervention or Allied action in the Balkans, Italian policy would not change. M. Paul Reynaud asked him then what attitude his country would take up towards the U.S.S.R. Signor Guariglia replied that it was not impossible for Italy to be induced to conclude with Russia arrangements similar to those which the Allies had done with Turkey.

'The Ambassador repeated on several occasions that too much importance should not be attached to Italian claims against France, such as were being currently expressed in certain papers of the peninsula. "On the other hand," he stated, "we cannot tolerate a policy which establishes the British as guardians at both ends of the Mediterranean. The fact that our ships are bottled up in this sea is considered to be a humiliation by the Italian people, and even by those who are not in agreement with the claims against France."'

In spite of the assurances of the Ambassador the tone of the Italian Press towards the Western Powers became more and more aggressive. In mid-April I instructed M. François-Poncet to protest to Ciano that this campaign did not correspond with the feelings of the French people towards Italy nor to the friendly understanding which the French Government had shown towards Italian interests since the outbreak of the war, nor to the official position of the Italian Government in relation to the French Government as the latter believed its nature to be. The British Ambassador was instructed by his Government to take a

similar step. For several days Ciano avoided this request for an explanation with the result that M. François-Poncet was finally compelled to
make the representations to the head of Ciano's secretariat. As can well
be expected, the reply of this official was evasive.

I decided none the less to persevere in my efforts at conciliation. I
made statements to this effect before the Foreign Affairs Committees
of both the Chambers,[1] and gave them immediate publicity. I reinforced these statements by writing on April 22 a personal letter to
Mussolini. Here is the text of it:

'I have just read your telegram to Chancellor Hitler. You have
expressed a public desire to see Germany victorious. I see in this gesture
a new demonstration of a historic misunderstanding, a misunderstanding about the relations between your country and ours, a misunderstanding about the relations between your régime and ours.

'Having been responsible for the Government of France for some
weeks, I am writing to you, without standing on ceremony, as one of
those leaders, rare in history, who hold in their hands the fate of
millions of human beings.

'I do not want to try in this letter either to supplicate or to threaten
you. The essential virtue which we should possess is to understand and
to tolerate each other.

'Perhaps this letter will not change the present state of affairs in any way.

'Perhaps, tomorrow, the mountaineers of my country will be fighting
against your people. Once the dice have been thrown we shall see who
turns out to be the stronger. Perhaps then we shall surprise each other.

'But perhaps also our destiny has not yet been decided.

'It may be that other means than war exist to reveal the true Italy to
France, to reveal the true France to Italy. In order to determine the laws
which will bind our children together, there can be other ties than those
of blood, and ties which are as noble.

'I believe in democracy. You believe in fascism. But neither of us
will repudiate our past history if we strengthen by our actions what are
the two glorious types of Mediterranean civilization, types which still
remain today as yesterday, worthy of inspiring the future of the world.
This civilization rests primarily on our two countries.

'It is as vital for Italy as for France that a balance of power should be
maintained in Europe. Without this, no peace, no prosperity can be

---

[1] The communiqué which was published on April 19 at the end of the meeting of the
Senate Foreign Affairs Committee ran as follows: 'Passing to relations with Italy, the
President of the Council recalled that the French Government before and after September 1
had informed the Italian Government that it was prepared to explore with the former, in
a friendly exchange of views, a basis on which would be planned a just settlement of
questions outstanding between the two countries. These overtures have remained until
now without response, but the attitude which the Italian Government has thought fit to
adopt has in no wise changed the opinions of the French Government.'

lasting. What are the disagreements which have been able to arise between us during the last four years, beside this fundamental fact?

'It is not too late to try and bridge this broad ditch which seems at present to separate us. Your frankness and my own should try to link a traditional régime like ours and a new régime like yours; each would, thereby, be reinforced in the future by the dissipation of this distrust of its neighbour.

'I am speaking in the name of a country which, I know, would entirely approve of the step which I am now taking, if it were brought to its knowledge.

'It will not be possible to say that France and Italy came to blows on the battlefield without a thorough discussion and a meeting on the part of their leaders.

'A war between us, and our people would feel the same as we do, would be a sacrilege against our common heritage and against the sacrifice of those who lost their lives at Bligny. In these days when peace is so much more difficult than war, I offer you the more difficult.'

Desiring that this step should not be interpreted as a confession of weakness, I kept it a secret,[1] and only communicated its contents to Chamberlain in my room at the Quai d'Orsay on the termination of a meeting of the Supreme Council which was taking place at Paris on the 22nd.

Mussolini replied in Italian to my letter.

'I hasten to reply to your letter of April 22 which was handed to me on the 24th through your Ambassador in Rome.

'First of all, may I term as unjustified the reason which inspired your message, namely, the telegram in which I expressed a wish for a German victory. This should not come as a surprise to you, nor make you forget that Italy is and means to stay the political and military ally of Germany in adherence to the Treaty of May, 1939, a treaty which Italy, like all nations who cherish their honour, intends to respect.

'Your remarks on the relations between democracy and fascism and the need for a European balance of power would require developing at length, and this is not the place to do so.

'You seem in one passage of your letter to allude to the possibility of a meeting between us. I must, to my deep regret, decline such an offer. You will have no difficulty in understanding the reasons for this.'

Italy's aggression against France aroused so unanimous a contempt

[1] That is why I instructed M. François-Poncet to deliver my message as a sealed communication. I regretfully resorted to this unusual procedure which, in my opinion, had nothing ungracious in it towards our Ambassador. The latter was not, therefore, justified in showing himself, as Ciano writes (*op. cit.*, p. 238), 'somewhat resentful that he, the Ambassador of France, should be the bearer of a message as to the contents of which he is kept in complete ignorance. . . .'

throughout the world that I did not think it worth while, when it did take place, to make use of my letter to Mussolini or his reply. Nevertheless, Ciano writes with justice:[1] 'It is clear that the Duce's letter can be used by Reynaud against the remaining pro-Italian Frenchmen as proof of our provocative attitude.' This was, in fact, exactly the aim which I had wished to achieve.[2]

It was in such circumstances, a few days after I took over the Ministry of War, when disaster was at its full height, that M. François-Poncet sent me two personal messages. These contained a suggestion, the object of which was to take advantage of a respite in the struggle in order to inform the Italian Government secretly, through the intermediary of the Pope, what sacrifices the Allies would be prepared to make to obtain a continuation of non-belligerency on the part of Italy. Our definite offers, in order to have, according to him, any hope of success, should deal with the status of Gibraltar, Malta and the Suez as regards Britain, and Djibouti and Tunisia as regards France. To support this suggestion and to press me into giving effect to it, our Ambassador sent one of his colleagues from Rome, M. Garnier, Secretary of the Embassy. And he constantly asked his emissary by telephone to return as quickly as possible to Rome, bearing concrete and substantial proposals to place before the Italian Government.[3]

It will be realized that this suggestion was contrary to my personal views about the predatory policy of Mussolini. But it had been put forward by our Ambassador who was on the spot and his emissary urged it with such insistence to me, that I did not believe that I had the right to neglect it. In the military situation in which we found ourself, the entry of Italy into the war would indeed fill our cup of tribulation to overflowing.

On the 25th, M. François-Poncet telegraphed us that Mussolini's decision to enter the war would be taken as a result of certain pledges which he had given at the Brenner Pass. There remained the chance, however, he said, that the Allies could still prevent Italy entering the war, but they would have to pay a very high price to do so.

As the suggestion of our Ambassador concerned the interests of Britain as well as of France, my first duty was to go, as a loyal but exacting ally, and consult with Churchill to ask him, in so far as he was concerned, whether he was prepared to make the sacrifice.

Therefore, after having discussed the idea with the War Committee

[1] *Op. cit.*, p. 240.
[2] When sending me Mussolini's reply, in a personal letter of the 27th, M. François-Poncet wrote: 'Ciano ingenuously confirms that the final attitude of his country will depend on our ultimate chances of victory or defeat.'
[3] The letters in question must have been handed over to me by M. Garnier whom I received during the morning of the 25th. As I was not able to find them amongst my papers I asked M. François-Poncet in 1946 if he had kept a copy of them. He replied that he had not.

on the 25th, as I have previously mentioned, I decided the following morning to go to London. This I did. I consulted first of all in private with Churchill. Then, Chamberlain, Lord Halifax, Attlee, the Lord Privy Seal, and Eden, Secretary of State for War, joined in the exchange of views.[1]

Lord Halifax told me that he had already initiated advances on the previous day towards the Italian Ambassador in London, Count Bastianini, indicating to him that the Allies would be ready to consider any proposal for negotiation both as regards Italian interests as well as the bases of a just and lasting peace.

During the course of a trip which he had just made in Europe as Roosevelt's envoy, Sumner Welles had told me that Mussolini had strongly stressed to him the humiliation which the presence of the British guard at both gates of the Mediterranean placed on Italy who, because of her coasts, had access only to this sea.

I asked the British statesmen if it would not be possible to find some formula which would satisfy Italian self-esteem in the event of an Allied victory, on condition that Italy did not enter the war. I told them of M. François-Poncet's suggestions on this score.

I revealed to them how dangerous Britain's position would be if the Battle of France was lost because of this new aggression, for the Germans would hold the French coast from Brest to Dunkirk. I added that I thought it my duty to warn them that I would have difficulties with my Government if the Battle of France were lost, for Pétain would speak in favour of an armistice. It can be guessed how painful this confidence was which I made to men to whom I was and still am bound by friendship and esteem, but I considered it my duty to take any step in order to defend the soil of France. I thought Lord Halifax was struck by my arguments. He expressed his willingness to suggest to Mussolini that, if Italy would agree to collaborate with France and Britain in establishing a peace which would safeguard the independence of these two countries, and was based on a just and durable settlement of all European problems, the Allies would be prepared to discuss with him the claims of Italy in the Mediterranean and, in particular, those which concerned the outlets of this sea. It was agreed that the British Cabinet would discuss the matter and that I should be kept informed.[2]

[1] These conversations took place at the Admiralty, where, to save the trouble of moving, Churchill had thought it better to stay, when he took over the leadership of the Government from Chamberlain. 'Early on the morning of May 11,' he writes (*op. cit.*, vol. II, *Their Finest Hour*, p. 10), 'I sent a message to Mr. Chamberlain: "No one changes houses for a month." This avoided petty inconveniences during the crisis of the battle. I continued to live at Admiralty House, and made its Map Room and the fine rooms downstairs my temporary headquarters.'

[2] In his account of this day Churchill writes (*op. cit.*, vol. II, *Their Finest Hour*, p. 109): 'The most we could promise was to bring the matter before the Cabinet and send a definite answer the next day. Reynaud and I lunched alone together at the Admiralty.'

But I saw that Churchill, whose leonine courage once more won my admiration, was in principle hostile to any concessions to Mussolini. So were Chamberlain and Attlee, the former, it is true, with some reservations.[1]

Churchill and I then came to an agreement about the text of a new proposal which, at our joint request, Roosevelt agreed to put to the Duce. The same day Washington telegraphed to Mr. Phillips the text of a new message from the President. Here are the important parts:

Washington, May 26, 1940.
15 hours.

I wish to thank Your Excellency for your courteous reply to my last message.

Events are following each other with rapidity, but I persist in believing that a clear appreciation of their long-term repercussions in the political field should prompt an endeavour to prevent the extension of hostilities to areas other than those which are at present affected by them. In the hope of helping Your Excellency to prevent this extension to the Mediterranean theatre and perhaps to other areas, I would like to submit to him certain considerations. . . .

I am prepared to inform the Governments of Great Britain and France of Italian aspirations in the Mediterranean zone if you desire to make them known to me. . . .

If you did wish to use my offer of mediation, it would be understood, should the three Powers come to an agreement, that France and Great Britain would be deemed, *ipso facto*, pledged to carry out immediately, at the end of the war, the conditions which had been agreed upon, and to accept the participation of Italy in peace negotiations on the same footing as that of the belligerent countries. Moreover, for her part, Italy would be deemed, *ipso facto*, pledged on the one hand, to accept the execution of the conditions stated above as satisfying her claims, and on the other, not to enter the war. . . .

After I got back to Paris I received, during the evening, the following telegram from Churchill:

Private and personal.

Impossible to send you a text before tomorrow, Monday, for I must consult my other colleagues. I shall do my best, but I am convinced that our safety depends solely on the resolution which we

[1] During the London talks on the 26th, I did not speak to the British statesmen about continuing the war in North Africa, because I did not wish to weaken the effect of my repeated demands made to secure the co-operation of their aircraft. They did not speak to me either about this question.

put into the fight. Here, we are all grateful for your visit and admire your calm courage in the storm.[1]

I answered him on the same day:

'Thank you for your cordial welcome and your telegram. As regards Italy, the most weighty of my arguments is, to my mind, the one that the help given by your country to mine by this step in this tragic hour will contribute to strengthening that spiritual alliance which I believe to be so essential.'

During the evening of the 26th I informed Daladier and M. Charles-Roux of my conversations in London.

I have appealed to the recollections of M. Charles-Roux; and he has been kind enough to draw up a note, which I am going to use in my account, of the final attempts to keep Italy from entering the war.

1. During the evening of the 26th M. Paul Reynaud summoned M. Daladier and myself to his house. He informed us of the conversations in which he had taken part in London. He had explained to the British statesmen the military situation of France, and had put before them the problem of examining whether it would not be wise to make approaches to Italy, in order to prevent her entry into the war. Lord Halifax was favourably inclined to such proposals, and had spoken of sending a dispatch to Rome on this line. Mr. Churchill and Mr. Attlee gave the President of the Council the impression of being hostile to such a step. The meeting came to no positive conclusion concerning diplomatic action in relation to Rome. But it seemed—and M. Daladier was struck by the fact—that Lord Halifax was personally inclined to such a move being made.

2. On the next day, the 27th, M. Daladier and myself were summoned by M. Paul Reynaud . . . to the Rue Saint-Dominique. We went together. The President of the Council read to us two private letters from M. François-Poncet which had reached him, one immediately after the other, and which stressed the necessity for France and Britain to make proposals to Rome. M. Paul Reynaud was sceptical about the result, but he did not think that he could override the advice of our Ambassador. He then informed us of the step which the President of the U.S.A. was making at that very time at Rome on behalf of the British and French Governments. This seemed to me a very well-conceived plan, and I was struck by the important advantages which Italy would gain from it, if her Duce still retained some glimmering of common sense. When taking me back to the Quai d'Orsay in his car, M. Daladier agreed that this approach of Roosevelt to Rome in the name of France and Britain and under the guarantee of the United States possessed a singular value.

---

[1] When once the armistice had been concluded by the Bordeaux Government Chamberlain remembered only my words which described Pétain's state of mind, but he forgot that, in uttering them, I had had the sole purpose of influencing my British colleagues. He was to write that, from this day, one could foresee the moment when France would give up the fight.

At this point let us interrupt M. Charles-Roux's account. On the 27th Mr. Phillips discharged the mission with which the President had entrusted him. Here is how he reported to Washington the circumstances in which he had to carry it out:

Rome, May 27, 1940, 13 hours.

I was received this morning at eleven-thirty by Ciano. I told him that I had a message of the greatest importance from President Roosevelt to give verbally to the Duce, but that I would be happy if Ciano took note of it for his own personal information. He told me that the Duce could not receive me, but that he, Ciano, would accept the message, and with my permission, would note in writing the gist of the text. This he did, so carefully and attentively that I refrained from insisting on being received in audience by Mussolini. I asked Ciano if it would be possible for him to give me some general idea of the reply. He told me categorically that 'it would be a refusal'. He continued by explaining to me that the Duce, far from limiting his objectives to the satisfaction of Italy's legitimate aspirations, had decided to discharge the obligations which were imposed on him by his alliance with Germany. Ciano stated that the Duce was not then at the Palace, but that he would be returning at any moment, and he promised to have me called immediately he found himself in a position to hand me the Duce's reply. I asked the Minister if he fully comprehended the importance and gravity of President Roosevelt's message. He replied to me that he understood completely its significance, but that nothing could now change the course of events. He added that he could not fix the exact moment of Italy's entry into the war . . . and that it was possible that the event might not take place for several weeks, but he stated that 'it would be soon'.

Finally he questioned me upon the position of the United States. I drew his attention to President Roosevelt's programme which provided for the manufacture of great quantities of defensive armaments. Ciano confined himself to expressing to me that personally he thought the United States sympathized with the Allies in the same way that Italy was sympathizing with Germany.

The Minister called me at 1 p.m. and told me that the statements which he had made to me during the morning had been confirmed by Mussolini. Ciano declared that Mussolini wished to preserve his 'liberty of action' and that the Duce was not prepared to enter into any negotiations whatsoever, for this would be contradictory to the spirit of Fascism. The Duce, he emphasized, had pledged his word, and any attempt to turn Italy from her path was destined to failure.

Ciano, in his turn, notes:[1] 'Roosevelt offers to become the mediator

[1] Op. cit., p. 255.

between us and the Allies, making himself personally responsible for the execution, after the war, of any eventual agreements. I answer Phillips that Roosevelt is off the track . . . what he [Mussolini] wants is war, and, even if he were to obtain by peaceful means double what he claims, he would refuse.'

And on the 29th our Ambassador in Washington telegraphed us that Roosevelt had told him that his message to Mussolini seemed to have produced no effect on a man who had definitely made up his mind.

Since the 27th, M. François-Poncet had, in his turn, reported to the Quai d'Orsay the check to the President's approach, and the conversation that he had had with Ciano on this subject. '. . . He first repeated to me what he had already so often said of the determination of the Duce to remain absolutely loyal and faithful to his duties as an ally, and of his repugnance at feeling himself thought capable of failing in these. He then stated to me that at the present time the problem was quite simple—either Germany would be victorious and the status of Europe would be overthrown or else the Allies would be the victors and Europe would not be less profoundly changed, and in both cases it was necessary to await the outcome of the present war. Finally Count Ciano remarked to me, observing that he was expressing a quite personal opinion and on the plane of our friendly relations, that, if I had many times assured him that we were prepared to consider in the most generous spirit possible, the settlement of Italian and Mediterranean problems and to grant Italy ample satisfaction, I had, however, never stated precisely the nature of this, nor to what extent our future concessions would go. Count Ciano hastened to add that he thought the richest gifts would not now change Mussolini's attitude. But obviously he was curious to know what kind of presents these could be; he sounded me as if to discover if I were in a position to tell him more. This very curiosity, which he had never shown in such a way and which I was easily able to answer in such vague and general terms that he himself did not insist, seemed to me a novel and notable fact.'

Ciano alludes to this interview:[1] 'May 27. My conference with [François-]Poncet is also important, not because of its results, but as a psychological indication. He made some very precise overtures. Exclusive of Corsica, which is "an integral part of France", he said that we can make a deal about Tunisia and perhaps even about Algeria.[2] I answered that he . . . is too late. . . . [François-]Poncet recognizes the faults of the French, attacks the governments of the past . . . May 28. My conference with Poncet, who is the picture of distress, and the events of the night (the Belgian capitulation) led Mussolini to speed up his planning, as he

---

[1] *Ibid.*, pp. 255-6.
[2] It is obvious that Ciano must have misinterpreted the scope of our Ambassador's words, for the latter could not have used language so contrary to the intentions of his government.

is convinced that things are now coming to a head, and he wants to create enough claims to be entitled to his share of the spoils. This is all very well as regards France. But England is still standing. And America? The Duce talks of June 10th.'

Roosevelt was not, however, discouraged in his efforts. On the 31st he made a fourth and final approach by sending to the Italian Government a Note which Ciano tells us[1] was 'this time more energetic'. In it the President said that Italy's intervention would have the effect of making the United States double their supply of arms to the Allies. There was an angry reply from Mussolini on June 15: 'The United States have no more concern with the Mediterranean than Italy has with the Caribbean Sea.' Ciano adds: 'It was useless for Roosevelt to insist. . . . On the contrary . . . his pressure only confirmed Mussolini in his decision.'

Let us return to M. Charles-Roux:

3. On the 27th, telegrams from Rome informed me of the totally negative results of Mr. Roosevelt's approach.[2] The American Ambassador, Mr. Phillips had handed to Ciano the presidential message. Shortly after, the French and British Ambassadors inquired at the Chigi Palace of the reception it had been given: 'The reply', Ciano told them, 'was that there was no answer.' Washington, London and Paris could not be told more pointedly that they were wasting their time and that it was useless to carry the matter any further. Those who understood the situation had no doubt from that time, and everyone has discovered since, that Ciano was not in agreement with his father-in-law and patron as to what policy should be followed. It was, perhaps, because of this that he employed all the more frankness when showing that the Duce's decision was irrevocable. At this time the British Ambassador in Paris, Sir Ronald Campbell, came each day to give me his news, and amongst other things, the telegrams from his Rome colleague, Sir Percy Loraine. He reminded me of the report of an interview,[3] on the 28th, during which Ciano had said to Sir Percy: 'Even if France were to offer us Tunisia, Corsica and Nice, we should declare war.'

To clarify the story, let us interrupt this account which we shall take up later.

The day of the 27th was a particularly sombre one. About seven in the evening, Weygand came to tell me of the impending capitulation of the King of the Belgians. The Council of Ministers met at 10 p.m

---

[1] *Op. cit.*, pp. 258-9.

[2] On the next day, the 28th, at one o'clock, our Ambassador in London told the Quai d'Orsay that he had asked the Foreign Office what effect this set-back would have on the views of the British Government, and that he had been answered that it tended to demonstrate the uselessness of any approach to Rome.

[3] M. François-Poncet, had, for his part, reported this interview to the Quai d'Orsay: 'Even if', Ciano is reported to have said, 'France were to offer Tunisia, Algeria and Morocco to Italy, Mussolini would decline these offers. . . . The Duce has made up his mind.'

in an atmosphere of gloom. Weygand informed it of a deterioration in the situation caused by the defection of the Belgian Army, and I of the conversations which I had had the day before in London about Italy. At Daladier's suggestion the Council studied means for keeping Italy out of the war. To this end we decided ourselves to make Rome offers to which we should be prepared to agree without resorting to the mediation of a third power, and without subordinating these proposals to corresponding British offers, but we were to keep Britain in touch with our negotiations.

Let us once more take up M. Charles-Roux's account:

4. The surrender of the Belgian Army had made the already critical military position worse. The Council of Ministers in France was living through anxious hours. During the night of the 27th and 28th it met after dinner, and its sitting was prolonged until very late. I had gone home to bed at my house. I was awakened at 2 a.m. Two of M. Daladier's colleagues, Lagarde, the head of his Secretariat and Daridan, the deputy head, had come from him to show me the text of draft instructions to our Rome and London Ambassadors, which he had drawn up on the conclusion of the Council's sitting. It was a question of putting concrete offers to the Italian Government: Djibouti and the Addis Ababa railway; cession of territory, whose area was to be divided between the Libyan hinterland and the Gulf of Guinea, or, but only if this cession were refused as insufficient, some change in the status of Tunisia. I noted immediately that, in spite of all the precautions which we might take, this proposed change would entail placing in jeopardy France's supremacy in controlling the affairs of the Regency.[1] M. Daladier wished to know what objections the submitted draft might raise.

It goes without saying that I had objections to make. But I wished to discuss them with my colleagues. I, therefore, went to the Quai d'Orsay and summoned Charvériat, Rochat, Lagarde, Hoppenot and Daridan. We read the text again, and agreed that it must be re-written. I undertook to tone it down as much as possible. Having done that, I still felt some qualms of conscience. A text which was handed to me in such circumstances, and to which I had expressed my objections, was really only a draft. At four in the morning, therefore, I rang up M. Daladier by the private line which we had to his home. I informed him of my objections, namely, the extent of the proposed concessions, the impossibility of agreeing to even a part of them without some previous consultations with London, because Anglo-Egyptian Sudan bordered on our Equatorial Africa, which would be affected by our territorial cessions. M. Daladier immediately agreed, and instructed me to make such alterations as I considered appropriate. He gave it as his opinion that the matter was not one of desperate urgency, and concluded that we should talk it over again in the morning. I then re-read the text carefully. I arranged, until further orders, for a postponement in the dispatch of the proposed telegrams, and afterwards went back to bed.

At nine o'clock in the morning I went back to my office; I called up M. Paul

[1] i.e. in Tunisia, which is a French protectorate [Tr.].

Reynaud, and informed him of my objections to the proposals of the previous night, stressing the absolute impossibility of not consulting London, before making any offer of this kind to Rome. He was not aware of the text in question, and he stated that he was in agreement with me. Moreover, he observed that nothing had been definitely settled at the meeting of the Council. When M. Daladier arrived at the Quai d'Orsay, I went to his room to see him. He also supported my remarks. We went straight away to M. Paul Reynaud. After a brief conversation, it was decided unanimously that London should be consulted, and any approach to Rome should, in the meantime, be postponed. In order to avoid the risk of any indiscretion which might come of some negligent handling, the telegram, which was to be sent to M. Corbin, would not be communicated to our Ambassador in Rome.

In London, Lord Halifax, who had received no reply from Count Bastianini, had approached Ciano through Sir Percy Loraine. Ciano had replied that he had indeed received a telegram from Bastianini on this subject, but that this approach was now under the general embargo which Mussolini had placed on all discussions with the Allies, whatever they might be. Ciano had added that, in such circumstances, it had seemed to him useless to reply to Lord Halifax's overtures, even out of politeness. The British Government had, therefore, decided to make no more new approaches to the Italian Government.

Let us interrupt M. Charles-Roux's account at this point to give the text of the reply which I received on the 28th from Churchill in answer to our communication:

1. I have with my colleagues examined with the most careful and sympathetic attention the proposal for an approach by way of precise offer of concessions to Signor Mussolini that you have forwarded to me today, fully realizing the terrible situation with which we are both faced at this moment.

2. Since we last discussed this matter the new fact which has occurred, namely, the capitulation of the Belgian Army, has greatly changed our position for the worse, for it is evident that the chance of withdrawing the armies of Generals Blanchard and Gort from the Channel ports has become very problematical. The first effect of such a disaster must be to make it impossible at such a moment for Germany to put forward any terms likely to be acceptable, and neither we nor you would be prepared to give up our independence without fighting for it to the end.

3. In the formula prepared last Sunday by Lord Halifax it was suggested that if Signor Mussolini would co-operate with us in securing a settlement of all European questions which would safeguard our independence and form a basis of a just and durable peace for Europe we should be prepared to discuss his claims in the Mediterranean. You now propose to add specific offers, which I cannot suppose would have any chance of moving Signor Mussolini, and which once made could not be subsequently withdrawn, in order to induce him to undertake the role of mediator, as the formula discussed on Sunday contemplated.

4. I and my colleagues believe that Signor Mussolini has long had it in mind that he might eventually fill this role, no doubt counting upon substantial advantages for Italy in the process. But we are convinced that at this moment

when Hitler is flushed with victory and certainly counts on early and complete collapse of Allied resistance it would be impossible for Signor Mussolini to put forward proposals for a conference with any success. I may remind you also that the President of the U.S.A. has received a wholly negative reply to the proposal which we jointly asked him to make, and that no response has been made to the approach which Lord Halifax made to the Italian Ambassador here last Saturday.

5. Therefore, without excluding the possibility of an approach to Signor Mussolini at some time, we cannot feel that this would be the right moment, and I am bound to add that in my opinion the effect on the morale of our people, which is now firm and resolute, would be extremely dangerous. You yourself can best judge what would be the effect in France.

6. You will ask, then, how is the situation to be improved? My reply is that by showing that after the loss of our two [Northern] armies and the support of our Belgian ally we still have stout hearts and confidence in ourselves we shall at once strengthen our hands in negotiations and draw admiration and perhaps the material help of the U.S.A. Moreover, we feel that as long as we stand together our undefeated Navy and our Air Force, which is daily destroying German fighters and bombers at a formidable rate, afford us the means of exercising in our common interest a continuous pressure upon Germany's internal life.

7. We have reason to believe that the Germans too are working to a time-table, and that their losses and the hardships imposed on them, together with the fear of our air raids, is undermining their courage. It would indeed be a tragedy if by too hasty an acceptance of defeat we threw away a chance that was almost within our grasp of securing an honourable issue from the struggle.

8. In my view, if we both stand out we may yet save ourselves from the fate of Denmark and Poland. Our success must depend first on our unity, then on our courage and endurance.[1]

This very fine message from Churchill strengthened my conviction. I felt I had sacrificed enough to the suggestions of those who favoured making concessions to Italy. M. Charles-Roux continues: 'When we received this reply from London, we gave up the idea of telegraphing Rome, for M. Paul Reynaud, who was backed up in this by M. Daladier, was opposed to any step of this kind. To return to M. Charles-Roux's account:

5. In the morning M. Daladier and myself were summoned to Rue Saint-Dominique. I left the Quai d'Orsay first, and when I got to M. Paul Reynaud's, I found gathered there in his room, Marshal Pétain, General Weygand, Admiral Darlan and M. Baudouin. The President of the Council held out to me a document and asked if I recognized it. I cast a glance over it. It was a draft Note for the Italian Ambassador. I said that I did not know anything about it. M. Paul Reynaud had received it from M. Daladier, together with a letter telling him that, in the present military situation, the Government ought to face up to its responsibilities, and that, in any case, he himself was fulfilling

[1] Churchill, *op. cit.*, vol. II, *Their Finest Hour*, pp. 109–11.

those which fell upon him. Whilst this was taking place, M. Daladier came into the room, and we began to examine the proposed text. The Note was skilfully drawn up. It expressed to Italy the readiness of France to examine with her Mediterranean problems in their entirety, and to support any feasible solutions. But it revealed too much of a tendency to promise what did not lie within our own power to carry out. I, therefore, remarked that we had no jurisdiction over Malta or Gibraltar and that, if it were not completely forbidden in diplomacy to dispose of another's property, at least it was necessary that the third party should not be an ally with whom one was collaborating at that same time. The terms of the Note were, therefore, toned down to meet with this observation. Then came the question. Should we send it to London before sending it to the Italian Ambassador? M. Paul Reynaud asked Marshal Pétain and General Weygand if it were not an impossibility, in the present circumstances, for us to do anything which might separate us from Britain. The two military leaders declared that this was so. On the threshold, as he was leaving General Weygand again said: 'Just a moment. Then we are agreed. We shall consult London. It is I who have need of the British.' He was promised that London would be consulted. Thus, the word 'support' was replaced by 'welcome', which removed any grounds for grievance by our ally, and the British Government was to be previously consulted.

Daladier summoned the British Ambassador at the beginning of the afternoon, and handed him the text of the Note. At six o'clock, Sir Ronald Campbell came to give him the reply of his Government. The latter did not object to the step, but it did not intend to be associated with it, and left us to bear the responsibility. Thus, if the overture did not produce any results, at least it had done no harm. At eight o'clock, Daladier, handed the Note to Signor Guariglia.

I must once more interrupt M. Charles-Roux.

Daladier, therefore, summoned the Italian Ambassador. By a coincidence Sir Ronald Campbell came during the day to confirm to the Quai d'Orsay that Lord Halifax's overtures had failed, and thus the British Government had decided to refrain from any new approach. The interview was a brief one. Here is the text of the minutes recording the interview:

'M. Daladier received Signor Guariglia on May 30, 1940, at eight p.m. When handing him the Note, a copy of which is appended, he stated in substance to the Ambassador that:

'"France is aware of the gravity of the hour. She believes that there exists no problem between herself and Italy, whose solution demands a recourse to arms. In this spirit she has decided to undertake a step of which the Government of the Republic has entrusted me to inform you.

'"France is the ally of Britain. She means to remain faithful to the pledges which she has given to Britain. It is on this basis that the suggested negotiations should begin in the future."'

Let us take up for the last time M. Charles-Roux's account. We shall see that the Italian Ambassador tried to exact from us a definite promise.

6. On June 1, Signor Guariglia came to see me: 'Are you aware', he told me, 'that the situation is developing very rapidly, and are you not going to do something to restrain Italy?'

'But', I said to him, 'is not this precisely the object of the Note which you ought to have received the day before yesterday?'

'Oh', he replied, 'the Note is not at all what I was expecting!'

The fact is that in Rome no attention was paid to it. Soon, Ciano, whose frankness was becoming increasingly disconcerting, warned Sir Percy Loraine that a declaration of war was now only a question of days, even of hours.

It was handed to the French and British Ambassadors in Rome on June 10, 1940.

The weight and tact with which M. Charles-Roux supported my policy of a close understanding with Britain is obvious to all.

Yet, during the night of June 1 to 2, Count Vladimir d'Ormesson, our Ambassador with the Vatican, visited Cardinal Maglione to examine with him the possibilities and prospects of a last approach by France or better still, by the Allies, to Mussolini through the intermediary of the Holy Father. It would be a case of asking the Pope, because of the menace of an extension of the conflict which would result in the collapse of Christianity, to make a supreme effort on behalf of a general reconciliation and peace. It was a pious intention, approved by M. François-Poncet, but unfortunately anticipated by the course of events.[1]

And this was not yet all. At midday on the 9th, the eve of the day on which Mussolini declared war on us, I received a visit from General Denain whom the President of the Republic referred to me, and whom Laval had sent to him.[2]

Count Arduini-Ferretti, who lived mostly in Paris and professed to

---

[1] The military plans of Italy gave rise to a corresponding number of conjectures, all equally confusing. Thus, General Parisot, our Military Attaché in Rome, telegraphed us on June 3:

'1. It is unlikely that Italy's entry into the war can be delayed any longer, in spite of powerful restraints; it will, however, I should say, probably be put off until the 15th—without, however, committing myself to absolute accuracy.

'2. Despite appearances, I confirm to you my belief that we have nothing to fear in the nature of an attack against France, Corsica or Tunisia.

'3. The reinforcements, whose dispatch to Libya has not been denied, are, I am informed, being sent as a precaution against our advance in Tunisia towards the frontier of Tripolitania, and especially against the threat of British motorized and armoured units, massed in the Matruh–Sollum area.'

It will be seen what a farrago of contradictory information the Government was receiving.

[2] This was by no means the first time that Laval had attempted, since war broke out, to offer his mediation in Franco-Italian affairs. He has related that, in March, 1940, Puricelli, an Italian Senator, who was reputed to be a friend of the King as well as of Mussolini, and

be a Francophile, was in the habit, so he told me of going to see Laval
when he returned from each of his trips to Italy. From the outbreak
of war he had never failed to do this, nor to deplore the growing intimacy of Italy and Germany. During the morning of the 9th, he went,
very moved, to Laval's office, to tell him that he had returned from
Rome, that Italy was going to declare war against France on the 14th
or 15th, but that, until then, there still existed the possibility of negotiating with Mussolini in order to dissuade him from taking this step.
According to this emissary, Italian troops would remain at the ready
on our Alpine frontier, even if war were declared. So that conversations could be opened and even continued after this declaration of war,
Mussolini wished, according to the report of Count Arduini-Ferretti,
that an anti-Fascist legion for fighting against Italy should not be
recruited. Questioned by Laval on the source of this information which
he was revealing, the emissary[1] answered that he represented a personality well known to Laval, the Italian Senator, Baron Aloisi, who
for a long time was the head of Mussolini's secretariat at the Ministry
of Foreign Affairs and had represented Italy, during the Abyssinian
campaign, at Geneva where Laval had been his colleague. Laval, in
any case, had gained the impression that the communication might
also be interpreted as coming from Mussolini. Believing it to be his
duty to inform the French Government of this approach to him, Laval
had asked Denain, who, in his capacity of Minister of Air in 1935, had

with whom he himself had for a long time entertained friendly relations, had come to see
him for the purpose of telling him that it was necessary, at all costs, to reconcile France
and Italy. Puricelli thought this reconciliation possible in certain acceptable circumstances
and expressly asked Laval, so the latter has stated, to go to Rome or some place in Italy
to meet Mussolini. The emissary also had added that he was empowered to make this
offer to Laval. Laval informed Daladier of this approach. After having asked for forty-
eight hours to think it over, he gave him no reply.

Daladier had his reasons for keeping silent. Amongst other things, he knew, through
M. François-Poncet, that Mussolini was opposed to the dispatch to Rome of any plenipotentiary extraordinary or any emissary who was charged with entering into negotiations
with the Italian Government. Rumours had spread on many occasions of the departure of
various personalities, political and otherwise, and often in conspicuous positions, who
loudly advertised their intention of going to Rome for such a purpose. On September 16,
1939, Ciano had notified our Ambassador of the Duce's opposition. Moreover, on
April 10, following a rumour spread by a Parisian newspaper, of the likelihood of Laval's
going to Rome, to which, it should be added, I had not given an instant's thought, Ciano
confirmed this attitude to our Ambassador by telling him of categoric instructions, which
he had sent on this matter to Signor Guariglia: 'Whoever the delegate may be', these
instructions ran, 'he will not be received.' I knew that Laval had been designated by name
as the one mentioned to our Ambassador. But the latter, and he himself has informed
M. Lebrun, Daladier and myself of this, during our joint captivity in Germany, suppressed
in the telegram which he sent me any reference to Laval, in order, he said, not to exacer-
bate the situation, and because the individual alluded to seemed to him obvious.
Nevertheless, this omission allowed Laval to prosecute his campaign.

[1] Count Arduini-Ferretti went the next day, June 10, to the Quai d'Orsay in order to
carry out what he believed to be his mission. On the very same day Italy declared war
against us, and as an Italian subject he was immediately interned. Laval, learning of his
internment, had him released.

signed with his Italian counterpart the agreements which I have previously mentioned, to pass the information on to M. Lebrun. I received
the General with the consideration due to a man who had just given
two of his sons to the country. He replied without equivocation to
the questions which I asked him. Laval, he told me, neither knew the
object of the negotiations, nor whether, in particular, they should
contain concrete offers on our part.

I observed to the General that Italy had already sent us an ultimatum,
and that M. François-Poncet had received this from Ciano himself.

'I am well aware of that', he replied.

I said that I regretted seeing him lend his collaboration to a manœuvre
in which it was obvious Laval wished to make use of him as a witness.

Laval telephoned me[1] at the beginning of the afternoon, somewhat
anxiously about General Denain's visit. I told him that it was obvious
that the die had been cast, and that, in these circumstances, any new
approach would be useless. Laval did not insist, but told me that he
was leaving for his estate at Châteldon in Auvergne.

On the next day, the 10th, Mussolini proclaimed from the balcony
of the Palazzo di Venezia: 'We have entered the lists against the pluto-
cratic and reactionary democracies of the West, which have always
barred the path of the Italian people. . . . Our conscience is absolutely
clear. The world is witness to the fact that Italy has done all that was
humanly possible to avoid war. But it has all been in vain. . . . Italians,
take up arms. There is only one word of command, *Conquer*. We shall
conquer.'

Such is the story of the last-minute efforts made by the Allies to
stop Fascist Italy from committing an act which shocked the conscience
of the civilized world, and which, by the just irony of fate, led finally
to her own ruination.

Let us acknowledge, today, that the attempts of Britain and France
were rendered hopeless for the reason which Ciano confided to M.
François-Poncet during the 'phoney war'. Mussolini was lying in wait
for the moment when he could knife France in the back, if, as he hoped,
she was brought to her knees. Nothing in the world would have cheated
him of this luxury,[2] or permitted him to let this 'fine prey', which he
so coveted, escape.

In the last days of May, 1940, our country experienced the most
agonizing period in her history. Whilst the German Army was penetrating deeply into her northern soil, she was at the same time threatened

---

[1] He had called me on five occasions during my absence, and only succeeded in getting
hold of me on the telephone at the beginning of the afternoon.

[2] This luxury was to manifest itself immediately after the Armistice under the most
hateful guises. A Fascist newspaper—I think that it was *Il Tevere*—was to flourish these
headlines addressed to us: 'And now, you riff-raff, get down on your knees, and stay there
for centuries.'

with an attack in the Alps. For us there was no possibility of withdrawal, and, therefore, we could not possess that equanimity of our
island ally. And yet, in spite of the manœuvres of his Ambassador,
Mussolini was unable to obtain any positive offers from the French
Government, which he could later employ against us as a weapon to
his own advantage. Confined as they were within restricted limits, the
last-minute overtures of France in no wise impaired the relations of
trusting friendship between her Government and that of her British
ally.

BADOGLIO'S REVELATIONS

After the shattering successes of the Wehrmacht in Flanders, the
Duce was seized with panic at the thought that he would enter the war
too late to snatch a share of the spoils.

Whilst I was in London on the 25th to inform the British statesmen of our Rome Ambassador's suggestions about the offers to be
made to Italy, Mussolini received a visit from Badoglio along with
Balbo, who had come to explain to him the critical situation in Libya.
Badoglio gives an account of this interview in his memoirs. The Duce
told them: 'Yesterday, I sent a written statement to Hitler, telling him
that I did not intend to stay idle, and that, as from June 5, I would
be ready to declare war against Great Britain.' Badoglio reminded him
that Italy was not ready, and added that entry into the war would
be equivalent to suicide. But Mussolini replied: 'In September it will
be all over, and I only need a few thousand dead to ensure that I have
the right to sit at the peace table in the capacity of a belligerent.' Can
a more shameful cynicism be imagined? But Mussolini's request was
not granted by Hitler, who was to authorize him to enter the war only
on the 10th.

MAY 27–8: LEOPOLD III CAPITULATES

Answering implicitly the criticisms which were levelled both at the
time and subsequently against his plan, Weygand stated, in his explanation on March 8, 1949, before the Committee of Inquiry that what
he asked of the Allied Armies of the North was 'perfectly feasible'.

'It was unattainable', replied Leopold III on October 16, 1949, in a
statement which he ordered his secretariat to make to the United Press.[1]

Whatever be the truth of this controversy, Leopold III—Gort
expressly notes this in his Report—was pledged to withdraw to the
Yser, whilst keeping contact with the British Army. During the
morning of the 26th, Gort asked Admiral Keyes to inform the King

[1] Mr. Bradford, Vice-President of this Agency, had asked Leopold III to make a statement for publication on the circumstances in which the Belgian Army had surrendered.
This, dated October 16, was published by the evening press on the 18th. *Le Monde*
printed extensive extracts in its issue dated the 19th.

of his 'strong desire' to see the Belgian Army retreating in the direction agreed upon.[1] Sir Roger, having discharged this duty, telegraphed to Gort that the Belgians would do their best, but that the King thought that the only method of avoiding disaster was a strong and immediate British counter-attack between the Schelde and the Lys. 'This was asking for the impossible', states Gort. During the morning General Michiels, Chief of the Belgian General Staff, warned Gort that the Belgian Army, having exhausted its reserves, would have to abandon the idea of withdrawing to the Yser. But Gort asked the War Office to insist on this to the Belgian Staff. On the next day, the 27th, at 12.30 p.m., the King telegraphed to Gort that his troops had been fighting without respite for four days under an intense bombardment, and that they were surrounded. Aware of the fact that the enemy held the mastery of the air, they were convinced that the situation was desperate. The message ended: 'The time is rapidly approaching when the troops will no longer be in a fit state to fight on. The King will find himself compelled to capitulate in order to avoid a *débâcle*.' But this message never reached Gort.

The capitulation of the Belgian Army and the speech in which I announced it to the French people have provoked numerous arguments. If I had committed a mistake, I should be the first to desire to make this good, for the Belgian people are the friends of France. The First World War has implanted deeply within both French and Belgian hearts a mutual trust which unifies our two nations. The sufferings which we experienced in common and the victory which we jointly gained have established unbreakable links between us. Personally I have a feeling of gratitude for the friendly and even affectionate welcome which I have always received in Belgium. I have admired Belgian resistance during four years of occupation, and I am deeply convinced of the necessity in the future of a close union in every respect between the two countries.

We have seen that, as regards the events which took place before the meeting at Ypres, I have adhered to the principle of sticking to a circumstantial account of the facts, supported by texts but without any commentary. Concerning the events which I am about to deal with, I have the firm intention of conforming still more strictly, if possible, to this line of presentation. I mean, therefore, to give the reader the means of forming an opinion for himself, and making sure that I myself do not in any way influence it.

I wish to say, first of all, that the attitude of the Belgian Government in this affair has been beyond reproach. It remained faithful to the

---

[1] On the 25th, Major Fauvelle, during the mission which I have previously mentioned, had termed the attitude of the Belgian Army as 'puzzling'. Weygand reports this fact in his above-mentioned deposition of March 8, 1949.

allies of its country, whom it kept loyally informed of the course of events which we are about to retrace.

On May 25, MM. Pierlot, Spaak and Vanderpoorten as well as General Denis[1] went at five in the morning to the Château of Wynendaele, where the King was. The latter received them immediately. This was the last interview which the King was to have with his Ministers. 'All of them remained standing', writes the King[2] in his account. He adds:

The Prime Minister spoke in the name of his three colleagues: the situation was desperate. The Army was on the verge of capitulation. Under these conditions the four Ministers in attendance on the King . . . realized that it was their duty to leave Belgium, for they could not allow themselves to be taken prisoners by the Germans.

The Ministers wished to make a last attempt with the King to beg him to leave with them, and to avoid at any price allowing himself to become a prisoner. . . . They called the most considered attention of the King to the fact that, by remaining in Belgium contrary to the unanimous advice of the Government, he was raising a very serious problem, for he was being responsible for the divisions which would arise in the country. Moreover, the King was deluding himself if he believed that he could exercise any influence whatsoever under an occupation. He would be degraded to the role of Hacha, or sent as a prisoner to Germany.

The King replied that, never in his life, had he lived through such agonizing hours. By deciding to stay in the country with his Army and the great majority of his people, the King considered that he was fulfilling his duties as Chief of State and Commander-in-Chief of the Army. His conscience compelled him to act in such a way. To leave would be to desert. He was convinced, moreover, that he could better serve the interests of the country from within than from without.

Contrary to what the Ministers said, he did not consider that, by acting thus, he was stimulating division in the country. It was, in his opinion, the only chance of ensuring the continuance of Belgium's independence and of the dynasty. If he left the country, he would never return.

The King noted that there still existed between him and his Ministers a basic difference of opinion: the Ministers thought that the Allies were assured of victory: the King did not share this optimism.

The Belgian Army had done and would do its duty. . . . It was still fighting; it was not today, the 25th, that it was going to surrender.

After the King had stated his case, M. Spaak asked permission to sit down as the nervous tension was insupportable. There was no opportunity of talking freely. With the permission of the King everyone sat down.

M. Spaak then began to speak. 'I am aware, once again, that when the King has come to a decision, there is nothing one can do.' He then continued by

---

[1] Of the ten other Ministers, nine had already left Belgian territory. M. Delfosse, Minister of Communications, had been surprised by the German advance when he was on the way to France. He returned then to Brussels.

[2] *Rapport, Annexes*, pp. 69–70.

developing M. Pierlot's point of view. And he protested that he would refuse to the very end to negotiate or conclude as Foreign Minister any agreement whatsoever with the enemy. M. Spaak was completely overcome: lying down, with his head thrown back in the chair, his arms hanging down, he uttered these disjointed sentences: 'Don't you understand that Belgium is ruined? . . . Out of fidelity to the King I do not want to abandon her, but I do not want to be a Minister under the occupation. . . . Let us all four resign. . . . Our colleagues will not resign . . . but so much the worse. . . . I don't know what to do. . . .'

The Prime Minister advised M. Spaak to think things over once more, and only to come to some decision that evening.

General Denis reminded the King that there were hundreds of thousands of Belgians in France who were fit to bear arms, that these were awaiting impatiently the hour when they could fight, and that the struggle was far from being finished.

The King was astonished at this remark, coming as it did from a soldier: to train men and to lead them into action, *cadres* were necessary; now these *cadres* were already in action. . . . The end of the interview was very disjointed. The Ministers were in a state of collapse. They did not know what to do. They talked of resigning. On the other hand they hesitated to abandon the King.

They left him at six-twenty.

A few hours later the King received a letter from M. Pierlot, which announced their departure for Britain: there was no longer any question of resignation.

During the interview the King read to the Ministers the text of a letter which he was going to send to the King of England. In this letter it was pointed out that nothing would be done which was contrary to the interests of the countries who had been Belgium's guarantors.

We have also M. Pierlot's version of this interview. Here it is:[1]

The Prime Minister stated: 'We have already told the King several times that, if the Belgian Army were completely or partly exposed to the imminent necessity of surrendering, the King ought to do everything possible to evade capture by the enemy. We have told the King the reasons for this. Capitulation, however grave an event, is, nevertheless, only a military act, but it would assume, of necessity, a political character if the King signed it or if he were at the head of the Army when it took place. On the other hand, if the Army had to surrender, the King's function as its Commander would be ended, whilst his function as Head of the State could continue to be exercised alongside Allied Governments, both in the political and the military sphere, by making use of Belgian war potential which is assembled in France. This is the King's duty. The Government is unanimous in a firm belief that this is so. Finally, it is impossible to contemplate, without grave apprehension, the return of the King to Belgium, under the authority of an occupying Power, especially if this were to continue in the exercise of certain attributions of the royal function under the control of this Power, attributions which would certainly be claimed even though the King decided to abstain from exercising them. As regards the Ministers, their attendance on the King at the time of any future capitulation would only contribute more strongly to give this happening a political aspect

[1] *Rapport, Annexes*, pp. 71-5.

which the Government wished to avoid at all costs. If the Belgian Army were
obliged to surrender, the proper place for the four Ministers who still remain in
the theatre of operation would not be there, but somewhere where they could
continue to exercise their duties—by the side of their colleagues and of the
Allied Governments. A final consideration of these factors together with the
decisive turn which events have taken makes it imperative to organize immediately the departure of my [the Prime Minister's] colleagues and their staffs.
This would make a total of some score of people whose journey to the coast
and embarkation might well become impossible within a short time. That is
why, unless the King has any formal objection, the three Ministers and their
staffs will leave today for Dunkirk, where transports are awaiting them. The
head of the Government, in accordance with the suggestion which the King
has already made during a previous interview, will stay behind until the King
has arranged his own departure. The King will choose this moment so that it
best reconciles the duties which he still thinks he must carry out with respect
to the Army, with his obligations as Head of the State. If the King so decides,
his departure will only take place after all resistance has ceased. But the Prime
Minister makes bold to ask the King to make a firm statement that he intends
to depart rather than allow himself to be taken prisoner. Failing such an
assurance, I should leave with my colleagues for reasons which I have just
recalled.'

After a moment's silence the King answered with an obvious effort. 'I have
decided to stay. Overriding the most substantial logical and political considerations, there are sentimental reasons which cannot be ignored. To leave my
Army would be desertion. I ought, whatever happens, to share the fate of my
troops. Moreover, in order to define more exactly what I think, and to reveal
the frame of mind in which I have come to decide on this line of conduct, I
am going to read to you what I intend to write to the King of England.'

The King read a letter in which he explained to the British sovereign the
motives behind his action, and in which he added, that, whatever happened, he
would never agree to do anything which was contrary to the interests of the
Allies.

Commenting on the last passage of this letter, the King added that, in his
opinion, this particularly applied to the case where the occupying Power tried
to make use of Belgian industrial capacity for the purposes of armaments. 'If I
were', he said again, 'driven to such a necessity, I would rather decide to go
into retirement.' In answer to a question from the Ministers, the King made
it plain that he meant by this that he would abdicate.

At this interview, as at that of the preceding day, we remained standing. The
King showed by his attitude, after expressing the intention of the above summary, that he did not wish to prolong the discussion any further.

But M. Spaak intervened to say: 'Sire, it is impossible for the King and his
Government to separate in this fashion. We would like to have a last talk with
your Majesty in order to explain all that we think. After that, the King can do
what he wishes. But he cannot refuse us this final interview. Is it not possible
for us to sit down, and carry on an exchange of views under conditions which
will allow us to explain fully what we think?'

These words were uttered with a mixture of respect and, so to speak, saddened friendliness. One felt there was an earnest wish not to break the threads, already become so taut, which still bound the Ministers to the Head of the State.

The King sat down after some hesitation, and, with a gesture, gave his Ministers permission to do likewise.

M. Spaak then continued the conversation:

'The King', he stated, 'is, in the unanimous opinion of the Government, about to commit a fatal error. By falling into the hands of the enemy, he is detaching his cause from that of the Allies. He is abandoning the prosecution of the struggle at their side, and this is contrary to the moral obligations which he has contracted by calling the Allies to his assistance. . . . The King will find in France troops whom he could organize. He could continue the struggle, not only with military means, but with those based on the economic activity of the country, which is still considerable abroad, with the resources of the Colony. He would be doing what the King of Norway and the Queen of the Netherlands have done. He would be remaining united to a cause to which the destiny of our country is linked. If the King stayed behind, what could he do? The King, contrary to the expression which he had used, would not, whatever happened, share the fate of his troops. His residence would not be a fortress in Germany but his palace. All that he tried to do would only compromise him and compromise the cause of our independence, because the King would be acting under the coercion of the enemy. As a result the conscience of the nation would be deeply disturbed. I would like the King to tell us what conception he entertains of the role, to which he has several times referred, which he would continue to play in Belgium.'

The King replied to this last question as follows: 'I do not know. I am unaware of what it will be possible for me to do. But I hope that I can continue to maintain in the country a minimum of economic activity, to assist, thereby, its supplies, and to spare my countrymen the worse sufferings such as deportation. If I do not stay in Belgium, I am convinced that I shall never return. The cause of the Allies is lost. Soon, within a few days perhaps, France will, in her turn, be obliged to abandon the struggle, for the disproportion of forces precludes any hope for her. No doubt, Britain will continue to fight, not on the Continent, but on the seas and in her colonies. The war may be a long one. But it will be one in which Belgium will have no opportunity of intervening, and, therefore, the role of this country is finished. For a period which might stretch to several years, Belgium will perhaps only enjoy a limited independence, but this will still allow her a certain degree of national life. Thus, she can await the day, if it should ever come, when, because of unforeseeable vicissitudes, circumstances become more favourable for her. This outlook gives no scope for any attempt to continue in the war beside the Allies. The decision which I am taking is grievously painful to me. Life will certainly be more easy for me if I withdraw to France, if I go and live with my children, whilst waiting for the end of this torture. But I believe, when two roads are open to us, that of duty is always the harder. This is the road which I have chosen.'

It appeared obvious that the King had made his choice. Nothing could turn him aside from his purpose. The Ministers then asked him: 'What does the King think we ought to do?' His reply was: 'As man to man, I tell you plainly that you ought to follow your inspiration, and, if you think you ought to leave, I shall offer no opposition.'

M. Spaak resumed: 'We cannot be satisfied with such an answer. . . . We wish for some instructions, but first we ought to know more of the role which the King thinks he will still be called upon to play in Belgium. Will the King have with him a Government in Brussels?'

Before replying, the King reflected. His attitude gave the impression that he had never asked himself the question. He replied, however, 'Obviously, for I don't want to be a dictator.'

'This Government', continued M. Spaak, 'is not intended by the King to be the present Government?'

The reply was: 'No, no by no means. It is certain that the occupying Power would not consent to that.'

M. Pierlot added: 'The King is aware that we ourselves would not agree to this. We are certainly disturbed by the thought of leaving the King in such tragic circumstances. For my own part, if I were a single man, I might allow myself to be governed by this feeling, and agree to remain, out of attachment to your Majesty's person. But I don't want my children to remember a name to which certain memories would be attached. However, if the King forms a new Government in Brussels, what will the position of the present Government be, not only as regards the Ministers who are present here, but also of those who are in France. Does the King think that they ought to resign?'

The King replied: 'That does indeed seem to me the logical outcome of the situation.'

Pursuing the line of his questioning M. Spaak then observed: 'We must envisage the reaction which would be produced amongst Belgians who are living in free countries, and the eventuality in which this present Government, or another which might be formed to take its place, would decide to prosecute the war at the side of the Allies, whilst, if I understand rightly, the King might have the intention of making peace, or would consider in any case that hostilities had ceased between Belgium and Germany. In my opinion this is a likelihood which we must anticipate, and it is one which, in fact, will occur.'

'If this present Government takes up the attitude outlined by M. Spaak, and carries on the war in France, will it,' then asked M. Pierlot, 'still be the King's Government?'

The King answered: 'No, such a Government would, of necessity, be opposed to me.'

These replies were given with decision, but, on each occasion, after a moment's reflection, which seemed to show that the different possibilities advanced by the Ministers had not hitherto occurred to the King, or, at least, had not been closely examined by him.

During this same interview the Ministers, who were painfully affected by the prospect of having to leave the King in such circumstances, wondered . . . if they should not stay with the King even if they had to shed any official capacity by giving in their resignations.

The King seemed to support this attitude: 'It would be an advantage', he said, 'to have in Belgium as many people as possible, having the moral authority which could be used to maintain the cohesion and unity of the country. On the other hand, even if the Ministers were to resign, and could not, therefore, participate in the Government, they could continue to collaborate with me by giving opinions and counsels. . . .'

But it did not take the Ministers long to see the moral impossibility of this hybrid solution: 'Our place', they stated, 'cannot be in attendance on the King, or, even though we resigned, our presence, as we have already stressed, would help to give to events that political character which we wish to avoid and which, at least, we do not wish to be of our doing. Our place is with our colleagues, with whom we have to co-operate, once a full Government has been constituted.'

The Ministers again took up a consideration which they had already stressed during a previous interview. 'Whatever', they said, 'the King's intentions might be, the line of conduct which he intended to adopt would be interpreted both in Belgium and abroad, especially in Allied countries, as a betrayal of the cause to which the King and Belgium had been morally bound from the time that they appealed to the guarantee of France and of Great Britain. Far from becoming a rallying point, the King would be amongst his countrymen a symbol of variance. The institution of monarchy, which had been the most potent symbol and medium of our national union, would be compromised without doubt beyond repair. Finally, when this news was known in France, where there were two million Belgian refugees, what would be the reactions of the population towards our countrymen?'

The King replied to this last point as follows: 'There are in Belgium six million other Belgians. It is not those who have left the country who are the most worthy of interest, but those who have stayed behind.'

The four Ministers who were present took a personal part in this exchange of views with the result that from it a feeling of complete unanimity emerged between them. But all their entreaties were to be in vain.

Before the audience came to an end, M. Pierlot took up another subject which was causing some preoccupation. 'According to the terms and the spirit of the Constitution', he said, 'the Ministers are responsible for all the actions of the King, whether they have formally assumed responsibility for them by affixing their counter-signature, or whether it is a question of public action carried out by the Head of the State in the exercise of his duties. Since the creation of the Belgian State in its present form every Government has considered that its essential duty was to protect the Crown. We have never failed to carry out this obligation. In the present case we are forced to say that our attitude will have to be different. The King has adopted a line of conduct which is opposed to the unanimous advice of the Government. The latter has not ceased to enunciate the most express reservations. It would be too unjust to place on us a responsibility for which we ought to bear no part. It is a question of an extremely grave problem, upon which hangs the existence of our institutions and our country. We consider that the way in which the King is acting is compromising everything. We have said this—we do not wish in the eyes of history to be considered as responsible for the catastrophe which is taking place. We shall, therefore, be forced, if the King persists in his intentions, not only to forsake the principle of protecting him but also to dissociate ourselves publicly from him. We know that such an action is contrary to established constitutional practice. It is without precedent and breaks the traditions of our public law. But we cannot see any possibility of adopting an attitude other than that which I have just stated.'

The King replied: 'I understand your position. This is what you believe. I know that it is a sincere conviction. You must act according to it.'

The end of the audience was approaching. The King stood up. Before leaving him the Prime Minister asked him yet another question. Alluding to a word uttered by the King during the interview, the sense of which had not seemed clear to the Ministers, M. Pierlot asked what the King had meant when he stated a few moments before that he would prolong resistance as long as it was possible, and whilst there existed the least hope that it would be of use. 'Does the King', specified M. Pierlot, 'consider that, apart from any completely unforeseen event which might modify the situation, the capitulation of the Army can still be avoided or, on the contrary, does he mean that it is certain?'

The reply was: 'It is not certain, it is inevitable.' 'How long', continued the Prime Minister, 'can it still be put off?'

The reply was: 'Twenty-four hours at the most.'

The King left after having taken leave of his Ministers by shaking their hand as is usual, but with a marked shade of uneasiness and coldness.

The inevitable had happened. The Ministers left the Château of Wynendaele at six o'clock deeply impressed by this dramatic scene.

At the end of the interview Leopold III, through Admiral Keyes, sent King George VI a letter in which he informed him of the line of conduct upon which he had decided. This letter, which he had drawn up the day before with the assistance of M. De Man and which he had read to his Ministers, expressed 'plainly what he was thinking and his own intentions' as the Committee of Inquiry stresses in citing the text *in extenso*.[1] Here are the essential points of this text:

Saint André-lez-Bruges,
May 25, 1940.

Belgium has fulfilled the promise which she made in 1937 to maintain her neutrality and to resist, with all the forces at her disposal, whenever her independence might be threatened.

Her means of resistance are now on the point of being crushed. . . .

It is impossible to withdraw any further.

As the entire cadre of officers and of staff are in action, it is impossible to create a new Belgian military force.

And so the assistance which we can give to the Allies will come to an end if our Army is surrounded.

In spite of the varied advice which I have been given, I feel that my duty impels me to follow the fate of my Army and to remain with my people: to act otherwise would mean desertion.

[1] *Rapport*, p. 53.

I am convinced that I can best aid my people by staying with them, rather than in trying to carry on abroad, especially against the rigours of a foreign occupation, the threat of forced labour or of deportation and the difficulties of feeding the country.

By staying in my country, I fully realize that my position will be very difficult, but my essential care will be to prevent my countrymen from being forced to join in any action against the countries which have helped Belgium in her struggle.

If I felt incapable of acting in this manner, and only then, would I abandon the mission which I have taken upon myself.

King George replied immediately. He did so both in his own name and in the name of his Government. For a long time the text of this reply was unknown to the public. It was only on December 23, 1949, that a translation of it was published by *Le Soir*.[1]

Whilst refraining from interfering in the sphere of Belgian domestic policies, the King expressed to Leopold III his 'serious concern at seeing him resolved to place himself under the thumb of the enemy', and warned him against any illusion that he might have the means of protecting his people against the rigours of a German occupation.

Dated May 26 this message was handed by Admiral Keyes early on the 27th to General van Overstraeten, who brought it to the attention of Leopold III. The latter was, therefore, aware of King George's objections well before he sent a flag of truce to the enemy. But *La Libre Belgique*, nevertheless, was to assert on December 24, 1949, that this message from the British King could have had no influence on the final decision of Leopold III because it only reached him after the capitulation.[2]

On May 26 in London towards the end of the afternoon when I was leaving the meeting which I had just had with Churchill and his colleagues, I was told that M. Spaak as well as M. Gutt had expressed a desire to go to Paris with me in the plane which was waiting to fly me there. I found them at the aerodrome. M. Spaak took me aside to tell me that he had some serious news to give me. He gave me an account of the interview at Wynendaele. He described to me the King's attitude, his categoric refusal to leave Belgian territory, his decision to remain there even under enemy occupation. He added that his three colleagues and himself had left Wynendaele inwardly convinced that

[1] The authenticity of this document was confirmed on the same day by the Foreign Office.

[2] In *Albert Ier–Léopold III: Vingt ans de politique militaire belge* (p. 703), General van Overstraeten gives an account of the day of May 27, 1940, which leaves no room for any doubt about this point. *Le Soir*, making use of this account, wrote on December 24, 1949: '*La Libre Belgique* is all the less to be excused for the falsehood which it has given its readers because it has published, in serial instalments, the work of King Leopold's military adviser.'

the King was preparing not only to capitulate but to attempt the constitution in Brussels of a new Government which would be entrusted with the mission of treating with the enemy and even of collaborating with the occupying Power.[1] When M. Spaak had finished his tale, I told him of my surprise. Was it, therefore, already too late to persuade the King to go back on a decision whose consequences must inevitably be disastrous? Was there not a last chance of averting so grave a danger which was threatening us? As I was in any case determined not to neglect the chance of doing this, I immediately instructed M. de Margerie to have a telegram sent, as soon as we arrived in Paris, to our Ambassador in Brussels, asking him to urge the King to escape to Britain.

As soon as they arrived in Paris, the Ministers went to their Embassy, where they held a Council in the evening. 'During its sitting . . .', writes M. Pierlot,[2] 'a telephone communication from the Count Guillaume de Grünne, transmitted from Bruges by the Embassy in London, reached us. The King was asking "for one of the Ministers to give his agreement and send his counter-signature as soon as possible, through M. Frédéricq[3] with a view to accepting the resignation of the Ministers and appointing new ones". What was the purpose of this demand for full powers? . . . It was on the advice of Henri De Man that this demand was made to the Government. . . . If they had agreed to it, the Ministers would have allowed the King to transfer the seat of the legitimate government to Belgium at any moment, and to reconstitute completely the executive power with all its executive organs in the occupied country. The reply of the Government was unanimous and negative.'

The Committee of Inquiry confirms this account. It records in its *Rapport* (p. 59): 'To designate a Minister, the King requires the signature of a Minister in office. The King took the advice of several notable people of whom M. De Man was the only former Minister available. The latter advised the King to ask the Ministers for one of them to agree so that his signature could appear on the instrument of resignation[4]

[1] Is it possible that the four Ministers who were present at the interview at Wynendaele could have formed a mistaken impression of the King's intentions? M. Spaak expressly denied that this could be so in the memoir which he drew up in July, 1940, on *L'Attitude du Gouvernement Belge*, the text of which is also reprinted in the *Annexes* of the *Rapport*. M. Spaak writes: '. . . The recollections [of the four Ministers] are so precise that even today it is difficult for them to admit that they made a mistake. . . . Amongst some of the remarks made by the King during this last conversation there were certain ones which showed a clear intention of constituting a new Government, and indicated that the possibility was envisaged of this Government acting in collaboration with the Occupying Power.'

[2] Pierlot, *op. cit. (Le Soir*, July 16, 1947).

[3] Head of the King's secretariat, who happened to be passing through Paris that day.

[4] In his speech at Limoges (*Rapport, Annexes*, p. 102) M. Spaak is still more categoric: 'On Sunday evening, the King telephoned to ask for a Minister to sign two blank decrees, one announcing the dismissal of the Government, the other giving the nomination of the

of the Ministers then in power, and on the nominations to a new Ministry. Count de Grünne, Controller of the Queen's Household, telegraphed to London in this vein.' Later, the Commission adds (p. 79): 'It was at the end of the meeting, that the Ministers were informed of the King's desire to have at his disposal one or some blank decrees which would allow him later to nominate the Ministers. From that moment, they no longer doubted that it was the King's intention to treat with the enemy.'

That it was in Leopold III's mind to 'treat with the enemy' and not simply to offer him the capitulation of the Belgian Army is affirmed by M. De Man himself in the memoir which he submitted to his country's Courts in order to explain his conduct during the hostilities.[1] He stated in so many words that the King's intention was to conclude an armistice. Now, an armistice, unlike a capitulation which is the exclusive resort of the military Command, is a convention which, like every act of this kind, can only be validly concluded by the Government. Hence the step which was made by the King, and the refusal of the Ministers. 'The King then asked me', continues M. De Man, 'if, assuming it was a question of signing an armistice, I would be ready to take on the political responsibility by becoming a Minister again, and even by forming an Administration. I said "yes" without any hesitation.' M. De Man adds that, for forming this Government the name of M. Hayoit de Termicourt was 'put forward with approval'. Thus, Leopold III had decided to treat: if he could not obtain ministerial sanction which was constitutionally necessary to the creation of a new government, he was determined to do without it. If he did stop half-way on this road, it was, as we shall see, because Hitler told him that he would only accept from him an unconditional capitulation.

On the next day, the 27th, I received in my room a visit from M. Pierlot and General Denis who confirmed the information which M. Spaak had given me.

M. Pierlot summoned the Council of Ministers in the afternoon. The President of the Chamber of Representatives, M. van Cauwelaert, and the President of the Senate, M. Gillon, as well as M. Hymans, Count Henry Carton de Wiart and M. Brunet, Minister of State, were present. At the end of the sitting, the Belgian Government issued through Havas a communiqué in which it 'proclaimed its unanimity in

new Ministers. Need I say that, out of the thirteen Ministers present ... not one consented to lend his name to this manœuvre, as we knew already the line of policy which was being shaped?' And in the above-mentioned memoir M. Spaak writes: 'All those who were present were agreed in seeing in this request the King's wish to carry out not only a military step by capitulating, but political steps, the first of which was to be a change of government.'

[1] M. De Man reports that, on May 11, the King had entrusted him with a special mission by whose provisions he was appointing him a member of his own entourage as well as that of his mother.

affirming its intention of continuing the struggle, whatever happened, at the side of the Allies until a common victory had been won'. It also asked all Belgians 'to maintain complete confidence in the destinies of their motherland', and defined its policy as follows: 'No peace until the independence of the country has been regained, and a respect for the laws and dignity of the country is again observed.' M. Pierlot himself spoke to his countrymen over the wireless to read them this resolution which the Government had just adopted.

And now for the dramatic event itself. At 7 p.m. Weygand came to tell me of the King's surrender. Baudouin writes:[1] 'General Weygand rang me up at 6.30 to say that he had very important news for the Prime Minister. I asked what it was, but he only answered, "It is very serious." A quarter of an hour later he arrived and gave the Prime Minister a telegram from General Champon timed at 6.5 p.m., which bluntly announced the total capitulation of the Belgian Army.'

Here is the text of this telegram:

From Lieutenant-Colonel Morel, north-east Front.

General Champon has telephoned to say: 'The King of the Belgians has sent an envoy to the German High Command to inquire under what conditions it is possible to conclude hostilities between the Belgian and German Armies. The King proposes that the cease-fire should begin at midnight tonight. I have taken note of the communication made by the Chief of the Belgian General Staff, and I have added that the discussion of this condition cannot validly be accepted, nor can it take place except in the presence of accredited representatives of the three Commands, Belgian, French and British, as the three Armies form an entity, and the Belgian Army cannot act alone.'

General Champon is going to establish contact with General Blanchard, but he has asked that the latter be also informed. He would like also to receive instructions.

In recounting the event Weygand writes in *Rappelé au service* (pp. 125–6): 'This news fell like a bolt out of the blue. There had been no warning, no indication which might lead me to anticipate such a step. General Koeltz, who had spent a part of the afternoon with the leader of the French Mission, had not given me any hint of it. The Belgian Command had, indeed, appealed for the support of one of our divisions in an area where it was finding itself in difficulties. . . . There had been nothing to lead me to anticipate the Belgian resolve to cease fighting during the night of May 27. The news only reached me after the request to lay down arms had already been sent to the enemy Command.'

[1] *Op. cit.*, pp. 59–60.

'I immediately warned the Government', such, in any case, was Weygand's reaction. This was, moreover, a perfectly natural one since he obviously could not leave the Government in ignorance of such a serious fact, about which, rightly considering it to be beyond his responsibility to tackle, he had immediately to ask instructions of this same Government.

It was, therefore, only from Weygand that I learned that Leopold III, without warning either Blanchard or Gort, had informed the enemy of his determination to cease fighting. I had the sad duty of bringing in my turn this news from Weygand to the knowledge of the French people. I was, as we shall see later, to do this on the morning of the next day, but not without toning down the energetic language in which Weygand had passed it on to me, and omitting above all the insulting opinion that this same man had, on his arrival at the Council of Ministers, passed on the Belgian Army.

Following the publication in *La Libre Belgique* of extracts from Weygand's memoirs chosen from the pages in which the latter attacks me, I had, in a reply which was published on February 14, 1950, in this newspaper, recalled the source from which the news reached me, and the point of conscience which was raised for me by the need to tell the country the truth and at the same time avoid wounding the legitimate pride of a friendly people. Commenting on the text of my reply, *La Libre Belgique*, whose fearlessness in supporting the cause of Leopold is well known, writes: 'The Belgian Command did all within its powers to warn the Allied Armies of the inescapable need for surrender.' This amounts to saying that the Belgian Command did not give the Allied Command the previous notice which the latter reproaches it for not having given. This admission was all the more valuable in that *La Libre Belgique* printed it on February 14, that is to say the date when the official *Moniteur* of the Kingdom published the law which decreed a referendum on the Royal Question. Thus, the controversy which had lasted so long on this point of fact seemed to be closed. As for specifying the obligations which the Belgian Command ought to assume in this particular case, it would have been in bad taste for me to meddle in a debate which, even if it was still not settled, was entirely of a military nature.

The supporters of the Leopoldist cause have, nevertheless, maintained, by *a posteriori* justification that warnings were duly given by the Belgians to the Allies. Thus, in *Le rôle de l'armée belge en 1940*, General Baron Verhaegen reproduces (p. 87) as an Appendix, a document from which it is inferred that M. Gutt, during a visit which he paid me on May 19, drew my attention to the danger which the Belgian Army ran at that time of being encircled and to the consequences which could result from such a situation. This is equivalent to saying that

M. Gutt gave me implicitly to understand that the capitulation of the Belgian Army was at hand. Now, I contend that M. Gutt limited himself during this interview to a description of the hardships of Belgians who, driven from their homes by the enemy invasion and seeking refuge in France, found themselves stopped at the frontier by the military authorities who were closing our roads. I had no difficulty in convincing my questioner that the Command, because of its responsibility for the conduct of the battle, must of necessity keep all avenues of communication free, and that, this being so, it was impossible for him to object to its arbitrary right to regulate civilian use of the roads.

The King had, thus, sent a flag of truce without even consulting General Blanchard to whom the Belgian Army was subordinated, and merely informed the French and British Missions with him of the fact. His envoy, General Derousseaux, left General Headquarters at 5 p.m. The immediate reaction, Champon's protest, will be well understood. Yet he was well aware of the state of the Belgian Army.

In his *Mémorandum sur les evénéments qui ont amené la reddition de l'armée belge,*[1] the King writes that he answered Champon 'a little later, that the mission was confining itself to asking under what conditions fighting could be suspended'. His envoy brought back Hitler's reply at 10 p.m.: unconditional surrender. At 11 p.m. the King accepted this, and proposed that fighting should cease at 4 a.m. At 12.20 a.m. the protocol for surrender was signed. At 1.30 a.m. Champon, who had already left General Headquarters to get to La Panne from where he hoped to reach France through Britain, was told of the surrender.

Weygand replied to Champon's message:

'1. I am immediately advising the Government of the fact.

'2. Pending new instructions, I order Blanchard to sever his contacts with the Belgian troops.

'3. In agreement with General Gort, Blanchard will take all the necessary urgent decisions to guard against this act of desertion.'

According to the *Mémorandum*, Champon at 3.15 a.m. on the 28th communicated a telegram from Weygand to the King's General Headquarters:

'The French and British Governments are in agreement that they must save the honour of their Armies by breaking off relations with the Belgian Army.'

Late on the evening of the 27th, Admiral Keyes made on behalf of the British Government a final approach in order to persuade Leopold III and Queen Elisabeth to go to London. Both refused.

[1] *Rapport, Annexes,* pp. 75-7.

The Admiral, who only managed with great difficulty to embark, sailed all night to regain Britain. At 11 a.m. on the 28th he went to Churchill, and gave him a report of his mission. According to the testimony[1] of a Belgian officer, Admiral Keyes appears to have found the Prime Minister 'very worked up about the failure' of the efforts made to persuade Leopold III to come to Britain.

We have, unfortunately, irrefutable proof that the King acted of his own free will behind the back of the Allies, and that his step was considered by his companions in arms as a defection at the height of the battle.

Baudouin notes on May 27:[2]

'General Weygand arrived at midday for the usual conference in the Prime Minister's room at which Marshal Pétain and I were also present. . . . He was very dissatisfied with the Belgian army, and he had just sent a strong telegram to General Champon, meant, in reality, for the King of the Belgians. He had also telegraphed to Lord Gort asking him to take some of the pressure off the Belgians by a counter-attack on the Lys.

'The General said that he had sent General Koeltz to the northern group of armies, and that at nine o'clock this morning General Koeltz had met Lord Gort at Cassel. General Koeltz had gone with wide powers, and Weygand expected from him some freely-made suggestions.'[3]

Baudouin notes on the 29th:[4]

'At 9.30 a.m. there was a conference in the Premier's room with Marshal Pétain, General Weygand, and Admiral Darlan. General Weygand . . . said that General Koeltz, whom he had sent to the northern group of armies and who had returned at 3 p.m. on Monday, had met the Belgian Chief of Staff, who gave him no inkling of the possibility of a capitulation on the following night. Quite the contrary, for this officer asked General Koeltz for the help of a French division for a counter-attack which he envisaged for the next day. It

[1] *Rapport, Annexes*, p. 113.   [2] *Op. cit.*, pp. 58–9.

[3] General Koeltz was, as we have seen, the Deputy Chief of Staff in charge of operations. This shows the trust and authority which he enjoyed with the three chiefs who formed jointly our Supreme Command: Weygand, Commander-in-Chief of all the Sea, Land, and Air Forces; Georges, Commander-in-Chief on the North-east Front and Doumenc, Army Chief of Staff.

[4] *Op. cit.*, p. 61. Baudouin had noted on the 28th (p. 60): 'General Le Rond . . . told me that in February, 1939, when Hitler had made up his mind to attack the Western Powers, King Leopold III had given Germany to understand that Belgium would allow her to attack Holland without intervention. It was only in November last that the King changed his mind.'

Sforza classes Leopold (*L'Italie telle que je l'ai vue*, p. 111) among the rulers of the post-war period who wished to play the dictatorship, the others being Constantine of Greece, Alexander of Yugoslavia, and Carol of Roumania.

would thus seem that the negotiations had been conducted by the King in the utmost secrecy.'

Weygand was to confirm these facts himself on October 29, 1940, in a speech which he gave at Dakar to the officers of the ground, sea and air forces in garrison there:[1]

'Two days later (May 27) . . . the Belgian Army . . . gave up the struggle without giving any warning, whilst at the same time General Koeltz was informing me that it was asking for a reserve division to help it to contain the German thrust. At six o'clock the King asked for hostilities to cease and for an armistice, without giving us any warning.'

Can one be astonished, therefore, that General Koeltz, on meeting Gort shortly after 11 p.m. learned with stupefaction the rumour which was being noised abroad? In Major Vautrin's report on the period during which he was in charge of liaison between our First Army and British Headquarters we read: 'I accompanied General Gort during the evening to Bastion 32 [at Dunkirk], where we arrived about 10 p.m. . . . There Lord Gort met General Koeltz. The latter asked him if he had heard that the King of the Belgians was said to have negotiated an armistice which was to enter into force that same night at midnight. General Gort was completely ignorant of the news which turned out to be correct. He left immediately for his Command Post at Houtkerque to prepare for the grave threat brought about by the Belgian defection.' Gort, in his Report, expresses himself in almost the same words. 'In the evening I left my headquarters at Houtkerque with . . . the French liaison officer. . . . I went on to Bastion 32 at Dunkirk to visit Admiral Abrial. . . . While I was at the Bastion, General Koeltz asked me, shortly after 11 p.m. whether I had yet heard that H.M. the King of the Belgians had asked for an armistice from midnight that night. This was the first intimation I had received of this intention, although I had already formed the opinion that the Belgian Army was now incapable of offering serious or prolonged resistance to the enemy. I now found myself suddenly faced with an open gap of 20 miles between Ypres and the sea through which enemy armoured forces might reach the beaches.

'Owing to congestion on the roads, I did not get back to my

---

[1] This was, in fact, a private meeting where statements could be freely made to an audience before whom Weygand could express himself frankly and fully. When he gave the Committee of Inquiry on April 12, 1949, a 'typewritten summary' of 'his words', Weygand stressed the 'improvised and unofficial' nature of his 'account, which was given without any manuscript' and 'was reproduced in the same form as he had delivered it'. 'It was not', he said, 'a written speech. . . . This was a typewritten version which has been given to me. . . . It was not a question of any meeting . . . it was rather a heart-to-heart chat.'

headquarters at Houtkerque until about 4.30 a.m. on May 28. There I found that a telegram had been received from the War Office at 1.30 a.m. saying that H.M. the King of the Belgians was capitulating at midnight.'

Here is a final testimony, and from one who was an eye-witness. General Champon, after having had to wait three days at La Panne, managed to embark on the 30th at 8 p.m. for Dover. The next day he gave to M. Corbin an account of the happenings of the 27th at Leopold III's General Headquarters. The following is a summary of it. At the beginning of the afternoon the King and van Overstraeten walked up and down the room which they usually used. They discussed matters with animation. Champon watched the scene from a neighbouring room, which was separated from theirs by a glass partition. The discussion between Leopold III and his A.D.C. concerned the dispatch of a flag of truce to the enemy. But it was only after the event, that is to say, after the departure of the envoy towards the German outposts, that Champon was informed of the King's decision to surrender.

I was certainly not aware in all their details of the circumstances in which Leopold III had taken his fatal step. But Champon's telegram left no room for doubt: the King had acted on his own responsibility and without the knowledge of the Allied Command.

As soon as the news was known, M. Pierlot came to see me at the Rue Saint-Dominique. He was accompanied by General Denis and M. Le Tellier. Baudouin writes:[1] 'At 7.10 p.m. there was a meeting of the Prime Minister, Marshal Pétain, General Weygand, M. Pierlot, the Belgian Premier, and General Denis, the Belgian Minister of National Defence. M. Paul Reynaud addressed them, and he did not mince his words. General Denis had tears in his eyes, and M. Pierlot declared that he was in complete disagreement with the King, who had betrayed Belgium.'[2]

---

[1] Op. cit., p. 60.
[2] The word 'treason', it will be seen, fell from M. Pierlot's lips. I do not deny that I myself, in my turn, took up this term in private conversations. But the reader will be satisfied, by what I say later, that, contrary to a rumour as persistent as it is calumnious, I refrained in my public statements from calling Leopold III's action by this name. This is a distinction of importance. Having thus clarified the situation, I will borrow from Herriot (Episodes, 1940–1944, pp. 40–3) the following account:

'On May 27, M. Frans van Cauwelaert, Minister of State, and President of the Belgian Chamber of Deputies, came to see me at 6 p.m. in order to assure me, following a meeting of a full Council of Ministers which he had attended, of the Belgian Government's fidelity to the Allies. But, at the same time, he told me that the Belgian Army was going to be obliged to lay down its arms, and that the King meant to allow himself to be captured with his troops. Stupefied and dismayed, I painted to him the extreme gravity of the situation which would thus develop. . . .

'Before the end of our conversation, I stressed to M. Frans van Cauwelaert the danger behind any future line of action which the King might take. . . . He told me that the Belgian Government unanimously repudiated the King. I answered him that this would

M. Pierlot, in his account[1] places the time of the interview at 8.15 p.m. He notes that both Pétain and Weygand kept 'obstinately silent', and that Pétain was 'obviously hostile'. He adds: 'M. Reynaud announced . . . that at 6 p.m. the King had sent an envoy to the German Command. He revealed forthwith the point of view which he was to develop a short time later over the wireless: capitulation in full battle without previously exhausting all means of resistance: desertion of the Allied Armies whom Belgium had called to her help: the campaign jeopardized through the fault of the Belgian Army. M. Reynaud stressed the fact that the Allied Command insisted that it had not been warned. Losing patience with these reproaches, General Denis energetically interrupted M. Reynaud to protest against his opinion of the Belgian Army's conduct. His clarification of the situation somewhat softened the aggressive warmth of the President of the Council, and the latter ended his statement with the question: "And now what does your Government intend to do?" I began by telling M. Reynaud that I could not accept his comments on the military events which had just taken place, and I stressed in this respect what General Denis had just previously said. . . . I then informed him of the decision of the Council of Ministers stating: "The Belgian Government intends to continue the fight at the side of France and Great Britain with all the means still at its disposal: troops under training, potentialities for economic activity . . . colonial resources. But I would like to know if, we, for our part, can count on the French Government." M. Reynaud promised his collaboration.'

I have no quarrel with M. Pierlot's account. It is probable that my reproaches were severe. But was not this one of my grievances, which was unfortunately well founded? Moreover, Pétain and Weygand were seated besides me. M. Pierlot has stressed their icy silence, their hostile attitude. Could I have shown myself less severe than they were?[2]

At the end of the meeting of the Council of Ministers in the evening at the Elysée, when I spoke of the King's surrender another interview took place between MM. Pierlot, Spaak and myself, this time at my own

not perhaps be enough to satisfy the French people who would with some reason be irritated.

'As soon as M. van Cauwelaert had left, I informed M. Paul Reynaud over the telephone of the conversation. He was at that moment talking with M. Pierlot, Marshal Pétain, General Weygand and the Belgian War Minister.

'About 8.30 p.m. Paul Reynaud called me up on the telephone. His first words were incisive. "The King of the Belgians has betrayed us. . . . M. Spaak, who came back with me by air, warned me of this yesterday." He told me that there would be a meeting of the Council of Ministers at 10 p.m.'

[1] Baudouin, op. cit. (Le Soir, July 16, 1947).

[2] I have reported above the words which Laure maintains that I uttered on May 18, the day when he entered my Government: 'The entry of the Allied troops into Belgium was a serious mistake. . . . We are being made to suffer through the actions of neutral States.'

home. We were faced by this undeniable and overwhelming fact: eighteen days after having entered the war, the King had capitulated in the full tide of battle at the head of an army of nearly five hundred thousand men, the largest army which Belgium had ever raised. Four years earlier, he had broken off the treaty which bound his country to France, its natural ally. On his appeal we had just undertaken, at a time chosen by the enemy, this disastrous Belgian campaign. And now. . . . My feelings can be well imagined! All the Belgian Ministers were filled with sorrow and indignation. We decided that M. Pierlot and I should speak on the wireless; he would announce the disaster which had befallen us to the Belgian people, and I should do so to the French.[1]

This event harboured for me another danger—which the Belgian Ministers did not suspect—since Pétain and Weygand were themselves desirous of capitulating and separating France from her allies, if the Battle of France were to be lost. I had, therefore, perforce to bring down the condemnation of the entire country on the surrender. To do this, I only had to tell the truth. I did not even tell all of it, for I refrained, naturally, from making the slightest mention of what the Belgian Ministers had said to me about their belief in the King's intention to form a new Government in order to ask for an armistice. Moreover, I gave them the main outlines of what I was going to say.[2]

At 8 a.m. I made the speech which later earned me the honour of attacks in the German Press of Paris, and the Press of Vichy.

In his speech on June 25, 1940, over the Bordeaux radio Pétain was to pass a judgement on the Belgian Army, for which I allowed him to assume responsibility, but whose insulting harshness I myself did not endorse in the slightest: 'The battle of Flanders has ended by the surrender of the Belgian Army in open battle, and the surrounding of British and French divisions: the latter have fought bravely.' But no doubt it was pointed out to him that he was the last man qualified to

[1] In his statement at Limoges, M. Spaak describes this interview thus:

'We were awakened . . . in the small hours of Tuesday by M. Paul Reynaud, who stated that he could no longer hide the news of the Belgian Army's surrender. As he feared that this news might provoke some reaction amongst the French against the Belgians, he asked us to make an immediate statement. We went to see him, intimated to him our intention of clearing up any ambiguities, and left on excellent terms. We went back to the Embassy, and drafted a preliminary declaration, the text of which was not quite the same as that read during the afternoon by the Prime Minister. I dictated it to a . . . boy-scout. As I was about to begin my dictation I said to him, "My poor child, I am about to dictate to you something which is not very pleasant or encouraging." He answered: "If it comes from M. Pierlot, it will in any case be honest." (Applause.) This well described our actions.'

[2] In a speech which he made at Montevideo, on August 27, 1942, Count Sforza declared (cf. op. cit., p. 219) that, if France had surrendered, it was chiefly because the King of the Belgians 'failed in his duty and, contrary to the wishes of his Ministers, refused to fly to the Congo in order to continue resistance there'.

censure the surrender, since he himself went further than the King of the Belgians had done, in surrendering France as he did, with her Army, her Fleet and her Empire. He wasted no time over his *volte-face*. On September 2, 1940, he rescinded the decree whereby Leopold III had been struck off the roll of the Legion of Honour, a step which had raised not the slightest objection from him or from Weygand, when I announced it to them at our daily meeting on the 28th. At the same time that Pétain rehabilitated the King, he had me reproached in his Press for having accused the monarch of 'treason' and 'felony'. If I had done this I would have seriously failed to observe the respect which the Head of a Foreign State, whoever he may be, is entitled to receive from the leader of a government. But, on this score as on so many others, Vichy took its customary liberty with the truth. The best answer to this allegation is to produce the text of my speech, which is given in the *Annexes* to the *Rapport* (p. 98) of the Committee of Inquiry itself:

'I have to announce a grave event to the French people. This took place during the night. France can no longer count on the assistance of the Belgian Army. Since four o'clock this morning the French and British Armies have been fighting alone in the north against the enemy.

'You know what the situation was. Following the breaking of our front on May 14, the German Army drove a wedge between our Armies, which were split into two groups, one in the north, the other in the south. In the south are the French divisions which are holding a new front along the Somme and the Aisne, and linking up with the Maginot Line, which is still unbreached. In the north were a group of three Allied Armies, the Belgian Army, the British Expeditionary Force, and some French divisions with whom many of us have some dear one fighting. This group of three Armies was under the command of General Blanchard. It was supplied through Dunkirk. The French and British Armies were defending the port to the south and west, the Belgian Army to the north.

'It is this Belgian Army which has suddenly surrendered unconditionally at the height of battle at the orders of its King, without warning its French and British comrades in the fight, and has thus opened the road to Dunkirk for the German divisions.

'This same King eighteen days ago, who until then had pretended to attach the same value to Germany's word as to that of the Allies, had addressed to us an appeal for help. Following a plan prepared since last December by the Allied General Staffs we answered this appeal.

'Now, in the full course of battle, without any warning to General

Blanchard, without, indeed, a thought or a word for the French and British soldiers who came, in answer to his anguished appeal, to the help of his country, King Leopold III of Belgium has laid down arms. It is an action unprecedented in history.

'The Belgian Government has told me that the King's decision was taken against the unanimous desire of the responsible Ministers. It has added that it is resolved to place at the service of the common cause all the resources of its country which it can still control and that, above all, it wishes to raise a new Army, and to collaborate in the task of arming France. . . .'

Baudouin writes[1] in an entry dated May 28: 'I went to the Prime Minister at half-past nine, and I suggested to him an appeal to President Roosevelt. I said, "When one is let down by one's relatives, the usual thing to do is to appeal to one's friends. What our pride prevented us from doing has suddenly become possible."'

In the evening of the 29th Weygand issued the moving communiqué:

'The French and British troops who are fighting in the north of France are maintaining, with a heroism worthy of their traditions, a struggle of exceptional intensity. For a fortnight they have been giving battle, detached from the body of our troops by German formations which are constantly reinforced. Attacked incessantly on the eastern and western flanks, they are contesting the ground with the enemy, clinging on to it, or counter-attacking with equal stubbornness and valour.

'Whilst they were facing these attacks, the Allied Army which was defending the positions of the Schelde and the coast to the north-west of Ostend under the direct orders of King Leopold III, received from the King an order to cease fire, and thus opened the road to Ypres, Furnes and Dunkirk.

'Since then our troops under the command of Generals Blanchard and Prioux, and in close collaboration with General Gort's British Army have had to face an increased danger. Displaying in this grave circumstance an indomitable resolution, they have done their utmost to manœuvre towards the coasts at the cost of severe battles.'

Churchill, in his turn, had asked the Commons on the 28th to allow him some delay before uttering judgement on the possible responsibility of the King, so that he could do this with a full knowledge of the facts. It was, therefore, only after a searching inquiry, and, moreover, after having heard Admiral Keyes plead the cause of Leopold III, with the warmth of friendship, that Churchill was, on June 4, to make his

[1] *Op. cit.*, p. 60.

noteworthy statement in the Commons. *La Libre Belgique* said of
this on October 22, 1949, that, 'going one better' than the complaints
which I had voiced a week before, it drew up an indictment of
'pre-war Belgian policy'.

Here are Churchill's words:

'But another blow which might well have proved final was yet to
fall upon us. The King of the Belgians had called upon us to come to
his aid. Had not this Ruler and his Government severed themselves
from the Allies, who rescued their country from extinction in the late
war, and had they not sought refuge in what has proved to be a fatal
neutrality, the French and British Armies might well at the outset have
saved not only Belgium but perhaps even Poland. Yet at the last
moment, when Belgium was already invaded, King Leopold called
upon us to come to his aid, and even at the last moment we came. He
and his brave, efficient Army, nearly half a million strong, guarded
our eastern flank and thus kept open our only line of retreat to the sea.
Suddenly, without prior consultation, with the least possible notice,
without the advice of his Ministers and upon his own personal act, he
sent a plenipotentiary to the German Command, surrendered his Army
and exposed our whole flank and means of retreat.

'I asked the House a week ago to suspend its judgment because the
facts were not clear, but I do not feel that any reason now exists why
we should not form our own opinions about this pitiful episode. The
surrender of the Belgian Army compelled the British at the shortest
notice to cover a flank to the sea more than thirty miles in length.
Otherwise all would have been cut off, and all would have shared the
fate to which King Leopold had condemned the finest Army his
country had ever formed. So in doing this and in exposing this flank,
as anyone who followed the operations on the map will see, contact
was lost between the British and two out of the three corps forming
the First French Army, who were still further from the coast than we
were, and it seemed impossible that any large number of Allied troops
could reach the coast.'

Was there a single word, either in Churchill's speech or mine, which
did not tell the truth? Let us, therefore, put aside these polemics about
the 'treason' and 'felony' of the King of the Belgians. They are expressions which were used at the time by newspapers which, under the
Vichy régime, found that the best way of changing their tunes was to
attribute them to me.

M. Pierlot had made that same day, a few hours after myself, a
speech full of dignity and moderation. Addressing his fellow countrymen, he told them in particular:

'Belgians, ignoring the formal and unanimous advice of the Government, the King has just opened negotiations and is treating with the enemy. Belgium will be astounded by this. But the fault of one man cannot be laid at the door of the entire nation. Our Army has not deserved the fate that has been imposed on it. The action which we deplore possesses no legal value. It does not pledge the country. . . . The King, by breaking the links which unite him to his people, has placed himself within the power of the invader. Henceforth, he is no longer in a position to govern, for obviously the duties of the Head of State cannot be exercised under the control of a foreign Power. . . .

'In a meeting in Paris, the Government, with the agreement of the Presidents of the two legislative Assemblies[1] and those Ministers of State whom it has been possible to consult,[2] and in confidence that it is interpreting the national will, has decided to continue the struggle for the salvation of the country. . . .

'Belgians, we are living through the most painful trial of our history. The time has come for us to remember the lessons of courage and honour offered by those who fought from 1914 to 1918. Whatever happens, we shall remain worthy of them.'[3]

The reader now knows all the details of the facts.

I, myself, shall confine myself to recalling that I have never held the Belgian people responsible for the grievous events which I have just related. A wave of indignation certainly did rise on May 28 in France and Britain. Because I feared that this indignation might translate itself into acts of annoyance directed against the Belgians who, driven from their country by the invader, had fled into France, I immediately ordered our censorship to see that the Press did not place on the Belgian nation the responsibility for the King's action. A leader of the Belgian Socialist Party has recently informed me that as a result of my words over the wireless, Belgian refugees did become the object of discriminatory treatment. I was deeply grieved by this. I am anxious to state that no one deplores more than myself such excesses, which were exactly opposite to my instructions, and which are explained but not excused by the confusion of the desertion and by the despair provoked amongst our nation by the defeat of its armies. Most happily, and this is the essential thing, the traditional friendship of Belgium and France emerged unimpaired from this test which was equally cruel for both our countries.

[1] MM. van Cauwelaert and Gillon, respectively Presidents of the Chamber and the Senate.

[2] The Ministers of State who were then in France were Count Henry Carton de Wiart, MM. Hymans, Brunet, van De Vyvere, van Overbergh and Poncelet. M. van Cauwelaert, President of the Chamber, was also, as we have seen, a Minister of State.

[3] *La Libre Belgique* of October 22, 1949, reproaches M. Pierlot for having in this speech 'gone even further' than my accusations, and for having 'subjected the King to the obloquy of the nation'.

MAY 29: THE FIRST WEYGAND MEMORANDUM

At our morning meeting on the 29th, Weygand gave me a note to read, which he had previously—according to his deposition at Riom—got Pétain to approve.[1] Here is its text:

'A determination to fight to the bitter end in our present positions, and the order that no subordinate commanders should consider retreat does not relieve the Commander-in-Chief of the task of examining, because of the grave circumstances, all possibilities.

'The French Army is staking, in the defence of its present positions, all the forces which are at its disposal after the reverses of the Meuse and in the north. If this defence is finally broken, the French Government will have to take vital decisions. It is important to plan these ahead, so that the Government will not be obliged to come to a decision under the pressure of events.

'Because of the enormous disparity between the attacking and defending forces and means—our defence being partly improvised during the course of the battle—it is possible that, despite the heroic efforts of all, the positions which we hold at present may finally be deeply pierced. In this eventuality the power of penetration and exploitation which the enemy derives from his armoured units and his Air Force might allow him to reach the vital centres of our country in a short time. Above all, the French Army might be powerless to stop an enemy thrust against the Paris region, where an important part of our war industries is concentrated. In this case, France would be incapable of continuing a struggle which ensured a coordinated defence of her territory.

'In the great battles of the last war it was always possible to close up the pockets made by attacks, because armies did not have at their service any weapon of exploitation comparable to the combination of tank and plane. During the 1870 war, it was possible for the Government of National Defence to build up again, once the armies in the

---

[1] Here is the text of the letter in which Pétain gave his agreement to Weygand:

Paris, May 29, 1940.
8, Boulevard des Invalides.

Marshal Pétain.

My dear Weygand,

I don't see that I can add anything at the moment to your memorandum, but it seems to me that it would be fitting to inform the British Government as soon as possible and invite it to come to Paris.

Accept my friendly and sincere wishes.

Ph. Pétain.

Let us note that Pétain, like Weygand, avoids writing the word *armistice*.

He sees nothing to add 'at the moment'. He thinks that it is necessary to invite the British Government 'to come to Paris'. This was what Weygand was already asking at the meeting of the War Committee on May 25.

field had been destroyed, other armies which could prolong resistance for another five months and thus save our honour. Today, even if France had at her disposal, which she has not, the necessary arms, clothing and equipment, the enemy would not give her the time to organize these armies and train them in the use of modern weapons of war.

'The Commander-in-Chief informed the Government of the military situation at a meeting of the War Committee on May 25. Since that date our Armies on the left flank have strengthened their positions on the Aisne and the Somme. But the defection of the Belgian Army in the north is speeding up the hour of decision, which will free the German armoured divisions to operate against our defensive line.

'The importance to be attached to a victorious resistance on this line is such that no effort should be spared in reinforcing it. That is why the Commander-in-Chief thinks it necessary that the British Government, which has been warned of the situation, should be advised to give all the assistance in its power to the defence of our lines, namely:

> two or three divisions formed in England;
> tank, anti-tank and anti-aircraft units;
> the support of aircraft based in England.

'It seems, on the other hand, also essential that the British Government should know that a moment might come after which France would find herself, against her will, unable to put up a fight which would be of any military use in the protection of her soil.

'*This moment would be marked by the final break-through of the positions, in which the French Armies have been ordered to fight without thought of retreat.*'

This memorandum was accompanied by commentaries from Pétain and Weygand about the need for soliciting an armistice in this likelihood, a need which I considered as contrary both to the honour and the interest of France.

MAY 29: MY REPLY TO THE FIRST WEYGAND MEMORANDUM

Faithful to my resolve to avoid a rupture, I replied that very day with the following memorandum:

'I have informed the British Government this same day through its Ambassador that the memorandum which you handed me this morning means:

'1. that, in conformity with the general instructions given by the

Government, you have decided to offer battle, without any intention of retreat, on the defensive line established by you between Abbeville and Switzerland;

'2. that, if the positions defended at present on this line are seriously breached, France would be unable to continue a struggle which would ensure the co-ordinated defence of her territory;

'3. that, because of the decisive importance that the resistance on this line has for the Allies, the French Government requests the British Government to comply with the demands enumerated in your memorandum.

'Because, in the eventuality previously mentioned, the whole of the national territory could no longer be defended does not necessarily mean that we would be able to suspend hostilities in circumstances which would be compatible with the honour and vital interests of France.

'Therefore, since, in view of this eventuality, the enemy would be in a position to make rapid thrusts over the whole area of the territory, I am asking you to have the goodness to study preparations for putting into a state of defence a national redoubt around a naval port which would give us the use of the sea, and especially lines of communication with our allies. This national redoubt ought to be equipped and provisioned—especially in ammunition—like a true fortress. It would comprise the Breton peninsula. Thus, the Government would remain seated in metropolitan France, and continue the war by using our naval forces and our Air Force, which would be employed in North Africa.

'I should add that it is my intention to raise two classes of conscripts,[1] and send them to North Africa so that they can contribute to its defence with weapons bought abroad.'

MAY 29: I PREPARE FOR THE CONTINUATION OF THE WAR IN NORTH AFRICA

It can be seen that I did not make either my intention to call two additional classes of recruits to the colours (this was technically the affair of the Army General Staff and not of the Command), or my resolve to continue the war in North Africa, conditional on the outcome of the battle.

Pétain, according to his biographer[2] and Weygand, through his

---

[1] One of the two classes would have been legally due for call-up in October, 1939, but this was adjourned. To the complaints of Gamelin about this, the Chief of Army Staff replied, on behalf of the Minister, that we must not cut our corn before it was ripe. We knew, however, that the Germans had then twice as many men of twenty years old than we had under the colours.

[2] Laure, *op. cit.*, p. 434.

friend, Charles Reibel[1] in *Pourquoi et comment fut décidée la demande d'armistice* (*juin 10–17, 1940*), stated that I passed from the solution of the 'Breton Redoubt' to that of continuing the war in North Africa, as if the two were contradictory. The two solutions were, on the contrary, complementary, and it was as such that I offered them to Weygand in the presence of Pétain.

I should add, however, that Mandel, whom I told about this plan for the 'Breton Redoubt', informed me that, as Minister of the Interior he was opposed to it. First, he considered that it was impossible to rule France from Brest, and secondly, the Government, in retreating to the extremity of the Breton peninsula would give the country the impression that it was being left to its fate. He was in favour of a withdrawal to Bordeaux. I was not convinced by his objections because I thought it was of great moral importance to the Government not to leave the country until it had resisted to the very last. We shall see why this stage of the 'Breton Redoubt' was abandoned.

I began to prepare for continuing the war in North Africa. Weygand, who was later to state in his evidence at Riom that the plan was 'absurd and repugnant', did not at that time object either orally or in writing. I was, nevertheless, to meet scepticism and apathy on part of the General Staff. When I told General Colson, Chief of General Staff of Home Forces, of my intention to raise two classes of conscripts to be sent to Africa[2] his reply was: 'It is useless. You won't have any rifles to give them.'

Thus, whilst Germany was forming successive armoured divisions, France, with the enemy at her throat, could not even raise one class of recruits, because rifles were lacking! The manufacture of rifles was not, however, grounds for controversy as were armoured divisions and fighter aircraft. . . . Darlan told me that it was impossible to ship two classes of recruits to North Africa, even if we had British assistance, and I, therefore, decided on calling up half a class (a hundred and twenty-five thousand men), and on buying rifles in Spain and the U.S.A.[3] The evidence collected on this subject by the Riom Court gives some impression of the disorder existing at the Ministry of War. In his evidence at Riom, Weygand stated there were at the time only five thousand rifles. At the hearing, when the Commander of one depot complained that he had not had enough weapons to instruct his staff,

[1] Reibel was a member of the Senate Army Commission. In his deposition of June 23, 1949, before the Committee of Inquiry, Weygand stated: 'I have told you of my friendship for M. Reibel. I knew M. Reibel when he was a close friend of Marshal Foch, and I have continued that friendship.'
[2] The last three months of the 1938 class were called up on June 8 and 9, a total of a hundred and twenty thousand recruits. In spite of the scepticism of the General Staff, Gras rifles were found in the end for arming territorial formations, and this allowed us to arm the recruits with Lebel rifles.
[3] I entrusted General de Gaulle with this task as soon as he joined my Government.

the Commander of an arsenal answered him amidst general mirth: 'If I had been asked for them, I would have sent them. There were as many as were wanted!'

It needed plenty of spirit to laugh at such a thing.

I ran into new difficulties about accommodation and training for the half class of recruits which I was raising. I was told that it was impossible from the point of view of billeting them, and because of sanitary difficulties. On June 2 General Noguès, Commander-in-Chief of the North African theatre of operations, sent the following telegram to the Ministry of War:

'In reply to your telegram . . . of June 1.

'Accommodation and training in North Africa of the French contingent to be called to the colours in June is meeting the following difficulties:

'1. as regards accommodation in barracks, etc., Algeria and Morocco have not the barracks, hutments, equipment for sheltering or encamping necessary for such a large number of effectives;

'2. as regards clothing, equipment and arms, there are no supplies in North Africa; all necessary equipment and arms would have to be supplied by Metropolitan France;

'3. as regards training, all cadres would have to be furnished by the Metropolis; the possibility of training is also greatly hampered because of a lack of special means for training in technical arms;

'4. as regards medical problems, calling to the colours in North Africa at a time when the hottest season is about to begin, which will last until the end of September, can only entail very severe hardship for young Frenchmen, who are not accustomed to the climate, and who, moreover, will be accommodated under very makeshift conditions. Serious difficulties were experienced in this respect last September when it was a question of effectives, older and more robust than young recruits. The medical personnel in North Africa is insufficient to cope with present needs, and would also have to be strengthened. Algeria has always asked for recruits not to be called up there in April.

'Under such conditions I do not consider the suggested substantial call-up is possible. However, about twenty thousand recruits could be accommodated and trained in Algeria or Morocco on condition that arms, clothing, equipment, tanks, material for mobile constructions, supplies for feeding, and the *necessary cadres*, including medical personnel, are supplied by the home country.

'Because of a dearth of training facilities, particularly as regards technical weapons, the majority of these recruits ought to be drafted into the infantry.

'Finally, it would be necessary to avoid sending them immediately after call-up so that we can have a certain period to make the required arrangements.'

On June 3, General Colson addressed the following 'verbal reminder' to me:

'The question has been verbally raised by the Minister's secretariat whether it would be opportune to dispatch and train in North Africa the French contingent to be called up in June, namely about a hundred and fifteen thousand men.

'The Commander-in-Chief of the North African theatre of operations, whose opinion has been asked, has sent a telegram . . . a copy of which is in the hands of the Minister's secretariat.

'There should be added to the objections offered by the General in command the fact that the transport of this contingent can only be made at the rate of twenty thousand men a week, and will thus be spread over about six weeks.

'Consequently the Army General Staff thinks it desirable that this contingent should not be brought on to the strength of the Army in North Africa.

'It should be noted, moreover, that the twenty thousand recruits, which the Commander-in-Chief of the North African theatre of operations proposes in Algeria and Morocco, represents not the number of French recruits living in North Africa (which is around five thousand), but a part of the metropolitan contingent.'

I summoned Colson, and made known to him my intention of overriding his objection: 'We are at war', I told him. 'We can manage to accommodate these recruits, if we make up our minds to do so.' The Director of Medical Services, whom I had summoned, had admitted that the medical objections were not insuperable. When he was leaving my room, Colson, from whom I did not hide my determination to break down any obstacles which might arise, said to the head of my military secretariat: 'Please draw the attention of the President to the fact that this is only a "verbal reminder" . . .'

The soldiers had borrowed from the diplomats their 'verbal reminders'.

Thirteen days later Colson[1] was Pétain's Minister of War. Laure gives us the explanation for this choice.[2] Pétain knew that he could rely on Colson, who was 'another of his men'.

When General de Gaulle joined my Government on June 5, it was essentially the problem of continuing the war in North Africa with

---

[1] In 1938 Gamelin had asked for Colson to be dismissed. This came to nothing. On mobilization he had also vainly asked for a General Inspectorate of the Interior, the division of the territory into several areas at a time when it was only one.

[2] *Op. cit.*, p. 267.

which I entrusted him. On this score I sent him on the 8th to London, pleased to take the opportunity at the same time of displaying to the British a resolute and energetic general, whose choice would have been senseless if he had not displayed my own determination to carry on the fight to the bitter end.

General de Gaulle, therefore, went to London on the 8th. He was accompanied by M. de Margerie, who introduced him on my behalf to Churchill, Eden and Dill. To Churchill, who received him in the Cabinet Room at Downing Street, he confirmed on my behalf my decision to continue the fight to the very end. He then asked for the assistance of the British Fleet in the transport of troops to North Africa as well as a more active share by British forces in the Battle of France, whose decisive phase was not far off. On the question of aircraft, Churchill said to him: 'When my fighter planes are fighting on the Continent, their losses are as high as those of the enemy, whilst when they are fighting over England, they bring down six times the number of Germans which they lose themselves. That is paying dividends.'

MAY 27–JUNE 4: DUNKIRK

Dunkirk was used as another *leitmotif* of German and Vichy propaganda against our ally! As was the case concerning the withdrawal of forty kilometres in the Arras area, the object of this propaganda was twofold:

1. to try and justify the Armistice demanded on June 16, 1940, despite our pledged word to our ally;

2. to sow the seeds of a lasting enmity between France and Britain so as to secure 'the isolation of our deadly enemy, France', the most essential condition necessary for Germany to establish her hegemony over the continent of Europe.

Let us add, that, as regards Dunkirk, there was also a desire to make out that the head of the last Republican Government had remained quiescent, and had not defended the interests of France herself because he was without doubt 'the slave of Great Britain'.

This propaganda was disseminated over the radio, in the Press and even through official Vichy communiqués in 1941 on the first anniversary of Dunkirk.

Let us now examine the facts in so far as I know them.

For in such an examination is to be found the truth, and the truth alone can disabuse French public opinion, crammed with lies by Vichy propaganda.

We know that the main provisions of the Weygand plan were based on the following suppositions:

1. that the French and British Armies, cut off by the scythe-like sweep of the Panzer divisions towards the sea, would be able to mount an offensive in the north towards the south;

2. that the Belgian Army, superior in numbers to the other two combined, would cover their rear.

But, attacked on three sides, from the east, south and west, the French and British Armies could not undertake an offensive, and, moreover, the Belgian Army capitulated at the height of battle, and opened thereby the road to Dunkirk.

From that moment the only chance of saving the two armies was to embark their men with rifles at Dunkirk and sacrifice all their heavy equipment and provisions. That is why the British abandoned thousands of trucks and a thousand cannon, in other words, double the number they retained.

Darlan, when I questioned him, stated categorically:

'It will be impossible to carry out the embarkation.'

It was, indeed, a miracle. It was accomplished thanks to a stupendous effort of the British Fleet, which used private yachts, most of which were sailed by the owners themselves, and thanks to the cover of British fighter aircraft, which showed themselves superior in quality, if inferior in number, to those of the enemy. It can be said that this was the first victory of the Royal Air Force, a portent of that crushing victory which it was to win four months later on September 15, 1940, in the sky over London. At Dunkirk the R.A.F. inflicted on the enemy four times the losses which it suffered itself. Our own aviation took a brilliant part in these fights during which it was not a rare thing to see French and British squadrons repel German formations of a greatly superior strength.

Let us recognize this as the most important fact.

A second is that the dispositions of the French and British Armies on the ground was such that normally the British were in a position to be embarked first.

As a result, there was a great disparity between the number of British and the number of French soldiers, who were evacuated.

This disparity was the first question which I raised before the Supreme Council at its meeting of May 31 at the Ministry of War in Paris. There Churchill represented the British Government and accompanied by Pétain, I represented the French.

I observed that, out of two hundred and twenty thousand British, a hundred and fifty thousand had already been evacuated, and out of two hundred thousand French, up to the present time, only fifteen thousand had been evacuated. I stressed strongly the fact that such a disparity, if it were not immediately corrected, might entail grave consequences in the political field.

Churchill admitted this. He remarked that British losses would exceed eighty thousand men, even if evacuation could be carried out under propitious conditions. He read a letter from Gort to Weygand, which stated:

1. that he would hold out as long as possible to cover evacuation by sea;
2. that this must be speeded up;
3. that it was necessary for the French Command to give orders to this effect.

Weygand stated that he was in agreement.

An understanding had been reached, he said, between Blanchard and Gort.[1] He stressed the vital role which Abrial, who was entrusted with covering the whole of the evacuation, would have to play. Backed up by myself, he asked that everything should be done to evacuate the eight French divisions which were farthest from the coast, and whose leader, General René Altmayer, stated that they were resolved to fight to the bitter end. 'Dunkirk should not', he said, 'be abandoned until it is known for certain that our divisions of the south are liquidated.' Churchill replied that, unfortunately, it was not possible to give them more than forty-eight hours, and that only the four divisions under Generals Fagalde and de La Laurencie, which were within the fortified perimeter of Dunkirk, could be saved.

In actual fact, I obtained from Churchill, as we shall see, an extension of the evacuation operations, which allowed the total number of French evacuated soldiers to be raised to a hundred and ten thousand.

I pointed out that orders must be given to Abrial, and I asked Churchill if he would like me to wire him what the Council had decided, namely:

'1. A bridgehead should be formed at Dunkirk to allow for the embarkation of the forces under the cover of three French divisions;
2. As soon as it is an established fact that it is no longer possible to

---

[1] This statement is important, for, on many occasions, Gort had shown signs of an independence, which aroused Weygand to complain. Bourget notes (De Beyrouth à Bordeaux, p. 60): 'On May 29, in the early morning, a telegram from No. 1 Army Group reached Supreme Headquarters, which stated that Lord Gort, ignoring General Blanchard's objections, was directing on his own initiative the withdrawal of his Army towards Dunkirk with the result that the flank of the First French Army was being uncovered, and that this Army was imperilled. General Weygand himself telephoned to M. Baudouin to ask the President of the Council to lodge a protest with the War Office against the too selfish attitude of General Gort.'

On May 31, Gort wrote to Admiral Abrial: 'As you no doubt are aware, I have received from His Majesty's Government an order to evacuate part of the British Expeditionary Force, and to leave in France a detachment, which will share in the defence of the Dunkirk bridgehead.'

concentrate any more troops outside the bridgehead on the point of embarkation, the units entrusted with its defence should embark, beginning with the British forces.'

I was certain beforehand of Churchill's reaction about this last point. With tears in his eyes, the Prime Minister stated that he did not wish to see French troops bear new sacrifices, and that it would be three British divisions who would make up the rearguard.

A telegram was drafted after the meeting, which laid down that the evacuation would be carried out with, 'British troops remaining, as far as was possible, to hold the rear.'

Churchill observed that, since there only remained a British Army corps and a French Army corps within the Dunkirk perimeter, there was no necessity for Blanchard and Gort to stay there, and that there existed justification for asking them to go to England after each had delegated command to a corps general.

I stated with relation to the immediate future of the war:

'Once the situation has been cleared up in the north, the enemy will attack on the Somme and the Aisne, and perhaps also in the area of Basle. . . . Let the R.A.F., therefore, bring an immediate attack to bear on the waterways, and let all available troops be sent there as quickly as possible. Great Britain has no need to fear that the enemy will begin land operations against her until the situation in France is liquidated. We must, therefore, in order to gain time, send back to the Continent all the troops evacuated to England, as soon as they have been re-equipped. The Germans will not delay in attacking us long enough for us to fortify the line of the Aisne and the Somme.'

Churchill and Sir John Dill showed some reserve on this subject. They feared that Britain would be immediately invaded. The evacuated soldiers would have to be regrouped, re-formed and restored in morale. But the British had one armoured division and one infantry division in France. Perhaps it would be possible for them to manage to send us one of the three divisions which they had in Britain. Behind these three divisions there were fourteen in training, but their only equipment was rifles and a few machine-guns. The Government was appealing to the whole military strength of the Empire. But the defence of the Empire itself exacted troops. There was in this respect a minimum below which it was absolutely impossible to fall.

I replied to this as follows: 'The battle of the Somme has also some importance. We ourselves are bringing here overseas troops, even from Tunisia, where we are threatened by the Italians. We are going to call two more classes to the colours, for whom we are buying weapons in Spain and America. We shall call up boys of eighteen and a half and send them to North Africa. Thus, they will be out of the way of the advancing enemy, and will be able to join in the war.'

Churchill promised to reflect 'on the proposals which he could put forward'. The entire discussion took place in an atmosphere of friendliness and mutual trust. At the beginning, Churchill had replied to a remark by Weygand, which, moreover, was a just one, in this very charitable strain: 'Let there be no argument between comrades in distress.'

But on the spot at Dunkirk, the situation grew rapidly worse: bombs and shells caused fearful destruction amongst the heterogeneous armada which was crowded in the roadstead.

On June 1, Churchill sent me this telegram,[1] which was destined for Weygand: 'Crisis in evacuation now reached. Five fighter squadrons, acting almost continuously, is the most we can do, but six ships, several filled with troops, sunk by bombing this morning. Artillery fire menacing only practicable channel. Enemy closing in on reduced bridgehead. By trying to hold on till tomorrow we may lose all. By going tonight much may certainly be saved, though much will be lost. Nothing like numbers of effective French troops you mention believed in bridgehead now, and we doubt whether such large numbers remain in area. Situation cannot be fully judged by Admiral Abrial in the fortress, nor by you, nor by us here. We have therefore ordered General Alexander, commanding British sector of bridgehead, to judge, in consultation with Admiral Abrial, whether to try to stay over tomorrow or not. Trust you will agree.'

At 4 p.m. on the same day, Churchill sent me the following message by telephone through the British Ambassador:

'It seems hardly probable that the embarkation can be prolonged beyond the course of tomorrow.

'It is, therefore, very desirable that the operation should end by tomorrow.

'Up to the present, two hundred and twenty-five thousand men have been embarked.

'By waiting until tomorrow we are running the gravest possible risk, that of not being able to save anybody else.

'Six ships have been sunk, of which several were packed with troops.

'Abrial strongly wishes that the embarkation should be prolonged, but he is hardly in a position to judge, since he is controlling operations from a casemate.

'We must leave the generals on the spot the task of settling the moment when it is suitable to bring the operation to a close.

'By waiting too long, we run the risk of losing everything.'

[1] *The Second World War*, vol. II, *Their Finest Hour*, pp. 100-1.

Spears informed me that General Alexander had decided to end embarkations after that night.

On the 2nd, Weygand cabled General Lelong, our Military Attaché in London, to ask him to insist to the British Command that the French rearguard should not be sacrificed.

Darlan in his turn telegraphed Abrial: 'Do everything possible to bring the evacuation to an end tonight. Five large torpedo-boats out of nine have been sunk.'

I did not dispute the gravity of the losses which the prolonging of the operation might cause us, but, even disregarding my feelings as a Frenchman, I thought it was of primary importance, from a military point of view to be able to send into the battle, which would rapidly be engaged on the Somme, as many French troops as possible, and also because of Anglo-French relations in general, to save the greatest possible number of French soldiers. I therefore insisted on the evacuation being continued.

I answered Churchill: 'My thanks for having given the order to send ships to save the rearguard, which has played a decisive role in the evacuation. I am giving Weygand and Darlan instructions that use should be made of them as quickly as possible in so far as the fighting allows.

'Paris, the Paris area and industrial targets have just been bombed by three hundred German planes. A similar treatment meted out to the Berlin area would be *greatly appreciated.*'

If I did not obtain satisfaction on this last point, the outcome of the evacuation resulted, by June 4 in no less than about one hundred and ten thousand French soldiers being saved. They had been saved, for the most part, by British ships, and the air cover of the operation had been chiefly provided by British aircraft. The essential thing, surely, was to afford those who had fought so bravely the means of escaping from the snare in which they had been caught.

Thus the Royal and British Mercantile Navies and the R.A.F. played the chief role, which naturally belonged to them, in the operation. But it is only fair to recall that we supplied three hundred war and merchant ships, two hundred other craft, and a number of naval air formations, and that our Navy lost in the engagement two destroyers, five torpedo-boats and a supply ship, without counting the number of craft which were damaged.

A year later, on May 31, 1941, Darlan, gathering around him the Press representatives in the Occupied Zone, was to tell them that 'our Navy had sacrificed itself at Dunkirk, Le Havre, Cherbourg and Brest to ensure the return of British soldiers to their island'. Was not one of the duties of our Navy, then, to help our Allies to escape, from the German claws?

Here now is how the German communiqué of June 5[1] describes the gigantic scythe-like sweep which the Wehrmacht had just made on Dunkirk: 'It was then that the enemy Command experienced a new shock which it had also thought impossible. Pushing to the sea, our armoured and motorized forces pounced with such speed that at Abbeville they even surprised troops who were on manœuvres on a training ground. The German Command had taken good care to guard its flank from the southern frontier of Luxembourg to the sea by a curtain of divisions, and thus ensured that the "miracle" of the Marne could not be repeated. The armoured and motorized column, thus having no need to worry about its rear, wheeled north, with its left flank based on the sea whilst its right crushed the armoured forces which, both at Cambrai and at Arras, the enemy sacrificed in desperate attempts to break out.' It is possible, added the communiqué, that, at Dunkirk, 'a few thousand men managed to save their skins'. And it concluded triumphantly: 'Material and equipment were strewn as far as the eye could see along the roads of Flanders and North France. On June 4, Dunkirk fell after a desperate battle. We have put the finishing touches to the first chapter of the campaign.'[2]

The communiqué detailed our losses as follows: a total of French, British, Belgian and Dutch casualties numbering 1,200,000. There was booty enough to equip between seventy-five and eighty divisions. Air losses were 1,841 craft shot down between May 10 and June 5, 1,142 in combat and 699 by anti-aircraft guns; between 1,600 and 1,700 were destroyed on the ground. On the debit side, the Wehrmacht admitted the loss, between May 10 and June 1, of 10,252 officers, N.C.O.s and men, and a total of 8,643 others missing. Of the latter, the number killed, stated the communiqué, was small. In addition, 42,523 officers, N.C.O.s and men had been wounded. Finally the Luftwaffe had lost, between May 10 and June 3, 432 aircraft.

Hitler had certainly just cause to boast a victory. He had beaten a powerful army, the best raised by the Allies. The latter had, however, inflicted casualties on him amounting to 61,000 men, if we accept his own figures.[3]

[1] I have quoted above, the preceding passage of this recapitulative communiqué which describes the forcing of the Meuse.

[2] Did not in actual fact the German Army of August, 1914, resemble a 'stage coach' beside a 'train', when compared with that of May, 1940? Or was Pétain proved right in his remark on the eve of war that: 'The swiftest attacker can only advance slowly'?

[3] We know that the official reports of the German Command on the 1870–1 war have been shown to be inexact in many details as is revealed by the testimonies of the German generals in their own accounts of the campaign, accounts which were published for the most part many years later.

In actual fact, the losses of the Allies were much less serious than the Germans claimed. The British lost, according to Churchill's estimate already reported, by May 31 between eighty thousand and ninety thousand men. We French lost, according to the Army General Staff in a note of June 6, around three hundred and seventy thousand men of the

JUNE 5: I RESHUFFLE MY CABINET

One of the items in the plan, inspired by my realization that differences existed btween Pétain and Weygand on the one hand and myself on the other, was, I have said, a reshuffling of my Administration.

Because I could not get rid of Pétain nor with him, Weygand, for reasons which I have already enumerated, I decided to eliminate those members of my Government who, I had reasons to fear, would be ready, when the time came, to join forces with these two, and to replace them by men whom I had cause to believe faithful. Faced with a compact and resolute bloc, Pétain and Weygand, even if they did not become resigned to changing their opinions, would at least have been made powerless. But it was important in the highest degree to handle the matter in a discreet way. For, preoccupied in avoiding anything that could endanger the restoration of the Army's and nation's morale which the arrival of Pétain and Weygand had gained for us, I had made a point of suppressing signs of any disagreement, the news of which would by itself have sufficed to nullify this invaluable advantage.

Such an operation is always a delicate one. One so often makes implacable enemies of the men from whom one parts. This was to be the case with Monzie, who, under the Vichy régime, was to write a book whose express intention was to avenge himself. He accused me in it,[1] not without some reason, of only having reshaped my Ministry to satisfy the wishes of those who were determined to fight on. 'Our exclusion from the Paul Reynaud Cabinet rejoiced the followers of Léon Blum. "A step for the public safety"', wrote La Lumière, Georges Boris's paper, and added: 'It is a question of organizing total resistance. The appointment of General de Gaulle, a soldier of an inventive turn of mind, is, in this respect, a tell-tale sign.' The organization of total resistance—could there be, indeed, any more abominable crime in Monzie's eyes?

This authoritative comment will enable me to dispense with the reasons why I had put Monzie at the head of the list of those to be eliminated. Monzie himself made no secret about his feelings. Thus it was that the British Ambassador had warned me a short time before that, during a dinner, Monzie had stated to him that, if Italy declared war on us, he would immediately resign his portfolio; he was, therefore, resolved to disavow his country at a time when Mussolini stabbed

---

Seventh, First and Ninth Armies. Our losses in material were heavy: a quarter of our field artillery, a third of our light and heavy tanks, the greater part of our transport, including, it is true, equipment lost in engagements fought along the rest of the front. These engagements, however, only accounted for a small item in this enormous booty.

But nearly three hundred and forty thousand allied soldiers escaped slaughter or capture.

[1] Ci-devant, p. 245.

it in the back. 'He will not be required to do this', was the sole reply which I gave to Sir Ronald Campbell. The position in which Monzie stood was, therefore, unambiguous.

There was equally no hesitation about that of Lamoureux. The remark which we have seen Monzie attribute to him depicts the state of mind in which he was.

In the case of Daladier things were different. The President of the Foreign Affairs Commission of the Senate came to notify me officially that this body had unanimously decided to have in future no further dealings with Daladier. This step forced me, therefore, to dissociate myself from him.

The ground, thus being cleared, it remained to rebuild. No doubt, the simplest means would have been to interrogate individually each of the men whom I contemplated including in my reconstituted Government about the attitude which he would adopt if the problem of an armistice were raised. We have seen the reason why such a method of action was *a priori* impossible for me. Therefore, I was obliged to do without the positive guarantees which such a method would offer me, and to put up with a rough-and-ready compromise, which left to chance an element that experience was to prove preponderating.

I had around me men whom I could trust: namely Mandel,[1] Rio, Campinchi, Monnet, Marin to cite only those who counted the most politically. The event was to confirm that my trust in them was well placed.

I was equally sure of Ybarnegaray. I had called him into my Government because I remembered hearing him say on February 25, 1938, when speaking in the Chamber, and (reports the *Journal Officiel*) amidst the applause of the extreme Left and Left as well as a part of the Centre and Right: 'Oh! I am well aware that men can be found amongst us to crowd into the ante-chambers of Ribbentrop, Goebbels, Goering, and who, without qualifications and without authority, are going like ingenuous pilgrims to seek for promises and for appeasement. Peace in slavery? No, a thousand times, no!' How could I possibly doubt such a man?

I thought that I could also count on Pomaret. Had not Monzie written[2] on August 31, 1939: 'I am making little effort to convince Pomaret; since August 27, I have lost faith in him. I think that he has been won over to Paul Reynaud's convictions'?

I took advantage of this reshuffle to create a Ministry for the Family.

---

[1] There existed between Mandel and myself on this point as on so many others a strict uniformity of views. M. Langeron, prefect of police in 1940, notes in his *Souvenirs* that he confided to Mandel his uneasiness that Mandel might not be included in the new team. Mandel confined himself to replying: 'But we have no intention of standing aside.'

[2] *Ci-devant*, p. 146.

For a long time I had been one of those who thought that our legislation, based since 1789 on the rights of the individual, should, after having brought the trade unions into existence, ensure the protection of the first social unit, the family. It was seen that, as soon as I became Minister of Finance in 1938, I had, in spite of the draconian measures which I had to take, succeeded in finding credits for encouraging larger families. When we were in the midst of war, I had, at the request of Adolphe Landry and Georges Pernot, applied the Family Code. The time had come to complete the work already undertaken.

The man who seemed most worthy of being selected as the first to hold this new portfolio, which was to include the Public Health Services, was Georges Pernot. Not only was this because he had become the apostle in this sphere, but he had also the reputation in the Senate of being one of those who were prepared to resist to the end.

In any case, one point is beyond dispute; a government whose leader had resolved, should the Battle of France be lost, to leave metropolitan France for North Africa to continue the fight, had, of necessity, to include within it one of the leaders of the Radical-Socialists. If Daladier were dropped, it was necessary to keep Chautemps. The latter's reputation, indeed, was great amongst the Left. As Vice-President of my Cabinet he had, as I have stated, shown proof of true loyalty towards me in the first difficult days of my Government's existence. But his previous record was not entirely reassuring: his attitude towards the *Anschluss* and Munich was such as to create within me a doubt upon the firmness which he would show in the hour of trial, that is, the hour when Pétain and Weygand would raise definitely the question of an armistice. The wisest course seemed for me to bare my thoughts openly to him. His reply was categoric: he assured me that he shared my views. Mandel told me that, on leaving me that very evening, Chautemps went to see him, and confirmed his opposition to any possible request for an armistice, ejaculating: 'It would be better for us to embark in a cruiser.'

Daladier's departure left vacant the Ministry of Foreign Affairs. Opinion about the problem of our relations with Italy was so jumpy that, if I had given the office to a strong opponent of conciliation, I would have been accused of provoking Mussolini. As I knew that he was determined to declare war on us within a short time, I was particularly desirous of not giving him a pretext which he would not refrain from seizing. However, I did not wish to entrust the Quai d'Orsay to an appeaser. I revealed my concern to Mandel, He answered: 'Give the post to Pétain.' Mandel's idea was obviously that Pétain would be only some kind of figurehead, and that I myself would in reality control foreign policy.

If Mandel was deluded by this hope, it was because Pétain seemed fairly harmless, especially in discussions within the Council of Ministers. In actual fact, Pétain followed the Council's debates with obvious difficulty. The interchanges of discussion escaped him. No doubt, his partial deafness alone might have been sufficient to explain his failure. But this infirmity did not seem to be the sole cause for a silence which Pétain only broke, it is true, very rarely, as he did, for example, at the War Committee on May 25 and at the Council of Ministers on the 27th, to utter often, moreover, remarks which seemed, to say the least, belonging to another age. Thus, he complained during a meeting of the Council on May 20 about the insufficiency of our intelligence about operations. His remarks aroused the interest of those present to such a degree that Marcel Héraud and Monzie each took notes of them, and the latter even retains no other impressions of the discussion.

Let us first read the remarks that Marcel Héraud puts into Pétain's mouth: 'We don't seem to be making use of carrier pigeons. There should be a dove-cote in the rear, which is permanently linked up with Supreme Headquarters.' And Monzie writes:[1] 'May 26, 1940. Marshal Pétain said very quietly at the end of the Council meeting: "We ought to use carrier pigeons. . . . It is regrettable that we have abandoned the use of carrier pigeons." This simple remark inspired in me a painful perplexity. Were our communications with the armies so deficient in spite of technical progress that we had to employ the methods of past wars? Carrier pigeons! We were back in 1870–1871!'[2]

It is obvious that Pétain's incompetence had not escaped my notice. I was, therefore, in agreement with Mandel that he could be considered as harmless in any discussion which would bring to a head the conflicting tendencies within the Government. I also agreed with Mandel in considering that it would be easy for me in actual practice to usurp Pétain's control over our diplomacy. But, on the cardinal problem, Pétain's views were none the less different from my own. Prudence, therefore, advised me to refrain from giving him a portfolio, the possession of which alone would have sufficed to consolidate his reputation in my Government. Thus, having been obliged to turn down Mandel's suggestion and lacking on the other hand a candidate who

---

[1] *Ci-devant*, p. 235.

[2] It is tempting to compare these remarks with those which Eva Braun, in her *Journal Intime* (*France-Soir*, May 5, 1948), ascribes to Hitler on the day after Montoire:

'Pétain is an old dotard. I never know if he understands what I say to him'; and with those which Pétain uttered to General Vlassov during an audience which he gave him at the end of March, 1943. Vlassov's account (*L'Intransigeant*, November 26, 1947) runs:

'Passing through Vichy, I was received by Marshal Pétain. Pétain surprised me considerably. He did not breathe a word about the war nor about present-day events. But he spoke at length to me about the visit of the Russian squadron to Toulon and the arrival in France of General Tatishtnev, A.D.C. of Tsar Alexander III, who himself died in 1894. I was really astounded to hear talk of all these events, the most recent of which was at least fifty years old. Truly, Marshal Pétain is living more in the past.'

answered the requirements which circumstances demanded, I had to take over the Quai d'Orsay myself.

It was also because of the Italian threat that I nominated Baudouin as Under-Secretary for Foreign Affairs, a post which he added to that which he was already holding in the Presidency of the Council. It will be recollected that it was on Mandel's suggestion that I had taken him as my subordinate. He was, moreover, *persona grata* with the Italians. I was not surprised, therefore, to receive a visit from Signor Guariglia the day after reshuffling my Administration. He came to inform me that his Government expressed their satisfaction at this appointment. The reader has seen that, in any case, it had no influence on my policy towards Italy. Various stories have painted Baudouin as the traitor in the melodrama. Certainly, his subsequent behaviour leads me to stress rather than to minimize the reponsibility which he bears. But the truth only is what counts. The importance of this person has been ridiculously exaggerated.[1] Because he was not a deputy he exercised no personal influence on Ministers. Moreover, I myself received Ambassadors. I *never* discussed with him the question of an armistice. I only remember that one day, at the beginning of June, he wished to steer the conversation upon Weygand whom he greatly admired. Now, Weygand had just repeated to me once again that it would be necessary to ask for an armistice in order to preserve an army which would ensure the maintenance of public safety. Cutting the conversation short, I replied: 'I am getting somewhat tired of this administrator of the Suez. I am not going to make war on the French.' The truth of the matter was that Baudouin exercised, on behalf of Pétain and Weygand, the duties of a busy and intelligent head of secretariat, and that, when M. Charles-Roux most commendably thwarted Laval's candidature to the portfolio of Foreign Affairs in the Pétain Administration, he (Baudouin) cleverly seized the opportunity to push himself forward. Whatever be the truth, the danger of these tales which have created a Mephistophelian hero of Baudouin lies in the fact that they pushed the chief culprits into the background when it was important, on the contrary, to keep them in the forefront.

The simplest thing to do as regarded the Ministry of Finance seemed

---

[1] Baudouin himself has, moreover, explained the conditions under which I entrusted him with the post of Under-Secretary for Foreign Affairs. In his deposition of July 26, 1949, he stated to the Committee of Inquiry:

'M. Paul Reynaud nominated me Under-Secretary of State for Foreign Affairs without any previous discussion between us about the post. If I am not mistaken he said to me at the end of the afternoon of June 5: "I am remaining at the Ministry of National Defence ... I am also taking over the Ministry of Foreign Affairs. I shall not have time to receive a certain number of people whom a Foreign Minister should receive. Take over in addition to your present functions those of Under-Secretary of State for Foreign Affairs. You will take up quarters in the Quai d'Orsay and according to my directives, you will have such and such a talk with this or that Ambassador."'

to be to hand over to the Secretary-General of the Ministry, Bouthillier, who had been my colleague for nearly a year and a half, and who had always held irreproachable opinions about the war. I considered him to be one of my men because I had dragged him out from obscurity at the Hôtel de Ville, where one of my predecessors had relegated him, to raise him to the high office which I gave him. He knew, moreover, the reason why I had broken with the man whom he was replacing. Could I honestly expect that this man would side against me, later demand my indictment as the leader of the 'war-mongers', and finally become, in the words which the Procurator-General of the Riom Court said to my friend Laniel, the 'most bitter' of my enemies? It was this deepest dyed ingratitude which inspired a President of the bar, Jacques Charpentier, in *Au service de la liberté* (p. 138) to call Bouthillier 'a bespectacled book-keeper, for whose advancement Paul Reynaud was responsible, and who did not forgive his benefactor for having dragged him out of obscurity'.

In my opinion the decisive factor at this time was the intervention of America in the war. Now, in this country where public opinion is supreme, our Ministry of Information was completely failing to achieve any results. I had learned of this from official reports, and also through the proprietor of several important American periodicals, one of which was *Life*, who had come to Paris several weeks before, and finally through Jean Prouvost, who, as editor of the review *Match*, had close relations with the United States Press. It seemed essential to me to entrust the Ministry of Information to a man who was really capable of influencing public opinion. That is why I chose Prouvost. I should add that nothing led me to doubt his sincerity when he told me that he approved of my policy. Moreover, he was only joining my Government as a technical expert. As he was not a deputy, he had no more influence on Ministers than had Baudouin.

General de Gaulle was appointed Under-Secretary of State for National Defence. He had just given proof of distinguished service at the head of the 4th Armoured Division. I have already stated that the merit for my amendment proposing an armoured corps in 1935 was his. During talks which we had since then, I had appreciated his high ideals which made him outstanding in technical matters. His appointment displeased Pétain, who told me a commonplace piece of gossip. It was even more distasteful to Weygand.

'What is your complaint against him?' I asked the latter.

'He's only a stripling.'

That same evening I asked General de Gaulle:

'How old are you?'

'Fifty.'

Weygand's grievance was, therefore, unjustified for, even if it were true that General de Gaulle was then the youngest general in the French Army, nevertheless Napoleon had ended his career when he was four years younger.[1]

I have also revealed that I entrusted General de Gaulle with the task of carrying on the war in North Africa, and that, on this score, he had gone to England, where he established contact with the Government. We know what was the outcome of this after the armistice, to the outstanding benefit of France.

The day after this reshuffling of my Cabinet, M. François-Poncet telegraphed that in Rome as well as in Berlin it was considered to be evidence of a tightening of the alliance as well as of my intention to fight the war to the bitter end. Thus, we see that neither Hitler nor Mussolini had the slightest illusion as to the significance of the move.

JUNE 5: I TELEPHONE TO ROOSEVELT

On June 5 I telephoned to President Roosevelt, whom I knew of old.

'In the midst of our struggle to the death, an irresistible impulse urges me to speak to you directly as man to man, because I feel across the ocean the immense power of your personal influence and of your support.

'I want to tell you that France will fight to the last man. The fighting qualities of our troops have never been higher and we are full of confidence. Our choice has been taken; our resolve has been made. We are going to fight until victory or death with all the strength which we possess. The destiny of this country, of democracy, of freedom throughout the world will be decided in the coming month.

'News from the front is good this evening, but, Mr. President, we need your assistance. We have in this critical hour desperate need of help from your great country to master and to destroy the enemy.

'Our men, our airmen are engaged in a struggle so heroic that they are bringing down three or four enemy planes for every one we lose. The enemy has a numerical superiority, but he is visibly tired and our men seem, at least for the moment, to be getting the upper hand.

'But, Mr. President, to continue this struggle during the decisive

---

[1] As soon as he took over command, Weygand recalled to active service General Dufieux, whose opposition to armoured divisions is known to the reader. A little later he gave the command of the Tenth Army to General Robert Altmayer who had been on the retired list for three years. When, as the situation became worse, the problem of defending Paris on the Pontoise line was raised, I proposed to him that General de Lattre de Tassigny should be named Military Governor. As we saw, he showed his worth at the head of the 14th Infantry Division, and we are aware of his later successes as leader of the Army of the Rhine and the Danube: 'He is too young', said Weygand. Napoleon's lieutenants Murat, Lannes and Soult, when they put to flight the septuagenarian generals of Austria and Prussia, had hardly reached half the age of the generals whom Weygand brought out of retirement.

weeks which are coming, to intensify it until victory, we have immediate need of all the available planes of your Army and Navy, which it
is materially possible for you to send us. Can you stretch a hand across
the ocean to help us to save civilization?

'Could you, in one way or another, either directly or indirectly, let
us have planes completely equipped and ready for battle?

'Can you get them to us as soon as possible at any point whatsoever
on the African coast?

'The problem of destroyers is equally urgent. Anything done about
all this would strengthen us very much. It could be decisive. It could
reverse the course of history.'

The President answered me with a touching cordiality that he would
send me to begin with and without delay, guns and munitions.

Roussy de Sales writes about this conversation (*L'Amerique entre en
guerre*, p. 72): 'June 7. . . . [Reynaud] telephoned directly to F.D.R.
[Franklin Delano Roosevelt] the day before yesterday, and, according
to various items of information (from St. Quentin and Noel Coward
who has spent two days at the White House) the effect has been salutary.
F.D.R., who was totally "deflated", has been cheered up by Reynaud.
Last night a hundred and fifty more bombers were sent to us. This is
a small beginning.'

JUNE 5: THE BATTLE OF FRANCE BEGINS

During the brief respite which the enemy gave us before opening the
Battle of France, I did all in my power to increase our chances of
offering battle under the best possible conditions. I said to General
Colson, but without success: 'Get me fifty thousand men to dig anti-
tank ditches, to mine the houses in villages which ought to hold out
against the Panzers.' On June 2 I sent the following telegram to
Churchill:

'The battle which is about to take place on our front possesses such
a supreme significance to our common cause that I wish to draw your
attention again to the necessity for the twofold assistance of the British
Army and Air Force.

'As regards the Army, General Weygand observes that the British
Expeditionary Force was supposed to be brought by today to a strength
of fourteen divisions. We are entitled to conclude from this that three
divisions ought to be available and ready to be embarked. I should add
that the hundred and ninety-four thousand men whom you have just
recovered from the northern front ought, it would seem, to allow you
within a short time to follow up the dispatch of the three available
divisions with some re-formed units of a tried fighting value. . .

'We would like British bomber aircraft to supply, before and during the battle which is about to be engaged, an assistance at least as powerful as that which it contributed during the battle of northern France. It seems possible for this collaboration to be given without your bombers being based on France.

'The role played by fighter aircraft is a decisive one since to abandon the mastery of the air to our opponent would be to jeopardize the outcome of the battle. I am asking you to give us greater help than that which you supplied in the north. It is obvious that these planes cannot operate if they are using English bases. You must, therefore, agree that they should be based on French airfields for the duration of the battle. Orders have already been given by us to place our own airfields at the disposal of British fighter aircraft. We are constructing new fields for our own planes. A note and map about this have been sent this very morning to General Spears so that he can immediately send them on to you.

'The usefulness of British collaboration on the ground and in the air will depend to a large degree on the rapidity with which it is given. We have received warnings that an attack is imminent at various points on the front.'

In a report on October 29, 1940, at Dakar, Weygand, having analysed the reasons for the Allied defeat in Flanders, describes the conditions in which operations on the Somme and Aisne front then opened:

'During the evening of June 5', he said, 'the battle began on the Somme–Aisne front, and I must say that, for three days I entertained a hope of coming through it successfully in spite of our numerical inferiority. Our troops stood very firm and fought very well on the front, but we had no reserves. The units in the line had to create their own reserves. The elements which were coming back from England were thrown into battle with vehicles straight from the factory, which were run in on the front itself. Thus, the battle began, and I for the first three days, as I have told you, was hopeful. I had had an opportunity during my trip to the southern area, of seeing officers whose units had borne the shock of the Panzer divisions, and I realized that these German units only advanced along the roads, thus not wasting their time in crossing fields; and they had their way cleared by aircraft. We adopted a new system; we set up a succession of support points where our men had the duty of holding out until death—which they did. But it would have been necessary to fight a battle in depth, and we had no reserves.'

Thus, however gloomy was the outlook, our Supreme Command had not lost hope. However, British assistance was more than ever necessary in order to make up for the numerical inferiority which our losses in the north had so dangerously aggravated. As soon as he had begun his preparations to receive the attack which he anticipated against this line, Weygand had insisted on the need for using all available resources to contain the enemy thrust. I have related how, at a meeting of the Supreme Council on May 31, I took the opportunity to show Churchill that, if we wished to engage in another battle with any hope of success, all the resources at the command of the two countries would be necessary. Since that date, not a day passed when, often repeatedly, I did not press the Prime Minister in order to obtain from him an increase of assistance given by the British forces, especially that of the R.A.F.

The documents bring out the pressing nature of these repeated appeals. At the time I often asked myself if the insistence which, at Weygand's request, I put into the demands for help from our ally were not excessive.[1] The outcome of events has indeed shown that Churchill would have committed the gravest of faults if he had sacrificed all his air strength in the Battle of France, when this was going to be indispensable to him several weeks later in order to defend Britain against German aerial attack. I do not feel certain today that I exactly sized up this peril, which was as vital to the fate of France as to that of Britain, since it threatened the fate of the coalition. But, during these first days of June, I was entirely preoccupied in the battle which we were waging to cover Paris. That is why, sharing the anxieties of Weygand, I did not cease, as we shall see, approaching Churchill.

On June 5 at 9.35 a.m. Supreme Headquarters learned that the British had already withdrawn some of their searchlights erected by them for the defence of Le Havre. Because we ourselves were lacking in equipment at this port, Weygand asked me to request the British Command to revise their intentions, and, in general, to keep at Le Havre both the anti-aircraft guns and balloon barrage which they had installed there.

At 9.45 a.m. Weygand sent me the following note:

> The Commander-in-Chief must point out that our appeals to the British Government have been of no avail. We are meeting the German attack without the advantage of any new British assistance. Neither fighter aircraft nor fresh divisions.
>
> Weygand.

[1] I found a note in my papers which was drafted after an oral communication from the British Ambassador, and of which the text is as follows:

'On the morning of June 3, the British Ambassador indicated verbally to the President of the Council that Mr. Winston Churchill had decided to do the utmost possible to satisfy the wishes of the French Government even beyond the point which his Generals thought reasonable, and that it was better, therefore, to trust in him, without multiplying appeals which, perhaps, might adversely affect the desired end.'

But France was invaded, and Paris was threatened!

At 11.45 a.m. on the same day, in the presence of Pétain, Weygand and Darlan, I received General Spears, who brought me the following reply, dated the 4th, from Churchill in answer to my message of the 2nd:

'In answer to the message which you entrusted General Spears to send to me on June 2, I assured you last Monday that we would examine immediately, without, however, giving a definite promise, the problem of the reinforcements which we could send immediately to France and the air assistance which we could give you in the coming battle.

'Let me first of all emphasize certain general points.

'1. The elements of the British Expeditionary Force which have been saved from the northern front can only be sent back into battle after they have been fully re-equipped.

'2. The three divisions which you mention as available in your message are not yet completely equipped. According to our initial programme, the first of them should be sent to France towards the end of this month. Almost all our fighter force was thrown into the last battle. Operations were carried out with an unprecedented intensity and the losses of the Air Force, particularly in pilots, have been consequently very high. I earnestly ask you to take into consideration the importance of these factors in affecting the scale of help which we are in a position to bring you in the immediate future.

'3. As far as concerns the ground forces, our anticipations are as follows: we shall reconstitute the British Expeditionary Force in France, including its Headquarters, as rapidly as we can. One division is ready to leave immediately, and we shall begin to send it overseas at the end of the week. A second division, one of the regular divisions saved at Dunkirk, is at present rapidly being re-equipped in order to follow the first as promptly as possible. A corresponding element of corps troops will be sent within the same time. It is not possible to give you a precise date when a third division can be sent, but we shall speed up things as much as possible. The date on which this division will be ready will depend to a large extent on the date when we can supply it with artillery. Can you help us in this respect? Corresponding supporting aircraft will also be sent to France.

'4. As for fighter aircraft, the three squadrons at present in France will immediately be brought to full strength. Because of the very serious losses over the last three weeks, a certain time will be necessary to refit our squadrons, to try to make up for our losses and to find out what future help we can send and when. We understand perfectly the urgency of the problem and I shall give you information on this subject as soon as possible.

'5. As for bomber aircraft, we intend to bring the six squadrons at present in France up to full fighting strength. The rest of our home air bomber strength will remain based on England but will continue to participate as in the past, priority being given to intervention in the battle itself as well as to attacking objectives chosen by your Supreme Command.'

I informed Spears on the 5th of Weygand's demands both as regards Le Havre and the general situation. Then I handed him on the spot, at midnight, my reply to the message which he had just brought. This was based on technical particulars supplied by Weygand.

'*Dispatch of British divisions*

'General Weygand is of the opinion that we run a very great danger of losing the battle unless he has the means to supply it. Therefore, it is necessary to speed up the dispatch of the British divisions.

'You inform me that the first division will only embark in a week's time. Now, another week must elapse between the embarkation and its employment on the front. This first division itself is likely to arrive too late. My conclusion is that the dispatch of British divisions should be speeded up as much as possible in view of the new fact that an offensive has been launched this morning.

'*Fighter Aircraft*

'You have pointed out to me that, because of heavy losses suffered by British fighter aircraft, you could only for the present bring up to strength the three squadrons which are at present in France. Therefore, you reject the request, which was drawn up by General Vuillemin and sent by me, yesterday June 4, to Sir Ronald Campbell, to dispatch to France:

'1. Ten fighter squadrons *immediately*.
'2. Ten other squadrons as soon as possible.

'These twenty squadrons represent half the fighter aircraft based in England. I cannot believe that you will persist in your decision in the new light of the German offensive.

'I remind you that General Vuillemin wrote in his letter of June 3 to General Weygand, a copy of which was handed to the British Government: "If, as seems likely, the enemy launches within a brief period a powerful attack with tanks and aircraft against the defensive front at present being organized, there is no reason why he should not succeed again in breaking through our positions, and proceeding quickly and deeply to exploit his success. It will be impossible to stop him doing this unless, at the very moment when the attack is launched, we are in a position to neutralize German bomber aircraft by a powerful employment of Allied fighters."

'General Weygand endorses this statement. It is useless to stress the extreme gravity of the situation. If British fighter aircraft do not give our Army the assistance requested by General Vuillemin, there is a possibility that the battle will be lost and Paris occupied by the enemy. The British Government is aware what the consequences of the loss of this battle and the capture of the capital will be.

'*Bomber Aircraft*

'Thanks for your statement which satisfies us completely.

'The French Government has complete confidence in the British Government and its leader's determination to remain solidly linked with us.'

Later in the day Spears sent me Churchill's first reply. Here it is:

'Very urgent.

'This morning we received a request, made in general terms, to give aerial support in the ground battle which is at present taking place between Abbeville and the second line of the front, but we have no precise information as to what should be the nature of this assistance or about the positions of objectives. We have available four bomber squadrons and two fighter squadrons at full strength, and ready to strike from this country (England). To obtain these we have had to break up numerous squadrons and suspend the process of reorganization which the severe trial of Dunkirk and resulting confusion made necessary.

'In the meantime, we are sending reconnaissance planes to survey all the German zones of the rear. If this reconnaissance can reveal worthwhile objectives, these will be attacked by bombers with fighter escort. Fighter craft will intervene, in any case, over the battle area.

'These operations will supplement those which are undertaken by British forces based on France.

'We have also strong bomber forces ready for an attack tonight against objectives already designated by you.'

On the same day, the 5th, at 8.45 p.m. Spears, in reply to a question put by us about the advantage there seemed to be in placing the air strengths of the two countries under a single command, stated that:

'1. Unity of Command is possible as far as bomber forces are concerned; command should be exercised by a Britisher.

'2. It is not possible in practice as regards fighter aircraft.'

Lastly at 10.30 p.m. he handed me the following reply about the defence of Le Havre:

'Urgent.

'For Colonel Redman from General Ismay.

'Please tell General Spears that the Chief of Imperial General Staff has this morning given the categoric order that the anti-aircraft defence of Le Havre must not be weakened in any way.

'Inform Darlan immediately of this, and also tell Darlan and Weygand that we are urgently studying the problem of supplying other ports with the means of anti-aircraft defence.'

I had also received the British Ambassador during the day, who had handed me the following telegram which he had just received from Lord Halifax:

Secret.

Telegram from Viscount Halifax to Sir Ronald Campbell, dated June 5, 1940:

His Majesty's Ambassador in Rome has received from a source which he considers trustworthy, a report which states that lack of petrol has become so great for Berlin that it may compromise imminent operations in France. The report adds that, for this reason, the conquest of Roumania is considered desirable so that Germany can be assured of control of all the stocks and production of petrol. The German High Command is reputed to be confident in the complete effectiveness of precautions already taken on the spot to prevent the destruction of oil wells before the arrival of German forces.'

In the evening Churchill gave his reply to my approach of the day before, in the following message:

Personal and Private.

Your comments will be examined by the General Staff, which has been ordered to send the two divisions as soon as possible.

May I observe that your divisions brought back from Dunkirk will not be fit to enter the line before a month is out. We are trying to send you one of our re-equipped divisions within a fortnight.

Fighter aircraft. The request of General Vuillemin was completely unreasonable, and his letter has created here the worst impression on everyone, and considerably increased my difficulties.[1] Refer, I beg you, to the paragraph in which he writes of the co-operation which we gave during the last battle. You appear to lose complete sight of the fact that our fighter aircraft have been strained to breaking point, and that their formations have been terribly mixed up by the need to maintain constant patrols of forty-eight fighters over Dunkirk, without which evacuation would have been impossible The mere repair of planes belonging to the differing squadrons practically paralysed the R.A.F. for four or five days. I have, however, cabled you this morning that we are reserving four squadrons of day bombers and two of Hurricane

[1] Indeed it was couched in inadmissible language.

fighters for this afternoon's operations, in addition to nine squadrons which you have already got. I shall try to keep up the same strength tomorrow. I shall cable you about this.

He completed his reply in the afternoon by the following telegram which was sent from London at 5.30 p.m.

Secret.

The movement of the 52nd Division has been speeded up to a maximum. Embarkation will begin tomorrow and, thanks to the use of two ports, disembarkation should be finished by the 13th. To assist you more rapidly than would be possible by the dispatch of a re-formed Dunkirk division, we are sending Canadians, who will begin to embark on the 11th. A division will follow as soon as possible if you can supply its artillery. Please let us know.

Our air forces, bomber as well as fighter, are intervening again today in the battle of the Somme, taking off from English bases. Fighters are filling up with petrol in France, and are thus able to undertake sorties of a longer duration. Moreover, considerable forces of heavy bombers will continue tonight their attacks on objectives designated by your Supreme Command.

Best wishes.

Coming back to the conditions of co-operation between the air forces, Spears handed me, also on the 6th, the following letter:

Confidential and Private.
Secret.   June 6, 1940.
My dear President,

In reference to what General Weygand told me this morning,[1] I should like to develop several points. I did not do this at the time, so as not to emphasize certain variances of opinion.

The views of the French Air Force are materially different from those of British. This difference, even if it does not affect the prestige of either, is none the less transformed into a lack of reciprocal confidence. The French Air Force is considered as an auxiliary of the Army. It is only one service amongst others, over which the Commander-in-Chief has complete authority. This conception only applies with us to a section of the Air Force, that which is attached to the Army. The remainder, that is to say by far the greater part of our Air Force has its own strategy, its own policy and its own doctrine.

It is inevitable that an air force having such a status should fear to be linked to a Command whose views are so different from its own.

I am obliged to say that I fear, if General Weygand were to insist

[1] At the daily meeting in my room, at which Spears had been present.

on his desire to limit the role of our Government and our Air Force to placing at his disposal the maximum number of our air formations to be employed as he wishes, according to his conception of the use of an air force, that we should be rushing into the most awkward difficulties. Our Air Force cannot be compared with a new machine, adjusted so that it can be handed over by industry to the army in order to be employed by generals as they think fitting.

I am very happy to see that you have put your finger on the most obvious fault in the present organization, namely, lack of liaison. I could hardly believe my ears when I learned that General Weygand had not yet seen Marshal Barratt. If, for any reason whatsoever, Barratt cannot be daily in close touch with General Weygand, a really capable officer should be entrusted with ensuring liaison. What is obviously necessary is that the essential needs and requests of General Weygand in relation to aircraft should be formulated in terms and spirit suitable to British aerial technique by someone who is attached to him. And it is also plain, as I said this morning, that our own Command would understand and appreciate the situation more exactly if it were explained to it by one of our own Air Force officers instead of being made as a simple request for support. Indeed, it is plain that the request made to it yesterday was put in such a way that it was misunderstood, and for this reason created a misunderstanding in our minds.

Yours very sincerely,
E. L. Spears.

It will be seen how the problem of relations between the ground Army and the Air Force[1] was creating difficulties.

At my request Weygand summed up the situation on the afternoon of the 6th. The following memorandum reveals in what terms he expressed his satisfaction. It will be also seen that liaison was finally established between the British and the French:

[1] The question of the co-ordination of the Army and the Air Force was one which had concerned me for a long time.

One of the results of the creation of a Ministry of Air had been to secure the independence of the Air Force from the ground command. The result was in practice a considerable lengthening in the time taken by the Air Force to carry out the operations requested by the Army. For example, the Air Force required forty-eight hours' notice to carry out a bombing sortie.

It is known that I had not ceased supporting, particularly, for example, in *Le problème militaire français*, the view that the armoured corps could only be used with its maximum effect in battle if its action was co-ordinated with that of assault aircraft. In 1937, I had called the attention of Laurent-Eynac to this point. At my request he had discussed the problem in an article which created some stir at the time.

In 1940, Laurent-Eynac was, as is known, Minister of Air in my Government. I pointed out to him the urgent necessity of ensuring that the Air Force Command should be effectively subordinated to that of the Army. I had no difficulty in getting him to agree to my views on this subject.

1. *British Ground Forces*

General Weygand received General Pownall, Chief of Staff to General Gort, this morning.

The latter told him of the arrival of the 52nd Division, which would begin to disembark in France tomorrow, June 7, and would have finished by the 18th. . . . An army corps commander would come to France at the same time, and take over all the large British units which were landed.

As soon as possible after this disembarkation a second and then a third division would follow. When the total figure of British divisions present on the French front had thus reached four, Lord Gort would resume command of the Expeditionary Force.

This is an excellent programme. It will be improved if its implementation is speeded up to the full measure dictated by the grave circumstances created by the new German attack, which is growing stronger every day.

2. General Weygand saw Air Marshal Barratt today. He has been assured by him, as also by Generals Georges, Besson and Tétu,[1] that a perfect liaison has been established between the British and French for using the British aircraft placed at the disposal of our battle line as effectively as possible, and in accordance with French plans.

Henceforth, *all* British *bomber aircraft*, whether they are based in France or England, will be employed for the purposes of our battle.

Nothing has been definitely settled about *fighter aircraft* as the British Government has not yet (according to information at hand, 5 p.m.) come to any decision. Air Marshal Barratt has explained the existing difficulties. General Weygand has asked him to bear in mind the crucial situation in which we are offering battle, and to plead our case with London.

To sum up, let the British Government give us planes, and they will be put to good use.

Weygand.

This note was written when I received the telegram which the Prime Minister sent today at 5.30 p.m. to the President of the Council.

Since the disembarkation of the 52nd Division will finish on the 13th, and since, from the 11th the embarkation of the Canadian division will start, we are beginning to get some satisfactory response. On the other hand, I am studying the possibility of giving artillery to the Dunkirk division. The solution of this problem is bound up with the arrival of five hundred American 75 mm. guns.

Weygand.

[1] General Tétu was in command of aircraft co-operating with ground forces on the north-east front.

By the 7th, British ground forces fighting in France comprised:

1. The 'Fortune' Division (twenty thousand men).

2. The armoured division which arrived in France on May 20 and was reduced to three thousand men and a hundred and eighty tanks as a result of the hard fighting which it had gone through on the 25th.

On the 7th I telegraphed to Churchill:

'The British effort in the sphere of ground operations is all the more important because General Fortune's forces have an important role in that they are protecting the road to Le Havre, which, as you will be aware, is necessary to the existence of Paris.

'I ought to tell you on this point that, although he has been placed under the orders of General (Robert) Altmayer, General Fortune withdrew the day before yesterday on his own initiative to the Bresle. Yesterday he allowed enemy elements to infiltrate to the south of the Bresle through the forest of Eu. When General Altmayer asked him this morning to drive out these enemy elements, he did nothing about it, and asked to be relieved. General Weygand reminded General Altmayer that General Fortune was under his command and that he should obey the orders given him. I would be obliged if you would see your way to confirming these instructions to General Fortune.'

On the next day I used Weygand's note of the 6th to enlighten the Army and Foreign Affairs Commissions of the Senate[1] at a joint sitting about the progress of operations.

I had, however, to refrain from telling them the full extent of British co-operation for, in the morning, I had received the following message from Churchill:

Very urgent.   June 7, 1940.
For General Spears from General Ismay.

The Prime Minister urgently advises against telling the Senate Army Commission of the exact strength of the forces employed in yesterday's battle, and even more strongly, that of those it is intended to use today.

[1] I explained to the two combined Commissions that, in the battle which was being fought, we had to deal at the same time with new material and new methods of waging war. Laval, forgetting that Mussolini had stated that he would refuse to receive him, wished to intervene with some words about Italy. The Commission did not allow him to do so. When I got back to the Rue Saint-Dominique, I received a visit from the President and a Vice-President of the Commission, Daniel Vincent and Chaumié, who asked me if I would agree to make the text of the communiqué upon which we had agreed more optimistic in tone. I told them, and they appreciated the fact, that I did not think I could do this.

However, so that M. Reynaud can form an opinion on the extent of our efforts, you can tell him for his personal information that a hundred and forty-four British fighters were employed in France yesterday, and an even larger number will be used today.

Britain, moreover, continued to increase her support. During the day Churchill informed me of this in the following words.

'I am now able to tell you that during the last twenty-four hours we have still further increased our efforts to help France in the aerial sphere. During the night, our heavy bombers have attacked in force (fifty-nine tons of bombs) all the objectives designated by the French Supreme Command. Moreover, our medium bombers, from bases in Great Britain, have during the day carried out sixty sorties up to the present.

'2. Fighters operating from their bases in England and using forward airfields situated to the south of the Somme have made a hundred and ninety-two sorties, both as medium bomber escorts and as independent patrols. This does not include missions to protect the transport of troops between Southampton and Cherbourg, etc. . . .

'3. By amalgamating three fighter squadrons we propose tomorrow to send two additional full-strength squadrons, which will be based on France within the forward area of air warfare, and under the orders of the British Commander-in-Chief of Air Forces. Thus, the strength of this fighter formation will be increased to five fighter squadrons at full strength. In addition, we hope to be able to place in action each day four fighter squadrons based on England and operating from advanced refuelling airfields situated to the south of the Somme.

'4. Recent experience has shown us that we cannot at present maintain a greater number of squadrons subject to wear and tear which is equal to that which they suffered in the battle of Flanders.

'5. As communications are today improved between Headquarters of British Air Forces and England we can now place the medium bombers based on England at the disposal of the Commander-in-Chief of British Air Forces, for the purpose of co-operating with French and British forces engaged in the battle.

'The heavy bomber squadrons will remain available for attacking night objectives designated by the Supreme French Command.

'6. I understand that, through the intermediary of the French Air Attaché in London, about seventy-four complete barrage balloons with their winches, etc., are requested for the defence of Paris. We are immediately allotting for this purpose twenty-four complete barrage balloons with their crews.

'7. It should not be forgotten that, during the last two nights enemy aircraft (about a hundred craft on each occasion) have made attacks on

England, and, in addition, have carried out large-scale operations for sowing mines.

'8. I informed the War Office of your complaints about General Fortune. He had to hold an extended front and has suffered heavy losses.'

But I was still not satisfied. On the 8th I returned to the charge with these words:

'Message from M. Paul Reynaud to Mr. Winston Churchill.

'Rouen and Le Havre are directly threatened and with them the supplying of Paris and of half the Army. I thank you for your efforts, but the situation requires more powerful ones still, including especially the basing of fighter squadrons on France so that they can give their maximum assistance, according to the advice of our technical experts.

'The new fighter squadrons which you are kind enough to promise us comprise only a quarter of the thirty-nine fighter squadrons you possessed on May 31, according to your statements at the last meeting of the Supreme Council.

'My duty is to ask you to throw all your forces into the battle, as we are doing.'

Churchill answered me the same day by this telegram:

'We are giving you all the support we can in this great battle, short of ruining the capacity of this country to continue the war. Today we have suffered very heavy and even disproportionate losses in the air. We shall nevertheless carry on tomorrow.'

As we know, it was on the 8th also that General de Gaulle was in London, and insisted on my behalf to Churchill on the urgency for a more active participation of British forces in the battle. Two days later I wrote to Churchill:

June 10, 1940.

My dear Winston Churchill,

General de Gaulle has told me of your talk with him. I am happy to see that our ideas coincide. I shall not return to the question of aircraft or of the new units which you are sending to France.

As far as the use of these units is concerned, I shall see that your remarks are taken into account.

Please accept my expression of friendship.

Paul Reynaud.

Thanks for the Merlin engines.

JUNE 10: SECOND WEYGAND MEMORANDUM

On the 10th, Churchill telegraphed me: 'British forces are giving their maximum support to the French Armies in the great battle which the latter are now offering with an indomitable courage. We are throwing in all our available resources to help you on the ground, on the sea and in the air. The Royal Air Force is continually engaged over the battlefield and, during the last few days, we have disembarked fresh forces in France, which are taking their place at the side of those which are already engaged in the common struggle, whilst new and powerful reinforcements are rapidly being organized and on the point of being embarked.'

On the same day at 10.30 a.m. Weygand placed in my own hand a 'very secret' memorandum which he had previously communicated to Pétain.

Memorandum for the President of the Council.

The Memorandum addressed on May 29 to the President of the Council pointed out to the Government the conditions under which the coming battle was to be engaged.

This battle began on June 5. Our armies are fighting heroically. They are inflicting on the enemy considerable losses. But the restricted number of our divisions does not allow them to be relieved. Fatigue, lack of sleep and losses are sapping their powers of resistance. During the morning of the sixth day of battle, I must note that the enemy attacks forced us into increasingly larger withdrawals. Each day our adversary is extending the scope of his offensive towards the East. Thanks to the number of fresh units which he possesses, he can still further extend his attacks, which already extend along a front from the Channel to the Argonne. At one point on this front, some German armoured units have succeeded, by a rapid exploitation which has been partially successful, in cutting into two the forces of our Army on the left, and in seriously threatening the lower Seine. Our armies have re-established themselves on the lower Seine front, in positions essential to the defence of Paris and along the Marne. This is the last line along which we can hope to put up any effective resistance.

I ended my Memorandum of May 29 by making it clear that 'a moment might come after which France would find herself, against her will, unable to put up a fight which would be of any military use in the protection of her soil'. I added that: 'This moment would be marked by the final break-through of the defensive positions, in which the French Armies have received the order to fight without thought of retreat.'

I am far from having lost all hope of stopping the enemy as my Order of yesterday shows. Our armies continue to fight and their operations are still co-ordinated. But events during the last two days of battle makes it my duty to warn the President of the Council that a final rupture of our defensive lines can happen any moment. The enemy may succeed in seizing crossings on the lower Seine and reaching the Paris area from the south, or he might make another deep thrust with armoured vehicles in Champagne, or lastly our divisions, broken by weariness and diminished by losses might be powerless under pressure of an enemy more than three times their strength, to re-establish themselves firmly on the lower Seine line, the positions defending Paris and the Marne.

In the case of such an eventuality, our armies would continue to fight until their strength and means were exhausted. But their disintegration would only be a matter of time.

Weygand.

Nothing could be more true. In this case, we should be defeated on the soil of metropolitan France. But our Fleet, perhaps a decisive factor for a victory for the coalition in which France was a partner, and our Empire, would remain intact.

In actual fact, at the time when I received this memorandum, the position of the lower Seine had already been forced, and Paris surrounded on the west.

JUNE 10: MUSSOLINI STABS FRANCE IN THE BACK

At 4 p.m. on the 10th I had a telephone call from M. François-Poncet. Ciano had just informed him in the name of the King that Italy would be in a state of war with France and Britain after midnight. He gave me an account of his conversation with Ciano:

'Why?' asked the Ambassador.

'Because of our alliance.'

'You are stabbing a man who is already on the ground?'

There was no reply.

From the balcony of the Palazzo Venezia, Mussolini vociferated the language which we already know.

Let us now hear from Ciano. He describes in his *Diary* (pp. 262–4) his final interviews with Sir Percy Loraine and M. François-Poncet. The phlegmatic behaviour of the former obviously impressed him.

'June 7. . . . An almost good-bye visit from Percy Loraine. He is sad and feels fully the gravity of the hour for his country, but talks with imperturbable firmness about a fight to the last, confirming his faith in victory "because the British are not in the habit of being beaten". He is personally worried about his journey home. . . . He is also worried about a colt he has to leave in Italy. . . .'

At the end of the afternoon I announced over the wireless Italy's declaration of war:

'We are now in the sixth day of the greatest battle in history. The conflagration has begun on the Somme and spread eastwards to the Meuse.

'For six days and five nights our soldiers and airmen, and the Royal Air Force have faced an enemy superior in numbers and weapons. In this war, which is no longer a war on a continuous front, but one of supporting positions stretching into the interior, our armies have fought in retreat. They have only abandoned each supporting position after inflicting heavy losses on the enemy. The kilometres gained by the enemy are strewn with destroyed tanks and fallen planes. In spite of any success in prestige which the enemy may gain, the effect of these losses on the outcome of the war remains to be discovered.

'Nothing will ever weaken our determination to fight for our country and our liberties. The trials which await us are harsh. We are ready for them. We shall not bow our heads.

'At this very moment when France, wounded but undaunted and upright, is struggling against the hegemony of Germany, when she is thus fighting for the independence of all other peoples as well as her own, Mussolini has decided to stab us in the back.[1] How is this act to be judged? France herself has nothing to say. The world, which is watching us, will pass judgement.

'You are aware of the efforts of reconciliation and the enduring patience we showed towards the Italian Government. You are aware that, on several occasions, I stated publicly, as did my predecessors, that there was no problem existing between Italy and ourselves which could not be settled by friendly negotiation. The most influential moral authorities in the world, the Pope and President Roosevelt, have tried on several occasions to prevent this war, which is a challenge to Christian ideals and also to the conception of human society. It has been in vain. Mussolini has decided that blood must flow. What is his excuse for this declaration of war?

'When, this afternoon at 4.30 p.m., our Ambassador, M. François-Poncet asked this question of Count Ciano, the latter replied that Mussolini was only carrying out the pledges which he had given to Hitler.

[1] In the text which I handed to the Press, I wrote 'declare war'.

'This same declaration of war has been sent to Britain. Hostilities will begin tonight at midnight. Appeal has been made to force. In the Mediterranean the Allies are stronger than anywhere else.

'France enters this war with a clear conscience, and for her this is not meaningless. The world will soon know, perhaps, that moral strength is also a source of power. During her long and glorious history, France has passed through greater trials. It has been then that she has astonished the world. France is indestructible.'

JUNE 10: MESSAGE TO ROOSEVELT

Before leaving Paris, I sent on June 10 the following message to Roosevelt through Mr. Bullitt:

I would like, first of all, to express to you my gratitude for the generous help which you have decided to give us as regards aircraft and weapons.

For six days and six nights, our divisions have been fighting without a moment's respite against an army which possesses a crushing superiority in effectives and equipment. Today the enemy is almost at the gates of Paris.

We shall fight in front of Paris; we shall fight behind Paris; we shall fortify ourselves in one of our provinces, and if we are chased from there, we shall go to North Africa, and, if need be, to our American possessions.

Part of the Government has already left Paris. I myself am preparing to join our armies.[1] This will be to intensify the struggle with all the forces which remain to us, and not to abandon it.

May I ask you to explain all this yourself to your people, to the citizens of the United States, and to tell them that we are determined to sacrifice ourselves in the struggle which we are waging on behalf of all free men?

At the hour in which I am addressing you, another dictator has just struck France in the back,[2] a new frontier is threatened. A naval war is about to break out.

You have generously answered the appeal which I sent you across the Atlantic some days ago. Today on June 10, 1940, it is my duty to ask you for additional and yet more ample assistance.

When you are explaining this situation to the men and women of America, I beg you to state publicly that the United States will give the Allies all the moral and material support within their means,

[1] I had to go and see Huntziger. It will be seen later what prevented me.

[2] Roosevelt, in a speech that same day to the University of Virginia at Charlottesville, said: 'Today, June 10, the man whose hand has never ceased brandishing a dagger has just struck his neighbour France in the back with it.'

short of sending an expeditionary force. I beg you to do this before it is too late. I know the gravity of such a step. Its very seriousness means that it should not be taken too late.

You yourself told me on October 5, 1937, 'I am forced, and you are also forced, to look into the future. The peace, liberty and security of ninety per cent of the world's population are endangered by the other ten per cent which threatens to bring about a collapse of the order that is based on international law. Surely, the ninety per cent who wish to live in peace according to the law and in conformity with moral principles which have received a more or less universal consent throughout the centuries, can and must find a means to make their will prevail?'

The hour has now come for this ninety per cent of the citizens of the world to unite against the mortal peril which threatens us all. I am confident that the American people are behind us in this vital struggle which the Allies are waging for their own salvation and also for that of American democracy.

Paul Reynaud.

Such was my last act before leaving Paris.

JUNE 10: DEPARTURE FROM PARIS

As the advance of the enemy army was still becoming more and more menacing, the representatives of Paris asked the Ministry of the Interior if the capital would be defended. I told Weygand of this step.

Vuillemin, for his part, believing that the bombing of Paris was imminent, wrote on the 7th to Weygand:

'Information from a source which has up to date proved very accurate indicates the imminence of Paris being bombed with the utmost severity. If this occurs, even though all French fighter resources were used in the aerial defence of Paris, we must anticipate very serious damage.

'Consequently,

'1. The problem of evacuating Paris has to be considered.

'2. To defend Paris, it will be necessary to withdraw our fighter craft for the time being from the ground battle, where they are now completely committed.

'I have the honour to ask for your decision on this last point; the evacuation of Paris lies within the province of the Government to whom I consider that the problem should, in the present circumstances, be submitted.'

Two days later, on the 9th, Weygand handed me this letter, and put the problem to me:

'I have the honour to send you the copy of a letter from General Vuillemin about the bombing of Paris.

'The first question concerning the evacuation of Paris raises a problem which seems to me insoluble.

'I cannot for myself advise any other step than a withdrawal from Paris of children under sixteen years.'

The advance of the enemy, moreover, raised the question of a departure from Paris. At 5 p.m. on the 8th, I informed the Council of Ministers of the measures taken for this purpose. When the Commander-in-Chief invited the Government to do so, the President of the Republic and the Ministers would leave Paris for places in Touraine, where their withdrawal had been settled and prepared for a long time in case of bombing.[1] I was to stay on in Paris together with the Ministers of the Interior, Air, and Marine, as long as the situation allowed. Delbos, amongst others, protested courageously against a plan which meant the departure first of all of the less important members of the Cabinet. But I was of the opinion that none of the arrangements settled should be changed.

On the 9th, Weygand, who had always been in favour of allowing public authorities to fall into the hands of the enemy, sent me the following note: 'If the President of the Council has decided on the principle of public authorities evacuating Paris, the Commander-in-Chief must point out to him that, in view of the military situation, he considers it wise to carry out this evacuation without including the Ministers whose presence the President of the Council thinks necessary in the capital up to the last moment.' The Council of Ministers met in the evening. It decided to leave the capital.

Here is an account of this Council's meeting by Lebrun:[2]

'General Weygand gave a complete account of the situation. It left us with a deep impression of sadness. Marshal Pétain said nothing. He seemed to be asleep, prostrated. I questioned him.

'"Don't you want to express an opinion, Marshal? These gentlemen are anxious to hear you."

'"I've nothing to say," he replied.

'He seemed from that moment to consider defeat as an accepted fact and the hope of doing anything gone. He had been called into the

---

[1] Instead of going to Touraine, Pétain followed Weygand to Briare, where General Headquarters had been established.

[2] Op. cit., p. 73.

Government by M. Paul Reynaud to put some backbone into it. In actual fact he seemed to gravitate into doing the opposite.

'The Council of Ministers decided upon the departure of the Government, and its withdrawal to the Loire to places previously arranged for each Ministry.'

The evacuation was to begin immediately. Mandel, who thought it undesirable to keep politicians in Paris under the rule of an enemy occupation, asked the representatives of Paris to follow the example of the Government. They met on the 10th at 6 p.m. in the Hôtel de Ville, and passed the following order of the day:

'The representatives of Paris, meeting at the Hôtel de Ville on June 10, 1940, at 6 p.m. under the presidency of M. Louis Peuch,

'After studying a letter from the Minister of the Interior in which the latter invited them to leave Paris in case of German occupation,

'Have decided to agree to this injunction with the following reservation:

'The representatives of Paris will appoint a permanent commission charged with remaining in Paris and representing the people of Paris whatever be the circumstances, together with the two prefects and working in close collaboration with them.

'This delegation, which will sit permanently at the Hôtel de Ville, will include MM. Jean Chiappe, Georges Contenot, René Fiquet, Maurice de Fontenay, Marcel Héraud, Noel Pinelli and André le Troquer.'

M. Peuch the President of the Municipal Council, sent the text of this motion to Mandel:

Paris, June 10, 1940.

M. Minister.

I have the honour to send you the order of the day adopted by my colleagues, who met in my room on June 10, 1940.

Please accept, M. Minister, my deepest regards.

Louis Peuch

The same day Weygand wrote to me:

'The city of Paris is an open town, but it is placed within a broad zone of armies whose front is about thirty kilometres distant from the capital. In order that Paris should preserve its character of an open town, it is my intention to avoid any defensive organization around the city on the belt of old fortifications, or on that of the old forts.'[1]

[1] Bourget (*op. cit.*, pp. 102–8, *passim*) relates that it was during the morning of the 11th that Weygand drew up the conditions for a future general retreat. 'A secret instruction was drafted to this effect and sent to General Georges with a formal notice that it should only be put into effect on a new order. . . . At 1.15 p.m. on June 12 he (Weygand) signed

In the process of regrouping his forces, Weygand created a new army, called 'The Army of Paris'. During the morning of the 10th, General Héring received the order to assume command of this Army. On the next day at eleven o'clock, he summoned the Prefects of the Seine and the police to tell them: 'The capital will be defended to the last.' Thereupon he sent General de Lannurien to Weygand to tell him that he could not devote himself to the organization and command of an improvised army, called upon to manœuvre continually and whose left flank was seriously threatened, and at the same time retain responsibility for the military Government of Paris. At 11 p.m. General de Lannurien reported to General Héring Weygand's decision, taken in agreement, he was told, with myself and Pétain. Here is the text of this decision:

'General Héring will assume command of the "Army of Paris" and will remain with it, whilst General Dentz, commander of the Paris region, will stay on the spot until and after the Germans enter the town, if this proves to be the case. Thus the continuity of the capital's life will be ensured without any break.'

So it was that General Dentz without being named Military Governor of Paris exercised the duties of this office after 6 p.m. on the 12th. General Héring, following the orders which he had received from General Besson, who, at this time, was commanding No. 3 Army Group, began, as from the evening of the 13th, to withdraw his Army on to the Loire. During the morning of the same day, he had placarded the following proclamation on the walls of the capital:

To the people of Paris.
General Héring, called to assume command of an army, has placed the military government in the hands of General Dentz. Paris is declared an open city, and every measure has been taken to ensure, in all circumstances, the safety and provisioning of its inhabitants.
General Héring.

Paris was already, as we know, outflanked towards the west. Elsewhere the enemy was advancing rapidly through Champagne, and reached Montlhéry on the 9th. We were no longer able to prevent the investment and siege of the city. Should we, therefore, in order to avoid seeing Paris fall without defending it, offer its population to massacre, its artistic and scientific treasures to destruction and pillage? Would it not have been playing Hitler's game to give him an excuse to sow devastation and death in a capital whose prestige he envied? I knew the

the order to put his instruction of the previous day into effect.' This order implicitly entailed the abandoning of Paris without any defence. In actual fact it was on the 12th that Weygand notified the Military Governor of Paris by telephone that Paris had been declared an open town (cf. Langeron, *France-Soir*, June 12, 1946).

people of Paris too well to feel the slightest doubt that they would not be ready to sacrifice everything for the welfare of their country. But what right had we to ask it of them when Weygand assured me that such an act of abnegation and heroism was useless, and especially when, convinced of the impossibility of dispelling military disaster on metropolitan soil, I only saw an escape in transferring the seat of public authority to North Africa, to continue the war from there?[1]

People of good faith have, nevertheless, stated that they heard me say on the wireless that Paris would be defended 'stone by stone'. I cannot understand what can have inspired this rumour for I have never spoken on the subject. I can only remind you, on this matter, about the communiqué issued on May 25 by the Presidency of the Council about German moves to 'spread . . . orders or instructions which they may or may not sign with the name of some French authority or even that of the President of the Council and the Minister of National Defence and War'.

Similarly I have been indicted about matters relating to the exodus from Paris. Now Mandel, who was in charge of the problem, had ordered the civilian authorities to oppose such a movement, and in any case not to take part in it. He acted rigorously against officials of the prefectorial administration and of the police as well as against the municipal magistrates, who did not conform to this expressed order. That is why the sub-prefect of Mondidier was relieved of his duties on May 21. On the 26th, eight police commissioners were dismissed in the Département du Nord. The same penalty was inflicted on several mayors on May 28 and June 3. On the other hand, on June 3 the Government elevated Cardinal Liénart to the dignity of a Commander of the Legion of Honour for setting an example of composure and calmness at Lille; and it also nominated as Officer M. Rochard, Prefect of the Pas-de-Calais, and as Knight, M. Poitevin, secretary-general of the prefecture of the Département du Nord.

JUNE 11–12: MEETING OF THE SUPREME COUNCIL AT BRIARE

Whilst General de Gaulle was visiting, on the Montmédy front, Huntziger, whom we were considering as a successor to Weygand, and of whom he said to me in the evening 'Good, but nothing more', I was delayed at Orléans by the news that a messenger from the British Government was arriving. He told me that Churchill wished to have a meeting of the Supreme Council during the day. The Council was held in the Château du Muguet, about ten kilometres east of Briare, that

[1] Weygand said at Pétain's trial (hearing of July 31, 1945) that he wished to avoid the useless destruction of the capital of France: 'I myself, therefore, assumed the responsibility for declaring Paris an open town. I took the initiative in this, and I claim full responsibility. I told M. Paul Reynaud what I had done.'

same evening between 7 and 9.30 p.m. and continued at 8.30 a.m. on the next day.[1] It was in this Château that Weygand and Doumenc as well as their staff officers, had just taken up quarters.[2]

Churchill stated immediately that, whatever the outcome might be, Britain would fight on, and that nothing would stop her. He added that he hoped the Germans would make an attack on the United Kingdom so that some stabilization of the French front might be gained. It is known that I did not share this hope. He announced that a Canadian division was disembarking that night. Another division would be disembarking around June 20. If the French Army could hold out until the spring of 1941, between twenty and twenty-five British divisions would once more be placed at its disposal, to be employed where it was desired, as, for example, in continental bridgeheads.

Weygand explained the military situation.[3] All his forces were engaged in the battle. He had not another available battalion. In the last two days the German offensive had spread to the Aisne front. The Army had fought well without any exceptions. Very considerable losses had been inflicted on the enemy, in infantry, tanks and also planes, thanks to the collaboration of the R.A.F. The Germans held two bridgeheads to the south of the lower Seine. Over part of the front we had only a thin curtain of troops. Our men were fighting during the day, marching during the night and falling asleep on the new positions which they took up. 'We are on a veritable razor's edge, not knowing from one moment to another on which side we might fall. There is no doubt that our opponent is very tired, and that he might be forced to stop for want of breath. That is why the General, in his Order of the Day, has spoken of the final stages. It is a race between the exhaustion of the French troops who are on the point of collapse, and a shortness of breath in the enemy.' If the battle could be prolonged for some days longer, then a new effort could be made. 'We entered the war too light-heartedly in 1939 without suspecting the power of German armaments.' His conclusion was summed up in these words: 'The God of battles will decide.' He added that he was ready to

[1] Those present at these two meetings were: British representatives, Churchill, Eden, Generals Dill, Ismay, Spears, Howard-Vyse, Brigadier Lund and Captain Berkeley; and French, myself, Pétain, Weygand, Georges, General de Gaulle, Lt.-Col. de Villelume and Capt. de Margerie. At the second meeting there was also present, Barratt (who attended part of the first), Darlan, Vuillemin and Koeltz, but neither Pétain nor General de Gaulle was there.
Contrary to what Weygand has stated in his deposition at Riom, and to what Baudouin has written (op. cit., p. 97), Mr. Attlee was not present at Briare.
[2] General Headquarters had moved during the night of May 10–11 from Vincennes to Briare where it installed itself 'hastily', writes Bourget (op. cit., p. 101), on the Varangeau estate near to the station. These quarters were not large enough, and Weygand went at the end of the morning to the Château du Muguet, leaving the various departments of G.H.Q. on the Varangeau estate.
[3] Weygand had issued his Order of the Day two days before: 'The enemy ... will soon have exhausted his effort. We are in the final stages. Hold firm.'

relinquish command. But since, according to his own statements all hope was not definitely lost, there could obviously be no question of relieving him.

Churchill asked that we should hear what Georges had to say. The latter was brought in. His account confirmed that of Weygand. In Flanders, he said, the Armies on the north-east front had lost at least thirty-five divisions out of a hundred and three, in addition to all the mechanized cavalry (three light motorized divisions) and a good part of the armoured divisions. The proportion which had gone represented the best units of the Franco-British Armies. Since June 5 the troops had shown a greater spirit of sacrifice in their resistance, but such a resistance was costly. Of the effectives engaged, twenty to twenty-five divisions had completely disintegrated. There was only a curtain of troops. Rheims was threatened in the east. The danger was the same in the west for the same reason; namely, lack of available troops. He could have also said, for lack of armoured divisions. He added that the entry of Italy into the war had necessitated the dispatch to the south-east front of a certain number of fighter squadrons at a time when our fighter strength had been reduced to between a hundred and seventy and a hundred and eighty craft, whose pilots were very tired. 'We are literally at the end of our tether' was his conclusion.

Churchill expressed regret that the British Army, 'which had come out of the Battle of Belgium literally naked' could not take a greater share in the Battle of France. He remarked that he had to keep a minimum of units in Britain to repel any attempted invasion. Now, he only had several territorial units, and hardly any regular regiments (two regular brigades, specified Eden). Churchill did not dismiss, however, the possibility of a quick change of fortune, such as he had witnessed during the previous war.

Weygand answered by insisting on the intervention of a new factor: the power of rapid penetration possessed by armoured units.

I intervened to stress that the only immediate assistance which our ally could bring us lay in his aircraft. Churchill replied: 'On the day after the Dunkirk operations, our aviation was in a state of great confusion, a confusion which has now nearly ended. British home-based aircraft are intervening daily with six to eight fighter squadrons, which are fuelling in France. There are also in France the forces of Air Marshal Barratt, six bomber and five fighter squadrons.' The Prime Minister promised to examine as soon as he got back to England the possibility of improving this situation still further. The hesitations of Great Britain were not the result of a mistaken selfishness but of a deep conviction that it would be impossible to continue the war if British fighter aircraft were gradually frittered away.

Georges observed that there could be no comparison between the usefulness of units which came from England and those which were stationed in France. He thought it scarcely possible that Britain would be attacked in the near future. In any case the massive employment of aircraft on the Marne could still retrieve the situation. For my part I stressed the considerable effect of enemy aircraft on the morale of the troops. Churchill answered this by saying that the infantry always thought it was insufficiently protected by aircraft. I insisted that British planes, placed at our disposal, should be based on France, and Churchill promised to study the question as soon as he got back to England.

'We shall always be grateful, but always asking for more,' I told him.

Weygand again intervened to say: 'We are in the final stages. There is no reason why we should not prevail in these final stages, and that is why all possible assistance which can be given us is really essential.' And he added: 'If we must anticipate the complete occupation of metropolitan France; we must ask the question how France will be able to carry on the war.' I interrupted him to state that, in his capacity as Supreme Commander, he had just given extremely competent advice about the military sphere, but that 'the question of continuing the war was a political matter, and depended on the decision of the Government'. The incident was a vivid one. It struck Churchill who in his memoirs relates it as follows:

'. . . General Weygand mentioned that the French might have to ask for an armistice. Reynaud at once snapped at him: "That is a political affair." '[1]

Churchill raised the question of finding out 'whether the obvious thing to be done was to wage a kind of guerrilla warfare in various parts of France, if co-ordinated war became impossible'. Pétain replied that this would mean 'the destruction of the country'. I toned down the statement by saying that 'the towns would certainly have to suffer a lot'. On the British Prime Minister's remarking that long years had been lost, but that the Allies were not far from reaping the harvest as concerned the manufacture of arms and munitions, I made this observation which was often quoted by the Vichy Press, ever greedy for anything which appeared to be a criticism against Britain: 'That may be true, but it is like talking of rain to a man who is in the middle of the Sahara.' It will be seen from the preceding conversation in what spirit these words were uttered.

On Weygand's emphasizing the difficulty of defending the 'Breton redoubt', I pointed out that General René Altmayer was on the spot as well as the Department of Public Works. I had, indeed, entrusted M. Borie, Commissioner-General in the Ministry of Public Works with

[1] Op. cit., vol. II, Their Finest Hour, p. 138.

the task of taking there the equipment used in building the fortifications of the Maginot Line.

Churchill expressed with eloquent warmth Britain's determination to continue the struggle. 'Great Britain', he said, 'wishes to share the sufferings of her ally. . . . She will not surrender until she is crushed. If the French Army is forced to break off the struggle, Britain will fight on, hoping that Hitler will be ruined by his own victories. With her Air Force and her Fleet, the Empire will be able to hold out for years, and impose the severest blockade on Europe. What is to happen, in such a case, to the French Fleet? These are real nightmare problems which we are forced to face. In any case Britain will fight on. If she is invaded, if she experiences the horrors of war on her territory, America will be impressed by this. Britain has command of the sea. Her Empire and the French Empire are intact. Belgian and Dutch possessions depend on her. This will quickly become a war of Continents. The Nazis might succeed in dominating Europe, but it would be a Europe in revolt, and all this could only end in the downfall of a régime supported above all by the victory of its machines.'

'M. Paul Reynaud stated that the French Government was equally resolute.' This is expressed in the minutes.

After the meeting, Vuillemin told me of a combined air and sea operation which was to take place during the night against the Italian coast. He asked me to put it off so that the Council of Ministers could discuss the consequences, which he said would be very grave, of the bombardments which the Italian Air Force might take against our towns by way of reprisals. As Darlan told me that he had no objection to a postponement, I stated that I was ready on the next day to put the question to the Council of Ministers. But, during the second meeting of the Supreme Council, I learned, not without a feeling of humiliation, that the British had carried out the operation without us. I explained to Churchill my excuses for our absence. As the Italians bombed Bizerta on the following day, the postponed operation was carried out. The postponement was the manifestation of a state of mind which Vichy was to appreciate, for Pétain and Weygand bestowed, as is known, the highest distinction on Vuillemin.[1]

The second meeting of the Supreme Council took place on the 12th at 8 a.m. It was brief.

[1] It was at the end of the first meeting of the Supreme Council at Briare that Churchill spoke to Georges about the plan for going to Africa, in the strain which I have reported previously. Here is what Churchill writes in his memoirs about this matter: '. . . I talked to General Georges privately, and suggested first the continuance of fighting everywhere on the home front and a prolonged guerrilla in the mountainous regions, and secondly the move to Africa, which a week before I had regarded as "defeatist". My respected friend, who, although charged with much direct responsibility, had never had a free hand to lead the French armies, did not seem to think there was much hope in either of these.' (*Ibid.*)

I asked for a greater collaboration on the part of British aircraft based in France.[1] I requested that they should be reinforced by four more fighter squadrons. Weygand asked for additional day bombers. Barratt recalled that, during the day, the bombers of Bomber Command operated in force from their English bases by attacking objectives designated by Weygand, and that, at night, a hundred of these planes were employed against the enemy rear. Churchill summed up the discussion in these words: 'We shall scotch the tail of the serpent with our aircraft.' Churchill promised to lay the problem before the War Cabinet on his return to London. At the same time he remarked that it would be a fatal mistake to deprive Great Britain of her essential defence. There could be no doubt about this. I said that the future problem which Great Britain and France had to meet was of armaments. Because of the enemy grip on a great part of French industry, the Allies could only hope to solve it by relying on the industrial potential of the United States. I recalled that the Germans, to our knowledge, had raised since the beginning of the war fifty-five divisions and built between four thousand and five thousand heavy tanks. Churchill admitted all this, and said that he was sending a personal message to Roosevelt on the subject. Weygand summed up the military situation by saying that an order had been given, should the external defences of Paris be broken, to declare the city an open one in order to avoid a useless shedding of blood and the destruction of the city. Paris, we have seen, was already outflanked as the Seine had been crossed in places around Rouen. The General then stated that he was entirely in agreement with the plan to counter-attack on the lower Seine, but for this, he would need about ten fresh divisions with full artillery and sufficient air support. For the present, the problem was to gain time. When we were breaking up, Churchill requested that he should be heard by the Council of Ministers before the latter came to any definite decision.

Darlan relates[2] that Churchill took him aside after the meeting to say to him:

'Darlan, I hope that you will never surrender the fleet.'

'There is no question about that', he replied. 'It would be contrary to naval tradition and to honour.'

---

[1] There were at this time eleven squadrons based on France, of which six were bomber and five fighter, or between seventy and eighty bombers and fifty and sixty fighters, which were always prepared for action. But Air Marshal Barratt thought that his bombers were less suitable for day than for night operations.

[2] Crusoé, *Vicissitudes d'une victoire*, p. 134 (letter from Darlan to Churchill, dated December 4, 1942). Churchill in his memoirs (*op. cit.*, vol. II, pp. 140–1) confirms this fact, which took place at the end of the second sitting. 'Finally', writes Churchill, 'I took Admiral Darlan apart and spoke to him alone. "Darlan, you must never let them get the French Fleet." He promised solemnly that he would never do so.' Churchill added later that Darlan had declared to him that he would never allow the French Navy to surrender to the enemy as he was fully resolved rather to sail to Canada with it, although, he emphasized, such a step ran the risk of meeting opposition from political circles.

944.0816 A769

H884

944.0815
W499

34.1 W855

944.08 R459

I went with Weygand to see Georges, in whose company was General Besson. Both were very gloomy about the military situation.

After luncheon at Supreme Headquarters, I had a short talk with Pétain and Weygand. With a view to restricting the number of prisoners, I asked them if, when it was established that the struggle in metropolitan France was useless, it would not be possible to take the Army into Switzerland, and even to discharge the men, who would immediately put on mufti. They answered me in the negative.

I remarked to them that, if we dissociated ourselves from Britain, whatever might be our agreement with her under the Convention of March 28, or whether we broke our pledge unilaterally, Britain would be, *ipso facto*, free of any obligation towards us. Our claim upon her, which this agreement gave us, would be broken. In this case, we should face Germany alone, both now and in the future. We should be delivered, bound hand and foot, to Hitler. To this Weygand, backed by Pétain replied: 'The country will not forgive you if, in order to remain faithful to Britain, you reject any possibility of peace.' I was so struck by this reply that I immediately noted it.

Why would France not forgive me? Obviously because the essential thing, in Weygand's opinion, as, moreover, in that of Pétain, was to bring the sufferings of war to an end. But what about France's independence? What about her moral grandeur, her faithfulness to the plighted word? What kind of a figure would she cut amongst nations, on the day after this betrayal? This seemed to count for nothing.

In the afternoon I crossed the loop of the Loire from Briare to Tours.

Then, I arrived at the Château de Chissay,[1] near to Montrichard, where I was going to stay a day-and-a-half, and which was bombed on the 14th, an hour after my departure. Hoping that the Council of Ministers would select Quimper as the place to which a withdrawal would be made, I asked my colleagues to hold themselves in readiness for going to Brittany. I then went to the Château de Cangé,[2] the provisional residence of the President of the Republic, where the meeting of the Council of Ministers was to be held.

I arrived there at 7 p.m.

---

[1] We have seen that a withdrawal of the Government to Touraine had been provided for on the outbreak of war. It should, therefore, have been prepared in minute detail. In actual fact, the quarters of the Presidency of the Council had only a hand-operated telephone and the post office of Montrichard, under which Chissay came, had only a dozen or so connections.

[2] The Château de Cangé belongs to the Pourtalès family. Built by the Captain of Louis XI's Scottish Archers, it was reconstructed during the Renaissance.

It was on the estate of Cangé that Paul-Louis Courier was killed one spring evening in 1825 by his gamekeeper's gun; the rumour ran that his wife was familiar with the latter.

CHAPTER XIX

I AM THROWN OUT OF OFFICE BECAUSE I OPPOSE AN ARMISTICE

JUNE 12: THE FIRST MEETING OF THE COUNCIL OF MINISTERS AT CANGÉ IN TOURAINE

AT the first meeting of the Council at Cangé, Weygand explained the military situation. He considered that a decision had been made by the 'God of Battles'. He drew thence the conclusion that the Government ought to ask for an armistice. All the commanders of Army Groups and Armies were with him in this, he said. Only the cessation of hostilities could allow us to preserve the cohesion of the Army. If the battle continued, our forces would be split up, disintegrate and fall into disorder. Not only would there be military disorder but also general disorder because of the influx and misery of refugees mixed up with soldiers and without food. It was clear that the protection of social order, which had preoccupied him from the day when he had succeeded Gamelin, became a fixed idea in his mind. The orator whom we had heard proclaim at Lille 'If we are forced into winning another victory, we shall win it' took up in conclusion the thesis which he had already put forward to the War Committee on May 25. And this was to supply Vichy, later on, with one of the most insidious weapons with which it tried to discredit the democratic régime: 'France entered the war unprepared.' Weygand complained finally of being 'dishonoured' by defeat. As if misfortune could bring dishonour.

Let us hear what he has to say. We know that on August 26, 1940, at the preliminary investigations before the Riom trial, he made a deposition in the form of an unusual memorandum in which he speaks of himself somewhat curiously in the third person. This was, therefore, a matter, and it is important to repeat this, not of an improvised deposition, but of a text drawn up at leisure. There we read:

'Marshal Pétain alone supported General Weygand's request. The President of the Council and the large numbers of Ministers who spoke and made what were in fact speeches, certainly prepared in advance, stated that they were opposed to such a request. What significance had public order when compared with honour? What would the Anglo-Saxon world think? France was an Empire. If France were lost, the Empire would save her. The sea and air forces would fight at the side of British forces. The United States would send tanks and planes. The Government would withdraw to the "Breton Redoubt" in order to direct the battle from there in conjunction with the British Government. If it could not hold out there, it would withdraw to North Africa or even to Central Africa, there to await the assistance which would bring victory, etc. . . .'

This account is incomplete, but what it utters is exact. It is true that I vigorously opposed an armistice, and with me a number of Ministers. I had said, it is true, that honour came before public order. And, since this statement provoked Weygand's sarcasms, I am prepared for my part that these two maxims should be engraved on the walls of Saint-Cyr:

> *Public order is more important than honour.*
> *General Weygand*
> *Honour is more important than public order.*
> *Paul Reynaud*

Does not the word 'Honour' come before even that of 'Motherland' on the flags of the French Army?

It is true we know Weygand stated on May 24 that France ought not to have entered the war on September 3. Why should our promise to Britain have any more value in his eyes than that given to Poland?

The argument about honour ought to have been sufficient reason. I could advance others. I have spoken of the need for France to remain united with the Anglo-Saxon world if she wished to safeguard her independence. I don't think that events have belied this prediction. Finally I said to Pétain and Weygand: 'You are taking Hitler for William I, the old gentleman who took Alsace-Lorraine from us, and that was that. But Hitler is a Genghis Khan.'[1]

Pétain was, therefore, clearly warned by me what an armistice would mean; Pétain who was, in his humiliating message of January 1, 1942, to speak of the 'semi-liberty' which was left to him, and who found himself shortly afterwards obliged to act as a recruiter for German war factories. Weygand, who was in November, 1941, to be deprived of his Command in French Africa at Hitler's order, after having been expelled by the Vichy Government, was also warned. That is what an armistice cost them; an armistice concluded 'in honour between soldiers'. But these arguments, which fell within the province of statesmen, had no more influence on them than that of honour.

Finally it is true that I had stressed the need for fighting as long as possible on French territory. Georges Monnet, who has kept a faithful record of these days, stated on February 3, 1949, to the Committee of Inquiry:[2]

'I can still perfectly well hear Paul Reynaud saying: "Gentlemen, we are about to withdraw into the 'Breton Redoubt'. When all defence has become impossible, we shall be forced to embark on a cruiser. We shall embark under bombing, and if some of us are killed, so much the better! This will prove that we only left the soil of our country when it was impossible for us to do otherwise."'

Here were words which Weygand found worthy of censure. Let us return to what he has to say:

'General Weygand opposed to this programme the exhausted state of the troops who had fought without rest and relief for eight days, crushed by enemy bombing which our Air Force was completely powerless to prevent, our decimated divisions reduced to a few battalions and guns, etc. . . . He also opposed the impossibility of

[1] It was revealed in November, 1945, at the Nuremberg Trial that, during a conference preceding the invasion of Poland, Hitler had aroused the enthusiasm of the Army leaders by comparing himself with Genghis Khan.

[2] It was at the first meeting of Ministers at Cangé that I uttered these words. Through an easily excusable mistake Monnet attributes them to the second.

holding out in the "Breton Redoubt" which only existed in the imagination of the President of the Council, and still had not troops available for its defence. Nothing could modify a decision which had already been made. The floods of eloquence continued on the same theme. There was no thought for those who were doing the fighting. The scene was heartbreaking.

'General Weygand should add that, if an armistice[1] had not been requested without delay, disorder would have overtaken the armies as well as local populations and refugees. Then he would have considered an armistice as having no importance for the evil would have been done.'

'Order, disorder'—the sole concern of this man who had, however, assumed an overwhelming mission, that of conducting the battle against the enemy.

Let us pass on. But may I be permitted to observe that it took a week for the Pétain-Weygand Government to obtain the effective cessation of hostilities. During the interim, what sorrows might it have been possible to spare mothers, wives, and orphans. This does not prevent Weygand from writing today:[2] 'I did not hear one word uttered of interest, gratitude or admiration for those who were fighting. . . . What can be said . . . of this hard-heartedness, the complete lack of sympathy and responsiveness for an army which was fighting under unbelievable conditions of inferiority!' It is true that six lines later he adds: 'If the Government had decided that the armies had to fight on to the bitter end, this decision *would have in no wise displeased me*.'[3]

Is one to ascribe such an inconsequential statement to bluster or to blindness?

As for the 'Breton Redoubt', let us remember that if, at this time, it only existed 'in my imagination', the fault for this was exclusively Weygand's for he was entitled, indeed it was his duty on May 29, namely the day when I asked him to study this plan, to put forward his objections to me. But Weygand preferred, first of all, to remain silent, then to do nothing and finally to indulge in sarcasm.

In any case the Ministers who opposed an armistice were numerous: Marin, Rollin, Dautry, Monnet, Campinchi, did so forcibly.

Prouvost alone allied with Pétain in supporting an armistice, but Chautemps drew attention to the fact that, since Churchill had asked to be heard, we were in duty bound to accede to his request. It was impossible for me to refuse this, and it was agreed that Churchill would be invited to attend the Council on the next day. It was 11 p.m.

[1] He was again to write in his deposition at Riom that when, at the first meeting of the Council at Cangé, he had asked for the cessation of hostilities, he had not 'considered Italy's entry into the war'. Now, she had been in the war since June 10.

[2] *Rappelé au service*, p. 213.   [3] The italics are M. Reynaud's.

THE 'BRETON REDOUBT'

About midnight I arrived at the Château de Chissay, where I found Bouthillier, General de Gaulle and my colleagues. The General, who had come from Brittany where he had seen General René Altmayer, spoke to me of the 'Breton Redoubt', whilst I hastily dined. He knew from my numerous talks with him that I had in mind a withdrawal into the peninsula as a means of holding out on national territory and of remaining in touch with Britain through Brest. I have said why Mandel was hostile to the operation, as, indeed, was the President of the Republic. I had raised the question with the Council of Ministers, and had not found a single voice to support me. Weygand had, as we have seen, pointed out the impossibility of holding out in the 'Breton Redoubt'. Hence, instead of the plan proving to be a moral benefit to the Government, would it not on the contrary lay us open to the discredit of making a precipitate flight? This is why I finally decided to abandon the idea of the 'Breton Redoubt'.

One of my colleagues drew attention to the strategic value of the 'Breton Redoubt' being all the more problematic because nothing had been prepared there, and because, under such conditions, the members of the Government, by seeking refuge there, might give the impression that they were allotting a part of the French Army to the protection of their own 'valuable' persons. General de Gaulle was not convinced by this argument, and our conversation had not ended when Bouthillier came, just as I was finishing dinner, to have a private word with me. We went together into my study. When I came out, General de Gaulle had left. I concluded from what I learned later that some keen exchanges had been made, around the table between him and my colleagues.

That is the gist of an incident which has been dramatized by certain people, as if the decision to go to Quimper or to Bordeaux was in itself the criterion of resisting or giving in to defeatism.

We shall see later on that, even if General de Gaulle had come into conflict with certain members of my staff as has been stated, he uttered on his own accord a public judgement on my attitude during these tragic days, which discharges me from the onus of stressing any justification of myself.

JUNE 13: MEETING OF THE SUPREME COUNCIL AT TOURS

During the morning of the 13th I received two messages from America. Roosevelt suggested to me that we should publish in the Press of our respective countries the message which I had sent him on the 10th, informing him of my decision to carry on the war in North Africa, and even, if need be, in our American possessions. This proposal possessed an immense political value for, in this message, I had thanked him for the assistance which he had promised in aircraft and arms.

I, therefore, gladly accepted the President's proposal. I saw in it the advantage of informing the French people that France would stay in the war, even if the battle was definitely lost on the soil of the home-land, and that it was in agreement with the President of the United States that I was making this known to the whole world.

In addition I got a message from Roussy de Sales. Backed by that authority which his exceptional position with the American Press and still further his personal friendship with Roosevelt gave him, he in-formed me that American public opinion was very disturbed, and 'strongly in favour of effective aid being given to the Allies'. He added that Congress was lagging behind public opinion, but that he did not think it would be impossible to obtain from the President 'the public statement that America would take her place by the side of the Allies in some way or other'.

What could I get which was more specific? I did not know exactly what, just as Roussy de Sales did not, but because I considered America as being the decisive factor in this war, I decided to speak on the wire-less to the American people and to Roosevelt at the same time in a last appeal.

About 1 p.m. I received Jeanneney and Herriot as well as Mandel, whom I had informed of these events, and with whom once again I observed that I was in complete agreement.

Going to Tours, where I was to meet Churchill at 3.20 p.m., I reflected on the words which he had uttered shortly before at Briare: 'If the French Army is forced to break off the struggle . . . what is to happen, in such a case, to the French Fleet? These are real nightmare problems. . . .' Such words, which were inspired by his nobility of soul and his affection for France, could, was it not a fact, be used against me by the partisans of peace?[1] Pétain and Weygand had heard them. The latter proved my fears to be justified when writing subsequently in his deposition at Riom about this statement of Churchill: 'He gathered the impression so clearly that a request for an armistice was impending, that he therefore expressed a wish that an irrevocable deci-sion should not be taken before he had been heard again.' Moreover,

[1] As regards this account of Bourget's (op. cit., p. 106), it describes the scene which took place, according to him, in the Château du Muguet at the end of the second meeting of the Supreme Council:

'In the hall of the Château, when on the point of leaving, the British statesman [Churchill] had a final private talk with General Georges whom he knew especially well. Questioned by him, the General repeated that the ability of the French Army to resist was approaching an end, and that, soon, the conclusion of an honourable armistice would be the only possible outcome. Mr. Churchill did not dispute this point of view any longer. As regards Britain, strong because of her insular position, she would prolong her resistance, and deal out some hard knocks to her opponent. Once her partner had been put out of the fight, she would, therefore, continue to fight on alone for the benefit of the alliance.'

would not consulting Churchill at a Council of Ministers, before coming to a definite decision, imply that the continuation of the war was not necessarily the only solution? I decided, therefore, to have a preliminary talk with him in order to come to some agreement about the statement which he was to make before the Ministers if he persisted in his wish to meet them. In actual fact our discussion dragged out, and he had to go back to London without speaking any further of his wish to see my colleagues.

I found him at the Prefecture of Tours, where he had just arrived with Lord Halifax, Lord Beaverbrook, the Minister of Aircraft Production, Sir Robert Campbell and General Spears, accompanied by Baudouin, who had gone to meet them.[1]

We went together to the Prefect's office, which Mandel relinquished to us. General de Gaulle joined us a few minutes later.

I intended to act as a loyal but exacting ally.

Loyal, in the first place. In acting thus, it was my first duty not to leave Churchill in ignorance of the position adopted by Weygand and Pétain, and the threat which it contained. I was, therefore, to paint the blackest picture of events, and even myself adopt the arguments of my adversaries. But, at the same time as I was warning Churchill, I was to reaffirm my determination to resist.

Exacting, in the second place. I was to use this threat to obtain the maximum amount of support from Churchill as regards Roosevelt. Since the Allies could not hope any longer to reverse the military situation by themselves, they must turn jointly to America for the purpose of getting from her in the immediate future the maximum assistance which she was in a position to supply.

Such was my plan at the time when this meeting, which was to be the last of the Supreme War Council, opened in a dramatic atmosphere.

We shall later hear the language which I used to Churchill. This was not my own, but that of my opponents! It was so far from my intention to ask Churchill to free us from our pledge of March 28 that, on the contrary, I stressed the need for safeguarding Franco-British solidarity, whatever might happen. This was the permanent security of each country's independence.

Churchill's touching statement, uttered with tears in his eyes, is enshrined for all time in the record of history: 'Whatever happens, France's cause will be cherished by Britain. If Britain emerges victorious from the struggle, she will restore France in all power and dignity.' But he added that there could be no question of absolving France from the pledge which she had given. That, in actual fact, went without

---

[1] I was coming from Chissay and my car had been delayed by congested roads, as a result I arrived after them.

saying. Churchill thought that, for the time being, the two Allies should appeal to Roosevelt, and postpone any decision until receiving his reply.

Could there be any more striking method of confirming the continuance of Franco-British solidarity than this approach to Washington?

After a brief suspension of the sitting during which he withdrew to consult with his colleagues, Churchill stated to me that the words which he had just spoken had received the approval of Lord Halifax and Lord Beaverbrook, and that I could consider them as expressing the views of the British Government itself.

Churchill then called my attention to the presence on French soil of several hundred German fliers who had been made prisoners by the Allied Armies. If we allowed them to remain on our territory, there was a likelihood of the Wehrmacht freeing them. It was, therefore, imperative to place them instantly in a safe place, namely to hand them over to Britain. I agreed forthwith to their immediate transfer to British territory. 'What is necessary', I said to Churchill, 'will be done.' And I immediately gave orders to this effect.[1]

Then we made an appointment for our next meeting twenty-four,

[1] When the meeting of the Supreme Council had ended, I entrusted General de Gaulle with the task of going to London in order to obtain from the British Government the tonnage which, together with that at our own disposal, would allow us to transport our troops to North Africa. He had also to arrange with those whom he was seeing immediate measures for the transfer of the captured German airmen to England. Such were the reasons why General de Gaulle went to Brest, where, during the night of the 13th he embarked on the destroyer *Milan* for Plymouth, then to reach London. During his journey he went through Rochefort to discuss the question of the transports with Darlan, who had just arrived.

With reference to the dispatch of the German fliers to Britain, the Ambassador handed me an *aide-mémoire* at Bordeaux, which ran: 'Do not forget your promise to send the captured German fliers to England.' Having given the order for this to be done, I wrote in red pencil on the *aide-mémoire*: 'Say where they will be embarked.' My staff immediately sent my instruction to the competent authority which was intended to speed up the execution of the operation. When they had done this, they handed me back the document, which I put amongst my papers. However, at the moment when I was thrown out of office, the prisoners had not yet been handed over to the British. The disorder which was then reigning had obviously something to do with this delay. But, after my fall, there was no longer any question of keeping my promise. In his speech of July 4, 1940, to the Commons, Churchill reproached the Bordeaux Government with this failure as follows: 'There were over four hundred German air pilots who were prisoners in France, many of them, perhaps most of them, shot down by the Royal Air Force. I obtained from M. Reynaud a personal promise that these pilots should be sent for safe keeping to England, and orders were given by him to that effect; but when M. Reynaud fell, these pilots were delivered over to Germany in order, no doubt, to win favour for the Bordeaux Government with their German masters, and to win it without regard to the injury done to us.' Hansard, *Parliamentary Debates* (July 4, 1940).

It should be noted that Baudouin, in a memoir dated October, 1943, which he distributed secretly, stated (*Réflexions sur l'armistice*, p. 12): that he had no knowledge of Churchill's request. It figures, on the other hand, in the account of the meeting of the Supreme Council which he was to give in another memoir of the same kind (*A propos d'un nouveau livre de M. Kammerer*, July, 1945), and which he was, we know, to reproduce in his book.

or, at most, forty-eight hours later. 'I feel', I added, 'that Mr. Roosevelt will take another step, and that I shall be able to come to some agreement with the British Government about the circumstances in which we shall be in a position to continue the war.' Churchill, for his part, assured me that Britain would in the meantime continue to disembark reinforcements in France. There was thus no alteration in the programme which was being put into effect.

The Council meeting ended with my reaffirmation that I had complete confidence in victory: 'If', I said to Churchill, 'I were to lose confidence in this, I should at the same time lose all reason for living.'

As we see the question of releasing France from her pledge was not brought up. Churchill even wished to exclude in precise words such a hypothesis. Vichy did not hesitate, however, to assert that Churchill had, at Tours, released our country from its obligation. During his trial, Pétain interrupted my evidence to make this assertion, but it only served to draw a final denial from myself.[1] Was it not obvious that Churchill would have begun by laying down conditions about our Fleet if he had freed us from our promise? Now, there was never any question of this, either during the meeting of the Council, before or after it.

I left this moving meeting with a belief that I had done everything that was possible as regards our Allies.[2]

In the corridor which was crowded with journalists, Elie-Joseph Bois got hold of me, although the ink of our reports was hardly dry. He had no doubt heard of Weygand's intervention at the Council of Ministers on the previous day, for he asked me if we were thinking of an armistice. My reply was summed up in two words: 'Surrender? Never!' Then I left with Mandel for Cangé, where we arrived about 5.30 p.m.

CHURCHILL AND TOURS

During the dramatic meeting did any misunderstanding arise between Churchill and myself? The account which he gives of it in his memoirs has left me with the impression that this was so. The reader of the account may indeed wonder if I had not abandoned all hope about the outcome of the war, and thus relinquished the intention of pursuing it. Churchill seems to be surprised, for example, that I refused

[1] Hearing of July 31, 1945.
[2] On leaving the meeting, Churchill talked for several minutes with Herriot and Jeanneney. He writes (*op. cit.*, vol. II, p. 162): 'At the end of our talk M. Reynaud took us into the adjoining room, where MM. Herriot and Jeanneney, the Presidents of the Chamber and Senate respectively, were seated. Both these French patriots spoke with passionate emotion about fighting on to the death.' Herriot has recorded this historic scene: 'I was introduced', he writes (*Episodes, 1940–1944*, p. 603), 'into a room where he [Churchill] was seated in an armchair, with tears in his eyes. I entreated him with all my power not to abandon unhappy France.'

his proposal to ask our Army to sacrifice itself 'from Paris to the sea' in a series of delaying combats. As if unfortunately there could be any further question of our unhappy troops carrying out co-ordinated actions! However, I was entitled to believe that my position could not appear to be in the slightest degree equivocal. No doubt I had been obliged to explain the conceptions of my opponents in order to impress on Churchill the full gravity of the situation. But I had taken the precaution of emphasizing that these conceptions, which it would have been disloyal for me not to reveal to him, were in no wise my own, and that they never would be, so unshakeable was my decision not to give in. In the minutes drawn up by M. de Margerie it is clear with what clarity I had on two occasions emphasized that whatever happened the government which might eventually accept that hypothesis, the intentions and scope of which I had outlined, would not be a government to which I belonged, and *a fortiori* not my own government.

The minutes which the British delegation drew up[1] and from which Churchill cites a passage in his memoirs,[2] however, put in my mouth words which gave the impression that, in stating the hypothesis in question, I had certainly alluded to some other government than my own, but that I had admitted that, at a pinch, the hypothesis could also be applied to my own. 'The present Government or another', such are indeed the words which this account ascribes to me. How can such a mistake be explained?

Already for more than three weeks I had brazenly kept on begging on behalf of France, who had exhausted herself in this advance-guard action which she was waging for the common cause, that of the democracies. How was it possible for me to suppress entirely my bitterness in seeing our Army, which had fought so valiantly, succumb, when the assistance which Britain had given it had been so weak? It is not improbable that this bitterness crept into my words. But Churchill could not see the situation with the eyes of a Frenchman. He was the inhabitant of an island which had remained unviolated, whilst the Panzers were tearing the body of France.

When he began to fear for the fate of his country, what did he himself do? Returning from Tours on June 16, he did not hesitate to hint to Roosevelt that there was a danger of the complete overthrow of British policy. 'A point may be reached in the struggle', he cabled him, 'where the present Ministers no longer have control of affairs, and when very easy terms could be obtained for the British Islands by their becoming a vassal state of the Hitler Empire. A pro-German Government would certainly be called into being to make peace.'[3] And

[1] The Foreign Office sent me the text in 1947, but asked me to keep it secret.
[2] *Op. cit.*, vol. II, *Their Finest Hour*, pp. 160–1.
[3] *Ibid.*, pp. 166–7.

on June 28 he was to cable to the British Ambassador in Washington: 'Never cease impressing on the President . . . that if our country were successfully invaded and largely occupied . . . a "Quisling" Government would be set up to conclude a peace which would make a German protectorate of Britain.' And yet, when Churchill was talking in this strain, not a German soldier had set foot on the soil of his country; his Government was solidly behind him, and the Fleet, which is to Britain what the Army is to France, remained intact. What differences were there between his situation and my own!

Let us take up again Churchill's assumption: he postulates Britain as invaded, and because of this, himself forced to resign and a 'Quisling' Government formed. There would be no lack of fine people to turn his telegrams to Roosevelt to his own disadvantage and to paint him as reconciled to capitulation. It was in this fashion that certain people acted towards me.

In any case there is one point on which the British text agrees literally with the French: the words on which the meeting ended. I repeat them. I affirmed in them my belief in victory: 'If I were to lose confidence in this, I should at the same time lose all reason for living.'

Is that the language of a man about to resign himself to abandoning the fight? Let us, therefore, relate this language to its setting.

In the morning I had made public the message by which I had three days previously informed Roosevelt of my resolve to continue the struggle in North Africa, and even, if it were necessary, in our American possessions. Had I not in some sort burnt my bridges at the same time as I was trying to burn those of Weygand and Pétain?

That evening, hardly had Churchill left Tours, than I got back to Cangé, where the Ministers were awaiting me. As soon as I arrived the Council went into session. We shall see if the attitude which I assumed was that of a man whose determination had been shaken by Weygand and Pétain.

JUNE 13: THE SECOND MEETING OF THE COUNCIL OF MINISTERS AT CANGÉ

The Council of Ministers' meeting had been summoned for 3 p.m. The order adjourning it to 5 p.m. had not reached most of my colleagues.

During his deposition of January 12, 1950, before the Committee of Inquiry, M. Matteo Connet related that the Ministers strolled in small groups through the park whilst awaiting my arrival. Pétain and Weygand talked together. Then Pétain went spreading defeatist rumours from one group to another—a provisional government headed by Thorez had seized power in Paris; the police had mutinied!

In such an atmosphere the meeting of the Council opened. Chautemps was the spokesman of his colleagues, who had thus been alarmed, and to whom I gave, into the bargain, the news that Churchill was not coming.

Convinced that it was in the interests of the coalition, and consequently in the interests of France, to keep what remained of French forces in the Allied camp, I stated, after I had outlined Churchill's position, that there was no question of surrender for France was staying in the war. Bouthillier protested that the Council had not voted against an armistice.

Let us again take up Weygand's deposition;[1] he, I have said, kept his diary daily. 'We waited until 5.30 p.m. for M. Paul Reynaud's arrival. He told us that a meeting of the Supreme Council had taken place, with, it seems, Mr. Winston Churchill and Lord Halifax. During this Council and in the presence of M. Mandel, who, said the President of the Council, had happened by chance to be there,[2] M. Paul Reynaud announced the intention of the French Government to fight on. There was a complete agreement between the . . . French and British Governments on this point.

'This statement aroused two protests from M. Bouthillier . . . supported then by M. Chautemps. . . .

'The first concerned the Supreme Council, which had met in a hurried fashion when, on the day before, the President of the Council had stated that the British Prime Minister would be heard by the Council of Ministers before any decision was taken.

'The second protest referred to the communication to the Head of a Foreign Government of a decision by the French Council of Ministers which, in reality, had not been taken.'[3]

After recounting this, Weygand continues in his ironical manner: 'A great uproar. The President of the Council, very embarrassed and evading the issue, stated that it was not his business to dispose of the person of Mr. Winston Churchill, who was in a great hurry to get to Britain. The President of the Republic intervened in the dispute to separate the disputants by saying that everyone had some justification.'

This last statement is inexact. I was in no wise embarrassed, and M. Albert Lebrun, on the contrary, verified the fact that a large majority had expressed themselves the day before against the armistice.

Weygand then gave the Council an exposition of the military situation.

'He reiterated . . . his request of the previous day concerning the need for obtaining the immediate cessation of hostilities. He added that

---

[1] At Riom.   [2] I could not have said this because it was not true.
[3] The decision to prosecute the war.

having made this without thinking about Italy's entry into the war, he had reflected on the fate of our naval Fleet. He suggested that we should take advantage of the delay necessary for Mr. Roosevelt's reply to send the Fleet . . . beyond the clutches of the enemy. Any measure of this kind ought to be taken before negotiations had begun for an armistice, so that we could not be accused of having failed to carry out any undertakings which, no doubt, the enemy would force us to give about our naval forces. This point was discussed without any decision being taken.'

Before asking for an armistice, Weygand admitted, therefore, that it was necessary first to dispatch our Fleet out of the way. Indeed, no precaution was more necessary in such a case. But why, then, did Weygand, having instigated the armistice and being its artificer, not give the order for the Fleet to weigh anchor when the time came?

Ever obsessed by the idea that revolution was coming, Weygand stated in a dramatic tone that Maurice Thorez was installed at the Elysée, and telephone communications with Paris were cut. In reply, Mandel got up, went into the next room, and came back, saying to the President of the Republic: 'The Prefect of Police is at the end of the line. If you wish to speak to him. . . .' The President declined the offer and the meeting continued.

Here is, now, the account, given by Weygand and also taken from his deposition at Riom, of what he said on that day to the Council:

'. . . Last night General Weygand said to this meeting that France no longer possessed the means to carry on the struggle with any hope of defending what remained of her territory. The Ministers who made speeches expressed a contrary wish. General Weygand found himself the only "blockhead" . . . in the presence of so many courageous men. General Weygand could also have availed himself of this type of verbal courage. He could easily have posed as a hero in the Châteaux which were his quarters; and, not bothering about the state of the troops, the obstacles they were meeting, their almost complete lack of ground and aerial weapons, give them orders which could not be carried out. Would these courageous Ministers allow him to tell them what he had on several occasions told the President of the Council? The Government should remain in Paris. The Roman Senate had not done otherwise when the barbarians entered Rome. Since Paris had been abandoned, they should at least have the courage to stay in France, whatever might happen.

'There were two reasons for this.

'First of all, Frenchmen would accept the sacrifices asked of them only at this price. The answer might be that it was still a greater sacrifice for these Ministers to leave the soil of the Motherland. No one would understand it in this way. They would be told that they were perpetuating the slaughter, the bombing, burning and suffering of our people, whilst they had taken good care to install themselves tranquilly in the sanctuary of Africa or somewhere else.

'In the second place, though admitting that they might be welcomed in one of our colonies—and this was not certain, for people preferred to receive conquerors—what authority did they think they could retain over France? How much time would they spend abroad? Enough time for American factories to produce the planes and tanks which would enable them to reconquer France? Then, that would be several years, and did they believe that anyone would remember them! And then, how would they recover France? By bombing our towns, our fellow countrymen? This was an absurd, hateful programme. Moreover, the Commander-in-Chief would not follow them. He would not leave the soil of France, even if he were put in irons.'[1]

To these categoric predictions and insolent remarks of this facetious General, I will confine myself to answering that France owes her salvation to this 'absurd and hateful programme'.

Here is how Georges Monnet in his deposition has retraced for the Committee of Inquiry this incident when Weygand endeavoured to teach the Government a lesson:

'Campinchi was amongst the Ministers who declared most bluntly, in opposition to Weygand, their opinion that we should not lay down our arms or ask for an armistice. It was, therefore, he whom Weygand took to task, by asking him: "But, Mr. Minister, if I had been a politician, if I had been the Government, I would not have left Paris. I would have acted like the Roman Senators at the time when the Gauls invaded Rome. In my curule chair, I should have awaited the invader. But there has only been one occasion on which the geese have saved the Capitol!" You remember this outburst, Mr. President?[2] I must say that I was a little surprised that General Weygand was not soundly put in his place.'

This attitude did not prevent Ybarnegaray from stating: 'I am a soldier. My leaders have spoken. I shall obey.'[3] A queer conception of ministerial function!

[1] Pétain himself termed as 'excessive' the 'nervousness' which Weygand showed. Baudouin tells us of this fact (*op. cit.*, p. 111):

'Friday, June 14. . . .

'I left the Château de Chemilly at 9.30 a.m., and I went to Marshal Pétain at the Château de Nitray, near Azay-sur-Cher. The Marshal received me alone in a vast room. . . . [He] told me that he had made up his mind to bring the present state of affairs to an end, and that he regarded the attitude of the Council as "ignoble and cowardly". He asked me to help him to obtain a decision, and he was not prepared to wait after noon on the following day. He was going to send a message to General Weygand (whose nervousness at the Council, he told me, was excessive) to tell him that his presence at Bordeaux was necessary. . . .'

[2] Marin was presiding over the sitting.

[3] Ybarnegaray was to state six years later to the High Court before which he was brought: 'When I heard Weygand, for me the incarnation of the great Foch, say: "We

After finishing his exposition Weygand left the room abruptly on the grounds that one of the Ministers—it was Mandel—had smiled. He was then in such an excited state[1] that any discussion was impossible with him. This is no doubt what induced M. Albert Lebrun to refrain from admonishing him when he stated that 'he would not leave the soil of France, even if he were put in irons'.[2]

Weygand stamped out of the room. In the hall of the Château he exploded into language which was both coarse and insulting. Georges Monnet states in his above-mentioned deposition:

'We could hear him shouting as he left the Council of Ministers with an amazing insolence and in front of all the ministerial secretaries. "They sit with their backsides in their armchairs, and they don't give a damn that, all this time, the French Army is in the process of being massacred!"'

After the sitting, I told the President of the Republic that I could no longer have Weygand at the Council of Ministers. Weygand would, therefore, have in future to stay in a neighbouring room, ready to come into the Council chamber if the Council wished to question him on the military situation. When he had given his explanation, he would immediately have to leave the room. This is, indeed, what happened at subsequent Councils in Bordeaux. No doubt, during the previous war Joffre had been admitted to the Council of Ministers when the latter wished to examine certain military problems of an especial gravity as, for example, the Salonica expedition. But what a difference there was between Weygand and this great soldier whose loyalty was only equalled by his coolness and moderation.

Indeed, Weygand's attitude to the Council of Ministers would have completely justified the Government in relieving him of his command. We have seen that I had not hesitated to take strict measures previously against both military leaders and Ministers.

Well, now that is all right as far as Paul Reynaud is concerned, said certain people. He whose appeal Weygand had answered, they added,

can no longer fight on. We are defeated"; when I saw Pétain rally to this view, my resistance completely collapsed. I asked Weygand: "Have we no reserves?" He answered me bluntly, "Yes, eight hundred thousand men in depots, but nothing with which to arm them!" Then, yes, I did vote for an armistice.'

[1] On entering the room where the Council of Ministers was meeting, he had spoken of putting General de Gaulle under arrest because of taking measures on my orders for continuing the war in North Africa.

[2] Weygand, in his deposition at the Pétain trial (hearing of July 31, 1945), acknowledged that 'the problem of continuing the war comes within the political sphere, and is subject to decisions of the Government'. He added: 'It is up to the Government to take a decision, as the President of the Council quite rightly declared at the Château du Muguet.' But at Cangé, Weygand warned the Government that he would refuse to accept the decision to leave France. Contrary to what has been said, no Minister advised me to relieve Weygand of his command as a result of this statement.

could at a pinch have some scruple in taking such action. But, they continued, there were around him men who, because of their duties, had their part to play in continuing the war: Mandel, to look after Algeria; Campinchi, the Fleet; Laurent-Eynac, the Air Force; Georges Monnet, the blockade. These men were not held back by any scruple of this nature. Why, they concluded, should these men who were all resolute in their opposition to surrender, have refrained from claiming Weygand's head?

Indeed, never in our history was a government faced with such a tragic decision: to abandon the soil of France, leaving behind Pétain and Weygand to call us deserters, as we were to see the former threaten us with doing; to embark amidst the howlings of a defeatist mob; to leave behind a country morally divided in two; such was the disaster hanging over our heads. Had we not the duty of doing everything possible to avert it?

Something had to be done. But the conditions under which the Government had to disperse its quarters over the four corners of Touraine[1] constituted in themselves a material obstacle to the necessary action. Since the Ministry was on the point of transferring to Bordeaux where it was to regroup itself, I could do nothing less than wait until then. As soon as we arrived in this city, I would, in any case, summon a meeting of the Council to demand of each a statement as to where he stood.

Let us come back to the present meeting of the Council.

After Weygand, Pétain had his say. He proceeded to read a statement. Having claimed that our troops, at present in complete disintegration, were not in a state to organize the defence of the 'Breton Redoubt', and that, under such conditions, the execution of such a plan would require fresh troops who could only be British, he said: 'It is impossible for the French Government, without emigrating, without deserting, to abandon French territory.' Following this pressure on the Ministers came the threat: 'The duty of the Government is, whatever may happen, to stay in the country, under the penalty of no longer being recognized as the Government. To deprive France of her natural defenders during a time of general disorder is to hand her over to the enemy. It is to kill the soul of France, and consequently to prevent its rebirth. It is necessary to wait for a French renaissance by remaining on the spot, rather than by a conquest of our territory through Allied guns in circumstances and after a delay, which it is impossible to foretell. I am, therefore, of the opinion that we should not leave French

[1] I have previously said that this decentralization had been decided a long time before by the military authorities, who feared that the attacks of enemy aircraft would quickly render impossible the maintenance in Paris of public authorities and central administrations. But the plan for their withdrawal, in spite of precautions to keep it secret, was known by the Germans who were aware in particular of the residence allotted to myself.

soil, and that we should accept the suffering which will fall on the Motherland and her sons. . . . I shall stay amongst the French people to share her pains and miseries.[1] An armistice is to my mind the necessary condition for the perpetuity of an eternal France.'

This position adopted by Pétain was all the more dangerous for those who wished to keep France in the war in that it coincided with the attitude which had won him his immense popularity. He was once more adopting the role of the leader desirous of husbanding the blood of the soldier, this blood of which we ourselves seemed prodigal. Later, we shall see why this demagogic argument was valueless.

Thus, Pétain knew that there was a chance of saving the independence of France, but he rejected it. Not only did he ask us not to clutch at this chance with an energy born of despair, but he summoned us to give up the struggle. He summoned us to lessen the chances of victory for the coalition to which France belonged by the defection of the intact French Fleet and the French Empire. Was the 'perpetuity' of Belgium compromised because this country was occupied for four years between 1914 and 1918? And to influence the Ministers, Pétain, like Weygand, used this demagogic argument, that those who left to continue the struggle in North Africa would be deserters, seeking to evade the sufferings of the French people. In their eyes it was only cowardice to remain at the side of one's allies, to keep one's pledged word and to leave France in order to save her.

When one of the Ministers took up this accusation, I replied that, if I believed that the Council could be influenced by this argument, I was ready to remain myself in metropolitan France whilst the Government could carry on the struggle in North Africa.

Pétain has told his biographer about this meeting at Cangé. There is a sober eloquence in this account. The text of Pétain's statement is, in fact, followed by a paragraph which reads as follows:

'After this text had been read, M. Paul Reynaud declared: "This is contrary to the honour of France."'

That is all.

Never in our history, I believe, had a marshal of France drawn forth a similar retort. Pétain had forgotten the entreaty of Fichte to the German nation after Jena: 'We have lost the war. Must we in addition lose our honour?'

I kept, indeed, coming back to the subject of France's honour in the spacious drawing-room on the ground floor of the Château de Cangé during these two evenings. It was this honour which I was defending against our 'glorious military leaders'. But it proved to be in vain.

[1] We have heard Leopold III use similar language before, when he was announcing his capitulation.

The war would go on, I added, whatever was our attitude. Whether we signed an armistice or not, the blockade of France by Britain, and the seizure of France by Germany were inevitable. Our people would be captive for a long time, and if we broke with Britain, it would be left without hope. To ask for an armistice would, therefore, be to lose both honour and hope.

Frossard, who was to vote later for an armistice at Bordeaux, made a warm appeal to those of our colleagues who were in favour of it, asking them to await Roosevelt's answer to my appeal. I did not oppose this for the reason which I have given.

JUNE 13: TOURS; MY CALL TO THE FRENCH PEOPLE AND MY APPEAL TO THE AMERICAN PEOPLE

On leaving the Council of Ministers I returned to the Prefecture at Tours to give a speech over the wireless.

Certain people have criticized the speech for having increased instead of quietening the anxiety of the country. It is true that such was its effect. But I was obliged to use this strain of language to prepare the French people for a fact without precedent in our long history: the Government abandoning national territory. I was all the more obliged to speak like this because I knew, from the attitude of Pétain and Weygand, that the members of the Government would be called deserters and cowards as soon as they had embarked. On the other hand, I counted upon speaking again at the moment of leaving metropolitan France in order to continue the war by the side of our Allies, so that I could emphasize as strongly as I could the good prospects which the coalition still had, and the reasons why France could still nourish some hope.

In my speech of June 13 I spoke successively to the American and the French peoples.

I did not lose sight of the fact that the electoral period was approaching in the U.S.A. Public opinion was, therefore, a more important factor than in normal times. Thus, it was to this opinion that I was, first and foremost, to make an appeal, by evoking the sacrifices made by France. 'We know what place ideals hold in the life of the great American people. The French Army has been the advance-guard of the democracies . . . France is entitled to turn to the other democracies and say to them: "I have certain claims upon you."' And I asked the American people to give us, even from afar off, the hope of a common victory, essential to every combatant. I thought of the message of Roussy de Sales. My object was to give Roosevelt the chance of doing everything he could which was compatible with the state of American opinion.

I then spoke to the French people. To them I said: 'I have seen men coming from the battle line, who have not slept for five days, harassed by planes, broken by marching and fighting. These men, whose nerves the enemy thought he could break, have no doubt what will be the final outcome of the war. They had no doubt about the destiny of the Motherland.' And, having offered the people the example of the soldier, I added: 'The soul of France has not been conquered: our race does not allow itself to be overthrown by an invasion. The soil on which it lives has seen many during the course of centuries! We have always thrown back or subjugated the invader!'

Was there reason to despair? Certainly not. 'The superior quality of British planes is becoming more obvious every day. Clouds of warplanes must come from beyond the Atlantic to crush this evil force which is dominating Europe. In spite of our reverses, the strength of the democracies remains immense. We are entitled to hope that the day is approaching when all this strength will be employed. . . . That is why we retain hope in our hearts. Whatever happens in the days to come, Frenchmen, wherever they may be, will have to suffer. Let them show that they are worthy of their country's past, let them become more brotherly, let them close ranks firmly about the wounded Motherland! The day of resurrection will come.'

JUNE 14: A FINAL APPEAL TO ROOSEVELT

On the next day, the 14th at 1 p.m., I drafted my last appeal to Roosevelt.

I was more outspoken than over the wireless, since the text was not intended to be published. What words should I use to influence his generous nature and induce him to make that public statement of which Roussy de Sales had spoken? I thought, not without deliberating at length, that the most powerful lever would be to get him to estimate the responsibility which America would bear if this gesture was not made, and to this end to show him the disasters which might result. Everything had to be done to obtain the maximum effort. Churchill as we know, set about the problem in the same way when in his message of the same day he gave Roosevelt grounds to fear that Britain would surrender and be enslaved.

Here is the text of my message:

'I thank you for having published in America the message which I sent you on June 10.

'I told you then that, for six days and nights, our troops had been fighting without an hour's respite, one against three, and with equipment a fifth as powerful as that of the enemy.

'Four days of bloody fighting have passed by since then. Our Army is now cut into several fragments. Our divisions are decimated. Generals are in command of battalions. The Wehrmacht has just entered Paris. We are going to try and withdraw our exhausted forces in order to offer further battles. It is doubtful if they can succeed in doing this after being at grips with the enemy, who is constantly reinforcing his troops.

'At the most tragic hour in her history France has to make a choice. Is she to continue sacrificing her youth in a hopeless struggle? Should her Government leave national territory to avoid surrendering itself to the enemy and to be able to continue the struggle on sea and in North Africa? Is the whole of France to live then, abandoned to her own resources in the night of Nazi domination, enduring all that this will mean as regards her body and her soul? Or shall she ask Hitler's conditions for an armistice?

'We can only choose the first path, that of resistance, if the chance of victory appears in the distance, if a light shines at the end of the tunnel.

'Now, in the present situation, despite a weakening of the enemy forces, which is due to the sacrifice of the French Army, the defeat of our loyal ally, Britain, left to her own resources, appears possible if not likely. Henceforth, France can only continue to fight if American intervention reverses the situation by making victory for the Allies certain. The only chance of saving the French nation, the advance-guard of the democracies, and thus of saving Britain, by whose side France can then remain with her powerful fleet, is to throw the weight of American strength into the scales. This very day. This is also the only chance of avoiding an attack by Hitler against America after he has destroyed first, France and then Britain, in emulation of Horatius' duel against the three Curiatii.

'I know that a declaration of war does not lie within your hands alone. But I have to tell you in this hour which is a grave one in your history as in our own, that, if you cannot give France in the coming days a positive assurance that the United States will come into the struggle within a short space of time, the destiny of the world will be changed.

'You will then see France go under like a drowning person after having thrown a last look towards the land of liberty from where she was expecting salvation.'

During the evening I received the following telegram from our Washington Ambassador: 'Your Excellency's message . . . reached the President this morning. The Under-Secretary of State who had just been in conference with the latter, told me that the tone and spirit of the document had made a deep impression.'[1] As we shall see, Roosevelt understood perfectly in what frame of mind I sent him this appeal.

JUNE 14: ROOSEVELT'S REPLY TO MY MESSAGE OF THE 10TH

I left Tours for Bordeaux during the morning of the 14th. On the way I stopped at Angoulême, where the Prefect handed me the following telegram from Roosevelt, which had arrived at 10 a.m. on the 14th:[2]

President Roosevelt to M. Reynaud.

Your message of June 10 has moved me very deeply. As I have already stated to you and to Mr. Churchill, this Government is doing everything in its power to make available to the Allied Governments the material they so urgently require, and our efforts to do still more are being redoubled. This is so because of our faith in and our support of the ideals for which the Allies are fighting.

The magnificent resistance of the French and British Armies has profoundly impressed the American people.

I am, personally, particularly impressed by your declaration that France will continue to fight on behalf of Democracy, even if it means slow withdrawal, even to North Africa and the Atlantic. It is most important that the French and British Fleets continue [in] mastery of the Atlantic and other oceans; also to remember that vital materials from the outside world are necessary to maintain all armies.

I am also greatly heartened by what Prime Minister Churchill said a few days ago about the continued resistance of the British Empire, and that determination would seem to apply equally to the great French Empire all over the world. Naval power in world affairs still carries the lessons of history, as Admiral Darlan well knows.

In his memoirs Churchill stresses the fact that he attached no less importance than I did to the immediate publication of this telegram because of the ray of hope which it brought us. Having insisted on this, he received Roosevelt's reply on the 14th. It was in the negative. During the night 14th–15th, Churchill returned to the charge: '. . . I

---

[1] On the next day M. de Saint-Quentin telegraphed to me:

'I have commented in urgent terms on the message. Mr. Sumner Welles has stated that the U.S. Government is determined to go as far as possible towards helping the Allies without coming into the War, for neither Congress nor public opinion would follow it to such a point. If war were declared, the President would have up against him not only the Republicans but also the more leftist trade unions and a certain number of dissident Democrats who would be only too happy to find a favourable excuse to attack.'

[2] The text give here is that given by Sir Winston Churchill in *The Second World War*, vol. II, *Their Finest Hour*, pp. 162–3 [Tr.].

have reported', he cabled the President, '[the] operative passages [of your telegram] to Reynaud, to whom I had imparted a rather more sanguine view. . . . I understand all your difficulties with American public opinion and Congress . . . but this moment is supremely critical for France. A declaration that the United States will if necessary enter the war might save France. Failing that, in a few days French resistance may have crumpled and we shall be left alone.'[1]

Churchill's attitude towards Roosevelt was, as we see, the same as my own.

JUNE 14: BORDEAUX

The Ministers arrived at Bordeaux during the evening of the 14th, and took up quarters in the public buildings; the lodgings of the Prefect, the military headquarters, the Prefecture, the law courts, chamber of commerce, university buildings, schools, etc. . . .

The President of the Republic occupied the Prefect's lodgings, Rue Vital-Carles, and I was lodged in the headquarters of the 18th Military Region. Mandel was at the Prefecture.

Laval, leader of those advocating surrender, was installed in the Hôtel de Ville, in the next room to Marquet, the Mayor of Bordeaux. The corridors and ante-rooms of the Hôtel de Ville became the meeting-place of the defeatist members of Parliament. Marquet was going to try, as I have since learned through Jouhaux, to organize a labour demonstration against the Government's departure from France. Jouhaux was to oppose it.

Charles Reibel himself also arrived on the next day in Bordeaux and placed in Jeanneney's hand a request to question the Government on its reasons why it thought operations should be prolonged, despite the unanimous advice of our military chiefs. He asked for the immediate summoning of the Senate. Jeanneney refused and merely promised him to inform me of this step. But even though Reibel could not ventilate his complaints on the floor of the Senate, he did not allow himself for all that to be stopped. He preached openly on behalf of an armistice; besieging M. Lebrun and then, in turn, each of my colleagues. I shall later return to his moves, which went as far as intimidation and even to threats.

The intrigue developed. Any method was good enough, even the most underhand. I have learned since that my telephone wires were tapped.[2] Deputies and Senators, arriving in a flood of refugees, were

[1] *Ibid.*, p. 166.

[2] That is why, as we shall see later, that the plan for a Franco-British Union on June 16 was known to the advocates of surrender before the meeting of the Council of Ministers.

In an alleged reproduction of these tappings of my telephone conversations errors have been made. I pointed out this fact during my evidence at Pétain's trial (hearing of July 25, 1945).

plunged into an atmosphere which became more pernicious with each succeeding day.

About 9.30 p.m. I received a visit from the British Ambassador. He was accompanied by Spears. They 'notified me orally' that Great Britain would exercise her rights to insist on the undertaking given by France not to negotiate separately with the enemy.[1] We know that I had never expected this communication to remind my colleagues of our pledge nor to tell them that our national honour was being questioned. That is why I received the approach with anything but good grace—at least, I fear so. I was wrong in this, for the British step was to offer me during later deliberations a valuable argument in my struggle against my opponents' case.

Churchill writes in his memoirs that, on the next day, the 15th,[2] during the course of the morning, I stated to the British Ambassador that I had 'definitely decided to divide the Government in half and to establish a centre of authority beyond the sea. Such a policy would obviously carry with it the removal of the French Fleet to ports beyond German power.'[3] Later he added, still in reference to this same day, 'Paul Reynaud . . . realized that the battle in France was over, but still hoped to carry on the war from Africa and the French Empire and with the French Fleet.'[4]

As soon as I got to Bordeaux I told M. de Margerie that I wished urgently to see Darlan about organizing transports for North Africa. He telephoned to Montbazon where the Admiralty was. They replied that Darlan had transferred his headquarters to Rochefort, but that they could get in touch with him. Half an hour later Darlan called M. de Margerie and told him that he would be in Bordeaux on the 15th at 9 a.m.

JUNE 15: MEETINGS

Darlan did indeed arrive at the appointed hour, and had a preliminary talk with M. de Margerie, who gave him a picture in broadest lines of the situation which I was going to discuss with him. Then he came into my office. Looking crestfallen, he told me that my scheme for transporting troops to North Africa was on too grand a scale, and that in any case he could not take charge of its execution. Later we shall see when and why he had changed his attitude.

'Do your best,' I told him. 'General de Gaulle is in London to get the ships.'

[1] It was during this visit that the Ambassador handed me a manuscript *aide-mémoire* about the captured German prisoners. This text included a second paragraph on: 'The necessity to destroy military as well as diplomatic archives.'
[2] As we have just seen, it was on the evening of the 14th and not the 15th.
[3] *Op. cit.*, vol. II, *Their Finest Hour*, p. 176.
[4] *Ibid.*, p. 177.

I then received a visit from the United States Ambassador. Afterwards I summoned M. Charles-Roux. I was in conference with him when Pétain was announced. We began talking in the presence of M. Charles-Roux, who has given a striking account of what we said.[1]

Pétain pulled out a memorandum, which he read to me but which told me nothing. It was, in actual fact, a re-edition of that which he had read at the second meeting of the Council at Cangé.

By way of reply I told Pétain the conversation which I had just had with Mr. Biddle. When I had said to him that I would send the Fleet, should the day come when everything was lost even in North Africa, to America to serve, at President Roosevelt's disposal, the cause of the freedom of the nations, the Ambassador uttered the words, 'You would do that!'

When Pétain had left, Baudouin came into my room.

'The President of the Council', writes M. Charles-Roux, 'repeated to him the brief account of his interview that morning with the United States Ambassador, and ended it by remarking: "We must have imagination in such a situation as we find ourselves!"

'This was true. He was right. M. Paul Baudouin agreed, but, in his answer, used the word responsibility, which M. Paul Reynaud seized on with great vigour.

'The Under-Secretary of State was no longer in agreement with . . . the President of the Council . . . Minister of Foreign Affairs. M. Paul Reynaud was steeling himself against an armistice. M. Paul Baudouin was becoming an avowed supporter of it.'

At the end of the morning I received a visit from the Presidents of the two Chambers.

It was later said that I had been asked by them to reshuffle my Government. This is inexact. We parted fully in agreement about the need for continuing the war, without the question of altering it being in any wise raised.

Here, moreover, is the account which President Jeanneney in his deposition at the Pétain trial (hearing of July 26, 1945) has given: 'President Paul Reynaud informed us of his deep apprehension concerning the rapid advance of the German Armies. He repeated to us what he had said at Tours; his annoyance with the Supreme Command which was most rebellious about the instructions of the Government; and we felt that there was a strong likelihood of dissension amongst the Administration. He emphasized to us, at that time, his unshakeable determination not to cease the struggle. We approved strongly of this attitude, and encouraged him in it.'

[1] *Op. cit.*, pp. 41–2. The interview took place on the 15th and not as M. Charles-Roux writes, on the 16th.

JUNE 15: FIRST DISPUTE WITH WEYGAND

Before the Council of Ministers had ended on the 13th, Weygand left Cangé to return to the Château du Muguet, which he reached a little after nightfall. He spent the day of the 14th there.

At 8.30 a.m. he received a visit from Lieutenant-General Sir Alan Brooke, who had just assumed command of the new British Expeditionary Force, and with whom he signed an agreement at 10.30 a.m. settling the co-operation of British and French forces.

At 5 p.m. a message was brought to Weygand by Major Minart, who was on Pétain's staff.

It ran as follows:

'The Council of Ministers has decided to make no decision about asking for an armistice from Germany until a reply has been received to a telegram sent to Mr. Roosevelt, last night, asking him to declare war on Germany.

'The Marshal considers that the utmost time limit in making this decision is Saturday midday.

'To do this, it is necessary to have a meeting of the Council of Ministers at the end of tomorrow morning.

'General Weygand's presence at Bordeaux is necessary.

'The Commander-in-Chief should be at 58, Rue Saint-Genès, Bordeaux, the domicile of M. Baudouin, telephone 868–20, *before 10.30.*'

Having decided to withdraw Supreme Headquarters to Vichy, Weygand got into his special train with three officers.[1]

[1] It was during the night of the 14th–15th that the British troops reassumed their liberty of action as regards the French Command. Brooke, in his dispatch writes indeed, that at 10.35 p.m. on the 14th, General Dill, in his capacity of Chief of the Imperial General Staff, advised him by phone that he was no longer under Weygand's orders except to co-ordinate as effectively as possible the action of his troops with that of our Tenth Army.

During the evening of the 14th, Brigadier J. G. des R. Swayne, head of the British Mission with Georges, left the latter to return with his staff to Britain. At 8.45 a.m. on the 15th Georges received from Swayne the message in which Dill notified Weygand of a repudiation of the agreement. Here is the text of the message:

'Due to the present situation and the difficulty in communications General Brooke can no longer hope to receive orders from the French Supreme Command.

'I have informed him that he need no longer consider himself under the orders of the Supreme Command, but that he ought to continue co-operation with French troops operating in his vicinity.

'I am taking your agreement as given as from now.'

Brigadier Sir Richard Howard-Vyse, head of No. 1 Mission (with Weygand) in his turn also left Briare for London, only leaving out of his staff Colonel Desheer, who followed Supreme Headquarters which, during the morning of the 15th, took up quarters at the Hôtel du Parc in Vichy.

It was there, during a brief stay which he made during the morning of the 16th that Weygand received at 8.45 a.m. Colonel Desheer, who, in his turn, was taking his leave of him.

'Because General Georges finds it impossible, owing to the departure of the British Mission, to give orders to the British troops, I give notice', Weygand told him, 'that I am freed of all responsibility as regards these troops.'

'The journey', writes Bourget (*op. cit.*, p. 128), 'was never-ending. ... At 7 a.m. the train ... had not even got to Châteauroux, and it was only at the beginning of the afternoon (of the 15th) that it entered the station of La Bastide.[1] General Weygand found Marshal Pétain at the Grand Hôtel in conference with MM. Baudouin, Bouthillier and Admiral Darlan. He gave them the latest military information, and went immediately to the residence of 18th Military Region's head-quarters, Rue Vital-Carles. There, around 3.30 p.m., the General met M. Paul Reynaud.'

Baudouin, who tells of this exchange of views (*op. cit.*, p. 112), notes that Weygand first of all 'apologized for his excitement on Thursday and promised to keep calm'.

We shall see how this undertaking was kept. Within a few minutes this '*tête-à-tête*', to repeat Weygand's expression at the Pétain trial (hearing of July 31, 1945), 'this private interview', to borrow that of Bourget (*op. cit.*, p. 128), lost the deliberate character which the exami-nation of a vital question more than ever required during these tragic hours. Weygand raised his voice. The interview soon turned into a dispute. And yet what was it I said to him?

Still tormented by a fear of seeing France cut in two, I tried to change his mind. Therefore, instead of pinning him down on a point of honour, I told him that, even if the situation was agonizing for the Commander-in-Chief, it was no less so for the Head of the Government, but that, if he wished to consider the two ways which were opened, he would realize that I was right in choosing to continue the fight—as I had warned him that I should do in my reply to his memorandum of May 29. I added that, in any case, I should not give way. It was necessary to cease fire, as the Commander-in-Chief of the Dutch Army had done. Weygand would have to settle the time when the struggle was to end, but he must not, in making this choice, lose sight of the need for the Government to reach North Africa, without any haste savouring of panic but in time to avoid the danger of falling into enemy hands.

'The Government cannot leave France,' he said to me.

'But what is Algeria but three French departments?'

'It is not the same thing.'

I came back to the question of a cease-fire. He offered me the objec-tion that an armistice was a governmental act, whilst a cease-fire would be an act of the Command, and he did not wish to assume respon-sibility for it. To this I answered: 'If that is stopping you I will take on the responsibility. I will give you a written order.' He declared that

---

[1] Weygand writes in *Rappelé au service* (p. 225): 'It was ... after 2 p.m. when we reached the station of La Bastide. General Lafont, Commander of the 18th Region, was awaiting us there. He was a very old friend. He took me to the Grand Hôtel, where I found Marshal Pétain.'

'the honour of the army' was at stake. Thus, on the excuse of not dishonouring the Army, it was necessary to dishonour France herself! For Weygand, armies which, succumbing under the weight of numbers, ceased to fight without asking for an armistice, committed an 'infamy'; 'covered' their flags 'with shame'. None of them escaped his condemnation. There were troops, however, in these unlucky armies, who had fought valiantly and who had only surrendered after completely exhausting their resources. That did not matter. None of them could find pardon in the eyes of Weygand. All, without distinction, he burned with the branding irons of dishonour.

Here, now, is how Weygand, in his evidence at Riom, describes this stormy *tête-à-tête*, not without some flight of fancy:

'General Weygand was received by M. Paul Reynaud.

'The President of the Council told him of the anguish he felt about the decision he had to take. In his opinion the question could be summed up in the following dilemma: either to act as Queen Wilhelmina had done, leaving for England and entrusting the Chief of Staff of the Dutch Army with the duty of laying down arms, or to follow the example of King Leopold, who remained in his country after surrendering. He had made his choice. He would not ask for the cessation of hostilities and he would leave France if necessary.

'General Weygand replied that there was no similarity between a monarch and a prime minister. The former could rightly claim to represent a country over which his dynasty had reigned from father to son. What similarity was there between him and a prime minister when the Third Republic had already counted more than a hundred in its seventy years of existence? Once the head of a Government in France had gone, he was soon replaced and forgotten.

'The President of the Council suggested in conclusion to General Weygand—and the latter rejected his suggestion both decisively and indignantly—that he should follow the example of the Dutch Chief of General Staff, that is, he should capitulate.

'General Weygand would never acquiesce in an action which cast such shame on the flags of the French Army.'

Thus, because France had committed the *unpardonable* fault of being a Republic, its honour and interest could not be defended in the same way as those of Holland! But Weygand boasts of having ridiculed democratic institutions in front of me by pretending to confuse the Head of the State with the Head of the Government, and drawing an unseemly satirical parallel between a monarch and the prime minister of a Republic. It is unnecessary for me to say that, if he had ventured in my presence to indulge in such excessive language, I should have called him to order.

In any case, the dispute strengthened me in my resolve to relieve Weygand of his command as soon as possible. This is what I decided to do at the meeting of the Council of Ministers to which I was going.

JUNE 15: THE COUNCIL OF MINISTERS: THE 'CHAUTEMPS MANŒUVRE'

The Council of Ministers met at 4 p.m. in the residence of the President of the Republic. It was a meeting of decisive importance. The problem of an armistice had to be settled, and with it the question of Weygand. Weygand gave some information about the military situation. He stated with more emphasis than ever that this was getting worse with each passing hour, and that it was necessary to ask for an armistice immediately. 'They wondered if I were mad,' he says with his customary exaggeration.

General Lafont asked for permission to come in, and brought news of the battle-front in a melodramatic tone obviously assumed for the occasion.

After this, Weygand and Darlan at the request of M. Lebrun left the Council.

I made known Roosevelt's reply to my telegram of the 10th.

I explained again that the honour and interest of France were in unison to urge us to stay in the war. But Chautemps appealed to the humane feelings of his colleagues. He depicted our soldiers 'as being exterminated in a rabbit drive'. I answered that, if the Command thought necessary, I was ready to give the cease-fire order. I observed that, even taking human considerations into account as Chautemps was doing, the fitting solution was not an armistice but a cease-fire.[1] It would be physically impossible to conclude an armistice in less than four days whilst a cease-fire could come into immediate effect. As everyone seemed to be in agreement, I said that no one was better suited than Pétain to tell Weygand, who was waiting in the next room, that this solution was in no wise contrary to the honour of the Army.

M. Lebrun who describes this meeting in *Témoignage* (p. 81) states: 'Marshal Pétain seemed convinced. He was asked to withdraw for a moment to persuade the Supreme Commander, who was holding himself in readiness for the Council. He came back fifteen minutes later, having unfortunately been changed in his opinion by his inter-locutor.'

[1] In his deposition at the Pétain trial (hearing of July 30, 1945) Herriot said in relation to this: 'I have told you why I myself never asked for the French Army to be sent into battle if it were incapable of fighting. I have told you this without any prompting. M. Paul Reynaud himself said, when an appeal was made to his humane feelings: "But I am going to do something better than conclude an armistice. I am going to order a cease-fire, and shooting will stop at once."'

What passed between the two men? They alone know, and we shall see that they both agreed not to reveal their secret.

Whatever be the truth, this abortive attempt strengthened me in the conviction that it was immediately necessary to relieve Weygand of his command. This decision implied a previous settlement of the question of an armistice. I, therefore, asked the Council to give an immediate opinion on the subject.

Then it was that there occurred a sensational turn in events which has been called the 'Chautemps manœuvre'. It was this, indeed, which opened the way to an armistice.

Chautemps carefully refrained from supporting the attitude taken up by Pétain and Weygand. But he remarked to me that, if the Ministers were prepared to follow me to North Africa, they should at least be protected with regard to public opinion. He himself was convinced that the enemy conditions would prove unacceptable, but there was only one means of finding out, namely to inquire what these conditions would be. Once this had been done, every Frenchman would understand that the Government had no other choice than to continue the war, a determination which implied the transfer of the seat of public authority outside metropolitan territory. Nothing, then, would prevent the Ministers, who would have regularized their position with public opinion, from accompanying me to Africa. It was, therefore, only a matter of getting Britain's consent to such a step, the object of which was to place the Government in a position to carry on the war. And Chautemps concluded that Churchill, who had shown himself accommodating at Tours, would not be able to refuse a demand which was presented in such a way.

Frossard, whom Pétain was to take into his Ministry, and who was to obtain from him permission to publish at Marseille the newspaper *Le Mot d'Ordre*, gave in this journal, on November 23, 1940, under the title 'La démission du cabinet Reynaud', an account drawn up at a time when his recollection of the events was still fresh, and when he had had the leisure to check it with that of former members of my Cabinet. He wrote: 'For the first time, most of the Council seemed to support the opinion of the military leaders. . . . I was convinced that the worst possible mistake would have been the transfer of the Government to North Africa. Rightly or wrongly, the country would have judged that its leaders were leaving it in the lurch. Moreover, the Government would have disintegrated at the time of departure, as the Marshal and several other Ministers refused to leave France. The only eventuality in which a departure could be contemplated was in the event of armistice conditions proving dishonourable. It was still necessary for us to find out what they might be. Chautemps found the formula. "Ask the Reich what conditions it would attach to the cessation of hostilities." The majority of the Council showed its approval of this step.'

We see that this was, indeed, a question of asking for an armistice, for is not asking for an armistice, strictly speaking, asking for the terms of an armistice?

In any case Chautemps' proposal was obviously playing the game of a number of Ministers who, convinced that the defeat of Britain was imminent, imagined themselves already forced after a very brief flight, to regain France amidst jeers, to be looked upon as deserters. It was only, indeed, after the armistice that I learned that Weygand's phrase, which, it is true, he denied at Pétain's trial,[1] but which nevertheless bears his stamp, was already being repeated: 'Before three weeks is out, Britain will have her neck wrung like that of a chicken.'

Churchill himself, for that matter, was not deceived about the nature of Chautemps' proposal. '. . . an insidious proposal', he was to write in his memoirs,[2] 'which wore the aspect of a compromise and was attractive to the waverers'.

Against this, Chautemps, in a letter published by the *New York Times* of March 3, 1949, opposed the opinion of Léon Blum, who stated to the Committee of Inquiry on July 30, 1947, that the proposal was a sincere one. Was Léon Blum aware at the time of the facts that I have mentioned above, which prove that Chautemps was acting in collusion with Pétain? It seems hardly likely. In any case he adds: 'The fatal mistake which they (Chautemps and Frossard) made was to have supposed that one could play with this idea of an armistice. . . . It was in not having realized that, as soon as one had put a finger in this mesh, one was caught. What was dangerous about the proposal was that most of the Council of Ministers were jolted out of their determination by it. I am forming this opinion from several of my friends, and I can cite them to you, members of the Reynaud Cabinet who had been firmly and even enthusiastically behind Reynaud, and opposed to Pétain and Weygand, yet who were, on the other hand, tempted and seduced by the Chautemps-Frossard suggestion because, first of all, it avoided the necessity of coming to a definite decision.'

Now let us come back to the sitting.

I considered for my part that to ask conditions of the enemy even with the assent of Britain would be to break the last element of resistance. It was, indeed, obvious that the Germans would answer: 'If the French wish to know our conditions, let them come and ask us for them in the Rethondes[3] railway coach.' Thus, I fought against the

---

[1] Hearing of July 31, 1945.   [2] *Op. cit.*, vol. II, *Their Finest Hour*, pp. 178–9.
[3] Near Compiègne. It was in a railway coach at Rethondes that Marshal Foch and General Weygand in 1918 dictated the armistice terms to the Germans [Tr.].

proposal.[1] But Chautemps and Frossard had now won over a number of the Left just as Pétain and Weygand, for their part, had already seduced certain of the Right. It was then that a Minister uttered the words which Weygand, in his talk with Reibel, attributed to himself: 'You have asked us', he said, 'to go on to the end. We are at the end!'

This was the real crux of the dispute. Some wished to fight on; others to lay down arms. The Pétain-Weygand clique coalesced with the Chautemps. I divided a paper in two from top to bottom, and one after the other I wrote on the left the names of those in favour of Chautemps' proposal, and on the right the names of those against it.[2] There were thirteen for and six against. M. Lebrun has stated (*op. cit.*, p. 85): 'At a meeting on the day before (that of June 15), M. Paul Reynaud placed before me a sheet of paper on which he had noted down the attitude of the Ministers; fourteen in favour of Chautemps's proposal, and six against it.' The majority, therefore, was in favour of asking for armistice terms. I then turned to the President of the Republic, and told him that, in the circumstances, I was resigning. He protested keenly, and even with violence, striking the table with his hand and threatening to resign himself. I told him that, in spite of this, he could not force me to act contrary to my policy. The President insisted that I should give way. I replied that, in any case, such a policy could not be conducted by me. Moreover, was it not in the interests of the country to keep the credit which I had gained in Britain and America? Not very many of us had such! I could not succeed in convincing him. I had, then, several moments of internal struggle, which were the gravest of my public life. I reflected that it was only, indeed, a matter of asking Britain if she would agree to absolve us from our pledge not to conclude a separate armistice; the step to be taken, amounted, therefore, to an implicit recognition that France had not the right without Britain's consent to ask for armistice terms. This was equivalent to acknowledging that, if Britain refused, France could not persist without forfeiting her honour. Thereafter, I had not the slightest doubt. My duty was to overcome the repugnance which the accepted step raised within me, and not to stand aside. It was obvious, moreover, that if I did resign, I should be playing Chautemps's game since the question of my succession would open the way to Pétain and his followers, and that certainly meant an armistice. Consequently, any chance for France would be lost. I could not leave my post in such circumstances. Moreover, the event was to justify me. We know that,

[1] In *Le Mot d'Ordre* of June, 1941, Frossard was to recall, under the title of *Les journées historiques de juin, 1940: l'heure du Maréchal*, the anniversary of these tragic events. He wrote: 'Most of the Council gladly supported the proposal of Chautemps. Paul Reynaud and also Louis Marin, Georges Monnet, Louis Rollin and Rio opposed it.'

[2] I have not been able to find this sheet amongst my papers. I cannot, therefore, give the names of those Ministers who were either for or against.

on the next day, Britain gave us her final refusal, and that, using their own argument as a weapon against my opponents, I countered them by the fact that we should forfeit our honour if we ignored this refusal.

It is true that there was another possible outcome. President Lebrun could have accepted my resignation in order to entrust me at the same time with the formation of a new Government which itself would be in favour of continuing the war.[1] But M. Lebrun had already dismissed this solution from his mind. Indeed, only one thing counted with him. In this problem, which was certainly more than a purely military one, but which was linked up with military considerations since the question was one of continuing the war or not, we have seen that most of the Council were against me. Now, this majority comprised Pétain, then at the height of his reputation, and Chautemps, a Vice-President of the Council, like Pétain himself, and moreover, it was supported by Weygand and the important leaders of the Army. For those who were seeking a way to justify altering their minds, could a better excuse be found, indeed, in such a controversy than to offer the authoritative opinion of our 'glorious military leaders'? Here one puts a finger on the responsibility of Pétain and Weygand. Their opinion was, indeed, to outweigh that of the Presidents of the Chambers.[2]

I, therefore, agreed to transmit the request, but on condition that I specified that it emanated from a majority of the Council.

At least I forced Pétain to admit that handing over the French Fleet to the enemy so that it could 'stab our ally in the back' would be an action contrary to honour.

After the Council I summoned the British Ambassador and Spears. I informed them of the full gravity of the situation, and I stated that it was in the name of a majority of the Council that I presented this demand.

That morning I had received a brief visit from Gaston Palewski, who, after having served Lyautey in Morocco and rendered me myself

[1] No one doubts that, from the morning of the 15th, this question was the chief concern of a number of my colleagues. The only proof I wish to offer is the following passage from the above-cited deposition of Georges Monnet: 'When I got to Bordeaux, I remember that the first person I went to see was Mandel, who had his quarters in the Prefecture. It was Saturday morning. We both reviewed the situation and we both reduced it to exactly this. "There are at present a certain number of Ministers who are clearly in favour of the armistice. Others are beginning to waver. Is there any possibility of cutting down the number of Ministers, and keeping only those who are in favour of continuing the war?" Mandel was convinced that this ought to be done. He said: "Everything depends on Lebrun. If Reynaud wishes to resign, Lebrun can only entrust the formation of a new government to Reynaud or another person equally determined to carry on the war. The thought that Lebrun, who will consult Herriot and Jeanneney, can hand over power to anyone who wishes for an armistice is . . . impossible to contemplate."'

[2] People who have entrusted power to their 'glorious military leaders' have little reason to compliment themselves on this. A marshal harnessed Roumania to the chariot of Hitler; another brought Finland into the war against Russia on the side of Hitler; an admiral, out of servility to Hitler, urged Hungary along the road which a Prime Minister of that country thought to be so dishonourable that he committed suicide.

most considerable services, left me in January to join the Air Force, in which he distinguished himself as brilliantly as he was to do later with the Free French Forces in Africa, before becoming the right arm of General de Gaulle. From Lyautey to Charles de Gaulle, what a career! He was opposed, it goes without saying, to an armistice. I had assured him that France would never surrender.

CHAUTEMPS' DOUBLE GAME

'Let us rather board a cruiser,' we have heard Chautemps exclaim, when he heard that I made his support to my Government conditional on an irrevocable pledge that he would stay by me in the decisive hour.

It was a necessary precaution in respect to a man who was reputedly inclined to subterfuge and weakness, but whom political considerations forced me to keep in my Administration.

The grandiloquent bravado of Chautemps' reply to Mandel certainly clashed with all that I knew about this person. It will be said that my suspicions should have been on the contrary aroused and not appeased. The truth is that Chautemps was trying to deceive me. I am obliged to admit that he succeeded. But, even if I had to protect myself against his weakness, how should I have known that this 'spoilt child' of the Republic had already entered into a close alliance with the opponents of the régime?

Today the proof is established. It was, we have seen, Baudouin who revealed that, on May 26, Chautemps decided to support Pétain. Six days later there came another approach. Baudouin notes (*op. cit.*, p. 74):

'Saturday, June 1, 1940.
'This morning I had a talk with M. Chautemps on the question of the evacuation of Paris by the Government. . . . He returned to the idea which he expressed to me a few days ago, namely, that at a given moment Marshal Pétain would make himself Head of the Government.'

What does this mean but that Chautemps, anticipating the political upheaval which was being planned, meant to be the civilian whom no military dictatorship could do without? But our man had too much practice in the moves of the political chess-board to be so naïve as to suppose that when the time did come he would be the only one to intrigue for this plum position. Therefore, he had to make himself indispensable. Obviously by remaining on the spot he could most effectively assist the move, and at the same time offer proof of his abilities. Thus, when Mandel and myself took the initiative by exacting from him a frank answer, Chautemps himself only thought of dissipating our vigilance. Whereas we believed that we had only to safeguard ourselves against his weakness, it was really against his duplicity that we should have been on guard.

We shall see presently how the intrigue developed. On June 7, Chautemps dined at Ribet's house. He was in the mood for uttering confidences. During the course of discussion he ended up by saying to his hosts: 'Reynaud does not grasp the position. He will be shoved out of power, and we shall have a military dictatorship.'[1] And Chautemps did not refrain[2] from hinting of successive purges.[3]

But he took good care to warn neither Mandel nor myself. What was his reason? It was because, after making advances to Pétain, he was now giving him pledges. But, still not daring to confide directly in him who, to his title of 'Victor of Verdun' was preparing to add that of 'Victor of the Republic', he approached Baudouin, an intermediary in whom he had reason to repose confidence. In actual fact he asked him to dinner on June 8. Baudouin notes:[4]

'Saturday, June 8, 1940.

'I dined with M. Chautemps at the Hotel Matignon. . . . He had no illusions as to the result of the struggle. "We must put an end to it. It is useless, and we ought to stop before the whole country is destroyed. Marshal Pétain sees the position clearest."'

Let us come to the decisive days. On June 12 we have seen that the Council of Ministers was in conference at Cangé. Chautemps put a request that we should hear Churchill. The insistence with which he made it did not fail to strike me. Mandel himself, wondering also if some move was to be detected in it, said to me on leaving the Council: 'Chautemps is hatching some scheme.' But, at that time, we were both far from suspecting that he had, contrary to his promise, passed into Pétain's camp. The latter knew that he could, henceforth, rely on Chautemps, and, consequently, took him into the conspiracy. Indeed, he treated him as one of his supporters on the 14th when we were about to leave for Bordeaux.

'On the morning of the 14th', writes Laure,[5] 'General Bineau and General Brécard (of the military secretariat), and M. Alibert (of the civilian secretariat) arrived at Nitray.[6] M. Chautemps and several

---

[1] I have these words from Maître Ribet. He informed Mandel and myself of them at Vals where, it will be later seen, we were imprisoned. Madame Bretty was present at the conversation.

[2] Maître Ribet also supplies this additional detail. He got it from M. Bouchardon, President of the Committee of Investigation to the High Court.

[3] Maître Ribet, entrusted with Chautemps' defence, expressed a wish not to be called to give evidence on the part of his client. He explained his position on this subject in a straightforward manner to me, emphasizing that his evidence would not, should he give it, add anything to what I myself said, and whose exactitude no one thought of contesting.   [4] *Op. cit.*, p. 88.

[5] *Op. cit.*, p. 434.   [6] At the Château de Nitray, near to Bléré in Touraine.

Ministers were talking with the Marshal. The general opinion was that a decision had to be reached on arrival at Bordeaux.'[1]

On the next day Chautemps took the initiative by proposing to the Council of Ministers that Hitler should be asked under what conditions he would grant us an armistice. Two days later he was to be Vice-President of the Council in Pétain's administration and expressly entrusted with asking for these conditions.

Then came Vichy. Pétain overthrew the Republic. Chautemps did nothing to defend the régime which had overwhelmed him with honours. His reply to Léon Blum laid bare his soul:

'I spent July 9 and 10 at Vichy,' stated Léon Blum.[2]
'. . . When I saw Chautemps for the last time in a corridor I said to him, "Well then. This is the end of the Republic?" He answered me: "I fear so."'

Chautemps was not long, moreover, in drawing his reward for this defection: a well-paid post in the United States. But a difficulty arose. Vichy decided to dissolve the Freemasons,[3] amongst whom Chautemps, it is well known, was one of the highest dignitaries. Was he prepared to leave the Brotherhood? Not only did he do nothing about it, but he told Pétain, who took a malicious pleasure in keeping him on a string, that he would welcome the measure as a 'veritable deliverance'.

Whilst I remained in ignorance of the intrigues in which Chautemps was involved, I put his change of face down to his weakness. Mandel and myself in our common prisons often discussed the problem. Mandel used to say to me: 'Men do not change. Chautemps acted in the same way at Bordeaux as he did in March, 1938, when he resigned at the time of Hitler's entry into Austria, and as he did six months later on the eve of Munich.'

But it is proved today that Chautemps, after having supported Pétain when it was a question of asking for an armistice, helped him at Vichy to strangle the Republic. Lack of resolution could at a pinch suffice to explain the first of these failures. This could not by itself explain the second, however considerable was the share it might have played in it.

Corroborative items of evidence now available to us give the key to what remained an enigma. Above all, it shows us that Chautemps,

[1] Chautemps was not, however, the only one to make the pilgrimage to Nitray. Bouthillier went there on the 13th. He writes (*op. cit.*, pp. 22–3): 'I found the Marshal alone in the spacious drawing-room of the Château. I hardly knew him. . . . His reputation was such in my eyes that his words seemed to be those of an oracle.' Pétain had just drafted the declaration which he was to read to the Council of Ministers on that same evening. Bouthillier read it: 'From that moment, I decided', he adds, 'to follow him with constancy and resolution.'
[2] Pétain trial, hearing of July 27, 1945.
[3] The law prohibiting secret societies was dated August 13.

like Pétain, saw in an armistice the means of overthrowing the régime.

JUNE 15: SECOND DISPUTE WITH WEYGAND

According to Weygand's evidence (hearing of July 31, 1945) it was at the end of the Council of Ministers' meeting on the 15th that the second dispute between myself and him took place—four hours after the first and still on the subject of a cease-fire.

Let us read Weygand's account, placing the scene in its setting as described by Bourget,[1] who states he was one of the eye-witnesses of this scene. Bourget writes:

'A meeting of the Council of Ministers opened in the drawing-room of the Prefect of the Gironde's quarters, next to the military head-quarters of the region, Rue Vital-Carles, and where the President of the Republic had his residence. . . . The room . . . was adjacent both to the winter garden and an outer drawing-room, both of which opened on to the colonnaded hall of the building. In these three rooms were the civil servants and officials of the President's household and the ministerial staffs of the Marshal and the Commander-in-Chief. . . . The latter took a stroll with his officers in the winter garden, and came and sat down in the outer drawing-room beside Admiral Darlan. . . . About 10 p.m. the communicating door between the two drawing-rooms opened: the members of the Government were leaving the Council meeting. M. Paul Reynaud came out last, and stopped in front of General Weygand. The latter was surrounded by three officers of his staff who had come with him to Bordeaux and several people who had waited for the ending of the meeting.' And Bourget goes on to describe the exchanges, which we shall find in Weygand's account. Bourget then adds: 'The Supreme Commander . . . disputed the fact in a raised voice, that he had uttered such words, whilst all around fell a complete silence. "I have never said that to you, Mr. Prime Minister," he repeated several times. M. Paul Reynaud . . . asked the General to calm down. . . . The word "responsibility" was uttered. M. Paul Reynaud asserted that he did not fear any responsibility and that he would assume all. Thereupon, he went towards the hall. The General walked in the opposite direction, towards the Council chamber, where the President of the Republic still was, to inform him of the incident. But M. Albert Lebrun stopped him with a word: he could only listen to what he had to say in the presence of the President of the Council. The latter had not yet left the building. He was informed. The discussion was resumed, but this time with MM. Mandel and Bouthillier as sole witnesses. . . . Once he was in his car with his officers he (Weygand)

[1] Op. cit., pp. 129–31.

calmed down. On the way to the Bastide station he stopped a moment at Marshal Pétain's to tell him of what had just passed. An hour later his special train was carrying him to Vichy.'

In his deposition at Riom, Weygand gives the following account of the scene which, as usual, he trims to suit himself:

'President Reynaud came up to General Weygand to tell him what had passed. The Ministers were in favour of an armistice only for the ground army and to be requested by the Commander of the ground forces. The President of the Council believed or pretended to believe at the meeting that the General would give his assent.

'The General treated him with scant consideration and raising his voice said: "I never said that to you." He added that he would never be forced to do such a thing, which was contrary to the honour of the Army. Let him be relieved of his command if necessary, for he was determined to refuse to obey such an order. This violent scene took place in the presence of several officers and officials belonging to the military household of the President of the Republic, to different ministeries and to the General Staff. The General stated that the cessation of hostilities fell, like a declaration of war, within the general conduct of the war and thus it was a matter for the Government. Let the Government shoulder its responsibilities! M. Paul Reynaud replied that an armistice meant handing over the Fleet, and that the Council was unanimous in its decision not to allow this. As for responsibilities, he would shoulder all of them.

'Before withdrawing, General Weygand wished to inform the President of the Republic about the incident. With this intention he went into the neighbouring room where the Council had just met, and where MM. Mandel and Bouthillier still remained. The President of the Republic refused to hear him except in the presence of the President of the Council. But the latter returned and General Weygand was able to explain what had passed to the President of the Council, and his own formal decision not to surrender. Was he to be taken for a child? Was it for this that he had been called back from Syria when the position was desperate? For twenty-three years he had followed the work of the politicians, and he knew what responsibilities they had to bear in the present tragedy. To the President of the Republic who wished to silence him, General Weygand recalled that, when he was in command of the Army, he had to appeal to him to fight against the dangers, which certain measures recently taken against his advice by MM. Daladier and Co., held for national defence, and that the President of the Republic had refused to listen to him. M. Albert Lebrun answered General Weygand that it was only a trivial question of manœuvres. The latter retorted that grave consequences were entailed:

the dismissal of five thousand officers carried out illegally by the Finance Law, and the refusal of several hundreds of millions credit specially intended for the construction of new equipment.

'This painful scene ended with General Weygand's renewed affirmation that nobody could force him to carry out an action which he refused to do.

'At 9.30 p.m. General Weygand caught the train for Vichy, where he arrived the following day at 7.35 a.m.'

Later Weygand was to take up this account again; on the first occasion at the Pétain trial (hearing of July 31, 1945) to intensify its tone, and on a second occasion in less aggressive strains, before the Committee of Inquiry (sitting of March 3, 1949). The reader will find in the note below the text of these two new versions.[1]

Whatever be the truth of the matter, this account, in which Weygand imagined that he was increasing his stature by assuming the attitude of a blusterer, was to leave a painful impression on whoever remembers the tragic character of the hours which our country was then passing through. What an example of aberration and also of degradation to try and derive glory from having lost his self-control to such a degree and at such a time, and from having forced me to call him sharply to heel.

In any case, this time it was no longer a question of a *tête-à-tête*. The scandalous scene took place before witnesses, and had two stages: first of all I was the only one who was attacked; then, it was the turn of the President of the Republic, who insisted that I should return, for he invoked his constitutional lack of responsibility to refuse to hear Weygand when I was not present.[2]

The second episode took place, it is true, before a more restricted

[1] The version given by Weygand at the Pétain trial ran:

'The President of the Council came to me . . . and said: "General, you will ask for the capitulation of the Army as we have agreed a short while ago."

'Gentlemen, I should tell you that at this moment I gave a genuine start of indignation. Were we really reduced to this? I took three paces backwards so that everyone could hear me. I was forced, I must confess, to give the President of the Council a resounding denial. I again stated that no human force existed which would make me sign the capitulation of an army which had just fought like ours had done.'

That given by him to the Committee of Inquiry ran:

'When the Council came to an end, M. Paul Reynaud came towards me and again spoke to me of this surrender in words which made me believe that he was under the impression that our private conversation had given him hope of seeing me make such an infamous decision.

'I then moved back so that the odd thirty people who were in the room . . . could hear me plainly in order this time to have witnesses, and I repeated to him that I could not agree to his request.'

[2] A third storm of the same kind was to take place, as we shall see, on the next day, the 16th, in M. Lebrun's study. Through an error at Pétain's trial (hearing of July 31) I ran the second and third quarrels into a single scene, which I placed on the 16th.

audience. Only Mandel and Bouthillier were present. Baudouin, whom the latter informed of this dispute, describes it in the following words:[1]

'At this, General Weygand had gone up in the air, and said that he would refuse to obey any such order. It was for the Government, which had declared war, to face up to its obligations. The General had addressed the most vehement reproaches to M. Albert Lebrun for having allowed the national defences to be compromised during the past few years owing to his fear of accepting any responsibility.'

These words were already assuming a menacing sound. 'Responsibility?'

For having declared war? We shall see the Pétain-Weygand Government define a new crime, that of having 'conspired to replace a state of peace by one of war'. We shall see that Mandel and myself were above all the objects of its attack. But, we shall also see the magistrates of the Riom Court, in a surge of patriotic indignation, thwart an intrigue which would have also injured the country.

'For having allowed national defence to be compromised.' This was to be, in substance, the accusation levied against Daladier, Blum and others.

Was not the Riom trial already taking shape?

When he was relating the second dispute of June 15, Weygand, we have seen, ascribed to himself these words, which, it will be agreed, tell a significant tale: 'For twenty-three years the General had followed the work of the politicians, and he knew what responsibilities they had to bear in the present tragedy.' When the Procurator-General, Mornet, asked him at Pétain's trial (hearing of July 31, 1945) to 'explain the significance which he attached to this phrase', Weygand was to reply:

'I stick literally to these words. In the present tragedy, politicians bore a responsibility and soldiers bore one. To try and deny this would be nonsense. Thus, I stick to everything which I said at that time.

'And as for saying that I was aware of this responsibility, I don't gainsay this at all since I had the honour of commanding the French Army in time of peace for four years. I had serious disputes with some Ministers on the gravest military matters. Consequently, I cannot withdraw anything which I have said.'

The politicians did, indeed, commit a capital error: that of deferring blindly to the military leaders.

But, for the time being, let us return to the scene.

I shall confine myself to saying that it is not possible for me to have used to Weygand the language he puts in my mouth for the simple reason that, hardly a few hours before, he had privately given me a

[1] *Op. cit.*, p. 114.

categoric refusal to order a cease-fire. What I said to him was that the Council entertained a different opinion from his own on this subject. But the scene had a conclusive significance: Weygand, it goes without saying, lost his self-control. His venom was overflowing. His attitude became aggressive and his tone provocative. Against whom? Against those who did not want France to give up the fight. This, in his eyes, was my crime. In his eyes it was also the most unpardonable one.

What I do not, in any case, dream of denying is that the conflict between Weygand and myself, the partisan of a struggle to the death, was to become one which could not be resolved.

JUNE 16: MEETING OF THE CABINET COUNCIL: JEANNENEY AND HERRIOT

At 10 a.m. the Presidents of the Chambers whom I had asked to come and confer with me came up into my room.

I reminded them that the Constitution required the Government to ask the opinion of the Presidents of the two Assemblies before removing the seat of public authority and I asked them to consent to its transfer into North Africa. They immediately agreed to this. I then asked them to come and give their consent in person to the Ministers in Council. They expressed their willingness, and thus gave me the support of their weighty influence, a support which, I am pleased to acknowledge, never failed me. They have both related this exchange of views in their evidence at the Pétain trial.[1]

At the Cabinet Council meeting, held at 11 a.m., the Presidents of the Chambers were introduced.[2] Jeanneney, on his own behalf and that of Herriot, gave an opinion in favour of the departure of the Government to North Africa. He made it clear that, in their opinion this departure was for the purpose of continuing the war. I thanked the two Presidents in the name of the Government.

JUNE 16: FIRST MEETING OF THE COUNCIL OF MINISTERS: PÉTAIN THREATENS TO RESIGN

Immediately after the Presidents of the Chambers had left, the President of the Republic joined the meeting and the Council of Ministers, thus constituted, began to deliberate. Before discussions

[1] Deposition of Jeanneney at the hearing of July 26, 1945, and deposition of Herriot at that of the 30th.

[2] Here is how Herriot describes the scene in his *Souvenirs* (*Ce Soir*, September 6, 1945): 'At the request of the President of the Council we repeated our opinion to the Ministers. In their presence, and in the name of the two Presidents—of the Senate and the Chamber —Jeanneney stated that, because of the enemy's advance, as well as to ensure the continuation of resistance, departure was necessary. I told Reynaud before leaving him: "I would rather be shot by the Boches than despised by the French."'

opened, Pétain read a letter of resignation.[1] Its reason was the delay in
asking for an armistice. 'Total destruction of territory, famine inevitable
in a very short time. . . .' (*These* were the dangers.)

'Final surrender of French sovereignty.' (That was how my fidelity
to our British allies was judged! Capitulation was evidently his idea
of restoring French sovereignty.) When he had finished, he got up, and
made a motion to withdraw. The President of the Republic, labouring
under a deep emotion, cried: 'Ah, you are not going to treat us in this
way at such a moment!' I told Pétain, in a tone intentionally dry, that,
since he had informed me of his decision in writing, he ought at least to
await my reply before putting his letter into effect. He agreed, not
without adding, however, that he would not sit down again, and he
remained standing with his letter of resignation in his hand. I remarked
to him that, since we had asked Britain to absolve us from the pledge
which we had given her, the least we could do was to give her sufficient
time to answer us about a problem which held such grave consequences
for her. Now, I felt certain that I should receive this reply during the
course of the afternoon, and would immediately inform the Council
of it. Rather crestfallen, Pétain put his letter back in his pocket and
went to sit down again in his chair. Thereupon, the Council adjourned
the sitting, and decided to resume its deliberations at 5 p.m.

JUNE 16: THIRD DISPUTE WITH WEYGAND

We have seen that Weygand who left Bordeaux on the evening of
the 15th for Supreme Headquarters at Vichy had only made a brief
appearance. On the next day, the 16th, at 10 a.m. he set out again for
Bordeaux. Bourget writes (*op. cit.*, p. 137):

'He [Weygand] ordered two planes to take him immediately with
two officers to Bordeaux. At 10 a.m. he took his place with the head
of his personal staff in the first plane at the Rhue airfield.[2] Captain
Gasser got into the second. . . . The Commander-in-Chief touched
down about midday at Merignac airfield, and was driven to the
quarters of the Prefect at Bordeaux. The meeting of the Ministers had
just ended.'

At midday the President of the Republic summoned me, and I found
in his room Weygand and Mandel as well as Paul Thellier, Minister of
Agriculture. Discussion was taking place on a cease-fire according to
the Dutch precedent.

This discussion in President Lebrun's room seemed futile to me, since
the opinion if not the move of Weygand was well known to me, and

---

[1] A facsimile of this letter may be found opposite.
[2] The Vichy airport, in the immediate vicinity of the town.

4

MARÉCHAL PÉTAIN
MINISTRE D'ÉTAT
PRÉSIDENT DU CONSEIL

BOULEVARD DES INVALIDES (7)
PHONE : SÉGUR 22·01 ET LA SUITE

PARIS, LE

Bordeaux ,le 16 Juin 1940.

N° ———

Monsieur le Président du Conseil,   P Reynaud

       La gravité ,chaque jour croissante,de
la situation militaire me convainct de la nécessité
pour le Gouvernement de mettre immédiatement fin aux
hostilités.

       Cette mesure est la seule capable de
sauver le Pays.

       L'avance de l'ennemi, si l'on n'y met
un terme, conduira à l'occupation et à la destruction
totales du territoire . Il en résultera une réduction
des ressources alimentaires de la Nation dans des
conditions telles que la famine est inévitable à trés
bref délai.

       Les délibérations quotidiennes du
Gouvernement m'apparaissent comme étant de pures
maneuvres dilatoires aboutissant à l'abdication définitive
de la Souveraineté française:

       Je ne puis m'y associer.

       Je vous remets donc ma démission des fonctions
de Ministre d'Etat et de Vice-Président du Conseil

Ph. Pétain

since the only way to get out of the impasse was to remove him from
his command, which I intended to do during the meeting of the
Council that afternoon.

'General Weygand tells us that a complete disintegration of the
Army is threatening us if we don't ask for an immediate armistice,' the
President of the Republic informed me.

'You are aware of my position.'

'But General Weygand states that capitulation would be contrary
to the honour of the Army?'

I turned to Weygand, and asked him:

'If capitulation is laid down in the conditions for an armistice, as it
is certain it will be, would you reject such an armistice as contrary to
the honour of the Army?'

'I will tell you that when the time comes.'

'No; you must tell us here and now,' uttered M. Albert Lebrun.

We were wasting our time. Weygand, having, however, objected
that an armistice was an act performed by a government, I told him
once again:

'I am prepared to give you a written order to this effect, if that is
what is stopping you.'

Weygand refused.[1]

The Council alone, at its afternoon sitting, could settle the difference.
If I were still in power that evening, Weygand would no longer
be Commander-in-Chief. It was necessary to put an end to this
situation.

I should say that my own military staff shared, for purely military
reasons, moreover, Weygand's opinion, and I had, therefore, to
draw up in my own hand the order for the cease-fire which I intended to give the new Commander-in-Chief as soon as I appointed
him.[2]

Weygand understood perfectly the supreme importance of these two
facts:

1. I offered on the 15th, privately, and on the 16th, in the presence
of the President of the Republic, to give him a written order to cease

[1] Thereupon, Weygand and his colleagues, on the invitation of Pétain, went to dine at
the private residence of M. Desbarrat, 54, Boulevard President Wilson, where Pétain had
taken up his quarters when he arrived in Bordeaux. Bourget (*op. cit.*, p. 138) informs us
of this fact. He adds: 'After the meal and some private conversation with the Marshal,
General Weygand was able to snatch a few moments' rest in a house in the Cours de
Verdun. About 5 p.m. he returned to the residence of the President of the Republic in the
Rue Vital-Carles; the Council of Ministers held a new sitting. The General waited in a
neighbouring room, but was not called in.

[2] I have since learned that, anticipating the eventuality of an armistice being asked for
by a new government, Lieutenant-Colonel de Villelume had, before my resignation, approached Darlan to ask him if he would be prepared to leave with the Fleet for America.
If he refrained from telling me of this step, it was, I am told, because he was aware of my
immovable opposition to any request for an armistice.

fire when he thought that resistance had become useless on the soil of metropolitan France;

2. Pétain had expressed an opinion that a cease-fire ordered by the Government would not bring the Army into shame.

Knowing these two facts condemned him, Weygand decided first of all not to speak about them in his evidence at Riom.

At the Pétain trial (hearing of July 31, 1945) he became bolder, and categorically denied them. He stated: 'People have talked about the authorization which would have been given to me. They have even spoken of an attempt by Marshal Pétain to influence me. Such an attempt was never made. This authorization was never given me.'

This is plain speaking.

But it is an imprudent denial. For it is an established fact that I proposed to Weygand that I should give him a written authority to cease fire, but that he declined my offer. Alluding to the interview of the 16th at midday, at which he was present in person, M. Lebrun has, indeed, stated at the Pétain trial: 'The President [Paul Reynaud] proposed giving a written order to the General so that he could take on himself the responsibility for surrender. The General refused.'

And yet Weygand denies this.

He also denies that the Council of Ministers was suspended on the afternoon of the 15th, the approach made at my request to him by Pétain, and lastly, Pétain's statement when he came back to the Council. It does not appear to matter that the whole of the Council was witness to this scene!

But then came the *coup de théatre*. Pétain broke silence, Pétain who had said that he remembered nothing. He recalled having left the Council Chamber to go and talk with Weygand in a neighbouring room on the question of a cease-fire. Then, making a right-about-turn, Weygand ceased further denials. He now remembered the discussion which he had had with me on this subject a few minutes before the meeting of the Council. But he had retained no recollection of the numerous events of the scene—that the sitting was suspended, that he had been approached by Pétain, that the latter had advised him to 'bring shame upon our Army'.

Here is the official shorthand report of this pathetic and painful scene, taken at the Pétain trial (hearing of July 31, 1945):

Marshal Pétain: 'There is one question which I should like to ask the General. When I went to find him in the neighbouring room, was I in agreement with him about the cease-fire? . . .[1] Perhaps we discussed the matter, but I cannot be sure that I came to any agreement on a cease-fire.'

General Weygand: 'You discussed, Marshal . . .'[1]

[1] The points of suspension are in the official shorthand account.

The conversation did, therefore, take place! The two men did, therefore, discuss a cease-fire. Weygand was beginning to remember. He was in a very dangerous position. The most brilliant of Pétain's lawyers flew to Weygand's rescue by interrupting him:

Maître Isorni: 'The question put by the Marshal is a very important one. For just a moment ago we were told the contrary, if I have understood correctly.'
General Weygand: 'Pardon. It is all quite clear.'

The only thing that was clear—I regret to bring it to attention—is that Weygand had just told the contrary to what was true when he asserted: 'This approach [of Pétain to him] did not take place.'
Pétain understood and stated:

Marshal Pétain: 'I cannot recollect anything at all.'
General Weygand: 'I do not remember having had a conversation with the Marshal on the subject, but I may be mistaken. I don't remember, either, but I may be mistaken again, that M. Reynaud gave me a document to cover me or even suggested that he should give me one.'

Thus, there was a complete breakdown of memory.

And we don't know what the end of Weygand's sentence would have been. We don't know what, according to him, Pétain discussed with him. Just when he was recovering his memory, nobody was curious enough to ask him, and he changed his tune in stating that neither Pétain nor myself could have been able to make him alter his mind.

And other things were taken up! That is how evidence at the Pétain trial was heard!

Yet, on his speech, M. Payen, President of the French Bar, was to consider that Pétain's approach to Weygand had been established.[1]

JUNE 16: THE CONDITION LAID DOWN BY THE BRITISH GOVERNMENT FOR ITS CONSENT: MY OBJECTION

On the morning of the 16th I received the British Ambassador and Spears, who told me that the British Government agreed to the French Government making inquiries about the conditions for an armistice, with the proviso that the French Fleet should weigh anchor for British waters. As I was not prepared to admit that France was leaving the coalition, I told them that this would be to lay North Africa open to action by the Italian Fleet.

[1] Hearing of August 13, 1945.

JUNE 16: ROOSEVELT ANSWERS MY APPEAL OF THE 14TH

After the meeting of the Council, I received the following telegram in which Roosevelt answered my appeal of the previous day:

Washington, June 15,
11 a.m.
Confidential.

I am replying to your message of yesterday, which has, you may rest assured, been the object of our most serious and friendly examination.

May I, first of all, repeat to you the increasingly deep admiration of the American people and its Government for the striking courage which the French Armies are showing on French soil in their resistance to the invader.

I would also like to repeat in the most solemn manner that, not sparing itself any possible effort in the present circumstances, the United States Government has allowed the Allied Armies to equip themselves in this country during these last weeks with planes, artillery and ammunitions of all types and that, as long as the Allied Governments continue their resistance, it will redouble its efforts in this direction. I think it is possible to say that, with each week which passes, a mass of more and more important war material will be dispatched to the Allied nations.

In conformity with its policy of non-recognition of territorial conquests by force of arms, the United States Government will refuse to recognize the validity of any attempt to strike at the independence of France or her territorial integrity.

In such heart-rending hours for the French people and for yourself, I assure you of my utmost sympathy, and I can promise you, moreover, that, as long as the French people continue to defend their liberty, and thereby the liberty of democratic institutions throughout the world, it can count on receiving from the United States an increasingly important volume of war material and supplies of every kind. I know that you will understand that these statements do not imply any pledge of a military nature. Congress alone has power to enter into such engagements.

JUNE 16: TWO TELEGRAMS FROM THE BRITISH GOVERNMENT:
CONSENT GIVEN AND WITHDRAWN

In the early part of the afternoon of the 16th, the British Ambassador and Spears brought me a telegram confirming their oral communication of the morning. Here is the text of this telegram:

Foreign Office to Sir Ronald Campbell.

Please give M. Reynaud the following message, which has been approved by the Cabinet:

June 16, 1940. 12.35 p.m.

Mr. Churchill to M. Reynaud.

Our agreement forbidding separate negotiations, whether for armistice or peace, was made with the French Republic, and not with any particular French Administration or statesman. It therefore involves the honour of France. Nevertheless, *provided, but only provided, that the French Fleet is sailed forthwith for British harbours pending negotiations*, His Majesty's Government give their full consent to an inquiry by the French Government to ascertain the terms of an armistice for France. His Majesty's Government, being resolved to continue the war, wholly exclude themselves from all part in the above-mentioned inquiry concerning an armistice.[1]

This telegram was quickly followed by a second, sent from London at 3.10 p.m., which was principally intended to emphasize that the condition laid down was as much in the interests of France as of Britain.

I repeated my objection of that same morning. But, an hour later, the Ambassador and Spears came to ask me to return the two telegrams, telling me that their Government had changed its mind.

What was the reason for this retreat? I thought it was because of my reiterated objection. But Churchill in his memoirs[2] gives us the explanation for this sudden change of policy. The British War Cabinet had, in actual fact, had second thoughts in the meantime. Instead of resigning itself to the rupture taking place, it had decided to try and keep France at Britain's side by reinforcing the alliance and transforming it into a 'union' within which the interests of the two nations should be amalgamated. Thus was born the conception of a general proposal, constructive and attractive, which was to be put before me a short time later, and which, taking the place of the conditional acceptance which the two telegrams had given me, was *ipso facto*, to render such an acceptance null and void. The War Cabinet, therefore, decided to cancel the submittal of the telegrams, and instructions were immediately sent to the Ambassador to this effect. But the latter had already handed the two documents to me. Hence, the only thing he could do was to get them back. I was pleased, in any case, to see the British Government revoking its consent, for this change in policy was to provide me with an argument to oppose, in the name of France's pledged word, any demand for an armistice.

[1] The text given here is that given by Sir Winston Churchill in *The Second World War*, vol. II, *Their Finest Hour*, p. 181 [Tr.].
[2] *Ibid.*, pp. 182 ff.

Certain disciples of Vichy have since reproached me, it is said, for having thwarted this British proposal. They point out that there could have been no surer method of placing the French Fleet out of the enemy's reach. My answer to this is that I thought it in the interests of the country to keep the French Fleet in the war. I refused, into the bargain, to believe that my colleagues, having admitted on the day before that the acquiescence of the British Government was necessary, would decide to ignore the British refusal, and to persist in asking for an armistice. Moreover, when the Pétain Government stated that it was necessary to cease fighting and ask for an armistice, could it be thought that the crews of our Fleet would have agreed to fight under the orders of the British Admiralty? What happened on those of our ships which were then in British waters does not lead us to believe this.

In my opinion the question of national honour outweighed everything. In addition, it seemed to me inadmissible that France could ask for an armistice, when she still possessed the second largest fleet in Europe and the second Colonial Empire of the world.

Moreover, if sending the Fleet into British waters was the duty of the Government which wished to ask for an armistice, it was for the Pétain-Weygand-Chautemps Government to take this step before asking for an armistice. It failed in this duty, and it was all the more blameworthy in that the British Government recalled to it several times immediately following the request for an armistice that it had only freed France from the undertaking of the 28th on condition that our Fleet sailed into British ports.

JUNE 16: BRITAIN PROPOSES TO US THE 'FRANCO-BRITISH UNION': I AM SPIED UPON OVER THE TELEPHONE; AN EXTRAORDINARY DOCUMENT

On the 16th, in the early afternoon, I received a telephone call from General de Gaulle in London. He informed me of the British intention to offer us an amalgamation of the two countries within a Franco-British Union. This was, indeed, a sensational turn of events, and one which could only fill me with joy since it was to give me a new argument for keeping France in the alliance. But I had to be in a position to put the proposal to the Council. Therefore, I asked General de Gaulle to urge our Allies to let me have a text of their proposals in time.

Without committing myself to the methods to be discussed, I accepted unhesitatingly the principle of a union of the two countries. Had I not always claimed that they could in the long run only safeguard their independence if they were bound by intimate links? Today it was Great Britain, who, under the stress of necessity, was proposing a union to us, the immediate result of which would be a unity of government and command. No doubt problems would arise, which it would be necessary to settle. And was it not bristling with difficulties for France, struggling as she was in such tragic circumstances? The essential thing was that union with Britain meant independence for us at exactly the time when we had only the choice between union or certain slavery under the German jackboot.

At 4 p.m. General de Gaulle called me up again on the telephone to tell me the text which the British War Cabinet had approved. The latter was, moreover, still sitting to continue its discussions. The draft, which he was submitting to me, was, therefore, only drawn up subject to revision. Minor amendments could be introduced into it.

I wrote in pencil under the dictation of General de Gaulle. On my return from Germany I had the good fortune to discover this historic draft amongst my papers. I reproduce it below:[1]

'At this most fateful moment in the history of the modern world the Governments of the United Kingdom and the French Republic make this declaration of indissoluble union and unyielding resolution in their common defence of justice and freedom against subjection to a system which reduces mankind to a life of robots and slaves.

'The two Governments declare that France and Great Britain shall no longer be two nations, but one Franco-British Union.

'The constitution of the Union will provide for joint organs of defence, foreign, financial and economic policies.

'Every citizen of France will enjoy immediately citizenship of Great Britain; every British subject will become a citizen of France.

'Both countries will share responsibility for the repair of the devastation of the war, wherever it occurs in their territories, and the resources of both shall be equally, and as one, applied to that purpose.

'During the war there shall be a single War Cabinet, and all the forces of Britain and France, whether on land, sea, or in the air, will be placed under its direction. It will govern from wherever it best can. The two Parliaments will be formally associated. The nations of the British Empire are already forming new armies. France will keep her available forces in the field, on the sea, and in the air. The Union appeals to the United States to fortify the economic resources of the Allies, and to bring powerful material aid to the common cause.

'The Union will concentrate its whole energy against the power of the enemy, no matter where the battle may be.

'And thus we shall conquer.'

After dictating to me the text of the *Declaration of Union* General de Gaulle told me that perhaps I would be the one called upon to preside over the War Cabinet of the Union.

[1] The text given here is that given by Sir Winston Churchill, *ibid*, pp. 183–4 [Trs.].

This plan, as grandiose as it was bold, aroused criticism against the British Government in Britain itself. One has only to consider the insular mentality, the particularism, and the pride of the British people, jealous of its independence and institutions, and reserved to the point of isolation.

Churchill then telephoned me. I told him that I gave my agreement in principle, and both of us, inspired by the same confidence, made an appointment in a port on the Breton coast, Quiberon or Concarneau.

It is interesting to observe on this subject that Churchill was not personally in favour of this fusion of the two nations. He gives his frank opinion about it in his memoirs.[1]

'I was not the prime mover,' he writes. 'I first heard of a definite plan at a luncheon at the Carlton Club on the 15th [June], at which were present Lord Halifax, M. Corbin, Sir Robert Vansittart and one or two others. . . . On the 14th Vansittart and Desmond Morton [my private secretary] had met M. Monnet and M. Pleven (members of the French Economic Mission in London), and been joined by General de Gaulle, who had flown over to make arrangements for shipping to carry the French Government and as many French troops as possible to Africa. These gentlemen had evolved the outline of a declaration for a Franco-British Union with the object, apart from its general merits, of giving M. Reynaud some new fact . . . with which to carry a majority of his Cabinet into the move to Africa and the continuance of the war. My first reaction was unfavourable. I asked a number of questions of a critical character, and was by no means convinced. However, at the end of our long Cabinet that afternoon the subject was raised. I was somewhat surprised to see the staid, stolid, experienced politicians of all parties engage themselves so passionately in an immense design whose implications and consequences were not in any way thought out. I did not resist, but yielded easily to these generous surges which carried our resolves to a very high level of unselfish and undaunted action.'

Since the publication of the French edition of this book, I have received from the High Court of Justice a document which figured in the dossier of the trial of Marshal Pétain. It concerned the listeners-in employed by General Weygand to report my telephone conversations to him. This extraordinary document, containing these revelations, proves that up to the very last moment I strove to keep France in the war, though certain advocates of the armistice have insinuated the contrary, hoping thus to associate me with them in their culpable weakness.[2]

---

[1] *Ibid.*, pp. 180–1.
[2] The reader will be able, therefore, to judge the worth of the assertion that I yielded to weakness on that very day.

The following are parts of the conversations overheard and recorded in the Palais Gallien, Bordeaux, on June 16.

16.6.40 at 12.30 p.m.

General de Gaulle in London to M. Paul Reynaud.

De Gaulle: I have just seen Churchill. There is something stupendous in preparation affecting the entity of the two countries. Churchill proposes the establishment of a single Franco-British Government, with you, perhaps, M. le Président, as head of a Franco-British War Cabinet.

Paul Reynaud: It is the only possible solution for the future. But it must be done on a large scale and very quickly, above all very quickly. It is a question of minutes. I give you half an hour. It would be splendid.

16.6.40 at 4 p.m.

General de Gaulle in London to Paul Reynaud.

De Gaulle: There is going to be a sensational declaration.

Paul Reynaud: Yes, but after five o'clock (17 h.) it will be too late.[1]

De Gaulle: I will do my best to bring it to you at once by plane.

Paul Reynaud: Yes, but that will be too late. The situation has seriously deteriorated within the last few minutes. Unforeseen events have occurred.

16.6.40 at 4.40 p.m.

President of the Republic to the President of the Council.

President Lebrun: Can I see you before five o'clock?

Paul Reynaud: Yes, certainly. I am making a note of the conversation I have just had with London. This goes far beyond what I led you to expect. It is extremely important.

JUNE 16: THE LAST MEETING OF THE COUNCIL OF MINISTERS

The Council met at 5 p.m. and sat until 8 p.m.

I opened with a reading of Roosevelt's reply to my last appeal.

It did not come up to the hopes which Churchill, Roussy de Sales and myself had entertained, but it possessed an immense political importance since America undertook to arm the enemies of Germany. The great Republic thus took with due deliberation a step towards war.

I told the Council the result of the mission to the British Government, with which a majority had entrusted me the day before. I indicated that the latter had at first given its consent and then withdrawn it.

I then read the offer which Britain had made me. I added to it the comments of General de Gaulle which accompanied it. I stressed the great importance which the proposal offered for the future. I concluded

[1] Because of the meeting of the Council of Ministers due at 5 p.m.

by announcing the visit of Churchill on the following day to a Breton port for talks with me on the subject.

My exposition aroused no response. Nobody in the Council spoke to express his adherence to Churchill's offer. Weygand, who had learned of the British Government's proposals from the listening-in posts, had been campaigning against these proposals among the supporters of the armistice. The latter, fully aware of General de Gaulle's communication, had hastened to lay siege to the Ministers before the meeting. It is probable, however, that, amongst those who kept silent, there were some who shared my feelings. It is none the less a certain fact that I was completely alone in supporting the proposal.

My opponents were thus to have the ball at their feet. It was Ybarnegaray who accused Britain of wishing to place our country on the level of a mere Dominion. Chautemps himself took up this imputation.

Such was the cavalier fashion in which was treated the proposal that Britain should unite with France to create the core of a new Europe. From the reluctance which our neighbours today show to be integrated in one, it can be judged what a windfall for us was this offer of 1940. Let Weygand,[1] who persists in justifying the treatment accorded to the proposal, go and beg Her Majesty's Government to repeat it today!

This error will, without doubt, out of all those committed by the advocates of capitulation, be the one which will have the most far-reaching repercussions.

But those who rose in indignation at the idea of union with our ally were the same individuals who were getting ready to bow and scrape to Hitler, and who were in actual fact a few hours later to deliver our native land bound hand and foot to him. Weygand was to state in his evidence at Riom: 'This proposal was received with indignation by all to whom the General spoke about it.' It is plain who were his interlocutors.

The following year I was to write to Pétain from one of my prisons in reply to an attack by his wireless: 'For my part I prefer to collaborate with my allies than with the enemy.'

Meeting complete failure in my exhortations, I came back to the vital question, that of an armistice. I was certainly not without the powder and shot to support my contention. But it is obvious that my position was weakened by the isolation in which I had found myself a few moments before. That did not deter me. In unequivocal words I invoked the honour of France. Addressing the Council, I told it: 'You have placed a statue to Albert I in the Place de la Concorde to honour his fidelity to his allies. Today, you have the choice of following two examples: that of Albert I or Leopold III.'[2] I observed that we could

[1] *Rappelé au service*, p. 233.
[2] The surrender of Leopold III symbolized for all of us the desertion of an ally by an ally.

not think of reconstructing France one day, if we banished the conception of honour.

But, in spite of the British Government's refusal to release us from our pledge, Chautemps again took up his argument of the previous day, the object of which was to ask the conditions under which Germany would grant us an armistice.[1]

I stated that the problem no longer arose since our approach to the British Government of the day before had come to nothing. Baudouin, who spoke for the first time in the Council,[2] tried to take advantage of the words uttered by Churchill at Tours. I answered him that I had just checked my recollections with those of M. de Margerie, and that both he and I were in agreement that at Tours Churchill had not authorized France to seek an armistice.[3] I added that since then the British Government had informed me of its wish to enforce the undertaking of March 28.

To a Minister, who asked me what was being thought in London, I replied: 'They are wondering whether we are going to act like Wilhelmina or Leopold.' In the fort of Portalet, where Pétain was to imprison me, as we shall see, Louis Marin handed me an extract of the private notes which he drew up on this historic meeting. Having recalled, he said, to the Council that it was myself who had concluded the agreement by which the two Allies renounced any separate negotiations, he asked me the following question:

'I ask the President of the Council if he considers, according to the dictates of his conscience as a responsible statesman, if the honour of France is still irretrievably pledged?

'Paul Reynaud, amidst complete silence, answered: "That is so. Up to the hilt."[4]

[1] M. Lebrun in his evidence at the Pétain trial has stated: 'M. Chautemps again took up his proposal of the previous day.'

[2] Baudouin was, therefore, in error, when he stated on July 12, 1949, to the Committee of Inquiry that he had never spoken at a meeting of the Council. The intervention in question, moreover, prompted me to remark to the President of the Republic that, if it was traditional that Baudouin should attend ministerial deliberations in his capacity as Under-Secretary of State to the Presidency of the Council, it was on the other hand contrary to custom that he should speak.

In his evidence of July 20, 1949, Baudouin was to state to the Committee of Inquiry: 'The President of the Republic asked me to attend the meeting of the Council of Ministers at Cangé. He had said to me: "War Cabinets will no longer be held. Now, there will be a Council of Ministers. You ought to treat meetings of the Council of Ministers like those of War Cabinets." Consequently, I used to take notes.'

But Baudouin had informed me that it was Chautemps who had told him that, in his capacity as Under-Secretary of State to the Presidency of the Council, he had a seat on the Council of Ministers.

[3] Baudouin was to state, again on July 12, 1949, to the Committee of Inquiry, that the word armistice had not been uttered at the meeting of the Supreme Council at Tours.

[4] Marin has related this episode in his deposition at the Pétain trial (hearing of July 26 1945).

Mandel, who spoke for the first time to the Council on the problem of an armistice, expressed his astonishment in a few scornful words that the Ministers who had entered my Government, knowing that it was a question of making war, should now oppose me. Then, in reference to the Chautemps 'manœuvre', he stated: 'The problem is simple. There are those here who wish to fight, and those who do not.' To this Chautemps replied bitterly that he had sons at the front. He added: 'In any case there is nothing that M. Mandel can teach me.'

Disagreement was turning into a quarrel.

I intervened in the hope of avoiding what seemed to me an outstanding danger for the future: the division of the Council into two camps; and Ministers calling each other 'capitulards'[1] and 'deserters'. It was clear in any case that I could not dream of remaining in power another hour under such conditions. It was, indeed, necessary to make immediate decisions, the first of which would be to relieve Weygand of his command. There was no longer a moment to be lost.

This was certainly the opinion of my adversaries, since Frossard was to write, June 15, 1941, in his previously cited *Mot d'Ordre*, that, after opposing a vote being taken, I said to the President of the Republic that I wished to discuss the situation with him. He added: 'I am giving away no secrets when I say that, if we had voted, Camille Chautemps, Ybarnegaray, Bouthillier, Baudouin, Prouvost, Pomaret, Albert Rivière, Chichery and myself would, with Marshal Pétain, have spoken in favour of an armistice. In all likelihood, Georges Pernot and Queuille would have rallied to this point of view, and it would have received a majority of votes. But Paul Reynaud well realized that his Administration, divided and racked, was on its last legs. The hour of the Marshal had sounded.' And he concluded that 'on leaving the Presidency each Minister knew that the Council had met for the last time', and that it was 'without surprise' that they learned two hours later that the Pétain Administration had been formed.[2]

This was also the opinion of Rollin, who gave evidence to this effect

---

[1] The term was applied to those who advocated the surrender of Paris in 1871 [Tr.].

[2] About to be indicted before the High Court and full of bitterness at the thought of going to sit 'in the dock alongside', as he writes, 'suspects and traitors', Frossard drew up a kind of apologia (*L'Aurore*, February 4–14 and 16, 1949), in which, forgetting the circumstantial details of which he had made use in his two articles in *Mot d'Ordre*, he took the opposite point of view to his own thesis, and maintained that 'nothing compelled me to resign'.

Frossard wrote this pleading 'some time before his death', *L'Aurore* tells us, in its introduction placed at the head of the document. He, therefore, composed it after the hearings of the Pétain trial. What does this imply but that Frossard was entirely absorbed in his spite against the men who had just denounced the misdeeds of the armistice? The best way of discrediting their opinions would be, is it not true, to make out that they were at variance with each other? Frossard tried to do this, but he only succeeded by his insinuations, which spared Jeanneney and Herriot no more than myself, in contradicting himself.

on January 20, 1947, before the Committee of Inquiry. Here is the question which was put to him, and his answer:

'Was it possible for Paul Reynaud, with the few colleagues who remained faithful to him, to remain in power?'

'I think that the President, Paul Reynaud, who had from the outset shown evidence of much courage, energy and firmness, would have found it impossible to govern from the moment that he was forsaken by his two Vice-Presidents of the Council, Pétain and Chautemps, and when a great number of his Ministers were, to say the least, in disagreement with him. All did not keep silent. There were some who declared violently against him, beginning with Bouthillier, and Pomaret, who said to him: "I have followed you. I was in agreement with you until these last days. But it is over. We ought to fall in line behind Weygand and our great military leaders." This was Chautemps' thesis who stated that "when we have the good fortune to have such glorious and renowned military leaders, we must give them our confidence". I was most decided in my opinion. I did not think that Paul Reynaud should continue in power.'

Certainly, it is quite possible for an administration to govern even if its majority in the Chamber is reduced to one vote. But, there is not the slightest analogy between such a situation and that of a government which, deeply divided on a vital question, finds itself, because of this fact, condemned to paralysis and inaction, and ceases merely because of this to be a government. Thenceforth, it is no longer a question of numbers which matters, and the problem for the President of the Council who takes note of this divergence of views is not to know if he has or has not a majority for the policy which he intends to pursue. Moreover, how could I ask myself such a question, when, faced with the exodus, the majority melted like snow in the sun? We have seen that the opposition of two at the first Council at Cangé had increased to thirteen at the first Council at Bordeaux.

I had, therefore, no other alternative to resignation, but I could leave things in their existing state, that is, I could refrain from forcing a vote on the vital problem under discussion. In this way, I would avoid putting myself in a minority within the Council, and, consequently, avoid compromising my chances of being called to power for the express purpose of carrying on my policy. This attitude also conformed to the custom which laid down that no vote should be taken in the Council of Ministers and that no minutes should be taken of its meetings.[1]

It will be seen, therefore, how groundless is the reproach which

---

[1] The Constitution of 1946 broke away from this custom. It ruled that minutes should be taken of discussions within the Council of Ministers.

certain people have levied against me for having committed the 'incalculable fault' of allowing France's fate to be decided by the vote of certain of my colleagues.

This is why, when one of the Ministers proposed taking a vote, I remembered the large majority who had supported Chautemps in the discussion of the day before, and I refused to lend myself to this departure from custom, so determined was I not to bend in any case to a hostile majority.

But Parliament was not assembled to make the choice between us. The Council of Ministers was not qualified to act in its place. The decision lay, therefore, with the President of the Republic. Later, we shall see that, in his reply to a question put to him by one of the jury at the Pétain trial, M. Lebrun expressly insisted on his constitutional rights as an arbiter.

M. Lebrun said in his evidence, given in the form of a memorandum, at the preliminary investigations of the Pétain trial: 'The interchange of remarks, the reflections of various Ministers showed that a majority had crystallized.[1] The President of the Council perceived this. He informed me of his decision. Since he was in a minority, he stated that he was handing in the resignation of his Cabinet.'

In actual fact, I brought the debate to an end by stating that I wished to consult with the President of the Republic[2] about the situation. However, I asked the Ministers to reassemble at ten o'clock. In actual fact, I wished to have them at hand in case M. Lebrun, following his consultations with the Presidents of the two Chambers, entrusted me with the duty of forming a new administration, or, if the alternative was the case, to put the collective resignation of the Cabinet into the hands of the President of the Republic.

M. Lebrun, in his above-mentioned deposition, alluded to the pressure brought to bear on him in order to make him give way. Thus, during this final Council of the 16th, Weygand handed him without my knowledge a copy of a message telephoned by Georges, which ran:

'17 hours. Situation still becoming worse. To the east, northern outskirts of Dijon and the Saône front reached by the enemy. In the centre, numerous armoured columns thrusting towards La Charité are threatening to envelop No. 3 Group of Armies. The forest of Fontainebleau has been occupied. Problem of feeding troops and civilian refugee population is very serious. Manœuvres have become difficult owing to

[1] Rollin also notes this fact in his *Journal*.
[2] In order to form a true estimate of the notes allegedly taken daily by Baudouin, it is sufficient to observe that he writes that I recommended at the end of .the Council meeting to M. Lebrun that power should be entrusted to Pétain. Most of those who attended the Council are still alive. They would, therefore, bear witness to the inaccuracy of this statement. How, moreover, could I have voiced such a recommendation when I had just told the Council that the honour of France was 'pledged to the hilt'?

the congestion of roads and the bombing of railways and bridges. There is an imperative need to come to some decision.'

I was to remain ignorant of this step, which was deliberately intended to spread alarm, until the day three years later when M. Lebrun, imprisoned with me, told me of it. Is it necessary to stress the incorrectness of this procedure, to recall that the essence of a representative régime is the limited power of the Head of the State? The correct procedure was to hand the President the message through me. But Weygand knew that I should have handled it in a way which was diametrically opposed to the line which he was taking. He had, therefore, to act without my getting to know about the message.

M. Lebrun himself admits that this step, taken to intimidate him, did influence his actions. His deposition, indeed, ends with this reflection: 'Who would dare to assert that men, even though they were as hard as rock or steel, could remain impervious to such an appeal at a time when they were about to make one of the gravest decisions?'

We have an eye-witness account of this last Council, which owes its distinctive reputation to the personality of its author. It is that given by Henri Béraud, of *Gringoire*, who undertook at Bordeaux his first campaign on behalf of the 'New Order'.

In his *Sans haine et sans crainte* (p. 8) he writes: 'But Reynaud, who was playing for his life, still fought on.' And he reproached himself for not having with his own hands strangled a Minister,[1] who, on leaving the Council meeting, uttered the words: 'I am for President Reynaud!'

A new era was beginning. The men of Vichy, indeed, were incapable of conceiving that my opposition to dishonouring the word of France could have any other motive than that of 'saving my neck'. The conclusion of an armistice might, certainly, imperil my life, for I had not the slightest illusion about the feelings which Hitler entertained for me, especially since my lecture in Vienna in October, 1937, on the eve of the *Anschluss*, and after Munich. If I had listened to the voice of fear, I would have left the soil of the motherland as soon as Pétain seized power to hand France to the mercy of the enemy. When I tried to convince the Council of the need for transferring the seat of public power to North Africa, Pétain, it will be remembered, uttered the word 'cowardice'. It will also be recalled that, in order to free my colleagues from the scruple of incurring such a reproach, I said that I was ready to remain myself on metropolitan territory whilst the Government left it. My readiness to carry out this sacrifice did not avail, as we know, in altering the course of events. Yet, although such a set-back would have given me complete liberty of action in this respect, I meant, by remaining in France, to face the danger to which I knew I was exposed.

---

[1] This was Rollin.

JUNE 16: I CONSULT WITH THE PRESIDENT OF THE REPUBLIC

I was, therefore, left face to face with the President of the Republic. Like myself, he was perfectly aware of the whole situation in all its details. The problem to be faced was crystal clear: should the country continue the struggle on soil outside France or should we ask for an armistice? For those who would persist in merely seeing the technical aspect, the problem presented itself as a military one. But, for those who agreed upon recognizing that it entailed the very future of the homeland, it was one of an essentially political nature.

The President was aware that the Government was split in two over this vital question. He knew that, though the two camps were numerically equally balanced, that of my opponents was led by Pétain and Chautemps, who joined to their influence as Vice-Presidents of the Council that which they enjoyed in their own respective spheres. He knew, and this was an important factor, that the Ministers who were ranged behind these two faction chiefs included men from groups of the Right and others from those of the Left. He was aware that Pétain had joined forces with Weygand, who, in his turn, was unanimously supported by the important army leaders. He knew the state of parliamentary opinion, the divisions of which mirrored the confusion felt by the nation at large.

It would, therefore, have been merely a waste of precious time to reiterate to the President those arguments which, since the 12th, he had heard me explain at every meeting of the Council of Ministers, or the remarks which had furnished the substance of my daily conversations with him. Consequently, I went straight to the heart of the problem. Two policies were clashing with each other: that of resistance which I myself embodied; and that of surrender which Pétain championed. It did not take me long to find out that M. Lebrun had made his choice. We now know that his anxiety, which I attributed to the threat of Pétain's resignation, was due to the alarmist trick which Weygand had just played on him.

It was clear that Pétain and Weygand had won the day. Our 'glorious military leaders' had thrown their influence into the scales. For the timorous souls such a sheltering cloak offered indeed a temptation and a godsend! Chautemps and Frossard, in giving the rallying signal, had pointed out the way to the clever ones; could there be a more solid security for these latter?

M. Lebrun informed me, therefore, of his decision. He pronounced in favour of an armistice. Yet, he asked me again, as on the day before, and as, moreover, he was to do a second time several moments later in the presence of the Presidents of the two Chambers, to give way to a majority of the Council—in other words, to side with the Chautemps proposal and to stay in power in order to put it into effect. But, on the day before, I had only given way to M. Lebrun's entreaties because an acceptance of this proposal had seemed to offer me a last chance of thwarting the move of those advocating an armistice. Since then conditions had drastically changed. To give way on this latter occasion could only mean in very fact asking for an armistice. M. Lebrun was urging me, therefore, to disavow myself. This inspired my reply: 'If you want such a policy carried out, go and ask Marshal Pétain!'

This talk with the President was of prime importance. To read M. Lebrun's book,[1] however, which is sparing in its details about this incident, one might well be misled about both his attitude and my own. Most fortunately M. Lebrun has been called to explain himself in the greatest detail on this point, in answer to a query at Pétain's trial (hearing of July 25, 1945) which was put to him by one of the jurors:

M. Pierre Stibbe: 'If I am not mistaken, M. Paul Reynaud stated yesterday that, when the first differences showed themselves within his Cabinet, he had, first of all, thought of resigning to form another Ministry from which defeatist elements would have been purged. But, he did not do this because he was not certain that you would entrust him again with the task of leading a Cabinet. When, finally, M. Paul Reynaud handed you his resignation, did you think of entrusting him again with the duty of forming a new Ministry, and did you ask him to do so?'

M. le Président Albert Lebrun: 'I told you that a moment ago. I have said that, at the end of the Council, when M. Paul Reynaud said, "You see I am in a minority. I cannot go on", I answered him. "But yesterday I tried desperately to prevent you resigning. I am asking you to refrain from doing so today." He said to me: "But what will come of it? I am in a minority. I cannot go out there and suggest the proposal in favour of which M. Chautemps has won over a majority of the Council. It is contrary to my policy. Therefore, I cannot do it. That is the position."'

Indeed, who was more hostile to this policy than myself, and who embodied it better than Pétain? Nevertheless, it was Chautemps who, with his dialectical virtuosity, was able to give it form. Since M. Lebrun had thus expressed himself in favour of the proposal which Chautemps was sponsoring, was it not quite natural that he should bethink himself that its author was the best qualified to carry it out? Now, Chautemps represented in my opinion a worse danger than Pétain.

I was, indeed, convinced that Hitler, obsessed with the vital need that he must not allow Britain any respite to recover from the Dunkirk disaster, and determined, therefore, to attack the British Isles without

[1] p. 85. Printed by September 20, 1945, the work was on sale by the end of the month.

delay, would impose a *sine qua non* condition on the armistice, namely the surrender of our Fleet. Failing the possession of our Fleet, he could not, in my opinion, dream of undertaking this great adventure. That my reasoning turned out right has been illustrated in no better fashion than by the statement of Field-Marshal von Rundstedt after the surrender of the Reich: if, on the morrow of the armistice, Hitler had to abandon his plan of invading Britain, it was because of the inferiority of the German Fleet.

I had explained these arguments the day before to the Council. I had concluded, as is known, that, for these reasons, France would dishonour herself if she agreed to deliver her Fleet to the enemy. I had persuaded Pétain to acknowledge this.

Therefore, in my own mind, I could not have any doubt that, whatever befell, Pétain was determined to refuse surrendering the Fleet. Because Hitler was not the man to be cheated out of it, I concluded that Pétain would have to renounce the idea of signing an armistice.

Chautemps' attitude during the last discussions, on the other hand, even without taking into account his weak-kneed behaviour at the time of the *Anschluss* and Munich, inspired me with a fear that he would in the end give way when he found himself at grips with such a determined opponent. If the President of the Republic ignored Chautemps and settled his choice on Pétain, the chances of an armistice would be lessened and correspondingly, those of France would be increased.

Eleven months later, from the prison where he was holding me confined, I was to write a letter to Pétain which held him up to shame for the policy which he was pursuing. In this letter, from which I give a long extract later on, I turned into a weapon against him my reply to President Lebrun of: 'If you want such a policy to be carried out, go and ask Marshal Pétain!' I had circulated at the time the text of this letter amongst my friends in the Resistance movement, just as I had previously communicated to them an account of the circumstances in which I had been forced on June 16 to relinquish power because of my opposition to the Chautemps proposal. It was, therefore, due to me that these circles were to gain knowledge of my reply to M. Lebrun. Is not this disclosure the best proof that it had never occurred to me that the meaning of my words could be twisted with treacherous intent so that they could be exploited against me?[1]

---

[1] Baudouin was one of those who most keenly devoted himself to this purpose. Here is what he said (*op. cit.*, pp. 115-16):

'Sunday, June 16, 1940.

'Bouthillier and I went at four o'clock to see the Prime Minister. . . . Bouthillier . . . left the Prime Minister's room.

'I remained alone with him, and we were silent for quite a long time. In the end I asked him what he intended to do. "What are you going to decide if at the end of the Council

My exchange of views with M. Lebrun was ending. However, before withdrawing, I begged the President to consult, in accordance with tradition, the Presidents of the Chambers, for I knew that their advice would be favourable to me.

But, before continuing the thread of my narrative, I wish to answer a complaint of another kind. Why, it is asked, when the meeting of the Council ended, did I not reshuffle my Cabinet on my own initiative? Why, in a word, did I not act as I had done on June 5?

The reproach is a curious one. Those who utter it forget, deliberately or otherwise, that on June 5 I had only been able to re-form my Administration because the President of the Republic shared my own views about the operation which I was proposing to carry out. Who other than the Head of the State is empowered then by the Constitution to sign decrees nominating Ministers, and, for that matter, decrees of any kind?

meeting there is a strong majority in favour of asking for an armistice?" His face showed only too clearly his sadness and weariness, and after a long silence he answered, "We are heading straight for a Pétain Government, and I have already discussed it with the President of the Republic." '

When he was giving evidence on July 26, 1949, before the Committee of Inquiry, that day presided over by Louis Marin, Baudouin was called upon to explain the significance which he attached to the words he put in my mouth. Here is an extract from this hearing during which Marin was to flatly contradict him:

M. Paul Baudouin: '. . . You are well aware, gentlemen, that the Government of Marshal Pétain was inspired by M. Paul Reynaud; I don't say in the choice of the Marshal's colleagues, but it was M. Paul Reynaud who, for twenty-four hours had believed that there was no other solution to the government crisis than an appeal by the President of the Republic to Marshal Pétain. M. Louis Marin, who presides over this sitting, knows very well what M. Paul Reynaud's attitude was, and he knows very well that . . .'

The President: 'I am completely in disagreement with you on this point.'

M. Paul Baudouin: 'Did not the last meeting of the Council of Ministers, M. le Président, close precisely with the clear indication that M. Paul Reynaud was asking for an interview with President Lebrun?'

The President: 'Yes, and in saying that we should meet again two hours later in Council.'

M. Paul Baudouin: 'That's right, but, during this interview, M. Lebrun received from President Reynaud the advice to appoint Marshal Pétain. Several moments before this Council of Ministers, I had asked M. Paul Reynaud "Where are we heading for?" and he said to me "We are moving inevitably towards a Pétain administration."'

M. Serre: 'That's not quite the same thing. . . . You have just told us that President Reynaud advised President Lebrun to call in Marshal Pétain and now you are telling us President Reynaud in talking to you said "The crisis is evolving in such a way that we are inevitably moving towards a Pétain administration." There is a vast difference between the two phrases!'

Is there any need for me to stress this myself? Will it not suffice, indeed, in order to show the extent to which Baudouin and myself disagreed, to give this other statement which he made to the Committee of Inquiry during the same sitting? 'When on the 12th [June], we [Reynaud and I] had had this conversation in which I told him very plainly that, in my opinion, there existed no possibility of France's prolonging the struggle, he immediately showed me that he did not think as I did.'

Moreover, M. Lebrun ought to know better than Baudouin what had passed between himself and me.

JUNE 16: BRITAIN'S LAST APPROACH

At this very moment the British Ambassador and Spears made a final move. They knew that, as my Government was no longer capable of surviving, a new Cabinet was in the offing. The President of the Republic was, therefore, going to call the Presidents of the Chambers for consultation. The Ambassador and Spears took counsel of Mandel, and at his instigation they went to ask the President of the Senate to persuade the President of the Republic to entrust me with the formation of a new administration.

In his memoirs, Churchill gives the text of a telephoned message by which Sir Ronald Campbell reported this step to him during the evening. Here is what he writes:

'. . . After seeing M. Mandel for a moment we then called for a second time today on the President of Senate, M. Jeanneney, whose views (like those of President of Chamber) are sound, in hope of his being able to influence President of Republic to insist on M. Reynaud forming new Government. . . .'[1]

The British Government was, therefore, of one mind with all those who, with Jeanneney, Herriot and Mandel at their head, only saw salvation in the formation by myself of a Cabinet prepared to resist. Is not this a decisive answer, if one be necessary, to those who insinuate that I had 'weakened' at the last moment?

Thus, we were to see Presidents of the Senate and of the Chamber, Jeanneney and Herriot, when consulted by President Lebrun, answer without hesitating, and then persist without budging that in their opinion the crisis should be solved by the formation of a government determined to fight to the end, and that the Head of the State should entrust me with the duty of doing this.

JUNE 16: CONSULTATION WITH THE PRESIDENTS OF THE CHAMBERS

At 9 p.m., Jeanneney, Herriot and myself went to the President of the Republic's room. This was the hour when the fate of France was to be decided, and when each was to shoulder the responsibility laid on him.

By now the problem had been completely explored just as sides had been taken. It was the moment for the President of the Republic to resolve the crisis by choosing between two diametrically opposite policies. When President Lebrun, in fulfilment of his duty, called the Presidents of the Chambers for consultation, there was one point about which he no longer had any doubt, namely, that I was irrevocably

[1] *Op. cit.*, vol. II, *Their Finest Hour*, p. 188.

hostile to an armistice. I gave the Presidents of the Chambers a full explanation of the situation, including the offer of a Franco-British Union, and I told them that the President of the Republic was asking me to retain power for the purpose of carrying out the Chautemps proposal. Judging this to be a policy contrary to the honour and interest of France, I had, however, given a categoric refusal.

The President of the Republic questioned in turn President Jeanneney and President Herriot. Both replied, as I had done, that they were opposed to a request for an armistice. They ended by asking President Lebrun to retain me in power in order to carry out my policy.

Revealing the fact that he had decided in favour of the Chautemps proposal, M. Lebrun was unable to win either Jeanneney or Herriot to his own point of view. Then, putting into effect his prerogative, he set aside the authoritative advice which each of the two Presidents had given him, and decided to call upon Pétain who, as he knew, would ask for an armistice.

After the conference between the President of the Republic and the Presidents of the Chambers, I crossed the room where the Ministers were waiting, wondering, wrote Prouvost in *Sept jours*, whether I or Pétain would be forming a new administration. I merely told them: 'Marshal Pétain is forming a government', and left. The formality of handing in the resignation of the Cabinet seemed to me a useless ritual. After I had left, President Lebrun asked the Ministers, so he told me afterwards, to hold themselves at the disposal of Pétain, just as I had wished to keep them at my own.

But, it will be objected, how could a man as scrupulous as M. Lebrun not have been restrained by the pledge of March 28? M. Lebrun anticipated this objection in his evidence at the preliminary investigations for the Pétain trial. 'From the moment', he has said, 'when one of the two countries signatory to a convention such as that of March 28 retains a part of its forces for its own defence instead of throwing them into the fight as its partner has done, it may still formally make use of a document to . . . recall the obligations which are recorded there. But, it has no longer the necessary moral authority to say: "I cannot release you from your pledge."'

Some light is, therefore, shed on the conditions under which Pétain came into power. However, M. Lebrun, who was so categorical in his explanations before the High Court, was to try three years later before the Committee of Inquiry to repudiate his first testimony. On July 25, 1945, we heard him state that, using his constitutional prerogative as an arbiter, he had refused to entrust me with the task of forming a government of resistance, and had taken, so he asserted, the initiative of calling upon Pétain as the majority of the Cabinet wished. Yet, on June 17, 1948, he stated that it was I who had advised him to do this.

But, following a question asked him by M. Gérard Jaquet, President of the Committee, the truth was immediately revealed. M. Lebrun was, in fact, to declare: 'Yes, no doubt. You are re-creating the scene. After a discussion of several hours, full of anxiety and at times turbulent, everyone was standing there, and Reynaud was able to say: "I shall meet you at 10 p.m.", under the impression that he would be given office again, and that he would need several of his former colleagues to reconstitute his Government.'

It was then that one of the Commissioners, M. Emile Kahn, struck by the contradiction, questioned M. Lebrun as follows: 'You have told us that it was he [M. Paul Reynaud] who advised you to summon the Marshal. How could he at the same time advise you to call the Marshal and retain the hope, on the same day, of forming a government of resistance?'

Pinned thus against the wall, M. Lebrun gave the same answer: it was for the President of the Republic to act as judge between the two camps.

To conclude, let us quote the argument which Louis Marin developed on many occasions before the Committee of Inquiry. Taking it up again on December 12, 1950, in my presence, he went as far as asserting that I would have been able to continue in power without reshuffling my Ministry. I had little difficulty in demonstrating the contrary. He replied that I could have 'changed the members of the Cabinet', that is to say, replaced certain Ministers by nominating others to their place, without bothering about the authorization of the President of the Republic. When I objected that he was reproaching me for not having violated the Constitution, Louis Marin replied that I ought to have forced M. Lebrun's hand. And he added: 'From what I know of M. Lebrun, he would not have done anything.' Louis Marin was merely forgetting that M. Lebrun only took his decision after consulting the Presidents of the two Chambers.

Certain other people also seem surprised that M. Lebrun showed in these circumstances a firmness which, they assert, was not natural to him. Reluctant though I am to take part in this discussion, I would observe that it is precisely this indecisive and timorous character that they attribute to M. Lebrun, which explains this firmness they find surprising. The guarantee of men who were at this time the incontestable 'glorious military leaders' of France, and perhaps, still more, the intimidating and even menacing tone of the summonses of Weygand, were, without doubt, the determining factors behind the resolve which M. Lebrun took. Could the latter be ignorant of the fact that physical force was behind Pétain and Weygand, and that, of the two, the latter, in any case, was reputed to be a man who would make use of it?

This will be my reply to the complaint that has been brought against me of not having taken a firm line with them.[1]

I should, for the sake of complete accuracy, add that M. Lebrun intended, as he has said in his book,[2] to return to a policy of resistance if the Pétain-Chautemps Government did not succeed in obtaining an armistice, and that, in such a case, he would have recalled me to power, entrusted with the duty of forming a government of resistance. Indeed, he spoke to me in this strain at Bordeaux after my fall.

We know why I myself thought that Pétain's approach to Hitler was doomed to failure.

Three weeks later, on July 10, during the few hours which I was to pass at Vichy on the day when the National Assembly met, I went to see President Lebrun to ask him not to resign as those who wished to overthrow the Republic were advising him to do. In seeing me off, he said sadly:

'Why did you resign?'

'How could I have pursued this policy, I who had concluded the agreement forbidding any separate armistice?'

'That is true.'

Why did so many other Ministers rally to Pétain and Chautemps? It was because, being only men, their nerves were broken by the sight of the exodus of refugees and by reason of the tragic character of the events which were taking place. In this state of prostration, which, unfortunately, it must be admitted was common to almost all the nation, they were perforce susceptible to the pressure which Pétain and Weygand, our two 'glorious military leaders', were putting on them.

But, outside the Bordeaux Hôtel de Ville, the confusion of ideas, which the pace of events had increased during the last days, was having its effect. There were, certainly, acts of treachery and deliberate desertion, but there were also examples of errors of judgement. On the day of my defeat, one of my colleagues, after describing to me the demoralization of the members of Parliament assembled in Bordeaux, asked me if I intended ruling against the will of the nation. I replied to him: 'If a referendum had been taken at the time of the 1917 mutinies, what do you think would have been its result?'

Certainly, men who remained unbroken by the events taking place were then rare. At the time of the debate on validating my election, I read to the Constituent National Assembly a letter sent me by Pierre Viénot on Sunday, June 16, which softened the bitterness I felt at the numerous deceptions inflicted on men. He developed in his letter an

[1] Chautemps wrote that Mandel and certain others 'were thinking' of arresting Pétain and Weygand, but they wondered if such a move would not inspire a civil war. Neither Mandel nor anyone else breathed a word about the plan to me.

[2] *Op. cit.*, p. 90.

idea which was similar to that which we have seen myself summarize at Cangé in the aphorism: 'Hitler is Genghis Khan!'

Here is its text, the nobility of which moved the whole of the Assembly:

Sunday.

Dear President,

Only one question and one criterion faces us.

How can we create conditions under which it will be possible for France to be reborn?

To put our signature to any terms, to endorse in any official way whatsoever our enslavement to Hitler would be to compromise this resurrection for ever.

Those who assert the contrary are fools, without *the slightest notion* of what Hitlerism means.

There will be no Rethondes for us. There will be the suppression of France under the weight of most abject dishonour.[1]

That will be the end.

Yours, P. Viénot.

The Paris correspondent of the *New York Times* telegraphed to his paper:

'Those who have seen the flood of refugees and troops rolling in confusion towards the south can only judge as fanciful the Reynaud-Churchill plan to cross overseas in order to continue the war. The collapse has been too widespread.'

My reply is that it was not on these fugitives that I counted to continue the war.

On the other hand, the problem of knowing whether Britain would hold out, as I affirmed would be the case, or if on the contrary she would be obliged to lay down her arms in her turn, played, I have said, a decisive role. The answers of our 'glorious military leaders' to this vital question was, we have seen, peremptory. Once again, Pétain and Weygand were deceived about a problem which fell within their own province. But, once again also, these two succeeded in gaining support for their views at the expense of my own.

Who were, therefore, the most to blame? The Ministers, who, under the pressure of the soldiers, lost sight of their own responsibilities to the country, or the soldiers who compelled these Ministers to share in their errors?

It must be realized that, to take such a grave decision as that of leaving France for the purpose of continuing the war, not merely without the public blessing of those two illustrious figures, Pétain and

[1] The words in italics are underlined in the text.

Weygand, but, in the face of their condemnation (which the enemy would immediately proclaim far and wide) was certainly not a negligible factor to men who, because of their political experience, were very sensitive to public opinion. This was all the more so from the fact that no section of public opinion had then begun to query the moral position held by these two great leaders. To override their opposition, to break with them, to run the danger of being termed by them (behind whom were solidly ranged the army leaders) as deserters, who had in Pétain's words 'handed France to the enemy' at the risk of 'destroying the soul of France', with the sole intention of 'escaping the suffering which would be imposed on the motherland and her sons', was the duty of the Government. But such a task was beyond the resolution of many Ministers.

JUNE 16: PÉTAIN ASKS FOR AN ARMISTICE

When the Presidents of the Chambers had left, Pétain was shown into the President of the Republic's room.

M. Lebrun has given an account of this historic scene at Pétain's trial (hearing of July 25, 1945). Here it is:

'It was perhaps 11 p.m. and my first thought was that France should have a government by the next day. . . . Therefore, I got hold of Marshal Pétain and I said to him: "Well, there it is. Form a government." Without hesitation the Marshal opened his brief case with a characteristic gesture, showed me a list and said to me: "Here is my Government." I must say that, despite the deep sadness of the moment, all the same I felt a small ray of comfort. I recalled those difficult negotiations about forming administrations . . . and here I had one given me ready made. . . . I thought that this was excellent.'

When Pétain read the name of Paul Faure, who symbolized the defeatist spirit of the extreme Left, the President of the Republic started:

'Paul Faure?'

'It is possible that his nomination will annoy Léon Blum!' was Pétain's reply.

Thus, at this unprecedented moment when a Marshal of France had decided to break the word of France, when, in the presence of the death-struggles of our homeland, we were all so untouched by considerations of domestic politics, the concern of this man was to 'annoy' Léon Blum.

In forming his Government, he called on Weygand and Darlan, to whom he had contracted a debt of gratitude of which we shall hear later, and he had only to take whom he wanted out of the large number of Ministers who had deserted me. It was to Chautemps that Pétain owed his accession to power; he nominated him Vice-President of the Council.

Here is the composition of the Ministry:

Marshal Pétain: President of the Council
M. Chautemps: Vice-President of the Council

Ministers:

General Weygand: National Defence
General Colson: War
General Pujo: Air
Admiral Darlan: Marine
MM. Frémicourt: Justice
 Pomaret: Interior
 Baudouin: Foreign Affairs
 Bouthillier: Finance and Commerce
 Rivière: Colonies
 Rivaud: National Education
 Frossard: Public Works and Communications
 Chichery: Agriculture and Supply
 Ybarnegaray: Ex-Soldiers and Family

Under-Secretaries of State:

MM. Alibert: Presidency of the Council
 Robert Schuman: Refugees

Sérol, whom Pétain approached, declined to join the Ministry.

Eleven members of the new Government had been in my own. A number of those who had deserted me were not in it.

Laval refused the Ministry of Justice and asked for that of Foreign Affairs, which Pétain gave him, then took away on the intervention of M. Charles-Roux, who told Pétain that the appointment would have a deplorable effect on Britain. Marquet allied himself with Laval, and refused the Ministry of Interior. Eight days later Laval was to be Vice-President of the Council; Marquet Minister of the Interior, and Prouvost[1] High Commissioner for Information. When another fortnight had elapsed, the parliamentary Ministers taken from my Government, with Chautemps at their head, were to be dismissed by Pétain, after having been implicated by him in the overthrow of the Republic.

During the evening I received the British Ambassador and Spears, and I related to them the circumstances in which I had been overthrown.

[1] The inclusion of Prouvost brought to twelve the number of members of my Government whom Pétain took into his.

I was so convinced at that time that I would regain power that I asked if I could not keep the meeting arranged for the next day with Churchill. But Spears rightly objected that this was not possible since I was no longer President of the Council.

At 11 p.m. the Pétain-Chautemps-Weygand Government met. It decided to ask for an armistice; this was the purpose for which it had been formed.

At 12.30 a.m. M. de Lequerica, the Spanish Ambassador, was received by Baudouin, who, writes the latter,[1] gave the Ambassador 'the manuscript note in which he asked the Spanish Government to make representations to the German Government' for this purpose. At 9 a.m. the Papal Nuncio was handed, again by Baudouin, our request to the Italian Government for an armistice.[2]

On the 17th at 12.30 p.m. Pétain, speaking to the country over the wireless, declared that France 'has fulfilled her duties towards her Allies', and then announced, 'I am dedicating myself to France in order to diminish her misfortune. . . . With a heavy heart I am telling you today that it is necessary to bring fighting to an end. I approached the adversary last night to ask him if he is ready to explore with me, as between soldier and soldier, when the fight is over and in honourable circumstances, the means of ending hostilities.'

'To bring fighting to an end.' This, before we even knew the terms of the adversary! This was a fine position to take up for negotiations! Baudouin tried to improve the phrase by altering it to 'try to bring fighting to an end'. It was too late! Pétain's words had been heard by soldiers as well as civilians. It was by this incredibly thoughtless action that Pétain inaugurated his régime.[3]

On 22 June, Weygand himself, in his capacity as Commander-in-Chief of French land, sea and air forces, and in the name of the Government in which he held the portfolio of National Defence, ordered Huntziger to sign with Germany (represented by the Commander-in-Chief of the Wehrmacht) an undertaking that France 'would end hostilities' both on metropolitan soil and in her overseas possessions as well as on the sea.

---

[1] Op. cit., pp. 118–19.

[2] It is said that, at Hitler's orders, Mussolini declined to accept the Vatican as an intermediary, and insisted on Franco acting as such.

[3] Here is what Tony Révillon says about the matter (Mes carnets (juin–octobre, 1940), documents et témoignages pour servir à l'histoire, pp. 58–61):

'Wednesday, June 19.

'. . . The news . . . from the front is very bad. . . . An orderly retreat was carried out until June 17. But Marshal Pétain's speech has demoralized our soldiers. . . . The phrase . . . "it is necessary to bring fighting to an end" has paralysed our soldiers. . . . Our country has had Lazare Carnot, the architect of victory. Now, it has Pétain, the architect of defeat; Reynaud was right. Weygand's Army should have ceased fighting since resistance in France was no longer possible, but the Government should not have asked for an armistice. This sorry retreat would have been avoided, and the future would have been still open.'

Without exception, therefore, our ground, sea and air forces were to 'end hostilities' in all territories throughout our Empire as well as on the seas. Under the pretext of avoiding the capitulation of our ground forces who were engaged in operations against Germany, what did we do? We ran headlong into a general surrender of our land, sea and air forces, wherever they might be, and consequently into a surrender of our Empire. Could we have concluded a more idiotic capitulation?

Let us return to June 17, 1940. The British Ambassador recalled on several occasions to the Pétain Government France's pledge not to treat separately with the enemy. Our ally would only consent to free us from this obligation if our Fleet joined its own. The Bordeaux Government concluded an armistice without troubling about this condition.[1] Weygand has, however, admitted in his deposition at the Pétain trial[2] that on June 17 the Ambassador handed the new Government the two messages which he had given me the day before and then withdrawn. Thus, Pétain and his colleagues deliberately broke France's word. It was on this day that they committed the crime from which so many others have stemmed. It was from this day that France ceased to be admitted to the meetings of the great Powers. It is through the fault of these men that France was to be absent from the Teheran, Yalta and Potsdam conferences. It was through their fault that Frenchmen were divided into two hostile camps.

It is with a blush of shame that we read the official communiqué of the British Government on June 24, stating with reference to the agreement of March 28: 'This solemn agreement has been broken by the Government of Marshal Pétain.' Happily, Pétain did not represent France.

But by good fortune on the 18th, General de Gaulle launched his historic appeal over the London radio:

'Leaders who, for many years, have been at the head of the French Armies have formed a government. The Government, using the defeat of our Armies as an excuse, has established contact with the enemy for the purpose of terminating hostilities. . . . Is defeat final? No. . . . For France is not alone. She has a vast Empire behind her. She can make common cause with the British Empire, which still holds the seas and continues to fight. She can, like Britain, use to the limit the immense industries of the United States . . . This war has not been decided by the Battle of France. . . . Struck down today by mechanized strength,

[1] The men of Vichy have asserted that Churchill had freed the signatories of the Armistice from any responsibility, by alleging on September 28, 1944, that he had authorized, in June, 1940, the French Government to conclude an armistice 'on condition that it sent its Fleet out of the reach of the enemy'. Sending it out of reach meant sending it into British waters. Such would at least have ensured that Britain could have used the vessels, if not the crews. This is what the anglophobia of Pétain's Ministers refused to accept. Darlan was saying at the time in Vichy: 'I have not created a fleet to offer it to the British.' That is why *this condition was not carried out.*

[2] Hearing of July 31, 1945.

we can conquer in the future by superior mechanized strength. The destiny of the world lies in this.'

German propaganda was jubilant on learning of my fall and the appointment of Pétain. Ciano notes on the 17th in his *Diary* (*op. cit.*, p. 266): '. . . Reynaud has fallen and . . . Pétain has taken his place. This means peace.'

Britain remained alone, standing four-square against the tempest. I thought of those words of Shakespeare in *Richard II*. . . .

> *This fortress built by Nature for herself*
> *Against infection and the hand of war;*
> *This happy breed of men, this little world;*
> *This precious stone set in the silver sea;*
> *Which serves it in the office of a wall;*
> *Or as a moat defensive to a house,*
> *Against the envy of less happier lands.*

This sea was to be an anti-tank ditch in 1940.

On the 17th, Churchill had sent this inspiring message over the wireless to the British people:

'. . . We have become the sole champions now in arms to defend the world cause. . . . We shall defend our Island home, and with the British Empire we shall fight on unconquerable until the curse of Hitler is lifted from the brows of mankind. . . .'[1]

JUNE 19: LAST MESSAGE FROM ROOSEVELT

On the day after my resignation I sent Roosevelt a telegram. We shall see if it is correct, as people have alleged (and what things have not been alleged?), that in this telegram I stood security with Roosevelt for Pétain's policy. Here is the text of this message:

> At the time when I am leaving office I would like, Mr. President, to tell you that I know the answer you gave to my last message went as far as present circumstances would allow you to go. I want to express to you my deep gratitude for your answer.
>
> Amidst the great misfortune which is afflicting her, France is aware that, because America exists, the kind of civilization which is her own will not perish, and that one day, liberty will relive in ancient Europe.
>
> Paul Reynaud

The President answered me on the 19th:

> Your very moving message has reached me, and I wish to tell you how deeply I am grateful for it.

[1] Churchill, *op. cit.*, vol. II, *Their Finest Hour*, p. 191.

The American people will not forget the brilliant, courageous and useful resistance which you have conducted at the head of your Government in the name of France.

The American people and its Government share the conviction that the ideals which France has defended for so many generations, the ideals of human liberty, of democracy and the noblest type of civilization, will triumph in the end, and that France herself will regain her full independence and her complete freedom.

Franklin D. Roosevelt

And these were not mere words.

Let it be said in passing that Roosevelt's reply is the best denial to offer those who insinuate that my appeals to the President were moves intended to cover up my own responsibility.

THE ORDER TO SCUTTLE THE FLEET

On the 21st I went to see Pétain and advise him to have Darlan order the Fleet to sail for the United States. Returning to my hotel, I sent him a written reply to the argument that the Germans would not hesitate, by way of reprisals, to pillage our cities if the Fleet sailed or was scuttled. I told him that, if, to prevent the enemy using our ships, we were forced one day to scuttle them, such an act of self-sacrifice would not gain us the slightest profit, while, on the other hand, France would, by ordering her Fleet to weigh anchor for the United States, secure, *ipso facto*, a substantial credit balance with the United States. To account for this action to the Germans, had we not a ready-made excuse—to say that it was due to Darlan's insubordination?

During this visit of the 21st, when I asked Pétain what his Minister of Public Education, Rivaud, a man knowledgeable in German affairs, whose book, in which he called Hitler and his accomplices 'adventurers', Pétain had certainly not read, thought of the situation, he replied, pulling out a paper from his pocket: 'This is most curious: Rivaud says that we can only save France from Canada, and that the Germans will demand the trial of those responsible for the war.' Three weeks later Rivaud had ceased to be a Minister. And on August 1, 1940, Pétain ordered the trial before the Riom Court of those who, by their acts, had contributed to the 'change from a state of peace to a state of war'. During this conversation I also asked Pétain if he was not forgetting that the Government, should it stay in Bordeaux, would fall into the clutches of the enemy. He cynically answered me: 'I believe the Germans will have some consideration for me.'

When I revealed my surprise that he was going to take Laval into his Government, he said to me: 'He has got plenty of people behind him.'

And what a class of people!

When the conditions of the armistice were known to those in official circles, I grew alarmed at the rumours which were spreading about the fate to be suffered by the Fleet. On the 23rd I went to see Pétain, in order to ask him to show me the clause dealing with the Fleet. This is what I read: '8. With the exception of that part to be left with the French Government for the protection of its interests and colonial Empire, *the French War Fleet will assemble in ports to be named later. It will be demobilized and disarmed there under German or Italian control. . . . The German Government solemnly declares to the French Government that it has no intention of using the units of this Fleet in its own operations of war* . . . except, however, such ships which are necessary for guarding the coasts and trawling for mines.'[1]

I said to Pétain: 'Everything depends, therefore, on Hitler's remaining faithful to his promise. What will the British do? Do they trust Hitler's word? Is it sufficient for them? And if it is not sufficient?'

Pétain kept quiet. Did he have a presentiment of the disaster to take place at Mers-el-Kébir? At my request he summoned Darlan. This ruddy-complexioned man paled when I said to him:

'I have just read Article 8. Does it suit you?'

'The Armistice Commission will modify it.'

'Do you really believe that?'

'In any case, the order will be given for the Fleet to scuttle itself rather than fall into the hands of the enemy.'

In actual fact the order was issued the next day.

Here it is:

> To Admirals: North; South; Africa; Antilles; Far East; 3rd Squadron; Force X; Levant Naval Division; Maritime Prefects, 1st, 2nd, 3rd, 4th and 5th maritime areas.

Armistice clauses will be notified to you elsewhere in clear. I am availing myself of these last messages which I can send in code in order to tell you what I think about this matter:

1. Demobilized warships must remain French under French flag, with skeleton French crew, stationed in French ports, metropolitan or colonial.

2. Secret precautions for scuttling must be taken so that neither the enemy nor foreigners who seize a ship by force can make use of it.

3. If the Armistice Commission charged with interpreting the Armistice conditions decides otherwise than in paragraph 1, warships will, at the moment when this new decision is to be carried out, and

[1] The italics are M. Reynaud's.

without further orders, either weigh anchor for the United States, or be scuttled, if they cannot otherwise escape the enemy.

4. Ships thus taking refuge abroad should not be used in action against Germany or Italy without the order of the Commander-in-Chief of French sea forces.

Admiral of the Fleet
12.45 p.m. 24.6

Leaving Pétain, whom I was only to see again when he confronted his judges, I was in anguish at the thought of a possible collision between the two Fleets, and the consequences which this would have on the relations of the two countries.

I should add that, as I had not been able to listen in myself to the wireless, I only learned second-hand that Churchill had, the evening before, made a speech which was said to be very violent.[1] I had advised Pétain not to reply, and I had understood him to give me a promise not to do so. Contrary to this undertaking he answered on the same day, and his speech helped to embitter still further relations between the two peoples. What could be done to avoid a conflict?

I hastened to telegraph to Churchill:

I am appealing to your friendship and the trust which you have always placed in me. Nothing would rejoice Hitler's heart more than a public and permanent quarrel between our two countries. Your statement of yesterday has so profoundly stirred me that I have discussed it with Pétain. I understand your anguish and I can visualize that the problem which is worrying you the most, as it also worries me, concerns the Fleet.

The stipulations of the Armistice agreement on this subject are, it is true, of a nature to make you uneasy. But, I have just questioned Admiral Darlan in the presence of Marshal Pétain. Darlan stated to me that, when the conditions for implementing this arrangement are discussed before the Armistice Commission, steps will be taken so that, under no circumstances [sic], will the enemy be able to make use of our Fleet against Britain in defiance of promises given by him in the text which has just been adopted.

This should set your mind at rest on the point.

You were good enough to tell me at Briare and at Tours that, if a Government other than my own, adopted a different policy and asked for an armistice, Britain would not waste her time in useless recriminations. But she would on the other hand take into account

---

[1] Similarly, I was unable to hear General de Gaulle's appeal on June 18 which Baudouin told me on the following day was insulting to Pétain. If I remained in touch with Baudouin, it was for the purpose of still keeping abreast with events, always with the thought that my recall to power was imminent.

the tremendous sacrifices which France had undertaken and which had immolated her as the advance-guard of the democracies; when final victory was gained, France would be re-established to her power and dignity. Such words touched us greatly. I am sure that you still feel them in the depths of your heart.

I send you my deep friendship,

Paul Reynaud.

Was the clash to be avoided. Unfortunately no. The frightful massacre of Mers-el-Kébir was to occur. Churchill, I realize, could certainly not, in this question of life and death for his country, put his faith in Hitler's word. But it was my duty to try and turn him from the fratricidal enterprise towards which I saw he was moving. How could I refrain from doing this when it was a question of the prior interest of my motherland? I therefore told Churchill of the solemn promise which I had just received from Darlan's lips, and I did not hesitate to commit myself strongly that such a pledge would be kept. Emphasizing deliberately the assurances which Churchill had given me at Briare and Tours, I seized the opportunity to remind him of the tremendous sacrifices which France had undertaken for the common cause, and because of these, the claims which she had acquired on Britain's gratitude. Was it possible for me to remain quiescent when I felt the danger which was threatening our Fleet and the future of the country?

In his memoirs Churchill writes that he sent a personal message on the 17th to Pétain and Weygand, to urge them to send 'the fine French Fleet' into the safety of British or American waters. The British Ambassador communicated a copy of this message to President Lebrun and Darlan. On the 19th a special mission arrived by seaplane at Bordeaux. It comprised the First Lord of the Admiralty, Mr. Alexander, the First Sea Lord and Admiral of the Fleet, Sir Dudley Pound, and Lord Lloyd. Sir Dudley and Mr. Alexander went to Darlan, who received them in the company of Admiral Auphan. The last named asserts, in his memoir (pp. 10–11) *Histoire de mes trahisons ou la Marine au service des Français*, that the British did not ask for the Fleet to sail for British waters. He disagrees on this point with his chief, who, in his letter of December 4, 1942, wrote to Churchill in reference to this same interview: 'If I did not consent to authorize the French Fleet to proceed to British ports, it was because I knew that such a decision would bring about the total occupation of metropolitan France as well as North Africa.'

Darlan rather than Auphan is to be believed on this point. The latter adds: 'He (Darlan) gave them his word of honour that . . . our ships would be used by none but ourselves; they would remain French or would be destroyed. The British left us, moved, friendly and apparently satisfied.'[1]

Apparently, as Auphan says. In any case, when Churchill heard the text of article 8 during the night of the 22nd–23rd, he stated on the wireless: 'If such conditions are accepted by the French . . . all the resources . . . of the French Navy would quickly pass into the hands of the enemy.' And, on the 25th, alluding to the Alexander-Pound mission he said: 'Solemn promises were given us that, in any case, the Fleet would not fall into German hands. . . . From this text (article 8) it is clear that French ships will pass, completely armed, under German or Italian control.'

Churchill's state of mind in these tragic days was certainly understandable. But the facts have not disproved the value of the advice which, in the interests of our two countries, I believed it my duty as an ordinary Frenchman to give him in my telegram of the 23rd. Darlan was, indeed, able to write to Churchill on December 4, 1942, again in his above-mentioned letter: 'The voluntary destruction of the Fleet at Toulon has just proved that I was right, because, even though I no longer commanded, the Fleet executed the orders which I had given and maintained, contrary to the wishes of the Laval Government.'

We know what the Armistice conditions were.[2] The *Mémoires* of Blum revealed that I was far from being the only one at this time to entertain illusions about Pétain and Weygand. Blum writes about this matter: 'I could not accept . . . the idea that the Marshal, that General Weygand, that a man like the Admiral, that certain civilian Ministers, had lost all will to struggle against the kind of demands which Chautemps and Frossard themselves had called intolerable but a week previously. . . . In less than a couple of days we had exchanged the Cabinet of Paul Reynaud, with its policy of resistance, for that of Pétain-Chautemps, with one of negotiation. And, in less than a week, we had abandoned the method of free negotiation (guaranteed, if there were need for this, by the departure of the Government and its determination to continue the war outside France), for pure and simple capitulation. It was all over. An irreparable step had been taken.'

[1] According to Alec de Montmorency (*The Enigma of Admiral Darlan*, p 92), the First Lord of the Admiralty is reputed to have made this insulting reply: 'We have no use for words.'

[2] Those of the Italian Armistice, dictated by Hitler to Mussolini were a cruel disillusionment to the latter. Ciano notes in his *Diary* (*op. cit.*, pp. 266–71):

'June 17. The Duce is an extremist. He would like to go so far as the total occupation of French territory and demands the surrender of the French fleet. But he is aware that . . . it is Hitler who will have the last word. . . . His reflections on the Italian people and, above all, on our armed forces, are extremely bitter this evening. . . .

'June 21. . . . Mussolini does not feel inclined to advance claims to territorial occupation. . . . June 25. . . . [The Italian people] were expecting immediate and gratuitous occupation. They thought that all the territory not conquered by force of arms would pass over to us anyway, in view of the agreement. When the document is made public, disillusionment will increase all the more.'

19

The spectacle of a panic-stricken flight from Bordeaux was so disgusting that I resolved to leave the city only on the same day that the Government did. But, as the Germans had asked for a list of people included in the official departure, I was asked to leave the day before.[1]

Several kilometres from Bordeaux my car had to stop in order to allow a column of artillery to pass. I heard a soldier say to one of his comrades in a tone of gloomy irritation, jerking his head towards me: 'That is one of those who wants us to break our necks.' However, it is by no means impossible that both of them became 'resisters' in the end.

After my departure from Bordeaux I became public enemy number one. I was to be calumniated,[2] imprisoned and finally handed over to the enemy.

---

[1] When the question arose of part of the Pétain Government leaving for North Africa, I decided to cross Spain to get there. The Franco Government forbade its Ambassador to give me a visa. Once the Armistice had been concluded, however, I no longer thought of leaving France. I have given the reason for this.

[2] The attacks upon me began on the 18th. Le Matin published on that day—immediately after its editorial staff came under the control of the invader—the following leading article, which, both in substance and language, bore a German imprint, and showed all the hatred which our enemies had stored up against me: 'The Reynaud Ministry, heedless of our soldiers' blood, continued without blanching to have them slaughtered by superior force, though the uselessness of fighting on was apparent to all. It is without regret and indeed with great relief that we hear that this instigator of useless massacre has at last retired.'

'What will happen to-morrow? No one can tell. But enough blood has been shed. Such is the situation to-day.

'When one makes the mistake of killing so many people uselessly, only one atonement is possible: to kill oneself. If Paul Reynaud still dares to remain alive after the machinations which we have just witnessed, history can duly accuse him of cowardice.'

Such is the relief with which the German Staff, through its spokesmen, greeted my departure—a confession, thereby, of the fears with which the prospect of the fight being continued inspired it.

CHAPTER XX

WHAT MOTIVES INSPIRED PÉTAIN, WEYGAND AND DARLAN?

The Mystery.—The Real Pétain.—The Real Weygand.—
Pétain's Manœuvres.—Pétain seduces Darlan.—What was Wey-
gand's Motive?—Weygand throws Reibel into action.—July 10,
1940, Pétain overthrows the Republic.

What we want is a kind of Consulate. Pétain.
That's a fine present which you wish to make me, Marshal. Darlan.
We must get rid of all these politicians. Weygand.

THE MYSTERY

How was it that Pétain, the 'Victor of Verdun', and Weygand, the 'right arm' of Foch, were able, in contempt of France's pledged word, to be the inspiration of her surrender? Caught in the vortex of disorderly retreat, were they, like so many others, the victims of a foolish error? That is the mystery.

It is difficult to detach from its legendary halo the image of a man who has won glory whilst still living like Pétain had, or that of one whom the rays of glory have touched as they had done Weygand. Truth is slow to reveal itself about those on such a plane.

Let us note one fact. Pétain and Weygand did not like each other. Weygand considered Pétain to be a man without fire, a man whom Foch had to push into victory. Pétain was slow, secretive, dissimulating; Weygand was impulsive, hot-headed. Yet they became allies. Let us try to see the reason for this.

THE REAL PÉTAIN

During several weeks of common captivity in Germany Signor Nitti, former Prime Minister of Italy, told me in his skilful Neapolitan way that, in 1919, when the Peace Conference was being held, Clemenceau paid a visit one day to his hotel. On arriving the Tiger said to him: 'I am coming to see you to get some rest from my friends.' Then, at the request of his interlocutor, he sketched in his biting voice the silhouettes of our victorious generals.

'What do you think of Pétain?' asked Nitti.

'He's a defeatist, who believes in nothing. He hates the British. He wished to surrender in March, 1918. It will be to France's great misfortune if he is ever to fulfil another role on her behalf.'

Such an opinion, though brutal, was just.

We have seen that the doctrine of systematic defensive action which Pétain based on his slogan 'It is the bullet which kills' was only an extension into the military sphere of his fundamental defeatism.

But it was when the catastrophic collapse of Gough's Army occurred in March, 1918, that this characteristic trait in Pétain's make-up was fully revealed. All evidence is in agreement on this point, both that of Poincaré and of Clemenceau, whose dislike of each other was obvious, as well as that of Joffre.

Let us hear what some contemporary witnesses have said:

Poincaré: 'On March 25, Clemenceau . . . went to see Pétain at Compiègne. He reproached him for utterances of an exaggerated pessimism. "Can you believe it," the President of the Council told me. "He said to me that if we were beaten, it would be thanks to the British."

'On March 26, Clemenceau . . . confided sadly to me that General Pétain was planning the withdrawal of the French Army to the south, whilst the British Army would retire to the north. Pétain had, Clemenceau added, given the necessary orders. Foch confirmed this item of information, and sent me the order of retreat issued by Pétain. . . . Clemenceau . . . said to me: "Pétain gets on one's nerves with his pessimism. Believe it or not, he said to me. . . . 'The Germans will defeat the British in the open field. After that, they will beat us.'" Milner spoke to me about Pétain without any trace of enthusiasm. . . .

'March 27: At 11 p.m. a meeting of the Council. . . . Before its sitting, Clemenceau informed me that Joffre had said to him: "Although I am left in the background, I see and know enough of the situation to understand that Pétain has committed the same errors as when he wished to evacuate Verdun. The situation can be saved if we set seriously about doing it!" Loucheur was very dissatisfied with Pétain, whom he found a complete defeatist, and who had said to him a few days before "We must begin negotiations for peace." . . .

'March 28: Marshal Joffre . . . stated that he had foreseen everything which Pétain would do. "Both Pétain and Anthoine", he said, "have no backbone."[1]

'June 1: Clemenceau . . . told me that he had found Pétain in a very gloomy state of mind, and envisaging the evacuation of Paris by the

[1] Poincaré, *Au service de la France*, vol. x, pp. 85–6.

Government. . . . Foch stated that he did not contemplate for a moment the idea of leaving Paris. At Pétain's insistence, Clemenceau warned Klotz, and asked him to take that night the most secret steps to transfer our gold bullion.'[1]

Clemenceau: 'It was at Doullens that Foch, without asking leave of anyone, demonstrated that he was the one to exercise supreme command. I shall remain grateful to him until my dying breath for that moment. We were in the courtyard of the town hall, watched by dumbfounded bystanders who were asking us on all sides: "Will the Germans reach Doullens? Do your best to stop them." The silence amongst us was suddenly broken by this exclamation from a French General (Pétain), who, pointing out (General) Haig to me, observed in a low voice, "There is one who will be obliged to surrender in the open field before a fortnight is out, and we shall be very lucky if we are not forced to do the same." . . . There was some commotion; Foch arrived on the scene . . . and, in his cutting voice which could be heard everywhere, said: "You are not fighting. I am going to fight until I drop. I shall fight before Amiens. I shall fight in Amiens. I shall fight behind Amiens. I shall fight all the time." There is no need to comment on this speech. I confess that I myself had the greatest difficulty in not falling into the arms of this worthy leader to express the gratitude of France in her darkest hour.'[2]

What a picture! And what a leader! With what an energetic arm Foch supported this faltering leader who had lost faith in France, and who was thinking of surrendering! In what tones he put him back on the right road!

Foch repelled the enemy at Ghent. Hence the reason behind Mangin's words to Michel Clemenceau on the day we entered Mayence: 'It was in spite of him (Pétain) that we won the war!'

Here is a final piece of evidence. I am borrowing it from the diary which General Brugère kept daily, and from which his son, M. Raymond Brugère, gave extracts in his book.

This is what we read:[3]

'April 28, 1916. The editor of *L'Echo de Paris* (Henry Simond) told me that Poincaré, in visiting Verdun, asked General Pétain what it was necessary to do in order to defeat the Germans. He replied: "Establish a military dictatorship."

'May 19, 1916. Pétain seems to have been over-praised. Operations are going much better since Nivelle took over . . . at Verdun. . . .

'May 10, 1918. Simond spoke to me about Pétain and Anthoine, who

---

[1] *Ibid.,* p. 205.
[2] Clemenceau, *Grandeurs et misères d'une victoire,* p. 23.
[3] Brugère, *Veni, Vidi, Vichy,* pp. 187–8.

are said to be in Painlevé's pocket, and to have been voicing for a long time the opinion that the only thing we could do was to make peace.'

There was unanimity also amongst his fellow soldiers. I have given Foch's judgement. As for Lyautey, he, as we know, only referred to him as *Monsieur* Pétain.

And what about Weygand? 'And to think that we have had to kick him into getting this,' was all he had to say about the ceremony during which Poincaré, in the presence of Foch and the Allied Commanders-in-Chief, handed Pétain his Field-Marshal's baton.

THE REAL WEYGAND

'And what about Weygand?' Signor Nitti asked Clemenceau.

'He is a frightful little fake, a regular church-goer. But, he's the most intelligent officer in the French Army.'

Weygand was in no wise a fake. It is true that Lord Lloyd said he looked like an aged jockey, but the breadth between his eyes, the quickness of his glance and the delicate shape of his mouth gave the impression of a keen intelligence. Was he intelligent? It depends how we define intelligence. He had one gift: he could explain things well. Neither Joffre nor Foch had this power. The workings of Foch's brain in particular erupted in outbursts which bewildered the unversed listener. 'Explain, Weygand', he would then brusquely say. And, in a clear, animated voice, expressing subtle shades of meaning, Weygand would make crystal-clear the thoughts of the great leader. Was it necessary for him to possess any additional qualities in order to secure attention in the conferences which, between 1918 and 1923, met, first of all to decide upon military operations, and subsequently to elaborate the arrangements for concluding peace?

With his eagle eye Foch had seen on the eve of the First World War whence came the peril. And what about Weygand before 1939? We have heard him deny in peremptory tones the revolution, which was patently obvious, that an armoured corps and dive-bombers were to introduce into the art of war. We have also seen him misjudge the scope of Germany's efforts to renew her military power.

But Weygand had the gift of explaining things clearly. And the person who can explain things intelligently is often more successful than the one who thinks intelligently. This is, no doubt, because he gives his listeners the impression that they themselves are intelligent. Between the two wars we have seen certain politicians who were regularly deceived about everything, succeed in making a brilliant career because they explained themselves in a way which carried weight. At the School of Warfare, Foch had chosen this maxim as the motto for his lectures on strategy: 'First of all, learn to think.' This great leader gave out rays of light. Weygand reflected them: he was a planet which France took for a star. Several years after his talk with Signor Nitti, Clemenceau passed a more profound judgement on Weygand, when he said to Emile Buré:[1] 'Look out. If ever a *coup d'état* is attempted, it will be by him.'

And later Daladier was to say to Tony Révillon:[2] 'He is a general who might inspire civil war.'

Untouched by the grandeur of republican ideals, Weygand was permeated by the spirit of the caste to which he belonged. He had made himself popular in the higher ranks of the Army by posing as the champion of the officer corps against the politicians upon whom he passed trenchant judgements in a language which was off-hand and vigorous. He was filled with a fanaticism for his profession, but it was the fanaticism of a partisan. He loved the Army, but he loved it as something to be opposed to the régime and its leaders. No one was farther than himself from the maxim uttered by Foch at the Invalides, on the day when he was handed the sword of Napoleon: 'More important than war, there is peace, and there are nations to be served as they think best.'

What counted with Weygand was being the 'right type'. Maybe for him any innovation had only to be supported by politicians to merit condemnation. Hardly had he succeeded Gamelin as Commander-in-Chief than, as we know, he called back General Dufieux to active service. No doubt this was because the latter, as we also know, had expressed in public his disapproval of armoured divisions.

No one will contest that Weygand had courage or the power to make a decision. But he was thoughtless, hot-headed and violent. Rudeness was for him a proof of spirit. He spent his life in running down politicians both of the Right and Left, and went as far as uttering, even in public, extravagances verging on vulgarity about them.

PÉTAIN'S MANŒUVRES

We have seen that, after the First World War, Pétain endowed us with an army which was incapable of permitting France to maintain her rightful place in Europe. We have also seen that he was opposed to a Franco-Soviet alliance. Had he any political views? Certain facts lead one to believe that he had.

In 1934, shortly after the riots of February 6, Pétain joined the Doumergue Cabinet as Minister of War. His political career was beginning. In this same year Jouhaux, Secretary-General of the General

[1] *L'Ordre*, August 26, 1945. [2] Révillon, *op. cit.*, p. 72.

Confederation of Labour, was the subject of a curious request; an industrialist invited him to lunch with Pétain. Jouhaux, from whom I have this, declined the invitation.

In 1935, Gustave Hervé launched in *La Victoire* the idea of a 'national rallying around the name of the illustrious soldier', a pamphlet entitled *C'est Pétain qu'il nous faut!* was circulated throughout the country, and particularly amongst certain Catholic elements. It suggested the institution of a 'national socialist republic' in which the power of the Head of the State 'would only be limited by his obligation to consult certain competent sections of his State Council'. Pétain was already called in it the 'man sent by providence'. Was not Joseph Barthélemy, Minister of Justice, to maintain at Vichy that Pétain's advent into power was a new proof of God's existence! Medals with Pétain's effigy were circulated throughout the country. Nobody will believe that such a campaign was undertaken without the one whose popularity it was intended to promote being aware of it. What is more, one could read the words, 'Pétain will not refuse', in the pamphlet itself. Pétain, in this very year, also strengthened his relations with Laval; he frequently received him in his office at the Invalides.

Shortly after the general election of April–May, 1936, the campaign was again resumed. Had Pétain any contact with the *Cagoule*? One fact is certain about this question: in the December of this year Pétain sent Major Loustaunau-Lacau, of his General Staff, to see General Duseigneur, one of the leaders of the *Cagoule*, in order to find out something of what was going on.

In April, 1939, a Nazi publication in French, *Le Grand-Occident*, headlined these words: 'Put Pétain in Power'. The editor of this paper was none other than Ferdonnet, who, at the beginning of the war, entered the pay of the enemy. On March 16 of this same year Pétain was nominated French Ambassador to Madrid.

The war broke out. In its initial stages Daladier decided to reshuffle his Government by bringing in prominent people in order to stiffen it. He thought of giving Foreign Affairs to Herriot and another portfolio to Sarraut. The first-named also advised him to call upon Pétain. Pétain came to Paris on Daladier's request. Daladier offered him a seat in his Cabinet. This was declined on the grounds that Herriot's presence at the Quai d'Orsay would antagonize Franco and Mussolini. Pétain's biographer was to write[1] later that the real reason was due to something else: 'Really, as he stated to his intimate friends, he had no confidence in Daladier being capable of running the war, and in the proposed ministerial reshuffle certain individuals with whom he did not, in any case, wish to collaborate, were being considered.' Let us not dwell on Pétain's hostility towards Herriot and Albert

[1] Laure, *op. cit.*, p. 428.

Sarraut, but consider his principal complaint. Pétain had no confidence in Daladier being able to run the war. Now, Daladier was offering him a seat in the Government. Within the Council of Ministers he could, thanks to the influence which his prestige gave him, fight against any methods which seemed to him injurious. He declined; he preferred to 'wait and see'. Subsequently strange rumours circulated with which the name of Pétain was always, expressly and implicitly, associated. Gamelin, as I have already said, learned of the 'existence of the Laval-Chautemps-Flandin peace offensive, backed by Pétain'. I discovered through *Mon patron, Georges Mandel*, by Francisque Varenne the following fact:[1]

'One day, towards November, 1939, he [Mandel] said to me: "What is Laval up to? There is almost nothing on which I can agree with him. However, it might be wise to have a word with him. Can you arrange a meeting?" A few days later we three dined together alone. During the meal the two men exchanged their points of view without stressing their differences too much. During February, 1940, the two politicians again met for dinner. Laval had attacked Daladier by an "interpellation" at a secret committee meeting of the Senate. The voting had naturally been in favour of the Government, but the President and the Council, directly challenged by Laval on their foreign policy, had been roughly handled, and the demonstrations of the Chamber during the sitting had been of a hostile nature. Daladier's fall from power seemed shortly possible, and a change of government appeared imminent. The conversation of the two men was full of interest on that particular evening. Mandel asked Laval how he thought things were going to turn out. . . . Laval made approximately the following reply, which I reproduce from memory:

'"I think that I have shaken Daladier. Reynaud may succeed him, but he will not prevent the military reverses which I see in store for us. When these reverses take place, I shall do my utmost to get a Pétain administration."

'"You see eye to eye with the Marshal?" interrupted Mandel.

'Laval gave a sign of assent, and continued to explain that it was only under the aegis of the "Victor of Verdun" that a government could be created, which would be able to deal with the grave circumstances inevitably bound to occur.'

In February, Vigne, secretary of the Miners' Federation, who, at the beginning of the war, had signed the appeal of the pacifists promoted by Jean Giono, predicted[2] to the secretary of the miners' syndicate at

---

[1] pp. 189–91.
[2] It was Jouhaux who told me about this prediction, when we were in Germany. It goes without saying that Vigne was one of the first to rally to Pétain after the Armistice.

Mulhouse that, before three months were out 'there would be an armistice and a military dictatorship'.

Now, here is something even more serious. When visiting Paris, Pétain went to see Monzie on March 30. The conversation of the two men is enlightening. Monzie, who refrained, and with good reason, from telling me about it, has given us an account[1] of the meeting: 'Marshal Pétain . . . came to see me at the Ministry of Public Works. Chatain, who was his official colleague in Spain, came with him to my room and then withdrew so that we could talk more plainly. The Marshal was hesitating about going back to Madrid. He was contemplating spending, alternatively, a fortnight in San Sebastian and a fortnight in Paris. I respectfully opposed this plan because of the fatigue it would mean for him, and because such divided effort would not serve any useful purpose. However, it did seem necessary that his mission in Spain should not be extended too long; the presence of our greatest leader in France was becoming increasingly necessary. We analysed discreetly an internal situation which, since the Finnish affair, was endangered by a spirit of weariness and uncertainty. The Marshal became confiding and told me "They will need me *during the second fortnight of May!*"[2] *They* signified the real civil and military leaders of the war—not us people who counted for little in the Government. On leaving the Marshal said to Chatain: "I am in agreement with Monzie about everything."'

The words spoken to Monzie were corroborated by those which Pétain said on May 5 to Darlan, when he went to see him at his head-quarters at Maintenon, about an hour's run from Paris. That day, the last page of the *Journal* was filled with a full-length portrait of Pétain.

Darlan has himself taken the trouble to tell us about this interview while he was, in actual fact, Head of the Vichy Government and was taking over several ministries, one of which was that of Information. He confided in Béraud, who published his words in *Gringoire* of May 30, 1941.

Pétain said to Darlan, when leaving him: 'We've got to keep shoulder to shoulder. Can I count on you?' Darlan, who at this time was speaking of Pétain without any appearance of goodwill, was taken aback: 'I must confess', he observed to Béraud, 'that on that day I did not seize the full significance of his request.'

He had so imperfectly 'seized' it that, when I asked him at the beginning of June in the presence of his Minister, my friend Campinchi, after a meeting of the War Committee at the Elysée, whether he would ever be the man to surrender the Fleet, he answered me: 'I would rather take to sea.'

He had so imperfectly 'seized' it that, on June 3, during a three hours'

[1] *Ci-devant*, pp. 207–8.   [2] The italics are those of M. Reynaud.

[*sic*] conversation which he had at the Rue Royale with Jules Moch, he told him: 'The Generals don't want to go on fighting and the soldiers are quitting. If an armistice is asked for one day, I shall round off my career with an act of glorious indiscipline; I shall sail with the Fleet.'

During this same period Pétain was obviously desirous of joining my Cabinet for he came to see me on the 6th to tell me: 'I am a member of the War Committee and I should like to attend its meetings. I should also like to visit the soldiers and the Armies.' I had been told that he had for some time been neglecting the duties of his mission in Madrid, that he was not even carrying out the steps which he was instructed to do. Therefore, I answered him:

'Nothing is more simple. Hand me your resignation as Ambassador, and we shall be happy to see you at the meetings of the War Committee.'

'But Daladier tells me that it is my duty to stay in Madrid, and I should like the Government to be unanimous in its wish for me to take my place on the War Committee,' was his reply.

I answered him that he was asking too much of me, and he took his leave. Shortly after, he received Gamelin, who relates this interview in *Servir* (vol. III, p. 381): 'On the 6th, meeting of the War Committee . . . I then went to Marshal Pétain's room, Boulevard des Invalides. He had been in France for three days, and I offered to explain the Norwegian situation to him. I stayed with him for nearly an hour and a half. But, at the end of our conversation the Marshal seemed hardly to be following what I said. He assured me, however, that he was in agreement with all that I had done. Similarly, I explained once again our plans for advancing into Belgium. He approved of them. These coincided, moreover, with his own former ideas, as soon as the Belgians refused to call us in as a preventive measure, that is to say, when we could not support them on the Albert Canal. He added that M. Paul Reynaud had wanted to take him into his Cabinet, but he did not wish to enter it. He gave me the impression that he wished to *hold himself in reserve for a more stable Cabinet*. "In any case", he stated to me, "if I entered the Government, it would not be to create difficulties for you, but, quite on the contrary, to give you my support."'[1]

Why, now, did Pétain twist the facts in the version which he put abroad, unless it was for the purpose of giving the impression that I was the one making the request, when it was he who had just done so? His docile biographer, Laure, became his accomplice in this pious lie, when he wrote:[2] 'Having seen various people and because of the gravity of the situation, Pétain accepted the offer which was made to him, and

[1] Pétain, on entering my Government shortly after the disaster [in Belgium], was not only to refrain from speaking one word in justification of Gamelin but, several months later, he was to put him in prison.

[2] *Op. cit.*, p. 429.

left on May 9 for Madrid in order to settle some urgent matters before he returned for good.' The truth is merely that I was only to agree to the wish which Pétain expressed to me on the day after disaster.

According to Maître Payen in his pleadings at the Pétain trial,[1] I am alleged to have 'begged and supplicated' Pétain to join my Government. The assertion, we can see, contradicts the very account of Pétain's biographer since Pétain's acceptance was, according to the latter, after the 9th.

Pétain joined my Cabinet, therefore, on the 18th. I sent General Pujo to bring him from Madrid, because I wanted him to get to Paris before Weygand. I had, indeed, some scruples. I wondered if it were not risky to relieve Gamelin of his command at the height of the battle, although operations only came, in actual fact, directly under Georges' control. Neither Pétain nor, a little later, Weygand saw any danger in this. The latter has, moreover, stated at Pétain's trial[2] that he retained the orders issued by Gamelin.

Let us remember from the talks of Pétain with Monzie and Darlan that, on March 30 and May 5, Pétain was convinced the French Army was exposed to a grave and imminent danger. At the time, as we have seen, the second edition of Chauvineau's book appeared, still preceded by the preface in which Pétain stated that the French Army was certainly equal to repulsing an enemy offensive. It is known that this book was the Bible of front-line staffs. The Army could, therefore, sleep soundly on. Moreover, had not *Paris-Soir* on January 3 published as headlines this aphorism: 'We possess all the requisites for victory: Marshal Pétain'?

In the depths of his heart Pétain was convinced that the French Army was in deadly danger. Why did he delay in telling Gamelin, Georges, Billotte, Corap and Huntziger that, with the arms which it possessed, the Wehrmacht would descend on us like a thunderbolt, and why did he delay in counselling them to avoid, as though it were the plague, undertaking an advance into Belgium which would certainly lead us into disaster?

We are faced here with grave questions. Is it honestly possible to pass over them in silence?

From whom had Pétain learned that it would be in May that, contrary to the conviction which he himself had implanted in our Supreme Command, we would meet with disaster? Germany was then dominant in Spain, where the Gestapo held sway—the price for the assistance which the Wehrmacht had given Franco. Even though Pétain does not seem to have been on terms of intimacy with the Caudillo, Madrid was, nevertheless, a notorious centre for obtaining information. Numerous Spanish officers had been trained in Germany. The General

---

[1] Hearing of August 16, 1945.   [2] Hearing of July 31, 1945.

Staffs of the two countries maintained intimate relations. From an authoritative source I have learned that the rumour spread through Madrid in April that the Wehrmacht would not be long in taking the offensive. The number of divisions to take part was even given. It was added that the Wehrmacht counted on breaking our front in three successive offensives. We realize, today, that the Germans were surprised by the devastating character of their initial success.

As we know, Colonel Beigbeder was Minister of Foreign Affairs. We are aware that he was well informed about the strength of the German Army, and that he made no secret of the information which was available to him on this subject. Nothing proves this better than the evidence offered by M. Paul Guillemet. He writes: 'In March, 1940, I was in Madrid, and I thought it was incumbent on me to pay my respects to Don Juan (Beigbeder), whom I had known when he was High Commissioner at Tetuan. . . . During our talk . . . Beigbeder told me amongst other things: "*Amigo*, may I observe to you that we know exactly what is happening amongst your enemies, through our Embassy Staff in Germany? In particular, we are aware that the striking power of the German armoured divisions exceeds anything which you believe possible. They will break through your front like a thunderbolt on the day they are hurled into the attack. Don't forget what I have told you. I don't ask you to keep it secret." Then, going with me to the room where the civil and military attachés were, he said to me in a loud voice: "As the Minister of a neutral country I am and I must remain neutral, but, personally, I wish from the bottom of my heart for the success of your country."'

Is it possible to believe that Pétain, whose duties placed him in direct contact with this Minister, received a less liberal treatment, in being given confidential information of this type, than a passing visitor?

Pétain began intriguing as soon as he joined my Government. He tried, as we have seen, to get round Mandel. He might as well have saved his time. It was quite a different matter with Weygand. Talking to him at the time about the military situation, Pétain said to him:[1]

---

[1] I have got this information from Michel Clemenceau. He had it himself from Pétain's own lips. Michel Clemenceau, who inherited from his father a striking similarity in his appearance and an equally uncompromising patriotism as regards his character, came to see Mandel and myself in September, 1942, at Portalet. After his visit he went to Vichy to express to Pétain, then President of the *Amis de Georges Clemenceau*, his indignation at the treatment meted out to us. Pétain said: 'Come and dine with me this evening.'

'I must decline the invitation. I've just shared the fare of my two friends at Portalet. I don't partake of the hospitality of two camps.'

It was then that Pétain, embarrassed by this rebuff, confided to him what he had said to Weygand.

Michel Clemenceau, moreover, repeated the account, which he gave to me during our joint captivity in Germany, during the Pétain trial (hearing of July 28, 1945). In his deposition (hearing of July 31, 1945), Weygand denied that Pétain said the words in question to him.

'Fight on as long as you can. When you cannot do so any longer, come and warn me, and I will see that an armistice is concluded.' A military dictatorship was already in the offing. Chautemps was also in the secret. He whispered the word in Maître Ribet's ear that Pétain had only to give me a push in order to overthrow me, and how he would begin forthwith the series of successive liquidations, whereby he would get rid of those whom he seems, from that moment, to have decided to eliminate.

Pétain was, therefore, working against me in an underhand way. He knew, however, that France and Britain had entered into a pledge that neither would desert the other, or conclude a separate armistice, or, *a fortiori*, a peace treaty. Knowing my own policy, we have seen that he was careful not to offer the least objection to it when he joined my Cabinet. If, indeed, an armistice already appeared inevitable, was not then the time to think of asking for it? The Germans, indeed, had not yet crossed the Somme. Why wait until they had taken Paris and advanced beyond the Loire? If Pétain did not speak of an armistice in May, it was obviously not because he entertained any illusions about our chances of avoiding disaster. Was it not because he wished to seize power, and because, in order to succeed in overthrowing me, he needed the co-operation of my Ministry? In order to secure such co-operation, he had to wait until we were completely routed. He delayed, as we have seen, until June 13 before asking the Government to bring hostilities to an end.

PÉTAIN SEDUCES DARLAN

Darlan had not 'seized', he has told us, 'the significance' of the invitation extended to him on May 5. At the beginning of June he made no secret, as we are aware, of his determination to refuse his consent to any request for an armistice as far as the Fleet was concerned. If he were to persist in such an attitude he would make it practically impossible to carry out any plan for separating France from the coalition. That is why it was essential for Pétain to seduce Darlan. Pétain, who was Darlan's evil genius, just as he was Weygand's, was, therefore, to play for high stakes. Darlan was, later, frank enough to make a clean breast of it in his statements to Béraud. As Darlan had not understood the hints dropped to him at Maintenon, Pétain unmasked his guns. At Briare on June 11 he took Darlan in his car to the aerodrome where Churchill was arriving. What better time could there be for exchanging confidences than during a ride? Darlan tells us that Pétain 'spoke very frankly'. 'He confided to me how disgusted he was at the Government's incapacity . . . to come to any decision whatsoever.'

By broaching the subject in this way, Pétain was deliberately twisting the truth. Let us restate the facts. Pétain knew better than anyone, from having been present at the conferences which were held in my room, that as soon as the question of an armistice arose I replied, orally at the time, and then on May 29 in writing, that I would call up two classes of conscripts in order to continue the fight in North Africa. He knew that the call-up of recruits had already begun. He knew that the Navy had already begun to ship arms and munitions to Bizerta. And, on June 10, I had telegraphed Roosevelt: 'We shall fight in front of Paris. We shall fight behind Paris. We shall fortify ourselves in one of our provinces, and if we are chased from there, we shall go to North Africa, and, if need be, to our American possessions.'

Pétain said he was 'disgusted'. A few hours previously he had been telling General Serrigny[1] of 'the great esteem in which he held me for the fighting spirit which I was showing'.

In reality Pétain's design entailed surrender, and he knew that he could only achieve this end by contriving my downfall. Therefore, any means were good enough to overthrow me. First of all, a campaign of calumny was begun.

He set about this behind my back and at the same time ostensibly lavished on me demonstrations of friendship. On the evening of the same day at Briare he went to the trouble of finding me a place in which I could spend the night. All these manœuvres surely were far worse than the 'political intrigues' which the Vichy Press and radio were later to place at the door of the *ancien régime*.

Let us take up Darlan's account once more. Pétain said to him: 'What we want is a kind of Consulate. And if I were asked my opinion as to who should be the First Consul, I would designate you, my friend!'

Darlan rejected this extravagant offer with understandable astonishment. It is true that we had not yet come to the time when admirals and captains, commanders and even lieutenant-commanders, thought they were fitted by nature to fulfil any duties. Moreover, Darlan was, at the time, completely unknown to Frenchmen.

'That's a fine present which you wish to make me, Marshal. . . . But I am not in the least desirous of it.'

'Come, come,' replied the Marshal. 'I have given it serious consideration. You are the only one who has carried out your duties successfully. Therefore, you ought to take this on your shoulders' [*sic*].

The two men separated, Darlan in possession of this amazing promise, which Pétain had obviously not for a moment any intention of keeping.

[1] Cf. the deposition of General Serrigny at the Pétain trial (hearing of August 2, 1945). Cited by Pétain's counsel as a witness for the defence, General Serrigny, former Chief of Staff to Pétain, had been one of the chosen collaborators of the latter. So close had he been, that Laure, retracing the military operations of 1915, calls him from that time the 'indispensable confidant', the 'favourite of the master' (*op. cit.*, pp. 52–3).

Now to start with, there was no mention of Darlan in *C'est Pétain qu'il nous faut!* On March 30, Pétain had said to Monzie: '*They* will have need of me in the second fortnight of May.' It was *of me*, not of Darlan. But Darlan was an obstacle in his path. This obstacle had to be removed. In other words, Darlan had to be won over. Pétain had certainly given the matter 'serious reflection', but it was not about Darlan that he was thinking; it was about himself.

This time Darlan did grasp the situation. His determination not to abandon the fight, and to 'take to sea', to perform an 'act of glorious indiscipline', suddenly vanished. Shortly after the entry of the Italian Fleet into the war, he decided to desert his companions in arms, the British sailors! The office of First Consul was well worth a mass!

Thus, Darlan, the man whose outstanding ability Churchill stresses on several occasions in his memoirs; whose 'remarkable' competence and 'continuance' in command, he writes, had given France a fleet 'of considerable strength and value', a fleet, in brief, whose 'strength had been unequalled since the days of the *ancien régime*', and whose 'support' was so vital to Britain; Darlan, the man whose vitality Churchill is pleased to recognize, and to stress that the Navy 'hailed in him its leader and its renovator', was preparing on June 10 to tarnish his fame by giving our squadrons, then at the height of their power, the order to withdraw from the battle! To the scrap heap with the *Richelieu*, *Jean-Bart*, *Strasbourg* and *Dunkerque*!

We can understand, now, why Darlan was to tell me in an embarrassed way on June 15 that he could not carry out all the transportation which I asked of him, and why, on the same day, he was to state to Jules Moch, who was dumbfounded at this change of tune: 'There is complete disorder! We are paying for the faults of the past twenty years. We must conclude an armistice.'

'The faults of the past twenty years': these were the very words which he also used to Béraud. During these 'twenty years' he had been closely linked with the action of the Ministers who had succeeded each other at the Rue Royale, and whose intimate collaborator he had been. But on June 11 it was solely a question of securing power. To attain it, a stepping-stone was necessary; this was to be defeat. On the 16th, Darlan was to become Minister of Marine under the orders of Weygand, who himself was to become Minister of National Defence.[1]

---

[1] In *Episodes* (p. 75) Herriot relates that, on June 16, when he was leaving the President of the Republic, he saw a number of people grouped together in the waiting-room. 'They were', he writes, 'obviously Ministers waiting to be presented. Admiral Darlan was amongst them, not in full dress. Remembering our conversation of the previous day, I went to him with outstretched hands, and said: "Well, Admiral, you are preparing the departure of the Government." "No," he replied. "A Government which departs never returns." This Admiral knew how to swim.'

In his memoirs Churchill mentions another fact which enlightened him also as to

Such an office was far from being the position which Pétain had dangled before Darlan's eyes. No doubt the two men had come to some agreement about the stages to be arranged. In any case, there could be no question of Pétain's effacing himself. The role of First Consul was one which he certainly counted on arrogating to himself, though he had to give Darlan hope that he would be his successor. Events at Vichy certainly marched step by step towards this end.

We have important evidence on the vicissitudes which marked Darlan's change of attitude. It was sent to me by Captain Pinguet, and concerns words spoken on June 22, 23 and 24 by Darlan to Commander Blanquet du Chayla, a member of his staff. Captain Pinguet asserts that these words were communicated to him by his friend Bordenave, Chief Commissioner of the Navy. The latter himself 'heard them directly from Commander Blanquet du Chayla'. Here is the evidence: 'This is the end of the exodus. The Government is in Bordeaux. The Americans have followed the Government. They will be ready in three or four years. They will never abandon us. But today they can do nothing. The war is inevitably lost.

'It was the intention of the Government to send all our warships to the United States. This decision was taken on June 22. It had still to be put into effect on the 23rd. By the 24th, time was pressing. Commander Blanquet du Chayla of Darlan's staff came to him to ask for orders to carry out the decision.

'"It is no longer a question of doing that," Darlan told him. "Everything has been altered. I am on the road to becoming one of the Consulate."

'The Americans did not understand this shocking statement. But they realized that it implied a change of policy. After a delay of a day or two, they warned the British of this. And, on July 3, came Mers-el-Kébir.'

What does this show but that Darlan, fobbed off by Pétain, was trying to force his hand? He was threatening to give the Fleet the order to weigh anchor. Pétain could see his plans tumbling to the ground. He came to terms. He would keep the most important position, but he promised the next important to Darlan, who accepted the alternative. On the next day, June 25, he entrusted to Laval this post which he had just promised Darlan. The latter, duped for a second time, was caught in his own trap, for it was now too late to begin intriguing all over again. During the night the Armistice came into force.

Darlan was to meet with another disappointment. On July 10 he was demoted to the rank of Secretary of State, and thus deprived of

Darlan's change of attitude. During the morning of the 17th he stated to Georges that he had made up his mind to order the Fleet to sail. In the afternoon of the same day he told him he had changed his mind. To his companion, who was astonished and pressed for further details, he merely replied: 'I am now Minister of Marine.'

access to the Council of Ministers. In order to achieve his ends he had, henceforth, to wait until Pétain had succeeded in shaking off Laval. We realize, now, that the two men applied themselves wholeheartedly to this task.

In any case, on June 11, Pétain triumphed covertly. He had seduced Darlan. At Bordeaux, his biographer tells us,[1] he waged 'a desperate battle against those who wished to prolong an impossible resistance'. He won this battle. In his communiqué of June 17 he asserted that my Government had asked him to take over power. But he neglected to suppress the publication of a semi-official account according to which, whilst I was conferring on the 16th with the President of the Republic and with the Presidents of the Senate and the Chamber, the Ministers in the neighbouring room were wondering if I was not going to be entrusted with forming a new Government, whose duty would be to continue the struggle. Such is the difficulty which those who twist the truth have in not contradicting themselves!

WHAT WAS WEYGAND'S MOTIVE?

Let us now consider Weygand. We have seen him back up Pétain in his manœuvres. 'If he did so', said his numerous admirers in emulation of each other, 'it was because he was convinced that all hope was lost, and that Britain herself was also going to succumb. He said at Tours and Bordeaux in his customary colourful phrasing: "Before three weeks are out, Britain will have her neck wrung like a chicken." He repeated this at Vichy. Numerous people heard him. He was honestly mistaken. Was not this, moreover, the unanimous opinion of the Supreme Command? As for his patriotism, his hatred of Germany, which was well known, offered the best surety for this. Weygand was a patriot who took the wrong path. Moreover, he belonged to that caste in whose opinion service as a soldier was the only possible career under a republican régime. He felt an instinctive aversion for a system which was essentially anti-clerical, and which he judged to be antagonistic towards a social hierarchy. After all, he was at perfect liberty to do so. But, he never meddled with politics. Did he not state at Pétain's trial:[2] "I defy anyone to discover any political action in my career."?'

Did Weygand really believe that Britain was about to succumb? At the time he did say so, and repeated his belief, although in various ways. First of all he expressed the opinion before the Armistice in the famous phrase: 'Before three weeks are out . . .' To Hervé Nader, Deputy for Finistère, who went to see him before the Armistice at Bordeaux in order to tell him that the Breton population was determined to resist and was awaiting 'directives for the struggle to be undertaken', he

---

[1] Laure, *op. cit.*, p. 434.   [2] Hearing of July 31, 1945.

replied: 'You are deceiving yourselves. You have no idea of Germany's strength. Her Armies will be in London within several weeks.' To Jean Borotra, who also went to see him at Bordeaux to inform him of his intention to reach England in order to go on fighting, he answered: 'It is useless. Before two months are out, Britain will have surrendered.' To an industrialist who told him, at the beginning of July, in Vichy, that he meant to begin making gas generators, he answered: 'I can guarantee to you that Britain will have asked for peace within a fortnight.'

Yet Weygand in his evidence at the Pétain trial denied that he believed, and much less said, that Britain was going to be defeated. When the President of the High Court said to him:[1] 'You are said to have uttered . . . a picturesque . . . phrase: "Britain will have her neck wrung like a chicken"', he answered: 'I formally deny having used these words. I have never uttered such words. If I had believed in final defeat, would I have asked for the Fleet[2] to be sent away so that it would not fall into the hands of the Germans? Do not all my actions belie the words which are attributed to me? No, I ask for evidence to be sought from people connected with me in order to discover what I was thinking.' He would only admit that he did not affirm a British victory to be certain. He added that he said to Laval when he was on the point of leaving Vichy on November 12, 1942: 'You have backed the wrong horse because Germany is beaten.' Again at the same hearing he stated: 'An Armistice (is) a kind of vigil of arms. . . . Fighting stops for a time. Why? In order to allow preparation for the future.'

There exists, therefore, a flagrant contradiction between the items of evidence which I have reported and Weygand's deposition. Let us examine the facts more closely.

Gamelin has described an interview between himself and Weygand which took place on May 20 at Vincennes in *Servir*:[3] 'General Weygand arrived punctually at nine o'clock. We closeted ourselves alone in my room. . . . The General seemed confident. I said to him: "I believe the execution of the order I have given is the only solution which can save the situation." . . . He answered me . . . "But I possess the secrets of Foch!" . . . Obviously he thought that he could succeed. Such faith did him credit for, if he thought the situation was lost, he would not have agreed to take it in hand. If he had, it would have been a grave matter, for what good could he have done?'

[1] Hearing of July 31, 1945.
[2] Weygand asserted during the Pétain trial (hearing of July 31, 1945) that he put forward this demand to the Government at the second meeting of the Council at Cangé. I cannot recollect this, nor can any of the Ministers there. But it was one above all to which a Government that had resolved to continue fighting could not consent. It is obvious, in any case, that the Fleet, if it continued to fight, would in no wise run the risk of falling into the hands of the enemy.
[3] pp. 435-6.

The two men then exchanged opinions on the military situation. But Weygand did not stop at that. Let us see again what Gamelin has to say: 'The conversation digressed . . . on to internal problems. . . . On this matter he remained intransigent: "We have got to change all this political business. We must get rid of all these politicians. They are, into the bargain, all as bad as each other." I was deeply shocked that he could think about questions of this kind at such a time as that, when soldiers should, more than ever, have been filled with other cares. General Weygand had certainly remained what one would call the "born enemy" of republican conceptions.'

What can this mean but that Weygand thought that he had at last found the opportunity and the means of overthrowing our republican institutions? Certainly, he would have preferred this opportunity and these means to be given him through victory. But, failing this, would not defeat do instead?

As our reverses became more serious, Weygand was emboldened. We know what kind of talk he was indulging in on May 26 to his visitors, and to Rollin in particular. It is instructive to take up the latter's account again:

'May 28, Sunday.

'At 11 p.m. I went to see General Weygand at his G.H.Q. . . . He greeted me cordially. He said to me . . . "Why was I not called in sooner?" I answered: "You know that Paul Reynaud earnestly wished to replace Gamelin by you, and that, to accomplish this against the opposition of Daladier, he had to stake his premiership and precipitate a ministerial crisis." "I am aware of that," he said to me. And, as I was stressing the absence of forethought and the inefficiency which characterized the preparation and the conduct of the war, he added: "Nothing has been done for these last eight months." Then he said to me: "Since yesterday I have thought a lot. I think that the Government should not, in any case, leave metropolitan territory." I believe that it was in his mind that the Government should stay on the spot in Paris, and await the enemy there unflinchingly.'

The reader knows the rest. Weygand recalled the famous scene which so vividly illustrates the majesty of the Senate; the conscript fathers, seated in their curule chairs, awaiting the arrival of the barbarians; the irruption of the latter into the curia; the massacre. Thereupon, 'General Vuillemin was announced', notes Rollin, and adds: 'I withdrew, and General Weygand politely begged leave not to see me to the door.'

Rollin told me, following my return from Germany, that Weygand, during this conversation, indulged in violent attacks against the régime, whose faults, according to him, were the root cause of our defeat, and whose overthrow he predicted. The country would find in this, he asserted, some compensation for its misfortune.[1]

For Weygand 'compensation' meant, as we have seen, settling his account with the 'riff-raff'. The duty of the Government, he asserted, was to stay in Paris, that is, it should *deliver itself up to the enemy*, and, at the same time, surrender the régime to Hitler. The latter certainly did not hope for such good fortune, not by any means! He obviously would not deny himself the pleasure of such a magnificent haul. But would he have been the only one to rub his hands with pleasure?

WEYGAND THROWS REIBEL INTO ACTION

Let us deal now with the question of the Armistice, in which Weygand played, as we have seen, a decisive role. We have some important evidence about this role; that of Weygand's friend, Reibel, who, as we know, revealed it in *Pourquoi et comment fut decidée la demande d'armistice*. In this book the author relates with a fidelity which leaves no room for any doubt the confidences with which Weygand entrusted him during the days of June 14, 15 and 16.

Reibel says that he was frightened when he heard me announce in my radio speech of June 13 the Government's intention to leave France. He went on the next day to the Château du Muguet, where we know that Weygand had taken up his quarters. On greeting him, the orderly officer of the Supreme Commander told him that 'for more than a week, he [Weygand] had been insisting as strongly as he could to the Government that they should ask for an armistice'. Moreover, all the Generals, Georges as well as Besson, Huntziger as well as Prételat, thought that it was high time to put an end to a struggle which contained no more hope.

Going straight to the heart of the matter, Weygand addressed Reibel in these words: 'I wanted to see you. After this frugal lunch, I shall tell you everything and support it by documents.' At table he 'launched a few cutting criticisms upon the obstinacy of the Government which was refusing to ask for an armistice'. Subsequently Weygand explained in a neighbouring room that the British withdrawal at Arras lay at the root of our defeat. Then he read to Reibel the two memoranda which he had sent me, the first on May 7 and the second on June 10.

Continuing this diatribe, Weygand described the Ministers to Reibel as insensible to the sufferings of the Army, and yet, on June 12, we know that, in agreement with Pétain, he rejected my suggestion that we should evacuate part of that Army into Switzerland. 'You wish', he said, 'to fight on to the end? You have come to the end.' On the

[1] Tony Révillon was aware at the time of this episode. He has chronicled it in *Mes carnets* (p. 16).

13th, Weygand is supposed to have exclaimed[1] on leaving the Second Council at Cangé: 'They are mad; they don't understand anything. They should be arrested!'

And what is said about continuing the war in North Africa? 'General Weygand demonstrated in vain the foolishness of such a plan; an air force cannot reconquer a country; it can only finish off its destruction.' Always decisive in his prophecies, he stated that it was unlikely that 'the Anglo-American Air Force could in several years become more powerful than the German'.

Weygand added: 'And then—above all—what will become of France and Frenchmen? Will the latter agree to such a desertion? . . . Ought we not to anticipate that, amidst ruin, misery and death, with our Army completely destroyed, small local governments will be formed as though by some process of a general sovietization?'

There we have it! In these tragic days, Weygand, obsessed by a fear of domestic chaos, discarded any idea of liberating France, the only consideration which was obsessing me.

Weygand threw Reibel into action: 'Bring home to the President of the Republic, to the Ministers, that this state of affairs cannot go on without the country running the gravest dangers.'

There was no question about myself in these words. And for a very good reason: Weygand knew that he would only be wasting his time in trying to win me over to the idea of an armistice. The aim to be achieved, therefore, was to secure the defection of a majority of the Ministry so that I should be driven into resignation and the President forced to entrust power to Pétain. In this arrangement everyone was playing his part: Pétain had just seduced Darlan; it was now up to Reibel to try his hand with M. Lebrun and the Ministers. 'And above all, Mr. Minister, act quickly, very quickly,' cried a general in Reibel's ears as he was moving off.

As soon as he got to Bordeaux, Reibel set to work. 'I buttonholed the Ministers at the end of meetings, and I tried to convince them, in turn, of the need for an armistice.' After persuasion came threats.

On the 16th, after the last meeting of the Council of Ministers, he attacked Campinchi and Rollin. We have two unimpeachable witnesses on this score: M. Matteo Connet and Rollin.

In his deposition of January 12, 1950, M. Matteo Connet stated to the Committee of Inquiry:

'At the end [of the second meeting of the Council of Ministers on June 16] two distinct groups emerged . . . those behind Paul Reynaud [Mandel, Campinchi, Louis Marin, Queuille, Rio, etc.], and those

---

[1] These words were uttered in the presence of Max Brusset, head of Mandel's secretariat. I quoted them at the hearing of Pétain's trial (August 1, 1945). Weygand interrupted me to say that he was *not at all* in agreement with Max Brusset.

behind Chautemps. Amongst these latter were numbered those who, for a long time, had made up their minds to follow Chautemps. Then, there were others who, during the course of the day, had perhaps allowed themselves to be enticed by this magic word. At that moment, Campinchi said to me: "Matteo, come along with me. We are going to walk." Chautemps remarked to him: "Campinchi, are you mad or thoughtless? Don't you realize that you are the most unpopular amongst us! Take care of yourself. Come in a car." . . . As we went out into the street, we found M. Charles Reibel at the door. I can still visualize the scene. Campinchi, myself beside him, and M. Louis Rollin . . . Charles Reibel, whom I had seen walking for a long time in the garden with General Weygand a short while before, approached Campinchi and said: "I was waiting for you. I have just been talking with Weygand. You are the most dangerous Minister. You want to leave for North Africa and carry on the war. We should get rid of you!" Campinchi answered: "I am not accountable to you for my actions, and I warn you that no one proffers such threats to me twice."'

Here is Rollin's account, January 20, 1949, before the Committee of Inquiry, of this shameful episode:

'I was leaving the house of the President of the Republic with Campinchi when we ran into M. Reibel who was waiting at the door; foaming at the mouth and with his eyes staring, he said to us, "You are a miserable lot and I've come to kill you. You will not leave Bordeaux. Do not imagine that you will leave Bordeaux. I have come to kill you."

'We shrugged our shoulders. We wondered if we were not in the presence of a man who had lost his reason, and went on our way.'[1]

Then Reibel went to Mr. Lebrun, who exclaimed: 'Could there be a more tragic hour than that when our military leaders refuse to fight?' The words are not literally those which M. Lebrun was later to tell me that he had uttered. He was to assure me that he said: 'It is a curious situation. In the Council it is the military men, Pétain and Weygand, who wish to stop the war, and the civilians, Paul Reynaud, Louis Marin and Mandel, who wish to go on with it.'

Weygand did not long enjoy the advantages which his struggle for an armistice earned him. Pétain, when reshuffling his Ministry on September 6, 1940, sacrificed him to Laval, and gave him the same

---

[1] Taking up, in *France-Soir* (February 4, 1950), certain allegations put forward by Weygand in his memoirs, I had made allusion to the activities of Reibel on June 15 and 16, 1940, and particularly to his threats against Campinchi and Rollin.

In reply to this indictment published by this paper on February 10, 1950, M. Charles Reibel again took up the defence of the cause which was dear to him, that of an armistice, but he did not, either contradict the facts or the remark cited by myself. Such silence was an implicit confirmation both of the former and the latter.

treatment as the parliamentarians, whom he had resolved to remove.
It is true that at the same time he entrusted him with the general delegation which he set up in North Africa and the post of Commander-in-
Chief. There, Weygand had the chance of coming back into the
struggle at the side of Britain. He deliberately refused to seize this
opportunity.

First, as we shall see, Catroux in agreement with Eden twice offered
him the chance in November, 1940. It was useless.

Then Churchill himself, as he writes in his memoirs, tried to give
Vichy the opportunity of 'profiting from the favourable turn of events'.
In November, 1940, he sent to Pétain through the intermediary of the
Canadian Chargé d'Affaires at Vichy a message in which he stated that
he was ready, should Vichy agree to re-enter the war, to send an expeditionary corps into Africa, whose strength would amount to six
divisions. Pétain left the offer unanswered.

This silence impelled Churchill in January, 1941, to turn once more
to Weygand, to whom he personally addressed the same message.
Entrusted with the delivery of the communication, the British Consul-
General at Tangier resorted to the intermediary of his French colleague,
M. de Castellane.[1] The latter urgently sent Captain de Lesparda, French
Military Attaché at Tangier, to Algiers. This officer handed the message
to Weygand himself. And did Weygand seize this godsend with both
hands? Not at all. He confined himself to acknowledging its receipt
through the same channel, but also hastened to send it on to Pétain.[2]

The matter did not rest there. Flandin, who was then Minister of
Foreign Affairs, took umbrage against M. de Castellane, for not having
refused to receive the British Consul-General. He immediately recalled
and dismissed him. Such severity is not even excused by a desire to
avoid offending Ribbentrop, since Berlin had not the slightest knowledge of the affair. What is more, this disgracing of M. de Castellane
deprived France of the services of a valuable diplomat. At Tangier,
where, since our defeat we had been hard pressed in defending our
rights against the covetousness of Spain, he had stood up to the
intrigues of this Power and showed the metal of which he was made.

How can such harsh treatment be explained? Perhaps Flandin wished
to vie in a display of zeal with Weygand, whom Pétain had preferred
to himself as head of the General Delegation in Africa. Indeed, it seems
to have been Flandin who was the author of the extraordinary pro-
consulate institution, which as Baudouin tells us[3] he canvassed for
himself:

[1] M. de Castellane had for a long time been a member of our Embassy in London.
During this period of service he had won the esteem of British circles.
[2] Cf. *Rappelé au service*, pp. 470–9. Churchill's letter is dated January 17, 1941. Weygand
states that he received it on the 20th.
[3] *Op. cit.*, pp. 164–5.

'Thursday, July 11, 1940.

'I had an interview with Pierre Etienne Flandin. . . . He told me that he was entirely at the disposal of the Marshal, but that did not mean that he expected to be in the ministry, but he would be glad to be of service to the Government. His ambition was an important position in North Africa as a delegate-general of the Government in the three countries.'[1]

But let us get back to Weygand. His contemptible attack against me will not prevent me from putting down to his credit his meritorious attitude in certain respects towards Vichy. One must, indeed, do him this justice, that he faced up courageously both to Laval and Darlan, and that finally he was deported by the enemy for having advised Pétain to protest vigorously against the Wehrmacht's occupation of our southern zone.

JULY 10, 1940: PÉTAIN OVERTHROWS THE REPUBLIC

Pétain summoned the National Assembly to Vichy on July 10, 1940, in order to obtain full powers from it with a view to reforming the Constitution which had governed France since 1875.

'Modify our Constitution? Perhaps, but it will be when you are gone', the Netherlands Prime Minister, M. Colijn, proudly answered the Germans. Pétain did not bother about this kind of consideration, and, under the cunning eye of the enemy, indictments were uttered in Vichy against this Republic which had given Alsace-Lorraine back to France and built up the second largest colonial empire in the world for our country, but which had erred, as we know, in accepting as gospel truth the doctrine of our 'glorious military leaders'.

Although grievously ill and in spite of the express ban of my doctor, I went to Vichy to attend the preliminary sitting of the Chamber, for I meant to be there in case Laval or any others attacked me.[2] On arriving I went to see Herriot, who said to me: 'Flandin, Candace (Vice-President of the Chamber) and Mistler (President of the Chamber's

[1] i.e. Algeria, Tunisia and Morocco which formed the French possessions in North Africa [Tr.].

[2] As I was not attacked during this preliminary sitting, there was no reason for me to prolong a stay against which my doctor had so strongly advised me. I, therefore, left Vichy without waiting for the meeting of the National Assembly, at which I had nothing to contribute. As I was not present at the debate, I was, in actual fact, placed amongst the thirty 'absent by leave', who were so designated by the *Journal Officiel*. Weygand has, therefore, perverted the truth when stating at the Pétain trial (hearing of August 1, 1945): 'He did not even dare to vote. He abstained.'

The question of the circumstances in which I left Vichy was raised at the Pétain trial (hearing of July 24, 1945) by the defence. It was put thus by one of the jurors:

A Juror: 'I am unable to appear as a witness but I should like to ask M. Paul Reynaud a question. Before lunch, did he not seek out M. Vincent Auriol (I cannot remember at which hotel) and say to him, "I cannot last out any longer. I must go. Please excuse me"?'

I answered this query in the affirmative.

Foreign Affairs Committee) have approached Lebrun with the object of getting him to resign. This has probably taken place by now.' I quickly left Herriot and went to the Sévigné Pavilion. I pointed out to M. Lebrun that his resignation would make it appear that the republican régime was being liquidated, and that it was important that the President of the Republic should only retire as a result of a constitutional act of Pétain's, which expelled him from his post. M. Lebrun remained silent. On seeing me off, he said sadly, in allusion to the visit of the British sovereigns to Paris: 'Do you remember that charming little queen a year ago!' And he added the regrets which I have already mentioned about my resignation.

M. Lebrun, who told me afterwards that he never thought of resigning, wrote in *Témoignage*[1] about this approach to him by Flandin, Candace and Mistler, in the name, as they alleged, of a group of parliamentarians, as follows: 'I certainly did not expect such a proposal from them. If I had given way to my first impulse, I would have vigorously rejected it. As I was very determined to keep calm in the most critical situations, I entered into discussion. . . .

'They told me that my voluntary resignation would be the more honourable course for me. They added that my effacement would be a very useful action in the present tragic situation, and might have very propitious results. It was essential to avoid any source of resistance or disturbance. They brought my attention discreetly but unmistakably to the division which had been hastily re-formed at Clermont-Ferrand, and which was defiling at intervals in the distance across the Place de Jaude amidst the demonstrations of the people.

'So we had come to this state of affairs. It gave some idea of the disturbance in people's minds in this unhealthy atmosphere of Vichy. A former President of the Council, a Vice-President (or former Vice-President) of the Chamber of Deputies, the President of one of the Chamber's important committees, were putting pressure on the Head of the State to induce him to desert his post. . . .

'I learned, moreover, on the following day, through a friend who was a deputy, that these three individuals had not been entrusted with the mission which they said they had to discharge.'

Bergery read a declaration in the National Assembly signed by himself, Déat, Montigny, Scapini, Vallat, etc., in which we find the following: 'On the day following our military defeat, two foreign policies became once more conceivable:

'The Reynaud policy of relying on Britain in the hope that the latter, with or without the help of the United States, would manage, not, of course, to reconquer continental Europe, but to obtain through naval and air action, a negotiated peace.

[1] p. 105.

'The alternative policy, that of Marshal Pétain, which entailed a degree of collaboration with the Latin Powers and with Germany herself and the establishment of a continental "new order".

'It is possible to argue about these two policies.

'As supporters of the second, we do not consider the supporters of the first *ipso facto* as lacking in feeling or as traitors to our native land.'

Pétain was asking for full powers to reform the Constitution, but he was not giving the slightest intimation as to how he intended to do this. He told the Assembly through Laval who was his spokesman that the new Constitution would be ratified. But by whom? Not by universal suffrage, because that would be a plebiscite, Laval replied to one question. Not by the present Parliament, oh no, he said in response to a question from Bergery. Well, then, by whom? No doubt by those caricatures of Councils which he intended to create and to pack with his tools. The Assembly was obviously averse from thus pledging itself in the dark. It was then, in order to rally the waverers, that Laval, I am told, discreetly made use of an argument which proved to be decisive. Knowing that Pétain had the reputation in parliamentary circles for being a man of the Left, he wielded the threat, which, after all, he may have believed in himself, of a Weygand setting up a dictatorship of the Right by armed force. How was it possible under such conditions not to hasten to grant Pétain full powers and thus to bar the way to seizure of power by a faction?

So emerged the New Order, on which it is not wholesome to dwell. One would prefer to go no further than the definition that M. du Moulin de la Barthète has, and not without humour, uttered:[1] 'white terror, black market, rose-coloured reading'.

[1] *Le temps des illusions: souvenirs* (*juillet 1940–avril 1942*), p. 189.

CHAPTER XXI

SHALL REYNAUD AND MANDEL BE SHOT?

Eight Items of Evidence.—May 8, 1941, Abetz offers my head and that of Mandel to Ribbentrop.—May 30, 1944, Hitler decides to hand over Blum, Mandel and myself to Vichy with the order to have us assassinated.—July 7, 1944, The assassination of Mandel.

EIGHT ITEMS OF EVIDENCE

A MAN who took before, during and after the war, such a decided attitude as I did, was inevitably bound to make a host of enemies. According to some people, I had been a Machiavelli who only appealed to Pétain and Weygand with the secret intention of throwing the responsibility for a disaster which I saw to be inevitable on our 'two glorious military leaders'. Thus, I was one of those whom Major Loustaunau-Lacau indicted at Pétain's trial when he denounced the people who tried to 'shuffle the blame for their errors on to an old man who was almost a centenarian'.

As for 'handing over to Pétain', the reader knows the true story about this. Pétain himself remained silent at his trial, but one of his defenders, Bâtonnier Payen, in his pleadings (hearing of August 13, 1945) reproached Daladier and myself and *above all*, he stressed, Louis Marin, for having made our confessions on the breast of his client. And then he added: 'Here, therefore, was M. Paul Reynaud who was proposing to appeal to the Marshal. Here were M. Herriot and M. Jeanneney who were stating: "We have no objections."'

Thus Presidents Jeanneney and Herriot were alleged to be accomplices of a crime which I had myself instigated.

But two years after his trial Pétain changed his mind. He did not wish to be left behind in the campaign which portrayed him as the victim of my Machiavellian behaviour. Suddenly abandoning his silence, he stated on July 10, 1947, to the Committee of Inquiry during his deposition: 'It was Paul Reynaud who had me nominated in his place, because he did not wish to ask for an armistice for France on account of her Fleet. He named me because he wished to pin on me the responsibility for the action.'

Let us pass over this reference to the Fleet. As for Pétain's being made a victim, we know on the contrary with what eagerness he aspired to power and with what cunning he manœuvred in order to seize hold of it.

Eight items of evidence, some of which, as we shall see, come from my opponents themselves, will enlighten the reader.

President Jeanneney said about my attitude on June 15:

'He emphasized to us at that time his steadfast determination not to give up the struggle.'

President Herriot remarked about June 16:

'He was waging an open struggle against the Marshal and against General Weygand.'

General de Gaulle, head of the Provisional Government issued the following statement on June 25, 1945:[1]

'A newspaper has recently published an article mentioning conversations, in which General de Gaulle is supposed to have taken part in 1943, concerning the last days of the Government of which he was a member in 1940. It is believed that this article was published without the President of the Government being told about it, and that it contains certain inexact statements.

'It will be recalled, on the other hand, that though General de Gaulle never did cease, as is well known, to advocate within the Paul Reynaud Administration that the struggle should be continued in North Africa, he himself expressed his opinions about the former President of the Council in a letter published in the periodical *France Libre* of February, 1943. In this he stated: "The only thing which I wish to say about this subject is that I have retained completely my respectful esteem for the man who was in this drama my leader and my friend, President Paul Reynaud. If he was at last submerged by the tide, this courageous and clear-minded man did not for one moment, and to this I can bear witness, cease to work and act on behalf of France's honour and interest."'

President Roosevelt wrote me on June 19, 1940:

'The American people will never forget the brilliant, courageous and useful resistance which you have directed in the name of France at the head of your Government.'

Winston Churchill said in the Commons on June 25, 1940:

'M. Reynaud, the courageous Prime Minister, after all, was the fighting spirit. . . .'[2]

[1] Official communiqué of June 26, 1945, to the *Agence française de presse*.
[2] *The Parliamentary Debates*, House of Commons, June 18 to July 11, 1940, Fifth Series, vol. 362, col. 303.

M. Paul Henri Spaak, then Belgian Minister of Foreign Affairs, remarked during a debate on July 25, 1945, in the Chamber of Representatives about the events of May to June 1940:

'The problem of knowing what the Belgian Government should do if France ceased to fight had to be considered by the Ministers on June 14 or 15, 1940. . . . General Denis and myself were convinced (from the statements of Reynaud, Campinchi, Mandel) that France would not surrender.'

General Weygand, General Delegate of the French Government and Commander-in-Chief in French Africa, said on October 29, 1940:[1]

'The Government of M. Paul Reynaud never consented to ask for an armistice. M. Paul Reynaud intended to retreat into the "Breton Redoubt" and to continue the struggle with the remaining forces at our disposal. . . . The other plan of M. Paul Reynaud was, failing the possibility of fighting on in France, to continue the war in the Empire, in North Africa and even in Central Africa.'

Marshal Pétain, Vice-President of the Council of Ministers, is reported as saying.[2]

'On June 11 . . . in the car which was taking us . . . he [Pétain] told me of the great respect in which he held his President of the Council, because of the fighting spirit which he was showing.'

And it is written about Pétain when he was Head of the State:[3]

'The very memory of the struggles, which set him in opposition to Paul Reynaud on the eve of the Armistice, made him more severe towards the clique of war-mongers, to "those who wished to fight to the end without guns", as he used to say, and who were headed in his opinion by Paul Reynaud and Mandel.'

As for Hitler, one of the best-informed men about my activities, he considered the creation of my Administration in March, 1940, so severe a blow to his plans that we see him in 1944 giving consideration to certain French people who tried to stop me at the former period from coming into power. And what did he think about my later attitude? He was to resolve, as we shall see later, to have me assassinated.

MAY 8, 1941: ABETZ OFFERS MY HEAD AND THAT OF MANDEL TO RIBBENTROP

I owe Hitler and his acolytes this justice that they did nothing to hide the feelings which they felt towards me. Every rumour which reached

[1] In his lecture at Dakar to officers of the Army, Navy and Air Force, then in garrison at that place.

[2] Through the words of General Serrigny at the Pétain trial (loc. cit.).

[3] From the pen of M. du Moulin de la Barthète (loc. cit.).

me in my prisons brought me proof of the fact that they wished to see me come to a violent end. I shall later cite some items of evidence in support of this. For the time being, I shall confine myself to that of Abetz, who, he himself stated, would not be able to get over having had to deny himself the pleasure of 'strangling me with his own hands'.

I was, therefore, permitted to labour under no illusion. However, if I was instructed about the fate which the Führer and his henchmen intended to reserve for me, I was, nevertheless, ignorant of the plots which some or other of them were weaving to get rid of my person. Documents discovered in the Chancellery of the Reich by the Allies have, a short time ago, put me in a position to fill in this gap retrospectively. These documents show that Abetz stood out by his determination and perseverance in this sinister task. Indeed, he neglected no opportunity to stir up the rancour which he, better than any other, knew Hitler cherished for me. He did not even shrink from using lies.

It was on March 8, 1941, that Abetz initiated his campaign by offering the Führer, through the channel of Ribbentrop, the heads of Mandel and myself. For Abetz pursued us both with one and the same hatred, because he wished, so he wrote, that Germany should 'through the persons of these two Frenchmen' strike at one blow 'two of the principals responsible for the war'. He told Ribbentrop this frankly in his message of March 8, 1941. He had not the courage to remain faithful to such frankness when the French military courts asked him to answer for his actions in July, 1949.

For a Hitler who was haunted by his own responsibility and was anxious like every criminal to lay a false scent, could there be a more convincing argument than that which Abetz took up against us? But would it not be still better to charge these two 'war-mongers' with every possible sin, and above all to make them seem so completely deprived of scruples as to have taken steps which exposed certain of their fellow countrymen to suffer the fate reserved by the rules of war for *franc-tireurs*? The affair of the territorial guards was to furnish Abetz with a pretext.

It is only necessary to hark back to the tragic days of May, 1940, in order to recall immediately the action of the German parachutists, sowing confusion in the rear of the Allied Armies and terrorizing the civil population. At the outset of operations we saw them in the Netherlands, Belgium and Luxembourg, wearing in defiance of the laws and customs of war, Dutch or Belgian uniform and even non-military clothing of the most unusual type. One of them, disguised as a Sister of Mercy, hid his sub-machine-gun within the folds of the robe in which he was garbed. I had already been briefed about these illegal ruses at first hand by Prince Bernhard of the Netherlands, who, passing through Paris at the time, had come to describe the invasion of his adopted country to me.

The laws and customs of war impose, as is known, the wearing of national uniform as one of the conditions which a combatant must fulfil in order to possess the right of having the status of a belligerent. The wearing of any other uniform, whether it is a question of the uniform of enemy troops or of civilian attire, is, then, incompatible with this status. As a result any combatant who breaks this rule is defined as a *franc-tireur*, and must expect to be treated as such when he is captured bearing arms, whatever be the channel (infiltration through the lines, landing on airports by parachute, etc.) which he has employed to reach the place at which he is captured.

Bound like France by these international regulations which govern the conduct of hostilities, Germany was in no wise ignorant of the fate to which the Wehrmacht exposed the men whom it entrusted with missions to be carried out under these conditions. Our armed forces were in any case justified in taking appropriate measures. However, despite the fact that nothing forced us to state publicly beforehand our intentions of exercising this right, I wished, on humanitarian grounds, to warn the enemy Command in good time of the instructions that we had given to this effect. Such was the object of an official communiqué that the Presidency of the Council published on May 13, and of which this is the text:

'During the ruthless attack which they have just launched against the Netherlands, Belgium and Luxembourg, the German Armies have employed parachutists who were often clothed, contrary to international law, in Dutch or Belgian uniform, or in various civilian attire. The French Government wishes to state publicly that any enemy combatant, captured in France, who is not wearing his national uniform, will be immediately shot. The armed forces of the territory have received all instructions necessary to this effect.'

The measures which, in conformity with the law of nations, we thus took against irregular parachutists became increasingly necessary in that, as the Wehrmacht advanced, these men pushed their forays more and more deeply into the interior of the country. The rumour spread that they hid themselves during the day in the woods, and emerged when night had come to pursue their enterprises under the cover of darkness. Spread from mouth to mouth, these rumours sowed alarm in the country districts. They reached such a pitch that Henri Roy, who, as Minister of the Interior, had to ensure the security of all areas of the territory which did not come under the authority of the operational armies, came to me on several occasions to point out the urgent need for special protective measures. Failing this, he told me, panic threatened to become contagious. He infused into his argument and insistence all the more heat since, as a senator of the Loiret department, he represented an area which was the special objective of the parachutists. Thus, he was prompted to voice to me an echo of the fear and even the 'panic' itself which, he assured me, reigned through all the Orléans district. Therefore, I gave my assent to the plan, the outlines of which he explained to me. Then Roy and Daladier took it upon themselves to submit the decree of May 17 for the signature of President Lebrun, which, published on the following day in the *Journal Officiel*, created 'for the duration of hostilities, military formations of territorial guards, to participate in action for the protection of national soil against the enemy operating to the rear of the front'.

The text stresses with good reason *military* formations. There were, in actual fact, no requirements demanded by the laws of war which the organic status of these formations did not, in this case, justify. They were either raised or demobilized by military authority, on the advice of the prefectorial authority. They were attached to the gendarmerie. They were openly armed, and finally, they were obliged to wear an armlet whose authenticity could be immediately verified. They were, therefore, formations which owed their existence to an ordinary regulation of the public authority, and which the latter had provided with all the attributes to give them their military character—enlistment, equipment, identification, officering, ranks, subordination. They were consequently regular troops, whose duty was to collaborate in the defence of the territory against the enemy, and especially against irregular parachutists.

These were formations which, reversing roles, the Wehrmacht called civilian formations in order to bring them on to the level of *franc-tireurs*! Now, some hundred and twenty territorial guards had fallen into the hands of the German forces; brought before courts martial they were liable to the death penalty.

It was then that Abetz intervened. Commiserating ostentatiously with the fate of these unfortunate men, he asked for them to be spared since they were in actual fact only instruments, and for the men who had raised these incriminated formations to be sent to the execution stake, that was, stated Abetz, myself as President of the Council and Mandel as Minister of the Interior.

I have called this a pretext. Yet it was a specious pretext since Abetz would certainly not have bethought himself of it if he did not believe he could find the means of crushing thereby the two 'war-mongers', whom he knew his master had sworn to eliminate. But it was a tempting pretext as well, since, due to its humanitarian veneer, it could be exploited in a demagogic manner. Such an exploitation Abetz intended in the immediate future to organize to his profit, though ready, should things turn out badly, to invoke it as a claim on the mercy of the vanquished if they became victors. Abetz, indeed, boasted at his trial before the military courts (hearing of July 16, 1949) that he had saved the lives of one hundred and twenty territorial guards.

So many advantages were after all worth a lie. Abetz uttered such a one in attributing to Mandel and myself the paternity of a measure about which we knew nothing, for the reader knows that the names at the foot of the decree of May 17 were neither that of Mandel, who, as we know, had not yet left the Ministry of Colonies, nor my own. Yet was Abetz right in thinking that there was infinitely little chance that the substitution which he was making would one day be discovered, that it would never be checked in the *Journal Officiel*?

Such were the conditions under which Abetz proposed on March 8, 1941, to ask Vichy for our extradition. Ribbentrop, evidently, shared his views, and he took steps to this end. But Vichy refused, and at the same time asked for clemency on behalf of the territorial guards. Berlin agreed, as far as we were concerned, not to insist, at least for the time being, but made the granting of the clemency asked subject to two conditions:

1. The Vichy Government was to condemn Mandel and myself to life imprisonment.

2. The Vichy Government which possibly had in its possessions documents proving that Mandel and myself had urged Roosevelt to enter the war, was to place these documents at the disposal of the Reich Government.

Darlan agreed. But how were we to be sentenced to life imprisonment? We shall see that there was no possibility of doing it legally. There remained a sentence by the exercise of arbitrary power; for was not the *lettre de cachet* the last recourse of dictators? By this method Pétain would pronounce our condemnation.

But Pétain, on reflection, changed his mind. Would it not indeed be better to have us condemned by the Riom Court? Perhaps the Court would prove amenable to instructions as to the methods to be followed. Perhaps it would even go as far as condemning us to death. For Pétain it would be a means of handing over to the Courts the responsibility for the condemnation, and, to borrow an expression dear to his friends, of shuffling the blame on to them. An admiral was obviously unsuitable for explaining these judicial manipulations to Abetz. A more tortuous mind was necessary, which was well versed in every trick of the trade. The obvious Machiavelli for this duty was Benoist-Méchin.

Here is the text of the discovered documents. 'State Secret' is the endorsement which all of them bear:

I
Abetz to Ribbentrop

Paris, March 8, 1941.

No. 780.   Urgent.

Amongst the French prisoners of war who have fallen into our hands are a certain number of men belonging to civil formations raised and armed in order to fight German parachutists. Because of this fact they should, according to the laws of warfare, be considered as *franc-tireurs*, and consequently shot.

It was Paul Reynaud as President of the Council who decided upon the constitution of these formations, and Mandel as Minister of the Interior who was entrusted with the implementation of the measure: I think that we ought to make the French Government extradite Reynaud and Mandel in order to have them shot instead of those who are only guilty because they acted as their instruments.

The execution of Reynaud and Mandel would be a just expiation of the crimes committed against the persons of our airmen and parachutists, but it will allow us at the same time to strike directly at these two Frenchmen, the two who are chiefly responsible for the war.

II
Ribbentrop to Abetz

No. 605.

On board the special train *Westfalen*, July 5, 1941.

In reply to your telegram No. 1,909 of June 26.

Please inform Darlan orally that, in spite of our right to treat the territorial guards as *franc-tireurs*, we are disposed to take Marshal Pétain's request for their pardon into consideration.

On the other hand, as we wish to agree to the desire which Darlan expressed to us, we are also prepared to let drop our demand for the extradition of Reynaud and Mandel, who instigated and are, therefore, morally responsible for the activity of the territorial guards.[1]

However, the granting of pardon to these latter is subordinated to the following conditions:

(*a*) the French Government is to imprison Reynaud and Mandel for life, and will assume full and entire responsibility for the means to prevent any attempt at escape on their part, which, if it were successful, would allow them to flee to foreign territory.[2]

[1] As it appears in *La France a sauvé l'Europe* (vol. II, p. 9), the translation of this passage, although literally exact, might be interpreted as signifying that Darlan had agreed to the extradition when the text wished to convey the opposite. The above translation leaves no room for ambiguity on this point.

[2] One can see the fear of the Nazis at the idea that one day or other we should get to London.

(*b*) the French Government will hand over to us all the documents it possesses, which prove the collusion between Reynaud and Mandel, and the American Government; we are already in possession of certain documents which prove that these two former Ministers tried to bring about war in connivance with Roosevelt and his acolytes, especially Bullitt, when the latter was head of the United States Embassy in Paris. But we are trying to fill in the gaps in our documents by completing them through means of papers which should still be in the French archives. These papers are probably more numerous and more conclusive than those in our hands.

France, as much as Germany, has the most vital interest in exposing to the world the inner facts of these warlike machinations, if it is only because this revelation would contribute to hamstringing the manœuvres of American war-mongers, and thus hasten a return to a state of peace. In publishing these documents which the French Government would supply to us, we would take care not to divulge their origin, and to give the impression on the contrary that they were part of those which we had ourselves discovered in France.

As soon as the French Government has agreed to the two proposed conditions above . . . the territorial guards will be collectively pardoned. Naturally, this pardon will not extend to offences which would be punishable if they had been committed by men belonging to the regular army. The territorial guards who may have laid themselves open to such offences will be judged according to the same procedure as if they had belonged to the regular army.

III
Abetz to Ribbentrop

Paris, August 8, 1941.

No. 2,364.

Very Urgent.

Darlan paid me a long visit this morning. . . .

As regards the territorial guards to whom, according to the terms in your telegram, No, 3,566 of August 6, the German Government means only to grant a pardon in exchange for the condemnation by the French of Reynaud and Mandel to life imprisonment, Darlan confirms that he is ready to accept a settlement on this basis. Consequently, Marshal Pétain proposes to take out of the hands of the Supreme Court of Justice the case now being examined before it, and, after having thus dispensed with judicial . . . procedure, to proceed by means of sentences . . . of a political character. The object of resorting to this step is to permit Reynaud and Mandel to be condemned to perpetual imprisonment.

IV
Abetz to Ribbentrop
Paris, August 18, 1941.

No. 2,540.   Very urgent.

Darlan came to see me this morning at the Embassy. . . .

He declared officially that, as far as the territorial guards were concerned, the French Government was prepared to fulfil the conditions which the German Government imposed for the granting of a pardon.

Marshal Pétain has decided that Reynaud and Mandel as well as other persons accused before the Riom Court should from October 5, 1941, be subject to a condemnation on political grounds.

As for the search for documents establishing collusion between Reynaud and Mandel and Roosevelt and Bullitt for warlike purposes, the investigations undertaken in the archives of the interested Ministries have borne no fruit. The French Government hopes, however, to be in a position to send us documents taken from the Riom dossiers, and, if possible, from private dossiers.

V
Abetz to Ribbentrop

No. 3,198.   Paris, October 17, 1941.

With reference to the decision made public today which increases the severity of the conditions to which the civil and military persons before the Riom Court are subject, I learn from one of the members of the Vichy Government that Marshal Pétain had at first intended to take out of the Court's jurisdiction the cases in question. He could then have judged them himself with the object of passing sentence, on October 15 [16], on the accused, and of making their condemnation a purely political matter. But investigation during these last weeks has raised, with regard to certain of them and especially Mandel and Reynaud, charges of such gravity that the Courts would find in them sufficient motives to pass a sentence as severe as one passed on political grounds. That is why Marshal Pétain has preferred to let the investigation, which has already begun, follow its course; he has, however, ordered it to be speeded up.

I have replied to my interlocutor that the speed with which this investigation opened against the French war-mongers is conducted would be the best means for the Vichy Government to prove that it was determined to carry out loyally its new policy.

VI
Abetz to Ribbentrop
Paris, October 31, 1941.

Benoist-Méchin came to confer with me today about prosecutions which we have begun in court martial against the territorial guards.

The French Government has agreed to the condition which we are imposing upon the granting of a pardon. It has, therefore, condemned Mandel and Reynaud to life imprisonment.

The first intention of Marshal Pétain was to pass, on October 15 [16], a sentence based on political reasons. But he had hardly made this decision when new charges were brought against Reynaud and Mandel, the gravity of which was such that they seemed sufficient to justify a legal judgement which would condemn these two individuals to life imprisonment and even, perhaps, to death. Marshal Pétain preferred in these circumstances to abandon the idea of removing the case from the jurisdiction of the Riom Court, and to allow the procedure already begun to follow its course. The judgement to be pronounced on Reynaud and Mandel ought to be given by February, 1942, at the latest. In the meantime Reynaud and Mandel are to be transferred to Portalet where they will be subject to a rigorous treatment.

I answered Benoist-Méchin that we were following with the greatest interest the penal procedure now being employed against Reynaud and Mandel. As the fort of Portalet was close to the Spanish frontier, and thus favourably situated for an escape, we expected the French Government to take appropriate measures for keeping a good guard.

As for the prosecution of the territorial guards, I proposed to dissociate them from the Mandel-Reynaud affair, advising the French Government that none of the death sentences which would be eventually pronounced would be put into execution before March 1, 1942, a date by which we expected that the condemnation by the Court of Reynaud and Mandel to life imprisonment would be an accomplished fact.

As we see, the fixed idea of the Nazis was to get rid of the responsibility for the war. Anything was good enough for them to attain this end. They were greedy for documents as proof. It is a miracle that they did not succeed in getting their hands upon my own papers.

I had them, as a matter of fact, in my possession within my cell at Portalet when the Gestapo came to seize me. When about to be handed over to the enemy, I placed them in the care of the fort's commandant, and entrusted him with the duty of sending them to the Ministry of

War at Vichy. This was done. Though the immediate danger was averted, it was, however, by no means eliminated. On December 4, 1942, Laval named a committee of three people to make an inventory of the papers which the military authorities had handed over to him, and to send 'to the Head of the Government proposals regarding the destination' to which they should be sent.

The committee met, went through the files, classified the documents. But where should they send them was the problem. Believing that it was essential, above all, to prevent them falling into the hands of the Germans, M. Ernest Lagarde, Director of Political and Commercial Matters at the Ministry of Foreign Affairs, and by this office, a member of the committee, stated that they were documents of a diplomatic character. He succeeded in having them, now they had been subject to a preliminary search, entrusted to his care so that he could have the leisure to study them at his ease.

In these circumstances M. Lagarde obtained possession of my papers, which were thus finally to be secure from the eyes of any indiscreet, or clumsy, not to say ill-intentioned, zealot. He only relinquished them on the day he handed them over to me on my return from Germany in 1945. Most of them have been incorporated in this book. It would have been a regrettable loss if they had disappeared for ever! It would have been a much more serious affair if they had fallen into the hands of the enemy!

Hitler, as we shall see, had certainly not abandoned his design of eliminating Mandel and myself. In his eyes we were to be the victims who would extirpate with our lives the insolence of having opposed Nazi ambitions. If, in 1941, he relinquished his criminal design, it was for him only something deferred, and in his innermost heart he made the reservation to take up his plan again as soon as a better excuse than that of the parachutists presented itself.

This excuse did turn up for him in 1944.

MAY 30, 1944: HITLER DECIDES TO HAND OVER BLUM, MANDEL AND MYSELF TO VICHY WITH THE ORDER TO HAVE US ASSASSINATED

Germany had raised in Tunisia a body composed of Frenchmen and especially of natives, who under the name of the 'African Phalange' had taken part in the campaign of 1942 to 1943 as a unit of the German Army. During the fighting a number of the men belonging to this formation had fallen into Allied hands. Others, infiltrating into the Allied lines or parachuted behind the lines to stir up political trouble or to carry out sabotage, had been arrested. The Algiers Committee had handed them over to military justice. Convicted of having borne arms against their country, most of them had been condemned to death, and certain of them had already been shot. Hitler intended at all costs to stop these executions.

Here was a fine opportunity. He threatened Algiers that he would shoot the men who had committed the crime of never resigning themselves to bowing their heads before him. The question of our execution, left in suspense, was therefore reopened. Archives seized in Germany have provided us with documents about this subject, whose cynicism is revealing. Their secrecy and 'ultra-urgency'—*supercitissime* is, indeed, an endorsement with which many of them are marked—are stressed in an imperative fashion.

A memorandum of a recapitulative nature which the services of the Wilhelmstrasse drew up on May 15, 1944, for Ribbentrop's use, reveals to us the deliberation with which the snare was constructed.

Laval declared himself ready on March 25 to arrest, with the object of making reprisals, two hundred adult males who were linked by family ties with members of the Algiers Committee, and on April 3 to agree, for this same purpose, to the execution of individuals guilty of Gaullist or anti-Government actions.

On May 3, on hearing news of the execution of Christofini, a member of the African Phalange, Laval summoned a court martial which condemned nine so-called leaders of the Resistance, five of whom were immediately shot. He had, therefore, stained his hands with French blood.

But, from a 'secret and infallible French source',[1] Berlin learned that these individuals were in no wise the true leaders of the Resistance Movement, and that there was nothing to show that the victims had not been selected from common malefactors. Ribbentrop telegraphed, May 8–9, to Abetz that 'the whole affair was a complete farce'. He demanded the heads of the real leaders of the Resistance, not only those who 'were notoriously known to be such', but even those who may have played a 'leading part in the movement'.

Abetz replied on May 13 in an 'ultra-urgent' telegram that Darnand was indignant at this reproach. Indeed there could be no question protested Darnand of giving up leaders taken with arms in their hands, liable on this account to summary jurisdiction and therefore shot on the spot. It had, therefore, been necessary to choose five sacrificial victims out of a bunch of 'maquisards' collected in a drag-net over the plateau of Glières. Though no positive charge could be laid at the individual door of such and such a man, their presence in these localities was sufficient evidence to prove their connection with the Resistance Movement. In addition, the five unfortunates were found to be officers

---

[1] This miserable individual, who found these executions an insufficient revenge and demanded more, is cloaked under the title of 'the brown friend' in the records of the Reich intelligence service.

of the 27th battalion of Chasseurs Alpins, the regiment in which Darnand himself had served and fought. And Darnand emphasized how much it had cost him to strike against men who, but yesterday, had been his own regimental comrades. And here, instead of being grateful to him for this choice piece of cruelty, Ribbentrop was calling this sinister massacre a masquerade! Pushing home his argument, Abetz remarked that the leaders of the Resistance Movement had taken the precaution in good time to send those relatives whom they held dear to North Africa, in other words, to a safe place. The result was that the hostages which Vichy had succeeded in seizing from amongst the people who were related to the Resistance chiefs, did not possess, except on rare occasions, the qualities which persons held as a reprisal should have, if the threat was to have any effect. And Abetz gave a dissertation on this macabre subject: the proximity of relationship, sentimental ties, political antecedents and affinities, the importance of the part played, the influence of the followers—each factor was weighed in the balance. From this detailed analysis, Abetz drew the conclusion that reprisals would be of no use unless those marked out to be victims were choice hostages, in other words, leaders of the Resistance Movement, and even further, unless they were leaders of the front rank or personalities chosen from 'those who were responsible for the war'—in other words, from those men on whom Germany was trying to throw her own responsibility for the war. Having thus defined the circle, Abetz threw the ball back to Ribbentrop. Men answering to the characteristics which he had just laid down were to be found not at Vichy, but only in Germany where they had already been deported. Therefore the Reich had within its clutches a reserve from which it was suitable to draw. One important fact remained. Who should be the first? There could be no doubt about that. The honour of initiating the series of massacres could only fall to Blum, Mandel and myself.

Ribbentrop showed his teeth at the news that Vichy was not detaining the principal leaders of the Resistance, although Berlin was indefatigable in ordering Laval to arrest all people suspected of belonging to the movement. He attached such importance to the matter that he sent Steengracht, Secretary of State for Foreign Affairs and his *alter ego*, post-haste to Paris. There was to be an end to negotiations: Abetz had only to execute the orders which were sent to him. The *missus dominicus*[1] did not mince his words. He overwhelmed Abetz with

[1] Steengracht had to deal at the same time with two other matters, which were linked up by their nature to the principal problem.

(a) The diplomatic courier service of Vichy; Ribbentrop stressed the importance of the use which the Resistance Movement made of this service to ensure liaison with Gaullist circles abroad.

(b) The Guy La Chambre-Jacomet affair: Abetz had stated that he was in favour of liberating Guy La Chambre and de Jacomet, both of whom, he said, had been indicted at Riom for having failed to organize the French Air Force with sufficient thoroughness. Guy

remonstrances; accused him of lacking backbone and even of cowardice. But Abetz stood up to him. Could it be wondered at, he answered back, angered in his turn, that Vichy had not one of the leaders of the Resistance in its hands when the German Counter-Espionage had, on Ribbentrop's orders, arrested and taken into custody about fifty thousand Frenchmen suspected or accused on this ground, and when it was detaining, either in a transit camp at Compiègne or in its camps in Germany, prominent personalities whom it had put in preventive detention and transferred to Germany? But the controversy was cut short. For Steengracht, the only problem which was relevant, was to decide on whose shoulders the execution of the sacrificial victims should fall, not who should provide them.

There was no doubt about this point. French authorities would have the exclusive burden of carrying out the duty.

Hitler's intervention brought the argument to a head. The seed sown by Abetz had germinated. On May 30 a top secret telegram came for Abetz. It bore the fatal superscription of, 'For the personal attention of the Ambassador'.

It ran:

'Concerning the question of reprisal measures to be taken in answer to the execution of members of the African Phalange, the Führer agrees to your proposal. On the first execution of another member of the Phalange, the French Government should, therefore, proceed to execute, as a reprisal, Léon Blum, Georges Mandel and Paul Reynaud. But the Führer thinks that it will be necessary to see that the French Government does not allow these persons to escape, once they have been handed over to it.'

The decision had been taken. At the first opportunity it only remained to take the victims out of their cage.

Then the Algiers Council of War condemned Lieutenant-Colonel Magnien, leader of the Phalange, to death. This time the execution bell had tolled.

On July 2, Abetz, in the name of his Government, warned Laval, who was in Paris that day, that Blum, Mandel and I were to be handed over to the Vichy Government in order to be shot as a reprisal for the sentence which had been passed. At the Pétain trial[1] Laval was to state about this subject: 'I immediately lodged a most vehement protest.'

La Chambre, added Abetz, might be said to have also assisted the Reich in other circumstances, and especially by joining up with a group of politicians who, in 1940, were coming round to the view of concluding a separate peace with Germany, and had succeeded in keeping Reynaud out of power to this end.

Naturally, I shall leave with Abetz the responsibility for these assertions.

[1] Hearing of August 4, 1945.

Laval forthwith summoned the Spanish Ambassador who was also in Paris that same day to the Hôtel Matignon, and handed him the following note:

Paris, July 2, 1944.

The Algiers Committee has just condemned Colonel Magnien, former leader of the African Phalange, to death.

Colonel Magnien had not committed any offence. He obeyed the orders of his leaders and of the Government.

The German Government immediately informed the French Government that it was prepared to hand over to the French authorities, MM. Léon Blum, Paul Reynaud, and Georges Mandel, who were to be shot as a reprisal.

This notification was made on the day following the assassination of M. Philippe Henriot at a time when indignation aroused by this hateful crime had reached its height.[1]

The French Government would be grateful to the Spanish Government if the latter would agree to approach the Algiers Committee to inform it of this communication from the German Government.

The French Government has not followed up the proposal, but the execution of Colonel Magnien would entail the risk of producing grave consequences.

The Spanish Government carried out the step which was requested. On July 27, Count de Bailen, Spanish Chargé d'Affaires at Vichy, informed Laval of this fact. The latter immediately drew up the following note: 'Count de Bailen, Spanish Chargé d'Affaires at Vichy, has, today, handed the following communication to the Head of the Government: "The despatch with which President Laval entrusted M. de Lequerica on July 2 on the occasion of Colonel Magnien's condemnation has been handed to the Foreign Affairs Commission in Algiers. The latter has replied that it is deeply grateful to the Spanish Government for this communication."'

Performed with the full knowledge of Abetz, this step of Laval's would have contained no significance if it had not automatically at least had a suspensive effect. It was in any case necessary to wait for the reply of Algiers, and it seemed to be implicitly agreed that, if Algiers consented to put off the execution of Colonel Magnien, Hitler, for his part, would give up any idea of carrying on with his design. And so Laval continued to assert that such was the conclusion which he thought he was entitled to assume from his exchange of views with Abetz.[2]

[1] As we know, Henriot had been killed on June 28.

[2] M. Jean Tracou relates in Le Maréchal aux liens (p. 322) that, on July 7 at 10 a.m., Laval said to Pétain: 'Hitler wishes to hand Blum, Mandel and Reynaud over to us in order to shoot them if a certain Colonel Magnien . . . is executed. This is a very dirty matter, Monsieur le Maréchal. I don't want to get mixed up in it, and that is what I said

JULY 7, 1944: THE ASSASSINATION OF MANDEL

On July 4, Mandel was taken out of his German prison and taken by plane to Rheims, and thence by road to Paris, where he arrived in the evening. General Oberg, head of the S.S. and of the German police in France, took custody of the unfortunate man and shut him up in a flat in the square of the Bois de Boulogne, which the occupying authorities had made into a prison. Colonel Knochen, head of the *Sicherheitsdienst*,[1] and by reason of this under the orders of Oberg, informed Knipping, head of Darnand's secretariat (Darnand being then at Vichy), that he held Mandel's person at the disposal of French prison officials for purposes which were known.

On the 7th, Knipping accepted the offer. Violating the law, he himself issued a committal order, although such an order fell within the exclusive province of the courts. But Baillet, director of prison services, refused to take custody of a man whose imprisonment was not ordered by a court warrant. Ignoring this, Knipping confirmed his order, and advised Baillet that he would only leave Mandel in the custody of the prison authorities for a few hours.

Mandel was, therefore, transferred to La Santé prison. He was taken there in a German car by a German officer, to whom a receipt was given. On the 7th at 2 p.m. Mandel thus crossed the threshold of his prison. In the prison register it was recorded that the detained was being held at the disposal of the Secretary of State in the interests of public safety. He, therefore, was the only one with authority to order the eventual release of the prisoner. Shortly after, Knipping authorized the delivery of Mandel to the 'militia' for transfer to a prison which the latter had set up in the Château des Brosses just outside Vichy. Neither Baillet nor Knipping thought of informing Laval. About 5.30 p.m. Mandel was told of the transfer order. Knipping signed the delivery order. Mandel was taken out of La Santé prison, and the 'militia' took custody of him. Mansuy, known throughout the 'militia' as being prepared to try his hand at any task, was chosen for the mission. Two

---

to Abetz. I have no blood on my hands and never shall.' On July 12, Laval gathered the Council of Ministers under his presidency. I extract the following passage from the minutes which have been published by M. Tracou (*op. cit.*, pp. 329–38):

Laval: 'A few days ago I was warned by the Embassy that MM. Léon Blum, Reynaud and Mandel were to be handed over to the French Government as hostages to be shot if Colonel Magnien . . . was himself shot. I declared emphatically to . . . Abetz that I refused absolutely. . . .'

Brinon: 'I should tell you, M. le Président, that M. Abetz is not in agreement with you on this point. He says you accepted their persons, simply saying, "You are not making me a present by doing this."'

Laval, turning to Brinon and striking the table with his fist, cried emphatically: 'I cannot allow such a thing to be said. Nothing is more contrary to my nature. I have no blood on my hands, and I will not have any.'

[1] Security Services, abbreviated S.D.

cars were waiting at the door of the prison. Mansuy put Mandel in the first, with two other militiamen by his side, and himself took the wheel. The second car followed, with the German officer inside. The convoy set out along the road to Fontainebleau. In the forest, Mansuy, pretending he had a breakdown, stopped the car. The convoy came to a halt. Everyone got out. Mansuy, with a burst of his sub-machine-gun at point-blank range from the back, brought down Mandel, who collapsed with six bullets in him. Mansuy sprayed the car with a second burst to make it appear that Mandel had met his end in an armed attack. Such was to be the version which the executioner and his accomplices tried to pass off when they had finished their job.

At 3 a.m. on the 7th, Laval left Paris to go back to Vichy. The latest information in his possession was the notification which Abetz had made to him on the 2nd. He thought, therefore, that it was only a question of a threat, whilst Mandel, whom he believed still to be in Germany, was already in Paris on the point of being handed over to his executioners.

Laval was to learn of the events in the drama around 5 p.m. on the 8th. It was Darnand, also at Vichy, who went to tell him about it. The latter declared that he had just been told the news by Knipping.

Laval immediately summoned Knipping by direct telephone from Vichy to the General Delegation in Paris. Knipping, who at this moment was at Brinon's very shoulder, told him as an explanation the trumped-up version of the murder.

'I found', stated Laval at the Pétain trial (hearing of August 4, 1945), 'this explanation . . . halting. I deduced from this . . . that Mandel had been murdered. I protested. I begged Darnand, I begged Knipping not to take charge of Blum and Reynaud if they were handed to them, because I believed that these other two would be the next after Mandel. I protested to the Embassy, and neither Blum nor Reynaud were handed over.'

Blum and I, in actual fact, were intended to meet the same fate forthwith. The order to this effect had been given. It would seem, therefore, that both of us owed our lives to Laval; 'I prevented', he also stated at the above hearing, 'Paul Reynaud and Léon Blum being murdered.'[1]

This was a strange vicissitude of political life. Since 1935, Laval had had no more determined opponent in Parliament than myself!

---

[1] M. Tracou writes (*op. cit.*, p. 324) that, on the morning of the 9th, Laval arrived at Vichy from Châteldon, where he went each night, and said to him: 'I have just put Abetz in his place, for telling me that another one, probably Blum, would be handed over. This dirty business is frightful. I told Abetz that he could not count on me. . . . He promised that he would do his best to avoid another tragedy. I have confidence in him; I think that Blum and Reynaud are not in danger.'

In . . . *Et Paris ne fut pas détruit* Taittinger gives[1] the following details which he has himself gathered about these terrible events:

For some time [he writes] the Germans had placed at the disposal of the French Government selected hostages so that they could be executed. Laval declined these frightful offerings . . . and I can state that Léon Blum personally owes his life to Laval. If hostages were arrested because they were bound by bonds of relationship to the men of Algiers, it was contrary to the wish of Pierre Laval, and each time that any one of them happened to escape, Laval openly showed his pleasure. . . .

The unfortunate Georges Mandel was put at the disposal of the 'militia' in order to appease the shades of the unfortunate Philippe Henriot. . . .

A German police car, escorted by another vehicle, delivered Georges Mandel in person to La Santé prison, where he was not expected. He was snugly wrapped up in his fur coat although it was still full summer. It is true that the trip from Germany to France had taken place by plane. . . .

The former Minister was put in a cell. He began to wash and brush up. In Georges Mandel's mind this was the toilet of a man already sentenced to death. . . . Moreover, he did not hide the deep contempt in which he held the Marshal's Government for having first arrested him, and then handed him over to the Germans. . . .

Two days later I was . . . at the Hôtel Matignon . . . a telephone call was handed, in my presence, to Laval by M. Gabolde, the Minister of Justice. The body of . . . Mandel had been in the morgue of Versailles hospital since the day before. . . . M. Gabolde asked for his instructions. Laval replied in a curt tone: 'I have requested an inquiry to be opened, and for the murderer to be prosecuted. The Prosecutor has only to carry out his duties.' When the Minister of Justice evidently persisted in stressing that the murder had been ordered, and that the Germans would not allow justice to take its course, M. Laval ended by saying: 'That does not matter to me; it is not my concern, and I hope, not yours. The investigation which has begun should be carried out, and if there is any interference with it of the type which you anticipate, where the responsibility for the crime lies will be clearly proved.'

Turning to me the President said: 'I was not particularly friendly with . . . Mandel, but I will not allow this policy of indulging in reprisals. In any case, I don't wish, directly or indirectly, to be mixed up in all this. It is up to justice to do its duty.'

'Even if the guilty person is a member of the Government?'

'Even if the guilty person is a member of the Government,' was Pierre Laval's straight answer to my query.

Moreover, the Germans did not try to hide their satisfaction over Mandel's murder. Here is proof. On July 8 around 5 p.m. M. Tracou was in Laval's room while he was studying the account which Darnand had just given him.

'There was a subdued ringing of a telephone [writes M. Tracou].[2] It was a call over the direct line which linked him with Brinon in Paris.

[1] pp. 286–9.   [2] Tracou, *op. cit.*, p. 323.

'Do you know what Brinon says? It seems that the Germans are very pleased with Mandel's murder, because he is a Jew and one of those responsible for the war. They think it will have a good effect. They are only sorry he was not officially shot by the French Government.'

But there is proof of a more condemning nature: The journal, *Je suis partout* openly rejoiced in the murder of Mandel, 'this war-monger'.

But let us ignore such infamous joy.

During his career Mandel proved a worthy disciple of his leader, Clemenceau.

What is astonishing is that I survived him.

In *The Last Days of Hitler* Trevor-Roper writes, that, on April 22, 1945, the Führer, realizing that he was lost beyond all hope, trembling with rage, shouted, 'Let them all be shot! Let them all be shot!' Evidently he was referring to political prisoners.

CHAPTER XXII

MY PRISONS

August 1, 1940, The infamous decree: France is responsible for the War.—September 6, 1940, Mandel and myself are imprisoned successively at Chazeron, Pellevoisin, Aubenas and Vals.—Vichy in search of an Indictment.—A trial for the crime of refusing to surrender?—Flandin at war with the war-mongers.—October 16, 1941, Pétain judges us without a hearing, and condemns us without giving a reason.—April to July, 1941, My letters to Pétain.—June to August, 1942, The findings of Bâtonnier Jacques Charpentier.— A year of Incarceration in Portalet.—November 20, 1942, Pétain hands us over to Hitler.—Five months in a cell at Oranienburg.— At Itter.—Liberated by the Americans.

AUGUST I, 1940: THE INFAMOUS DECREE: FRANCE IS RESPONSIBLE FOR THE WAR

ON August 1, 1940, Alibert, the Inquisitor of the régime, got Pétain to sign a decree to bring before the Supreme Court of Justice those who had committed 'crimes and offences, or betrayed the duties for which they were responsible, by actions which contributed to a transition from a state of peace to one of war before September 4, 1939, *or those who had later aggravated the consequences of the situation thus created*'.[1] This Supreme Court of Justice was a judicature which the New Order had just instituted, and which, reminiscent of the 'Grand Jours d'Auvergne',[2] had its seat in Riom.

This subtle language was intended to lay down three avenues by which prosecutions might be instituted:[3] 1. direct or indirect responsibility for the war; 2. lack of military preparedness, that is to say, responsibility for defeat; 3. opposition to the request for an armistice; in other words, prolonging the suffering attendant on hostilities.

---

[1] The italics are those of M. Reynaud.

[2] The popular name given to the courts set up by Louis XIV to restore the power of the French monarchy in Auvergne which had lapsed during the Wars of Religion into a state of anarchy [Tr.].

[3] Is there any need to observe that this text violates, at least to a large extent, the principle of the non-retrospective action of laws?

Let us pause for a moment at the first of these complaints. In Vichy's eyes the France of 1939 was responsible for the war. Hitler's provocations were thus only the inventions of 'war-mongers'. But the France of 1940, whatever she might be, was indissolubly linked to the France of 1939, just as the Germany of 1918 was to the Germany of William II. Thus it followed that Vichy laid the responsibility for the war at the door of France. And Alibert stated in his pedantic fashion to the Press: 'People must in future be made to realize that a declaration of war is a very serious matter.'

On the morrow of Jena, Fichte abjured the 'German nation' to act so that it never aroused the scorn of the conqueror. At Montoire, Pétain confided to the Führer that he had always been against the war; he allowed him thus to fob off the responsibility for this war from Germany's to France's shoulders. And yet Pétain had been warned, immediately after the request for an armistice, by Rivaud, to whom he entrusted the Ministry of National Education, that Hitler would force him to open a trial to determine the responsibility for it.

Caught in the net, Pétain allowed himself on several occasions to censure France's entry into hostilities in his messages. Several times also he went as far as to order his Press to accuse M. Lebrun of permitting the Constitution to be broken by not requiring a declaration of war to be made conditional on a vote of the Chambers. As we have seen, however, there was really no declaration of war since the aggression of the Wehrmacht against our ally, Poland, automatically placed us —as Georges Bonnet pointed out to Berlin—in a state of war with Germany. Moreover, we know that the voting of credits took place in such circumstances that a special vote on a declaration of war would obviously have been only an idle repetition. Therefore, it was not honest to maintain that the Constitution had not been respected.

The Riom Court carried out its investigation into this war guilt at the same time as into our unpreparedness for war. I must, on behalf of accuracy, recognize that the members of this Court and especially M. Cassagnau, the Procurator-General, felt the odious nature of the task which had been thrust upon them. The preliminary investigation lasted, however, a long time. I was myself interrogated as a witness on these matters in February, 1941, by M. Henri Lagarde, then President of the Court. I remarked to him that the Chamber had acclaimed Daladier when, taking up the theme which I had already broached before the Chamber, he had declared that, if France allowed Poland to be crushed, a day would come when she would be thrown into a war 'without honour and without allies'.

The matter is made all the more serious in that Bonnet[1] had warned Pétain and his entourage against the dangers that lay in opening such

[1] Cf. Bonnet, *op. cit.*, p. 391.

a trial. On July 25, 1940, he obtained an audience of Pétain during which he protested against what was still only a project. He handed a memorandum to Pétain in which he had no difficulty in demonstrating the gravity of the evil which such a trial would inflict upon the country. M. du Moulin de la Barthète has placed on record this step of M. Bonnet's. He writes:[1] 'Bonnet, who was then the object of violent attacks for not having agreed in 1939 to a new Munich and who feared that a new trial would indict not only the Government to which he had belonged, but the whole of France, sought out the Marshal, Baudouin and Bouthillier around July 25. He gave them to understand that France had no responsibility for the origin of the war. . . . A trial for war guilt, inadmissible, whatever the circumstances, in an occupied country, would, therefore, only play into the hands of France's opponents.' Vichy, nevertheless, persisted in its intention.

Daladier entrusted Maître Ribet with his defence. Bonnet states that, at the beginning of the trial, he got in touch with Ribet to let him know that he would be pleased to help him in his task. What exactly happened? Daladier told us in Germany that, after Bonnet's first depositions at the investigation, he had intimated to him that someone was going to be amused at the hearing. Bonnet,[2] informed by Ribet of what Daladier meant to say, would seem to have withdrawn his first evidence.

When Pétain was in the dock, he defended himself against the suggestion of ever having thought of opening a trial dealing with war guilt. In a memorandum which he handed to the investigating committee of the High Court he wrote:[3] 'During June, 1940, France was dumbfounded at the rapidity and completeness of her defeat. The Chambers became the interpreters of the emotion felt by the nation. M. Herriot asked for the responsible persons to be discovered and punished. It was for this purpose that I created the Supreme Court. . . . There was not the slightest question . . . of getting a Court of Justice to declare that France was responsible for the war. It was solely a matter of discovering the errors committed and who were their authors.'

M. Caous, who presided over the Riom Court, has declared in his evidence at the Pétain trial:[4]

[1] Op. cit., pp. 375–6.

[2] According to Bonnet, there was a misunderstanding. 'At the end of a year, towards the termination of the investigation, the Riom Court', he states, 'tried to make use against Daladier of the minutes of the Chamber's Finance Committee (from which it appeared —in spite of some alterations which it had undergone—that Daladier had promised not to declare war without facing Parliament). I was warned of this', continued Bonnet, 'by his colleague, Genebrier, and I said that I was ready on this particular matter to answer any queries which could be asked. M. Daladier's lawyer informed me of these. I answered them at Périgueux, where I was living, in front of a judge who examined me by a rogatory commission. This evidence, which dealt with a new subject, had nothing to do with war guilt, on which I had at the outset adopted a categoric attitude.'

[3] Les Silences du Maréchal, p. 263.   [4] Hearing of July 28, 1945.

'I can report . . . a definite fact, a saying of the Marshal . . . which was addressed to me in private . . . on the only occasion . . . that there was any talk between us of the Riom trial. . . . Immediately after the hearings of the Court had been suspended . . . by a law . . . of August 12 or 13, 1942, there was . . . a series of Press articles. There was also an interview granted to *Le Petit Parisien* by the Minister of Justice at that time, whose object was to force the Court to extend its prosecutions to other matters besides those it had dealt with up to then . . . and specifically to the declaration of war so as to demonstrate that France was guilty of having made this. I had the feeling—the trial had ended, otherwise I should not have done what I did—. . . that the Marshal was doubtless not aware of all this, which was happening without his authority, and I wished to go and tell him about it. I asked for an interview. I saw the Marshal. I explained to him why we did not wish to hold the trial which his Government seemed to want at that time. Having unfolded what I was thinking, I said: "Monsieur le Maréchal, nobody can expect the highest court in France to state that France was guilty of provoking the war." The Marshal answered me: "But, surely, one would be mad to think otherwise."'

In any case the Court has to its credit the fact that it quashed by decree the investigation which it had opened into war guilt. It is true that it still had some ammunition in its locker, namely, the trial on our unpreparedness for war.

SEPTEMBER 6, 1940: MANDEL AND MYSELF ARE IMPRISONED SUCCESSIVELY AT CHAZERON, PELLEVOISIN, AUBENAS AND VALS

On September 6, 1940, the Vichy wireless published extracts from an article which had appeared several days earlier in *L'Eclaireur de Nice*, under the title 'Si on avait écouté Weygand, l'Italie ne serait pas entrée dans la guerre'. It was the refusal to ask for an armistice in good time that was the reason for Italian intervention, maintained the author. Therefore, the wireless drew the conclusion that here was to be seen new proof of 'the ignorance and incapacity of our rulers'. Now, Italy entered the war on June 10, or three days before Weygand had asked the Government to beg for an armistice.

Under the censorship then in force it was clear that this article had been inspired by a high authority. It was none the less clear that it was not a chance happening that the wireless had reproduced it after a few days delay.

In the evening I realized why. About 10 p.m., when I was in my old family home on the mountain-side near Barcelonnette, I heard steps outside. A divisional commissioner from the *Sureté Nationale* came to tell me of an order issued by the Prefect of the Basses-Alpes, M. Babillot, that day. This important official, invoking the law of September 3, 1940, 'relating to steps to be taken in the maintenance of national defence and political security on government orders with regard to dangerous individuals', and basing his action on the instructions of the Minister of the Interior, ordered my administrative internment[1] in the Château de Chazeron, in the commune of Loubeyret (Puy-de-Dôme), an establishment appointed for this purpose by the Minister of the Interior.

Recalling the attack on the wireless, I was not a little proud of being arrested for the crime of not having surrendered. I immediately wrote a letter to Pétain in which I told him that I was leaving my house under an escort of his policemen with my head held high.

M. du Moulin de la Barthète attributes[2] the initiative for my arrest to Laval and to Alibert. Marquet admitted to him, he says, that Laval saw in Alibert's proposal a means of eliminating his political opponents. 'For Laval, just as for Alibert and Marquet . . . Paul Reynaud remained, with Mandel, public enemy Number One. Pétain allowed himself to be convinced, for he had been told a ridiculous story of secret funds, in which Paul Reynaud was most wrongly implicated and about which I considered it a point of honour to give evidence myself at the Riom Court.' Nevertheless, Marquet asserted at his trial before the High Court that, in determining upon our internment, he only obeyed a desire to 'protect us against certain excited people'. Yet this step, which he meant to be chalked up to his credit, was one of the last which he took in his capacity as Minister of the Interior. For, on September 5, he went, he has said, to find Pétain and tell him that he 'had had enough', that he did not wish to have a hand in prosecutions against freemasons. The next day, the day of my arrest, Pétain put his signature to Marquet's resignation from office.

In the middle of the night of the 6th, I left under a strong escort of five police cars. We spent three hours in an hotel at Gap, and then retook the road for the Château de Chazeron. The Château was built in differing architectural styles. The main building dated from the Middle Ages. Two wings had been added to it in the seventeenth century for Louis XIV, during one of his journeys, had given warning that he intended to stay there, but he passed by without stopping, and the lord of the Château was put to an expense for no purpose.

I was held in solitary confinement as if I were a conspirator. Two policemen slept in the room adjoining my own chamber. Night was falling as I arrived. One of them, very embarrassed, came to tell me that he had received an order to stay beside me until the workman,

---

[1] This was a form of detention, ordered by the Administration and particularly used in the French colonies, against individuals alleged to be a political danger to the State. It corresponds roughly to confinement under our own Regulation 18B [Tr.].

[2] *Op. cit.*, p. 379.

occupied in fixing bars to the window, had finished his task. I was a prisoner of the State. On the following day *Paris-Soir* explained that it was a case of 'expiatory detention' [*sic*].

A stroll could be taken in a neglected garden. Going down the stair-case which led to it, one caught sight of the Auvergne countryside with its prominent round hills under a sky which was often filled with beautiful clouds. I had in my luggage a small wireless. What happiness I derived in hearing the moving eloquence of Maurice Schumann, or the restrained feeling with which Pierre Bourdan pilloried the double-dealing and blighted hopes of Mussolini! I used to read. I did physical exercises. Daladier and Gamelin had arrived on the same day as I did. Léon Blum followed shortly afterwards.

At the end of several days I saw through my window the arrival of Mandel with his customary very high, detachable collar, muffled up in a thick maroon overcoat, with his keen look from under his small blue soft hat. He told me later that he had been made to travel by plane for the first time in his life in order to get from Morocco to France. He had a room above me, but I waited in vain for him to lower a paper at the end of a string when night had fallen. He never thought of having recourse to a prisoner's tricks.

Vichy dared to assert that my imprisonment was intended to ensure my safety. Now, Professor René Courtin, at that time head of security in the department of Basses-Alpes, had already received, at the end of July, 1940, an order to have all aerodromes watched, even those of a temporary nature, because the Government, he was told, had reasons to fear that I might be carried off by a British plane.

In November, Blum, Daladier and Gamelin were, under a committal order of the Riom Court, transferred to a dilapidated country house at Bourrassol, about three miles from Riom. Vichy then came to the conclusion that the Château de Chazeron, upon which considerable money had been spent, was too costly for the confinement of two prisoners.

Mandel and I were transferred to Pellevoisin, an hotel for pilgrims, near to Châteauroux. It gave us a most unfavourable opinion of the comfort with which this type of customer put up. A sickening smell hung about part of the corridors. Exercise was only to be got in a dirty courtyard between barbed wire. The policemen had received from our former subordinates, now with Vichy, an order not to allow us the privileges which it is usual to grant former ministers. The Germans themselves never stooped to such pettiness. A commissioner, called C., found in the handbag of my daughter, who had come to see me, a letter from her husband, a prisoner. He kept her standing in front of him whilst he read carefully through it from one end to another. But there is one weapon which no one can take away from a prisoner, scorn.

Former Ministers of Léon Blum's administration were at Pellevoisin: Vincent Auriol, Marx Dormoy and Jules Moch. Pomaret was also there. The reason for his imprisonment was because, after having been dismissed by Pétain from the post of Minister of the Interior, he had spoken about him in terms which were insufficiently congratulatory. There were two aircraft manufacturers, Paul-Louis Weiller and Marcel Bloch, and last of all a stockbroker who had been arrested in error and who was released in error a few weeks later by Peyrouton, Minister of the Interior, under the impression that he was one of his former fellow-students of Sainte-Barbe. We were still kept in solitary confinement, and, if we were occasionally able to communicate with each other, it was due to some Alsatian police officers, who made no bones about their indignation with Vichy. In the sentry-boxes an order of the Ministries of the Interior and of War was posted, indicating to all military and civil officials that the order not to fire on prisoners had been cancelled. After a single summons 'officials were to open fire on the prisoner without any hesitation if he did not obey this summons'.

On what grounds could I be indicted before a court? It would have seemed too paradoxical to include me in the trial for unpreparedness for war! The only counts then left were 'war-mongering' and 'refusal to surrender'. We shall see that Vichy tried to proceed against me on these strange charges.

However, it was essential to give the public some immediate food for consumption. The Press of the Vichy régime, and especially the weekly Press, took upon itself this sordid task. Hardly a week passed, indeed, but *Gringoire* or *Je suis partout* used me as a target. These two papers had been entrusted with the mission to drag through the mud a man whom they knew was not in a position to defend himself. They both performed their task brilliantly. Need I recall in relation to this the regularity with which they studded their miserable diatribes with quotations extracted from my war speeches, after having artfully taken them out of their context? In their joint outrageous attacks the words, 'We shall conquer because we are the stronger' and 'The road for iron ore', served as an everlasting refrain.

Such was the treatment to which Vichy had resolved to subject me. I wrote to Pétain summoning him to bring me before the Riom Court and to place me thus in a position where I could publicly answer these attacks. It was to no avail. I then began compiling a report called *Je m'accuse*, which I had circulated in Resistance circles, and which was the origin of *La France a sauvé l'Europe*.

Let us get back to Pellevoisin. On December 31, 1940, at midnight, there was a general departure by car to Aubenas in the Ardèche. Following a move by my defending counsel, Maître Jacques Charpentier, bâtonnier of advocates in the Appeal Court of Paris, and brought face to face with its responsibility, Vichy decided on this transfer. The bâtonnier writes:[1]

'I went to see my client at Pellevoisin. . . . I found him in a broken-down building. It was the first time that I had seen a man of this importance . . . subjected to physical coercion as a Common Law criminal. . . . This impression was soon replaced by another more emphatic. I had noticed with genuine fear that the prison was only a few kilometres from the line demarcating the Occupation Zone. A raid carried out by half a dozen motor cyclists would have placed the accused in German hands within half an hour. . . . The danger seemed so urgent to me that I immediately took the train for Vichy and asked for an interview with M. Peyrouton, Minister of the Interior.

'I was lucky enough to meet him in the Chantecler restaurant. I went quickly up to his table and questioned him urgently. He interrupted me, saying, "I had thought about it."

'This might have been true. What is certain is that Paul Reynaud and Mandel were immediately afterwards transferred to . . . Vals in the Ardèche.'[2]

At Vals, Darlan permitted us to live under a political régime, which allowed us to establish friendships with men whom we had rubbed elbows with in the Chamber, without getting to know them personally.

Finally, in April, Darlan freed the other prisoners, and asked from the Germans authority to place Mandel and myself under house arrest still in Vals. The proposal was rejected.

VICHY IN SEARCH OF AN INDICTMENT

On June 24 the *Massilia*[3] arrived at Casablanca. Mandel disembarked and went immediately to Rabat. He visited the British Consulate-General. The Consul-General gave him information about the situation.

On the 25th, Duff Cooper, Minister of Information in the Churchill Cabinet, and Lord Gort arrived by aeroplane at Rabat. They tried to persuade the Resident-General to keep Morocco in the war, but it was useless.

Asserting that it saw a link between the arrival of the two British leaders and Mandel's visit to the British Consul-General, the Pétain Government decided to open an inquiry on grounds of a conspiracy against the security of the State. The case was referred to the permanent Military Tribunal of Meknès, which, on the outbreak of the war, had

[1] Charpentier, *op. cit.*, pp. 139–40.
[2] As is known, we were first taken to Aubenas, together with our companions in captivity. All of us were only transferred to Vals in March.
[3] The *Massilia* was a ship which took a certain number of French parliamentarians in late June to Casablanca [Tr.].

been empowered to try matters concerning espionage and treason in the territory of the Protectorate.

The alleged motive was indeed only an excuse. This is obvious from statements which both Duff Cooper and Gort made independently shortly afterwards. Here is a translation of Duff Cooper's statement:

> With reference to Press reports about the charges which are to be brought against M. Mandel, Mr. Duff Cooper thinks that he ought to state that his visit to Casablanca in June was in no wise inspired by M. Mandel, who had no previous knowledge of it, no more than any other French statesman had. During his stay at Casablanca Mr. Duff Cooper did not come into contact with M. Mandel.
>
> Duff Cooper

> I certify that Mr. Duff Cooper has signed the above statement on August 16. 1940. Signed [illegible]
> 29.9.40.[1]

The investigating magistrate of the Meknès Military Tribunal was at that time Major Joulin, judge of appeal at Rabat. On mobilization he was appointed to exercise these functions with the rank of judge-advocate of the third class. This official showed himself somewhat awkward. He jibbed against pressure exercised on him by the military command in Morocco, which wanted him to issue a warrant for arrest. He, however, issued a mere summons to appear before the Court on July 18, which he had served by the military prosecutor. Mandel, who was still at the Hotel Aletti in Algiers, arrived in Meknès on the 23rd.

But Vichy was not going to tolerate the scruples of this independent magistrate. On July 12, Major Joulin was relieved of his duties, and replaced by Lieutenant-Colonel Loireau, who was also in the judge-advocate-general's department but as a regular officer.

The investigation of the case fell, therefore, on Lieutenant-Colonel Loireau. It was a difficult task, for the Command, making clear to this regular officer that it counted on his sympathetic collaboration, pointed out to him, Mandel was later to tell me, that he was expected to secure, purely and simply, a capital sentence. The officer was in no doubt, therefore, that his career was at stake. Nevertheless, he listened to the voice of his conscience. After hearing Mandel and provisionally releasing him, he dismissed the charge. Vichy's reaction was emphatic; it forbade the Press to mention the decision; it opposed the dismissal of the charge, and finally it relieved the officer of his duties, and then retired him. The only thing left to Lieutenant-Colonel Loireau was to sell part of his property to buy an insurance book and thereby gain a livelihood for himself and his dependants.

[1] I have a photostat of these two statements in my possession; I got it from Mandel.

But Vichy had not finished with its dubious tricks. Why, indeed, should it not prosecute Mandel and myself for misappropriation of public funds? On July 3, 1940, Bouthillier, in his capacity as Minister of Finance, opened fire by laying a complaint before the military courts against me on this score. The case was taken before the permanent military tribunal of the 13th Division. Its investigation was entrusted to Lieutenant-Colonel Leprêtre. Would he dare to refuse the Marshal of France, and 'Victor of Verdun', who had saved France on two occasions, the service of indicting a politician, if he were told that the higher interests of his country demanded it? He had, indeed, the perilous audacity to refuse. Lieutenant-Colonel Leprêtre heard me, and after he too had taken counsel of his conscience, he gave Pétain a negative answer. What did Pétain do? He took the matter out of military jurisdiction and placed it in the hands of the Riom Court by a law which Alibert submitted for his signature on September 24, 1940. We, Mandel and I, were, therefore, handed over to the latter for misappropriation of public funds.[1]

To Bâtonnier Jacques Charpentier, who expressed his astonishment at seeing such an accusation brought against me, Alibert answered: 'I have proof of Paul Reynaud's dishonesty. He invested fifty million in an aircraft company. Where was he able to get all those millions?' Of course, a paragraph in *Gringoire* accepted the story as gospel truth. Now, these fifty millions had been invested in a nationalized aircraft company by Guy La Chambre acting in his capacity as Minister of Air and by myself as Minister of Finance!

Vichy knew very well that, though a prosecution for misappropriation of public money could only be instituted on the initiation of the Minister of Finance, based on a judgement of the *Cour des Comptes*, such a procedure was not applicable in the case of secret funds. The reason for this lay in the obvious fact that the Minister responsible for funds of this type was under certain restrictions because of their secret nature, and, as a consequence, he was only accountable to the Head of the State who alone was qualified to establish any possible deficit. But what did this matter, especially if, by announcing such a prosecution, it was possible to dishonour the men who wished to pursue a policy of honour and whose very existence appeared a living reproach to Vichy! The Procurator-General vainly observed that the prosecution presupposed a complaint from the Minister of Finance, and the latter could not lodge such an accusation because he had no control of these funds. Vichy insisted that he should prosecute without bothering about these trifles. The Procurator-General maintained his point of view. Alibert informed him in writing that the Minister of Finance was

[1] Mandel was also indicted for other equally invidious crimes: corruption, extortion, currency speculations, misuse of funds in his charge.

'absent from Vichy' [*sic*], and insisted that he should nevertheless continue.

So it came about that Mandel and myself were charged on the formal order of the Minister of Justice. What judge was to be entrusted with the trial? A Master of Requests of the *Conseil d'Etat* was expressly seconded to the Riom Court. He was M. Devémy, who, because of his devotion to extreme Right-wing opinions, had formerly pushed his scruples so far as to decline an offer which a Minister of the Republic had made him to join his staff. To him, the case of the two politicians was plain. But, unfortunately for Vichy, like the three officers, the Master of Requests showed himself to be an honest man. As for M. Cassagnau, this Minister of Justice vainly ordered him to request the Court[1] to issue a committal order for Mandel and myself; he refused to comply. But Vichy took no heed. Could it not resort to a *lettre de cachet*, that is to say, imprisonment ordered by the Administration?[2]

It was then decided to have Mandel's private fortune and my own valued. Notaries, currency dealers, bankers and stockbrokers were questioned and summoned to say if we did not hold secret funds, either in our own names, or in joint accounts or those of nominees. I had been Minister of Finance and, in this capacity, I had carried out certain conversions. If I had done so in order to make certain of enriching myself or if it had been discovered that one of my income-tax statements had been inaccurate, Vichy would have had a piece of luck. In the end, the account of a certain Reynaud was discovered in one bank, in which an item concerned a large transfer of funds to Tangier. 'This time, we have him', thought Vichy. Unfortunately it turned out to be someone who had my own name. Finally, the expert submitted his report. It turned out that I had impoverished myself in the service of the State; that on becoming Minister of Finance, November 2, 1938, at a time when the franc appeared, as we have seen, in such danger that my predecessor only saw salvation in a control of exchange, I ordered my banker to sell the foreign securities which he had bought on my account.

As for Mandel, the valuation of his private fortune was still continuing when we were handed over to the enemy. Need I say that it revealed nothing out of the ordinary? Naturally, Vichy did not take the trouble to send him any document whatsoever, nor, moreover, to interrogate him.

Such were the customs of the New Order. They were inspired by one principle: despotism.

[1] By its organic statute, the Court itself carried out a preliminary investigation of trials. It was, therefore, because of this statute, competent to issue its own warrants.

[2] In actual fact Mandel and I were subjected to this type of confinement, and remained under such until we were transferred to Portalet.

A TRIAL FOR THE CRIME OF REFUSING TO SURRENDER?

Vichy, I have said, had decided to open a prosecution against those who had opposed the request for an armistice, namely, Mandel and myself. Why was Mandel chosen? He certainly merited this honour for his constant opposition to France's shirking of her international obligations. Yet, after all, he had only spoken on this subject at the last meeting of the Council of Ministers, whilst Rio, Marin, Campinchi and Monnet had expressed themselves in this strain at nearly all Council meetings. Was it to give the Resistance Movement a semitic taint at a time when Jews were declared to be responsible for all the misfortunes of the country? I don't know, but the fact remains.

Unfortunately for Vichy the Procurator-General stated that a condemnation was impossible. No doubt he observed that there had been many trials in the past for surrendering, but never for the crime of 'refusing to surrender'. It was an injudicious proceeding! And no doubt he added that the members of a government were jointly responsible and that Pétain had been a member of my own. This indictment was, therefore, abandoned. The Germans certainly complained about this, as the Paris Press reveals, but they had a second string to their bow, to which they had attached still more importance since it involved France's responsibility for a declaration of war. They wished us to be condemned for 'war-mongering', at least in order to establish the fact that it was France who was responsible for the war.

In November, 1940, Bouthillier filed a long indictment of the 'war-mongers' with M. Cassagnau. He stated that I was their leader, and that I was the one who should be prosecuted. Was it not necessary for him to purge away the blemish which was afflicting him, namely, that of having been my creature?

FLANDIN AT WAR WITH THE WAR-MONGERS

Bouthillier then asked, in November, 1940, that I should stand trial as head of the war-mongers. Was it not a strange thing to see this man, a complete stranger to the political life of the country, push himself forward and take such a step? Indeed, the complaint which he uttered against me was certainly far from being original. We must, therefore, get to the roots of this campaign to which Bouthillier was giving voice.

Now, a document has just been published by the British Government which throws an especial light on the inner workings of this intrigue which was woven against me. In a telegram of September 2, 1938, to Lord Halifax,[1] Sir Eric Phipps, who was, as we know, British Ambassador in Paris at this time, reports that Etienne Flandin was spreading

[1] *Documents on British Foreign Policy, 1919–1939*, (Third Series, vol. II, 1938, pp. 219–20).

the rumour that war was inevitable, and that MM. Edouard Herriot, Georges Mandel and Paul Reynaud were doing their best to bring it about.[1]

Thus, in September, 1938, Flandin was accusing me of provoking a war. From that time he did not cease to maintain this accusation. A few days later, on the eve of Munich, came his startling poster: 'You are being deceived', in which, as we have seen, he attacked the 'hidden forces' which were trying 'to make war inevitable'. It was these same words which Sir Eric Phipps had just placed in his mouth. On the day after Munich he was to send, as we have also seen, his telegram to Hitler 'for the maintenance of peace'. A collation of these three documents is illuminating.

War broke out; defeat and the armistice ensued. Flandin came out of the shadows. These were the days of Montoire: a honeymoon spent by Vichy and the conqueror. Then came a change of scenery. The play was now to be continued in Paris. People contested for invitations from Abetz. The Embassy's Golden Book was filled with signatures. Pétain's Ministers made the Rue de Lille a home from home. They rubbed shoulders there with men who, evicted by the new team, were burning with a desire to return to office. In this atmosphere of intrigue tongues began to wag. Digging into his past, each exaggerated the claims of which he could boast in forwarding Hitler's interest. There were more timorous spirits who, anxious in spite of everything to guard against a turn of fortune's wheel, hesitated to burn their boats, and confined themselves to speaking off the stage. There were bolder ones who did burn their boats and gave their pledges in public.

Flandin was one of the latter. On November 15, 1940, he summoned the Press at Dijon: 'It was a curious speech', writes M. Maurice Martin du Gard,[2] 'in which there was no question of Laval, (and whence) it appeared . . . that it was he, Flandin, the man of peace . . . who had worked more stubbornly for peace than any other, and that everything was quite settled as regards the impending peace.' M. Maurice Martin du Gard adds: 'At the end of the meeting at which fifty editors and members of editorial staffs representing fourteen French departments attended, a telegram was sent to only the Marshal, with all the customary tributes to the national revival, the confidence of the country, the great European family (no one was excluded). If the cap fitted. . .!'[3] There is nothing surprising in the fact that Flandin was speaking in this strain, no more than in the language which he had been using against me for the past two years, and to which may be added particularly his refrain on the 'hidden forces' which had thrown France into the

[1] Sir Eric Phipps adds that M. Georges Bonnet, when questioned by him, denied M. Flandin's statement in so far as it concerned M. Herriot and myself.
[2] *La chronique de Vichy: 1940–1944*, p. 111.
[3] The points of suspension are in the text.

war.[1] In any case, such was the language which the contemporary Press was unanimous in attributing to him, without provoking any denial from him.[2]

It is clear that, through his Dijon speech, Flandin was hoping to draw upon himself the attention of Hitler and Pétain. For those who were scanning the horizon, he was the coming man. Bouthillier, who had conceived a taste for power, was not deceived about this. He turned deliberately to him. Let us hear what he has to say.[3]

'In July, President Flandin . . . had been left out of a government in which the master of the hour had meant to be the only former President of the Third Republic.[4] The time had come for the Marshal to give him a position. I visited M. Flandin in Paris on November 21. I was not in a position to give him any promises as the Marshal had not given me any message.'

Bouthillier nevertheless took it upon himself to urge Flandin 'to go to Vichy as quickly as possible'. But Laval, who was looking out for squalls, was on his guard. It was, therefore, necessary to circumvent his distrust. Bouthillier watched for an opportunity. Pétain's journey to Marseilles on December 3 and to Toulon on the 4th was to give him this.

Bouthillier rejoined Pétain at Toulon and went with him in the train which was taking the latter back to Vichy. Let us see again what he says:

'The Marshal . . . was wavering. . . . Fortunately I had adopted a very decided and positive position. . . . Now, here I was, near to the Marshal. In the dark saloon coach there were two settees. I sat down on the one to the left, on the right of the Marshal. In the opposite corner I saw Admiral Fernet, crouched in the dark . . . I brought up . . . the question of a successor. The Marshal answered that he was thinking of M. André François-Poncet.'

Bouthillier proposed Flandin. The portrait which he gave of him was etched in a way to please Pétain. There was nothing lacking. Morvan, Domecy-sur-Cure, the family estate, the family itself, the

---

[1] The analogy did not escape Mandel, who observed to me one day at Portalet that the Dijon speech was in the same strain as the notorious poster of the eve of Munich. In both, Flandin, Mandel stressed, attacked the 'hidden forces' which he accused of pushing us into war. And Mandel concluded: 'Four weeks after the Dijon speech Flandin was a Vichy Minister.'

[2] When he was prosecuted before the Supreme Court, Flandin, it is true, was to deny using this language. But why wait six years to do this? And how can he explain that M. Maurice Martin du Gard who himself never denied his sympathy with Vichy, published his book in 1948 without making the slightest allusion to this tardy correction?

[3] Bouthillier, *op. cit.*, pp. 220–65, *passim.*

[4] The reference is to Laval, Pétain's chief minister. The only former President of the Third Republic means President of the Council of Ministers. Both Flandin and Laval had been pre-war premiers of the Third Republic [Tr.].

home, the ivy and the virgin vine, Milly and Lamartine, Barrès Vauban, Cluny, Clairvaux and Abelard himself. 'He's not what one can call a cosmopolitan or in other words a wanderer.' Then Bouthillier's tone became elegiac: 'I went one summer day with the President [Flandin] to the shadow of the basilica of Vézelay, and contemplated the hill on which St. Bernard preached his crusade.'

How could such a litany be resisted, especially if one felt sleepy?

'All right, I agree', said the Marshal. 'Let us settle on Flandin. . . . Ask him to come to Vichy.' So the matter was arranged. On Saturday morning, the 7th, Flandin was with Pétain. He left him with the promise of the Ministry of Foreign Affairs in his pocket. He was to set out for Paris on the 10th, and was to return to Vichy on the 14th in order to receive out of Laval's heritage this 'mere post of Minister', to adopt an expression which dropped from Bouthillier when Darlan secured the larger share of the succession.

Bouthillier had guaranteed to Pétain that Flandin's presence in the new combination would be sufficient to appease the resentment which Hitler would feel on the ousting of Laval.[1] Bouthillier can flatter himself today for having sized up this problem correctly since, he says, Abetz, once the first feeling of anger had passed, asked Pétain to govern with both Laval and Flandin.

Thus, on Bouthillier's own confession, there existed in November, 1940, a real sympathy of opinion between himself and Flandin. Is it stretching truth too far to say that the two men had at the time joined forces? Is it not in any case obvious that when Bouthillier denounced me as leader of the war-mongers, he was reinforcing the campaign which Flandin was to persist, as we shall see, in prosecuting?

Flandin, indeed, profited by his accession to power in order to put his shoulder to the wheel. It was he who inspired Constitutional Law Number Seven of January 27, 1941, whereby Pétain assumed the right of 'supreme justice' over all whom he called 'responsible for our disaster'.[2] Incredible though it may seem, I was one of those who came under this jurisdiction which resembled a resurrection of the royal prerogative. Pétain was not unaware, however, that the power which he was arrogating to himself, or rather reassuming, overlapped with that which he had already placed within the sovereign competence of the Supreme Court of Justice. Had he, therefore, regretted delegating authority to the Riom judges, and decided to revoke it? This was by no means so. The exercise of the power which he had arrogated to himself ought not (and the law expressly states this) 'to place obstacles

[1] Referring to this period, Brinon, in his evidence at the Pétain trial (hearing of August 9, 1945) was incidentally to allude to the high 'esteem' which Flandin enjoyed with the 'German authorities'. He talked about it as if it were a very well-known fact.

[2] Although setting himself up as 'supreme judge', Pétain refrained from passing on those he condemned a penalty more severe than life imprisonment in a fortress.

in the way of ordinary legal prosecutions', which might be undertaken against the same people for the same 'crimes or offences'. The jurisdiction of Riom remained, therefore, valid, whatever happened, and that Court was bound to judge the justiciables on whose case Pétain had already passed a verdict. It is true that the Vichy régime alleged that this was a matter of two distinct spheres of authority, which, consequently, only appeared to infringe one upon the other. Pétain was basing his action on political grounds. The Court itself could not step outside the judicial sphere. It ought not to take cognizance of the sentences which the first-named would pass. It, therefore, kept intact its freedom of judging and giving a decision. Let us leave these quibbles to those who indulge in them. In actual fact, there existed only one question, and it depended on common sense. The people who fell under the jurisdiction of Pétain and of the Court were the same men, and the facts which they had to answer for before Pétain and the Court were the same. How could it be thought that the Court would acquit these men when Pétain had just condemned them!

It is sad to note that, in a country like our own, where a devotion to justice has never ceased to flourish, the despotism introduced by Law Number Seven aroused practically no indignation. Monzie writes:[1] 'The Constitutional Law Number Seven aroused no feeling amongst the lawyers, so disillusioned have we become.' But this passiveness inspired Jean Zay to utter this cry of pained surprise:[2]

'October 16 (1941).
'The trial of "those responsible for our defeat" has not taken place. . . . But, within forty-eight hours . . . the Head of the State himself is to pass a condemnation by law. . . . We learn at the same time that the trial will nevertheless take place. The accused are simply to be judged after being condemned. . . . Nothing in all this is very remarkable. Here is something which is more so: no judge of the Supreme Court has offered his resignation.'

It would be cruel to push things any further. Yet this Law Number Seven was one of those of which the Vichy régime boasted. Finally, to stress its importance, Vichy immediately issued the following instructions:[3] 'Newspapers are required to present Constitutional Law Number Seven as an event of capital importance. Number of columns unlimited [sic]. The news must be preceded by official commentaries.'[4] Now, the Information Services also came under Flandin.

[1] La saison des Juges, p. 114.   [2] Op. cit., pp. 144-5.
[3] They were dated January 28, 1941, and numbered 128.
[4] Le Temps, setting the tone, wrote on the 29th, under the title of Retour à la Logique politique: 'In reading Constitutional Law Number Seven, which was published this morning, some ingenuous people, though of an upright mind exclaimed: "But has not that been so before now?"'

After he left the Administration, Flandin continued his campaign. The only proof of this which I wish to cite is an interview that he gave in his villa of Saint-Jean-Cap-Ferrat to Roger Stéphane[1] when Mandel and I were imprisoned in Portalet. Declaring war once more against the 'clan of war-mongers', he attacked first of all Louis Marin, then Mandel, who, he said, 'unfortunately is a Jew, and placed his interests before those of the country', and finally myself, 'one of those directly responsible', he declared, 'for the war and our defeat'.

Flandin remained, therefore, consistent in his actions. For him it was still not Hitler who was responsible for the war. As for our defeat, he still thought along the same lines as when he told Mandel, as we have heard, that my proposal to form an armoured corps was idiotic.

OCTOBER 16, 1941: PÉTAIN JUDGES US WITHOUT A HEARING, AND CONDEMNS US WITHOUT GIVING A REASON

Hitler wished the Riom Court to state that Mandel and myself were responsible for the war. As soon as he saw that the prosecutions begun against us deviated from this objective, he stormed and threatened. Abetz, in 1941, stated to Maître Ribet: 'The Riom trial interests us only very slightly. It is those who were responsible for the war in whom we are interested: Reynaud and Mandel. . . . If I had these two in my clutches, I should strangle them with my own hands.'[2]

In L'Œuvre, Déat made himself the echo of the ill-temper of his masters. He wrote one day: 'Good lawyers are wondering if MM. Paul Reynaud and Mandel are not going to get out of this business with excuses and congratulations.' And on December 4, 1940, taking up the same theme he again wrote:

'As for Reynaud and Mandel, war-mongers by doctrine, born slaves of Britain, ready to shed French blood to the last drop, resolved to

[1] *Chaque homme est lié au monde*, pp. 102–10, *passim*. On leaving the interview, Roger Stéphane polished up his notes and sent them to Flandin, who could see them again at his leisure. The author goes to the trouble of setting out in his book his own text side by side with that corrected by Flandin.

[2] To prepare their defence before the Riom Court, the accused needed files which, on leaving Paris, they had placed in safe places at various spots within the zone which was later to be occupied. But permission had to be got from Abetz for the transfer of these files to the unoccupied zone. Abetz agreed to the request made to him, but on condition that it was the Embassy which should take charge of this transfer, and which could thus find out their contents. Ribet, in his capacity as Daladier's lawyer, protested to Barthélemy against this claim which was prejudicial to the rights of the defence. Following an approach by Barthélemy, Abetz agreed that the files should only be handed over to him after they had been sealed, and promised to dispatch them in this state to their destination. Having summoned Ribet to inform him of these arrangements, he uttered then the words I have given above. During a visit to Portalet, Ribet recounted the scene to Mandel, who, in his turn, told me of it. In July, 1949, Bâtonnier Ribet confirmed to me this account, which I used in my evidence at the trial of Abetz (hearing of July 19, 1949), and Abetz, questioned by the President of the Court about my evidence answered, 'The facts which he has related are true.'

make France a dominion of His Majesty, to abandon the forty million French to their sad fate and to prolong the war in the shade of African palm trees, it is not known on what grounds they are indicted.'

Between April and May, 1941, Vichy, striving not to lag behind, launched in its turn an extremely violent campaign against me. Its wireless denounced me as 'a docile tool in the hands of Churchill, who had sacrificed thousands of French lives' by refusing to ask for an armistice, and wishing to continue the war against the advice of Pétain and Weygand. It was on the occasion of this campaign that I wrote a letter to Pétain from my prison in Vals on April 5, which[1] made him beside himself with rage, because, in picking up the lies of his wireless, I passed judgement at the same time on his own policy.

On June 20, 1941, *Gringoire*, the only newspaper in the unoccupied zone which the Germans allowed to enter the occupied one, went one better: 'All France is demanding that Paul Reynaud, the tool of Britain, should be brought to justice.' Indeed, explained *Gringoire*, if the first 'important crime' had been to unloose the war, the second had been to prolong it, and 'this is what Reynaud did'.

All this was extremely fine, but I had not yet been charged in the political trial.

Therefore, the Paris Press roared louder. *Je suis partout* wrote on August 4, 1941: 'Between these people (Jewish-Masonry, Reynaud, the British, the Communists) and ourselves it is a trial of strength.'

This was indeed talking!

On August 12, 1941, Pétain announced his intention of using this strange prerogative which he had arrogated to himself, as we have seen, by Constitutional Law Number Seven. He was, therefore, to pass judgement himself on 'those responsible for our disaster'. Everyone knew that it was a question of Daladier and his colleagues who, for a year already, had lain under accusation on this score.

But this did not suit the book of the Germans. They wanted the heads of Reynaud and Mandel.

Thus, Déat worked himself into a frenzy. He wrote on August 14, 1941, in *L'Œuvre*: 'But what about Paul Reynaud and Mandel? Are they to be judged, though not indicted? It would certainly be rather strange if the new Council of Political Justice did not take cognizance of their case.'

Let the accounts of these two be settled! Let them be indicted, demanded *Je suis partout*, or let them undergo the fate of Marx Dormoy, who, this newspaper revealed, on this occasion, 'was executed semi-officially'! And for an epitaph it suggested: 'They were allowed to expire without a tear being shed.'

[1] I shall give the text of this letter later.

21

On October 2, Déat wrote: 'The condemnation of Reynaud and Mandel will supply proof that we have realized the necessities of this continental revolution.' To 'make a Europe' it was essential to have us shot! On the 4th, Déat resumed his attack against 'the two men . . . who had driven the country towards disaster at a crazy rate . . . and delayed the request for an armistice as much as possible'. Certainly Hitler wished action to be taken against us! Vichy gave way.

Then Pétain summoned the Procurator-General to the Hôtel du Parc. He had Darlan, Barthélemy and Bouthillier with him.

'M. Procurator-General,' said Pétain, 'M. Bouthillier will tell you about this trial the Government means to open.' And my former Minister of Finance took up the subject: the trial to be instituted was, he stated, the trial of the 'war-mongering clan', and it was the leader of this clan—that is myself—who had to be prosecuted.

After this explanation the following discussion was begun:

'Can Reynaud and Mandel be condemned without being charged?'

'That is impossible,' answered the legal officer.

'Well then, charge them.'

'With what?'

'With . . . war-mongering.'

'What do you mean by war-mongering?'

'The crime of having unloosed the war.'

'But Hitler did that. You won't find a judge in France who will lend himself to a proceeding which tries to absolve him of this responsibility.'

'Then indict them for having opposed the request for an armistice, a crime which falls under the decree of which you are aware. Need I remind you that we passed such a decree expressly to deal with them?'

'But I have already told you, a government assumes joint responsibility with its head. How, therefore, can you dissociate Marshal Pétain from the Reynaud Administration?'

'Yes. That is true. Well then, charge them without giving the nature of the indictment!'

M. Cassagnau was equally blunt. 'There is nothing,' he kept repeating, 'against either Reynaud or Mandel.'

Under such conditions the last resort was to do without an indictment. This is what Pétain was to do. He created a council which he called 'The Council of Political Justice'. The words clashed but they well describe the summary and expeditious task entrusted to this peculiar institution: to deliberate in secret and without intermission in order to submit to Pétain an opinion on which he could base the condemnation which he had decided to pass himself. Eight people were chosen to compose this 'Secret Council', one of whom, it is true, namely M. Percerou, Professor in the faculty of law at Paris, excused himself at the opening of the deliberations. The most influential of the seven acting members was M. Emmanuel de Peretti de la Rocca, one of Pétain's few friends and one of his predecessors at our Madrid Embassy. This same man, in 1924, when he was welcoming Herriot to the Quai d'Orsay, took the opportunity of leading him into his own room, and of showing him the photograph of his son, saying 'I introduce to you, Monsieur le Président, a young Radical-Socialist.' Forthwith and authoritatively, the retired diplomat took charge of the conduct and presidency of the hearings. Under his inspiration, the matter was smartly dispatched.

M. du Moulin de la Barthète relates[1] the story of this judicial farce. Like well-schooled courtiers, several of the members of the Council inquired of 'certain ministers', M. du Moulin tells us, what Pétain expected of them. The Council, thus enlightened about its duty, summoned M. Cassagnau. The latter informed it of the indictment which he had drawn up following an investigation of Daladier, Blum and Gamelin. But he stated that he had no charge to formulate either against Mandel or myself.

Without hearing us, the Council, by four votes to three,[2] voted, however, in favour of condemnation. And one of the four persons who voted in this sense was President of the Council of State!

M. du Moulin tried to get Pétain to accept the opinion of the minority. 'But', he writes, 'Pucheu and Bouthillier (the latter actuated by a prejudice, inexplicable in my opinion, against Paul Reynaud, his former chief) brought pressure to bear on the Marshal, who, neglecting the scruples of the minority, declared the two former Ministers guilty —by an *ad hoc* ruling which was based upon no previous preliminary investigation.' This was an obvious abuse of the law,[3] a violation of the rules of all procedure (even exceptional) against which the bâtonnier of the Paris lawyers, Maître Charpentier, was moved to protest immediately to the Head of the State. Above all, it was to reintroduce, in a significantly oblique manner, a trial for declaring war into a trial for entering the war unprepared.[4] In Pétain's opinion it was certainly as war-mongers that we were condemned.

When questioned by a juror of the Supreme Court upon the reason

---

[1] *Op. cit.*, pp. 382–3.

[2] MM. de Peretti de la Rocca, Ripert, Audollent and Colonel Josse were in favour of a condemnation. MM. Charles Vallin, Félix Aulois and Drouat were for acquittal. 'The Marshal had given me to understand that he would enforce a penalty, whatever our judgement was', wrote M. Aulois to M. Cassin, President of the Jury of Honour, on September 29, 1945.

[3] The words 'deliberate flouting' were certainly those which the author had in mind.

[4] It was during its meeting on October 4, 1941, that the Council of Ministers conferred on what action it should take as a result of the judgment given by the Council of Political Justice. It voted, by a majority, in favour of our condemnation. Need it be said that, amongst those who were in the majority, Bouthillier stood out by the vehemence of his attacks against me?

for which he had 'advised Pétain to condemn Georges Mandel and Paul Reynaud', Berthelot, the former Vichy Minister of Communications, replied: 'Because they were held to be enemies of the régime.'[1]

Such are the circumstances in which Pétain set himself up as a judge in order to condemn both of us to life imprisonment. Pétain thus carried out the pledge which, as we know, he had given Hitler, to condemn Mandel and myself for war-mongering by October 15, 1941, at the latest.[2]

Let us see now the circumstances in which Pétain condemned us. The reader will receive shock after shock.

The docile Court of Political Justice asked Pétain what he wanted of it on October 6, 1941. Pétain sent the following questionnaire to the President of the Council 'in order to take into account your wishes' as he told him:

'2nd. Do you think that these penalties (in Constitutional Law Number Seven) can also be applied to

MM. Paul REYNAUD,
Georges MANDEL,

not by virtue of the special charges levied against them which have as yet only been the subject of mere investigations, but because of the responsibility which they assumed in our defeat by the way which they feed and personify the campaigns of a war-mongering propaganda?'

It was, therefore, for the crime, unknown in the Penal Code, of 'war-mongering', that is to say, acting on behalf of the honour of France, that we were to be condemned.

The Council of Political Justice, which was unanimous as regards 'the others who were responsible for the war' divided over Mandel and myself.

A majority (composed of MM. Peretti de la Rocca, Audollent, Josse and Ripert) was not inclined to show itself independently minded. It considered that if Pétain was absolutely convinced of the guilt of these two men, 'they ought then both to be immediately indicted for the same facts (responsibility for our disaster) before the Supreme Court'.

It is true that, in civilized countries, it is not customary to condemn people unless they have been charged.

Having said this, the majority was convinced that 'the severest punishment would not be too harsh for the grave events—due to them'.

---

[1] 'In view of the fact, on the other hand, that Berthelot advised Pétain to condemn Georges Mandel and Paul Reynaud, "held to be enemies of the régime"' read the judgement of the Supreme Court of July 10, 1946, when condemning Berthelot.'

[2] In a speech which he gave on the 13th, Funck, Hitler's Minister, mentioned this pledge by which Pétain stated he was ready within an agreed time to declare us guilty of 'having pushed France into declaring war on Germany out of affection for Britain' and to condemn us on this account.

What was my own crime?

'When military defeat was certain, he refused to consider the cessation of hostilities, and was thus prepared to subject the whole of France to invasion, then to total occupation, and what remained of the Army to captivity. At the final stage of the enemy advance [a month before this stage] he resolved to take his Administration from French soil in order to continue overseas a useless struggle, thus leaving the metropolitan territory without any government.' He was going to do all this in 'the firm belief that France could not continue to live under a foreign dominion'. Consequently, 'Paul Reynaud betrayed the duties which fell to him.'

I was, therefore, being reproached with the crime of refusing to surrender. No doubt it was the first occasion in the history of any country in the world that a man has been condemned for such a crime.

And what about Mandel? Here is the judgement passed on him:

'He shared in all the designs hatched by his leader in the Government, and in all his tricks to link the fate of France with foreign interests, and to induce the Government to leave metropolitan territory with this intention.'

As for the three minority members of the Council of Political Justice, they also declared that Mandel and I had not been charged by the Riom Court, and that, in the burlesque prosecution for misappropriation of secret funds, the Public Prosecutor's department had not at the time sufficient proof to justify placing the matter before the Court. Moreover, the Court had not issued a committal order against us, and consequently we had, therefore, been imprisoned 'by order of the Administration'. It was a question of facts being 'insufficiently established' (what a delightful euphemism) and 'moreover being irrelevant to the reasons for our national disaster'.

Proceedings designed for condemning us on a charge of warmongering were stated to be 'inopportune'.

'The only grounds for blame . . . sprang from their action in the critical hours of May to June, 1940.' But if French public opinion was 'unanimous as regards the responsibility for the nation's lack of preparation for war, it was still divided on the events of June, 1940'.

This was a source of great dispute between the Gaullists and Pétainists.

In any case, concluded these worthy lawyers, 'if, despite the opinion which we have just expressed, the Head of the State decides to condemn them, it would, in this case, be desirable, if not indispensable, for the Supreme Court of Riom at least to open before this a new inquiry upon this fact, and to issue a warrant for their arrest'.

On this point at least the minority was in agreement with the majority.

But Pétain paid no heed to either of them, and condemned both of us to life imprisonment without hearing us and without even charging us, an action which had no precedent in the legal history of any civilized country.

On the day following our condemnation, the Press published a list of the sentences of those 'responsible for our disaster'. Above each name was a space in which were printed the reasons for the condemnation. The spaces above the names of Mandel and myself were unfilled.

Pétain had condemned us without daring to give any reason.

APRIL TO JULY, 1941: MY LETTERS TO PÉTAIN

I have said that I sent a letter from my prison to Pétain on April 5. Here is the text:

It is already known that you imprisoned me for refusing to surrender and to conclude an armistice last June. . . . But what is still surprising is that, after having shut me up for seven months, you have me attacked by all the wireless stations of the national network on the occasion of an argument with General de Gaulle. I should not even have thought it necessary to protest if this campaign, for which it is said, you are giving your word as a bond, were not based, in so far as it concerns me, on a series of dishonest allegations. . . .

1. It is inaccurate to say that it was the British Government which asked us to continue the war in North Africa. You know better than anyone else, because you attended the meetings which were held every morning in my room, that this decision was taken by myself. This decision sprang from the pledge entered into by the Allies not to abandon each other, a pledge of which you were aware when you entered my Government and . . . I do not know that you ever asked me to repudiate it.

2. It is inaccurate to say that M. Charles Reibel was an 'eyewitness' of anything. He made use of blameworthy items of information, which were for the most part, fantastic.

3. It is inaccurate to say that, on May 29 and June 7, General Weygand wrote me letters which became increasingly urgent in their demands for me to conclude an armistice. On June 10, on the contrary, he wrote that he 'was far from having lost all hope. . . .' . . . A falsehood of such a flagrant nature . . . is all the more inexplicable in that I wrote to you on September 6, 1940, in order to point out that the national broadcasting service had just . . . reported it. At that time the wireless drew from it this conclusion; 'if we had listened to Weygand, Italy would not have come into the war'. This was a falsehood since Italy declared war on June 10, and in passing it may be observed that it showed a curious misapprehension about the minds of the Italian rulers. They would not have given up the idea of sharing in spoils to be got from us because we requested an armistice from Germany.

4. It is inaccurate to say that, 'the Armistice spared French families from sacrificing their children as hitherto they had done in vain'. As soon as our Command stated that the struggle was to no avail, I proposed ending it 'on the soil of metropolitan France' just as the Dutch had done. This would have

spared us the losses we suffered during the long delay necessary to obtain the Armistice. Such an event would have taken place, but for the fact that I had to relinquish power because I was defeated by a coalition of yourself, Weygand and a majority of Ministers. . . . It is not, therefore, the Government of which I was the leader . . . which can be accused of the belief that 'not enough French blood had been shed. . . .'

5. It is inaccurate to say that the conditions of the Armistice 'would have been less severe' if it had been asked for earlier. When General Weygand asked the Government to conclude an armistice on June 12 at Cangé, our Armies had been finally defeated on metropolitan territory. Germany showed, and shows with every passing day, that she means to exact the maximum price for her victory within and in addition to the terms of the Armistice.

6. It is inaccurate to say that, in the Supreme Council which was held on June 11 (and not the 13th) at Briare (and not at Tours), Mr. Winston Churchill refused any further co-operation on the part of British aircraft. He promised on the contrary to study the problem as soon as he was back in London. It is equally inaccurate to say that 'for weeks, our soldiers waited in vain for British aircraft', for we received, as a result of my daily entreaties, considerable assistance from the R.A.F. In the light of what has taken place since, nobody can reproach the Prime Minister for not having thrown into the Battle of France, all the aircraft on which, today, our hope of victory depends. . . .

7. It is inaccurate to say that President Roosevelt replied 'in a somewhat evasive manner' to the message which I sent him on June 14. This is to misinterpret completely the importance of his reply and the generosity which had prompted it. . . .

8. It is inaccurate to say that the offer of a Franco-British union which was made to us on June 16, 1940, would have 'degraded us to the rank of a Dominion'.

9. It is inaccurate to say that the text . . . was 'telephoned from London by General de Gaulle under the dictation of Mr. Churchill' . . . In actual fact General de Gaulle telephoned its text to me and Mr. Winston Churchill then telephoned to ask me how I felt about it. . . . But this is something more slanderous: 'a striking detail is that, at the other end of the wire, sitting next to the French Premier, as if by chance, was General Spears who was President of the Franco-British Committee'. This is a calumny, first of all, on myself, who am made out to be without that dignity required by my office. I say no more about this. But this attack on Spears, who is one of the oldest and most faithful friends of France[1] in the House of Commons and whom it is strange to treat as a suspect, is as unjustified as it is unseemly. He had been officially accredited to me, when Minister of War, by Mr. Churchill, and he visited me on that day in the company of his Ambassador. His attitude was, therefore, as always, perfectly correct. . . . Nothing is more contemptible or more contrary to our national interests than these insinuations—against the rulers of a nation whose heroism will bring about our salvation. We know only too well those who rejoice in this damage done to our interest.

All these inexactitudes . . . count for little compared with the statement that General de Gaulle added nothing as regards the employment of assault tanks

---

[1] It was only later that General Spears' attitude in the Levant gave grounds for criticism on our part.

to the contribution made by the late General Estienne. For, here, we touch upon the essential reason for our defeat. And here again, I am intimately concerned.

Can it be believed that French people are still unaware that our highest military experts stated that a continuous front . . . was unbreakable and that the enemy would only make break-throughs which would be more dangerous for them, the deeper they became? Can it be believed that they are still unaware that General de Gaulle stated on the contrary that an armoured corps, whose composition he laid down, would be an instrument capable of breaking this continuous front at a certain point?

Can it be believed that they are still unaware that, on March 31, 1935 . . . I tabled in the Chamber an amendment for the creation of an armoured corps; that I stated that the German Army would pass through Holland and Belgium; would thrust aside the Belgian Army on the Albert Canal and would attack our northern frontier, which the Supreme War Council had refused to fortify; that we would be invaded by an army . . . composed of armoured divisions, supported by fighter aircraft, if we did not possess an armoured corps which alone could allow us to mount a victorious counter-offensive?

Can it be believed that they are still unaware that my amendment was rejected in France as 'contrary to logic and to history' but adopted in Germany? . . .

Can it be believed that they are still unaware that it was the German armoured corps which cracked our front on the Marne in May, 1940, then won the Battle of France and smashed the French Army, preventing it, through speed, from taking up new positions anywhere?

You know better than anyone, because of the great influence which you exerted in the Supreme Council of War of which you were a member, why my amendment failed to secure acceptance. You know better than anyone how my amendment was opposed since, on the eve of the war, you introduced to the public a book dealing with principles in which could be read . . . 'As for tanks, which were to shorten our wars, their failure has been startling.'

Certainly, this is not the time to begin an argument, when the enemy occupies two-thirds of our territory. But, whilst awaiting . . . silence is better than lying, and discretion than defiance. . . . Truth is like a gas which explodes with greater violence the more violently it is compressed. I warn you solemnly of this fact. Reaction will be strong. . . . I am telling you this because I know you are capable of rising above the acclamations which greet your official visits.

Because I have not belonged to any political party, I have always been outspoken. Seven years ago I asked the Government of which you were a member to peg the franc to the pound sterling and to the dollar which had been devalued. I warned this Government that this was the only way to avoid social and political upheavals which would be dangerous to our safety. During these years, I tried to open the eyes of our highest military authorities, and of our Ministers who were their spokesmen in Parliament, as to the deadly peril which threatened our country. I was refused a hearing. France paid the penalty.

I don't ask anything of you for myself. We collaborated closely when I was in power, and even if I refused to follow your policy, I have done everything I could to assist you in your task when you took over from me. I did it in the interests of the country. Nobody owes me any gratitude for this.

Your attitude has been quite different towards me. You have kept me in prison, in solitary confinement for the last seven months. In your name, the defamatory weekly Press has then been told: 'You see this man behind his bars? You can, if you wish, spit in his face, as you pass by.' Courageously the Press has done this . . . during these months, with the approval of your censorship. It has even uttered falsehoods to try and strike at me. In France, that does not matter now. . . .

You have had a Minister of Justice who has told the world in an official communiqué that it is 'known by all French people' that I have made my fortune. On the word of a defamatory newspaper, and despite the fact that all my career has given the lie to this silly insinuation, the Minister of Justice stated that I had certainly enriched myself since I had invested fifty millions in an aircraft company. Now, I made this investment in my capacity of Minister of Finance in a nationalized company! There might have been reason to smile at this, but for the fact that this successor of Daguesseau, convinced about the truth of my explanation, tried to justify my imprisonment after it had taken place, and to discredit the leader of our Resistance by the lowest of political moves. This was by getting you to pass a law for the deliberate purpose of removing me out of the jurisdiction of the Court and of a judge who refused to prosecute me, and placing me under that of the Riom Court, charged with such an absurd offence that the Court itself refused to make my internment legal. . . . The latest sign of his lack of balance are the words, which created a scandal in the south, that he uttered about you, who had once raised him from obscurity. I do not possess such an outlook on public life. I never thought of throwing into prison those of my colleagues who, like yourself, did not share my own opinion about the Armistice. Instead of trying to dishonour them, I happened to shield the name of one of them, unknown to himself, in the past—perhaps you will learn about it one day—from any attack.

Keep me in prison if it suits you. Our own persons count for little. It will be my crowning honour to have suffered for having placed such a high value on the word of France, and for not having wished to diminish the chances of victory for the coalition to which she belonged.

But listen to the advice of a Frenchman to whom it would have been better, in the interests of his country, to pay more frequent attention.

Make people stop telling this nation that the honour of France does not count; that it was necessary for her to break her word to Poland on September 3, 1939, that it was necessary for her to break her word to Britain on June 16, 1940. Having 'lost everything except honour', what has our nation left, if it is deprived of honour?

Make people stop creating as an ideal for our youth, the idea they should collaborate with an enemy who annexes Alsace-Lorraine in contravention of the Armistice, and whose flags float over Paris, for one cannot raise oneself at the same time as one bends.

Make people stop running down that stoical race, our ally, on whom our salvation depends.

There can be no greater danger to a nation than to see its soul being degraded. Resurrect those feelings which certainly, as a Frenchman, remain in the depths of your heart.

As the Vichy wireless renewed its attacks, I wrote, to my great peril, two letters in the same strain but more sharp in tone to the 'Head of the French State'. In the last which was dated May 18, 1941, I recalled to him that I had called him into power and designated him to the President of the Republic—we have seen why I preferred him to Chautemps—when I chose to resign rather than ask for an armistice. And I said to him:

If it were true that, after having concluded an armistice with the enemy despite our pledged word, you were now preparing to reverse our foreign policy without consulting the French people, which has constantly endorsed it, and that you would grant no citizen the right to express an opinion as if we were a nation of helots;
If it were true that your policy might be aimed at stabbing our ally in the back, our ally who alone remains in the struggle and fights heroically on, in Egypt, Abyssinia, Iraq, the Mediterranean, Britain and the Atlantic, an ally whose seven hundred and fifty thousand sons fell during the last war defending the soil of France, and whose victory can alone give us back our lost freedom;
If it were true that your policy was in the process of breaking the precious friendship which, for a century and a half, has united France to the greatest people in the world, whose ideals are our ideals;
If it were true that your policy was to have the disastrous result of enslaving a France, thus isolated, to a nation whose ideals and beliefs are violently opposed to our own, whilst the war is not over, and whilst, after these days of trial, the final victory of the Allies looms in the distance;
If it were true that you might be contemplating the conclusion of a peace of Brest-Litovsk;
If all this were true, I should not repudiate the liabilities which I have incurred; on the other hand I should beg France's pardon for them.

On July 26, 1941, Marx Dormoy was assassinated in a cowardly manner at Montélimar, where he had been sent to live. This was used as an opportunity to make the circumstances of our confinement more rigorous. I sent a memorandum to the Vichy Government, from which I give several extracts:

I have heard of the assassination of M. Marx Dormoy, senator and former minister. . . . This crime fills me with feelings of indignation and shame for my country, but it does not surprise me in the slightest.
Since it is intended that I shall suffer from the murder of M. Dormoy, I have the right to ask the question, what inspired this murder, and also why my life is thought to be in danger?
M. Dormoy had been publicly denounced by his arrest, his imprisonment and supervision in an appointed place of residence and recently by dismissal

from his office as a departmental councillor. Official censorship indulged in a campaign of invective against him, which he was not able to answer. It is obvious that he would not have been murdered if, after being released from prison, he could have retired to his home town, his own house, and been surrounded by his family and friends, instead of being obliged to live at Montélimar in this public place which is an hotel for travellers, without being provided with effective protection by the authorities who forced him to live there. His assassination has been provoked, and conditions ideal for his removal have been engineered. This crime is, therefore, a direct outcome of the method of government instituted in France by the present régime.

Does the Government believe that my life is in danger? If this is true, whose fault is it?

Then, after having alluded to the campaign which was being waged against me, since arbitrary imprisonment, by the Press, radio, cinema, and even the theatre, and to the judicial penalties which had been perpetrated against me, I concluded:

If I have taken the trouble to write these lines, it is because the Government, which tells me it is concerned about the threat to my life, knows very well that, in so far as this may be so, it is only due to the fault of the Government. History will pass judgement.... It will be less merciless towards those arbitrary executions carried out in circumstances which are truly revolutionary than to these proceedings of unremitting defamation, of unwearying calumny, which I have just summed up, and which have never, to my knowledge, been employed before.

I have nothing to ask of the Government. It can persevere in its attitude, finding in the danger to which it subjects me an excuse to prolong endlessly my imprisonment on an arbitrary warrant such as is not permitted in any civilized country.

It can also scotch the danger which it has created by revealing the truth.

I leave it to the Government to decide which of these two methods is the more honest.

We know which method was chosen by Vichy.

JUNE–AUGUST, 1942: THE FINDINGS OF BÂTONNIER JACQUES CHARPENTIER

We have seen previously that the expert entrusted with verifying how I had obtained my money had proved how empty were the charges to which I had been subjected.

Using the results of this expert examination as a basis, Bâtonnier Jacques Charpentier deposited in June, 1942, findings which offered grounds for dismissing the indictment. In these findings, full of talented pleading and of courageous spirit, the bâtonnier stigmatized the dishonesty of the prosecution and the campaign of calumny which Vichy had unloosed against me. The President of the Court stated to Maître

Bétolaud, who defended me with the bâtonnier, that the matter was outside his province. He refused, in these circumstances, to put these findings before the Court. Maître Charpentier went to see Barthélemy, who, after having alleged that I was not suffering as a result of any charge, advised him to give up his request for a dismissal of the indictment if he did not wish to have 'trouble' with Pétain's 'staff'. Meanwhile the bâtonnier came to see me in my cell at Portalet. I told him how greatly I admired his findings but they had the fault in my opinion of making me appear to take the Riom Court and the trial which Vichy was instituting against me seriously.

It was then, on August 14, 1942, that the bâtonnier placed new findings[1] before the Riom Court. He demanded that legal acknowledgment should be made that certain arbitrary acts 'had been committed against me by the judiciary'. Here are some brief extracts from his deposition:

May it please the Court:
In view of the fact that M. Paul Reynaud has been refused a trial, it is fitting to reveal the successive arbitrary acts which have been employed in an attempt to attack him for being a statesman guilty of the following sins, namely, having demonstrated the revolution introduced by science into the art of war; having predicted whence and how France would be invaded; having stated how she ought to rearm and with whom she should ally to escape the deadly peril which threatened her; and finally of opposing, on June 16, 1940, the Armistice, because he wished to remain faithful to the pledge of France, and did not desire to lessen the chances of victory for the coalition of which France was a member. . . .
May it please the Court to declare officially to the petitioner that the following five arbitrary acts on part of the judiciary have been perpetrated against him:
1. In that his case was transferred by a special law from the Court of the judge before whom it should legally have been heard, because he refused to accept an indictment;
2. In that it was insisted that the petitioner should be indicted before the Supreme Court without being heard, though the judge who had examined him refused to accept an indictment against him. Moreover, this indictment was illegal, and its illegality had been concealed by a suppression of vital items of evidence in the files of the case;
3. In that the course of justice has been interfered with to prevent a judgement being given in the case of the petitioner;

[1] The complete text of these will be found on pp. 178–88 of the above-mentioned work of Jacques Charpentier.

4. In that the petitioner was imprisoned in a fortress for an unlimited term as responsible for our defeat, without being informed of the evidence supporting the accusation, without even being told what charges had been laid against him;

5. In that he was imprisoned for twenty-three months without a warrant.

Jacques Charpentier.

On August 26, Laval withdrew from me the right to communicate with my lawyers. This was another violation of the rights granted to the defence in all civilized countries. This decision was made known to me at Portalet, on September 1. I took official steps about it. The bâtonnier went to ask Barthélemy for an explanation. On November 16 he protested to him in vain in an official letter. At the same time he informed me of the failure of his approaches: 'These miserable individuals', he wrote to me, 'have already lost face. Now, they have lost their heads.' After having quoted this extract from his letter, he adds:[1] 'I was certain that the envelope marked "Personal" would be opened, and that a copy would immediately be sent to the Minister. This is exactly what happened. . . . Joseph Barthélemy . . . was very much irritated by my findings, and complained about them to Bâtonnier Payen, who sent me on his complaints. I played the innocent: of what was the Minister of Justice complaining? . . . I could only suppose that he had been unscrupulous enough to open a letter which was not intended for him.'

On September 3 the President of the Court informed me of his refusal to add to 'the file on the investigation opened against me' the findings which Bâtonnier Charpentier had placed before him. His reason was that these principally concerned facts whose investigation and evaluation did not fall within the province of the Court; moreover, they did not show that proper 'respect which was due to the law'.

Let us hear what Jacques Charpentier has to say on this matter:[2]

'This time, the denial of justice was signed. The President of the Supreme Court coldly informed the accused that he would not submit to the Court the findings which he acknowledged he had received. As if he had the power to refuse to do this!

'If the facts contained in the findings fell outside the competence of the Court, it was the duty of the Court to say so, and for it alone.

'If the findings failed to pay due respect to the law, it was again the duty of the Court to say why.

'It could reject the findings, but first of all it had to take cognizance of them.

[1] Charpentier, *op. cit.*, pp. 192–3.   [2] *Ibid.*, p. 189.

'The problem was never brought up. Nothing demonstrates better the depths to which justice had descended under the Vichy régime than this example of how the foremost magistrate of France was able to evade a request which was legally brought before him.'

A YEAR OF INCARCERATION IN PORTALET

It is here that my father would be if he were alive.

Michel Clemenceau

On November 14, 1941, we were informed of Pétain's sentence.

We, Marshal of France and Head of the French State:

In accordance with Constitutional Law Number Seven of January 27, 1941;

And of the Law of October 29, 1941, appointing the Fort of Portalet a place of detention within a fortified area:

Have decreed:

First Article: MM. Edouard Daladier, Léon Blum, General Gamelin, Paul Reynaud and Georges Mandel will be incarcerated within the fortifications of Portalet. . . .

Given by us at Vichy on November 7, 1941.

Philippe Pétain.

The sentence was silent upon the duration of the penalty. But there was no doubt that it meant detention for life. Indeed, Pétain had stated in his speech delivered on October 16 that the penalty which he inflicted on Daladier, Blum and Gamelin was 'the most severe' of those laid down by Constitutional Law Number Seven. This penalty, as we see, was one of detention for life within a fortified place. Now the sentence condemned Mandel and myself to the same punishment as the other three. Therefore, we too were imprisoned for life. And we have seen before that Benoist-Méchin told Abetz on October 30 of our condemnation to perpetual imprisonment. In addition, he anticipated more, for he dangled before the eyes of the latter the prospect of seeing the Riom Court itself condemn us to death.

On November 15, 1941, Mandel and myself were transferred from Vals to Portalet. The Press complacently described the isolated nature of the fort, constructed under Louis-Philippe, which lay in a gorge on the Spanish frontier and faced a rocky wall which deprived it of the sun. The water streamed down so abundantly that gutters had to be hollowed in the rock which served as a wall. *Sept Jours*, on November 9, gave details of life in this residence; one read that the temperature fell in winter to thirty degrees below zero; the condemned were shut up in cells, and watched by keepers through spy-holes.

One hundred and fifty steps had to be climbed to reach the small platform where we took our daily walk. My cell looked over a sheer drop of some sixty metres, at the foot of which ran the mountain torrent.

The stay of Daladier, Blum and Gamelin in the fort was only to last a few weeks. They were then taken to Bourrassol in order to appear before the Riom Court. For Pétain, although he had passed sentence on them, meant that a trial should take place.

'A country which has felt itself betrayed', he said on October 16, when rounding off his speech, 'has a right to the truth, and the whole truth. The sentence which will bring the Riom trial to a conclusion must be passed in the light of all the facts.' It is clear, indeed, that Pétain considered this exceptional judicature, the Riom Court, to be an instrument of the régime. This explains the cavalier fashion in which he treated it, asking it to begin proceedings whose outcome he had himself just prejudiced, and publicly dictating to it the sentence which he expected from it. The importance which Vichy placed on the trial lay in trying to prove that it was not the soldiers but the civilians who were responsible for our defeat. To defend the Army, it was, therefore, necessary to charge Daladier and Blum. What a windfall if Gamelin himself could assist in this manœuvre! But Gamelin was not to allow himself to be persuaded to assist in this. He remained deaf to the suggestions and advances of which he was the object, and decided to remain silent during the discussions. All Vichy's attempts to make him change his decision were to fail. 'I was resolved', he writes,[1] 'that the charge should not be based on certain points in my defence in order to set me in opposition to Presidents Daladier and Blum. . . . The second personage of the State at the time, Admiral Darlan, warned of the stand which I intended to take up, brought influence to bear on me so that I should speak with the purpose, so he had me informed, of "defending the Army". . . . Naturally, it was intimated that the attitude which I adopted in the circumstances would be taken into account. The very fact and nature of these approaches seemed to dictate, without any question, the line of action which I ought to pursue. . . . There is a kind of bread which a man of honour, even if he is starving, will certainly not deign to eat.'[2]

Let us get back to Portalet. Mandel and I stayed there for a year. After having been subject for seven months to solitary confinement, we were permitted to see each other every evening.

Relations and friends came to see me: Joseph Laniel, Champetier de Ribes, Pierre Viénot. Finally, I made the acquaintance of the Reverend Father Carré, of the Order of St. Dominic, whose nobility of soul I came to admire during the course of his visits.

[1] *Op. cit.*, vol. I, *Introduction*, pp. ix–xiii, *passim*.
[2] I heard from Gamelin that the approaches in question were made by General Revers.

Mandel, for his part, received almost daily visits from Mme Bretty, whose praiseworthy devotion was equalled by her talent.

My friends in France and in Britain were thinking of my escape.[1] The rumour of this reached the ears of Vichy, who decided to tighten up my guard. Barbed wire entanglements, pill-boxes, all the apparatus of permanent fortifications were constructed. The façade of the fort was subsequently illuminated by a searchlight during the whole night. The General Staff drew on the supplies of the Army services for equipment and ammunition which it used for the defence of the fort, 'the internment place of politicians'. In doing this, it was so certain of anticipating the wishes of its masters that it only asked the approval of the latter after it had taken this glorious initiative. The steps which it took to solicit this approval were contained in 'most secret' instructions given on September 25, 1942, to General Beynet, head of the French Delegation to the German Armistice Commission.

In spite of these precautions, Henri Aubry, whose *nom de guerre* was Avricourt, the hero of the Resistance Movement in the south-east, whom my friend and former colleague, Raoul Anglès, had alerted, drew up a plan for escape with Henri Frenay. He had made a very thin cord of sixty-five metres in length by which I was to be lowered to the road which ran alongside the torrent.[2] He was to blow up the electrical transformer so that the façade of the fort would be suddenly plunged into darkness during the night on which I was to escape. I was to remain hidden for a certain period in a neighbouring farm. Alfred Reynaud brought me in my cell two metal saws which, when I made a visit to the fort in March, 1948, I found between the plinth and the wall, where I had hidden them.

The plan attracted me by its sporting character. But how could I bring myself to abandon Mandel? We then thought of getting him out of the fort on the evening of my escape, disguised in the cloak of Mme Bretty, who would remain in his place inside the cell. But settling the arrangements for this took time.

The British Government in its turn did not forget me. My friend, Maurice Sigoret, received a visit from a South American diplomat, posted to London, who came to ask him, on behalf of the British Government, if I was prepared to escape. The emissary gave proof that his mission was a bona fide one by having a phrase, which my colleagues had given him, broadcast over the wireless by London for several days.

But the Germans upset these plans.

[1] Whilst I was at Vals, my cousin Alfred Reynaud had already rented a villa in the neighbourhood where I was to hide, and then to escape under the noses of the police in a furniture removal van.

[2] I told Maître Jacques Charpentier at the time of my plan; he speaks of it on p. 191 of his book.

NOVEMBER 20, 1942: PÉTAIN HANDS US OVER TO HITLER

On November 16, 1942, the same day as the Wehrmacht proceeded to occupy the southern zone, a squad of S.S. came to the foot of the fort at 9 a.m. The officer in command ordered the governor to hand the two prisoners over to him. We know now that the order came from Himmler.[1]

I telegraphed to Pétain: 'You are faced with a problem of honour. Are you going to hand your former leader over to the enemy?' And to Laval I said: 'Your Government is detaining me without a warrant. When the question of whether I am going to fall into enemy hands because of its action, hangs in the balance, I mean to call in question formally your responsibility, so that you cannot plead ignorance when the day of reckoning comes.'

Nothing was easier than for the French authorities to contrive our escape. I explained this to the governor of the fort, but with no other result than to see, when evening came, two German sentries in the corridor leading to my cell.

The next day I again addressed Pétain: 'Armed German soldiers are occupying the fort of Portalet. Thus, after having sentenced me your-self a year ago to imprisonment in this fort, unheard and without even knowing the charges formulated against me, your former chief, because I refused to surrender, you are now handing me over to the enemy. This new crime will find me prepared, for I have at least the pride of being able to say that my policy would have preserved intact French honour, the French Fleet and Empire.'

I had forbidden any of my sympathizers to make any approach to Vichy. Inspired only by his friendship for me, Champetier de Ribes went to see Laval. The latter spoke to him in a familiar way as was the custom of the Chamber. Champetier answered him so icily by calling him 'Monsier le Président' that it earned for him the penalty of being sent to join Herriot and Jouhaux at Evaux. 'They still have not been shot then?' answered the Head of Laval's staff to Champetier, who got nothing more out of Laval.

The Reverend Father Carré, for his part, went to see the Papal Nuncio, who received him courteously.

On the 18th, Colonel Knochen, head, as we know, of the *Sicher-heitsdienst* in France, came into my cell. The governor of the fort followed him with his head lowered.

That same evening my secretary, Mlle Mabire, was arrested in a neighbouring village.

On the 20th at 1 a.m. the warder knocked at my door. He came

[1] When prosecuted by a French military court, General Oberg stated, at his investiga-tion, that our deportation to Germany had been decided by Himmler.

in: 'Good news,' he said. 'We have received a telegram. The two Governments have agreed for you to be transferred to another place. Perhaps, you are going to join the others at Bourrassol.'

At seven o'clock he came back, pale with emotion. 'The other place is Bordeaux.' We were to be handed over. I wrote with deliberation on an empty sheet of paper: 'Marshal Pétain, Vichy. At the moment when you are handing me over to the enemy, I answer you with "Long Live France!"'

M. François-Poncet had told me in Bordeaux at the time of the Armistice: 'If they lay hands on you, they will treat you like Schuschnigg.' We were certainly to find out. At 9 a.m. the Colonel of the S.S. arrived. He had to wait until 11.30 a.m. I took my time. I burned all my papers which could compromise relatives or friends. Two gendarmes packed my things. Mandel came to see me. The night before he had told me: 'They won't dare to do it. There is no precedent for it.' And he had spoken to me of his daughter. Believing that he was going to Bordeaux to live in confinement under political conditions, he asked for permission to take his negro servant, Baba, an old Senegalese rifleman. His wish was readily granted. Nothing further was heard of this unfortunate man, who died in Buchenwald.

Transferring us to Bordeaux was quite a military operation. We arrived at night at the fort of Le Hâ. The governor of Portalet accompanied us, and said to us on leaving: 'I must return to Portalet. You will get some privileges here.' But he believed nothing of the kind. Knochen promised me that my secretary would be released that same evening. When she was taken on September 30 to the Rue des Saussaies, the headquarters of the Gestapo, she asked the reason for her arrest. The reply was: 'This is war. Paul Reynaud is our worst enemy.' Mlle Mabire was imprisoned in Fresnes and then deported to Ravensbruck; she was to spend two and a half years in Germany.

We passed through the grille doors of the fort. The door of the cell opened. There was a table fastened to the wall, a stool fixed to the paving by a chain, and bowl dish to serve both for toilet and food. That was all the furniture which I had. I threw myself on the bowl, which had just been filled with a thin gruel, for, after all, one had to keep alive. I stretched out on my mattress. The light was in my eyes. Thank God it went out when the alarm siren went.

At midnight we left. We did not know where for. An ambulance took us into a barracks. We changed vehicles. We crossed the river and took the road for the north. A few hours later we stopped. Here was another prison. I asked the German warder, whose pallor resembled that of the actors in Grand Guignol, and who was flattened against the wall: 'Where are we?' The reply was: 'I don't know.' This was henceforth to be the eternal answer to all my questions. Two days later about

765/   20 Nov. 42

Monsieur le Maréchal,

Au moment où vous me livrez à l'ennemi, je vous réponds :

Vive la France !

Paul Reynaud

CHAMBRE DES DÉPUTÉS

R URDOS 550

Le maréchal Pétain
Vichy
765

My letter to Marshal Pétain of November 20, 1942

1 a.m. we left in a reserved coach with blinds drawn. Towards the end of the morning we arrived at the Gare d'Austerlitz. Were we to be shut up in the political wing of La Santé prison? But we circled Paris and headed for the east. We were certainly bound for Germany.

Mandel, muffled up in his fur coat, was at the other end of the coach. At Vitry-le-François one of the S.S. officers who was guarding me brought me a paper. In the middle of the first page I saw this: 'Since there has been a change in circumstances, when will these two gentlemen of Portalet be shot?' We got out at a station near Berlin. I climbed into a vehicle whose side windows were covered. We stopped at the Gestapo headquarters in the Wilhelmstrasse. I was taken into a large room with two doors. I could not refrain from remarking, half serious, half joking: 'On which side is the torture chamber?'

When night had fallen, I set out again. This time we were half an hour on the road. We came to a camp entrance. There were hutments. The vehicle stopped before a one-storey pavilion. It had a central corridor, and on the right and left were doors with spy-holes. I learned later that we were at Oranienburg, twenty-five kilometres to the north of Berlin. The small florid S.S. colonel who commanded the camp as well as the high-ranking Gestapo officials who brought me were there. I was put into a small cell. There was nothing on the wall: not even a water tap.

'Is this where I am to live?'

'Yes.'

'Will I get any news of my family?'

'None.'

'Can one take any exercise?'

'No.'

'Ah. I understand. Well, I am sorry for Germany.'

'What about our plenipotentiaries at Versailles?'

'I am not aware that they were imprisoned.'

'The Russians would have shot you long ago.'

'I did not know that you took them as mentors.'

The colonel became apoplectic. The door closed on me, just like the lid of a watch.

FIVE MONTHS IN A CELL AT ORANIENBURG

At 9 p.m. the light went out in my cell. In this kind of confinement every familiar sound assumed a most intense significance. How sympathetic the barking of a dog seemed to me. When I came out for a shower, there were guttural cries of 'Somebody is coming.' The fatigue men, dressed in coarse canvas with blue and white stripes, fled, for none of them was supposed to be aware of my presence there. The official version was indeed that I had not left the Bordeaux area, and that a château in the outskirts of the town had been allotted me for my residence.[1] My luggage which came to the Gestapo headquarters in Bordeaux was never sent on to me.

Why was I not shot immediately? I asked myself the question in my cell. Perhaps they first wished to tear out of me some statements which would be harmful to my country? Would they torture me? How would I stand up to this? I could not say. I had, therefore, to find a means of avoiding this. I was escorted each morning to the shower and the barber. When he had shaved me, the barber would open the door of the cell in which he worked, and call the guard. I remained seated with a magnificent row of razors in front of me. From that moment I formed my plan. If I was asked for a damaging statement, I should answer: 'Give me time to think. I shall give you all you want tomorrow.' On the following day, when the barber went to call the warder on duty, I should seize one of the razors which lay in front of me, and before the mirror I should cut my carotid artery, according to the formula of Professor Farabœuf: 'To cut it, you must saw through it.' Looking at my hand, I thought with satisfaction of the anger of the Nazis when it was cold. I had found a moral escape.

At various times I received a visit from a S.S. major who acted as liaison officer with the Wilhelmstrasse, no doubt with a view to informing Hitler of my reactions in my cell. I set myself to demonstrate to my benevolent listener the overwhelming superiority of America. I had the satisfaction of noting that I had convinced him of an Allied victory. My arguments gained such an ascendancy over him that in the end he got me a wireless set. Pétain's police had taken away my own!

I wrote to the German Government in order to shame them about the treatment to which they were subjecting me. I touched them really on the raw without expecting to do so. A few weeks later I received my baggage. My conditions were transformed. I had my books, a fountain-pen, some odd sticks of furniture, and, finally, my solitude. A travelling clock enlivened this with its 'tick, tick'. I had left Portalet without even a watch.

In the end I obtained permission to take half an hour's exercise in the courtyard. I was alone there. There was not another soul except the sentry in the distance on his observation post. Sometimes I saw a flock of rooks in the sky. They were free!

I worried about Mandel's fate. Was he in a concentration camp for Jews? One day I passed an N.C.O. The death's head which decorated the lapel of his jacket was a bad omen. So much the worse! I took the chance of asking him if Mandel was here. 'Mandel? I don't know him.'

[1] Gamelin told me later that, at Riom, the Germans circulated this information. They even went as far as to say that I rode on horseback in the park of the château.

I later learned that we were given false names. Mine was 'Richard'. I succeeded, however, in establishing contact with Mandel. No one would be more astonished by this than the commandant of the camp, if he is still alive.

One day when, through negligence, the warders left me alone for a few moments in the shower-bath, I had time to open the fanlight which, however, was removed the next day, and to note that only two cells, my own and another, were hidden by screens. Who then was this other occupant—the object like myself of such especial care? Could it not be Mandel? Unfortunately this second cell was a long way down the corridor, so that I had little hope of being able in passing to lift the cover of the spy-hole, whilst the warder was taking me back to my own, and going in front of me instead of following me. To have the opportunity of finding out who this comrade in misfortune was, we should, therefore, have to be both changed into the opposite cells, facing on the courtyard, and which, by good fortune, looked south. Immediately I asked to be transferred, giving as an excuse my need for the sun, as my treatment at Portalet had given me rheumatism, and also shingles on the head. I should soon see if the other prisoner also changed his cell. The fanlights facing the court were indeed also provided with screens, but two of them were slightly different from the others. I knew that the cell housed a mysterious personage. I noted that the fanlight of the cell which intrigued me was always closed. Mandel, I knew, lived in fear of draughts. One day as I passed in front of the cell during my exercise, I uttered the syllables *Man-del*. For I also knew that Mandel was somewhat hard of hearing. However, I made out a face in the fanlight. I went nearer.

'Who is there?'

'Mandel.'

I was so moved that for the first and last time in my life I addressed him in a familiar style. 'It is you, Mandel?' I saw him through the fanlight and the wall. I saw he was very pale. He said to me:

'I am suffering cruelly from being without news.'

From that time we had one or two minutes' talk almost every day. That was in February.

This régime of complete isolation had no effect on my morale, but it did impair my physique. My nails became soft. Profiting from the state of my health to find an excuse for some alteration in the conditions under which I was confined, which would enable me to live with Mandel, I sent a note on March 22, 1943, to the German Government, which ran: 'The professor . . . who examined me . . . has noted . . . symptoms of excitement and blood pressure which is above normal. Since then these symptoms have become worse. . . . This deterioration in my health is due to the conditions under which I am imprisoned.

... For four months I have lived in complete isolation, shut up in a cell. the door of which is opened without any knocking, like that of a kennel, and I have received no news of my relatives. . . . Now, however long this war may last, it cannot go on for ever. . . .'

What was the result of this step? One day at about two o'clock during the following month, I was paid a visit.

'You are leaving at four o'clock.'

'Where to?'

'We don't know.'

During my last walk I saw Mandel through the opening in the fan-light.

'I am leaving. I want to tell you that I have no wish to die.'

Mandel wrote in his diary:

'Reynaud has gone. I feel so very lonely.'

At 4.30 I arrived at Saxenhausen not far from Oranienburg. Here there was a large hut encircled by high-voltage wires. I felt more cut off than in my cell because I was deprived of my daily talks with Mandel, however brief they might have been, and also because the familiar sounds of men living together is company. But what a childish joy there was in being able to open a door by oneself.

One day I saw Borotra arrive. He proved to be an excellent companion. Shortly afterwards I read in the infamous *Echo de Nancy*, printed for the benefit of prisoners, that Blum, Daladier, Gamelin and Jouhaux had just been transferred to Germany,[1] where they were imprisoned under the same conditions as in France. I asked to be able to enjoy such a régime. Thus it came about that Borotra and myself were transferred on May 12 to Itter in Austria. When we left, we passed before a row of large huts similar to our own. At the door of one of them I noted a thin, exhausted-looking man.

'Is that Schuschnigg?' I asked the officer who was escorting us. I gathered from his smile that it was, indeed, the Chancellor. What had he felt like, I thought, on the day when he was present at the talk which I had gone to give in Vienna, in order to infuse heart into the Austrians? I was later to learn that other huts housed Breitscheid and his wife, Prince Xavier de Bourbon-Parma and his wife, Captain Churchill, Thyssen, etc. We slept at Weimar in the same hut as Léon Blum and Mandel, who were kept apart from us for racial reasons.

I had not seen Blum since catching sight of him in a corridor of Portalet during December, 1941. When I left them on the following morning Blum was full of affectionate warmth, as was his custom. As for Mandel, he looked at me for a long time as if he had a feeling that we should not see each other again.

[1] In actual fact it was in April, 1943, that Blum, Daladier, Gamelin and Jouhaux were transferred to Germany, the first three from Bourrassol, and the fourth, from Evaux.

AT ITTER

The castle of Itter, a dilapidated building in Rococo style, is perched on a peak of the Tyrolean Alps, which dominates a tributary of the Inn and the railway from Innsbruck to Vienna. Bestriding a ravine, a bridge links the castle to the flank of the mountain. Over the entrance of the castle, the phrase of Dante on the gates of hell, 'Abandon hope all you who enter here', was carved.

Daladier, Jouhaux and Gamelin had been there for some days. I fear that I must have shocked them when I cried out: 'This is paradise!' In actual fact, life was incomparably less hard for me, and the habit of work returned to me easily.

I spent two years there, during which we saw several birds of passage come and go: there was M. Nitti, who, to my deep regret and in spite of his wishes, left us. M. Lebrun, who was soon sent back to France for reasons of health; M. François-Poncet, who was the first to leave for a residence that he was assured ought to be more comfortable.

In December, 1943, Weygand arrived,[1] and Michel Clemenceau shortly afterwards. How could a man like Michel Clemenceau, bearing such a name, reconcile himself to eating peacefully the bread of servitude? I have already related how he had protested to Pétain about the severity of the treatment to which Mandel and myself were subjected at Portalet. He again protested to Pétain when the latter handed us over to the enemy. Later, when, in order to justify its sorry task, Vichy covered the walls of Paris with placards in which it had the impudence to recall the name of the Tiger, Michel Clemenceau pointed out to Laval in a vengeful letter that, as he held him personally responsible for this outrage against the memory of his father, he counted one day 'on demanding satisfaction from him for it'.

This time the cup was thus filled to overflowing. Laval complained to his masters. And so Michel Clemenceau came to share our fate and to bring us at the same time the reassurance of his unshakeable confidence.

When Weygand arrived, I asked Borotra to tell him that I was most determined to take no notice of the man who had forced France to surrender, thus breaking her word, and that I should, therefore, refuse to sit at the same table with him. Gamelin adopted the same attitude as did Michel Clemenceau. The result was that one table was formed at which Weygand, Borotra and Colonel de la Rocque, who himself had arrived in the meantime, took their places. Michel Clemenceau, Gamelin and myself dined at another.

---

[1] When announcing the arrival of Weygand to me, the S.S. officer who came periodically from Berlin to inspect our camp said to me: 'I think you will be pleased by it.' I said to this: 'Why do you want it to be pleasing to me?'

LIBERATED BY THE AMERICANS

As they saw the end of the war approaching, my friends at Itter grew increasingly alarmed at the fate which they imagined Hitler might have in store for me, when the worst came to the worst. Clemenceau, who spoke German as well as he did French, one day summoned the S.S. commandant of the castle, and in the presence of Gamelin and myself told him: 'It is possible that you may shortly be told to hand over President Paul Reynaud. Berlin is soon going to be encircled. Indeed you ought to take on the duties of the Allied military authorities. You will be accountable to them. If President Reynaud is taken away, you know for what purpose it will be. You also know that the Allies will hold responsible all those who help in an action of this nature. What do you mean to do?' The captain replied, not without dignity, that he was only accountable to his conscience, but, as he did not think it compatible with the interests of his country that I should be shot, he would help, if necessary, in my escape if that were possible.

Each time a car arrived my friends were on the alert. Had I finally been forgotten in the confusion? In actual fact I was never sent for.

During the last days we saw a succession of cars belonging to S.S. officers in the entrance courtyard. These officers were most often accompanied by their wives, and with their weapons and luggage were fleeing to the east. In the panic they kept their discipline. After staying for a night they left.

On May 1 I heard in the next room to mine a couple of shots: the adjutant of the camp commander of Dachau, a camp under which Itter came, had just shot himself near the heart, and then finished himself off with a second shot behind the ear. We learned that he had in his luggage four kilos of scrap gold which came from his victims at Dachau. Next day we saw his coffin come back into the courtyard of the castle. The village priest had refused to bury a suicide in sacred soil. To assure ourselves that he was really the officer who had come to inspect us several months earlier, and to establish the identity of an important 'war criminal', Gamelin, Jouhaux, Clemenceau and myself demanded that the coffin should be opened. This was done in the garage. It was a frightful sight. Soldiers had stolen the dead man's boots. His bloodstained shirt was half opened to show his breast; his head was thrown back; his mouth was wide open and his eyes staring. This torturer looked like one of the damned. When the coffin was closed up again, the soldiers dug a grave in a field, and over the newly turned earth they threw some branches. These were the only honours given to one of their former chiefs by the S.S. men of Itter. We drew up a report of these facts for the future help of the leaders of the Allied Armies.

At 3 a.m. the captain told us of his intention to leave the castle, and asked us for a certificate of good behaviour. My opinion was that we should refuse it to him until the Americans came. However, we gave him one, but not before we had got hold of some weapons. I myself took a tommy-gun.

Then Clemenceau and myself, now freed, went for a walk in the village, where Austrian flags were flying, and on whose roads the columns of the Wehrmacht ebbed in march towards the east. In their ranks were boys in uniform, who seemed to be hardly more than ten years old. In the afternoon we got a bicycle from a village shopkeeper. On this we sent our trusty friend, the Czech cook, André, to Woergl, the neighbouring village, so that he could establish contact with the American Army if it was already there, and inform it of our presence in Itter.

When he got to Woergl where he knew nobody, André was, and for a good reason, in great difficulty. There were no Americans. As the S.S. had begun to fire on windows draped with Austrian flags, all of them had disappeared in the twinkling of an eye. André spoke to a passer-by whom he picked on because of his friendly appearance. He pulled out of his pocket the end of an Austrian flag. He was, therefore, a friend. André told him about our position. The passer-by explained to him that the Wehrmacht wished to stop fighting by applying the convention agreed in Italy between Field-Marshal Alexander and the Commander of German troops in Italy and Austria. 'What do you know about that?' replied the S.S. 'You have not received any orders from your leaders. If you have heard of it over the London radio, you deserve to die for this very fact alone.'

Thus, there arose a conflict between the S.S. and the Wehrmacht. The stranger took André to a colonel of the Wehrmacht, with whom was Captain Lee of an American assault tank unit.

In the evening we saw Captain Lee arrive with some American soldiers. They left their tank before the entrance of the castle. There was also the colonel of the Wehrmacht with a lieutenant and some fifteen men who had come to shelter with us from the vengeance of the S.S.

But the drama had not yet come to an end. On the morning of the next day, at an early hour, several bullets splattered on the façade of the castle. We did not think much about them, believing that some of the Wehrmacht and the S.S. were settling their differences in the neighbourhood. But, around 11 p.m., we were out strolling when a broadside of shells hit the top of the castle. The upper wall collapsed in front of us whilst the American tank, which was guarding the entry, flared up like a punchbowl. More dangerous was that the machine-guns joined in, and we had to shelter behind the parapet of the encircling wall. I soon saw that, as the tank was burning, the attackers could penetrate from the other side into the courtyard by the bridge which linked up with the flank of the mountain. I dodged into the castle. I got my tommy-gun out of my trunk, and went down to the courtyard, where I found some soldiers. Clemenceau had already calmly posted himself at a loophole in case the attackers wished to take possession of the tank. I myself took up a position near to him. The colonel of the Wehrmacht left the castle at this moment. He said that he had campaigned in Russia during the winter of 1941–2, that he had been at Stalingrad, and that consequently he had a charmed life. 'I am going to parley with them', he said.

But, just as he was leaving the courtyard to cross the bridge some twenty paces from us, this strongly built man collapsed, killed stonedead. One of his men was seriously wounded. Seeing this, the other Wehrmacht soldiers, knowing what to expect if they were taken with weapons in their hands by the S.S., vanished. The situation of Clemenceau and myself was not happier.[1]

Captain Lee put a man with a tommy-gun at the window of my room from which hung a long tricolor that we had made out of a sheet, the red cloth of a Hitler flag and the blue of a woman's skirt. The man swept the entrance court with his fire. We ran to the other side of the castle in order to defend the surrounding wall against possible attack, although the ground fell in a steep slope. A young Austrian patriot with a white and red brassard showed himself very active. The Wehrmacht lieutenant, glasses to his eyes, pointed out targets against which to direct our fire. In my role as national guard, I regret that I cannot affirm that I killed one enemy.

The situation was dangerous, for the S.S., who had left us on the previous day, had alerted elements of the *Grossdeutschland* division, which was in the valley. André, dodging through the fir trees, reached Woergl, where he, in his turn, gave the alarm to the Americans. Borotra, who also had gone there, came back in an American uniform. With a prodigality which alarmed me in the end, Lee scattered grenades in the wooded ravine whence an attack was likely to come.

Finally, we heard the noise of a fight taking place between the advancing American tanks and the S.S. below. The battle was won. At the beginning of the afternoon we were free. Near the entrance of the courtyard the American tank continued to burn.

The following day we crossed Germany by car.

At Ulm the spire of the cathedral still stood, but around it, as far as one could see, were ruins. From time to time handfuls of civilians silent

---

[1] I was later to learn from a report sent to General Béthouart that it was the intention of the attackers to shoot all the prisoners at Itter.

and dazed came out of cellars. 'That is war,' answered a Gestapo officer in a dry and sarcastic tone to our complaints.

At the end of the day we reached the shores of Lake Constance. In the courtyard of the hotel an infantry battalion in white gaiters paid honours to us. There was no dinner at the Headquarters of General de Lattre de Tassigny, who knew how to give a suitably warm welcome, but had received during the afternoon a telegram from General de Gaulle, ordering him to receive some of our party with certain reserve.

I was pleased to find Maurice Schumann here, with whom I had become friendly formerly during the Abyssinian affair, and whose warm eloquence expressed from London during the war years the spirit of Fighting France.

Next day we went by car through the Black Forest, and then, skirting pitiful columns of German prisoners, we entered Strasbourg. Strasbourg! I had visited it, deserted and tragically silent, in January, 1940. Now here today was a festive crowd, celebrating victory in streets beflagged with tricolors. I mingled with the crowd under the cathedral arches. Devout Christians, insensible to the noisy demonstrations of joy, were praying with uplifted eyes.

In the private plane of General de Gaulle, the Cross of Lorraine marked on the gleaming fuselage of this powerful bird of the sky, we flew towards Paris.

What kind of a France were we to find?

Would she understand better tomorrow than yesterday the demands which her rehabilitation would require, the sacrifices to be made for her defence? Would she acquiesce more readily to these sacrifices? Or would she show towards her new problems, whose solution would determine peace or war, victory or defeat, the same former lack of understanding? Would she realize that today she must steel herself as Prussia had done on the morrow of Jena?

How was it possible not to find confidence restored at the sight of these cherished landscapes, however small the height at which we flew reduced them? Here was the Champagne of Diderot, the Ile-de-France of La Fontaine, of Racine, Molière and of Voltaire.

This was France, our France.

BIBLIOGRAPHY

ENGLISH BOOKS

Baudouin, Paul, *Private Diaries 1940–1941* (1948).

Churchill, Sir Winston, *The Second World War*, vols. I and II (1948–50).

Ciano, Count, *Diary, 1939–1943* (1947).

Feiling, K. G., *The Life of Neville Chamberlain* (1946).

Francois-Ponçet, André, *The Fateful Years: Memoirs of a French Ambassador in Berlin, 1931–1938* (1949).

Hull, Cordell, *Memoirs* (1948).

Langer, William, *Our Vichy Gamble* (U.S.A.).

Liddell Hart, B. H., *The Other Side of the Hill* (1948).

Montmorency, A. de, *The Enigma of Admiral Darlan*.

Rauschning, H., *Hitler Speaks* (1939).

Trevor-Roper, H. R., *The Last Days of Hitler*.

U.S. State Department, *Nazi-Soviet Relations during the Years, 1939–1941*.

Welles, Sumner, *The Time for Decision* (1944).

Woodward, E. L., and Butler, R., *Documents on British Foreign Policy 1919–1939*.

Falsifiers of History (Soviet Publication, *New Times*, 1945).

FOREIGN BOOKS

Auphan, *Histoire de mes trahisons ou la Marine au service des Français*.

Badoglio, Pietro, *Memoirs*.

Baumont, Maurice, *La faillite de la paix*.

Beneš, Eduard, *Memoirs*.

Benoist-Méchin, *Histoire de l'armée allemande*.

Baudouin, Paul, *Reflexions sur l'armistice*.
    A propos d'un nouveau livre de M. Kammerer.

Béraud, Henri, *Sans haine et sans crainte*.

Blum, Léon, *Mémoires*.

Bonnet, Georges, *Défense de la paix: I. De Washington au Quai d'Orsay. II. Fin d'une Europe (de Munich à la guerre)*.

Bourget, *De Beyrouth à Bordeaux*.

Bouthillier, Yves, *Le drame de Vichy: I. Face à l'ennemi, face à l'allié*.

Braun, Eva, *Journal Intime*.

Brugère, Raymond, *Veni, Vidi, Vichy*.

Cartier, *Les secrets de la guerre, dévoilés par Nuremberg*.

Champeaux, Georges, *La croisade des démocraties*.

Charles-Roux, François, *Cinq mois tragiques aux affaires étrangères, 21 mai–1er novembre, 1940*.

Charpentier, Jacques, *Au service de la liberté*.

Châteaubriant, Alphonse de, *La gerbe des forces*.

Chauvineau, *Une invasion est-elle encore possible?*

Clemenceau, Georges, *Grandeurs et misères d'une victoire*.

Crusoé, *Vicissitudes d'une victoire*.

Fabry, Jean, *De la Place de la Concorde au cours de l'Intendance*.

Ferré, *De défaut de l'armure.*

Flandin, Pierre-Etienne, *Discours* (Collected edition published 1937).
   Politique française.

Frossard, Luc-Olivier, *Les journées historiques de juin, 1940: l'heure du Maréchal.*

Gamelin, *Servir.*

Gard, Maurice Martin du, *La chronique de Vichy: 1940–1944.*

Gaxotte, Pierre, *Le siècle de Louis XV.*

Herriot, Edouard, *Episodes, 1940–1944.*
   Souvenirs.

Hitler, Adolf, *Mein Kampf.*

Jodl, *Journal.*

Kammerer, Albert, *La verité sur l'armistice.*

Kerillis, Henri de, *Français, voici la vérité!*

Langeron, Roger, *Souvenirs.*

Laure, *Pétain.*

Lazareff, Pierre, *Dernière édition.*

Lebrun, Albert, *Témoignage.*

Léger, *Les cahiers de la quinzaine, été-automne.*

Lyet, *La bataille de France (mai–juin 1940).*

Maassen, *Par delà la Meuse.*

Mazé, Pierre, and Genebrier, Roger, *Les grandes journées du procès de Riom.*

Monzie, Anatole de, *Ci-devant.*
   La saison des juges.

Mousset, Albert, *Histoire de Russie.*

Murawski, *Der Durchbruch im Westen.*

Nemanov, *La Russie et les problèmes de la paix.*

Noël, Léon, *L'agression allemande contre la Pologne.*

Overstraeten, van, *Albert Ier-Léopold III: Vingt ans de politique militaire belge.*

Paul-Boncour, J., *Entre deux guerres.*

Pierlot, Hubert, *Pages d'histoire.*

Poincaré, R., *Au service de la France.*

Potiemkin, V., *Histoire de la diplomatie.*

Prouvost, Jean, *Sept jours.*

Reibel, Charles, *Pourquoi et comment fut décidée la demande d'armistice, juin 10–17, 1940.*

Révillon, Tony, *Mes carnets (juin–octobre, 1940), documents et témoignages pour servir à l'histoire.*

Reynaud, Paul, *Jeunesse, quelle France veux-tu?*
   La France a sauvé l'Europe.
   Le problème militaire français.

Ribet, Maurice, *Le procès de Riom.*

Rivaud, Albert, *Le relèvement de l'Allemagne.*

Rollin, Louis, *Journal.*

Roussy de Sales, *L'Amerique entre en guerre.*

Rucart, Marc, *La dépêche de Paris.*

Sforza, Count, *L'Italie telle que je l'ai vue.*

Spaak, Paul-Henri, *L'attitude du gouvernement belge.*

Stéphane, Roger, *Chaque homme est lié au monde.*

Taittinger, Pierre, *Et Paris ne fut pas détruit.*
Tardieu, André, *L'année de Munich.*
Tracou, Jean, *Le Maréchal aux liens.*
Varenne, Francisque, *Mon patron, Georges Mandel.*
Verhaegen, *Le rôle de l'armée belgeen 1940.*
Vlassov, *J'ai choisi la potence.*
Weygand, Maxime, *Rappelé au service.*
Wullus-Rudiger, *Les mémoires de P. Reynaud et la Belgique.*
Zay, Jean, *Souvenirs et solitude.*
   Carnets.

INDEX